No Place to Call Home

The 1807–1857 Life Writings
of
Caroline Barnes Crosby
Chronicler of Outlying Mormon Communities

Edited by
Edward Leo Lyman, Susan Ward Payne,
and
S. George Ellsworth

UTAH STATE UNIVERSITY PRESS
Logan, Utah
2005

© 2005 by University Press of Colorado

Published by Utah State University Press
An imprint of University Press of Colorado
245 Century Circle, Suite 202
Louisville, Colorado 80027

 ASSOCIATION of UNIVERSITY PRESSES The University Press of Colorado is a proud member of the Association of University Presses.

The University Press of Colorado is a cooperative publishing enterprise supported, in part, by Adams State University, Colorado State University, Fort Lewis College, Metropolitan State University of Denver, Regis University, University of Colorado, University of Northern Colorado, University of Wyoming, Utah State University, and Western Colorado University.

∞ This paper meets the requirements of the ANSI/NISO Z39.48–1992 (Permanence of Paper)

ISBN: 978-0-87421-601-1 (hardcover)
ISBN: 978-1-64642-155-8 (paperback)
ISBN: 978-0-87421-524-3 (ebook)

Library of Congress Cataloging-in-Publication Data

Crosby, Caroline Barnes, 1807–1884.
 No place to call home : the 1807–1857 life writings of Caroline Barnes Crosby, chronicler of outlying Mormon communities / edited by Edward Leo Lyman, Susan Ward Payne, and S. George Ellsworth.
 p. cm. — (Life writings of frontier women ; v. 7)
 Includes bibliographical references and index.
 ISBN 0-87421-601-X (alk. paper) — ISBN 978-1-64642-155-8 (pbk) — ISBN 978-0-87421-524-3 (ebook)
 1. Crosby, Caroline Barnes, 1807-1884. 2. Crosby, Caroline Barnes, 1807–1884—Diaries. 3. Mormon pioneers—West (U.S.)—Biography. 4. Mormon women—West (U.S.)—Biography. 5. Frontier and pioneer life—West (U.S.) 6. Mormons—West (U.S.)—History—19th century. 7. Salt Lake Valley (Utah)—Biography. 8. Middle West—Biography. 9. San Francisco (Calif.)—Biography. 10. San Bernardino (Calif.)—Biography. I. Lyman, Edward Leo, 1942– II. Payne, Susan Ward, 1942– III. Ellsworth, S. George (Samuel George), 1916– IV. Title. V. Series.
F593.C897 2005
917.8'042—dc22
                    2004026228

No Place to Call Home

The 1807–1857 Life Writings
of
Caroline Barnes Crosby
Chronicler of Outlying Mormon Communities

Volume 7
LIFE WRITINGS OF FRONTIER WOMEN
A Series Edited by
Maureen Ursenbach Beecher

Volume 1
Winter Quarters
The 1846–1848 Life Writings of
Mary Haskin Parker Richards
Edited by Maurine Carr Ward

Volume 2
Mormon Midwife
The 1846–1888 Diaries of
Patty Bartlett Sessions
Edited by Donna Toland Smart

Volume 3
The History of Louisa Barnes Pratt
Being the Autobiography of a Mormon Missionary Widow and Pioneer
Edited by S. George Ellsworth

Volume 4
Out of the Black Patch
The Autobiography of Effie Marquess Carmack
Folk Musician, Artist, and Writer
Edited by Noel A. Carmack and Karen Lynn Davidson

Volume 5
The Personal Writings of Eliza Roxcy Snow
Edited by Maureen Ursenbach Beecher

Volume 6
A Widow's Tale
The 1884–1896 Diary of Helen Mar Kimball Whitney
Transcribed and Edited by Charles M. Hatch and Todd M. Compton

Caroline Barnes Crosby, 1855, from print of
daguerreotype with shattered glass cover. Courtesy of Special
Collections and Archives, Utah State University Libraries.

CONTENTS

Maps and Illustrations

FOREWORD

Maureen Ursenbach Beecher

Two events in the young life of S. George Ellsworth were turning points leading to the great legacy left behind with his death in 1997. The first, while he was a student preparing to become an architect, was his coming upon his grandfather's handwritten autobiography. That moment persuaded him to spend his life researching and writing the history of his people, the Latter-day Saints, and their antecedents. The second significant event was his meeting and marrying Maria Smith, an Arizona school teacher. Together they created the exemplary teamwork in home, family, church, community service, and professional productivity without which he might never have become, as he did, a historian of note and mentor to the subsequent generation of writers of Utah history.

Being forerunners and nurturers was part of the Ellsworths' contribution to Utah history. If, as George once observed, Juanita Brooks was "the queen of Utah historians," then he and Maria were their nurturing parents, George in the professional limelight, Maria unpretentiously by his side, usually offstage. Stories are told of the study groups they fostered during their early years in Logan. George and his colleagues would read to each other papers of shared interest, often having to do with Mormon studies. From that group, as from George's classes at Utah State University, came many of the luminaries who began in the 1950s to fill the gap in scholarly exploration of the history of the Latter-day Saints. There was hardly a writer of Utah and Mormon history of the years of George's tenure at USU but came under their influence. The story is also told of George's generous coaching of such colleagues as Leonard J. Arrington, who once stayed so late in the Ellsworth house that the gracious Maria was forced to remind him that it was well past supper time and he should go home so George could eat.

The photo opposite best illustrates the *modus operandi* by which George and Maria worked: side by side, he the researcher-writer, she the confidante, assistant, editor, critic, source and inspiration. The eight

Maria and George Ellsworth, 1994.

books and uncounted articles, lectures, and reviews bearing the Ellsworth name can be to a greater or lesser degree attributed to them both.

George's early bibliographic research in Mormon collections had made him aware of the rich vein of gold among the records: the diaries and autobiographies the early Saints had written. Like Davis Bitton, under whose direction the landmark *Guide to Mormon Diaries and Autobiographies* was compiled, and Juanita Brooks, who earlier had found, transcribed, and published some of the early gems of the genre, George recognized in his grandfather's memoir and in the letters and diaries of Maria's ancestral family, the literary and historical worth of these life writings. His 1974 volume, *Dear Ellen: Two Mormon Women and Their Letters*, from documents in Maria's family collection, was an early inspiration for the creation of the present Life Writings of Frontier Women series. Such texts, the letters demonstrated, are much, much more than mere sources of historical evidence; they are a literature of their own.

From that same collection of the Pratt/Hunt/Smith/Udall papers came George's 1990 publication, *The Journals of Addison Pratt;* Maria's 1992 *Mormon Odyssey: The Story of Ida Hunt Udall;* the 1998 *History of Louisa Barnes Pratt: The Autobiography of a Mormon Missionary Widow and Pioneer;* and the present text, the writings of Louisa's sister Caroline. Maria and George had collaborated in George's editing of Louisa's writings, in the production of which George acknowledged Maria's "help-ing me much, and saving me from errors." Both texts were, after all, those of Maria's family members, and George depended on her to "master . . . family relations."

But George died in 1997, and *The History of Louisa Barnes Pratt* appeared posthumously. Maria, in the meantime, had for years been focusing her attention on the Caroline diaries, adding to George's volu-minous research her own insights and discoveries. She, however, followed him in death in 1999, leaving the task of editing the diaries undone.

It is to our immense satisfaction that E. Leo Lyman and Sue Payne came forward to complete the preparation of the text. With the same rigorous adherence to historical and editing standards, they have added the Ellsworths' files to their own extensive research and transcriptions and, with scrutiny and attention to detail, carried on.

Despite differences in background and approach, both Leo and Sue are well prepared for the work at hand. Leo, now wrapping up a forty-year-long career teaching American history at high school and col-lege levels, is well known among his colleagues for his publications: five books, twenty-plus scholarly articles, as well as many reviews and doc-umentary appearances. His 1996 *San Bernardino: The Rise and Fall of a California Community* established his reputation in that piece of history in which the Crosbys played such a role. He goes on now to complete a biography of Amasa Lyman.

Sue Payne came to the Caroline Crosby diaries by a more circu-itous route: originally a student of foreign languages, after a year's study in France, she returned to the University of California at Berkeley, mar-ried, and while rearing her two children, earned her teaching creden-tials in history as well as foreign languages. Switching gears, she worked in the medical field for twenty years as office manager and assistant to an ophthalmologist. Following her love of reading and interest in his-torical research, Sue found herself a volunteer in the San Bernardino library transcribing the diaries from a microfilm holograph—"a trea-sure hidden away on a shelf waiting to be deciphered."

Retracing a part of the old Mormon Road on an excursion headed by Dr. Lyman, Sue entertained the group by reading excerpts from the dia-ries. The shared bond was created, and these pages, cooperatively incorpo-rating George Ellsworth's research and Maria's concern, are the result.

It is with great pleasure that we offer, as volume seven of the Life Writings of Frontier Women series, this collaborative editing of the diaries of Caroline Barnes Crosby. Meet her in her own words and rec-ognize, as we all have, the strength and splendid simplicity of her unwav-ering faith, her devout soul.

ACKNOWLEDGMENTS

No publication of this scope and character can be accomplished without the ongoing assistance of numerous caring individuals involved in such an endeavor. As current editors, we were inheritors of a project already underway in the capable hands of S. George Ellsworth and his wife, Maria S. Ellsworth. We are particularly indebted to their son, Mark A. Ellsworth, who invited us into the family home in Logan, Utah and entrusted us with documents, photographs and personal papers that he and his mother spent many hours working with together. According to Mark, his father always said that Caroline was truly the saint in the Crosby family. We share his parents' admiration for her, and our commitment has been to finish the work George and Maria began with the same meticulous attention to accuracy, scholarship and clarity that they would have demanded of themselves.

We owe Mae Crosby White, deceased in 1987, a special note of recognition. Granddaughter of Caroline and Jonathan Crosby, she became the family historian and record keeper. As guardian of the Crosby journals she placed these valuable papers in the hands of Dr. Ellsworth for his use, who in turn entrusted them to the Utah State Historical Society.

Donna Naegle of Provo, Utah, and other descendants of Lois Hunt West, grand-niece of Carolyn Crosby, generously assisted with the project's publication costs.

A very special note of appreciation goes to Lorin K. Hansen, who gave us a historic tour of the East Bay region of Northern California. He also provided time-related maps of the bay area, shared his knowledge of the local history of the Church of Jesus Christ of Latter-day Saints, and encouraged our efforts at every step.

Janell Tuttle of the Utah State Historical Society offered her services many times, and Stephen Sturgeon assisted us early on at Utah State University. No one has been more helpful than John R. Alley, executive editor at Utah State University, who never failed to immediately answer a question or fulfill a request, and who has guided us patiently throughout the process of preparing this manuscript for publication. It is an honor and a privilege to have the commitment of Maureen Ursenbach Beecher, general editor of this series of women's writings, supporting us throughout. Her confidence in our efforts has been gratifying.

We are indebted to the staff and docents of the Feldheym Public Library in San Bernardino and its California Room, where Caroline was first introduced to Sue by special friends Chris Shovey and Will Bagley. Thanks go also to our cartographer, Norman Meek, professor of geography at California State University San Bernardino. Also we express great appreciation to our families, who have encouraged and supported us in every way possible, with good humor and patience and love.

Finally, a very special acknowledgment belongs to Kerry Petersen, who in innumerable ways helped us to see beyond Caroline's words into the spirit of her writing. Thank you.

Editors' Notes

Description of Manuscript

The manuscript pages of Caroline Barnes Crosby's journals are of several colors, white to creme, grey and light blue, and are of two basic sizes. The majority of the pages are approximately 8 ½ x 11 inches, with others 8 ½ x 14 inches. Generally, each page features small, neat handwriting covering virtually all of both sides of the paper. There are yet remnants of thread and string and small holes in the paper from when the pages and folios were more carefully bound.

The memoirs and journals published here comprise a dozen file folders of varying numbers of pages and folios. The memoirs, begun at Tubuai, Society Islands, in January 1851, retrace her life to September 1846. The ensuing segment, carefully blended into the reminiscences preceding it, is actual diary, covering the pioneer trek to Salt Lake Valley. The residence at Salt Lake City is summarized in another brief memoir. The next portion of the journal recounts the trip from Utah to San Francisco in the summer of 1850. There is then some mixing of memoir and daily journalizing from early in the Tahitian mission (January 1851) until some months into their ensuing California residence (February 1853). From 10 February 1853 onward the manuscript features detailed diary entries on California life to January 1858, the conclusion of this first volume. Caroline Crosby's journals, recounting her experiences in Beaver, Utah, continue with some interruptions until two years before her death in 1884. They will be published in a second volume.

Provenance

The holograph journals of Caroline Crosby were passed to her son Alma, and in turn to his daughter, Mae Crosby White, both of Beaver, Utah. In June 1957 Mae White placed them in the hands of S. George Ellsworth for reference in his preparing the journals of Addison Pratt for

June 27th 1844, we arose with heavy hearts, full of doubts and fears
respecting the safety of our beloved Prophet and Patriarch who were
then incarcerated in Carthage jail. The city was full of rumors concerning
the mob who were assembling at Warsaw and Carthage.

Mr. C. and his Morris set off in to find cousin Jane. We talked out
to the young Marks on the prairie, but found she had come into the
city. They left her letters, with directions for her to call and see us.

That P.m the governor with a large posse came to Nauvoo, and
requested the legion to deliver up their arms, which they did. He then
made a lengthy address to the saints, exhorting them to keep quiet &c, which
they obeyed to the very letter, but felt greatly insulted by him, knowing
that there was no occasion for his remarks, or counsel.

The next morning at an early hour, the news of Joseph and Hiram's massacre
was spread throughout the length and breadth of the city, we would not
believe the first report, but finally it was confirmed to us beyond a doubt;
And Oh the sorrow and sadness of that day, many were made sick by the
intelligence, others deranged, many walked the streets mourning and
wringing their hands. I lost my strength and appetite, could not attend to
any business for several days. P.m their bodies were brought home, and arrangements made for their burial. Every body was invited, or rather had the
privilege of seeing them by walking through the house, we went in at one
door, passed by their coffins, gave them a short look, and then went out at the
opposite side. They were much disfigured, I thought they did not look natural
in the least, could scarcely tell them apart.

I shall not attempt to describe the confusion and doubts the church was thrown
into for a short time, with regard to our leader, or president, until the
return of bro. Brigham Young, and other members of the twelve, when
all, or nearly all were at rest upon that subject.

Page of holograph (memoir) 27 June 1844. Used by permission, Utah State
Historical Society, all rights reserved.

Jun 22nd, I felt very unwell this morning, but had everything to do before meeting time. My head was so distressed that I went to my chamber before the A.M. meeting closed. Afternoon Alma kindled a fire, put on the tea kettle, and I made a cup of tea for sister Hollenbeck, and myself and by raising a little perspiration, my head soon became relieved, and I enjoyed the P.M. meeting very well. Mr. Hollenbeck called with the carriage for her, while she was sitting at dinner, which deprived her of the the second meeting. She went away rather reluctantly.

Capt. Hunt spoke to us, in his plain shrewd manner. He with Bro Lyman and Badlam took supper with us. Bro Badlam has stayed with us two nights back. A number of the brethren spent the evening with us, among whom was a bro Meder from Santa Cruz, one of the Brooklyn co. He talks of helping he at Lyman in paying for the San Berdino rancho.

Mon 23rd cloudy and unpleasant. Some rain in the night sufficient to wet the planks considerably. Bro Hunt and Lyman took breakfast with us. Sister Combs called in, and sat some time with me. Chevy went home, took letter for Frances. I did a job of sewing for colored man Bro Dodge and Badlam supped with us. Mr. Neddy called a few minutes enquired after the friends at San Bdo. Said he had been to the mines.

Tues 24th This is the 7th anniversary of the Saints arrival in the valley of the mountains. Very dull cloudy day. I washed and baked. Bro Badlam left for Sacramento. Henry Wilkins ate at dinner with us. Elder Lyman, Capt Hunt, and Badlam breakfasted with us. Mr. Crosby and Alma papering the Bedroom. Judge Stiles called today. Evening it playing the violin.

Wed 25th Ironed. Bro H Wilkins called again, brought me a nice boquet. Sat and conversed a while, informed me that bro J. M. Horner, family had gone over the bay to their ranch again. Bro Nathaniel B. Jones, missionary to the Indies returned from Sacramento, and called on us. I thought I should know him by his portrait which bro Fotheringham had left with us, but I could see little or no resemblance between them. I never had any acquaintance with him, but knew his wife very well. I asked him if he was any connexion of the Jones that married Rebecca Burton. He answered not nearly only happened to be the same ones I was pleased, and told him I knew his wife another sister.

Page of holograph (diary) 22 July 1854. Used by permission, Utah State Historical Society, all rights reserved.

publication and to prepare a typescript that would be useful to her, as well as to preserve them in an archive.

The Crosby journals were microfilmed by the Latter-day Saint Church Historian's Office, and a typewritten transcription was begun in 1957 under the direction of Dr. Ellsworth at Utah State University, Logan, Utah and completed several years later. Bound in four volumes, Mark A. Ellsworth eventually passed on the original set to co-editors Leo Lyman and Sue Payne. The holograph has remained for the last several years at the Utah State Historical Society in Salt Lake City, Utah.

The Editors

S. George Ellsworth spent years researching and writing on many aspects of the lives of Caroline Barnes Crosby, her sister Louisa, and the sister's husband, Addison Pratt. Knowing historical documents well, Professor Ellsworth viewed the Pratt-Crosby papers a most significant collection. After publishing the journals of Addison, and as he completed the editing of Louisa's journal, he and Maria commenced work on the Caroline Crosby journals. Professor Ellsworth had already performed a most important preliminary task of having the manuscript transcribed. An essential editorial contribution by both Professor Ellsworth and his wife Maria, was the extensive study and writing on the Pratts and Crosbys during their years in the Society Islands. In June 1996, the much-honored scholar informed friends he intended to become fully involved with its publication. However, within weeks, medical problems forced George to alter those plans. Although there were continued efforts on the Crosby journals, the subsequent deaths of both himself and his wife halted the project. The work of Professor Ellsworth was important and all those involved with later editing and publishing the Crosby manuscript desired that his name be included as one of the editors. Mark A. Ellsworth, after conferring with Leo Lyman and Sue Payne, expressed assurance that they had the interest and skill necessary to assume the important task commenced by his parents.

Leo Lyman, a longtime scholar of Mormon history, was initially mentored on that subject by Leonard J. Arrington and Thomas G. Alexander, making him a second-generation Ellsworth student. He had discovered the value of the diary in assisting him to recount various aspects of life at San Bernardino as he wrote a monograph on that subject. Throughout this process, Professor Ellsworth expressed warm support and, following completion of *San Bernardino: The Rise and Fall of a California Community*, he wrote a complimentary review of the book. He appreciated the treatment of the Pratt and Crosby families in the work and might well have approved of Dr. Lyman essentially inheriting the opportunity to see the Crosby journal project to fruition.

Sue Payne, a lifelong resident of California, who studied history at Dr. Ellsworth's alma mater, the University of California at Berkeley, was introduced to the Crosby diary while serving as a docent in the California Room at the Feldheym Public Library at San Bernardino. Sue's transcription of the San Bernardino years from the microfilmed holograph pages, independent of Ellsworth's work, gained the attention of some historians in Utah. Like Lyman, she fell in love with Caroline. Her recounting of incidents from the chronicler's life became important campfire and lecture features among historical groups. As an experienced editor, Sue enthusiastically tackled the "labor of love" of bringing these journals to eventual publication.

In preparing this volume, Leo and Sue have primarily studied scrupulously the handwritten manuscript, both in the original and on microfilm. The typewritten transcription has also been of invaluable assistance in interpreting the original documents.

Editorial Procedure

Our goal as editors has been to reproduce the diarist's handwritten pages with as few modifications as possible. Caroline, with her education and ease of expressing herself, has essentially produced a manuscript, which is notably readable. Any alterations between the written text and the printed page are done solely to facilitate the presentation of the manuscript.

It is not our intent to correct misspellings; occasionally we have inserted missing letters or completed words with brackets and in Roman type. Words—e.g., *valley* and *vally*—will be seen interchangeably; note especially *Tuesday* and *Teusday*. Some spellings—e.g., *verander*—give us a hint of her regional background. Variations in spelling of proper names and places are common, and we have added in brackets the current or most common spelling of a proper name when it initially appears, e.g. Br Hide [Hyde].

Italics are the editors'. Parenthetical explanations are bracketed and italicized, e.g. [*spelling unclear*]. Dates have been italicized to distinguish them from the body of the text. In addition, names of ships have been italicized.

Capitalization has been difficult to reproduce with certainty. Letters at the beginning of a sentence or phrase, especially *s*, and *r*, are often written in the lower case but are over-sized, while *w* and *m* often start a sentence with a flourish but are diminutive in size. Generally, we have interpreted these variations as capitals.

We have attempted to replicate Caroline's marks of punctuation as they visually appear. It is sometimes difficult to distinguish between a comma and a period in the manuscript, or if there is any punctuation mark at all. Usually, Caroline ends her sentences with a distinct period, particularly when writing in apparent comfort and not in haste—or in a moving wagon. Abbreviations are generally not punctuated.

We have converted apostrophes, which she writes as a firm stroke at the bottom of the line—e.g., *Mary,s river*—to the standard position. (An interesting note is her placement of the hyphen, which appears at the left-hand margin at the beginning of the second half of the word following the line break.) We have not closed any open parentheses.

We have retained Caroline's dashes, or ellipses, an expressive and constant feature of her handwriting. They commonly denote an incomplete word (e.g., *S—— L—— city* or *Mr C——*) and vary in length; we have reproduced them here with a standard-sized two-em dash.

Paragraphs are for the most part Caroline's. In the instances where her writing continues without breaks, we have done little to divide the unbroken text. Most daily entries have a morning and an evening component, which often begins on a new line. In the interest of conserving space, we have generally combined single-lined sentences or short entries into one paragraph.

Our intention as editors is to interrupt the reader as infrequently as possible. Thus, we have dispensed with [*sic*] to denote apparent "slips of the pen," e.g., *mysefl*. Nor have we added any text where words are missing, allowing our readers to interpret the document as written. Words repeated unintentionally—e.g., *the the*—have been silently omitted.

Multi-word phrases and sentences appearing as superscripts or squeezed between lines or along margins have been designated with carets. Superscripts of one or two words have been brought to the line. Partial words or phrases are often squeezed above the line and into the right-hand margin of the page to complete a sentence. These have also been brought to the line.

It was our original intention to omit crossed-out words and phrases, as the author obviously intended, but after due consideration, we realized that it was more enlightening to gain an insight into her own editing process.

Underlined text is presumably the author's. Occasionally, a date is underlined or duplicated in a margin or as a superscript, in a different-colored ink and in a notably shaky hand. These entries were undoubtedly made at a much later time than the original writing. We have included these underlines without comment and have bracketed the text and indicated it was added later.

As co-editor S. George Ellsworth stated so succinctly in his introduction to volume 3 of this series, *The History of Louisa Barnes Pratt*, the editorial policy overall has been guided by an attempt to present the author as she presented herself, with as much convenience as the printed page allows but as little interference as possible. That each reader might spend long sessions with the original notebooks might be preferable, but we trust this will prove to be a reliable and enjoyable second-best reading experience.

Introduction

Despite the existence of a vast, but until fairly recently, relatively untapped body of documentary material reflecting on the lives of mid-nineteenth century American women and their attitudes toward their lot, the editors know of no single source from the general period, including a favorite, Mary Boykin Chestnut of the South, which better accomplishes offering such insights than the one presented here. John Mack Faragher long ago noted the inherent problems in writing the history of the "inarticulate," meaning mainly the lower economic classes.[1] While Caroline Crosby was far less well-off financially than was typical even of the working class, she was certainly far from inarticulate. Thus, perhaps the greatest contribution of her journal is the rather rare, for her class, detailed word-picture of everyday life and thought this candid and impressively uncomplaining woman left, even though she was usually in the depths of poverty. As she and her husband understood, their circumstances were largely the result of frequent relocations brought about by their absolute faithfulness to their ecclesiastical leaders of the Church of Jesus Christ of Latter-day Saints. Caroline's observations of the church and its leaders, plus her commitment to them, present an invaluable commentary on the impact of this new American religion on its members. The Crosbys' willingness to sacrifice for the cause and to go obediently where directed, without reservation or complaint, on numerous occasions, makes this document an outstanding record of the fervency that powered the growth and development of nineteenth-century Mormonism. In fact, there are few documents which more fully illustrate total commitment to such a cause.

Through her personal recollections and diaries, a young schoolteacher emerges, marries a favored cousin, and becomes an early convert to Mormonism, one of many "sects" of the time, despised in its inception but destined to become a world religion. A compelling portrait of a dedicated wife and mother and resolute pioneer missionary companion unfolds as Caroline recounts her life experiences. Doubtless like most women of her day, Caroline fully embraced the values of the so-called "cult of true womanhood," piety, purity, domesticity, and submissiveness.

1

In contrast to her sister, Louisa Barnes Pratt, Caroline displayed no perceptible independence. In fact, another notable aspect of the chronicle of her life is the absolute harmony and commonality of purpose between her and her husband. As a historical reflection of American women of the time, the manuscript is important; as a personal narrative, interesting and engaging. Rarely does so appealing a woman come to life across the pages of her journals as does Caroline Barnes Crosby.

Essentially, the diarist and her husband cast their lot with one of the most unpopular religious movements of their time and their lives and experiences reflected absolute commitment thereto, despite many to whom they were close who concluded church membership was not worth the costs. From the time they moved to Kirtland, Ohio, to be at the center of the infant Church of Jesus Christ of Latter-day Saints, they obediently moved as the changing circumstances of that often-beleaguered church demanded and its leaders dictated. Caroline's experience with the church covers over a half-century of its initial, most eventful years as a religious movement, which also entailed geographic movement west and other journeys into various corners of the globe.

What most struck the editors about this woman was her equanimity in facing whatever circumstances arose. The only real complaint recognizable in the entire journal was Caroline's exasperation with the three-day dust storms then endemic in San Bernardino and what this did to her usually immaculately clean house. About these she confessed "It makes me feel rather impatient, but I try to bear it as easy as I can." At another time, when she was "somewhat inclined to murmur at [her] poverty and lack of enjoyments which many of [her] brothers and sisters [in the church-community] were blessed with," she took down a piece of verse previously selected on the theme, "It is All for the Best," and read and sang it several times. She thereafter recorded her "spirits became cheered and enlivened thereby." And when she and her husband became aware that through a market glut in gold rush California, the price of potatoes and grains they had grown were not worth the expense it had taken to produce them, literally wasting a year's efforts, she commented philosophically "it would not be wise for us to give way to dejection or suffer ourselves to be cast down on the account. We have had quite a struggle in refraining from it, and for myself I think I have nearly overcome it." She then revealed the key to her success in dealing with all such trials when she concluded "What the Lord has in store for us I know not, but I pray Him to give us strength to endure all things." Life to a committed Latter-day Saint was much a testing ground through which faith was to be developed. She added at that time, "where another year will find us I know not,"[2] but she and Jonathan were certain they would not be again engaged in farming.

Lillian Schlissel, in her extensive study of diaries of women involved in the westward movements, discussed the reluctance of many to engage in those journeys, primarily because of concerns over safety and survival.[3] While Caroline Crosby made at least three such treks, there is no evidence she apprehended them (other than hints of regret at leaving friends and loved ones behind). It might be too much to call her adventurous, but there are several evidences of quiet courage and many of an abundant measure of faith in Providence to oversee the lives of her and her family. Caroline's diary accounts of her pioneer travel, including the later account, to be published in the second volume of her writings, of her family's move from southern California to southern Utah in 1858, are among the most vivid and detailed in the period. There, her journal rises to the level of classic of its kind and purpose.

Equally valuable is Caroline's treatment of the inner workings of what was one of the most successful American communities (in the truest sense of the word community) in the nation during that era—San Bernardino, California. She documented the great degree of neighborliness there, most visible in the visiting back and forth between households, but also in such acts as sewing and quilting for others with little regard for remuneration. The network of compassionate care of the sick and dying (and dead)—quite clearly outside the realm of any church directives or assignments—is truly impressive. Others have documented the considerable amount of dancing, which was probably the most popular recreational social activity of the time, but few have noted as much of the related preoccupation with music, both vocal and instrumental, as the present journal does. Similarly, few, if any, others so fully detail community fruit and melon "feasts." These included a clear refusal to take money for commodities regarded as a community resource to be shared. Thus Caroline provided a truly rare glimpse into the exceptional atmosphere and attitude of that time and place. To a lesser degree, she likewise described social interaction and everyday life in most other places where she resided.

Born in Warwick, Massachusetts in 1807, Caroline Barnes grew to maturity in the "cold wilderness" of East Canada, where her father relocated his large family in hopes of better farming opportunities. In October 1834, at the relatively late age of twenty-seven, she married her first cousin, Jonathan Crosby, from Massachusetts. He had already joined a controversial new religious denomination which became the Church of Jesus Christ of Latter-day Saints. She soon followed the same course, establishing a set of goals and a lifestyle that the two embraced throughout their long lives together.

The Crosbys gathered to Kirtland, Ohio, the center of Mormondom at that time. En route to Ohio, they stopped with Caroline's sister, Louisa

Barnes Pratt, and her husband, Addison. While visiting, Jonathan and Caroline introduced the Pratts to Mormon doctrines, which they too subsequently accepted. Addison would become a successful missionary to Tahiti and important church leader. Louisa and her four daughters would remain an integral part of Caroline's most personal history throughout her lifetime.

At Kirtland, Ohio, the Crosbys met the founder of the church, Joseph Smith, to whom they would remain dedicated. Here Jonathan was ordained a Seventy in the Latter-day Saint (LDS) priesthood. Learning the carpenter trade, he helped construct the church's first temple. The family witnessed the painful disruption within the church when several affiliated businesses collapsed amidst the national economic panic of 1837.

Many church members then gravitated to Missouri, the new Mormon Zion, where they confronted even more bitter persecution and conflict, but the Crosbys and Pratts stopped midway on the National Highway in Indiana. There they farmed and manufactured furniture, maintaining homes that became havens for both local Latter-day Saints and prominent church leaders passing through, some of whom stopped with them overnight to preach in the vicinity.

The Crosbys moved on to Nauvoo, Illinois, in June 1842, after that city became the primary gathering place for the Latter-day Saints. Soon thereafter, Jonathan answered a call to serve a mission and headed east to preach, staying for more than a year. In the meantime, Caroline attended to their young son and taught school at her home. When her husband returned he was ill with smallpox. After a difficult recovery, Jonathan worked on the Nauvoo Temple. In late June 1844, Joseph Smith and his brother, Hyrum, were murdered while jailed at nearby Carthage. In subsequent years Caroline would recall regularly in her journal the anger and sadness that event brought.

Like many early reminiscent accounts of the time, Caroline's is often discreet and staid, protective of her privacy and that of her family. We must read "between the lines" to gain knowledge of the Crosbys' brief experience with polygamy. Caroline's diary alludes to their cousin, Amelia Stevens, coming to reside in the Crosby home in September 1845. It is clear from other sources that she became a plural wife of Jonathan during that time. Caroline only briefly mentions her husband later corresponding with the former wife (probably already voluntarily released from further marital obligations) after they moved from Illinois, where Amelia chose to remain, at Nauvoo, when many Mormons, including the Crosbys, subsequently moved west. That marriage quietly dissolved, and Amelia later remarried. Polygamy was not discussed openly during the Nauvoo period. However, on several occasions later in her life, Caroline

Crosby defended the principle of plural marriage with some fervency, certainly seeing nothing immoral in what she considered a commandment from God.

Because Jonathan was ill, the Crosbys remained in Nauvoo after most other Latter-day Saints had already moved out onto the prairies of Iowa. Caroline cursorily mentions the violence that then erupted as the city was abandoned. Her husband's own brief memoirs conveniently bridge a subsequent gap in his wife's account, including time spent attached to the "poor camp" gathered on the west side of the Mississippi River opposite Nauvoo.

Jonathan, Caroline, and their son, Alma, did not immediately travel with other church members all the way across Iowa to the Missouri River, but stopped on the Des Moines River at the village of Bentonsport. Jonathan obtained employment making furniture and doors as he acquired livestock essential for the subsequent journey west. The family moved on to Winter Quarters on the Missouri River in June 1848 and joined the church emigrant companies forming to cross the plains to Great Salt Lake Valley that summer. Brigham Young and many others had made the initial trek the previous season. The family traveled in the last company that second year, led by Amasa Lyman and Willard Richards, both general church leaders.

During the journey west, Caroline penned a detailed firsthand account of life in a wagon train. While many diaries focus on the geographic features encountered en route, Caroline's daily log provides valuable descriptions of the women's activities during the migration. She socializes and sightsees while walking with her friends. She washes in the soft water of the Loup River, bakes a mince pie, cares for a sick woman's children, carries a newborn calf on the trail, gets a fire to boil the teakettle.

Caroline concisely summarized the following year and a half at Salt Lake City. Even so, there are entries detailing social occasions such as Christmas, a wedding, schools, and something of the mud of winter. Jonathan again engaged in the furniture and cabinet business, prospering well by catering to the needs of emigrants heading for the gold fields that season. However, they were soon called to accompany missionaries being sent to the Tahitian mission previously opened with great success by Addison Pratt. This took them to the Pacific island of Tubuai in the Society Islands of French Polynesia in 1851.

Again with the intended move to Tahiti we encounter the recurrent theme of the lack of a permanent home that pervades these journals. Caroline strives not to complain, but we can feel her distress when "after labouring and toiling so long to get to a place where we could feel ourselves at home," once more she is directed "to take another and even more tedious journey . . . for the gospels sake."[4]

Caroline again takes up a daily log, documenting the journey from the Salt Lake Valley to the Pacific Coast during the high point of the Gold Rush, including interaction with non-Mormon travelers, often low on food supplies, and encounters with Native Americans. Descriptions of the desert around the Humboldt Sink and of the road through the Sierra Nevada Mountains are well recounted, as are her contacts with Mormon gold miners and church agents including Amasa Lyman, Charles C. Rich and Porter Rockwell. Surprisingly, the most difficult portion of the trip was what would seem the easiest, down the mosquito-ridden Sacramento River on a small sailing ship.

Proselytizing opportunities were few for a missionary wife, so Caroline determined "to write a brief Sketch" of her previous history. Her narrative skills are apparent from the start, and her voice is that of a formally-schooled lady of nineteenth-century New England working-class roots. She is articulate, and her vocabulary is extensive. Her sometimes ornate phrasing evokes patterns of fashionable gentility, evidence of the popular romantic style of the period. Some stiffness of expression is to be expected, but she clearly elucidates traditional values of sympathy, kindness, understanding and sensitivity. As opposed to her historical sketch, Caroline's daily journals are less formal and more reflective. Reading her day-to-day entries is akin to sharing a conversation with a close friend or family member. The daily weather becomes more relevant when we realize she is waiting for a chance to hang the wash out to dry. If several days of entries seem tedious, we sense her own ennui. Occasionally, personal angst and emotional outpourings jolt the rhythm of her narrative. For the most part, however, not only her expressive style but what she chooses to write reflect the conventional proprieties of her time.

During the two years spent in the Society Islands, Caroline described the people and places she encountered with memorable detail. She made the best of the totally unaccustomed but not unpleasant circumstances. This was in marked contrast to her more complaining sister, Louisa. Yet both women made significant contributions showing Polynesian women how to quilt and care for their children and homes according to American customs and standards, and while learning the Tahitian language, they sought to teach them concerning religious conduct and practice according to the fervor of that time period.

Separated from her husband for almost a year while he preached on neighboring islands, Caroline took a young mixed-blood girl into her home and her heart, and the eventual separation of the two exposed a longing in Caroline that would resurface often in the years to follow, evidenced by the number of children she was willing to take and raise (albeit temporarily) as her own. Caroline would have loved to have had another child.

The Society Island mission essentially disbanded when French officials were unwilling to cooperate with the LDS missionaries. Thus the jobless Crosbys headed back for California "to provide ourselves a home and the necessaries comforts of life, with nothing but our constitutions, (and as regards my own a wornout one) to depend upon."[5]

The approximately five hundred pages of diary which follow, detailing her half-dozen years in California, are unquestionably the most valuable contribution of Caroline's work. Her record of the three years' sojourn in the San Francisco Bay area, from September 1852 through November 1855, is a unique and comprehensive treatment of a crucial segment of the region's history. First residing east of the bay in the vicinity of present Fremont, California, she chronicles life among the founding Anglo-Americans, many of them Latter-day Saints who arrived in 1846 from the ship Brooklyn or who came overland with the Mormon Battalion. She details church activity, social interaction, schools, and some of the first agricultural enterprises in the newly admitted Golden State. Latter-day Saints and anyone interested in California history will find new material and perspectives of the lifestyle of this period.

Similarly, when the Crosbys move to San Francisco in January 1854, her diary entries prove to be some of the most vivid accounts known of everyday life in that burgeoning metropolis. Her interactions with other Mormon members of the infant church branch struggling for permanency offer intriguing insights. She befriends Eleanor McLean, victim of a husband's abuse and eventual wife of Parley Pratt. She enjoys the visits of Mrs. William Pickett (widow of Joseph Smith's brother Don Carlos) with her two daughters, Agnes and Josephine Smith (later the poetess Ina Coolbrith). She is a guest at Samuel Brannan's home in the high-fashioned Rincon Hill district, and she entertains such notables as Orson Hyde and George Q. Cannon. She travels into the city by omnibus, takes excursions to Lake Merced and to South Park, and frequently walks "over the mountains," relishing the scenery from the tops of the peaks on the Noe land grant. This document is precious as a source of study of San Francisco in its early years.

There may be no record that better traces the details of Horner's Addition, when one of the most prominent contemporary citizens of the region sought to subdivide the sand hills south of the city, adjacent to the present-day Mission district. Caroline's husband worked for John Horner and the two families resided for some time in the same house. Frequent references to his plans and ultimate failures capture one of the most significant early attempts to extend San Francisco into yet undeveloped sectors, some of which still retain the names Horner placed on them.

Disappointed in not receiving proper remuneration from the almost-bankrupt Horner, the Crosbys concluded to gather to the recently

Jonathan, son Alma, and Caroline Crosby with niece Frances Pratt, San Francisco 1855, from print of daguerreotype with shattered glass cover. Courtesy of Special Collections and Archives, Utah State University Libraries.

established Mormon colony of San Bernardino. They traveled by coastal steamer and freight wagon to the growing community some fifty miles from the coast, to what was not only the largest Mormon town outside of Utah but also the largest Anglo-American settlement in Southern California at the time.

Jonathan built the family a much-admired home, while also serving as a town handyman and finish carpenter. Caroline became deeply involved in assisting in the care of the sick and elderly in her extended neighborhood. Her effort to improve the unhappy living conditions of an alcoholic mother and her wayward children is especially poignant.

This diary is undoubtedly the best source available of the amazingly extensive amount of social interaction among the few Mormon plural wives and other town women. An average count would indicate Caroline called on or was visited by one or two persons a day for two years, recording a remarkable degree of neighborliness. Finally, she reports the growing amount of dissension in a community formerly noted for impressive harmony at a time when the Latter-day Saint church, facing increasing apostasy, instigated its own reformation on the populace.

They had just finished what was perhaps the most admired home in a town of three thousand inhabitants. Yet when the directive came to move to Utah, in keeping with the call of Brigham Young to have all faithful Saints gather to Zion during a time when the church was supposedly threatened by an approaching United States army, they traded the house for a wagon, a team of oxen, and a few provisions and moved out with no complaints.

The account of the difficult trek back to Utah is one of the best by any woman ever to travel over this southern route. Included is an extended stay at the abandoned Mormon Indian Mission fort at present Las Vegas, with unique descriptive details of the Native Americans and the lone missionary remaining among them, Benjamin Hulse. This significant subsequent period of Caroline's life is chronicled in the second volume of this work.

There are few, if any, women's diaries that recount such a long and varied breadth of experience among the Latter-day Saints in the early years of the church. In numerous instances, this diary looms as one of the most instructive sources available for Mormon and community social history in California and, later, southern Utah.

At no point after the move from Ohio were the Crosbys long at the center of Mormondom, although there were brief residencies at Nauvoo, Illinois and Salt Lake City, Utah Territory. Rather, just as Jonathan and Caroline established themselves in comfortable circumstances, they were directed by church leaders to move on. As mentioned, their situation when abandoning San Bernardino was the most vivid example. After San

Bernardino, they would never again reside in such comfortable circumstances, even though they both lived many more years in Beaver, Utah. The accounts of their seven or eight moves makes the title to this volume, *No Place to Call Home*, most appropriate.

This sincere and dedicated woman spans the generations with her gift of narration, imbued with dignity and expressive appeal. By entrusting her diaries to future readers, Caroline Barnes Crosby very fortunately has left a legacy of lifetime travels, observations, and experiences to share and to enjoy.

Family of Jonathan Crosby and Lois Barnes

Jonathan Crosby m. Lois Barnes
1778–1839   1776–1818
fa: Jonathan Crosby   fa: Abraham Barnes
mo: Esther Osgood   mo: Mary Stevens

- David Crosby m. Marial Thompson
  1805–1844   1808–1893
- Jonathan Crosby m. Caroline Barnes
  1807–1892   1807–1884
- Emily Crosby
  1814–1833
- Lois Crosby m. Harvey Thompson
  1818–   1810–

Alma Crosby m. Mary Kelly
1836–1897   1850–1925

Sources: Pedigree chart listing Temple Record and Family Bible of Jonathan and Alma Crosby. See also *Early Settlers of Rowley, Massachusetts*, compiled by George B. Blodgette, A.M. (Rowley: Amos E. Jewett, Publisher, 1933).

Family of Willard Barnes and Dolly Stevens

Willard Barnes m. Dolly Stevens
1766–1848   1771–1852
fa: Abraham Barnes   fa Joseph Stevens
mo: Mary Stevens   mo: Dolly Sawyer

Lavinah Barnes 1795–1879	Horace Barnes 1797–1878	Dolly Barnes 1799–1880	Cyprian Barnes 1800–1878	Louia Barnes 1802–1880	Lyman Barnes 1804–1884	Caroline Barnes 1807–1884	Lois Barnes 1809–1835	Catherine Barnes 1812–1838	Joseph Barnes 1814–
m. Stevens Baker	m. Lucretia Susan Cone	m. Walter Lockwood	m. Sarah Chadsey	m. Addison Pratt	m. Dolly Sikes	m. Jonathan Crosby			

Family of Addison Pratt and Louisa Barnes

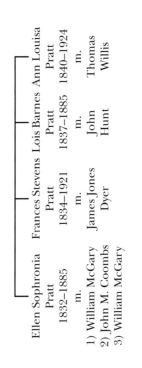

Ellen Sophronia Pratt 1832–1885	Frances Stevens Pratt 1834–1921	Lois Barnes Pratt 1837–1885	Ann Louisa Pratt 1840–1924
m. 1) William McGary 2) John M. Coombs 3) William McGary	m. James Jones Dyer	m. John Hunt	m. Thomas Willis

Sources: Family Register. LDS temple records, St. George, Utah. All Saints Anglican Church records, Dunham, Quebec, Canada.

Family of Joseph Stevens and Dolly Sawyer

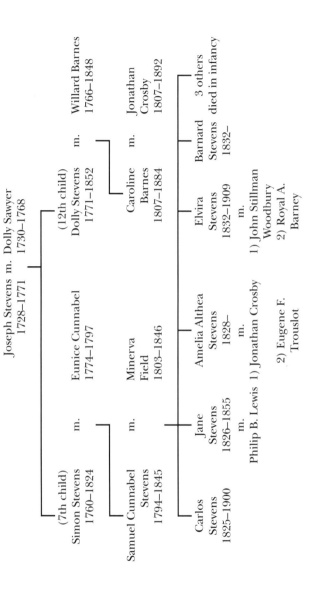

Joseph Stevens m. Dolly Sawyer
1728–1771   1730–1768

(7th child)
Simon Stevens
1760–1824

m.

Eunice Cunnabel
1774–1797

(12th child)
Dolly Stevens
1771–1852

m.

Willard Barnes
1766–1848

Samuel Cunnabel
Stevens
1794–1845

m.

Minerva
Field
1803–1846

Caroline
Barnes
1807–1884

m.

Jonathan
Crosby
1807–1892

Carlos
Stevens
1825–1900

Jane
Stevens
1826–1855
m.
Philip B. Lewis

Amelia Althea
Stevens
1828–
m.
1) Jonathan Crosby

2) Eugene F.
Trouslot

Elvira
Stevens
1832–1909
m.
1) John Stillman
Woodbury
2) Royal A.
Barney

Barnard
Stevens
1832–

3 others
died in infancy

Sources: The Stevens Genealogy, compiled by Dr. Elvira Stevens Barney (Salt Lake City: Skelton Publishing Co., 1907). Nauvoo temple records.

PART ONE

Beginning Life's Journey

Youth to Arrival in Salt Lake Valley
January 1807–May 1850

CHAPTER ONE

Youth to Marriage

Memoirs, 1807 to October 1834

[Memoirs Begun]

Island of Tubuai, Society group, South sea Islands *Jan 1851*

 Sometime has elapsed since I drew a determination to write a brief Sketch of my history. Being banished as it were to this retired island for the word of God and the testimony of Jesus Christ, And ~~also~~ in some device relieved from the cares which naturally arise from an association with civilised and enlightened society, I have thought that the improvement of my few leisure moments to this purpose might perhaps hereafter prove a source of satisfaction to myself at least.

[Move to Dunham, Canada]

I was born on *monday Jan the 5th AD 1807*, in the town of Warwick Franklin co Mass Where my parents resided after their marriage untill I was nearly 3 years and a half old, when they removed to East Canada. My father was in rather low circumstances, having set out in life with little more than a good constitution and a general knowledge of farming, which knowledge he found to be of little use to him on the barren soil of Warwick, and he came to the conclusion in compliance with an invitation received from a brother in law residing in Canada, to try his fortunes in that <u>then </u>cold wilderness part of the country. He had already arrived to his 44th year and had a family of 8 children; His friends however persuaded him to leave two of them with them, untill such times as he should find himself comfortably situated in his new home. They left Mass sometime in the month of June and arrived in Dunham ~~New~~ Lower Canada *July 4th 1810*, the distance being 230 miles. Instead of getting his land for little or nothing as many had done before him, he was persuaded to take a small farm with a

17

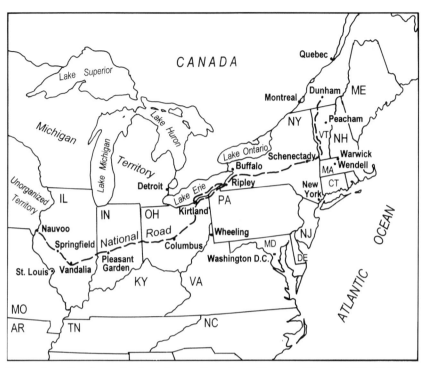

Route from Dunham, Quebec, Lower Canada, to Nauvoo, Illinois, 1835–1842.

little improvement, at a large price. Several cold seasons coming on immediately after his arrival to that country, in which he was unable to raise his
bread, his children also being small and unable to render him much assistance, the oldest son being only 13 years, he was necessarily reduced to
rather straightened circumstances, being a man unaccustomed to trade
or to accumulate property otherwise than by the sweat of his brow. I have
many times heard him speak of hoeing corn all day while the snow was
falling fast around him in the month of June. They used to plant a small
early sort of corn that would grow and ripen in 90 days.

The war of 1812 between Canada and the United States was also
one cause of provision being dear, and a source of misery to the poor
people. My father was one that was called away to guard the lines, where
he was taken prisoner and carried to Burtington [Burlington, Vermont]
but he was not detained long in consequence of his being afflicted with
rheumatism and meeting friends from his native state who assisted him in
gaining his liberty. I was then very young and have a faint recollection of
what happened, however I well remember that we all had sad hearts in his
absence and joyful ones on his return.

[Family]

My father was born in the town of Marlborough Mass near Boston ^in the [year] of our Lord 1777 [1766],^¹ he was the second son of Abraham ^and Polly^ Barnes ^formerly Polly Stevens,^ of that town, who was a man famed for honesty and piety. My grandfather had seven children, of whom my father was the third. What time he moved to Warwick I cannot tell, but I have heard it observed that his children all married in that town and settled so near him that he could ride to the farthest of them, in one hour; my father was the first, and only one, that moved any distance while their parents lived. And if I am not mistaken he and mother were both homesick for a number of years; as well as the oldest children. My mother was born in Petersham Worcester Co. Mass Nov 19th 1782.² She was the 15th child of Joseph and Dolly Stevens, formerly Dolly Sawyer. 10 of their children lived to be married, and had children, 6 sons and 4 daughters. My mother and grandmother Barnes were cousins, brothers children. Grandmother's father's name if I am not mistaken was Abraham Stevens, and her mother's maiden name Polly Martin. She (Grand) had a number of brothers, their names as near as I can recollect were as follows. Abram, Wilder, Gove and Nathaniel; she also had two sisters, one married a man by the name of Bass, the other Woods, who having deceased, she married Levi Benjamin. Grandfather Barnes had brothers, I am not however certain of any of their names but one, that was David, who was a Presbyterian priest 52 years in the town of Scituate, near Boston; he was considered a worthy man and a great preacher. I myself, have seen his sermons in print. One was an oration delivered on the death of Washington, whom he called the great man of the West, and compared him with Moses whom he considered the great man of the east.

My father had two brothers Samuel and Abram and 4 sisters, the eldest Polly, who married Cyrus Pomroy. The 2nd Lucy, married Joel Jennings, 3rd Lois married Jonathan Crosby³ 4th Catherine whose husband's name was Wm Burnet. Mothers brothers names were as follows, Lemuel, Gardner, Simon, Oliver, John, and Cyprian. The two last named died young men, but left families. A number that died in infancy their names I am not certain of, though I think one was a Simon, Thomas, and one daughter, by the name of Dolly I believe they died before the birth of my mother. Her sisters, the eldest Eunice, husbands name was Wing Spooner; the 2nd Damaris's, husband's name was Daniel Ward, 3rd Polly married Joseph Baker.

I will also mention that I think Grandfather Barnes' mothers name was Willard, and that my father received his name from her. The Barnes's originally were of Scotch descent; The Stevens's english.

My parents had 10 children, 4 sons, and 6 daughters. The eldest Levina married her cousin Stevens Baker. The 2nd a son named Horace wifes name Susan Cane [Cone], 3rd a daughter name Dolly, who married Walter Lockwood. 4th a son named Cyprian, wife's name Sarah Chadsey. 5th a daughter named Louisa married Addison Pratt[4] 6th a son named Lyman wife Dolly Sikes 7th myself Caroline, husbands name Jonathan Crosby. 8th Lois who died of consumption the 12th of April 1835, being 26 years and 1 day old. 9th Catherine who also died with the same disease Aug 3rd, 1838, 26 years the March previous. 10th Joseph Willard unmarried. The two last named were born in Ca—— the others in Warwick Mass.

Nothing occured in my fathers family, that I recollect, worth noticing, untill I was 10 or 11 years old. When my brother Lyman, who was two years older than myslf, had a feversore on his knee, with which he was afflicted about six months. He lost several pieces of bone, from his leg, and became much emaciated. However, through the attention of a skillfull physcian, ~~he was~~ and the blessing of God, he was restored to perfect soundness.

The winter that I was 12 years old, we were visited by a cousin from massachusetts by the name of William Ward, A very fine looking young man about 25 years of age. We were highly pleased with his ~~society~~ appearance, and had no doubts but that he would prove a blessing to his parents, and an ornament to society. But alas the inebriating cup proved his overthrow, and he died a premature death.

About a year after another cousin came to Canada from the south of Vermont, by the name of Simon Stevens. He was a middle aged man had a wife and several children, had been unsuccessful in business in his native state, came to try his fortune in cold canada. And a cold fortune he made of it. However he staid near ten years and moved to York state. He was an int[el]ligent kind hearted man, too conscientious and benevolent to accumulate property in that cold unfeeling country.

His wife also was one of the excellent of the earth, a pattern of piety and virtue. They were our nearest neighbours for 7 or 8 years. Their two oldest children were twins a son and daughter, 4 years younger than myself. We grew up togather, and were intimate companions, untill I was 25 years of age. The young man became noted for genius and learning, and delighted in making a display of his talents. The daughter was not inferior to him in either, but was endowed with that meekness which is in the sight of God, of great price. Cousin Simon taught school nearly all the time he staid in Canada. The winters that I was 14 and 15 I attended his school.

[Children Reunited]

I have forgotten to mention that the winter I was 8 years old, father went after his daughter and son whom he left behind when we moved to Can.

I well recollect the delight we all experienced at the time he set off with his horse and sleigh to go for them; and also the still greater delight on their arrival, although they had grown entirely beyond our recollection. ^He was gone six weeks^ Just before they came in sight of the house, my sister proposed to father to halt a little and let her go on alone, to take us by surprise; Accordingly he did so, but mother whose mind had been constantly upon her absent children for 5 years, knew her the moment she saw her, although she had grown from a small girl to be considerable taller than herself. I need not say that we had joy and rejoicing over them for a long time. And more especially on sisters account, as she had been homesick and quite discontented. I reccollect the sympathy my eldest sister felt for her when she heard from her lips the story of her discontent; and the offer she made her; which was that she should have the privilege of staying at home as long as she pleased; and if she wanted any article of clothing which father did [not] feel able to obtain for her, that she herself would willingly work for it.

[Activities in Dunham]

Sept 15th [1821] I think, was the dedication of Allsaints Church, in Dunham.[5] I was then in my 15th year. The same fall I believe, an old man by the name of Hubble died, was buried in the churchyard, and his body was stolen for dissection, the grave being left entirely open, the clothes and coffin ~~being~~ were scattered about in a most shameful manner, to the great mortification of his children, and friends. He was very aged and remarkble for piety.

The same fall[6] a young woman by the name of Polly Broomley died, she was 18 years old, 2 years and a half older than myself, we had lived nigh neighbors for several years, and were very intimate friends. I never mourned the loss of a companion more in my life. She was a lovely girl; gentle as a lamb. Soon after her death my sister Louisa went to Bakersfield [Vermont] to learn the tailoress trade, was gone 3 months. ^My second brother Cyprian also lived there the same winter.^ I was very lonely a greater part of the time.

January 1st 1823. I attended a new years ball at the tavern house in the centre of Dunham, kept by Mr Nath Stevens. I tried to enjoy myself as well as I could, but the church was near by, just in sight, where my young friend was buried, and the thoughts of her made me sad, in spite of all our diversions. We had a very agreeable company, my oldest brother Horace was one of the managers The same winter my mother and oldest brother went to Mass on a visit. Sister Dolly, now Mrs Lockwood, kept house in mothers absence. They were gone 6 weeks, had good sleighing all the time, and a very pleasant journey. They were highly pleased with their visit, had some presents made them by some of the friends. They also brought some to cousin Simon Stevens and family. Cousin S was confined to his house that winter, with a lame foot, occasined by a bad cut in chopping. The corner of the ax went entirely through his foot, and boot, leaving a gash 3 inches in length on the bottom of the boot. His circumstances were rather bad and feeling the need of a little assistance, and as his father was a wealthy Dr in the state of Vermont, he thought to excite a little pity from him, by sending his boot, as a witness of the wound he had received. The old man was very sorry for the accident, called him a poor unlucky fellow, but offered him no assistance. The spring following, another cousin, a connexion of my father, came to Canada peddling leather and stave bonnets. His name was Humfrey Stevens, A young man of 26. He staid about the vicinity untill the following fall when he returned and father accompanied him to visit the remainder of his connexion that were living many of them having deceased since he had been there. They were absent only 3 weeks. Humphrey returned and spent the winter in Can——, taught school about 8 miles from fathers. Sister Dolly was married that fall, and a cousin of ours, Mrs Guy died about the same time, leaving a family of 8 or 10 children to mourn her loss.

The winter of *1824* Edward Baker taught school in our district. I attended a short time, but was confined at home with sickness, a greater part of ~~the time~~ it. I went 12 miles to a new years ball, on Dunham east road ^that winter.^ My partners name was Robert Atkins. I was then 17 years old.

[Family Events]

In the same spring my oldest br Horace left home, and went with cousin Humphrey Stevens to Mass——. His leaving was a source of great grief to us all, and more especially to mother as she had expected him to stay at home and provide for her in her old age ^he being her choice in her sons.^ And father previously had made over his property to him. But some dissatisfaction arising between them H concluded to give up the writings and leave. He stoped in Mass untill the following fall and then accompanied cousin H S to N York state, Livingston county, where he resided a number of years and taught school, he also attended school one year, to qualify himself for teaching.

Louisa kept school in our schoolhouse that summer. I attended some. The younger girls went regularly and also Joseph the youngest br Levina's two sons Wm, and Charles B staid at fathers the most of the summer, and went to school.

Aug 14th Sister Lockwoods oldest son Frederick was born. I staid with her 3 weeks. She took cold, had a sore breast Mother took her home, and nursed her 6 weeks, she was under the Dr's care a good share of the time.

The next winter *1825* Joseph Baker, another cousin taught our school. I attended in co with my brs and sisters. We had a large school, several young ladies and gents attended. In the course of the winter some french musicians came along through the district, and put up at Mr Towners, near the schoolhouse. They also carried with them pictures, pupet dancers, &c, which they wished to exhibit. The young men and our teacher thought it a good time to have a dance. They accordingly obtained leave of Mr Towner, and had a fine party. At the same time the english missionaries were preaching in town, and proclaiming against dancing in the strongest terms. So that we were not without some remorse of conscience even while trying to enjoy our selves in so simple amusement.

The following season also sister Louisa taught the district school. And in the fall she accompanied Unkle and aunt Baker, and Mrs Simon Stevens to Mass——

About that time we all became quite seriously impressed with a sense of religion. I united myself to the church of Eng. My brs Cyprian and Lyman joined the Methodist church.

Sept 5th br C was married to Sarah Chadsey.

We had a fine infair [infare: wedding reception], but did not witness the marriage ceremony, as the parties went to the <u>priest</u> the previous evening and had it performed at his house, in consequence of his being unable to attend at her fathers.

I formed an acquaintance with and an attachment <u>to Lucy Chad</u>[sey] which I cultivated for several years, untill she married and left the place.

[Becoming a Teacher]

The winter of '25 *and 26* I attended the district school which was taught by ~~Heman Allen, a fine young man, and a Methodist exhorter~~ James Brown, son of Elaxander Brown esq. They had frequent prayer meetings at the schoolhouse. Br Cyprian brought his wife to fathers and kept her several weeks previous to their going to housekeeping.

Young Mr B paid considerable attention to us (myself and sisters) took us to his fathers on a visit, and brought his sister Catherine to visit us. I just commenced that winter to realize the importance of learning as I intended the next season or summer to offer myself as teacher. Accordingly the summer following I appplied and got the district school, which I taught 4 months.

1827 this winter Mr Fassett taught singing school, and his daughter <u>Minerva</u> taught a small day school in our neighborhood. I attended singing school, and was much pleased with it.

March 20th of this year David Lockwood was born. I staid with my sister several weeks. They lived in a house belonging to Mr David Ricard, an old bachelor, who lived with them. In May of the same year br C——s oldest daughter Levina was born. In the course of the summer following they br Lockwoods moved to live with Mrs Towner, her husband having died the winter previous.

The winter of *1827 and 8* our school was taught by Heman Allen, a fine young man, and Methodist exhorter. We had a very good school, and frequent meetings at the schoolhouse. I boarded with my sister Lockwood, and went from there to school. In the spring the widow Towner died. I was still staying with my sister, and staid for some time after.

Sister Lois had a run of fever this spring.

Immediately after the death of Mr[s] Towner her heirs came on to settle the estate, and my sister had the notary public Esq Leland and his son to board. In the meantime I became disgusted with the conduct of the old Esq towards me, and left my sister to get another girl. This summer cousin Eliza Baker was very sick, came near dying. I staid one week with her. At the turn of the disease we all thought she was dying, she bid us all farewell; and we wept bitterly thinking we were soon to be deprived of her society. But toward morning she revived, and called for food, which the Dr ordered to be given her, saying it was death hunger. But she continued to improve from that time onward, and recovered her health.

Winter of *'28 and 9* I did not attend school, except singing school, which was kept by Mr Fassette. I went once or twice to the north part of Dunham with himself, and son, and daughters; where he had a large school in a public schoolhouse. We had a fine sleighride of it, and returned, much pleased with the excursion.

We were on terms of intimacy for many years, and my heart now yearns over those friends of my early youth. Would to God it were in my power to bless <u>them</u>, for their love and friendship to <u>me</u>.

[Teaching School]

The next spring I went to stay awhile with my sister Levina, thought perhaps I should spend the summer with her but when I had been there 6 weeks, I had a call to teach a school in the west part of Dunham, which I engaged, and left. Commenced the second day of July 1829. I continued five months, when the roads became very bad, and I was tired of the school. My sister Louisa returned from Mass and wished me to sew with her as she intended opening a shop. Accordingly I engaged a young man by the name of Nathaniel Chadsey to take my place. I boarded near the schoolhouse, at my br Cyprians. I left about Chris[t]m[as] and went to sew with Louisa. We had a room and boarded at Hiram Larkins, his wife was a cousin of ours. They had been latly married. We enjoyed ourselves finely. Toward spring she returned to fathers where we continued tailoring through the winter.

1830 New years I attended a baptist quarterly meeting at the baptist meeting house, St Armand N J Sears was my escort, there were quite a co of us, we went to the hotel and took dinner, had a pleasant ride home. Sears taught the winter school that I kept in the summer previous. This summer of 1830 I taught school at Bachelors, north part of Dun—— 6 miles from the Methodist chapel commenced the 24th of April, kept 6 months. I enjoyed myself well, was pleased with the children generally, made a good many new acquaintances. Visited my young friend Lucy Chadsey who was teaching at Ellisen's neighborhood. I generally boarded among my schollars, but made my home at Bachelors tavern. Where there were a number of young girls; a widower and widow had married and brought their families together. Soon after I closed my school in the fall, cousin David B Crosby[7] came to Canada, from Mass—— staid at father's through the winter. Lyman was married this fall. ^Soon after I commenced my school Mrs B's daughter Juliann was married to a young man by the name of Jathem Austin who was living in her family. They removed to Broome township, I visited them in co with Rebecca Bachelor soon after they went to housekeeping, found them pleasantly situated and enjoyed a fine visit.^

[Sister Louisa's Marriage to Addison Pratt, April 3, 1831]

1831 Sister Louisa also lived at home that winter. There were a large family of us, and we had some lively times several fine visiting parties. I sewed with sis L—— 3 months, but as my health became poor, mother thought I better give it up and accordingly Lois my younger sister undertook to sew with her. She sewed untill Louisa was married, which occured on the *3rd of April*, and one week after she left with her husband Addison Pratt for the west part of York state, she lived six months in Buffalo, and then removed to Ripley Chatauqua Co where br P bought land in co with my br Horace Barnes.

[Agreeable Acquaintances]

My health was very poor at the time sis L was married and had been so all the winter previous occasioned by taking a cold in the fall, going to singing school in a cold house. The school was held in the church. I frequently walked two miles on the frozen ground, and sung untill 9 oclock and walked home again, so anxious was I to attend the school.

Shortly after sister Louisa was married I took a school in churchville Dunham northpart, where our church of England minister resided. I had a large school and my health being poor at the commencement I several times almost decided on giving it up, But after worrying along with it 3 months, my health began to improve, and at the close of six months the term I engaged for I was in usual health. I made my home at Kathans, and Capt Churches, but boarded among the schollars. I enjoyed myself finely in that place, formed some very agreeable acquaintances. Among whom was a young lady from Vt. by the name of M M Westgate, who was teaching school in Farnham, an adjoining town. She was a highly accomplished an intelligent young lady, had been raised and educated in Saratoga, by a wealthy unkle, who had unfortunately lost his property and became a bankrupt, which cast her upon the world to seek a fortune for herself. We corresponded and visited each other considerably, untill she married and left the province. I also became acquainted with a Miss Wood, daughter Esq Wood of Farnham, who was a fine amiable young lady. Mr Kathan had several daughters and sons who were interesting society. In about two weeks after I left the place Capt Jos Church took sick and died very suddenly. I received a letter from his wife soon after requesting me to come to her and sympathize with her, as she was almost inconsolable. I however did not go untill the next winter, when priest [Charles Caleb] Cotton sent his son Charles after me with a horse and sleigh, requesting me to come and spend a week with them, and attend to some business respecting the school money, which was to be received from the government. I went with him, he was then a young man only 16 years of age, but very forward and self sufficient. I enjoyed a visit among my new acquaintances and returned.

[Visiting Cousins]

1832 shortly after this visit I accompanied my cousins Levi Roany and Simeon Sikes to Stukely Bremton [Brompton] and Durham to visit the cousin Steven's. I was gone 4 weeks when I returned with cousin Lemuel Sikes, who was married and lived in Bremton but the company that went with me, all staid among their friends several weeks longer. ^Sister Lois kept school at Fordice's a few miles below me. She taught 3 months and tired of the school, but Catherine went and took her place. Cousin David C visited me and took me to see Catherine. She was boarding at John Riters.^ I had a fine ride, a nice pleasure sleigh covered and cushioned. The first night we staid at Stukely with cous. Artemas Stevens. Oldest son of my mothers oldest brother Lemuel Stevens. They lived in a large new house. As soon as his wife saw us she commenced crying as it brought to mind the death of her oldest son Simon who died a year previous. Soon after we arrived, we were informed that a party were soon expected to assemble there for a ball, as cousin Stevens had a large hall in his chamber which he rented for such purposes. I was then so very superstitious that I considered it almost a sin to go into a ballroom, but as rest of my company desired to go up I concluded to accompany them and sit a few minutes. We admired their dress and manners. Cousin Nathaniel Stevens was one of the managers, and afterward married the young lady that he waited upon to the ball.

We travelled several days by the side of the St Francis river which was then frozen so that we crossed it on the ice once or twice, going and coming. We staid only one night at a public house and the next arrived at cousin Gardner Steven's where we found a family of girls, who were second cousins to me, but first to the Sike's. Lemuel S—— had married the oldest daughter Amanda. The country was new and very hilly, besides the weather being very cold, I almost thought I had paid dear for the whistle but for the most part enjoyed myself very well. We went to Durham to see cousin Simon S—— who lived with my father a number of years after the death of his mother, which occured when he was 14 years of age but previous to my recollection. They had two daughters much younger than me. I admired the place and family very much. We visited cousin Thomas Stevens who lived in Brempton. Their oldest son's name was Cyprian, and a fine looking fellow. He afterwards visited us in Dunham, and was considerably admired by his friends in that place. Cousin Gardner Stevens afterwards moved his family to Ohio Trumble county, where he visited us in Kirtland.

[Sister Lois Barnes's Move to Ripley, New York]

This winter sister Lois lived with sister D Lockwood and attended school at Lavery schoolhouse. Cousin Dana Stevens taught. In the spring I think about the *first of May* she went to Yorkstate to live with sister Pratt. She had promised sis P—— before she left home that she would come in one year. Father was quite opposed to her going but as she was decided in so doing he finally consented and carried her to St Albans where she took a steamboat to Albany and from thence to Buffalo on the canal, and took a steamer to Dunkirk, which was only 5 miles from Ripley where br P's lived. We all felt very sorrowful after her departure, but she tried to keep her spirits up, altho I saw as I followed her to the carriage that the tears were in her eyes, and her tongue almost refused utterance. Mother comforted herself with the idea that she was going to live with an older sister, and brother who would be to her as father and mother. Little thinking that she would never see her again in this life. When she left St Ableans she fell in company with a very good family who were moving to that part of York state, and went as one of them which was a great gratification to her, as she was naturally very diffident among strangers, and felt the need of a guardian. We received a letter in a month or two stating that she had arrived in safty and in good health. Our hearts were then at rest, altho we missed her society, we felt willing make the sacrifice for Louisa's sake as she complained so much of being lonesome and homesick. Mother now had only two daughters at home and one son, sister Catherine had poor health, and as I had been absent the two previous summers she thought I had better stop home and assist her with the work, to which I willingly consented. We milked 5 cows, made butter and cheese for sale, besides doing a great deal of spining and weaving.

[Cholera in Lower Canada]

This summer the cholera raged very furiously in Montreal and other places, some two or 3 cases in our town, one young man by the name of Jerome Kingsbury of our acquaintance died with it.

Our good Methodist preachers were untiring in their exhortations to us, to prepare ourselves for sudden death, as the Judgements of God were abroad in the earth, and the inhabitants thereof, ought to learn wisdom. I was many times almost afraid to sleep at night fearing I might be suddenly seized with it. Weekly reports were 60 and sometimes more in Mont. but it raged only a short time. The cool weather coming on, it disappeared. The gov of L——— C [Lower Canada] then issued a proclamation for a day of thanksgiving to Almighty God for removing that fatal disease from among the people.

[Meeting Jonathan Crosby, 1832]

In Oct of this year Jonathan Crosby, my husband came to Can——— to visit his br David who had then been there 2 years. He spent one month in visiting his friends, took some very pleasant rides, one I recollect to cousin Simon Stevens, they then lived on Mr Bachelors farm at the north part of Dunham. Lucy taught school there. Br and sis Lockwood went with us. We formed our intimacy while he was there, which finally resulted in our marriage. The next winter br David Crosby went home to Mass. Father let him his horse and sleigh. He was gone about one month. While he was there his sister Emily took cold, which terminated in consumption, and she died the next June 1833.

This summer I taught school in St Armand, in what was called the Lavery schoolhouse. I enjoyed myself very well. Cyprian lived about one mile from where I kept. Two of his children attended school. I made my home at Thomas Reynolds, and E——— Dunings. I taught 4 months the school was small, in consequence of the people living scattered. David C called down to see me and brought me a letter from Jon——— which informed me of the death of cousin Emily.

Towards the close of my school one of my schollars died very suddenly with scarlet fever, her name was Elizabeth Duning, she was seven years old.

[Visit from Louisa]

Louisa Pratt came home from the western N Y, brought her oldest daughter E S P [Ellen Sophronia Pratt], spent 3 months. I closed my school, went home and staid one week in the time. She and Levina came to visit me at br Cyp. I was boarding at Mr H Bakers. They called for me, and took me with them to brs——. Augusta Johnson taught in fathers district that summer. I formed some acquaintance with her, found her quite agreeable. Louisa left in Sept for her home in N Y state. It seemed very hard to part with them. We had all become much attached to Ellen and especially her grandfather Barnes. He named her the queen of N York. Whenever he inquired after her afterwards, would say "How does the queen do".

[A Disappointed Suitor]

This fall we became acquainted with a young man by the name of M S Drury, a cousin of Mrs Meiggs, one of our neighbors. We prized his society very much, as an acquaintance and an associate. He was a member of the methodist church a fine young man. He escorted me to singing schools and frequently accompanied Catherine and I to prayermeetings.

We believed he intended to form an intimacy with one of us, but he never decided which he prefered untill, after I my marriage was published. He then talked to me with tears in his eyes for deceiving him. I told him that he never had asked me whether I was engaged, and I had had no occasion to tell him, and finally he acknowledged himself all the one to be blamed.

1834 This winter our school was taught by a young man whose name was Phillips, a son of Dr Phillips. My youngest sr attended.

In the course of the winter Miss A Johnson came to visit us and spent a week. We attended prayer meetings, singing schools and spelling sch and enjoyed ourselves quite well. The next spring she beame the mother of a son, but was deserted by a falsehearted lover, and left to the mercy of strangers. Sister Dolly Lockwoods daughter Ellen was born in *March '34*. The next summer I taught school in father's district, 4 months.

In the course of the season Sylvester Ricard came down from U[pper] Can, called at my schoolhouse several times. I always esteemed him as a virtuous honest young man, but some were suspitieus that his visit to the Province was not altogether on honorable principles, as he was known to associate with a company of counterfeiters. He returned to U

C in the fall. My school closed the last of Aug, and I went to weaving for mother.

[Marriage to Jonathan Crosby, October 26, 1834]

About the *1st of oct* Jonathan Crosby arrived from Mass. We had been corresponding then two ~~long~~ years, and <u>long</u> years they seemed to us, as our hearts were united in the strongest union, altho we had not seen each others faces, but had read each others hearts in many a welcome letter. In less than a month after his arrival we were married. *Nov 3rd* we set off for his fathers in Wendell Mass We were married Oct 26th. There was a very little snow fell during the day, but upon the whole it was tolerably pleasant. Our minister of the church of england Mr Cotten performed the ceremony. My oldest sister and husband were bridesman and maid, and everything passed off very well. I was happy in many respects, knowing that I had married a man who loved me, and would do all that he could to promote my happiness. The idea of parting with my near and dear relatives would sometimes distress me, but it did not mean that I was going among strangers, as it was near my native place, and I had still many relatives living there. The distance was only 230 miles, could easily be performed in one week. Levina told me if I was homesick I should write her and she would come and bring me back. My friends shed many tears when I left, sister Catherine wept aloud, and refused to be comforted, mother also. Br David C was married about one month previous in Peacham Vt, his wife was still there with her mother.[8] Accordingly he accompanied us to that place, where we made a short stop, took dinner and proceeded on our journey.

CHAPTER TWO

Conversion, Baptism to Arrival in Kirtland, Ohio

Memoirs, November 1834 to January 1836

[A Strange and New Religion]

My husband had been a member of the Church of Jesus Christ of Latterday saints one year previous to our marriage. His religion was strange and new to us, and some of our friends seemed to feel very sorry that I had fallen in with such a society of people. Some said they would rather bury me if I were their daughter. Others told strange stories of Jo Smith walking on water &C. But they all seemed like idle tales to me, as I was disposed to listen to my husband and believe what he said concerning the doctrine and characters of the people. I could find no fault with the doctrines he taught knowing they were purely scriptural, yet I felt sorry that he should take so decided a stand against other sects of Christians. At the same time my conscience told me that there must be a wrong somewhere in modern christianity, and possibly he might be right in trying to expose that wrong.[1] We travelled in an open carriage, with two horses one before the other. The weather was very pleasant and warm for the season, no rain in the course of the week.

[The Crosby Family]

We enjoyed the journey finely, reached his fathers in the course of the evening *Sat—— night the 10th of Nov 1834*. His father and stepmother were sitting alone by the fire. Sister Lois had gone to bed. It looked rather lonely to me to see so small a family in a large house, it being so different from my own fathers family and house. I did not see sister Lois untill the next morning when we introduced ourselves to each other, by saying we supposed that we were new sisters, or something of that nature. My

31

husband was not very ceremonius on the occasion. But we soon became familiarly acquainted, and much attached to each other. It was the sabbath, but as I had been travelling every day through the week my husband thought I had better rest at home. Accordingly he went to meet his little society over whom he then presided.[2] His father and mother went to their church, which was the orthodox. Lois and I were left at home alone, we had a very sociable time, and were no longer strangers after that day. Altho there was some difference in our ages, yet she seemed like a sister indeed. [Lois was 16, Caroline 27.]

She soon learned me to braid palm leaf hats, which was then quite a profitable employment. Shortly after my arrival, we were visited by an elderly gentleman from Vt, by the name of King, who was a elder of the church of Jesus Christ of Latter day Saints. He put up at father Crosby's, and staid some 3 or 4 weeks in the neighborhood, held frequent meetings, had formerly been a methodist preacher. I was soon convinced of the truth of his doctrine, but considered it best to read the book of mormon, and search the scriptures untill I was thoroughly convinced that it was the work of the Lord.

Christmas day I well recollect it was rather a gloomy day to me, Being removed from all my former associations. Notwithstanding I had discovered that they were in darkness, and error, yet it seemed that I almost regreted leaving my prison, so firmly were my feelings rooted to it. Reflecting that they were still together enjoying themselves as usually, and how many years I had been with them in their worship, but now in all probablility I should never meet with them again. These were the train of my refletions, as I silently looked abroad and saw the snow falling in profusion around, and whitening the ground ready for the sleighs, and bells. My husband had promised me, and also my mother, that he would take me to my old church, the episcopal, or church of england, if I desired it. And therefore proffered his services on Christmas day, if I chose to go. But I knew I should not see my old friends, and associates at Greenfield Mass if I went, and as the weather was stormy we gave it up.

[Baptism]

About the *1st of Jan 1835* came elder [*blank space*] Bent and his wife to visit their friends in Wendall, from Michigan, where they had resided for many years. They had recently joined the church, and were now on a preaching and visiting tour to their old native state. Br Bent had two sisters living in Wendell, one of them was his wife's stepmother Mrs Kilbourne her husband was the orthodox preacher in W—— for many years previous to his death. Shortly after elder Bent came I was baptised *Sunday morn the 18th of*

Jan 1835. The ground was frozen and partly covered with ice and the ice was very plenty in the creek where I was baptised. But my heart rejoiced in the Lord, and I went forward with good courage.

Sister Lois wished to be baptised with me, but her father objected to it on account of her poor health, as he said then, but afterwards he utterly refused her on any consideration, and she said she would wait until she was of age to act for herself, and then do as she pleased, which she accordingly did. We had some very interesting meetings, and visits, as br and sister Bent were both good singers, and old associate of father and mother Crosby's. Altho they would not believe their faith or receive their testimony yet they treated them with much respect on account of their youthful associations. One of my husbands cousins had married a nephew of father Bents. His name was Wm Bent his wife was Lucinda Armstrong. We visited them in co with br and sister Bent. Lois also accompanied us, and we had a very fine visit.

[Gathering in Kirtland]

The next spring the members of the church began to talk of gathering to Kirt[land] Ohio. Br Bent left for that place, and from thence proceeded to Missouri. I did not feel much of the spirit of gathering untill after they left and I found we had lost a great help in them. The day before they left br Jason Ballad was baptised, also his mother and aunt. We all felt very severely the loss of their society. The church was reorganized, and now was in quite a flourishing condition. Several elders called in the course of the season, among whom was Haslow Redfield from Vt He called himself a pedlar of Kanklin salve, Said he had heard there were mormons in that vicinity and wished very much to see them, and attend their meetings. Asked me if they were hospitable people and would keep a person at night without pay, as he had very little money, and was on a journey to Conn. I assured him they would. He then commenced questioning me with regard to their faith, whether they believed in the bible, and what they were gathering togather for. All of which questions I answered to the best of my ability, thinking him a stranger to the work. Shortly after he went to the field where the men were at work, and commenced in the same way with my husband, but he soon discovered his policy, which was merely to find out whether we were strong in the faith. He told me afterwards to go on, that I should make a good preacher. He baptised several persons, and we were all very well pleased with him.

Bishop Partridge and elder Isaac Morley[3] also visited the branch in the course of the summer. Our meetings were held the most of the time at the house of br Joel Drury, as he was a cripple at that time, and it was difficult for him to get out from home. He had been afflicted for years, and although he always seemed strong in the faith, yet he was not healed, which proved a great stumbling block to many unbelievers.

[Visiting Family in Massachusetts]

I formed a number of very interesting acquaintances while I lived in Mass—— which was only one year. We visited many of our friends. Unkle Abram Barnes and family Uncle seemed very much like father, he had a cancer on his face which was afterwards the cause of his death. His wife was sick in bed had then been confined a number of years. I liked the appearance of their sons and daughters, two of each were at home. Their sons names were I think Wm, and Aaron, the daughters Phebe and Mary, who were the 2 eldest chidren; the third daughter Clarissa was married, I did not see her. The youngest Louisa died a short time before.

We also called on a Mr Henry of Gill, his wife was a cousin of mine formerly Eliza Stevens, eldest daughter of Dr Simon Stevens of Guilford Vt. We took dinner with them, and proceeded on our way home. I accompanied my husband to Templeton to visit an aunt of his, sister of his fathers, her husbands name was Jennisen.

On our way we called to see aunt Spooner, mothers oldest sister she was then 76 years old. I think she was the oldest looking person I ever saw. She appeared very childish and broken. Was much pleased to see me, although she could not recollect my parents for sometime. She said she could not remember that she ever had a sister Dolly, but when I told her who she married she then said "O yes, I used to be well acquainted with them when they lived in Warwick". She took both of my hands in hers and drew me close to her, saying " I should know you was some of my relation, you look so natural." Her son and family invited us to stay and make them a visit, but we declined, being in some hurry to proceed to Templeton. We stoped only one night. I was much pleased with aunt Jennisen and her eldest daughter, who was married and lived with her husband at her fathers. We returned home through Athel, had a very pleasant ride. We also visited Irving, and Warwick my native town. Staid one night at uncle Burnet's, and one at Mr Lesure's, I think we spent the sabbath, and went to the church where my father and mother used to belong.

Uncle and aunt Burnet treated us with much kindness and affection their children were all absent from home. Aunt seemed very near, and reminded me of aunt Baker. After church we went to aunt Jenings, where we had another good visit. Aunt seemed so much like father I think I should have judged her to have been his sister. We had a very pleasant visit there. Her son Samuel, and daughter Lucy lived with her, the former was married and had one child, the latter single, near my age.

After we left there, we called on several of unkle Samuel Barnes family, found them in rather low circumstances, but seemed pleased to see us, and invited us to stay which we declined doing, as we wished to reach home that night. We went in sight of my fathers old place, where I was born, but did not pass near it. I had no recollection of anything I saw. We arrived at Irving near 12 oclock. Called at Mr Clapps, Mrs C was formerly cousin Emily Burnet. We met a cordial reception there, and were treated with much politeness. Mr Crosby and Clapp, soon got upon a religious discussion which as they were determined to disagree was anything but interesting to me. I admired Mrs Clapp very much. She was really a nice pleasant woman. Her youngest brother Abram Burnet was living with them tending store. They occupied a very large house, and had previously kept boarders. They had never had any children

Mr C[lapp] was very fleshy then, but soon after was taken sick, and lingered for several years. He also became a bankrupt, and his wife was obliged to work very hard for their suppport. So we were satisfied that his rejecting the gospel was not a blessing to him. But I think he was not a persecutor. We there met a Mrs Gage and her daughter. The former was the eldest daughter of unkle Samuel Barnes. We formed an agreeable acquaintance with them altho very short, for I never saw any of them afterwards. Soon after that visit we began to make arrangements to move to Ohio. It really seemed a great undertaking to me, but I had become so homesick that I could not think of staying there another winter. We therefore decided on leaving the *first of Nov 1835*.

[Moving to Ohio]

When my husband first broke the subject to his father, he seemed very much distressed, and used all the persuasion he was master of, to induce him to stay, but all in vain; we had set our faces as a flint Zionward and were ready to forsake all to gain that port.

When he saw that we were determined to go, he did what he could to help us away. We bid farewell to the brethren and sisters who wept freely and mourned our departure, but not as those without hope for they intended many of them to join us again at some of the gathering places of the church before many years if it was the Lords will.

Poor old grandmother Crosby felt very bad, and was rather inclined to blame me on account of Jonathans leaving, as he was all the son his father had with him, David the eldest having been away for several years. But sister Lois plead my cause, or spoke in my behalf to <u>her</u>, and aunt <u>Lucinda</u>, who was a little <u>cripple</u>, that had lived with her mother, untill she was then near 50 years of age. Father Crosby had had the care of them. They had a house and farm of their own near by his.

My husband sold what little stock he had, fixed his buggy in order for travelling with a cover to it, and *Nov 2nd 1835* we set off toward Canada. Lois wept bitterly when we parted with her, but there was not that deep heartfelt sorrow which her father expressed. I shall never forget how he looked. A solemn deathlike paleness pervaded his countenance and rendered him almost speechless. Alas, poor man, he had rejected the call of the gospel, and hardened his heart in unbelief, and where now could he look for comfort in such a time of trial. He merely shook us by the hand with[out] uttering a word. I surely felt to sorrow for the friends we left behind, but we had much the advantage of them, for we had the consolations of the holy spirit, and the fond anticipation of meeting with the saints of God in a far off pleasant land. We bent our course toward Canada as I was not willing to go west untill I bid them farewell at home.

[Farewell Visit to Canada]

We had been informed that there were some few brethren in Vt, and decided on visiting them on our way. Accordingly we proceeded to Brattleboro and Bennington, called in Shaftsbury on a family by the name of Bowin the man was a member of the church but was absent. And his wife was a bitter enemy to the cause, and did not ask us to stop, or treat us with common civility, consequently we went on our way, having ascertained that the other brethren were some distance from our road, and we had not time to search them out, as it was late in the season, and we had a long journey before us. We left our goods, or the greater part of our loading, at a public house in Arlington, near the church. It was a very pleasant town, and a pretty church. We intended to be there again in two weeks, as we were merely going to Canada to say goodbye to our friends, and bear our testimony to them of the truth of the gospel as restored to us in the last days. We found the roads rather muddy in some places, and did not reach fathers untill 12 oclock in the night saturday ~~Saturday~~ I went into Catherines sleeping room. She and Malvina were alone, as I opened the door she awoke. I said <u>Catherine</u>, she answered "is it you Caroline" I assured her it was. She soon spoke of our dear sister Lois who had died far from home, since I left her. I told her I was faint and weary, and did not wish to converse about her then. By this time the family was all aroused, and soon dressed, I had been absent one year, and had returned to bid them a <u>long</u> <u>long</u> <u>farewell</u>. We spent a week very agreeably with them. Conversed much upon the subject of our religion, found some of them very hard hearted, while others and especially mother was much inclined to listen to our arguments. Sister Lockwood was also quite favorably inclind. I had the second trial of parting with them Mother and Catherine wept as before, but I told them it was unnecessary as I thought perhaps I might return in another year as I had then. The zeal and love for the cause in which I was engaged supported me beyond everything, and I only felt to mourn for them because they had not the same consolation that I had. My two youngest brs Joseph and Lyman accompanied us to Franklin Vt on business, where we parted with them, and pursued our course back to Arlington, reloaded our goods and bent our way westward into Yorkstate.[4]

[Traveling to Ripley, New York]

I think we had some rain the first night we staid in Y St and night coming upon us suddenly we called at a private house and were made welcome to stay. They were people from Jersey, and very good farmers, they had a plenty of apples and hicory nuts. The family consisted of the man and his wife and one son, a young man some 25 or 6 years of age. The old gent was a baptist by profession, and he and Mr C soon got quite engaged on the subject of religion, which the young man did not take much interest in, and he got out his fiddle and commenced sawing on it, in order to turn the subject. It had the desired effect, for Mr C soon got hold of it, and played the accompaniment to several hymns, while the young gent and I sang. They all seemed much diverted, and appeared to enjoy our accidental call, as though we ~~were~~ ^had been^ old acquaintances. The young man took us to his room to lodge, which was very nicely furnished, and carpeted in style, made us welcome to the best the house afforded, and the next morning would accept no money, excepting for horsefeed, which my husband bought of them. After we got into our carriage he came with a panful of hickory nuts and turned them into the bottom for us to eat. Also gave us some very nice apples, and I carried some to Ripley. The snow commenced falling when we got to the hudson river, and the ground was frozen. We had some idea of going on board the canal had we reached it in season, but it froze up and was stoped when we reached Schenectudy, consequently we were obliged to proceed on at a slow rate. In Casenovia we lost our way, and a hard storm of snow and hail ^coming upon us^ we were again compelled to call at a private house. It was Sat night. They had formerly kept a public house, and very willingly took us in, and kept us over Sunday.

The mans name was Farnham. The lady told us that she had a br among the mormons, but I do not recollect his name. She had a son who was a cripple, had two crooked feet, could not walk at all, but rolled himself about the house in a little carriage, he was very intelligent and interesting. They also had a large family of girls. I admired the lady much, she certainly for a stranger seemed very kind and friendly. We generally found very good entertainment at the hotels. We kept the south roads below the lakes, in order to shun the snow which was not much untill we arrived at Cataraugus co. Where we found brethren, in ^the town of^ Freedom, and staid 3 days. We first called at Dr. Warren A Cowdry's, and introduced ourselves as saints on our way to the place of gathering, at Kirtland, and were made welcome and treated kindly. They had sold their inheritance in that place and were intending to emigrate west in the spring themselves. Had rented a small house for the winter, and were not as comfortably situated as they had been. We staid one night with them, and then went to br Heman Hydes where we staid two nights. We had a very interesting time there. They sent for their oldest sons wife, who was at her fathers, staying while her husband was gone to Kirtland. She was a young woman lately married, had the gift of tounges and interpretation. They sang talked in tongues and interpreted. It was quite a curiosity to me as I had seen very little of it before. Charles Hyde, the cripple, was full of the spirit of the work, seemed to want to speak in tongues all the time.

Suffice it to say we felt that we had got home again, and rather dreaded leaving, and going off in the snow, of which there had fallen a new recruit while we had been stopping there. We waited one day for the snow to settle a little, and then set forth towards Lake Erie, found the snow very deep, in some places. Mr Crosby walked nearly all the way; our pretty black horse began to get thin, and look sober. We came across a man who was going on our way with a span of horses and sleigh, and Mr C hired him to take our carriage, and fasten on his sleigh; tied our horse behind, and so carried us on one days travel, much faster than should otherwise have done, in consequence of the snow being deep and bad for wagons to encounter. After we got on the lake road the snow was not so deep, and we got along very well. We stoped the last night in Freedonia, and the next night, arrived at br Pratts in Ripley *Dec 12th.* My mind was gloomy, notwithstanding my anxiety to reach there, but the thoughts of our dear sister dying, and being buried there about 6 months previous, was a sufficient cause for sadness to overspread my mind.

[A Visit with the Pratts]

We reached their dwelling, as twilight was declining, having called at the hotel in the centre of the town, a mile and a half back, and inquired the way. Mr Rice was the landlords name, he had a daughter a young lady, who had been an associate of Lois's. They were intimately acquainted with my br Horace Barnes, and Pratts people, thought my voice, and speech, were very like my sisters. Jon—— left me sitting in the wagon, while he went in to see if they knew him, I overheard sis P say "Jonathan Crosby," and soon they came out to me. I had not seen my br Horace in 12 years, but could not discover that he had changed very materially, looked very young, I thought. After a few days my husband concluded to go to Kirtland, and see what prospect there was for us there, while I staid to visit my friends as they invited, and urged us to stop with them, untill spring at least. I

A painting by modern Mormon artist, Valoy Eaton, of the Kirtland Temple under construction. Jonathan Crosby helped build this first Latter-Day Saint temple. His family resided within sight of the structure. Walter Rane, courtesy of the Museum of Church History and Art, Salt Lake City.

had a sick turn when we had been there a few days, which terminated in a miscarriage. I soon recovered however, and enjoyed a very good visit with them. Frances was then a babe,^one year old^ and Ellen was near 4 years, and a very interesting little girl. Mr C was gone 10 days, when he returned bringing a very favorable report, said he liked the brethren and especially the prophet very much, had engaged us a boarding place and got a place for himself to work on the temple. I was highly pleased with the intelligence, and even felt anxious to go on immediately.

Accordingly we set off *tues the 5th day of Jan, 1836*, my birth day. I was 29 years of age. We found the roads almost impassable, the mud was up to the horses knees. We had a hard time, was nearly a week going 100 miles. Our horses breast became very sore. It gave me very unpleasant feelings to see him work in such misery.

CHAPTER THREE

Kirtland to Pleasant Garden, Indiana

Memoirs, January 1836 to June 1842

[Arrival at Kirtland, January 9, 1836]

We reached Kirtland the *9th day of Jan.* The first person that we saw was Evan M Green,[1] ^one of^ the young men who first brought the gospel to Mass at the time my husband was baptised. He assisted us in getting our wagon up the hill near the temple, which we found very difficult in ascending, in consequence of the ground being clayey. We went directly to Parley P Pratts, where they had engaged to board us awhile; and were soon introduced to a score of brethren and sisters, who made us welcome among them, and I ever felt myself quite at home in their society.

Shortly after our arrival my husband was ordained to the office of an elder [seventy], and chosen into the second quorum of seventies. I well recollect the sensations with which my mind was activated when I learned the fact that my husband had been called and ordained to the Melchisedek priesthood and would undoubtedly be required to travel and preach the gospel to the nations of the earth.[2] I realized in some degree the immense responsibility of the office, and besought the Lord for grace and wisdom to be given him, that he might be enabled to magnify his high and holy calling. The brethren had meetings of some kind almost every evening in the week. Besides singing schools in which all ages took a part, from the young adult to the old gray heads. Consequently we also took a part with them, and met two evenings in a week. The quoir was large. Meuriel C Davis was our leader for a year or more.

[Patriarchal Blessings]

Father Joseph Smith sen, was ~~then~~ the first and ^then, the^ only patriarch in the church. Acordingly we went to him for a blessing, and received as

40

good, and as great promisses, as any mortal beings could ask. I will therefore record them, for the perusal of my posterity, and friends

A Patriarchal Blessing,[3] by Joseph Smith Senior, Kirtland *Feb 21st AD
1836* Jonathan Crosby jun, born in Wendall, Franklin Co Mass. July
20th 1807 Recorded in book D. of John Smith Patriarch. Page 238.
No 721.
    Albert Carrington Recorder.

    Brother Crosby, I lay my hands upon thy head in the name
of Jesus, and confirm the blessings of a father upon thee, and for
thy posterity also, for thou shalt raise up children, and the Lord
shall bless them, and they shall be kept in the covenant of Abraham,
and receive the holy priesthood. And thou shalt have great joy over
them, if thou wilt discharge thy duty unto them.
    Thou hast been called with an high and holy calling. The Lord
hath looked upon thee in past days, and thou hast obeyed His voice,
even the voice of the good Shepherd, in obeying the gospel. Thou
art of the seed of Israel, even an Ephraimite, and the Lord shall give
thee power to claim thy father, and all thy connexions according
to the flesh, that thy joy may be full. The visions of heaven shall be
open unto thee, and the voice of thy God shall speak unto thee, so
that thou shalt know for thyself.
    I seal all former blessings, even the blessing of the holy anoint-
ing, which thou hast received, and the most holy priesthood, which
has been confirmed upon thee. Thou shalt go from land to land,
and preach in large ships of the ocean, and have power over the
winds and waves. Be wafted from place to place, by the power of
God. Be caught up to the third heavens, and behold unspeakable
things, whether in the body or out. Thou shalt see thy Redeemer in
the flesh, and know that He lives. Angels shall minister unto thee,
and protect thee from thine enemies, so that none shall be able to
take thy life. And when thy mission is full here, thou shalt visit other
worlds, and remain a Priest in eternity.
    Thou shalt stand upon the earth 'till the Redeemer comes,
See the end of this generation, and when the heavens rend, thou
shalt rise and meet thy God in the air. And thy thousands shall be
with thee. Thy family also, and thy posterity also. If thou wilt live for
these ~~things~~ blessings, thou shalt receive them. And I seal thee up
unto eternal life, in the name of Jesus. Amen.
    Also Caroline his wife. Born in Warwick Franklin co Mass Jan
5th AD 1807 Sister Crosby, let thy heart rejoice. Thy name is written
in the Lambs book of life. Thy heart is pure, and thou shall be blest.

Thou shalt never want for blessings if thou wilt keep the commandments I seal blessings for thee in common with thy husband. Thy life shall be as his life, and thy years as his years, And thou also shalt see thy Redeemer come in the clouds of heaven, and thy joy shall be full.

When thou prayest in faith the Lord shall answer thy prayers. Angels shall minister unto thee. And thy husband shall receive strength from thy prayers when he is absent from thee. And you shall know each others state by the spirit when in far distant lands, and be comforted.

Thou shalt receive an inheritance in Zion, for thee and thy children. See the glory of God fill the house. Even the glory of the kingdom of heaven And if thou desirest thou shalt bid the grave adieu, and never sleep in the dust, but rise to meet thy Redeemer at His coming, and shalt then be forever with the Lord.

I seal these blessings upon thee in the name of Jesus. Amen.

Sylvester Smith—scribe

Recorded in book D of John Smith, Patriarch. Pages 238 and 9. No 722. Albert Carrington Recorder.

These blessings cheered and rejoiced our hearts exceedingly. I truly felt humble before the Lord, and felt to ~~be~~ exclaiming like one of old, "Lord what am I, or what my fathers house, that Thou art thus mindful of <u>us</u>."

They led me to search into my own heart, to see if there was any sin concealed there, and if so, to repent, and ask God to make me clean, and pure, in very deed. The Patriarch conversed with us sometime, told us we had come to gather right. And when we told him our ages, and places of birth, he observed that he thought we were both born under one planet. But merely by way of merriment. Mother Smith was in the room. She also added her blessing, or confirmed what we had already received.

[Living in Kirtland]

Our meetings were held in the printing office, or rather in a room under it. The room was not large enough to convene the people who came. It was quite a curiosity to see them coming so early, almost as soon as light in order to get a seat. And finally they decided on taking their turns in staying away, as the weather was cold, and it was unpleasant for those who stood outside. The females usually had seats. My husband worked 3 months on the temple before it was dedicated, which was nearly the first he had ever done at the business.

I enjoyed myself well with sister Thankful Pratt. She was a very sociable interesting woman, but had very delicate health. The brethren attended meetings almost every evening, which left us togather considerably. When they all left us, she would look about her and say, "Well, it is you and I again, Sister Crosby" She was afflicted with severe spells of sick-headache, which came upon her monthly.

[Dedication of the Kirtland Temple, March 27, 1836]

About the middle of March, we went to Harpen Rigg'ss to board. They were a young, lately married couple, near our ages. They lived in a new house, which was situated on the cross street, which led from the Boston house, to bishop Knights. It was quite a pleasant situation. Sister R was a Mass woman, and seemed very near to me. We enjoyed ourselves togather finely. Chapman Duncan also came and boarded there several weeks, before, and after, the dedication of the temple, which transpired on *the 27th of March AD 1836.* I believe however, it was continued several days. In which time the spirit of God was manifested in healing the sick, casting out devils, speaking in tongues, interpretation &C.[4] We had some glorious preaching, that cheered and animated our hearts. How often while listining to the voice of the prophet, have I wished Oh! that my friends, parents, brothers, and sisters, could hear the things that I heard, and their hearts be made to rejoice in them, as mine did.! And I would frequently be led to exclaim with Dr Isaac Watts,

Why was I made to hear thy voice, And enter while there's room. While thousands make a wretched choice, And rather starve than come.

We had some joyful times that spring and summer. Many strangers came from various parts of the country, to see the prophet, and the temple. It certainly was a very pretty building, but my powers of description are inadequate to describe so complex a ~~building~~ structure. Immediately after the dedication, many of the elders were sent on missions, some went to Missouri with families. My husband purchased a lot west of the temple and began to make preparations for building. I followed braiding palm leaf hats for eight months after we came to K——t——l——d. ^Braided near a hundred the first season, which brought me 75 dolls.^

[Brigham Young Family Blessing]

We had an invitation, and attended a family blessing meeting, or feast that was held at the house of John P Greene.[5] It was appointed for Father Young to bless his family, and as sister Greene was his eldest child (as I think she was) it was held at her house. The house was crowed full, we had nice wheat bread and sweet wine all we wanted to drink, it was also called a feast, and so it was a feast of fat things. The brethren and sisters blest one another, but father Young I believe concluded to defer blessing his family untill he could have them by themselves. He seemed rather diffident in regard to speaking, or his mind so much affected by the subject, that he could not express his feelings. Brigham therefore arose and spoke in his behalf. The old gentleman wept freely, as well as many of his family, so that we had weeping, and rejoicing, nearly at the same time.

It was a general time of rejoicing for several months among the saints. They frequently met from house, to house, to break bread, and drink wine, and administer to the poor and afflicted. We also attended a blessing at Dr Frederick G Williams. His eldest daughter had been lately married, and was about to leave for Missouri. He therefore blest his family previous to their leaving. He laid his hands upon each of their heads, and the scribe wrote them. The prophet Joseph was present, and had a vision of their journey, saw their wagon turn over, but no one was injured. It came to pass even as he said.

About the last of May, elder Parley P P went on a mission to Canada, and took his family. Mr Crosby rented his house, and accordingly we went housekeeping. *May the 27th*, we moved our effects back again into br Pratts house, and commenced providing for ourselves. We had then been married a year and a half, and had not kept house before. I felt like a child with a new set of toys. I cleaned the house from stem to stern, and arranged everything in the best of order.

[Visit from Horace Barnes]

Soon after we commenced housekeeping, my brother Horace Barnes came to see us from York state Chatauque co. He spent a week or more with us. We went with him to see the prophet, but I think he was absent; he saw father Smith, and Emma, who showed him the records of Abraham, that were found with the mummies, and explained the characters to us, as she has heard her husband explain them.[6] We said all we could to enlighten his mind. We also invited a br who had formerly been a member of the presbyterian church, to come and converse with him. He never seemed disposed to <u>contend</u> against it. Br H brought me the melancholy news of sister Catherine's sickness, with consumption, or liver complaint. We had a very good visit from him. It was in the month of june. He left quite undecided in his mind with regard to the truth of the work. I had some lonely hours after his departure.

[Housing Accomodations]

Several families came in at that time from Y——k st, and as houses were very hard to be rented, every place being filled, Mr C—— rented the cellar kitchen to a man, and wife, with two small children. His name was Lewis, a blacksmith by occupation, and very poor people. But they found it rather uncomfortable, and staid only a short time. About the middle of July a co came from Boston Mass. Among them was John Boynton's parents, brothers in law and sisters, Br Henry Herriman and Jonathan Hail [Hale]. And no house could be found for their accomodation. John was building, but could not get it ready in season, he therefore came to us and offered to give us four times the amount of rent we paid, if we would go in with sister Sabre Granger, a maiden lady near by us, who was living alone, and let him have our house for his friends. My husband left it with me to say, to which I hesitated some time, but at length consented, rather reluctantly. The remuneration I considered no object; to leave my pleasant little house, and go in with another, after living by ourselves so short a time; but the idea of accomodating friends, stimulated me to make the sacrifice.

Sister Granger's house was small, only one room, besides cellar, pantry, a small closet, and chamber. She had however a stoveroom, outside where she cooked her food. She had many peculiarities, which in some respects were not as agreeable to us, as we could wish. Notwithstanding being kindhearted, and friendly, atoned in my estimation, for many imperfections. My husband attended a Hebrew school[7] that summer, and made some considerable improvement. I also learned to read, but not translate. He bought a nice set of books, consisting of bible, lexicon, and grammar. We had a small feast in co with sis Grainger while there. Father Morley presided. There were some great blessings pronounced upon some heads. One by father M—— upon Mr Crosby, was that he should have a son a foot taller than himself, that he would be obliged to sit while his father blessed him. There was also a wedding there while we lived in her house. A br by the name of Foster married a widow from Boston, her name I do not recollect. Shortly after we went in, sister Mariann Sterns, came from the State of Maine. I think came with Lyman Johnson, and put up at his house. She had one child, a little girl 4 years old. She soon became discontented there, and thought she was not welcome any longer, Sister Granger very kindly offered her a home, untill she could do better. Accordingly she came and stoped one month. Sis G—— was very kind in her rough way. She brought home work, sewing and knitting for her, and fed her on vegetables, hard corn, and tough string beans. We made her welcome to a share of what <u>our</u> table afforded, which was not very <u>bountifully</u> supplied at that time. I admired her very much, thought her an amiable, interesting woman. From there she went to housekeeping. Sister Granger had a sister come from Boston, who made her home there, a good share of the time.

[First Home]

The middle of Nov we got our house enclosed, and a loose floor, no windows, but my anxiety was so great, to get away by ourselves, that I determined to move in at all events. I truly felt rejoiced beyond measure, to get into a house of our own after so long a time.

My husband continued his labors incessantly, untill he got the doors and windows in; and then we thought ourselves highly blessed. We had a nice cooking stove, a good cellar, and well, close to my door, which <u>certainly</u> were <u>three</u> <u>great</u> <u>conveniences</u>. But as yet we had no partition in the house.

[Birth of Son]

The weather continued very pleasant untill the middle of Dec, when a snow storm came on, which lasted sometime. The *14th of Dec* ^4 oclock PM^ Alma was born. That day, and night, the snow fell in profusion.

Dr W A Cowdry was my physician. Sister Warren Smith, Sherwood, Vincent Knight, and sis Drury were with me. The lattter staid one week, and then intended sending her daughter, but as I did not get along as well as I could wish, we concluded to get a more experienced person. Sister John Goodson, understood my situation, and very kindly offered her services, for one week. I found her to be an excellent nurse, as well as an interesting young woman. She had come from U Can—— a few weeks previous and had been married, but a short time. We were much surprised at her offer. But I think she did it as a sort of joke on her husband, more than anything else. After she left, Ruth Drury came, and staid two weeks, and I then thought I could get along alone. I tried one month, took cold, which settled in my left breast, and caused me a severe sickness, ~~accompanied~~ with a broken breast, and all the disagreeable accompaniments, of that distressing disease. We then hired a young woman by the name of Susannah Hidden, afterward the wife of Stephen Perry. After she left I had Lydia Chapman, quite a young girl. I did not attend meeting untill the next April. My babe was then 4 months old. While I was sick I sent for father Smith to lay hands on me. When he came he questioned us with regard to our faith and feelings towards the first Presidency, said there were many murmurers about, and a spirit of dissension in the church. I told him I had been confined at home, and had neither seen or heard scarcely anything of it, that I desired to continue in the truth, and keep the commandments of God. He then said he would shut the door and keep the devil out, after which he in co with another elder laid their hands on me, and prayed. I felt that I had received a great blessing.

[Troubles in Kirtland, 1837]

^*AD 1837*^ Times became very hard ~~about these times~~ in Kirt——. It seemed that our enemies were determined to drive us away if they could possibly, by starving us out ~~or rem~~ None of the business men would employ a mormon scarcely, on any conditions. And our prophet was continually harassed with vexatious lawsuits. Besides the great apostacy in the church, added a duble portion of distress and suffering to those who wished to abide in the faith, and keep the commandments. We became very short of provision, several times ate the last we had and knew not where the next meal was coming from. We then had an opportunity to try the charity of the brethren, who were many of them in the same predicement as ourselves. I recollect that Wm Cahoon called into see us one night, as he was going home with a few quarts of corn meal, and enquired if we had any bread stuff on hand, we told him we had not. He said he would divide what he had with us, and if my husband would go home with him, he would also divide his potatoes and meat, which bore the same proportion to his meal. Joseph Young[8] also divided with us several times in the same way, and we with him. We had numerous opportunities of dividing almost our last loaf with the brethren. Mr C worked on br Joseph's house, as he was building tolerably large, but frequently got so straitened that he had nothing to give the workmen, when saturday night came, and they were obliged to borrow, or do without. They all left at one time, except Mr C——, he worked on for several days alone. Sister Emma observing that he was laboring there alone, came in one day, and enquired of him, whether or where he got his provision. He told her he was entirely without, and knew not where to look, as he had no money, and the boss who employed him had no means in <u>his</u> hands. She then went into her chamber, and brought him a nice <u>ham</u> weighing 20 lbs, ^~~and brought him~~^ telling him <u>that</u> was a present for his faithfullness, and that he should bring a sack, and get as much flour as he could take home.[9] Accordingly he came home rejoicing, considering it a perfect God send. It was beautiful white flour, and the ham was very sweet. I thought nothing ever tasted half as good. About this time the Kirtland bank failed, which caused a great deal of distress among the brethren.[10]

We had a little garden which was a great help to us, we had no cow, and were obliged to buy milk for the babe. My husband was sued once, by the men who kept the meat market. Leonard Rich, and Roger Orten, and was obliged to sacrifice twice the amount ^of the debt^ in property,

to raise the money. Alas thought I! the trials that I had heard the elders
preach of, were in reality coming upon us. As to poverty we could endure
that patiently, but trials among false brethren, who can endure with
patience? Many of our most intimate associates, were among the apostates. Warren Parish was a sort of leader of a party of some 30 or 40 persons, among them was John Boynton and wife. Luke and Lyman Johnson,
Harpen Riggs, and others whose names I do not recollect. These were
some of our nighest neighbors and friends. "We had taken sweet counsel together, and walked to the house of God as friends." They came out
boldly against the prophet, and signed an instrument got up as I understood by W Parish and others, renouncing all their alliance with the
church. I met sister Riggs afterwards, and asked her if it was true that
she had apostatized. She said she was dissatisfied with somethings in the
church, but that she still believed the book of Mormon, and thought she
always should. I felt very sorrowful, and gloomy, but never had the first
idea of leaving the church, or forsaking the prophet.[11] I was very feeble
all through the summer, but Alma grew, and was quite fleshy, began to
walk when he was ten months old. As the fall advanced I began to gain
strength, and felt much better.

[Jonathan Sent on Mission, 1838]

We got our house a little more comfortable, the floor plained, and made
very tight, a partition through, and floor overhead. It began to seem
more like living. About the *first of Dec* a number of elders were sent on
missions My husband was one that was appointed to go. He made what
preparation he could, and the *7th of Jan 1838*, in company with Warren
Smith (who was afterward martyred at Hans [Hauns] mill by the missouri
mob[12]) he set off toward the east part of the state of Ohio, and went into
Pennsylvania.[13]

[Breaking Up of the Church]

We had contentious times immediately after they left. The apostates commenced persecuting the church, and especially the Smith family, and
nearly all of them left, and went to Missouri.[14] Elder Sherwoods family
lived opposite of me, and Jane their youngest daughter, with Henrietta
McBride, used to take turns in coming to sleep with me. Sometimes I
staid alone with a little boy James McBride only 7 years old.

About the *15th of Jan*, I was awakened one night near the middle of
the night, by sister Sherwood calling to me, and Jane, crying fire. I awoke
and as I lay near a window I looked out, and beheld the ground as light
as day, while the sky was as black as a thundercloud. A deep solemnity

pervaded my mind, and a very strange sensation ran through my whole system. We arose immediately, and opened the door, and beheld the printing office all in flames, and men assembling from every direction, in great haste. But they were all to late. They merely threw out a few books, and some of them were scorched. The sparks and shingles were carried To an immense distance. It was the nearest building to the temple but the wind was favorable in protecting it from the flames. The burning of that building seemed to be the breaking up of the church in Kir[15] Directly after, the seventies decided on moving to Missouri in company.

The seven presidents were to lead us. Benjamin S Wilber and family came to live with me. He was chosen to officiate in the place of one of the counsellors who was absent. They appointed capts of hundreds, fifties and 10s.

[Jonathan's Invitation to Ripley]

Mr C—— was away at the time of organization. He was appointed a capt of 10, however and his co set off to him. He was absent only 7 weeks, hearing of the troubles in the church he returned to assist if possible in making preparations to remove. Not long after his return, we received letters from my sister, wife of Addison Pratt, who then lived in Ripley, Chatauque, co York state, inviting my husband to come and see them, told him that if he considered his religion of so much importance, she wondered why he did not take more pains to convert his friends, or something of that import. Accordingly taking advantage of her invitation, he set off on foot, with no money, the roads still quite muddy, and begged his way through a land of unbelievers, to make them as he thought a farewell visit, and leave his testimony with them, perhaps for the last time. He felt that he had already rid his skirts of their blood, by reasoning with them out of the scriptures, left our books with them, when on our way to K. Besides we had written to them frequently, and done (as we thought) all in our power to enlighten their minds, but apparently to no purpose. Yet as she had invited him to come and continue his persuasions, he determined on doing so immediatly. He arrived just at the close of a protracted meeting of 18 days. They were so happified, and filled with religion, that they had very little room for the truth, and acknowledged that they were not much pleased to see him, knowing that his arguments would be in exact opposition to their present state of mind. They continued to oppose his arguments for several days. He finally succeeded in getting up a public meeting, and after hearing one public discourse, they began to listen attentively. My sister became convinced of the truth, but was not wholly ready to obey the gospel, thought she must come to Kirtland and see the witnesses to the book of Mormon, and get all the testimony she could on the subject, before she embraced it.

[Arrival of Louisa Pratt and Horace Barnes in Kirtland]

Mr Crosby was gone about 4 weeks, and returned feeling quite encouraged, with regard to his success; informed me that my brother and sister
were coming out to see us, as soon as the springs work was through. Br
Wilber had been wishing for Mr C's, return, to assist in preparing wagons,
tents, &C, preparatory to our journey, consequently he immediatly went
to work with all diligence. We had our tent nearly ready, when my brother
and sister arrived. I think it was in May. The weather was rather unpleasant, but still we went about some with them; took them to see Martin
Harris, who was all the witness there was in K—— at that time.[16] And he
was then at variance with Joseph, and had been disfellowshiped by the
church. Notwithstanding he bore his testimony to the book of Mormon in
the strongest terms, and that was sufficient to satisfy my sister, the remainder of the doctrine she could read very plainly in the bible. She however
chose to defer being baptised untill her husband had been to see for <u>him-
self</u>. As to br Horace Barnes he never opposed it, but still I think he had
the least faith of any one of them.

[Addison Pratt's Baptism, June 18, 1838]

Immediately after their return home, br Pratt came. We had moved from
our house into br Joseph Smiths. They had all gone previously, and his
house was unoccupied. Br B S Wilber and we, lived together as one family, had each a little boy. Mine was a year older than hers. We enjoyed ourselves finely. Br Pratt found us in that situation when he arrived, I think he
stoped one week, and in the meantime was baptised, I think by br Josiah
Butterfield, who was then one of the seven presidents of the seventies.

[Removal to Ripley, June 1838]

As soon as br P—— became convinced of the truth, he determined to go
with us to Missouri; but could not get ready to go before fall. He therefore invited us to come out to his place, and wait till they could get ready
to remove, and in the meantime, either himself or br H B would accompany my husband to Mass—— and Can—— to carry the gospel to our
friends, and try if possible to persuade them to embrace the truth. Mr
Crosby went to his counsellors for their opinion, and they told him to go.
Accordingly we gave up all our interest in the company, took our leave of
the brethren and sisters; some of them did not like the idea of our going
back, but still did not blame us, as we were counseled to do so.

Old br Lamoreaux took his horse and wagon, and carried us to the
harbour at Richmond Ohio. Br Pratt gave me two dollars and a half at

Kirtland, towards bearing our expenses to Ripley. And said he or br H would meet us at Erie Penn—— with his horse and carriage to convey us to their place. Br Lamoreaux was very sociable, and friendly, conversed very familiarly with us, wished us many good wishes, and blessings, assured us that the hand of the Lord would be with us for good, and seemed to have a sort of fatherly feeling for us, which I shall never forget. When he left the hotel, where we stoped to await the sailing of the steamer, he took us each by the hand, and blessed us in the name of the Lord. I truly felt that we were then alone, as it were, and a desolate feeling seemed to pervade my mind, untill we returned to Kirtland the next fall. We went on board of the *The new Erie*, at 12 or 1 oclock, and arrived at Erie about 5 oclock, where we found br H Barnes waiting for us. We took a little refreshment and left in his carriage, had 25 miles to ride, did not reach home untill 9 oclock, I think it was near the middle of *June 1838*. Br H—— had the sickheadache and was unwell several days after. & 3 or 4 days after our arrival he and sister Pratt were baptised in Lake Erie. Mr Crosby officiated. And soon after he and br H set off on their mission. I think it was *the 2nd or 3rd of july*.

Sister and I were full of hopes and fears concerning our friends, wondering whether they would receive or reject their message. We knew they had always respected br H's judgment and testimony in worldly matters, and thought they might perhaps in that case. He had been from home 14 years. They were all much pleased to see him, Father and Mother were willing to receive their testimony, and even willing to sell and follow them to the church if br would come back, and assist in helping them off, which he agreed to do. Sister Catharine was then very low, had been sick over two years.

Mr Crosby thought if the friends would unite their faith, and receive the gospel, she might be healed; their sudden arrival almost over came her. They staid about two weeks. My husband preached 7 or 8 times, but no one obeyed the gospel. They left and came to Mass—— where ~~my husband~~ he held a number of meetings, and I think baptised some, preached in Winchester. His father gave him a horse and wagon, both of them old and of little value, but still they were very acceptable, as he was far from his family, without money and br H had very little. He also received some few presents from the brethren and sisters in the church. They then put their means together and returned to York state where they found us all well, and pleased to see them.

[Moving West]

Sister P and I had worked very hard in their absence to get things in as good order to leave as we could, hoping to get away immediatly on their return, but we found it was a harder, and more difficult job than we had an idea, to dispose of stock, fowls and hogs, houses and lands, ^household furniture^, all to advantage, and prepare for so long a journey. Sister had a large quantity of wool to work into cloth, made her a nice carpet, coleured the yarn all at home, had 14 or 15 differnt colors and shades, and many other things too numerous to mention. The weather was remarkably warm, I had not been accustomed doing much housework, and especially over a fireplace for several years. Which made it rather hard on me. I was troubled with a prickly heat occasioned by over heating my blood, suffered severly with it.

My husband and br Horace reached home the *first of Sept*, and commenced operations for moving west. *Nov. 20th 1838*, we set off accompanied by br Pratt Addison, and family, expecting br Horace Barnes was going directly to Canada, to assist father and mother to dispose of their effects, and come to the church, but shortly after we left, the news of the brethren being driven from Missouri reached him and entirely discouraged him from going to Can—— or assisting our parents to come west.[17] His old presbyterian friends in the meantime gathered around him and told him back into their church again. Shortly after he married a young lady by the name of Susan Cone, a member of that society.

[Stopping in Kirtland]

We had a very good journey to Kirtland, where we stoped one week, rested our teams, and visited some of the saints that were yet remaining there. One family of eastern people, by the name of Hobert, who had joined the church since we left. We formed a short acquaintance with them, and found them very zealous in the cause, but heard afterwards that they apostatised from the truth.

On returning to K—— we found our things that we left in a house formerly owned and occupied by Vincent Knight, had been disturbed, and some of them were missing. One trunk covered with oilcloth, and marked with the initials of my name, in brass nails, was gone and with it some articles of clothing, crockery, knives and forks, &C. Mr C employed a constable to assist him, got a search warrant, and found the transgressor, with the articles. He was very humble, when exposed, and offered anything they had in the house to settle with them, but they had taken the law in hand; and could not settle with him on any other terms, Accordingly he was put under bonds to appear at court in the following March. While there we visited old Mr Branan, father of John and Samuel Branan, who was a revolutionary soldier, and said to be an hundred years old.[18] He was sick, but had a great desire to go to Missouri to join his wife and children, who had gone and left him to wait untill the ensuing spring, when he would draw his pension money, and by that means get a fit out to the far west. He requested us to tell his children that he wished them to come after him in the spring ~~without fail~~, but before that time arrived he was gone to his long home. We enjoyed our visit in Kirtland finely, altho it seemed rather desolate with so few brethren in it, and so many vacant houses.

[Continuing West]

Br Hiram Kellogg presided, who was a very friendly, peace loving man. We left with many blessings and good wishes for our welfare, and prosperity in travelling ^to the land of Zion.^ While we were there, the report arrived of the church being driven from Missouri, but we were not inclined to give credence to it, and pursued our course onward. Before we got out of Ohio we met some who had been brethren, going back to K, who confirmed the report, and assured us that it was even so. My husband and br Pratt counseled together about what was best to be done in regard to travelling further west, untill we heard from the church, and found where they intended locating. Mr C's counsel was to travel on as near to the brethren as we could before we stoped, or as long as the roads continued good. Accordingly we continued our jouney to Indianapolis, when it commenced raining, and the roads became very bad, so that we travelled only 45 miles west of the metropolis of Indiana, and stoped at a little town by the name of Pleasant garden, in Putnam co, 25 miles east of Terrahaute.[19]

[Pleasant Garden, Indiana, January 1839]

We put up at a hotel kept by Peter Barnet, a Stammering man. In the course of the evening a gent called at the hotel by the name of Chester L Heath, who told us that he had once belonged to the church but had been disfellowshiped, for not receiving the book of Doctrine and Covenants.[20] Said he still believed the Book of Mormon. He was quite anxious that we should stop in that place, and as the road had become very bad, we all concluded it would be best to do so. Br Heath directed the men to a house which they rented, and after staying one day at the hotel we removed our effects to our stopping place, and commenced housekeeping. Br Pratt took an upper room with a verandah in front of the house, and we took one large room that had previously been used for a Dr's office, and court room.

And there we found ourselves in a land of strangers, with little more than one dollar in money, very few clothes, one horse, and an old one-horse wagon. But we trusted in God, and were not confounded.

[Jonathan's Cabinet-Making Shop]

In passing through Putnamville the day previous to our arrival in the place, my husband found a young br, from N Y, by the name of Ross R Rogers, who had stoped there some weeks previous, and in conversation with him, found he was a Cabinet maker by occupation. He therefore decided on proposing to him, to come to our place, and open a shop in co with himself. Accordingly the next sabbath he visited Putnamville for that purpose, and obtained a promise from br R—— to that effect. In the meantime br Pratt went to Clay county, and purchased government land, to the amount of some one thousand dolls worth.[21] I lived in the shop sometime. We found br Heaths people very kind and neighborly. They offered to lend us anything they had to spare, in the housekeeping line. It was sometime before my husband got his business started sufficiently to earn much money. I therefore proposed washing for sister Heath, as she had poor health, and was obliged to hire; which brought us in a little money every week, and provided us with meat and butter.

We found our neighbors very kind and sociable. They were mostly from N C—— and K——y. After living several weeks in the shop, I moved into an upper room, where br Pratts stoped, on our first arrival. I found it much more pleasant and agreeable. Here we resided for several months, untill the families all left the house, and then we took possession of all the lower part, and converted the upper room into a furniture room. I then had three tolerably nice rooms. But as yet were unable to have furniture, as they had nothing but their hands to commence with, not even tools. Wm Watkins esq, who lived nigh us, lent them what he had. I think however that my husband had a set of bench plains of his own. They got in debt for lumber, house rent, tools &C so that it took them sometime to work it out. In the meantime Mr Crosby was in debt to br Pratt for his assistance in bringing us from York state, to Indiana. And he, br P, in consequence of having paid out all his money for land, had become quite needy, and it proved quite a trial to both parties. But after having some few unpleasant words with regard to our situations, they agreed to leave it to br Rogers to say how they should settle, and it was managed satisfactorily to both. In the course of the summer Dr Knight bought the house we were living in and the one adjoining, and moved into the next door. We found him a very kind neighbor, ready to lend them money to carry on their business in the shop, and manifested a desire to assist them in many respects. His wife was much younger than her husband, and of quite a different temperament. Was fond of society and religiously inclined, but <u>he</u> seldom or never attended religious worship.

[A New Branch Organized]

The Sept following A W Babbit[22] came along, on a mission to Cincinatti. He put up at the hotel kept by a Mr Freeman. Mr Crosby accidentally chanced to see him and knew him, went over and invited him to bring wife and put up with us, which he did very readily.

Mr Crosby and Rogers were anxious that he should preach that evening, to which he consented, and they notified the neighbors. The house was filled, and all seemed highly interested; insomuch that he appointed another the next evening, and then continued his lectures every night (but one) for two weeks. Some two or three came forward for baptism, and several others were almost persuaded to obey the gospel. Among them was Dr Knight, who finally promised elder B that he would go forward before he left, and requested him to stay awhile longer; untill he should have time to ponder it over in his mind, and weigh the matter thoroughly. Babbet therefore concluded to defer going to Cincinatti, as long as there was so good a prospect of doing a work there. He also had a dream that encouraged him to stay. He dreamed that he baptised eight persons, and organised a branch in that place. As soon as some few were baptised, the evil geniuses began to operate against us. A set of rowdy fellows took off one of his carriage wheels and carried into the woods, where they hid it so securely, that it was not discovered, untill after he had another made. The more respectable part of community, Sympathised with him, and contributed towards getting him another in its stead. He staid in the country 3 months, preached 80 discourses, baptised 8 persons, and organised a branch of some 25, or 30 members.[23] Appointed Mr Crosby to preside, ordained br Rogers a teacher, and then pusued his journey to Ohio. Previous to leaving, the people became satisfied with his preaching, and very few, except the members, attended. The meetings were held in our house all the time or nearly so, while we lived there. My husband held meetings every other sabbath, for sometime, previous to our leaving the place at the house of Thomas McCully, a remarkably tall man, whom he baptised, And who lived in another part of the township.

["Mormon Tavern"]

This was in the *fall of '389*. While br Babbitt was still there, br Joseph Smith and Hiram, Sidney Rigdon, Brigham Young, H Kimball, G A Smith, Orson Hide, Reuben Hadlock, Dr Foster, and many others whose names I donot reccollect, came through our place, and stoped with us awhile.

We had some happy meetings, especially when br Joseph called and put up with us. Dr Knight invited him to go into his apartment to sleep, but br Joseph told him to take Sid Rigdon, as he was sick, and needed more attention than he did. After they were gone he told me that he prefered stopping with us, that he felt more at home, and was very willing to let elder Rigdon go in his place. Our accomodations were rather coarse, but we made all <u>welcome</u>, to our homely fare.

There was scarcely a week passed after the organisation of the branch, but that we had one, or more of the elders, or brethren of some description with us, and sometimes a half dosen at a time. Our house was called the Mormon tavern, all the time we lived in Indiana, which was 3½ years.[24]

In the *winter of '40* Mr Crosby bought a small house at the west end of the town, and in March, we moved into a house of our own, with a half acre of land attached to it. They again rented a shop of D Knight, that stood near us, so that we were very comfortably situated again.

[An Attempted Assassination]

Sister Knight was taken sick a short time previous to our moving, and became quite low. The first night that we slept in our new place a very exciting circumstance transpired in the town. Dr M Shepherd was assassinated, by someone, and left for dead. But toward morning he revived, and succeeded in crawling across the street to his boarding place, but was so dirty and his face and eyes so swollen that they did not know him, and he could not speak plain enough to be understood. He remained very low for sometime, but recovered at length. Soon after he began to ride again, there was a letter found at the door of his boarding place, advising him to leave, as his life was in danger.

That letter also created a great excitement. The mormons were suspected by some, and the grand query was whose writing that was, as it was an anonymous address. Every merchant, tradesman and bookkeeper in the place were called upon to bring forward their books, to compare with that letter, in order that some clue to its author could be obtained, if possible. But all to no purpose. Previous to this exitement Dr Knight moved his family to Greencastle, the county seat; and shortly after sister K died, of a quick consumption. The Dr was heartbroken, and almost distracted. In the course of the season Dr Shepherd's br from Illinois came, and persuaded him to go home, to his friends in that place. Accordingly he left.

Dr Mahan came to Pleasant garden; his wife was a cousin of Dr Knights and a very agreeable, fine lady. The Dr was also an honorable man, and a friend to our people. Dr Knight also returned after Shepherd left, and kept house in the place where we once lived in the old tavern stand. He hired Elizabeth Egbert to keep his house, had it repaired and put in good style.

~~This fall br Pratts moved to Nauvoo.~~

[Dissolution of the Business]

June '40 came brs Hide [Orson Hyde] and [John E.] Page, going on their mission to Jerusalem. They stoped some 10 days with us, and then proceeded on their way. Br R R Rogers accompanied them as far as Kirtland, on his way back to N Y after his wife. He and my husband dissolved com[pany]. Mr C—— bought his share in the shop, or business, and paid all demands against the firm of Crosby, Roger, and co. Br Pratt Addison, moved his family in town and staid a short time.[25] In *Sept '41* they removed to Nauvoo. Mr Crosby also went up to conference and carried a load of furniture to pay his tithing, in co—— with br Busby. He likewise went the previous fall in co with Dr Knight.

Louisa Egbert staid with me and Alma in his absence the last time he went and Almira Heathe staid the first time.

My husband was holding meetings every other Sabbath at Tho McCully's. I accompanied him once. Chester L Heath was also preaching in an adjoining co, and we went once to see them and attended meeting.

In the *winter of 42* My husband began to settle up his business, and prepare for removing to Nauvoo. I had a sickness which lasted me 3 or 4 weeks, in Apr, and May. Matilda Scott staid 2 weeks with me. Alma was also sick with chills, and fever.

CHAPTER FOUR

Nauvoo, Illinois

Memoirs, June 1842 to September 1846

[Departure for Nauvoo, June 14, 1842]

June 14th We left for Nauvoo. We were in hopes of finding co— but as none presented itself we set off alone. Our neighbors accompanied us to the creek, which was a large millstream that we had to cross, by fording, it was then quite high, we had waited a week or more for it to fall, and it then barely fordable. Mrs Thompson was very kind to me in my sickness, offered me any assistance I needed, and in getting ready to move she was also willing to assist me. They invited us to come and take breakfast with them the morning we left. Br Busby came with us to br Dentons who then lived on the farm in Clay co, that Addison Pratt formerly owned then sold to Dr Knight. We found a br Biby there when we arrived who accompanied us to Terrahaute. While we were waiting at br Duncans and consulting what we could do for company a young by the name of Andrew St John came along from the south of Ohio. Said he wished to go to Carthage Ill, and would like company, would drive a team or work his passage some way for the sake of his board. Accordingly my husband made arrangments with him to assist us in driving our cows, and we boarded him. We got along very well on our journey. Just before we reached Terrahaute we were met by a large co of the citizens who were going out to meet expresident Van Buren. Who was on a pleasure tour, through the western states. He was escorted from village to village, from city to city all the way to Vandalia which then was the capitol of the state, but afterwards was changed to Springfield. He passed us several times on our way, and we had an opportunity to witness the great attention paid him by his courtiers.

We found our strange travelling companion quite an honest sort of a fellow; he was entirely ignorant of our faith, but no way prejudiced against us. On arriving at Carthage he left us and we proceeded on alone to Nauvoo.

My husband sold the horse that St John rode, in Carthage, tied the other to the wagon, and the cows followed, so that he managed to get along alone, very well untill we came to the settlements when the cow was somewhat troublesome, and he found an acquaintance who offered us some assistance.

[Arrival at Nauvoo, June 1842]

On reaching the temple we found br Pratt at work raising the large stones, on the second story. He left his work and escorted us to his habitation. Where we found them all rejoiced to see us, and welcomed us with smiles and kisses. And then we found ourselves the second time gathered with the church, and a temple being building to the Lord. We naturally felt to rejoice, and praise the Lord, for his mercy to us, in preserving our lives, and forwarding us on our way, in keeping his commands.

Every house was occupied, and we were under the necessity of going into a cellar kitchen belonging to Benj Clapp who was himself on a mission to the south. It was directly opposite br Pratts, I spent the most of my time in their house for 2 weeks when my husband bought a house of Benjamin S Wilber, on main street. It was a small frame on maine and cutler. I was well pleased with the place, altho the house was small and unfinished, yet it was situated in a pleasant neighborhood, where we could see the great mississippii, with its numerous steamboats passing and repassing. Besides we had fine prospects of the temple could distinctly see the men at work, and hear the sound of their hammers, while cutting the stones.

Br Wilber had a nice garden growing, and we had one half of it with the improvments, for 220 dolls, he also had several peach trees, which bore fruit before we left there.

He agreed to give us possession in two weeks, but did not get his new house ready to move in that time and offered to let us come in with them. We accordingly lived together awhile. My husband worked in a shop with McArthur at cabinet ware.

[Sister Lois Crosby's Arrival at Nauvoo]

In about one month after our arrival in Nauvoo Sister Lois Thompson and her [husband] came from Mass, we had not seen her for nearly 7 years and were certainly much rejoiced to meet her at the gathering place of the Saints.[1] Her husband however was an unbeliever in the gospel which was a source of unhappiness to her as well as to us.

She had fondly hoped that on arriving at the church he would be more believing, but it seemed to have a contrary effect, for he certainly became more and more hardened, continued so dissatisfied and homesick that he threatened to leave, and would have done so, if she had been willing to follow him, but she told him if he went he must go without her, and by that means she kept him.

[Jonathan Sent Again on a Mission]

The next fall there were numerous elders sent to different portions of the states. My husband was among them; he left his home in 3 months after our reaching Nauvoo, and was absent 13 months. He had very little means to leave with us, but trusted us in the hands of the Lord, in whose work he was engaged, feeling sure that we should be provided for in some way or another.[2]

[Opening a School]

He left about the middle of *Oct. '42*. Shortly after I opened a school, as the only means of raising a little fund to support myself and son, who was then 6 years old. My house was small, and cold. His sister and husband lived with us, and when the children all got together we were too thick to be agreeable to each other.

We had one of the coldest winters that was ever known in Ill. The Miss——— was frozen 5 months, or from the last of Nov——— to the 6th of Apr——— so that teams crossed it on the ice.

Mr Thompson was very unhappy, and was continually cursing the place, and people, which made it very unpleasant for his friends. It was nearly all he could do, to get wood to keep us comfortable. I taught one quarter, and then closed untill warm weather.

In *Apr '43* I opened school again, and taught another quarter. I had 27 schollars. Sis T——— assisted me some.

[Joseph Smith Kidnapped]

In the course of the summer, br Joseph Smith was kidnaped by a number of missourians, while on a visit to the north part of Ill— with his wife. He was rescued by the authorities of Dixon, and a company of the brethren went out to meet him, and escort him home. A great many of the citizens also went out to meet him, after he came near home. As they came down to maine street I let the schollars out to go and join his train, which filled the road to a great distance, all rejoicing to meet their prophet once more alive, and welcomed him to his beloved city and friends.

[Jonathan's Arrival Home with Smallpox]

As the sickly season drew near many began to feel its effects, and H Thompson and myself shared the general fate. Both of us were sick at one time, with chills and fever, and none but Lois to take care of us. Alma was then in his 7th year, and assisted his aunt in waiting upon us. I received several letters from my husband in his absence, and wrote often to him, Informed him of my sickness and requested him to come as soon as convenient. We looked for him in *Sept——* but to our great disappointment he did not arrive untill *Dec——* and then came sick with Smallpox. His bro David and family came with him. He was attacked with the disease while on the Ohio river, but knew not what it was. Began to breakout at St Louis. There was a young Dr on board who travelled some distance with them, and prescribed medicine for him, but did not define the disease if he knew what it was.

We often thought it a mercy that he did not, as he would no doubt have been put off the boat, and left to the mercy of Strangers, or sent to some hospital. The Mississippii being very low the boat could [not] come over the rapids and they were obliged to take land conveyance from Warsaw, and did not reach home untill after dark. We were rejoiced to meet him, and the rest of the friends, but sorry to see him so afflicted. He had suffered greatly on the boat from the noise and confusion which surrounded him, and felt extremely thankful to get into his own house, where all was peace and quietness. The next day we sent for the elders of the church to administer to him, and they advised us to call a physician to know what ailed him. Accordingly we sent for Dr John Weld, and he pronounced it the Small pox, but somewhat modified by the kind pox.

We also sent for elder Sherwood, who said he had had it twice; once by vaccination when a young man, and again that same winter, by being exposed to it while moving a family out of the city, that had it. Mr C was confined to his bed 4 weeks; his bro David was in every day and waited upon us faithfully. I also stoped with him continually with Alma, but none us had it excepting sis Thompson. She was confined with a son, and the next day she had several pox on her face, which however did not fill, but in 4 or 5 days the babe broke out very badly only lived untill the 10th. He was one complete blotch The conclusion was that the child nursed it all from its mother which saved her from being sick but proved his death. Myself Alma and bro Davids wife felt the symptoms considerably, but nothing further.

[Nauvoo, 1844]

Jan 1844 Nancy Henderson came to live with us. She was ten year old a very healthy fleshy girl. Her father had died not long previously, and her mother died a year or two before. Her Grandmother Henderson brought her to me, and wished me to take her and do by her as I would if she were my own child.

Soon after Mr C recovered from the Smallpox he commenced work on the temple. Alma and Nancy went to the masonic hall to school. Bro Hathaway was teacher. When my husband returned from Mass—— he brought me a hundred weight of palm leaf; all prepared, ready for braiding. I learned the children Alma and Nancy to braid on the sides of the crowns, and they soon began to help me.

[Samuel Stevens's Family]

In the course of the spring or summer I was informed by a sister Empy that a young lady by the name of [Jane] Stevens (had been stopping with her) late from York state. I told her that I believed she was a connexion of ours, as I had seen the name Samuel Stevens in the *Times and Seasons*, whom I believed to be a cousin of mine and sister Pratts, and thought probably she was his daughter. She told me that she had gone out to the prairie and was stopping with a br Marks, son of elder Wm Marks. I requested her to inform the said young lady when she saw her, that she had connexion near her, who wished her to call on them. Shortly after the church were in great trouble. Bros Joseph and Hyram were taken prisners to Carthage, and many of us passed restless days, and sleepless nights. Mr C—— went to elder Marks to enquire for cousin Jane Stevens, and left word with them to her to call on us the earliest opportunity.

June 26th 1844, a man by the name of Capt Morris from Moira N York, called and put up with us. My husband I think baptised him, when on his mission the year previous. He gave us an account of our cousin Simon Steven's family who lived in Moira, and also informed us concerning cousin Carlos, who he had accidentally fallen in co with on his travels to the west. Said he left him at work up in the north part of Ill. Said C wished him to visit his sister Jane, and take a letter to her from him. Mr C concluded to go with him next day in search of her.

[Carthage Jail Massacre]

June 27th 1844 we arose with heavy hearts, full of doubts and fears respecting the safety of our beloved Prophet and Patriarch who were then incarcerated in Carthage jail. The city was full of rumors concerning the mob who were assembling at Warsaw and Carthage.

Mr C—— and bro Morris set off in to find cousin Jane. Walked out to the young Mark's, on the prairie, but found she had come into the City. They left her letter, with directions for her to call and see us.

That Pm the governor with a large posse came to Nauvoo, and requested the legion to deliver up their arms, which they did.[3] He then made a lengthy address to the saints, exhorting them to keep quiet &C.

which they obeyed to the very letter, but felt greatly insulted by him, knowing that there was no occasion for his remarks, or counsel.

The next morning at an early hour, the news of Joseph and Hiram's [Hyrum] massare was spread throughout the length and breadth of the city. We would not believe the first report, but finally it was confirmed to us beyond a doubt. And Oh the sorrow and sadness of that day! many were made sick by the intelligence, others deranged. Many walked the streets mourning and wringing their hands. I lost my strength and appetitet, could not atttend to any business for several days. Pm their bodies were brought home; and arrangements made for their burial. Every body was invited, or rather had the privilege of seeing them by walking through the house, we went in at one door, passed by their coffins, gave them a short look, and then went out on the opposite side. They were much disfigured. I thought they did not look natural, in the least, could scarcely tell them apart.

[Leadership of Brigham Young, August 1844]

I shall not attempt to describe the confusion and doubts the church was thrown into for a short time, with regard to our leader, or president, untill the return of bro Brigham Young, and other members of the twelve, when all, or nearly all were at rest, upon that subject.

Sidney Rigdon came to the stand and tried to show to the people that he was the rightful successor of Joseph. And his arguments were so powerful, that many were almost persuaded to believe him such. But as soon as the twelve apostles with bro Brigham Young at their head took the stand, it was shown conclusively where the power rested. It was the first time, that I ever thought he resembled bro Joseph. But almost every one exclaimed that the mantle of Joseph had fallen on Brigham. For one I never had any doubts afterward.[4]

[David Crosby's Death, Oct 1844]

We all soon became comforted concerning our leaders, but perecution continued all around us. The brethren were obliged to be on guard all the time. The sickly season soon commecnced. I was sick several weeks. In the meantime bro David B—— Crosby took sick and died. He was much exposed by being on guard, and going from home to work for his living. Times were very hard for the poor brethren. He went out to the prairie to cut hay, where he took his last sickness. I had not seen him in two weeks when he died, having been confined to the house with chills. He was mild and gentle, an industrious honest saint, and bro. Died *Oct 29th 1844* Peace to his spirit. His family mourned his [*illegible crossout*] theire loss extremely. My husband labored on the temple, which was prosecuted with renewed vigor, after the death of Joseph and Hiram.

The church renewed their zeal for the cause by holding frequent meetings from house to house and exhorting the brethren to set their house in order, according to the order of God. The twelve and high council were appointed to that office. Father Bent came two or 3 times to our house.[5]

Sister M[arial] Crosby moved in with her bro H[arvey] Thompson. Thus passed away the year 1844.

[Nauvoo, 1845]

1845. Came cousin Jane A Stevens to live with us. I learned her to braid palmleaf hats. Nancy H—— and Alma also worked some at it.

Carlos Stevens was a regular visitor. We admired him much. He and his sister had left their parents the spring previous, had been keeping house on the prairie, previous to her coming to live with us. In june or july the rest of the family arrived in Nauvoo.

Their mother was sick and had been all the way up the mississippi Had been sorely afflicted with musketoes, had large sores on her limbs which continued to run for a long time. They all came to our house, stoped a week or more. When they rented a house east of the temple Jane commenced a school in the upper part of the house, but taught only two weeks. She afterwards went to Dr Phinehas Richards, where she stoped awhile, but her health being very poor, soon returned home. Sister Lois Thompson gave birth to her son David

Sept—— Amelia [Stevens] came to nurse her. After staying one month, she came to live with us. This fall the seventies completed their hall. The dedication continued several days untill all the different quorums had each had a feast, and rejoicing in it.

Early in the fall the persecution was renewed in the surrounding settlements, insomuch that the branches were advised to move into Nauvoo. Bro Bullocks from Lima came in, and stoped a week or two with us. They lost a considerable property by the removal. They with a number other families moved into the then called Foster house, which bro Joseph used to call the Mammoth home.

[Death a Frequent Visitor]

The upper part of the temple was finished this winter, and endowments were given to the majority of the brethren. We received our washings and anointings sometime in *Jan.* Afterwards were sealed by bro Kimball.[6] I had forgotten to say that bro Samuel Stevens died after a short illness in

Oct—— 45. His wife was taken sick in Jan '46, and after about 4 weeks sickness she also died, having been only 6 months in Nauvoo.[7]

I went to visit her, washed and anointed her from head to foot, with sister P's help. She seemed very anxious to live to receive her endowments in the temple and we also felt very sorry that she could not. I anointing her, inadvertently told her, that it was for her burial. Notwithstanding my anxiety to have her live. But the words some way pressed themselves out of my mouth.

She died in the faith of the evelasting gospel, her last words were those of counsel to her family about preparing to go with the church to Cal——[8] Her children were almost inconsolable at her death. Amelia came to live with us sometime previous to her fathers death. We both visited them often in during their illness.

A sister Newel who was near neighbor to us died the same day that bro Stevens did. I was present at her death. She died with chills conjestive chills. Left a number of small children, and husband to mourn for her. Death became so frequent a visitor in Nauvoo that we were perfectly familliar with it. Amelia lived with us all winter.[9]

Carlos and the other children kept house a few weeks after their mothers death, but finally Jane got married to Kimball Bullock, and went to the west or winter quarters.[10] Took Alvira [Stevens] with her Carlos and Barnard came and lived with us.[11]

We enjoyed ourselves very well for awhile. Haying season coming on the boys left us, and went to Alton where they worked about 3 months. Did very well, staid untill after harvest. When they returned found us all sick. Barnard assisted about house Carlos went to work for Mr Kenny at the stone house; staid 2 or 3 weeks and then returned sick.

[Mob Attacks in Nauvoo]

The mob soon commenced operations against the few remaining saints[12] and new citizens, who were determined to stand their ground as long as they could; every instrument of warfare was called into requisition. My husband being sick at that time, the [militia] of the city came and took his rifle, and bowie knife, promising to return them, but he never saw them again.

They resisted the mob for several weeks. I could sit, or lie, in my house, and hear the canons roar, and count 40 in succession. Our healths were miserable all the time. Still my mind was quite calm and tranquill untill toward the last. 2 or 3 of our brethren were killed, which caused my heart to sink, and I began to fear we should be overpowered by our enemies. Our officers reported many of the mob killed, but the exact number was unknown. Various reports were in circulation. Sometimes we were expecting friends to come to our relief, at others the mob was gaining numbers. But pen cannot describe our feelings and situation.[13] Being annoyed as we were with sickness, fleas, bugs, and musketoes. No one to come into wait on us, and we unable to wait on one another. In the meantime there was a Dr Wm Smith come in from Laharp, and stoped with his family in a house just opposite of us. He showed himself very friendly, gave us some medicine, and receipts to make more.

Amelia Carlos and Barnard, had their lodging in Thompsons chambers. Sometimes came to our house to eat, and at others cooked and ate there. The war was finally concluded, by a party of mediators from Quincy, who professed to do justice, but the concessions were all on the side of the Saints. They were to lay down their arms, and leave the city in ten days, with a promise of receiving their arms again on the Iowa side of the river. The mob was then allowed to come into the city without destroying any property, or molesting any one.

Accordingly on the *17th* (I think *of*) *Sept——— 1846*, they came in and patrolled the city, wherever they pleased. Mr Crosby was then able to walk about, and was out in the street and saw them.

Caroline ends her memoirs of Nauvoo here in September 1846. On the 17th of that month the last of the Mormons were driven from the city by mobs after a three-day battle culminating in the surrender of Nauvoo one day earlier. The next existing folder of her writings begins 10 May 1848 and is a diary of her journey from Bentonsport, Iowa to Salt Lake City.

Fortunately, Jonathan Crosby's own memoirs bridge the gap here in Caroline's writings. Of the fourteen thousand or more Saints who left the Nauvoo area for the West in 1846, it is estimated between two thousand and three thousand lagged behind, halting temporarily in southeastern Iowa and northern Missouri.[14] Suffering from poverty and ill health, lacking food, funds, good wagons and teams, many sought housing and jobs, among them the Crosbys. The following is extracted from Jonathan Crosby's "Biographical Sketch Written by Himself."

In *February 46* the Church began to move. A large company left, crossed the River & went on to Garden Grove & Pisga. We stayed in Nau——— untill after the mob came when we were all sick & in poverty also, tormented with musketoes, flees, & bedbugs, we could lay abed, & hear the roar of cannon & guns in time of ware. & when the mob came into the City, one of them a old Missourian mober came into my house leveled his gun at me to shoot, demanded my armes but I had none but a pistol, I gave him that & he left, shortly after 3 or 4 of the mob came in & talked quite friendly said we should'nt be hurt, but we might stay as long as we pleased. Although I was sick I made out to get a waggon fixt up & loaded our things in to it & got a yoke of oxen of a brother & hauled it down to the river & thare we lay 2 or 3 days sleeping in our waggons, awaiting to be ferried over; at length they took us over the west side of the big slue whare we stayed a week or more & the quailes were very plenty.[15] I had a gun that I got towards our place I sold to German he gave me a coat a gun & an old watch for it; it was worth several 100 dols. & with the gun killed some of the quailes, which was a great help to us in our poverty. In the time of the ware we were out of anything to eat, & all sick with the ague, I was just able to walk about, so I cald on bro Joseph L Haywood[16] & made know our Condition, & he in much kindness provided some food for us, which was verry thankfuly received. . . . While we were lying by the big Slue I killed many quails others that were camped thare did likewise. After a week or more I borowed a yoke of oxen & moved up to Jackoak grove, thare we camped a week or more in company with severel others; then I got a brother to take his team & hawl us over to Sugar Creek a few miles further. (Whare Pres. B Young & company camped in winter after leaving Nauvoo) Quailes were very plenty every whare som have said that they went out & picked them up alive,[17] but I saw no such thing with me they so wiled I could hardly get near enough to shoot them.

Shortly after arriveing at Sugar Creek a man came to us. (A gentile.) & learning our situation, said he wanted some work done on his house & if we would go, he would come the nxt day and hawl us thare, a few miles further on. The next day he came with team & hawled us to his home. (His name I forget) We were quite unwell I had a chill every other day, but nevertheless I went to work, some of time I had to stop. Several weeks we stayed thare & were treated verry kindely, but the ague hung on to us, & as winter was coming on, he was affraid we would be a burden to him. So he proposed to take us to Bonypart, 5 or 6 miles further, & we were quite willing to go. In Bonipart we found brother Melvin Wilber with his family, with them we stayed a week or 2. We had 2 cows that we brought from Nauvoo, only one gave milk, the other was quite fat so I kild her & sold some for bred stuff, so we had enough to eat. (It was in November I think) Soon we moved into Bentonsport,[18] into a house with a brother Cheney; David Moore a mechanic worked in one room of the house, but did'nt stay but a day or 2, we mooved into a little shanty a little way off, but I worked in thare with Moor a while made a few bedsteds; then I got chance to work on a house makeing sash & Doors at a very low rate. So we lived, provisions were very cheep & I made out get aplenty, & with my work I got a yoke of oxen, a yoke of 2 year old steers & cow, got fitted out with provisions, & in May[19] fore part I think I yoked the cows & steers, started of for Kanesvill or some whare else, did not know whare. About the middle of the day we came to slew, & in crossing it got stuck; unhitched the teem & commenced unlodeing the waggon, When on looking back saw a yoke of oxen comeing all yoked up, so I hitched them on with my one & pulled out, turned them loose again, put in things we took out, & went on, we looked upon that as favor & blessing from Father.

At this point Caroline's journal of reminiscences begun in Tubuai in 1851 is replaced with a daily log begun 10 May 1848 of the trip from Bentsonsport, Iowa to Winter Quarters and on to Salt Lake City. After reaching the Salt Lake Valley on 12 October 1848, her journal records a synopsis of events until 7 May 1850, at which time a daily record of the trip to California and the Society Islands begins.

CHAPTER FIVE

Across the Plains to Salt Lake Valley

Journal, 10 May to 12 October 1848

[Leaving Bentonsport, Iowa]

Wed May 10th 1848 left North Bentonsport crossed the Desmoine put up at Br Moore's waited untill the next Monday for com, but no one being ready we concluded to [*illegible crossout*] proceed alone. Accordingly about 9 oclock we started, br and Sis Moore accompanied us almost to Merits. Bathia came down to bid us farewell, came with [us] beyond the school-house. I felt bad to part with her, could not refrain from tears, was also much affected when I parted with Sis Moore, she was very kind to us while we stayed there. My health was poor, scarcely able to wait on myself sis M treated me with the affection of a sister, which I hope I shall never forget.

Our team was rather wild we were fearful that they would not be sufficient for our load, but they did much better than we expected travelled on untill 3 or 4 oclock when it commenced raining which made it muddy and slippery, we concluded not to travel in the rain, but just before we were ready to stop the cattle landed us safely into a mud hole from which we could not extricate ourselves untill the next morn. while he was meditating where to go for help he accidentally beheld a large old yoke of oxen grazing near us, and after consulting a couple of german who were at work near by took them as they were ready yoked and with the help of our old cattle hauled out the waggon. We then came on smoothly to indian creek where we put up for the night in hopes some one would come along to accompany us, but no one arrived, we accordingly proceeded on our way to fox river had some difficulty in the forenoon got set once had to partialy unload the waggon, loaded up went on a piece got hitched against a root hindred us some time arrived within a mile of String town a little before sunset stoped for the night found brother Levi Allred living close bye.

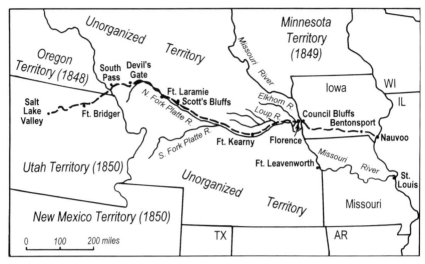

Route from Nauvoo, Illinois, to Salt Lake Valley, 1848.

Thursday morning had an addition of a calf to our stock which hindered us through the day. *Friday* morning started on, carried the calf a greater part of the day, Friday night stoped on the prairie near a well, got mired in a mud hole just this side of the well. unloaded part of our things. *Saturday* came on through Drakesville lost our way, went down to Fox river bottoms got stalled again, had to unload, ~~again~~ it rained while we were there, such a time as we had I never experienced before, it hindred us half a day; got back into the right way came on to a new road staid over night near an old farmers, very friendly people, offered to let us sleep in their house, let us through their field to shun a bad hill. *Sunday* morning pursued our journey fell in co with Kire and Dukes son were glad to find co. Jimy swung his hat when he saw us and rejoiced. Sunday we had a good day's travel came within 4 miles of soap creek staid near a farmer by the name of Foster late from Missouri very sociable and friendly.

Monday about 9 oclock PM arrived at Soap, found a tremendous bad hill to come down got through safely, found a co camped there from Iowaville passed them and went on to the open prairie stop'd over night took a cold supper and breakfast next morning, came on to a spring where was a man building a house, found br Jolly and Millets family there, stoped and got a warm dinner, rested our teams and then came on to another farmhouse, put up for the night, soon after our arrival, we were joined by 8 waggons, 5 from Iowaville and 3 from near Montrose, which with our two, made 10 in all.

Wed 24th came on with our large co stoped at noon in the prairie to bait and rest our teams, the wind commences blowing looks likely to rain, high wind all the afternoon & much rain. Wed night staid at Sheridan point found Dack and one other family living there.

Thursday 25th came on to another point of timber near Sheridan river, very warm day some of their cattle gave out had to stop till near night.

26th Friday morn one of our oxen went off had to hunt a long time, found him on a mile ahead of us. Friday forenoon passed the road that led to Garden grove came onto a bad ravine had to get help'd through, came on till noon, <saw the place where a woman was killed by a waggon running over her, and buried by the side of the road,> stoped to rest in the open prairie, no water near came on to a little stream called white breast put up for night, had a little prayer meeting, it seemed quite natural to get to a mormon meeting once more they all seemed to rejoice that they had got liberated from the gentiles once more.

Saturday very windy, felt quite unwell all day. Sat night staid within 7 miles of Pisgah.

[Pisgah, Iowa]

Sunday, came on a way hard rain accompanied with thunder and lightning, stoped near little creek 4 miles from Pisgah untill the rain was over, Came on through Pisgah road very muddy nothing seemed very pleasant to me, called at Cluff's saw br Grover which were all that I knew Jimmy Duke and br Kire got in just before us and took another road so that I had no chance to bid them farewell.

Crossed a branch of Grand river very bad bridge had to ford. a few miserable looking log cabins in P[isgah], and some of the raggedest children I ever saw, I went into Cluffs they were all very comfortably clad Sister Cluff shed tears when she told me she had heard by some of our co that her son Moses who had been at work in Iowaville was going off on a steam boat. In P—— we passed Merkly and Conly who had been waiting a day or two for com. came on seven miles stoped near a stream staid one day to wash and bake.

Monday were joined by Merkly and Conly, two br father Shearer and Gould met us direct from the bluffs[1] had a meeting father Shearer spoke some time on the necessity of prayer and other Christian duties after which fa Gould gave us a brief sketch of his travels, to the valle which was very interesting, and concluded by exhorting us to be of one mind, and keep the commandments of God.

Tuesday proceeded on our journey about 20 miles fine day for travelling staid in the great prairie where was no wood we all brought a little enough boil tea kettle. Tunigth met another waggon from the bluffs.

Wednesday the last day of may pleasant cool day for travelling have just stoped for noon all in good health and spirits crossed seve[r]al bad ravines to day, just crossed quite a stream fork of grand river another broad prairie before us, staid in the great prairie Wed night.

[A Visit to the Indian Graves]

June 1st Thursday drove very hard all day crossed several bad ravines and bridges arrived very late at Indian town, staid near to the Misery Botoms. Visited the indian graves, curiosities to me.

Friday morn June 2nd, visited the indian graves the great curiosity respecting them was that of two infants coffins which had been put up in trees, one had fallen down and broke open, they were each made of two troughs, the child was laid in one and the other composed the lid, nothing remained of the child but some few bones, the skull was very plain to be seen, the blanket and beads and a ladle were also in complete preservation.

We crossed the Misery bottoms again and traveled on very smoothly met two brethren from the bluffs. Phineas Kimball was one he brought me a line from sis P. the other I did not know. stoped for night near where some brethren have stoped to make claims.[2]

Saturday morn all hands in search of cattle, looks likely to rain, two days drive from the bluffs. Saturday night stoped at Silver creek had a hard rain to day roads very bad arrived late at our stoping place found quite a settlement of brethren here, a fiddler came in to the camp, set some of them to dancing. I have had the headache all the afternoon cannot enjoy their mirth very well.

[Arrival at Winter Quarters (Kanesville), June 4, 1848]

Sunday June 4th arrived safely in winter quarters, camped two miles from the tabernacle.[3] feel very anxious to go on but fear we are not suitably prepared. Met br Phineas Young just moved over from the other side of the river. his wife is sick been so for more than a year, looks very bad.

Monday morn very cold wind, disagreeable being out, heard sis P has gone. expect I shall not see her untill we get to the valley.[4] *Tuesday* washed and ironed think we shall go ahead at all events. br Draper called on us told us where Marial Crosby lived. *Wednesday* we visited her found her quite comfortably situated, appeared very glad to see us. made her a short visit. Harlan came home with us and staid over night.[5]

Thursday brother Merkly gone to winter quarters to get counsel whether to stop here untill the company gets ready to start, or go over to winter quarters and wait there.[6] We understand the indians are troublesome there, have killed one of our brethren and wounded another.

Sunday June 11th Father Bullock and wife came along and offered to carry me to meeting, I went heard [Almon] Babbitt speak on the origin of the priesthood, and the proceedings of the trustees in Nauvoo. After which Br [Joseph L.] Haywood spoke, and was followed by George A Smith, who justified them, and said he believed they had done the best they could. All hands requested to go and hunt Indians. *Saturday* previous Merkly returned, his horses stolen by indians. had been trailing them 2 days, nothing to be found of them, has to part his family, sends his wife and son on to the vally, stays himself untill another year. *Tuesday* Hutchinson and wife called to see us, promised to come and make us a visit the next day, next morning Huchinson had a bad fit, could not come, she came in the afternoon, made us an agreeable visit. *Wednesday* a company of 13 wagons arrived from Montrose among which was Daniel Jackson's *Thursday* left Musketoe creek, came within 2 miles of the ferry, found a good camping place, where we stoped untill Saturday. A sister Tanner who had been over to the council house on a visit on her way home staid with us over night, and rode with us part of the afternoon. had quite an agreeable time with her found her an intelligent interesting woman.

[Crossing the Missouri]

Saturday june 17th arrived at the ferry had to wait untill sunday morn Merkly and Conly gone over our turn comes next. Found Samuel Richards and wife just came over from the other side going down 60 miles in Mo to live on a farm. he has latly returned from Europe on a 2–years mission, had the small pox is quite disfigured with it, her health very poor had the chills and fever for sometime. The wind rises begins to rain fear it will be bad crossing. went into the store this morn in co with sis Merkly, found nothing that I wanted.

[Arrival at Winter Quarters (Nebraska), June 18, 1848]

Sunday morning arrived safely at winter quarters called at br Hewitt's, staid, till towards night, came up to the camping ground, stoped near an old chimney where they told us John Parker formerly lived. *Monday* washed *Tuesday* commenced braiding a hat. *Wednesday* made crackers. *Thursday* rainy day, cold and unpleasant, felt sick all day in consequence of the hard days work the day before, *Friday* finished my hat, sis Merkly and I took a walk about town. Called at Phinehas Richards saw B Johnson's Also called at Nathan Tanner's, had quite an agreeable time. *Sunday 25th* very windy, baked bread in br Robinson's and prepared to leave on *Monday*, but did not get started untill Thursday, feel very anxious to get away from the flies and dirt which are almost intolerable.

[Leaving Winter Quarters, June 29, 1848]

Thursday all hands begin to roll out, great rejoicing among us. All seem pleased to leave the Omahaw's lands, and the dirt cabins, which are only fit for such a race. *Thursday* night 29th stop'd on a high prairie very pleasant arrived late probably about 80 wagons. 6 miles.

    Friday morn expect to stay here today, the co waiting for Dr [Willard] Richards.[7] Br Amasa [Lyman] is addressing the brethren. Sister Merkley and myself been taking a walk; yesterday her husband parted with her probably for a year, she feels quite dejected and unwell.

[Elkhorn River, July 1, 1848 *27 miles from W.Q.*[8]]

Sat——July 1st today all hands rolling out, going onto the horn [Elkhorn][9] leave Dr Richards to come with another com. Br Lyman waited as long as he dares to, fears cold weather will over take us before we get through, last night we were much disturbed with the cattle, the guard had as much as they could do to keep them within bounds.

    Sunday the 2nd all crossed the horn formed a large circle with the sheep fold in the centre everything good order and harmony.

    Monday all washing and baking expect to wait 2 or 3 days for Dr Richards

    Wednesday a messenger arrived from him requesting us to wait untill Friday. Br A Lyman has consented to it *Thursday* night Dr R arrived with quite a large co and I understand not much order in it.[10]

[Liberty Pole, July 7, 1848]

Friday morn 7th day all preparing to go ahead, it appears that the 1st are to be last, and the last first as the scripture says. The camp are all in tolerable health I believe two children born since we stoped here. My health been rather poor, ~~since~~ It is a cool windy day good weather travelling *Friday* camped near platte river close by the liberty pole, sis Merkley and myself with several others inscribed our names on it. I understand it was erected by P P Pratt and J[ohn] Taylor, it is now filled with names nearly as high as they can reach, the platte is good water but rather rily.

    Saturday, July 8th 1848 all preparing roll on. When I first awoke this morn I imagined myself on a large farm with numerous flocks and herds about me of all descriptions, cocks crowing cows lowing sheep bleating and pigs squeeling, and to crown the music, children crying. Sat night staid near the platte again.[11]

    Sunday 9th rested and attended meeting. Br A Lyman read the rules of the camp and exhorted us to attend to religious duties and strive to live in peace one with another. Sunday night sister Tanner called to see us. Sis Baily sick with teethache had hands laid on her, I was called on to assist in taking care of her children.

Mon 10th cool pleasant morn the old cow strayed from the camp probably gone to the other co.

[Shell Creek, July 11, 1848 *62¼ mi*]

Tuesday morn 11th cool air, very pleasant Last night the old cow had an heir, shall be obliged to carry it a day or two. Yesterday Nelson Merkly broke his wagon tongue, made a new one last night. We staid at a very pleasant camping place called shell creek, plenty of grapes. I gathered quite a quantity

Wednesday the 5th co went ahead, the heat and dirt was almost insufferable, several pigs died and cattle almost gave out, we staid close to a little lake southside the road, having travelled 11 miles and ¾.

[Beaver River, July 13, 1848 *103¾ mi.*]

Thursday night staid at Beaver river, a very pleasant stream some of the cattle strayed to the other camp which caused bad feelings, but they were all in vain for they found them again before night, the next ~~night~~ day *friday* came to cedar creek, pass'd the indian settlements, or where ~~the Omahaws~~ [*illegible crossout*] they had been burnt out by the sioux,[12] several of the Omahas came to our camp staid overnight. Capt [William] Crosby[13] fed and kept them to prevent their stealing.

Sat 15th one mile from loup fork, it commences raining. crossed over the fork near an indian settlement, had plenty of visitors but not very agreeable ones, came on a mile or two staid over *Sunday* expected to have meeting, but all had to go and help Dr Ric[hards] co over, and the women had a washing party at loup fork beautiful soft water. *Monday July 17th* very warm morning, quite an alarm raised about indians thought they were driving off cattle several men went armed on horseback, but it was a false alarm. (Last night called on sis tanner her oldest daughter sick with ague, she gave me a piece of good cheese.)

[Upper Ford of Loup Fork, July 17, 1848 *133¾ mi.*]

Monday came on to loup fork near the upper ford the heat and dust almost suffocating Brs Lyman and Capt Flake went ahead and found a letter from the other comp. Found they were just one month before us, we have gained three days of them in coming from the horn. *Tuesday* morning cool and cloudy, have 20 miles to go to day and expect find no wood to night. Teusday night arrived in good season at our stopping place near prairie creek, having had a cool comfortable day for travelling. *Wednesday* very warm have 10 miles to go to day, had a beautiful camping place last night, on a high prairie, entirely out of sight of tim[ber]. Wednesday night arrived late at our camping place having travelled much farther than we expected to in the morning we stoped about 4 miles west of wood river in an entirely new camping place, being almost worn out with the heat and dust. Capts Lyman and Flake went on a hunting excursion, got so far from the camp and being destitute of water they nearly perished with fatigue and thirst, their horses broke from them by being frightened with an antelope, which they caught they were discovered by Dr Richard and rescued from their almost perishing condition, br Lyman I understand was so far exhausted as to be deprived of reason.[14]

[Platte River, July 20, 1848 *183¼ mi.*]

Thursday July 20th 1848 came to the platte again, where the road descends to the low lands, having travelled 8 miles.

Friday 21th[st] this morning they have been repairing wagons, have spent nearly half of the day, which has given us time to wash; the platte is rather hard or at least not as soft as loup fork. yesterday and today the weather has been quite comfortable. I understand that br Lyman is quite low yet, not able to speak above his breath. Our camping place is very beautifully situated on the platte, an excellent chance for cattle. Yesterday the prairie took fire by Capt [William] Crosby light a pipe and spread with great violence, the wind however being in our favor it passed by us without doing any material injury. Friday night stayed on the platte again, plenty of grass but no wood short of going to an island just opposite our camping place, it was quite a curiosity to see the men and boys wade the river, which is very wide, and return with old trees on their shoulders, so that we had a good supply of wood. *Sat 22nd* cool and cloudy, the camp preparing to take an early start. Last night the girls sung me to sleep with songs and hymns, quite a mixture of moral and religious music. Saturday travelled 20 miles, which kept us out untill near nine oclock at night, we then stoped far from timber, and were forbidden to make fires, on account of high winds and dry grass.

Sunday morn 23rd winds still high were afraid to burn what little wood we picked up here and there probably flood wood, some went and dug fire places in the river's bank, it however abated towards noon so that by diging holes in the ground we ventured to make fires. Sunday the brethren killed an immense sight of wild game I believe 4 buffaloes and some 12 or 15 antelopes and deers which supplied both camps abundantly with fresh meat, and a great deal was dried to carry along. This morn we met a company returning from the Valley, principaly soldiers returning for their pay.[15] some of them left the vally the 8th june which make 45 days they have been coming.

Monday morn 24th this morn they talk of dividing the companies into three division, the prospect is we shall have warm day. *Tuesday 25th* contrary to our expectations yesterday morn we have stay untill today, the council was sometime deciding upon our manner of travelling, none of our com were willing to leave and go into Dr Richards, they therefore decided that we should all travel together in a large body, for the present. We have 23 miles to go today, my health is quite poor, was very unwell yesterday, but feel better today.

Wed 26th last nigth we arrived late at our camping place, had some rain towards evening, had to go to bed on a cold supper after being sick all day, took pills last night, feel better this morning, think I am troubled with the kidney and liver complaint. Yesterday I invited sister Riettchie [*spelling unclear*] a doctress woman to come in and see me: She thought she could help me if she could find the roots she wanted, but feared she could not. This morning the weather is remarkably cold for the season, have 20 miles to go.

[Tragic Accident]

Thursday 27th Yesterday a very sad accident occured in the camp one of Sidney Tanner's little boys was killed almost instantly by a wagon wheel runing over him, he appeared like a very forward smart child for one of his age, was between 6 and 7 years was driving team sitting on the tongue and fell backwards.

Friday the 28th cool and cloudy, correlled near the river last night, plenty of buffalo chips, but no wood. This morning they are burying the child, have brought it thus far along to find a proper burying place. There are high bluffs here some distance from the river. Friday came a short distance correlled near the river ^tremendous hard shower.^ *Saturday* all hands washing, baking and hunting. Satu eve terrible storm of wind and rain, hunters had a bad time, did not return untill late at night, sis Merkley slept with me in consequence of her wagon being gone after buffalo

Sunday we still continued our labours ^washing and cooking^ as we expect to see no more wood at present. In the evening the counsel held a meeting to organize travelling companies. We are in the second co led by Capt [Andrew] Cunningham I believe there are some little feelings, with some of the old women and girls, for one I am quite passive on the subject, notwithstanding my former acquaintances are principly in the other co's.[16] *Mon 31st* All preparing to leave Dr Richards takes the lead, we are in the centre; br Lyman brings up the rear. Mon night camped on skunk creek a very pleasant little stream. Dr R's co just opposite us, a plenty of buffalo chips to cook with, and fine chance for the cattle.

[Buffalo at the Platte, Aug. 1, 1848 *295 mi.*]

Aug 1st; this morn we were visited by a large herd of buffalo, but they all escaped unhurt. It is a fine pleasant morning. Tuesday night, came 15 miles correlled close to the platte, heard the buffalo bellowing, and wolves[17] howling all night, thousands of them to be seen on the opposite shore, but out of the reach of the hunters, had a hard shower of rain. We however succeeded in getting a fire made and teakettle boiled. Br Luce's wagon broke down to day had to distribute his load among our ten.

Wednesday 2nd cool and pleasant, teamsters preparing to leave.

Thursday 3rd Soon after we started Yesterday we were met by a large band of Sioux warriers going to battle with the Pawnees. They were dressed in very spendid indian style, appeared very friendly to us, traded some with our people, swaped horses &C. We crossed black mud creek a little before night, came to where the road and river joins and camped; passed Dr Richards co a mile or two back. Last night some of the brethren worked all night mending wagon for br Luce.

Our co trying to get away before Dr's comes along. We understand that his co have voted him in sole leader their band, which I suppose constitutes them a separate party.

[Sandy Bluffs, Aug. 4, 1848]

Friday 4th Yesterday we crossed the sandy bluffs which are very curiously formed. I took a walk by myself; passed through some of the most singular looking places I ever saw; it seemed to me that nature in her playful moments had formed curiosities for her own sport. One I observed which was particularly interesting. It was formed in the shape of a bowl, and I presume 20 feet deep, and so steep that it was hard climbing up the sides, it had no entrance only at the top, with not a stick or shrub of any kind but lined with clean white sand, almost as white as snow. In the course of my walk I saw a large buffalo which had been to the river for drink, he was just rising the bank as I came in sight of him. It appeared that his curiosity was as much aroused as mine, he gazed at me for a moment as I did at him then shaking his head and switching his tail, started toward me in great haste, but as there were several deep gulfs between us I was not much afraid of his reaching before I could gain the wagons, however I concluded it was best for me to be leaving. We arrived at our camping ground in good season, found a very pleasant bottom with plenty of feed and water, and dry willows for fires.

[An Encampment of Sioux]

Saturday 5th last night we staid near spring creek very good camping place plenty of buffalo, our boys killed one. Met a company of soldiers returning from California. We understand there are lots of indians a little ahead of us, expect to meet or pass them to day. Saturday evening arrived at the indian town where were quite a large body of Sioux. They seemed much pleased to see us, commenced beging immediately and offering their skins and mockasins for sale, would give a good pair of mockasins for a slice of bread. Their curiosity was much excited at seeing our wagons and the variety of animals we had. They were willing to trade us anything they had even to their squaws, offered my husband a young one for me, wanted to buy our children, but notwithstanding their professed friendship they stole a number of articles from us before we could get away. Their chiefs tried hard to keep them back from our wagons but it was almost impossible. We did not intend to travel on *Sunday* but in consequence of being so annoyed, our Capts thought best to travel on, and rest the next day. Accordingly we came 7 or 8 miles (escorted by some of their young warriors half that distance) and put up untill *Monday* noon, we then proceeded to shoal creek, staid on the ground where the forward companies had staid found buffalo chips [al]read[y] gathered.

[Lone Tree, Aug. 8, 1848 *378 mi.*]

Tuesday 8th came 15 or 16 miles ^passed the lone tree^[18] staid on the bank of the river, excellent feed for the cattle. *Wednesday* cool wind, just visited by an indian, preparing teams to roll out. *Thursday* morn, we had not proceeded far yesterday when we were met by a number of Indians on horseback some of the same we passed a day or two before, they dismounted and asked a present, the same as they had done before, probably thinking we should not know them. The company nearly all gave them something, they followed us 2 or 3 hours, traded some mocasins and buffalo robes for bread and meal. At night we staid where the road and river joins. Yesterday we found several buffalo skulls with inscriptions on them which gave us intelligence from the forward co's, We found they were a month wanting four days before us. This morn is very cool and cloudy. *Friday* morn we have a prospect of a warm day.

[Sightseeing at the Ancient Bluff Ruins, Aug. 10, 1848 *419 mi.*]

Yesterday we passed what Clayton[19] call the cobble hills, and as the road was sandy and hard on teams, we all concluded to walk that were able to. Sis Merkley and myself took it into our heads to take an excursion over

~~the hills~~ ancient bluff ruins. I presume we travelled 5 miles over some of the greatest natural curiosities our eyes ever beheld, they resembled very much the ancient ruins I which I have heard discribed by travellers in central america and other places. We climbed several steep ascents where we would have thought it almost impossible for persons in our feeble health to have ascended, but curiosity lent strength to our limbs, and our ascending one only added fresh desires to attain that of another, and thus we were led on from one to another untill we began to fear we should be left far in the rear of our company who already feared we were lost or taken captive by indians. But we had no such fears as we were nearly all the while in sight of the wagons. One singularity we noticed was several old cedar trees growing at that great height just between those barren rocks, and now and then a low shrub a little wild sage and one article we called wild camomile. The tops of the rocks were bespangled with a red moss wrought into many curios flowers and also scatered over with a variety of pebblestones resembling those in the beds of our eastern streams. ^They extended over many acres and were as level on the tops as a floor, the edges projected over in many places and under them were dens and haunts for wild beasts^[20] Between the immense piles of rocks were several dry creeks, and the whole land for many miles had no doubt been once the bed of some mighty stream probably connected with the platte. We were led many times admire and adore the God of nature who in his mighty power formed such wonderful curiosities. Marvelous are thy works thou Lord of hosts.

^We found several places where there were stairs formed by nature quite convenient to descend. Our minds were so much delighted with the novelty of the surrounding scenery that we almost forgot we were a little past the meridian of life, and for a moment imagined ourselves mere children, sporting at leisure. All the animal we saw was one little rabbit which ran from us in great fear and a few very pretty birds that seemed make homes in the old cedar trees.^

Saturday morn cool and cloudy, last night met another company of Sioux beging for something to eat, a comp of them on the opposite side the river this morn, they have come again asking for sugar, brought letters from the leaders of the forward companies. I gave them a little they appeared very thankful said we would all go togather and dance togather. *Sunday 13th* last night corralled near the river, many indians around us. Our company rests today. Dr Richards co came up with us. It is a pleasant place here but no wood and few buffalo chips. No chance for washing or baking.

[Spring Creek, Aug. 14, 1848 *476 mi.*]

Monday. Yesterday we had a cold rain, it is remarkbly cold for the season, we expect to cross the river today. *Tuesday* morn very pleasant We still continue on the north side of the river. Staid at spring creek last night, a very pleasant little stream, water clear as chrystal.

16th wednesday, last night staid at a small creek which runs near the river very good water, but no wood short of wading the creek and river to an island.

[Road to Laramie Fort]

Thursday 17th Yesterday we crossed the platte, found plenty of good dry wood but poor feed for cattle. Dr's co are on the opposite side, last night had music and dancing inside the carrall, expect to reach Laramie to day.

Friday morning last night staid in sight of Laramie fort three gentlemen from there visited our camp, we found good roads the most of the way yesterday after crossing the river, it seemed like the eastern turnpikes.

Last night my favorite pet sheep was destroyed by wolves. My heart ached when I saw the bloody rope which was round her neck and I could not refrain from tears. I feel like waging a war of extermination against those ferocious beasts of prey. But her destruction was occasioned by neglect or carelessness. I sincerely wish we may learn wisdom by the things we suffer. *Monday morn 21st* We have been staying here on the bank of the river since Friday noon, about 7 miles from Laramie. I understand the Dr camp has passed us. The brethren have burned a tar kiln [charcoal pit?] and made some repairs on their wagons.

[Warm Springs, Aug. 21, 1848 *536¼ mi.*]

22nd Yesterday passed the warm spring, heavy sandy road our Capt intended us to keep the river road, he therefore called us back 2 or 3 miles through the sand, brought us up several bad hills, we travelled untill 9 oclock and then found no feed for cattle. The herdsmen took a different road and staid out all night with nothing but milk to eat from one morning untill the next, excepting a little bread which sister Merkley sent them by Nelson who went in search of them after sunset in co with br Luces boy and staid untill morn. They arrived at the camp about breakfast time in good spirits, said they had not suffered for victuals as they had the cows and bells to drink out of. *Wed* yesterday we came only 4 miles in consequence of the hard jaunt the day before, found good water wood and tolerable feed for cattle. *Thursday* last night stoped in good season very good feed plenty of water wood and thousands of choke cherries and the largest black currants I ever saw, besides hops in abundance. We all gathered as many as we could, in so short time. One of our oxen gave out ye[s]ter[day] in consequence of having a very sore neck, Capt Clark let us have one of his and got a loose one out of the herd to put in his own team. *Friday 25th* Remarkably cold east wind, we staid on a very high prairie last night, having travelled quite late; creek close by, pretty good feed on it for cattle. Yesterday we passed a singular looking place where the platte runs through the high bluffs, they were several hundred feet perpendicular on each side, the bluff being of a reddish color gave them quite a curious appearance. I wanted to visit it myself but my health would not admit. *Saturday* Yesterday we accidently left the river road came on the hill again, pass'd Dr Richards co, they however passed us again this morn. Br Lymans co close by us, some of them visited our camp. Homer Duncan, Charles Burk, Oliver Mcbride. Our oxen have sore necks and feet so that they are hardly able to travel.

Sunday 27th of Aug very warm and pleasant, camped near small creek last night, no feed of any account near. Yesterday passed the red sand which had a singular appearance, our wagons and teamsters were covered with red dust.[21]

[Box Elder Creek, Aug. 28, 1848 *607½ mi.*]

Sunday night staid at box elder creek plenty of wood and water but poor feed. *Monday 28th* came to deer creek where Dr Richards co were camped. *Tuesday* morn I called to see some of them. Phineas Ric[hards], B Johnson, found them well, came on ten miles our team very weak for want of feed, hardly able to travel. ^staid at large grove near platte north side the road.^

Wednesday 30th cold wind Came only one mile in hopes to find better feed but found none of any account. *31st* This morning the men are holding council in the carral, Some hardness between some of them I believe. Bro Alexander left Capt Martin's ten, came and joined ours.

["2 Ravines, Near Together," Sept. 1, 1848 *644 mi.*]

Sept 1st yesterday passed the two ravines mentioned in the guide, carraled near the river Br Alexander broke one of his wagon wheels, had to stop with Huntsucker to get it repaired. Very windy and cloudy this morn. Yesterday found an inscription from br H C Kimball from which we learned that his co passed here Aug 11th.

Sat 2nd crossed the platte came to the mineral spring and lake, travelled in the rain, the 1st we have had in several weeks, very hard wind in the night. *Sun 3rd* very cool wind, some fear concerning the bad water. Cap Martin had a cow die yesterday, very strangly she crossed the river well enough in the morning but soon after commenced swelling and laid down and died.

Monday 4th Staid at grease creek very good water. Monday night Sis merkley's cow died with the murrain. Several cattle sick. Met a co of brethren returning to winter quarters, some from Francisco some from the Valley of salt lake, others from br Youngs co. Recd a letter from sis P. *Teusday* I passed the salaratus lake which was a great curiosity to us, all filled sacks with it; it resembled a lake of ice covered with snow, Came on to the sweet water river staid close to Independence rock.[22]

[Devil's Gate, Sept. 6, 1848 *704 mi.*]

Wednesday came to the devils gate a place where the sweet water river runs through the rocks which are 400 feet perpendicular. ^morn took a walk upon the rocks saw many curiosities, many names engrave upon it the most of us left ours there,^ we went into a den or cave in which resembled a room several names were engraven there in, we found on the top of the rocks a hollow filled with clear cool water in which we washed our hands and face, and returned much fatigued to our wagons.

Thursday sept 7th rested from our travels to wash bake and hunt, the most of our ten went out, but had no success, they have not been prospered in the hunting line for some reason or another. *Friday* morn, very warm sun, all preparing to roll on, one of our oxen is missing. *Friday* night staid at alkali lake.

Saturday Sept 9th very warm sun. Yesterday met two wagons from the valley, they brought rather an evil report. Were going back to winter quarters, thought they could not live there, said the crickets destroyed their crops, said they came in great droves. *Sunday* came 8 miles rested *Monday*, the men all gone hunting, hope they will be successful, as it is nearly their last chance at cathing buffalo. We are now about 300 miles from the valley.

[Along the Sweetwater to South Pass, Sept. 12–18, 1848]

Tuesday Last night the brethren returned much fatigued having spent 2 days and one night and obtained only one buffalo, the wolves destroyed a part of that. On their return home they lost several articles which caused my husband a walk of 12 or 15 miles this morning to find them. He started as soon as it was light, alone through a rout thickly beset with wolves and bears, it gave me great concern of mind fear it for his safety, but he returned about 10 oclock with all the lost articles, said he saw neither bears nor wolves.

Friday morn Last night the express [*word unclear*] returned. Br Foscrin took supper with us, My husband treated them to a drink of whisky alcohol. We had a very sociable time with br F who staid with us untill bedtime. I sent a letter by him to sis Pratt, baked them a mince pie to take with them. My husband also lent them a sack of corn to feed their horses, with the promise of having it again when we get to the valley.

Saturday and *Sunday* staid on the sweet water.[23]

[Across the Divide, Sept. 18, 1848 *802½ mi.*]

Mon came to the Pacific creek[24] travelled late, cold wind. Albert Tyler's ox died with blind staggers. We all felt bad as they had only two yoke and know not how to get along without it.

Tuesday 19th Sept cold east wind have 20 miles to go.

Wed 20th arrived late last night at our camping place I was much fatigued, besides being afflicted with a bad headache. Yesterday met a co from fort bridger and the Valley among who was a br Ludington and family who were going to Ohio. I understand they inquired for me but I saw no one that I knew. They were principly fur traders going to Laramie. We are now 204 miles from the Salt lake valley. *21st* day fine pleasant morning, we had a pleasant camping last night, but not very good feed for cattle.

Friday 22nd last night staid on big sandy again tolerable feed; ten miles to green river.

Every day wafts us so much farther from the land of our birth and home of our parents. The idea frequently causes a deep drawn sigh to escape me and almost every morning I find my spirit has been wandring back to the scenes of my childhood and youth, and mingling with the companions of my early days, But ah! those days are past never more to return.

[Blacks Fork, Sept. 25, 1848]

Monday ^*Teusday*^ *26th Sept,* warm pleasant day last night staid on Blacks fork, very muddy water. Yesterday a young english woman in co with br Martin got hurt in getting out of the wagon, but providentially escaped material injury. We met two men from the Valley, said Br Young's co had gone in last week, also that Br A Pratt was on his way would probably be there about the time we arrived.[25]

Thursday Sept 28th remarkably warm pleasn weather, the camp all well and prospering. Last night camped near a very pleasant stream of water clear as chrystal, name unknown; it was really like water to thirsty souls as we had none the night before that could scarcely be called water but rather mud.

[Fort Bridger, Sept. 29, 1848]

Fort Bridger *Friday 29th Sept 1848* Arrived here between 3 and 4 oclock yesterday. Our Capt concluded to stop and trade some. It is quite pleasant place here, but so cold that they say they can raise nothing, have not so much as a garden. Mrs Vascan [Vasquez] (the woman whose husband owns a share in the fort) told us that she had sent her oldest son to the valley to go to school. They have one of our mormon brethren and wife living with them, expect they will stay untill next spring. Mrs. V appeared very friendly and sociable.

~~Saturday~~ *Friday* found a very rough road, came 12 miles descended a very stony hill or mountain, staid in a canyon, very pleasant place. *Saturday* rose a long hill and descended the opposite side found rather poor camping place no water near.

[Bear River, Oct. 1, 1848 *80¾ mi.*]

Sun Oct 1st fine pleasant morning going on to bear river where we expect to stop a day. ^*Monday* staid on bear river washed and baked, met a co from the valley with teams going to meet Dr Richards.^26 *Wednday [Thursday] 5th* Staid last night on echo creek 10 or 12 miles from Weber river, good water and grass; two indian families tented near us going to the valley to spend the winter. One of the men is of spanish descent, and is going to teach the spanish french and several of the indian tongues. He has a squaw for his wife who appears to be quite a modest intelligent woman. *Tuesday* night [*Oct. 3*] we staid close by Cache cave which is a great curiosity. I visited it in com with several others, saw several names engraven therein, it is said to be 30 feet from the entrance to the back side, it has an oval roof, and a hole in the centre resembling a chimney. We saw tracks of wild beasts, and holes under the rocks where they doubtless resort.

Thursday night we camped in a canyon on Weber river rested *Friday* from our travels, or at least let our teams rest, after much consultation among the brethren on the subject, the majority were in favor of staying in opposition the capt and several others whose teams were not so weak.

[30 Miles from Salt Lake Valley, Oct 8, 1848]

Sunday morning Oct 8th 1848 Yesterday came ten miles, staid near a small creek, had some very bad places to pass; br Barnard's buggee capsised but did no injury of any account. This morning is very pleasant and warm. We are now almost thirty miles from the valley. Three days more will (we hope) land us at our place of destination. I hope I shall be truly thankful to God for his preserving care through so long and tidious a journey. *Monday* morn. Yesterday we travelled about 9 miles through very bad roads camped in a valley or canyon entirely surrounded by mountains. Soon after we stoped we were joined by a frenchman and an indian with their families, who were going to the valley to buy provision. The frenchman has a squaw for his wife, they also had a young man and girl from the valley which they had hired, the young woman had been making butter and cheese for them. ^Monday we came only a short distance. Father Luce's wagon tire got broken had to stop to get mended. Br A Lyman, Flake and two other men came by us on horseback going on to the valley.^

Tuesday we ascended and descended a very high mountain[27] the teams had all they could do to draw the loads, on arriving at the top we had a glimpse of the valley of salt lake which we had so long been striving to reach. We all rejoiced and thought we were the same as there, but when we came to descend the mountain we found we had one of the worst and most crooked roads to pass over that ever was seen, we however got through safely and arrived within 14 miles of our place of destination before dark. *Wed—* 11th warm and pleasant we some expect to roll into the valley to day.

[Arrival at Salt Lake Valley, Oct. 12, 1848]

Thu Oct 12th, Yesterday we were detained by rain, we travelled untill 3 or 4 oclock and then stoped, this morning is very pleasant, intend to make the best of our way into the valley, a little after noon we ascended and descended the last hill, found two families living in tents close the mouth of the canyon. I understood they had salt for sale, I went and bought some for salaratus. About 4 oclock we arrived within the fort the first we saw of our acquaintances Phill B Lewis[28] he told us sister P was at his house close by the gate we had just come through.

Caroline's initial daily journal ends upon completion of her venturesome wagon trip from the Des Moines River to the Great Salt Lake Valley. What follows is a fairly brief reminiscent account of the subsequent two years spent in Utah.

CHAPTER SIX

Salt Lake Valley

Memoirs, 12 October 1848 to 7 May 1850

[Reunion with the Pratt Family]

They soon came runing out to meet us, all hands
Ellen Frances Lois and Ann Lousia Elvira Stevens among the rest, all
looked very natural, only sister had lost her front teethe which disfigured
her some, and the children had grown considerably larger. We intended
to go on to the camping ground with our Co, but sister P turned us up to
her place of residence where we staid two weeks before we got into a house
by ourselves. At evening br P[ratt] returned home from work, I had not
seen him for more than five years yet he looked just as natural as though
I had seen him every day. They were thronged with company, day and
night, people calling to see br and hear about his mission to the islands.
Oct 18th we received a visit from br B Young and wife. Br P exhibited his
shells and other curiosities besids interesting us with numerous anecdotes
respecting the islands and natives The next day were visited by W Phelps
and wife. We also made several visits in the time we staid there, one at br
Bailes with B Young and 3 of his ladies or wives. *Oct 25* we moved into br
[John] Eagers house which he purchased of br Edmund Elsworth.[1] Br
Eager boards with us Lois P also came with us, expect she will stay with us
for the present. It is determined that we accompany Br Pratt and family to
the Islands of the Pacific. We therefore feel ourselves still in an unsettled
state. After labouring and toiling so long to get to a place where we could
feel ourselves at home, we have now got to take another and even more
tedious journey and take up our abode among the wild sons of nature
perhaps for several years, but it is all for the gospels sake, therefore we do
not wish to murmur, but keep our eyes upon the recompence of reward,
that rest which remains for this people of God. *Nov 26th* we all were baptised in city creek for the remission of our sins according the counsel and

custom of the church. I felt quite released from a burden of sorrow and dejection, which had been hung over my mind for several months, and rendered me almost miserable.

[Salt Lake Valley, Winter 1848–49]

Nov 28th Elvira S came to live with us to assist me in attending to my domestic concerns. We have very cold weather which disappointed a greatt many as they were unprepared for winter, Chrismas and new years [*1849*]. The weather was very cold and snow abundant, we however had some good parties, Chrismas night at our house and new years at br Pratts, we enjoyed ourselves very well, notwithstanding the intensity of the weather. The winter continued remarkbly cold, many families lived in their wag-gons all winter some suffered very much, some were very short of food had to live principly on meat, which caused them to be sick as soon as the warm weather came on, a number died out of one family, but for the most part they were remarkbly healthy in the valley while we staid there. John Eagar boarded with us and kept a school. We found him quite inter-esting and agreeable, besides a good saint, Alma attended <u>his</u> school, but Lois went to Sister Zina Young.[2] Our time very busily employed through the winter, we had quorum meetings almost every Sunday night at our house, beside meeting at different places through the week, and native school at br Pratts 3 evenings in a week, which I attended very little my health being rather poor some of the time and my eyes weak;

[Salt Lake Valley, Spring and Summer 1849]

March 20th we moved into the adobie house formerly occupied by Sister Cobb. We made a very good exchange as ~~the house~~ it was much warmer than the one we left, but the cold weather left about that time, And spring came with its busy bustle, and as the islanders say (Mea rahi ahipa). My husband hired a shop near by and set up the cabinet business, had tried to work some through the winter, but as there was no chance for him to get his bench under cover, could do but very little. When spring came a great many moved on to their farms and some took their houses with them, but there were many empty ones left, The forts were really almost a desolation, after having been crowded to overflowing through the winter, it made them look very desolate to be so suddenly evacuated, but there were enough left to be neighbours and truly the summer passed away very agreeably with me. Indeed I think there was never a more lively place for business than was the Salt Lake vally while we staid there, there was evry thing to be done, farms to be made, houses built, fencing done, ~~and~~ roads and bridges made, all in one short season, and notwithstanding all this, some thought they must surly go to the gold mines; and accordingly left And now the great crowd of emigration came pressing through on their way to the mines, some of them almost famishing with fatigue and want of food, and notwithstanding their former prejudices towards our people, they proved their saviors in ma[n]y instances by taking them into their houses and administering to their necessities in every possible manner. Some expressed much gratitude, saying they much disappointed in finding us to be a very different people from what they had formerly imagined. And in some instances they proved a blessing to <u>us</u>, by bringing clothing, groceries and many other articles which were much needed by us; as no merchandise had yet been brought by our people. The *1st of June* Sariah Johnson came to sew for me, she staid 2 weeks in which time a correspondence commenced between her and John Eagar, and in one month from that, namly the *1st of July*, they were married, at her fathers Sunday morning before meeting, and came direct to our house. The *4th of* [*July*] I made a sort of infair for them, Br and sister Young, Sister Cobb, Eliza Snow, br and sis Lewis, br A Pratt and wife, and br Parley Pratt, with what belonged to our own family composed the co. We had a very agreeable time and a good supper, The variety of which it was composed (considering that harvest time had not fully arrived) drew forth a number of compliments from the company.

Br John staid about one month after he was married and then went to housekeeping a few doors west of us. He made considerable money that season in selling guides to the gold mines.[3]

My husband kept a number of hands in the shop and was much hurried with business all summer. Thousands of the emigrants left their wagons in the Vally, and got packsaddles made, which brought a great deal of work to the shop.

In the meantime our mission to the islands was given up for that season, excepting br Pratt and two young men,[4] in consequence of the great emigration to California and the report that many were suffering on the way by losing their teams for want of feed and so forth. Accordingly my husband commenced building even at that late season, about the *1st of Oct 1849.*

[Pioneer Day Celebration, July 24, 1849]

But I am proceeding a little too fast, passing over the *24th of July*, that was truly a season of rejoicing with us all. It was the second anniversary of our arrival to the Valley, every possible means was used to render the meeting and scenery delightful. Large boweries were formed around the main ave by the Bishops of the different wards, and long tables set. The wards were then divided into cos of ten families each, with their captains at their heads to prepare the tables, a large com—— of emigrants partook with us, some of whom were gentlemen from Boston, who appeared perfectly astonished to see the abundance and variety with which our tables were loaded, and said they did not believe that a greater variety could have been produced in that city. ^Boston^ They had new and appropriate hymns composed for the occasion. The 24 young men and women dressed in white, the latter with wreaths of white on their heads all marching in perfect order and singing one of the most splendid anthems sung in the church, was really delightful.

[Building a House and Shop]

Oct 13th we moved onto our lot or building or building spot which Br Young gave us near his own residence and just opposite John McCuen's, on the side of the bluff on the north side of the city it is in my estimation as pleasant a place as there is in the whole city, being very sightly, the salt lake is very plain to be seen and more than one half of the city is in full view. My husband built a shop in co with Calvin Reed.

He also built a small house 16 ft by 18, which we occupied through the winter for dwelling house and shop together.[5] The cold weather coming suddenly upon us prevented us getting it plastered. We found it rather cold through the winter, being very large for one room. Elvira Stevens came to spend the winter with us just before Chrismas, she stayed the greater part of the time, and left 2 weeks before we did in the spring.

[Called to the Island Mission]

We had pretty much given up the expectation of coming on the island mission as br Young had told several times spoken in favor of our staying, and even a short time before Conference said at our house that he thought we should not go, that as Mr Crosby had so much business engaged, and his work greatly needed, some other had better go in his stead, and under those expectations conference arrived his name was not called with the first that received an appointment, nor untill the last day of Conference and it took us at last by surprise.[6] The thoughts of being so suddenly broken up in all our business affairs occasioned no small degree of confusion in my mind, having as well as my husband got my business laid out for summer. Myself and girls had gotten a large quantity of straw prepared for braiding, and were calculating to do business on a large scale. But accustomed as I have been for many years to disappointments and hardships of various kinds it took but few moments reflection to reconcile my mind to another sacrifice of house home and friends for the sake of the gospel.[7] And now it was that friends began to seem nearer than ever. Many of them came to bid us farewell and wish us much success Among them were Br and sister Young, Sister Cobb, sister Joseph Young, br Addison Everet and wife, sister Heman Hyde, with whom I have been acquainted for many years and who has proved herself a faithful friend. We were much affected when we parted even to tears, she is considerably advanced in life and thought in all probablity she should not live to see us again.

Brother Young proved himself a father and friend indeed to us on our leaving, by assisting us in getting a team and flour for our journey, and wishing us many and great blessings. Sister Young likewise manifested much feeling for us, she offered me anything she had that I needed for my journey. She gave me a bottle of bitters, a bottle of pepper sauce, a jug of good vinegar, and a box of mustard. I gave her my bonnet in return.

Brother Young took nearly everything we had, house, shop, tools, and many articles of furniture, and gave us the money for them. The shop was converted into a storehouse, and Esq Wells intended moving into the house as soon as he could plaster it.

PART TWO

Mission to the Society Islands

To French Polynesia
Return to San Francisco
May 1850–September 1852

CHAPTER SEVEN

Overland Journey to San Francisco, California

Journal, 7 May to 16 August 1850

[Leaving Great Salt Lake City, May 7, 1850]

Left Great Salt lake City and pursued our journey towards San Francisco, in co with brs [Joseph] Busby, [Simeon A.] Dunn & [Julian] Moses;[1] called on several of the sisters to say farewell, found it hard to take the parting hand of those I long had loved, and more especialy when I considered the great extent of the journey, and the long lapse of time which we were doubtless to would necessarily be separated. Found sister Pratt at br [William] Hendricks, called and bathed the warm spring.[2] Called on Mother Gibbs, she took hold of me with both her hands prayed for and blessed me with a great deal of zeal and affection. Called at the settlement about a mile north of Sessions, took supper with sister Tiler. Ann rode a ways with us, I made her a present of some pictures, came on to br [Thomas] Tompkins, found them packing and preparing to set out on the following day.

8th day, left br Tompkins about noon, travelled ten or a dozen miles, camped near a small stream. Br Hatey called on us in the evening.

9th day arrived at Ogden City near noon, dined at Br [James] Browns, the female part of us with sister [Abigail] Abbot who was very pleased to see us, and treated us with a great deal of warmth and politeness. We found the waters of Weber and Ogden very high the banks overflown for some distance, a part of the bridge over weber left that night. ^my husband got his legs badly poisoned in waters of Ogden.^ As soon as our wagon was over Ogden I set out in search of brother David More, called on a br Chase's for information, was kindly assisted over a creek by sister Chase and son, and directed on my way to br Mores. Arrived there

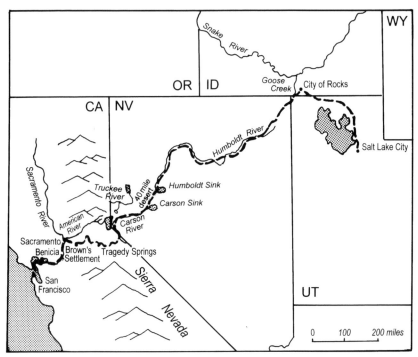

Route from Salt Lake City, Utah, to San Francisco, California, 1850.

about sunset having near a mile, found myself somewhat fatigued but pleased to meet my old Bentonsport neighbors and friends who received and entertained us very cordially. My husband got ^his legs^ badly poisoned in crossing Ogden.

10th We were delayed by rain untill noon consequently made but a few miles, found the roads bad, and streams very high.

11th cold and windy bad roads was much fatigued had a shower soon after camping which made it difficult for us to cook supper.

[Bear River Ferry]

12th day we reached bear river, near 4 oclock, found the ferrymen had been waiting for us several days and were on the point of leaving, as their provisions were nearly exhausted. We were soon to be over the river in safety, but it was rather a difficult task to make the cattle swim the river and their boat was not sufficient to ferry them over, they however succeeded in getting them all safely across. ^and we there joined Capt [William D.] Huntingtons Co consisting of a dozen waggons.^3 We found the United States surveyors camped on the south side of the river. My husband received an invitation from Mr Gunnerson [John W. Gunnison] the Lieutenant to come over with his family and take supper with him.[4] ~~Accordingly~~ We very pleasurebly accepted the invitation accompanied by Br H[iram] Clark Were treated with much kindness and politeness by the Lieutenant, he is a ^native of^ Newhampshire ~~man~~ and very much of a gentleman, he dined once with us in the fort and seemed anxious continue our acquaintance, he complimented us on the great importance of our mission and the vast amount of good we should undoubtedly accomplish, wished much success thought possibly he might see us there as he was a great traveller.

13th Left Bear river crossed Malad, very muddy stream, took six yoke of cattle to haul the wagons out the teams being very tired we traveled only a few miles and camped for night. Find the roads much better west of bear river.

14th Came 16 miles camped near a warm spring ^or rather in warm spring valley,^ the water quite brackish, nothing but sage brush for fuel. There are ~~waggons~~ 18 waggons in co. *15th* Travelled 12 miles and camped near the spring of the mountain had quite a time singing hymns, br Tompkins was mouth in prayer.

16th Came 12 miles camped in a pleasant valley about 36 miles from bear river, about half a mile to water, plenty of sage brush for fuel. Mr [John B.] Bader the socialist set forth some of his principals to us,[5] we sung two hymns, prayer by Busby. Camped on deep creek.

17th Travelled 20 miles arrived at the mountain spring our camping place at 3 oclock found good roads, fine day for travelling, had quite a pleasant time in singing round a large fire, prayer by br [Sherman A.] Gilbert. Our camp ground was very pleasantly situated, ^there were a number of acres^ surrounded by cedar trees, plenty of wood and very good water.

18th Found rather rough roads, travelled 8 hours, came 20 miles, camped on Casier [Cassia] creek, between two mountains; good feed and water; all joined in washing.

Sunday evening *19th* finished our washing this morning and prepared for meeting, at 2 oclock the trumpet sounded. Meeting opened by President Clark, ^prayer by Crosby^ who was followed by remarks from a number of the other brethren. We find the ford so bad that we are obliged to go around a mountain some out of our way to find a better passage.

[City of Rocks]

20th day We went some seven or 8 miles out of our way in getting to the ford, found a very stony piece of road, arrived at the steeple rocks at half past 4 oclock, find them to be a great curiosity.[6] We all walked nearly a mile and a half to see them, a number of boys ascended the highest point of one of them, it almost frighened me to see them. Alma was one of the first who ascended them. The men and boys joined in rolling down one very large one, which made a tremendous crashing and burst into a great many pieces. There are a number of names inscribed on them. This a very good place to camp, good water and dry cedar for firewood. I understand the emigrants to the goldmines, had a battle with the indians at this place last season.

[Goose Creek]

21st day we came 15 miles over some very high hills which afforded us a very grand prospect of the surrounding country, they appeared at first sight to be almost impassable for wagons yet we all descended them in perfect safety, and arrived at goose creek about 4 oclock, found good water and wood. Had lecturing again from Mr Bader on socialism.

22nd Travelled near 20 miles to get 12, in consequence of high water we were obliged to go over and around mountains to shun mud holes; arrived in camp at half past 4 having travelled 8 hours, stoped again on goose creek. The co all in tolerable heath and good spirits. My health is not good I am affected just as I was when I came the valley, with something similar to seasickness.

23rd Arrived in camp about 4 oclock again on goose creek, had a snowstorm which prevented us from travelling untill afternoon, came only 7 or 8 miles. I find myself sick with headache.

24th Cold morning, I had a very restless night, felt very miserable, got the elders to lay hands on me, felt better afterwards. Arrived in camp at halfpast 3 oclock, having travelled 20 miles, stoped in warm spring vally good water and wood.

25th day very cold and stormy, left camp at half past 7 oclock, found roads very muddy, saw two indians on the way. We stoped in hot spring vally at half past 2 we expect to stop here over sunday.

Sunday 26th Cold windy day all busy in preparing for travelling tomorrow. In consequence of the wind we were not called together for meeting untill near night, when the wind ceased, and we had a short one. The good spirit was with us and we all felt to rejoice. There were many appropriate remarks made by the brethren, and we all felt glad that we came together even at that late hour.

Monday morn 27th we proceeded on our journey Came 20 miles, stoped at half past 6 oclock in a very pleasant place. We were hindered considerably in crossing a creek, the men had to make a bridge with their wagon tongues, and fill in willows and then take the wagons all over by hand. We camped again in a warm spring vally, beautiful water, and plenty of sage brush.

[Mary's (Humboldt) River, May 28, 1850]

Tuesday 28th 3 weeks to day since we left the city of the great Salt Lake, we have been blest and prospered exceedingly thus far. We have passed some lofty mountains covered with perpetual snow, and some pleasant little valleys, interspersed with a variety of flowers and watered by pleasant streams, the feed is generally very good. Camped tonight at the head waters of Mary's river.[7] Traveled nearly 25 miles, stoped at half passed 6 oclock.

29th Left camp at nearly 8 oclock, travelled some 10 or 12 miles camped at 2 oclock on Mary's river, good roads with the exception of a miry stream, where they had to double teams. We have had quite a warm day. My health seems to be improving. I think the camp appears almost universally in good health, and spirit.

30th We travelled some 7 or 8 miles, arrived about 11 oclock at a branch of Mary's river, where we were detained a half day in getting across. The capt made a ferryboat of father Clarks wagon bed and took the goods over, at least all that would be injured by getting wet. Two of the brethren swam across the steam with a rope, which they attached to the waggons; then hauled them across with teams, it rained some, and the wind was quite high, we however all got safely across by half past 6 oclock The wind rain ceased and the evening became quite pleasant. The brethren had ~~quite~~ a sort of a shooting match. I had quite an intercourse sister [Elizabeth] Gilbert, lately from England. She appears to be a person of great faith, has seen some trials for the short time she has been in the church. She was on the boat where 59 persons died with cholera. She represents it as being the greatest scene of distress she ever witnessed, they were nearly all of them saints from the old countries. She was attacked with it herself, but was instantly healed.

31st Left camp between 8 and 9 oclock, it took us half the day to get across two miry creeks, we traveled about 10 miles, camped again on the head waters of Mary's river, good feed and water, wind and rain this afternoon.

[An Exploding Stove]

June 1st Left camp at 8 in the morning travelled 20 miles crossed the river, it was so deep that we were obliged to raise our goods to the tops of the wagon beds to prevent them from getting wet. We arrived camp at nearly 7 oclock. One young man killed an antelope which was divided among the co. There was quite an excitement raised in camp this evening in consequence of a canister of powder being accidentaly discharged. Some of the boys had carelessly set it in sis Pratts stove and it was not discovered when the fire was built. The teakettle and coffeepot were both on the stove at the time of the explosion the teakettle was severly bruised, they were both however found standing near the stove right side up ^the top of the stove was taken entirely off^ no one happened to be near at the time, so that no material injury was done. Sis Pratt left the stove not more than two minutes previous, upon the whole we considered it a very providential escape.[8]

Sunday the 2nd we had a pleasant camping place all hands were employed in the forepart of the day in washing and baking, the afternoon we had meeting, opened by singing and prayer by br Dunn. Remarks by Mr Crosby, who was followed by several others. A number of hymns were sung, and a good degree of the spirit of God seemed to be present with us. In the evening a br Mills made quite a display of his phrenological talents, upon a number of the co—.

[Following Mary's River]

Monday 3rd we left camp at a few minutes past 8 oclock were detained about a half hour in consequence br Tomkins's horses getting a little frightened and refusing to be caught. We traveled on, the weather very pleasant and warm, stoped to eat dinner a few minutes before 12 excellent feed and water. Arrived in camp about 6 oclock having traveled 20 miles.

Tuesday eve June 4th. 4 weeks today since we left the vally. Left camp this morning at 20 minutes past 7. We crossed quite a high mountain, passed through a very pleasant canyon, variegated with flowers of almost every description. The sunflower sundial, hollyhock, marygold, foxglove, sweet william and a number of others which I cannot name we have seen through almost all our journey thus far. We have been blest and prosperd exceedingly, no accident of any account ^has occured to detain^ We truly have reason to rejoice and be glad.

Wednesday 5th This morning br Clawson got his wagon axle tree broken by our oxen starting forward and locking wheels with his, we were consequently detained an hour or more as he was obliged to unload his wagon and store his goods in other wagons, We started on at half past 8, had a remarkably dusty time, and rough roads, arrived in camp a few minutes before 7 in the evening, excellent feed for cattle and good water. Some of our cattle drank so freely after going all day without any that it made them sick.

6th Left camp at 7 oclock this morning found the roads very dusty. The middle of the day was very warm, and the dust was almost suffocating, we travelled untill after 5 oclock, ^came 20 miles^ when we camped again on Mary's river, it seemed to me that I could not have endured another hour's travel, I was so much fatigued and my head ached all day.

7th Left this morning a few minutes before 7, found the roads very dusty & the forenoon I prayed earnestly for rain, in the afternoon we had a small shower. I believe was never more revived or more thankful for anything, I was as much refreshed as a drooping plant would have been. We traveled 20 miles camped at 6 oclock.

8th day Left camp at 7 oclock we had a good day to travel cool and cloudy came 20 miles camped at about 6 oclock in a pleasant place a little distance from the river expect to stop here over Sunday, the musketoes seem determined to wage a war of extermination against us. They act as though they considered themselves the original owners of the country, and looked on us as great intruders.

Sunday the 9th They were quite annoying this forenoon, but we were favored with a strong cool wind this afternoon which drove them all away. We had a good meeting at 4 the spirit God was with us, and we all felt comforted. There was one of the sisters, viz Sister Gilbert delivered propesy in the name of Jesus that if the camp did not seek peace and union and strive to keep the commands of God, we should be afflicted with sickness or some other trial. But if we maintained union and the love of God in our midst we should be abundantly blest, It was confirmed by Captain Huntington who said it was true in the name of Jesus.

Mon 10th we came 20 miles camped near the river had a very comfortable day quite cool this evening.

Tuesday the 11th we left camp at 7 oclock, the weather quite comfortable and cool arrived at 2 oclock a branch of the river found it very bad crossing, took us nearly 3 hours to get all over as we were obliged to double teams. Sister Gilbert rode with us yesterday and today, in consequence of some little difficulty between the company who belongs to the waggon she travels in. In the evening the brethren had quite conversation with regard to our manner of traveling and also standing guard, some fault was found with a man by the name of Wanaska a Norwegian by birth, for not doing his duty while on his watch tour. He was very much offended and refused to stand on guard any more for the future but he however repented and ~~went on guard~~ stood again the same night. ^he has been a catholic priest, but has lately joined the saints^ We camped as soon as we got over the river, in consequence of it being near night, but there was no feed of any account, Accordingly they concluded to yoke up this morning *Wed the 12th* as soon daylight and travel about a mile and half to where was good feed. Arrived at 6 oclock, stoped and got breakfast, set off again at 9, traveled 2 hours when it commenced raining, which we were all glad to receive, and we camped not far from the river where was pretty good feed. I believe we pretty much all of us slept untill the rain was over, we then arose and went to cooking and washing. I made some pies for brother Moses who was unwell. He is one of the elders who are appointed to the Island mission has been quite unwell for some time past; brother Busby has attended principally upon him and thereby received the tittle of Dr.

[Feeding the Gold Diggers]

Thursday 13th We left camp near 8 oclock, rested awhile at noon, arrived in camp again at 4, had a cold rainy day and a little lecturing from the Capt on early rising and retiring to rest in the evening. About eleven oclock ~~14th~~ we were overtaken by a number of gentlemen from Ohio who were on thier way to the mines, they camped a number of miles behind us, and seeing our lights, they resolved to come on at least 4 of them and over haul us.

They arrived at 11 in the evening, tarried overnight, breakfasted this morning the *14th,* They are from Waine Co Ohi fine gentlemanlike appearing men. The one who eat with us was a sandy, complexioned young man by the name of Flack; appeared very grateful for our kindness, and desirous to reward us. I gave him a piece of cheese to carry to a sick man whom he said they had with them for which I understood he afterwards remarked he would willingly give me a piece of gold shoud it ever lay in his power so to do. In the evening the remainder of their co came up, and as they were quite destitute of provision the capt got them places to eat among us. Capt David Peffer ^from Worcester Ohio^ took supper with us, appeared to be a very fine man, also breakfasted with us next morning. I let him have 2 loaves of bread and a little salaratus, and he gave me a half pound of tea. *15th* We travelled from 8 in the morning untill 4 in the evening, the morning was very cold and wet we went out of our way travelled 18 miles to get 10.

Sunday 16th very cold and windy, we were surrounded by gold diggers who were almost entirely destitute of provision. They offered us almost anything they had for flour or meat. Several of the brethren bought boots and shoes of them in exchange for flour. In the afternoon brother Clark preached to them on the first principles of the gospel,[9] and was followed by br Busby. They appeared very attentive and friendly.

Monday 17th Cold wind my health not good, in the evening had the sick head ache, went to bed with out my supper, we camped late.

Tuesday 18th Quite pleasant day We set off at half past 7 and travelled untill after 3 camped near another company from the Vally also a large co of packers from the states. A number of our women were engaged in baking for them. We also have to bake enough to serve us across the desert. One young man came up to us who said he had nothing to eat all day, and all he had had for two weeks, he got from our companies from the Valley.

Wed 19th We set off at 8 oclock, the morning quite warm and dusty, we came onto the desert. In the afternoon we (~~passed the sink of Mary's river~~) were favored with a cool wind. We travelled late untill 7 oclock, camped on a high bluff, near the sink of Mary's river, the water is quite brackish.

[The 40-Mile Desert]

Thursday the 20th We set off across the desert, brought wood water and feed for our cattle. The weather was quite favorable for us, it being somewhat cloudy; and a cool wind. Our astonishment was quite excited to see the vast number of wagons and frames of cattle that were mouldering on the desert. We stoped awhile at noon, near a well which some travellers had dug, the water was cool but so salt we could not drink it, and there were but few of the cattle that would drink, altho they were very thirsty. In the course of the day we passed through a singular looking place, at a distance it resembled a mighty river, but as we approached it still kept ahead of us. We found it to be what the philosophers describe it the Aosis [mirage rather than oasis], Caused by the reflection of the sun on the heated air which arose undoubtedly from the alcali with which the surface of the earth is partialy covered. At 6 in the evening we rested our teams and got our suppers, just before sunset we set off again and traveled by the light of the moon untill 12 oclock when we came to a fire where some wagons were burning we rested again a few minutes, in the meantime the boys made a great fire of an old wagon which illumined the desert for miles around. started on again and traveled untill half past one when they providentially found a spot of feed, they then turned out their teams untill daylight.

[Salmon Trout (Carson) River]

We arrived at Salmontrout[10] river a little after sunrise where they stoped and watered their teams, but the feed being poor they concluded to go 5 miles further to camp. Arrived *Friday 21st* at 10 oclock at a little valley on said river, happy and thankful for having been preserved, and brought in safety through so dismal and dreary a place which from every appearance must have been the cause of great suffering to many of our fellow beings who had previously passed through.

The Salmontrout is very winding in its course, but rendered pleasant by the large cottonwood trees, which adorn its bank, It is also stored plentifully with fishes, which are easily caught when the water is low, We have not obtained any, as the water is very high. *Saturday 22nd* set off at 8 oclock found the roads dusty in the forenoon, and very rocky in the afternoon, camped on the river bottom, where were some beatiful shade trees. Sister Gilbert rode with us all day, was quite unwell. Some difficulty between him Gilbert and Bader.

Sunday 23rd very warm day. The camp that was ahead of us camped near us last night and went on this morning with the exception of one wagon, the occupants of which intend to travel with us, Grant Teeples.

At 3 oclock the trumpet sounded for meeting, which was very well attended, and we had quite a lively time. A good spirit pervailed. In the evening a number of us took a walk to the grove, made a new discovery, found where the buffalo gnats breed, that is, in the bud upon the cotton-wood trees returned to camp had music in the evening, Tomkins horses st[r]ayed all hands went in search returned with them at 11 oclock *Monday 24th* left camp at 8 oclock, the weather remarkbly warm and dusty, travel-ing hard we were untill 9 oclock in the evening getting 17 miles. It was 12 before we went to bed Baders team failed some went back to meet him he did not arrive in camp untill 12 oclock. Sister Gilbert made herself very sick by walking untill she was nearly exhausted and drinking too much water. *Tuesday 25th* we tarried at our camp to rest our teams; a very pleas-ant place close to the river where were beautiful shade trees, I washed baked and Ironed. In the evening the boys made a swing, all hands [*illeg-ible*] down and swung by moonlight. But the exercise did not altogether agree with me, it gave me a sick headache. ^[Pegleg] Smith the mountain [man] passed us about sunset with his co choosing to travel in the night and lay by in the light of day, we passed them again today, expect they will pass us again to night.^

Wed 26th We set off at half past 7 oclock found the road very dusty in the forenoon, stoped at half past 10 feed and water. I walked up into a little canyon for exercise, found a sort of wild plumb although they resembled peaches in their outside appearance having a thick rough skin. I think they would be pretty good if they were ripe but at present they are very bitter. ^They grow on a low bush not higher than a current bush.^ We rested near an hour and then came on to a very rocky hill the worst I every saw, it seemed to me that we should all be shaken in pieces. I walked some distance up the hill, arrived in camp a few minutes past five, a very pleasant place on the river bank, about 142 miles from the goldmines.

Thursday June 27th left camp at half past seven, found roads sandy and dusty, I walked near an hour and half in the morning. Saw some indi-ans direct from California, said there were lots of snow on the mountains; they had been there to work in the mines and were on their way to visit their tribe on Mary's river could speak some english brought consider-able news from Cal—— We stoped for noon where were good feed and water. This afternoon we traveled through the richest valley I have seen since we came to the western country, such tall thrifty, grass and beautiful streams of cool soft water pourring down from the mountains, which are covered with lofty cedars and pine, and whose tops are white with snow, was enough to make our hearts dance for joy. Our brethren think it will be a splendid place for a stake of Zion, What a blessing to travelers to have settlement here where they could recruit their provisions and teams, about a hundred and 18 miles from the mines.[11] The salmontrout river flows through enriching the soil by overflowing its banks in many places in the spring of the year, its banks adorned with beautiful shade trees. Arrived here at 5 oclock having traveled 18 miles. It did our hearts good to see the poor beasts lay hold of the grass as though they meant to pay themselves for the deficiency they had suffered. Sister Pratt Tompkins and myself with the girls took a walk after sunset towards the mountains but we found the distance so much greater it appeared to us from the camp that got discouraged and came back.

Friday 28th we left camp at half past 7 oclock Sis Pratt and myself set off on foot stoped for the teams under the shade of the largest pine trees I ever saw, they were realy a splendid sight. We proceeded on through the most luxurient growth of grass I ever saw. Stoped to feed and water a little before 11 oclock on a beautiful little creek, where we understand the fore-most com found gold. We passed a company just before we stoped. We learn that a company of prospecters have been over from the mines into this valley, and have found gold here. Captain [Sidney Alvarus] Hanks co is camped on one side of us, and peg leg Smith (as he is called) is on the other. Capt H has been out prospecting several days. We arrived in camp at 4 very pleasant place about 8 miles from the canyon that leads up the mountains. We understand there is snow on the mountains yet.

Sat 29th laid by Tomkins Hanks and [Joel] Tarley set off with the intention of crossing the mountains to see whether they were passable, they had not proceeded far before they returned having met Barnard who had been over them, he satisfied their curiosity, thinks we can go without any difficulty. *Sat* afternoon Moses Martin[12] and wife visited us from Hanks co, took tea with us, were friendly and sociable, ~~but~~ think they have made a very lucky escape from Salt lake Valley. Martin said he intended to get every person who was any way connected to him, out of the vally. Said he should never come into the church again while Brigham Young presided. He talks of going to Italy, requested my husband to write him from the society Ilands, and let him know what our prospects were there, and thought he might come to settle in that place. Crosby thinks when he encourages him to come to us it will be after this. *Sunday June 30th* we were surrounded by the packers from the states who were all out of provision, they surrounded our wagons almost with tears in their eyes beging for bread. They all got supplied from the 3 co who were camped near each other. At 2 oclock our meeting commenced, a number of them attended and appeared well pleased. Br Julian Moses spoke to them on the first principles of the gospel, he set it forth in a very clear light, was followed by Br Clark. *Monday the 1st of July* we staid in camp washed baked, the men cut hay to carry along for their cattle, some of the co talk of stoping on this side the mountain to dig gold. *Tuesday 2nd* the company moved on to the mouth of the canyon with exception of 3 wagons which have gone back 15 miles to join the company who intend to try their luck on this side of the mountains. Arrived about 2 oclock to the mouth of the canyon, and camped by the side of a foaming torrent, which came pouring down the side of the mountain with great velosity, and roaring like distant thunder.

[Ascending the Sierra Nevadas]

Wed 3rd We set off at 6 oclock passed through the canyon and ascended the mountain, over the rockiest road that ever was or could be traveled by human being with wagons. We crossed the stream three times on bridges, at the first crossing br Dunns cow fell accidently in and was carried down near half a mile by the foaming torrent over the rugged rocks. We all watched her with longing eyes and fearful apprehensions for her life, but through the ingenuity and perseverance of some 4 or 5 brethren she was rescued without any material injury to the great joy and surprise of all of us. Camped at half past 2 in a little valley at the head of the canyon, having traveled about 7 miles. We were all so weary, that could scarcely stand on our feet, but thankful that no wagons were broken nor any loss of any account sustained by any one. *Thursday 4th July.* Set off about 7 found the roads very good for awhile, we had not however proceeded far untill we came to a stream which was rather difficult to cross, and our forward axle-tree broke, we were obliged to stop where we were, just out of the mud untill my husband went on and got the brethren to come to our assistance. Br Tompkins came back with Padro a yoke of cattle and two forward wheels to bring us up to the camp which we found waiting for us a mile ahead in a very pleasant place, they all concluded that it broke in the right place as there was plenty of good feed and water Capt Huntington and George Clawson went back in search of an axeltree returned about 5 oclock with a very good one, having traveled some ten miles, we have snow in spots all around us which renders the air cool and pleasant. I think we have attained the highest point of our journey, although they say we have another mountain to ascend. We met men from the mines, or rather they passed us about noon today, by whom we sent letters back to the vally.

Friday the 5th We moved on at 7 oclock roads tolerably good untill we came to the foot of a mountain where was a large snow bank and mudhole, our wagons all went safely over, but br [Samuel] Hall had a pair of worn out horses that he bought of the emigrants to the gold mines which were very weak and getting a little scared they fell into the mire, from whence they were unable to extricate without assistance he however got them out and washed off the mud and I believe he got them up the mountain.

I walked up the first notch which was very steep and think I was never so nearly exhausted in my life they stoped a few minutes for the teams to rest, and I got into the wagon with a determination to ride at all events, but I found it nearly as hard work to ride as walk, and soon relinquished my determination and got to my feet again. I climbed over snow bank higher than any mans head, and scrambled up the sids of huge rocks which I think must have bothered a goat. I found I was much mistaken in thinking we had got to the utmost height, and perceived that the top of one hill was only the bottom of another, as was the case with the hill of science. Our wagon got considerably racked which hindered us some, one side of the projection was badly broken, they tied it up and got along very well untill we stoped for night in a little vally. My husband then took hold and with the assistance of br Hanks fixed it pretty solid. We passed one pretty lake today which was quite a curiosity to see so high up in the mountains, we camped on a sidehill in the woods where was a little feed. *Sat 6th* we came down a very steep hill into a vally where was a stream and miry ground; br Hanks' horse was missing, he and Busby were some time in searching for it, they found it hitched by his lariette in the brush, we traveled over a very rocky mountain in the morning, br [John] G[h]een's wagon got broken which hindered the company a couple of hours. In the afternoon we ascended a snowy mountain. I presume the snow was 3 or 4 feet deep on a level, and the wind was very cold and piercing we camped on the hightest point of our travels, where the wind was so severe that the snow was all blown away, there were no trees and nothing but rugged rocks, we had a tedious night of it indeed, they chained up their cattle and fed them with hay which they brought from Salmon trout valley.

[Descending the Mountain]

Sunday 7th morn. ^2 months since we left^ the cold was very intense, and we concluded that we should be perfectly justified in travelling to a warmer climate before we stoped to rest, accordingly we set off at a very early hour and descended the mountain on snow, such a rough cold time as we had baffles description we traveled untill 7 oclock, then stoped to bait our teams and get breakfast on the snow. We found naked spots round the roots of trees to make our fires, my appetite was entirely gone, being wearied and sick with the headache. We traveled on untill noon, stoped an hour and then descended the worst road I ever saw or any body else, it was so bad that I could not stay in the wagon and so mudy that it was impossible to walk, I got out several times and got my feet wet, and then tried the wagon again, and thus we worried along untill we got to quite a warm comfortable place in plain sight of our camping place the night previous. There was a lake between the two places which caused us to go around some 20 miles to get 8 or ten. We camped on the top of mountain, and drove the cattle and horses down to a valley for feed and notwithstanding they had a strong guard the indians stole br Tomkins horse.[13] *Monday* morn were detained untill 9 oclock in consequence of Tomkins horse being gone he and Hanks went on ahead in order to overtake some emigrants that passed us, thining they might have taken it.

[Tragedy Springs]

We passed Traggedy springs about noon or a little before where 3 of our brethren were killed by indians 2 years ago I got out of the wagon and went to the tree, read the inscription which was carved I understand by br Pratt.[14] It was a melancholy sight. A large pile of stones covered their grave as they were all laid in one, we rested at noon in pleasant little opening where was a little feed, then came on to leak valley where we camped for night. Tomkins returned soon after without success. Hanks went on still in pusuit. The way the emigrants crowded upon us was not slow, all out of provision offering almost any price or any thing they had for it. Some were entirely out of money and were obliged to beg. *Tuesday 9th* 10 men were dispatched to an indian camp in search of the stolen horse. They found a number of squaws gathering pine buds, took them prisners, but sent one of them down into a deep valley where the indians were to ask them to bring the horse in exchange. In the meantime Tom and Padro (Tomkins 2 indian boys)[15] went down into the valley without premeditation, the brethren above hearing guns fired concluded they were certainly killed. In the meantime an indian from the camp came up and showed them fight, he aimed his arrows at them which Tomkins wrested from him, he then tried to get br [Josiah] Arnolds gun and he wounded him in the hip, ^tried to decoy them into the valley by telling them the horse was there but the bushes being very thick and not knowing their number there thought it not wisdom to go down^ they called to the boys several times but received no answer, the squaws all the time kept such a screeching that nothing else could be heard. They finally returned to camp about 4 oclock with fearful apprehensions for their safety. Some of them believed we should never see them again, others thought they would return, we were all lamenting their fate, when suddenly the sound of guns off in the woods attracted our attention they were answered from another camp and instantly to our almost irrepressible joy Padro and Tom made their appearance among us the men women and children all gathered around them to learn their history. They stated that they saw but 5 indians the remainder of them were off hunting, that 2 of them wanted to kill them, but feared their rifles. They spoke spanish and probably reasoned with them. This night we met some of our young brethren from the mines going on a trading expedition, back to salmontrout valley with provision and groceries, Among whom was Albert Tyler, Judson Stodard, Ervin Stodard, Wm Bears, and others that I didnot know, also father [Solomon] Chamberlain who left the valley only a few days before us, he only staid 2 weeks in the mines and finding the times not as good as he expected got homesick was on his return to the Salt lake city.

[Passing Through the Gold Camps]

Wednesday 10th left camp a[t] 8 oclock traveled 10 miles passed a trading post where they had a table set under a tree with liquors groceries and provisions of almost all kinds to sell. We passed on a mile or so by them and stoped for dinner at half past one, close to a pleasant cool stream. We pursued on over a very rough road untill 6, camped in the woods, poor feed and little water; found roads very dusty. *Thursday 11th* the trumpet sounds for prayers. Set off at 8 oclock roads very rough and dusty camped on a sidehill, 2 greenies close by us. The houses were made of posts set in the earth and covered with cloth, they look very comfortable for summer,[16] traveled 16 miles. *Friday 12th* some of the oxen gone were detained by hunting for them. Started at 8 very warm dusty traveling. Stoped at noon on a ridge, took the cattle down the hillside to water came down into pleasant valley,[17] met lots of traders going on into the mountains to speculate off of the emigrants. Pleasant Valley is in reality pleasant place, such beautiful groves and splendid shade trees I scarcely ever saw. There are 3 or 4 trading establishments here, Among the rest Mr [Louis C.] Bidamen.[18] from Nauvoo in company with a young man from Keokuk [Iowa] by the name Wm Stead have quite an extensive house. In the evening a number of us took a walk to see what they had for sale, bought a little tea at a dollar and half pr pound, and dried pears at 75 cents. Found father [Samuel] Burton and wife [Hannah] there employed in cooking; they came out in Br Hanks co and stoped to recruit their teams, accordingly Mr Bidamen employed them to cook and gives them a share of the profits. We received an invitation from the old gentleman to come up and take tea Saturday evening as we were intending to stop untill Monday. We accepted the invitation in com with Br and sister Tomkins, Br and sister Gilbert, Sister Pratt and her girls. We were entertained in very good style for this wilderness country. A long table set under a bower formed of pine boughs was well filled with warm biscuits, butter, cheese, sweet cakes, and pies made of the sugar pears, together with dried beef and good tea, and I might add a plenty of good brandy for those who chose to partake of it, but which added nothing to the entertainment in my estimation. Upon the whole we had quite an interesting time and returned home a little after sunset accompanied by Mr Bidamen; he seems very friendly and sociable stoped untill we had prayers and singing; was much delighted with some of our hymns, told us he had received late intelligence from Nauvoo, his wife is living there; himself and br own a large store in Sacrimento city.

Sunday the 14th We had singing and prayers after breakfast the brethren concluded best to discontinue our meetings, as br [Charles C.] Rich and [Amasa] Lyman[19] we understand hold none here, however a number of them ~~brethren~~ spoke around as we were collected together, we were dismissed by prayer. Soon after the attention of the camp was called to the correction of children, by one of the brethren [Sherman A. Gilbert][20] whipping his little son very severly, he was spoken to several times and told to desist, but he paid no attention untill a young man threatened him very hard. The brethren collected together to reason with him upon the subject, they got him to confess that he was too severe. In the meantime the sisters were busily engaged in conversation upon the ~~subject~~ topic, There was considerable warmth of feeling manifested by several of the brethren and sisters, but upon the whole concluded that every one would take their own course.

Monday 15th Left camp at 8 oclock pursued our journey on through Weaverville [Weberville].[21] Br Gilbert and family stoped there. Also [Henry H.] Harrisons, their cow was taken sick a little way the other side, and soon after we came through the town she laid down. They stoped their team and concluded to stay. The next morning the boy came to the camp and said she was dead, we all felt very sorry as she was all the cow they had, and a large family of little children were depending on her for nearly half their living. *Tuesday 16th* We left mudspring [El Dorado] at 8 in the morn. Came 10 miles through the mines where the men were digging passed several comfortable looking houses, one was in building, was intended for quite a nice house, Arrived at Browns settlement at near 3 oclock.[22] Met father Clark and Huntington today. They left us a week ago have been at Lathrops and other places waiting to see Brs Rich and Lyman.

[Brown's Settlement]

Brownsville *Wednesday 17th day of July 1850* We tarried in camp having a very pleasant shady grove with a small stream running through it. Two of our co set off this morning for Sacramento city Viz Tompkins and Busby in order to try and ascertain where would be the best and most proper place for us to stop untill such time as we could make preparations to pursue our journey the Islands. There are two large co's camped on this stream near here waiting as it were for the moving of the waters. Some of them seem almost discouraged as gold is not so easily obtained now as it has been; provision and other things are very high. Keepers of public houses ask 1 dollar and half for a meal of vituals.

Wed evening We have just heard that brs Rich and Lyman have arrived at the city, and are expected to be at [Asahel] Lathrops[23] tomorrow. We shall undoubtedly get some counsel from them in regard to our mission.

Thursday 18th Bro Rich and Lyman arrived, their counsel to us is to go directly to the bay. They brought a letter from br [Addison] P[ratt] ^to his wife^ he sailed the 21st of April, writes that he wants us to come on as soon as convenient, he thinks the brethren at Francisco will receive us kindly, and furthermore that the natives of the Islands are anxiously waiting to receive us. *Friday 19th* Br Rich and Lyman are with us, we expect to leave tomorrow for Henry Jacob's[24] He lives about 9 miles from here, Friday evening we had a very agreeable time in singing hyms. Brs Rich and Lyman were with us and expressed much pleasure to join us in our evening devotions. They told a great deal of their travels in California and warned us of the great wickedness and corruptions of the people. It increases our anxiety to pursue on our journey as soon as possible.

Sat 20th We still concluded to stay where we were untill Mon——, brs R—— and L will preach to us on Sunday. Sat morn Sis P and myself, ^accompanied by a sis [Iris] Chase^ took a walk to Brown's establishment in order to trade a little and see the place. Sisters Edmunds and Jacobs (two of Henry Jacobs sisters) received us very politely, and we staid and spent the day with them; and as we had no work of our own with us we sewed ~~with~~ for them Sister Edmunds rewarded us very liberally for our assistance, besides giving us a good supper and we returned home much pleased with our visit.

Sunday 21st Tomkins sold his oxen and waggons for 1075 dollars. We had a very good meeting in the afternoon. Brothers Rich and Lyman said a great many good things to us, concerning our mission, and also counseled those who expected to stop in California to abstain from the vices of the country viz gambling drunkenness and every other that can be named. *Monday the 22nd*, one of our oxen were missing, which hindered us untill noon, We then set out and came 9 miles to ^white rocks^ the place where Henry Jacobs had previously kept public house, but left the same day. Sister Pratt and myself set off in the morning went and bid

the other camps goodbye and walked on to Browns and sewed a while
for Sister Edmunds. When my husband came up, he sold his oxen and
waggon to Brown for 225 do he received one hundred dollars down and
expects the remainder when they take the team. *Tuesday 23rd* We proceded on our way through a very dry dusty part of the country but rendered rather pleasant by frequent public houses and nice shade trees,
came to the American fork, called to water our teams at [J] Lewis and [A.
D. and William] Pattersons, ~~the company~~ Mrs Lewis came out and spoke
us and invited us into her house, she was a member of the church of
saints, had lived in Nauvoo with her first husband by the name of Sexton
who being deceased she was married to Lewis who does not belong with
us, however she said she intended to go to salt lake city sometime if she
lived. She has a very pleasant situation, said they were making money
quite fast, We came down to the neighborhood of Roots,[25] about 5 miles
from Sacramento, good feed camped near the river, a little tavernhouse
close by us in the evening Sis P. and myself went in a few minutes, they
are lately married quite young, the Lady came here last fall from Ill is a
very good looking genteel woman. *Wednesday 24th* remained in camp, all
hands washing and baking, Tomkins went to the city to engage our passage to the bay, We expect to move on tomorrow. Wed—— evening brs
Rich and Lyman called on us and took supper. They stop at Roots ^the 6
mile house^ The next morn *Thursday 25th* their mules were missing, they
were tied close to our camp through the night, and in 15 minutes after
they were loosened the next morning they were missing. They searched
for them several days, sent back to Browns, but heard nothing of them
only that 2 men were seen riding bare back towards the mines. They were
very nice animals and the brethren felt very sorry to loose them.

[Sacramento City, July 25, 1850]

The same day we came down in to Sacramento. We left our oxen and
waggon at Roots put our things in with Sister P and Tomkins. There
are some very pretty houses on the way from Roots to the city, especialy
the 5 mile house is quite a splendid building, we halted a little below
it to unload our wagon, and while we were stoping a couple of ladies
late from Missouri who were boarding there came out to see us thinking we might be from their state. One of a Mrs White had a babe which
she said was born on the road to California and lived in a wagon untill
she was 4 months old, ^she seemed quite at home in our wagon and
rather unwilling to leave^ she was a fine looking child; they called her
Kate. The ladies were quite genteel in their appearance. We came on
to the city found it to be as it had been previously represented to us an
irregularly built dirty place full of dead creatures bones and all manner

of uncleanness. We stoped a few minutes under a shade tree untill the men went to get us a boat. My husband went and borrowed a tent of br [Levi] Dorotty [Dougherty] and set it up close to the side of the river, where were a number of others, and we staid there 2 nights. Immediately after we loaded our things on the bank of the river a number of young gentleman who had just come in from Boston or New York called on us and brought a half dozen bottles of wine and beer with as many mince and apple pies and made us a present of them. They were quite a treat to us as the day was very warm and we were all fatigued. *Friday* we spent in baking and preparing to go on board the bark Wm O Alden Captain. In the evening Mr Hughs called on us, and introduced himself as the husband of Mary Parker, he had just landed in California and finding the times rather dull was nearly homesick. He had been living in St Louis, had sent his [wife] to Nauvoo to stay with her sister Mrs Kenny while he came here to make his fortune, he informed us of the death of his wife's mother, who died with Cholera last summer after a sickness of sixteen hours illness. In the eve my husband and self visited br Doroty's who were our old travelling companions from the states to the Valley, they arrived in Cal a few days before us, were living a new unfurnished house built for a store, and were selling milk for a living, have 5 cows and from them sold from 8 to ten dolls pr day of milk and butter.

[Aboard the Bark]

Sat 27th We went on board the bark, found it very dirty and unprepared to receive passengers, but as the captain was friendly and offered to take us free of expense our men concluded to go with him. We found the muske-toes on board before us and standing ready with open jaws to devour us, our cabins were very small and as for sleep the first night we got none at all, such scratching and groaning I ne'er saw before, at first in the births and then on the floor, one man thought in the ladies cabin to find sweet repose but soon found his mistake and without ceremony arose. And thus the night passed between hope and despair, one moment in the cabin then out in the air.[26]

Our Cap found it impossible to work the boat to any advantage (the wind being opposed to us) and sent back to the city to hire a steamer to hitch on to us, he at first offered 300 dolls they refused to go for that, and he sent the third time, offered 4–5 and finally 600, and they refused to go for that. They continued trying to get along but all to no purpose all day *sunday*, and *monday* made 10 or 15 miles. *Tuesday morning 29th* [*30th*] a steamboat captain sent word to him our cap that he would come the next morning and take us down for 600. So now here we are lying on the Sacramento waiting the arrival of the steamer. The women and children fighting musketoes, cooking and moving about, the men employed in filling the water casks and preparing to go out to sea. We all forsook the cabin after the first night and took our beds on deck, where the wind kept the musketoes a little at bay, but my blood is so poisoned that whenever I get a little warm they pain me the same as at first.

Thursday Aug—— 1st still trying to work the bark, but all seemingly to no purpose as the wind is still against us. The musketoes are making such unmerciful havoc with our hands and faces that we are actually afraid there will be little or nothing left of us many days longer, but we desire to let patience have her perfect work. *Friday the 2nd* nothing transpired worthy of notice, made little or no head way.

3rd Sat. Our Captain determined to make another attempt to raise Steam Sufficient to take us through if possible, Accordingly deputed Tomkins to go back to Sacramento for that purpose, he started off on the first steamer that came along.

[A Fortuitous Steamer]

4th Sunday towards noon the steamer *Hartford* hove in view rang her bell and gave us a call, inquiring of the Capt if he wanted steam, the capt answered in the affirmative, concluding that Tomkins had of course engaged her assistance. We all rejoiced at our apparent good fortune, expecting very soon to be taken beyond the reach of the musketoes. She hitched on to us and for a few minutes took us along finely, but immediately to our surprise her capt came on board and enquired for passengers saying that bro Tomkins had engaged him to take some sixteen or seventeen of us, that he Tomkins was detained at the city on business would be down the next night, he was in a great hurry to get the baggage on board, Accordingly men went to work getting baggage out of the hole without stopping to ask questions, The women folks also flew about in the greatest confusion all except myself. I had just got my hands in dough was going to make up some fried cakes consequently did but little towards picking up my things. My husband in the meantime began to mistrust that all was not right. He could not see the propriety of bro T's sending a stranger here to take us off and himself stay behind, knowing also that he settled all his business before he left that place. And furthermore if he the capt of the steamer intended as he said he did towing the Bark down, why should he take away the passengers? After a few minutes reflection he told them his things should not be taken off the bark. Bro Dunn, Tomkins family, Sis Pratt and family, the whole consisting of 12 persons, went on board the steamer *Hartford*. No sooner had he got the passengers than he droped the Bark saying he could take us no further then but would hitch on to us again when we got through the slough or the next time he came down;

and some were left in the worst place for musketoes in the whole route. Our Capt did not seem to discover the trick in getting the passengers untill he found himself left in the rear. The brethren had worked their passage on the Bark, and then to leave and go down on a steamer would cost the same as if they had started from the city, 17 dollars a person. In the night Tomkins returned with the *Star*, a boat that he had engaged to take us down. She was rather a weak sister could do but very little with us especially when the wind was high. In calm weather she took us along finely. Her capt worked faithfuly 4 or 5 days was apparently a fine man. I felt sorry that he should laber so long for so little. Our Capt was to give him 600 dolls if he took us through but if he failed in the undertaking he of course did not expect it; he staid by us untill *10th Saturday* morning when we arrived at [*spelling unclear*] he then left, our capt paid him only half price. ^[Tomkins] was quite surprised to find his family gone, said he made no such arrangement with that capt, only asked him his price for taking passengers, told him if he could not get the bark towed down he should be under the necessity of taking off the passengers, he staid with us untill the week following he got a little lonesome and left for San Francisco. My husband offered to let me go with bro T if I chose but he was determined to stick by the Bark; I concluded I could gain but little in leaving and as the Musketoes had left and I had the cabin all to myself I was quite content to stay.^

[In Sight of San Francisco Bay]

Taking advantage of the tide we floated along untill *Sunday morn 11th day* about 9 oclock we hove in sight of the town of Benecia,[27] the place we had so long been wishing to see. As the capt and crew had told us if they could only get there they could go to San Francisco in one day, We passed the town a mile or so and then stoped to take in Ballast. A few days previous to our arrival here the capt of a schooner saluted our capt as he was passing and informed him of the failure of Barton and Lee, two traders at Sacramento who were owing him 5000 dolls for the lumber he brought from Maine; he also a few days previous heard of the total wreck of a brigg in which he was a large sharer. It served to make him curse a little, but upon the whole I thought he bore it quite patiently, I understand he has heard since that there is a prospect of his getting what is due him from Barton and Lee.

Monday 12th ^*and Tuesday 13th*^ also we lay in harbor at Ben[i]cia taking in ballast Bro Busby been very unwell for several days, the pilot likewise has had the ague, and my husband is complaing today. My health is tolerably good considering the privation of sleep which I suffered for ten nights almost in constantly fighting musketoes. My blood became so poisoned by them that I was under the necessity of taking medicine. I bathed my sores in camphor which healed them immediately. Our arrival at Francisco seems to be delayed far beyond our expectation this is now the 18th day since we came on board the bark. *Wed 14th* we expected to reach our destined port, but failed. *Thursday* 20th [day aboard the bark] arrived; they told us the sailors the day before that we should be sure to get there Thursday night, but now they are obliged to defer it one day longer; the wind and tide being against us the greatest part of the time. Our capt is now very sick in consequence of trying to work the first day they spent in getting in ballast, he had just recovered from a fever when we came on board, and was unable to do any hard work, the sailors cautioned him against it, but his ambition exceeded his strength, and he soon found himself overcome with fatigue. The other men who were sick on board are improving quite fast. Bro Busby is still quite unwell and I think a little homesick with all. Charly the 2nd mate complains of being lonesome since the girls left, is in a great hurry to get down to San Francisco. Says he shall leave the bark if we do.

I have enjoyed myself remarkably well since we got away from musketoes. I never knew how to price quiet sleep before. I have read all my eyes and head would allow me to, and slept when ever I chose had not much to do but cook our victuals.

Another proprietor of the Bark came on board, last Sunday, a fine looking man by the name of Crosby. Also another sailor whom they call pilot.

Thursday morn we hove in view of the shipping at San fra. Alma came in great haste to inform me of it, and ask me to come and enjoy the sight with him. We expected to anchor among the many hundred vessels in a few hours, but the wind dying away and the tide soon rising against we were compelled again to cast our anchor where we were, some ten or twelve miles from harbour.

CHAPTER EIGHT

San Francisco to French Polynesia and Return

Journal and Memoirs, August 1850 to September 1852

[Arrival in San Francisco, August 16, 1850]

21st [day] ^of our embarking^ *Friday* We arrived among the vessels but not near enough to shore to see much of the town. The great collection of vessels here resemble as near as I can describe them a body of dry cedars in some of the eastern countries. Our men are preparing to go on shore in search of the balance of our company. It looks rather lonesome to me, to think of staying out here in the water very long but dont know (as house rent is very high here) but that I shall conclude to do so, unless we should be detained longer than we now expect. Friday night my husband returned to the brigg, saw Tomkins, but sister Pratt and girls were at St Joe's mission on a visit.[1] he now expects to leave the Bark, as br Tomkins has partially engaged another boat, Tomorrow morning I expect to leave the Bark and enter into the golden city, which is built on hills of sand.

Sat morn Aug 17th we were landed safely on shore, and commenced our walk towards the centre of the city found the streets very narrow and crowded with people from allmost all parts of the earth. The 1st house we called at was a br Griffith's found them living very genteely, she is a very tall plain looking woman she treated us with common civility, asked us to be seated and lay off our things.

We concluded to walk on to br Nicol's where we were received with more familiarity, found Tomkins there also br Dunn who had been very sick ever since his arrival to the city. Mrs Corwin was there. In the evening

117

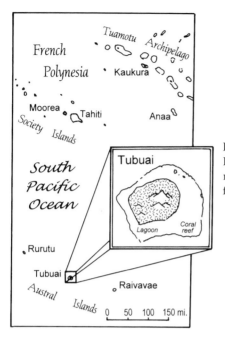

French Polynesia: Society and Austral Islands, 1850–1852. Tubuai, approximately fifteen square miles in area, lies four hundred miles south of Tahiti.

Mrs Eagar called and invited us to go home with her. She was remarkably friendly to us, I presume on account of our being particular friends of Johns, I staid 2 nights with her.[2]

 Sunday 18th we were invited to visit at br Jonh Robins. Mrs Eagar accompanied us with her carriage, we had a fine visit, returned ~~to Mrs Eager's~~ with her in the evening accompanied by Mrs Pratt and 2 of her daughters. *Monday morning 19* she sent her son Wm with the team to take us up to br Nicols. She has two sons living with her, the eldest Thomas has the appearance of being a very modest genteel young man, he treated us with much politeness. Monday I made some calls traded some in the evening Sister Corwin called again, Sis Tomkins and myself sang some of our hymns to her with which she was so much pleased that she called again shortly and invited us to accompany her to a particular friends of hers ^by the name of Lockwood^ where she was visiting, said there was a sister boarding there late from Boston who wished very much to hear our hymns. We went and found them very agreeable, sung the pioneers hymn. Being invited we took supper and returned at 8 ck. The next morning *tuesday 20th*, I called and was introduced by sister Tomkins to br Skinner's.[3] They I understood had offered to take in one family of us while we were obliged to stay in Francisco. They made us welcome to their house, gave us a room in their chamber to put our bed, and treated us with every attention we could wish. We found Br Skinner to be a

person who bears acquaintance remarkbly well, his health was poor when
we first went there which made him rather unsociable, but his usual health
returning he became more agreaeable and interesting. Sister Skinner is
one the best of women was to me a sister indeed.

I made several very agreeable visits with her among the brethren. We
staid there 3 weeks and became very much attached to each other. Sister S
had a brother living with her by the name of Alphonzo Farnsworth who was
also a member of the church and in good faith, he left while we were there
and removed to Santiago in co with a number other brethren who intend
locating in that place. I must also mention a brother and sister [George
K. and Hanna] Winner who were very kind to us, they made us a present
of 50 dollars in money.[4] I made her a silk dress and she rewarded me for
that also very liberally. We received presents from several of the brethren
there Brother John Robins and wife, Capt Everet from Boston, he is rather
sceptical with regard to religious opinions, but his wife is a member of the
church. They gave us quite a quantity of crockery and 3 smo[o]thing irons.
The capt is a lively agreeable sort of a man, we made them a visit on *Sunday
the 8th* [*September*] in company with br and sister Skinner and sis Robins.
They made us a good dinner, and wished us many good wishes. I found
she was acquainted with several of my acquaintances in the vally, and upon
the whole we had a very agreeable time and returned in season to attend
meeting at Winners, br [Charles C.] Rich was there, he happily arrived just
in time to bid us farewell. Sister [Ruth] Morey [Mowry] I found to be a
good saint, also sister [Caroline] Thorp I was much pleased with.[5] Suffice
it to say I enjoyed myself remarkably well in Francisco, the *monday* succeeding the meeting at Winners I spent at Fa—— Morey's. *Tuesday* returned
to Winners baked me some bread and cakes, called at Dr Jones with sis
Corwin and took dinner, from thence proceeded to brother Thorps where
I spent the afternoon in co with sis Skinner and Sis Mory, she sis Th gave
me a dress pattern a pair of stockings and towel. Bro Skinner came for
us in the evening with his carrage. *Wednesday* I spent a part of the day at
brother Morey's staid at Skinners every night.

[Aboard the *Jane A. Hersey*]

Thursday morning I came on board the Brigantine *Jane A Hersey*, sister
Pratt and [Ann] Louisa came with us they however returned to the city,
but I concluded to stop over night, intending to return the next day
but feeling quite unwell I defered it another day and finally concluded
it was too long a walk to take merely to say goodbye. *Friday* Frances and
Lois came on board. *Saturday* eve Sis P—— Ellen and Louisa came.
Tomkins came on *Sunday* morning a few minutes before the vessel set
sail. She hoisted her sails and launched forth in to the broad ocean, on

Sunday morning the 15th Sept. 1850. The winds being in our favor we were soon out of sight of the city and also the land. It was something pleasing and new to us to see a vessel under full sail bearing out into the mighty deep, but our feeling were soon reversed, All faces became pale, and soon after the heaving up commenced, such times I never saw before, Some however soon recovered their usual health while others were sick all the passage. It seemed to me, I never was sicker in my life I threw up everything I ate the first week. In 8 days having pleasant weather and fair wind I began to feel a little comfortable, but it was of short duration. I became so weak from loss of appetite, and constantly throwing up my food that I could scarcely walk without help Sister Pratt Brother and sister McMurtray, and Br Tomkins and myself were sick nearly all the way. Our Capt's name was Salman, an Englishman from Tahiti, he is a very pleasant good natured sort of a man apparently a well bred gentleman, no religionist but inclining to infidelity. He treated us as well as his accomodations would permit, was very sociable and friendly. I must also mention Capt Hall an associate and particular friend of Capt Salman's who also belongs to Tahiti and accompanied us from San Francisco to the Islands, he is a man considerably advanced in life but very pleasant and cheerful, We found his company very agreeable, he ~~seemed to~~ manifested a good deal of sympathy for us in our sickness and a degree of friendship.

Mr Pool and wife from Tahiti were also on board he is an Englishman claiming relationship to the royal family of england She is the daughter of Capt Henry of Tahiti, her grandfather the oldest missionary on the islands, her father was the first white child born on the islands, she is very young and quite agreeable.

We made the passage in 35 days, had very pleasant weather all the way, there was one week that the winds were contrary and we made but little headway, but upon the whole we were regularly blest through the whole of our journey. Our capt spoke a vessel near the Marquesus islands a whaleship Capt. Nicols master. They both raised their flags, Capt Nicols was from boston; proved to be an acquaintance of Capt Hall's, our capt sent out a boat to the whaler and bought sweet potatoes oranges and several other articles. Capt Nicols came on board of our vessel and brought his little daughter about 5 years old he had his family consisting a wife and 4 children the youngest a pair of twins, born on the ocean. They had been 9 months at sea and expect to be 4 years from home.

[Arrival at Tubuai, October 19, 1850]

We hove in sight of Toubouai on *Saturday the 19th oct,* all eyes were on the alert to behold the little speck as it appeared to us at a distance, and as it really is when compared to America. The wind being contrary we were unable to land untill *monday the 21st.* Our capt and crew being unacquainted with the harbour were obliged to use a great deal of precaution in landing and notwithstanding all *Saturday* evening while the capt was below we were near being driven on the reef, he was much alarmed and blamed the mate and crew very much said that in one half hour more as the wind was then blowing it would have been impossible to have saved the vessel from being dashed against the rocks; But Providence was in of our favor, *Monday* morn before breakfast a comp left the vessel ~~accompanied by~~ consisting of Mr Pool, Osborne and a number of the crew, they had a very hard task in finding the harbour, it kept them untill afternoon at hard labour. Immediately after they landed, a boat from the island was seen coming to us we watched it with great anxiety in hopes of seeing brother Pratt but it proved to be two natives, they informed us that br Pratt was at Tahiti.[6]

The second boat that came out brought br [Benjamin F.] Gr[o]uard[7] We were rejoiced to see him as our fears were in a measure dispelled on learning from him the state of affairs on the Island. Sister Pratt and girls was much disappointed at not seeing him, but our hearts were all revived and comforted by a welcome reception from the natives who met us at the waters edge to shake hands and say your honour, meaning peace be with you, untill our hands and arms were actually tired as some of us were very weak from seasickness.

Brother Gruard led us on to his dwelling followed by a large com of natives where we were introduced to a great com of them. Their curiosity was as much excited to see us as ours would have been to have seen a caravan of animals. They prepared us a supper consisting of the fruit of the island fish and fresh pork, and we all ate with greedy appetites every thing was new to us and happened to please our tastes remarkbly well. Evening came the house continued filled with natives all seated on the ground gazing at us with eagar eyes. We proposed singing which they readily complied with. We sang a number of our hymns and they in return sang theirs accompanied by br Gruard. We were much delighted to hear their musical voices singing the praises of God. Such perfect ~~tune keepers~~ harmony I never heard before; especially from those who never learned rules of music.

[Living Accomodations]

We retired to rest at a late hour. The next day our goods were brought off the ship, and each family began to lookout a location Sister Pratt concluded to stay with Gruard. Tomkins got a house close by belonging (I think to [John] Layton who is now in Califor) Br McMurtrey and ourselves stoped in a house belonging to a native br, by the name of Tahoetau, which he had prepared on purpose for the missionaries, it consists of 3 rooms, we occupy the two ends and the middle one contains articles belonging to the owner of the house and also seems to be a place of resort for loungers. We found 4 bedsteads 2 settees and a table in the house Which is considerable furniture for this country as chairs are entirely out the question, the natives sit or recline upon hay floors, they also spread their food upon the ground on leaves A day or two after we got settled we gathered up our dirty clothes which of course made a large pile as I had done no washing of any consequence since we left California. A brother and sister from Anna [Anaa] offered their assistance which was very acceptable, as I was very weak myself. Sabbath morning arrived which here comes the 7th day instead of the 1st. The bell rang for church at 7 oclock, we all repaired to the <u>Fare</u> <u>bure</u> <u>ra</u>,[8] or house of worship, where some 80 or a hundred persons were collected for worship. We were highly pleased to see the decency and order which prevailed among them, allmost all of them with bibles under their arms ready to follow the speaker where ever he might appoint them. They have 3 meetings and a school in the course of the day, besides our white brethren have one expressly for ourselves, which keeps us very busily employed through the day.

Captain Salman staid here with his vessel untill some time the next week, he and co called on us several times and congratulated us on being so well situated. But our minds are not entirely free from dubiety respecting our long continuance here, as the French Governor at Tahiti appears to be jealous that we are taking too much liberty in his dominions, and fearful that we shall excite rebellion or something of that nature; which we think is the reason of brother Pratt's being detained there. He had previous to our arrival called for the elders who had here a number of years to come and give an account of themselves and the doctrine they taught, they found br Pratt and [James S.] Brown there, had their trial before the Governor, and were honorably acquited, and for what reason brother P was detained they could not tell.[9] The church here are building a vessel which they expect will be ready to sail in two or three months from the time of our arrival here.[10] They the elders promised capt Salman that they would all come to Tahiti as soon as it was done; and he in return promised to exert his influence with the Governor in their favor. He has promised them his protection if in case their teachings are such as merit his approbation On our arrival here we found a number of white men who had been here sometime. Br Gruard has been here 7 years, Br [Ambrose] Alaxander some longer, br [Thomas] Whitaker[11] came last spring. He was ordained by br Amasa Lyman in California and sent here to assist br Gruard in his labors among these islands, he has lived at tahita a number of years has a native wife.

[Tomatoa, King of Tubuai]

Tomatoa the King has a number of white men living with him, some of whom have been here 19 or 20 years. He is remarkbly fond of papai's as they call white foreigners, we live close to him he is very neighborly, but also very fond of intoxicating drink. The queen his daughter and one or two of his sons in law are members of the church.[12]

About the middle of December a vessel hove in sight, which was saluted with shouts of welcome from the shore by the natives, but for some reason they did not call, probably not understanding the harbor were afraid of getting on the reef.

Dec has been a very rainy month, it commenced about the 15th and rained nearly every day for 2 weeks. Christmas came and with rain. The elders were at Mahou[13] at work on the vessel. We were expecting to have a lonesome day of it but in the afternoon Sister Pratt and girls came in with their supper which we put with ours and sister McMurtrey's and the whole formed quite a variety, We had baked pig salt pork fish and goat meat, stringbeans, radishes, lettuce rice pudding, tarrowy fayees [*feii,* "plantain"], mummy apples baked—also pies made of mummy apples and banannas, and finally the day closed with quite a merry crismas. I spent the evening at sister P's had very sociable time we called to mind our last crismas anniversary, and the immense distance which time had boarne us from that place.

The rain continued untill after New Years which passed off with nothing worthy of remarking.

[An Island Feast]

Jan 4th 1851 being Br Gruard's birthday he made us a feast which was as great a curiosity as I ever saw. The natives were 3 or 4 days in preparing it, they had every variety the island afforded together with rice pudding and mince pies which the white sisters assisted in making. The victuals were served to us in native style (with the exception of our having plates knives and forks of our own), being placed on the ground which was covered with large leaves in the form of a table ^[*illegible crossout*] and extended the whole length of a long house^ We were all seated in turkish style on each side while another large company partook of theirs in the open air. It would require more patience than I am now in possession of to describe their variety of dishes and manner of compounding them. Suffice it to say they are all very palitable to the most of us foreigners, for myself I have not yet commenced eating raw fish ^or dog meat^ but believe some of our co—— have. In the evening after the feast a number of us took a walk on the beach which is rendered very pleasant being shaded with large trees.

We passed several fresh water streams on their way to the ocean, and as they were too wide for us to jump we submited ourselves to the conveyance of a native sister, who ~~offered~~ kindly offered to carry us across. We returned before dark and spent the remainder of the evening in singing with the violin and accordian.

January 6th we were awakened by shouts of Sailo from a number of voices, and rising saw a vessel in sight. It proved to be a french man of war from Tahiti bound to Valparaiso she sent on shore and got the King to come out to her, ^had letters for him^ they fired two canons while he was there.

Jan 13th the rain still continues, but the soil is so sandy that it does not affect the roads so as to make them muddy like most of other countries. Last night we had thunder and lightning it raind nearly all night. We have been here now nearly 3 months. have all enjoyed usual health, mine has been unusually good. Brother McMurtrey's is about the same, sometimes thinks he is better and at others not. Br Busby is ~~also~~ troubled some with the Phthisic [tuberculosis] he begins to think this is the wrong place for him I believe he intends going to Tahiti the 1st chance and probably from there home unless he should recover from that complaint.

21s Tuesday 3 months to day since our arrival, Last sat a schooner Capt—— [*blank space*] gave us a call they were whalers who have been wrecked near the Navigators island, they are now trading among the islands buying hogs to take to California. The capt and crew consisting 8 men attended our meeting on the sabbath. Br [Julian] Moses preached to them on the subject of charity, and spoke very much the purpose Br Gruard succeded him on the same subject, They paid very good attention and seemed to acquisce in the sentiments that were advanced. *Friday* Capt Scott returned with the Kings boat had been to a small island near by to buy hogs.

The arrival of a vessel raises quite an excitement here. The boys set up the greatest screaming I ever heard and continue it untill every person is warned. Scot now talks of returning to Tahiti soon. Busby and McMurtrey's talk of going with him. B——y thinks the bad state of his health a sufficient apology for leaving the island. he intends to see br Pratt and get his counsel upon the subject.

[Addison Pratt's Arrival from Tahiti, January 28, 1851]

Capt Scott sailed for Tahiti *Jan 28th* Busby accompanied him free of expense, but McMurtrey, concluded to wait for a more comfortable vessel as his was very small. The next day after he left br Pratt arrived in Capt Jonsons direct from Tahiti.[14] There was much rejoicing by his family and friends but we were sorry for br Busby knowing he would be disappointed, br Pratt was also sorry that he did not see him, I believe he thinks he could have persuaded him to stay, thinks if he had gone to Anna or should stay at Tahiti his health would be better; as those Islands have a much dryer atmosphere.

Br [John] Layton also came with br Pratt and brought letters to us from the elders at the Sandwich [Hawaiian] islands, which gave information of the cholera having been at California, it was not altogether unexpected to us, knowing the vast emigration to that place and the immense amount of wickedness among the inhabitants, it seemed to me that the judgments of God must necessarily be poured out upon the place, to stop their wild curses. We understand that the city of Sacramento was almost entirely depopulated. Br Pratt saw the Governor previous to his leaving Tahiti, and got his mind in full concerning our mission here, which proved more favorable even than many of us anticipated. He however sent a long list of written restrictions for us to walk by, so that we shall be compelled to walk in a straight and narrow path whether our hearts incline us to do so or not. but if in the end it leads us to everlasting life I suppose we must thank the French Governor.[15]

[Luna Williams]

Feb 18th Capt Jonson sailed for Tahiti. McMurtrey bargained for a passage with him, and even commenced loading his things into the boat and then some difficulty arising between them concerning their baggage prevented them from going. We had a number of letters written to California and other places which we declined sending untill Mc leaves, as he is expecting to do so the first convenient opportunity. Capt Jons's left his little daughter about 6 years old with br Pratt to be educated. I also took a little girl about the same time a cousin to that of Jonsons, about 3 years old they are both quadroons, Jons's one quarter black and mine one qr White. little Maryann Jonson or rather Cain had lived a year with an english family at Tahiti, and can speak tolerable english; she is a very sober, modest child, but the one I took which I call Luna Williams is perfectly wild, having never been accostomed to wearing clothes or being confined to stay at home only as fancy inclined her.[16] I have had her now about 5 weeks she has become considerably domesticated.

The natives met in counsel upon the Governor's message and their conclusion was that we should be welcome to stay with them, and that they would assist us in building us houses, [*illegible crossout*] that we Should Have the privilige of occupying what land we needed for farming purposes. and in fact their liberality many times is quite affecting.

[Launching the *Ravaai*]

March 16th we white women all went in the boat to Mahu, to witness the launching of the vessel which was commenced the *18th* and was one week in being accomplished.[17] The natives prepared food to last several days, and laid it in a large pile on the ground when each family was served according to their number There were two large companies of natives dressed in uniform with officers at their heads accompanied with music and dancing in their rude manner, the music being made on old tin pails for drums and bamboo fifes, besides a number who belonged the church that did not join either party. They had quite a distance to pull the vessel in consequence of the ground being very level where it was built and they had no machinery to forward it off with, it being their custom to all join together at anny such time and make a company business of it, accompanied with a great deal of noise and feasting. There were a number of persons belonging to Tahiti who came here with brother Pratt and established an order of dancing among the natives of Toubuai. whereas previous to their coming they were very still and sober.

[A Missionary Disfellowshipped]

April 4th Capt Jonson arrived from Tahiti and brought Elder Hiram Clark a missionary to the Sandwich Islands he had been there in co with 8 or 10 others and not meeting a very welcome reception, left for the Society or Marquesian, while 4 of the company returned to America, he was here the *6th April* and attended meeting with us, but immediately after commencing improper conduct towards the native sisters was disfellowshiped by our brethren and sent home. & was the cause of great grief to us all, having previously had great confidence in him.[18]

About the middle of April Capt Scot prepared to sail for Tahiti with King Tomatua's vessel, br Clark and MacMurtrey and Whitaker preparaed to sail with and even got their goods on board the vessel. But the night previous to the day they intended sailing the anchor chain broke and let the vessel against the rocks which injured it in such a manner that the voyage was given up, besides their goods were all or nearly all wet which made them some trouble but they called it a fortunate escape and let it pass. Our white brethren then set themselves to work with renewed diligence to finish the *Raveai Ns Tubuai,* as br Mac was in a great hurry to get away and offered to give them 40 dollars towards towards finishing her if they would get it ready to sail in 2 weeks.

[Dispursing the Missionaries]

They accomplished their object and sailed the *10th of May.* The brethren held a counsel the *Sunday* previous to their sailing to decide on their different places of location. It was determined that Brother Gruard take charge of the new ship untill such times as the brethren are located on their several islands, and that br Layton and Alexander accompany him. Brother Whitaker and Moses stay at Tahiti ——. Br Dunn and Hawkins go to the Pomutu's [Tuamotus]. Hanks and Brown to Rimatara and Ruruta. Pratt and Crosby sustain the mission on Tubouai and Livewy [Raivavae].[19] Bro Tomkins as he was unwilling to subscribe to the restrictions laid upon us by the Governor was counseled to return to California to make inquiries concerning the intended location for the saints in the lower country, and also to raise some means to assist the mission in these island. The vessel was crowed to overflowing with passengers and goods, the families from the Pumuta's nearly all went in her, and all the white men except 2 left the island, br Hanks concluded as he did not intend preaching in the french dominions that it would be unnecessary for him to go to Tahiti, Accordingly he came to board with me *Saturday May 10th,* The Anna boat sailed the same day of the *Ravai.* We accompanied the brethren and sisters to the harbour went on board and rode home with them. The harbour being 2 miles above the town, but small boats frequently go out to vessels from here. Tomatua went on board here, and we returned home at the same time. Our curiosity was excited on returning to the shore to witness the lamentations of a mother for her son who went on the new vessel to Tahiti it was the first time he had ever left the island and I suppose it seemed like death to her She sat upon the ground, wrung her hands and wailed like one in the deepest agony, Crying in the native toungue We Tamaite no'u, which being interpreted into english, is (Alas my son).

[A Retired Corner of the Earth]

Returning to our houses we found them looking quite desolate, so many of our brethren having left and above all our companions being absent. Myself and family took supper with sister Pratt and the day passed off quite comfortably. The sabbath day arrived accompanied with its usual exercises; the native officers of the church conducted the meetings in perfect order. *12th* day they commenced preparing to gather their Arrowroot. A com of them went with a boat load of material for house building to the west end of the island where they intended locating themselves for several weeks, while the remainder were busily engaged in cooking food. In a few days they nearly all of them left for the digging, a few old people and children stayed behind to be company for us. One would certainly imagine that persons so much accostomed to com—— as we are having for a number of years lived in large towns or villages, would be very lonely in so retired a corner of the earth, but this island is so pleasantly situated, such a calmness and serenity pervaiding it, together with the great variety of fruit with which the it is loaded loaded, that a calm contemplative mind could not in my opinon be unhappy.[20]

May glided away almost imperceptibly.

The natives came home occasionly with boat loads of pear, which some of those who remained at home commenced scraping and preparing as we do irish potatoes for making starch, only on a larger scale— they strain it into canoes, and let it settle then spread it out to dry. After which it is used similar to flour. It is very saleable at Tahiti. The natives use but very little of it themselves being under the necessity of selling it to buy their clothes. *June 1st* arrived, the weather very cold for this country. Almost feel the need of a fire in our houses. This day I attended meeting 3 times, Once before breakfast. The members of the church mostly came home to attend church on Sunday

[A Walk Over the Mountain]

Saturday the 7th we took a walk over the mountain, The children being desirous of a little recreation and recreation indeed it proved to be to us. We climbed some of the steepest and highest mountains that I nearly ever saw went even to the highest ascent of the goats, of which we saw a fine flock. And which I think was all the living creature we saw in our rout, with the exception of a couple of dogs which I presume were watching for a chance to feed themselves upon some of them. We returned home much fatigued almost thinking we had paid dear for the whistle, and I believe Sister Pratt came to that conclusion altogether as her weak limb which has troubled her for many years, well nigh failed her before she got home. We saw many curios looking trees. One was our common brake grown up into a large tree a foot in circumference, with no leaves or branches only on the top, where it spread out like an umbrella, the bodies of those decayed, also excited our curiosity, being hollow and full of holes like a lantern. We observed a number of dead trees covered with moss on which were growing even on the highest limbs the same herbage with which the ground was covered under them. In climbing over the rocks we saw the bodies of two kids which had fallen into places where they could not extricate themselves and consequently died.

Brother Alvarus Hanks and Hiram Clark were our conductors. Br Hanks left us after taking us to the top of the highest mountain, to find our way back the best we could. I proposed taking a strait shoot down the side of the mountain which would lead us through a dense thicket of trees and shrubbery not forgetting the rocks which served us for stairs, (but as I was tired of walking I didnot like the idea of going around). We caught hold of limbs of bushes in many places and swung ourselves down some distance, and in fact got along easier than where there were no trees to support ourselves against, but we found more danger from rocks, in coming down than in ascending the mountains, we were obliged to use considerable precaution to prevent them from rolling after us.

After getting through the thicket Hiram Alma Frances and Lois left Sister P, Louisa, and myself, and according to our request made the best of their way to the nearest stream of water, struck up a fire and made us a cup of tea, which Sis had been thoughtful enough to provide, and which with a little scraped opa or cocoanut meat afforded us no small refreshment, And after resting ourselves sometime and bathing our hands and faces in the cool stream which flowed over the rocks in copius effusion we proceeded on our way home where we arrived in safety a few moments after sunset so that the day proved to be just long enough for our expedition ^or rather excursion.^ On arriving to my house we found that br Hanks had been at home some little time before us, and to our great joy had a good supper nearly ready; had killed a wild hen in his travels, and a tame one at home; had two native boys assistance and the table all in readiness. We ate a hearty supper and soon forgot the fatigues of the day.

[A Great Disappointment]

Sunday the 15th arrived nothing transpired worth relating, the natives still working at their pear, br Hanks joins them occasionally in scraping. *Friday 20th* just before dark the shout of Pahi O was made by a number of voices near our house. We had been expecting the arrival of the *Ravai Ns Toubouai* and were not taken by surprise. Sis P, and girls were soon on the beach looking out for the vessel, but it being near dark and coming round the upper end of the Island we could not or at least I did not see it, untill the next morn—— The evening was spent in making little preparations for the reception of our friends the next morning, knowing they would not attempt to come through the pass into harbour in the night. ~~The night~~ [*illegible crossout*] When we arose She was in full view nearly opposite our house, Our hearts rejoiced exceedingly at the sight, feeling that our prayers had been answered in her behalf, as it was her first trip we had entertained considerable anxiety for her safety. She was soon safely moored, and the native canoes commenced running to her. I delayed my breakfast expecting that my husband would much rather wait for his untill he got home than eat on the vessel, but the first return ~~brought~~ boat brought me word that he was not on board, but had stoped at one of the Pumutu's. It truly was a great disappointment to me, as there was no talk of his staying when they left, but when I understood that great anxiety of the people of the Island for a missionary, I [i]mmediatly consoled myself with the consideration that he was on his Masters business.

[A Letter of Consolation]

They brought me a letter and package of goods which he had purchased at Tahiti, which were also a great consolation to me.

The letter read as follows.

> June 7th 1851 Pomutu islands, in the ship
> Dear Caroline, unexpectedly I sit down to write a line to you, which will be but short, as I have but a short time to write. I have much to say but have not time to say it. We have been drifting about among the islands for 2 weeks, in storms and calms. One night in a severe gale, and have come to the conclusion that we cant get to Anna this time. And Tanoa and his family are going to stop on an island called Kaukura, br Gruards wife also. And the brethren of the island are very anxious to have one of us stop with them. They appear to be good friendly people, and it ~~appears to be~~ is the counsel of all hands that I should stop, untill the ship comes back again, and then if all is right return to you ~~For~~ further information concerning our voyage there are enough to tell you all about it. I bought some things for you at Tahiti, a dress, pair of shoes, cloth for pantaloons, one bt bleach muslin, cotton thread, pins, kneedles, and a knife for Alma if has been a good boy. I will send them to you with all the good wishes and blessings I am master of, and you can make what use you think proper of them. I have made me a pr of pantaloons by the help of br Pratt and Ellen, br Gruard cut them. This is all I can write this time. Be faithful and remember me in your prayers, May the Lord bless you and keep you from evil, and from the hands of wicked men. Peace be with you, is the prayer of your husband Jon—— Crosby Write to me when br Gruard comes back.

Notwithstanding all I could not help feeling a little heavey hearted. Br James Brown came here in the ship on a visit, it is determined that he and br Hanks also go to the Pomutu's, when the vessel goes out again. She touched at 5 different islands on this first trip, and they were all very desirous for preachers. Br Pratt has promised to go to livewy and intends taking his family, says I may go with them if I choose, or to the one where my husband is, if he thinks proper, or stay here, the latter proposal seems the most agreeable to my present state of mind

[James S. Brown's Visit]

Sabbath morning June 22nd arrived; br James preached to the people in the morning, br Gruard, the next, and br Pratt in the evening. Br

Brown has made great proficiency in the language, has been here just one year.

Capt Gruard intended sailing again in one week, but circumstances being against him did not untill the *2nd*. We had a very agreeable visit from br James. They sailed the *4th of July*, his birthday, he is 23 years old. Capt Gruard took the cattle off to Tahiti this time, by King Tomatua's request ^who is still staying there awaiting his return. Capt Jonson's vessel returned the same day from a three months excursion among the islands.^ It really seemed very lonesome to see the brethren all go off except br Pratt and Alma, who are all the white brethren there are left on the island. I hardly dare anticipate being left here alone with my little family, but yet I know the Lord is able and willing to sustain us, and preserve us from all evil even among the wild sons of nature.

[Brother Pratt's Missionary Work]

Sabbath day July 6th Br Pratt officiated in the religious services, administered the sacrament, the day passed away very agreeably. ^In the evening I attended a marriage at his house, the young man was from Livewy, and the woman from Tahiti.^ *Monday 7th* he commenced a school, teaching them the arithmetic, which they had never known anything about before, They seem much pleased to learn, and some of them appear to understand it very quick. As for myself I do not understand their language well enough yet to assist them much in that branch, but can teach the younger ones to read.

July 10th Ellen came to live in the west room of the house which I occupy, and board with me. We white washed our walls and cleaned up the best we could. Thinking that as we had no man for company we would try to make things look as pleasantly as possible, as a sort of Substitute for their society. She has Br Gruards little girl [Sophronia] for company, and I have Alma and Luna Williams.

Our native friends are very kind to provide us with food; are much pleased to call in occasionally to converse with us, and hear Ellen play the accordion.

Sabbathday July 20th Quite warm and pleasant. We have had a long rain storm the past week. Yesterday Capt Jonson sailed on another trading expedition to the Gambia and other Islands. He was detained here several days in consequence of head winds.

To day br and sister Pratt came home with us from the second meeting, and a number of the native brethren and sisters called in to talk with him on his discourse to them The days are now very short and seem to glide away almost impercetibly. We somehow find plenty of employment for every hour. We can say with the poet with us no melancholy void, no moment passes unemployed, or unimproved below Our mornings are mostly spent in the schoolhouse, the evening is all we have to ourselves.

Tuesday morning the 22nd Capt Harrington from Tahiti arrived with King Tomatua, who has been absent since the 10th of May. His friends were much pleased to see him, he called to speak with me in a few minutes after his arrival, expressed some disappointment at not finding my husband here. I understand the vessel came to buy pia, or Arrowroot. *Saturday 26th* Br and Sister Pratt went to Mahu on horse back to spend the Sabbath. *Sunday 27th* cold rain and a strong east wind continued all day. I attended the 2nd meeting, preaching by Mabotu.

[A Frightful Storm]

Sunday evening we had the greatest storm of rain and wind I had ever witnessed in this place. It really was quite alarming to me. I presume we felt its effects more sensibly than any other of the inhabitants, as our house is nearer the shore. ~~than~~

I was truly thankful that we were not on the ocean, for the sight of it was enough to strike terror into the stoutest heart. As the Psalmist says the sea roared and made a noise". The wind roared frightfully as it retired from the east to the south, it reminded me of some vanquished beast, which had spent its strength in vain, and reluctantly retired to hide itself, or seek a new field of action. The tide rose higher that night than it has been before since we have been here, it came even with the level ground, it continued very rough all the next day. Capt Harrington's vessel [brig *Ann*] was driven upon the sand, but no material injury done to it.

August 3rd. Sabbath morning. Another week has passed away nothing having transpired worth relating. In so retired a corner it is quite seldom that I find anything which I consider worth recording.

Capt H has I understand purchased an immense sight of Arrowroot of the natives, and paid them in cloth. We fear they will have but little left for br Gruard; although he has paid them for it in advance by letting them have cloth before they had their pia made. *Friday the 8th* Capt Harrington sailed for Tahiti. Br P received letters from br Whitaker by his ship stating that there is a prospect of his doing something towards spreading the gospel in that place. He also informed us of a report ~~in that~~ there were 30 or 40 elders from Salt lake city on their way to these islands, and would probably be here in 2 or 3 weeks, but doubt its being true.

Saturday the 9th another severe storm of wind and rain

10th Sunday morning I felt very unwell, was considerably disturbed by the storm last night, notwithstanding I attended meeting today and thought I understood more of the discourse than I had ever done before.

br P—— appointed a meeting for us papa's next Sabbath, he intends taking up the first principles of the gospel, for the benefit of the children, and thinks of inviting Mr Bourne to meet with us.[21]

[The Queen's Son]

Friday 15th the queen Peto mai vahine brought her oldest son Darius to us, desiring us to instruct him in the english language. She requested that he might be constantly with Alma, and be an assistant to him in his manual services and he in return is to assist in learning him to speak english. He is a very good boy for a native but rather inclined to play or, hare noa, speaking after their manner.[22]

    Sabbath day Aug 17th Very pleasant weather This day have had 4 meeting, I attended 3 of them. the 3rd was in english. Mr Bourne, and another white whom we call paddy, Br P's family and my own were all that understood our language. Br P took up the first principles of the gospel and spoke well he intends continuing it. He also baptised one native woman to day.

[Jonathan's Return from the Tuamotus]

Friday 22nd the *Ravai* arrived from its second expedition, my husband also returned, rather contrary to my expectations; having been solicited to come to Anna, he concluded to return here and perhaps take us with him, as he thinks it rather improper for us to stay here alone if Brother Pratt should take his family to Livewy.

    A number of persons came here from Tahiti, among them were Hamatua and family who are members of the church. One young woman of the family came to live with Ellen, is apparently a sober good girl.

    Sunday 24th, Br P continued his lectures upon the gospel, we had a very good day. *Monday 25th* I had a large washing of ~~his~~ my husbands clothes which he brought from Pamutu, he is very well pleased with the Pamutu people, says he fared equally as well there for food as he has here, ^he baptised several some of whom had been cast off^ but as there were so few people there that belonged to that island, the majority of them having come there from other islands, and returned to them while he was there, he thought it best to leave the few with their native elders, of which they had several, and go where there are a greater population.

    Sunday morning Sept 7th A vessel arrived from Rurutu. They are quite respectable looking people; I understand they came to get timber to build a ship, some of them are from Laivavae [Raivavae], they inform us that the missionhouse at L is nearly completed, with the exception of the floor.

Monday a number were baptised, some for the remission of sins, others for their health; one of the men from Laivavae for the remission of sins; they state that it is very sickly in that place, and that a number have died lately.

Tuesday an infant died belonging to Mahu, which is the second death which has taken place among the people of this island, since we came here, the other was a very old man who died soon after our arrival.

Sunday 14th cold rainy day, several were baptised. Brother P continued his lectures in english.

Monday 15th One year this day since we sailed from Francisco. Our hearts were then full of expectation, whether good or evil we knew not; but we trusted in God and were preserved. And I can truly say that the Lord has been better to us than our fears. Time has glided away almost imperceptibly.

Friday 19th a native brother by the name of Jesse died; he had been partially deranged for several years, but was still very friendly and devoted to his religion.

Sunday 21st Br Gruard preached a funeral discourse

Sunday 28th arrived, times very dull, nothing having transpired worth relating; very rainy the past week. Sister P and Frances complain of being very lonesome; the remainder of us seem to endure our state of exile with a good degree of patience.

5th Oct Sunday being the first in the month the sacrament was administered according to our usual custom.

[Excursion to the Matu's]

Wednesday 8th We white people accompanied by Hamatua. Sister Gruard and the native children which reside in our families went on a pleasure excursion to the Matu's a cluster of small islands lying about 5 miles NE of Tubuai. We carried provision and bedding sufficient for one night. We found a small cabin erected; and our men built another sort of a shed and covered it with cocoanut leaves which answered to shelter us from the night air. They also caught fish and pahua's, which our faithful friend Hamatua cooked for us in good style. The islands produce a plenty of cocoanuts which with the tarrow and papoi that we took with us afforded a very comfortable supply of food. We walked around the island, found some very pretty specimens of coral and shells. On our way we saw several large turtle which was a great curiosity to us, or many of us, having never seen one swimming before. It surprised me to see with what velosity they move in the water. We also saw a number of beautiful large fish of which there are large numbers around those islands of nearly every hue from black or dark purple to light pink blue and green, The children diverted themselves by tilting on the limbs of the large Ito trees which grow in every direction. We had a very pleasant time the wind being in our favor going and coming.

Sunday 12th very cold and rainy, Br and sister P are gone to Mahu.

Our young prince Darius begins to become a little civilized; speaks a few english words, can understand considerable but is still so wild that it requires one each side of him to keep him strait when we get him into the house, which is rather seldom. *Wed 15th* Capt Johnson arrived To the great joy of his family and friends; some fears had been entertained for his safety, he having been absent much longer than they expected, besides the weather had been remarkably stormy. Report says that 100 sail of vessels were lost off Valpariso in a late hard storm. *Monday 20th* Capt J—— sailed again for Tahiti with his family. We were quite sorry to part with Mary as she had been so long with us.

[The Business of Teaching]

Teusday 21st One year to day since we landed on this island The time seems very short having had a plenty of business with which to occupy ourselves, both mental and physical. Our teaching has been mostly by example thus far, being unable to use precepts to their understanding.[23] We have sought for an understanding of their language both by study and by faith, and have been enabled thereby to obtain a partial knowledge of it, and we trust that ere long we shall be able to make known unto them the wonderful works of God among the children of men. Our female meetings are becoming tolerably interesting, Sister Ellen Pratt has obtained a sufficiency of the language to be able to act as an interpreter for her mother and myself.

Friday 24th a vessel arrived from the Pamutu's, Capt James Harvey Master; been to Lavavai and going to Tahiti. They informed us that the wind had entirely demolished br P's house on Lavavai, which a native brother had been building for him, with the expectation of his bringing his family there to reside among them as soon as it was completed. It was a little disappintment to them as they were expecting to sail the next day for that place. They also stated that the wind had nearly destroyed their standing fruit such as cocoanuts bread-fruit fei's [plantains] banannas &C. Which I think will probably prevent his taking his family with him. A large company from this place were intending to sail there on a visit, but the wind being against them had been detained several days. This night the dancing community of the island held a regular powwow at Tamatoa's house in which the ships crew joined, the capt brought rum with him and many of them became intoxicated, a fight between the capt and a white man residing here by the name of Bourne was the result. *25th* a trial ensued in which the capt was fined 20 franks

Monday 27th The *Ravai* sailed for Lavavai She was crowded almost to overflowing with passengers. Br P took all his family except Louisa and a little girl by the name of Auhura who had been living with them. They came to live with us. Tamatoa's vessel also sailed the same day for the same place and was also loaded with passengers. I should be lonesome were it not that I am so remarkbly fond of quietness, for it seems that there are scarcly enough left to keep the place. Tamatoa and a part of his family remained behind at home; he is very kind to us, tells us that whenever we want food to come to him.

Thursday 30th was the day appointed for our female prayer meeting. I opened the meeting by singing a native hymn in company with 2 sisters read a chapter in their bible and prayed in my own language. There were ten women of us with A Louisa. The most of them spoke and prayed, and the good Spirit of God was with us. We closed by singing a hymn and shaking hands all round. Saying ia orana ["wishing health and all good"] 2 or 3 times apiece.

Capt Harvey informed us that in the course of his voyage he found Brother Hanks in an open boat in co with 3 or 4 natives cast away or lost at sea, without food; said they attempted to go from one island to another and got lost, that he took them in and landed them safely in their desired haven. He further informed us that br James Brown had had some difficulty with the catholic priests on Ana, that he, the said priest had written to the Governor at Tahiti, the result of which is yet unknown.[24]

Saturday, November 1st a large schooner hove in view. She raised her flag by which we discovered she was an American. We flattered ourselves that we should certainly get news from home if not receive an addition to our number of labourers in this field, but we were disappointed in respect to both. The capt called in soon after he anchored, and introduced himself as Master of the *Velaska*, said he was a native of Long Island had been a sailer since he was sixteen years of age, was a very interesting and apparently well bred young man about 25 years old, by the name of Worth. He spent considerable time with us while he stayed, which was about 3 days Came here with the intention of trading some with the people as he was cruising among the island, but did not succeed, in consequence of so many being absent.

He had been 2 years from home, spent one year in the gold mines. My husband and son went on board of his vessel and took dinner, they say he has a fine ship indeed of a 139 tons burthen, he bought it in California in co with the mate who was also a very pleasant man by the name of Ludlow. They stayed one day and night to see Capt Gruard and his company, but they did not return as soon as we expected into one day, and therefore missed of seeing them.

The *Velaska* sailed from here *Teusday* about 2 oclock Pm *Nov 4th*. *Wed 5th* The *Ravai* returned in about 24 hours from Ravavai. Br P remained behind but his family all returned not very well pleased with present appearances in that place. They say Br P baptised 5 persons the first Sunday, but was treated rather cooly by the deacons of the english church, notwithstanding there were a sufficient number in favor of his staying to persuade him to do so. I received a number of presents from Queen Pitomai on her return; a nice pair of english ducks, a native cloth bedspread, a bunch of pearies, one bunch of banannas, hair oil &C. She likewise presented me with a dress pattern the morning she sailed for that place. The *Ravaai* sailed again for Tahiti and Ana *Friday 7th*.

But to return *Sunday Nov 2nd* Mr Crosby preached for the first time in the native tongue, and administered the sacrament, to what few there were of us.

The brethren came over from Mahu which formed quite a congregation. He has continued to preach once on the Sab since. Times continue very dull, nothing to be heard but but the pounding of the old women making tappa.

Saturday 16 [15]th in the evening Tena the daughter Maipuai came accompanied by her mother, and desired rebaptism, she had formerly been a member of the church but had left and followed the dancing party, she confessed her sins and said she intended to do so no more.

Her apology for coming in the night was that if her former associates knew it they would ridicule her. Her mother Ellen P and myself were all the witnesses.

[Problems for the Missionaries]

Sunday 30th day Capt Gruard returned from Tahiti bringing with him br James Brown whom he found imprisoned at that place. He had been informed against by the Catholic priests at Anna, and sent for by a french man of war, was accused of creating incitement among the people about going to a new country preaching doctrine detrimental to the french government and ^getting his^ living off of the people. Brother Gruard and the American consul counseled him to leave their dominions rather than wait there any longer for a trial, consequently he was a prisner while here which was one week; from here he went to Raivavai, to see Br Pratt; where his next location will be at present we know not.[25]

They sailed on monday *Dec 8th*, having been detained several days in consequence of ill winds.

Wednesday 17th Tutuilane died at Mahu, she was a worthy member of the church, and noted among the natives for piety and virtue. She had been sick several months with the consumption. Her friends (as their custom is) sent native cloth which they call tappa to wrap around her. They somtimes bury large quantities of it according to the number of their friends. But they begin to think it a <u>peu</u> <u>ino</u> that is to say <u>a</u> <u>bad fashion</u>. One of the sisters in the church observed that while she lived and was sick and cold and needed the cloth they gave her none.

Saturday 20th We took a walk of about 3 miles on the beach to Tuaknai where Br Layton is building a ship, there were 13 of us in co. We had one horse which sister P—— and myself rode by turns. We admired the place very much. They made us a dinner in true native style, with ground for the table, leaves for the tablecloth and for plates, and the old-fashioned knives and forks ^as they called them^ viz thumbs and fingers. *Chrismas day* arrived, the native brethren and sisters made us a little feast at sister P's. She white washed her house and trimmed it with green bush viz Ito, limes, and Burau [Purau *(hibiscus tiliacevi)*] flowers which are very beautiful when new, resembling hollyhocks. We all dressed ourselves in our *Sunday* clothes, and treated the day with that respect which we had been accustomed to in our childhood. It was a new idea to the natives, they gathered around to see how we trimmed our houses with a great deal of curiosity. We explained to them the importance of the day and they seemed highly gratified and pleased. It happened to be *Thursday* our prayer meeting day, the supper being over we repaired to the meeting house, the good spirit attended us. In the evening we returned to sister P's, and spent a few hours in singing and music with the violin and accordion Closed by prayer

[A Party on New Years Day, 1852]

Newyears day 1852 Queen Pitomai made us a party at our house, principally on account of her little son who is living with us, and who has had a turn of being rather homesick, occasioned by his being restricted from running at large, as he had done previously. My husband concluded that he would make no improvement in that way and thought proper to keep him in, or near, the house, which is very unnatural to children here. We whitewashed the house inside and outside, got new grass for our floors, trimmed the it with green bushs and ornamented it with pictures to the best of our ability, it was much admired by all who saw it. There were some 40 persons who ate with us.

We had not so great a variety as we might have had if we had given her longer notice. She had only one day to prepare the food, We had baked pig, fish, tarrow, popoi, tupinu, taiero, sweet potatoes, bananas, faii's, cabbage and tea, with cocoanut water to drink, she dressed her son very prettily, ornamented his head and neck with wreaths of flowers, and also brought wreaths to Alma and the little native girl. The day passed away very agreeably. Towards evening we resorted as usualy to the church house to sing and pray. *Jan 2nd* another sister died at Mahu Viz Tere vahine, with what the natives call the rotten throat, She left a husband and 3 or 4 children, who came over this side to live with a connexion of theirs as soon as she was buried. *Monday the 5th* was my birthday. 45 years of my short life have elapsed. I commenced writing a brief history of my life which I have long anticipated doing.[26]

Tuesday the 7th sister Pr and family went to Mahu on a visit intending to stay untill the ship arrived. Alma and Darius also accompanied them and stayed one nigth to assist them in taking over their clothes.

Friday the 10th the ship arrived having been gone 4 weeks and 4 days, had a very disagreeable time, storms and calms continually, did not succeed in getting to Tahiti, nearly lost his voyage excepting he got his little boy which had been some time at Anna. Br P also returned with him from Ravavai and left J Brown there in his stead, he finds the people of that island rather obstinate, being bound by the english missionaries. Our prospect for spreading the gospel in the French dominions seems rather dark at present. The catholics are building forts at Anna, and it is presumed that they will come here soon. My husband received an invitation from the people there to come, but he considers it useless to go, thinks if they would not allow br James to stay neither would they him.[27] *Tuesday 13th* Br P's returned from Mahu Br Elexander took a great deal of pains to make them comfortable, by whitewashing an empty house, and putting in new grass, setting up bedsteads, &C.

Wed—— 14th Capt Mayo arrived direct from California by way of Tahiti. With a vessel belonging to a br Richmond who also accompanied him, In the evening they called on us, br P and family were all present, Capt Gruard, br Elexander, Mr Bourne, and a number native sisters were in and we had a very sociable time. Tamatoa also returned from Tahiti with them. The next morning he called in with a present of tarrow and baked pig, he is very pleasant and sociable with us. Br Richmond brought papers from the coast which gave us much intelligence concerning our native country, he is a lively sociable man, has a native wife and children at Tahiti. The next evening we visited with them at br P's. We treated them with as much politeness as our circumstances would admit, and received their compliments in return notwithstanding we had great reason to regret their coming here, in consequence of their dispersing ardent spirits among the native which caused a regular powwow, that lasted for several days, almost every man and woman excepting the church members were drunken. Several were tried for misconduct. 3 men and their wives parted, one young man and woman quite severly whipped, and many other evils undoubtedly resulted therefrom. They sailed again for Tahiti

Sunday morning the 25th br Richmond when he left told sister and myslf that if we would tell him of anything we wanted of clothing kind he would endeavor to get it for us at Tahiti and send by the *Ravaai*. We thanked him I told as I was not suffering for anything I should prefer trusting to his liberality and whatever he was disposed to send would be thankfully received.

Tamatoa is desirous to have the sabbath day changed from Saturday to Sunday to correspond with the custom of other countries Accordingly it was decided in their public meetings that henceforth we observe the christian sabbath instead of the jewish. He Tamatoa returned again to Tahiti with Capt Mayo and took his wife.

[An Island Marriage]

Sunday morning Feb 1st Capt Grouard sailed again for Tahiti and Anna. Mr Crosby, Ellen, and Frances P accompanied him as passengers, also a number of natives, viz Mrs Bourne, Piatilai, and a woman from Tahiti by the name of Luna, a connexion of Piatila, who came here somtime since, to visit her friends, but in consequence of bad conduct was sent back. Last night she was married to Harpinae, the youngest son of Tamatoa, contrary to the law of the island, and in opposition to the will of his friends, it being contrary to law for a woman to marry without the knowledge, or consent of her parents, if she has any living. She has been mistress to a frenchman several years and is probably considerably older than the young man but I understand he was completely captivated with her and married her in the absence of his parents.

[Alone with the Children]

Alma and myself are left here alone to preside over our little family consisting of four children, viz Pitomai's oldest boy, 2 of Capt Grouards children, and the little quadroon daughter of Tummy Williams. I expect the time will seem long to us in their absence, but I think we shall be perfectly safe, if there is no ardent spirits brought here. *Monday the 2nd* last night on going to bed I reflected for a moment whether I should feel safer with a pistol or knife under my head, I went into Ellens room, found her knife and pistol both under her pillow I first thought I would take one of them but while stoping to consider which I should prefer, concluded I should feel safer with neither, and consequently left them and went to bed trusting in the Lord for protection. The moon shone very pleasantly all night, every thing in nature seemed to wear an air of cheerfulness, I arose in the morning with a grateful heart, and could say with the Psalmist, "I laid me down in peace and slept, and rose up again, for the Lord sustained me."

I also had entertained some fears respecting Darius; fearing he would take advantage of my husbands absence, and pursue his old habit of running away. I called the children all around me and talked with them upon the subject of obedience, they all promised due submission, he in particular said, "No me run away". Alma and he went this morning with Br Pratt to get a sort of fruit which the natives call Ahiias, they set off quite early and returned a little before noon, the fruit resembles our american apples in appearance the nearest of anything, and also in taste.

Tuesday 3rd the weather is now very clear and pleasant. January has been (as it usually is in this place) very rainy. Several of the native females called in to see me to day. Otioti vahine, Telii, and Pitomai vahine, she seems to be a faithful friend, and I believe a good saint. *Wednesday 4th* fine and pleasant, this evening is as light as day or nearly so, had a pleasant walk on the beach with sister P and the children. *Thursday 5th* evening, we have had some showers of rain today, as well as of food, the Lord opened the hearts of Avae, and Momai vahine to bring us fish papua's popoi and bananas So that we can truly say, He has given us <u>this</u> day our daily bread.

Our prayer meeting passed off as usualy, with the exception of Ellen's absence, it appeared rather dull at first untill sister P determined to speak to them in her broken manner. She spoke very much to the purpose, and I presume they understood her tolerably well.[28]

Friday 6th Nothing worth relating. I finished washing my shawll, which is considerably admired by those who have seen it. *Saturday 7th* very pleasant. This morning my little Luna arose with a high fever. I was somewhat alarmed on finding her very nervous and pulse high, I gave her a large portion of spirits of turpentine, and in two hours she was apparently well, her father called in and brought us a fish, found her on the bed, he told her it was "maitai parahi taoto" that is good to lie in bed. Alma and Darius gone after opa's. *Sunday* evening. Last night I had a dream that caused me considerable reflection, I dreamed of pulling loose hair out of my head by hand fulls, and throwing it on the floor untill I had quite a pile of it, I awoke immediately after and it was sometime before I could sleep again. I finally dropped to sleep and slept so late that I was unable to get ready in season for the forenoon meeting. I had breakfast to cook with Alma's help, for six of us in family, four children to wash and prepare for meeting. 3 of the native sisters called on me at noon to inquire if I was sick. *Sunday* evening took a walk on the beach with brother and sister P and the children. *Monday* spent a greater part of the day in reading a romance of Irish life headed Father Connel. The reading of romances is a business I disapprove of, never read but very few in my life. And especially late years I have found little time, and had still less desire to do so. *Tuesday 10th* last night was qite disturbed with Sophronia. She has a very sore ear occasioned by having it pierced, to day I went and washed, left her with Sister P. *Wednesday evening 11th* feel quite unwell, troubled with dizziness in my head and sick stomach.

Last night sister P and Taati Vahine called on me to sympathize with me in what they were pleased to call my state of widowhood.

Thursday 12th Extremely warm day, feel very unwell attended prayer meeting as usual, after supper went up to br P's, he gave us a duck for our breakfast the only one he had the good luck to obtain in his expedition for the day, but they had a couple of fowls given them so that they said they could very well dispense with it. Pitomai brought us Feii's and banannas this evening. Sophronia sleeps with Sister P'. *Friday 13th* very warm day, nothing transpired worth noticing. ^One year to day since Luna came to live with us.^ Soph—— sleeps there again tonight, I feel rather lonely, read a little before going to bed heard some one round my windows, trying to make discoveries, but I had them well secured, and a pistol under my pillow. *Saturday 14th* did some small jobs of sewing, read and cooked, in the evening went up to br P's, Luna and Darius went home to sleep, which left us quite lonely. Alma and Benjamin F in one room. Soph—— and myself in another, all quiet and safe.

[A Vessel from Ravavai]

Sunday 15th a little before breakfast the cry of "Pahi o," was made by a number of voices near by. I gave no credence to it at first, but it was soon confirmed to me by Darius. We much rejoiced at the news thinking it of course the *Raivai*, but on arriving in the harbour found a vessel from Ravavai. A br Ratcliff master, quite a large co from that place are out on a visit to the neighbouring islands many of whom never before left their island. They attended our meeting in the afternoon, and conducted themselves very respectably, although br James writes by them that they are in general very unbelieving on that island, however he has baptised 8 since br P left and a number more desire to be baptised, but are females whose husbands oppose them.

He writes that there is a great excitement among the people in consequence of the religious part of the community's closing their meeting houses against him. The Queen (by whom the island is ruled) was in favor of his having the house of worship, and said she would like to be baptised, but her family opposed her, and so great was the contention between the religious and irreligious party that they came to blows and it was with much emotion that he (br J) could possibly calm them. The church there now consist of 26 members who are very strong in the faith and even ready to fight for it, he talked of leaving in the ship as a party of them had threatened to drive him off the island, but the brethren told him if he did they would surely fight.

Monday morning 16th, a large co of the newcomers called in to see the vahine papa ma, as they called me, but as I could not talk much with them they staid but little while, and left, however called again in the course of the day and tried to make further discoveries; they are in my estimation very good looking people, rather lighter complexion than the people here, but not as much civilized as these are.

Tuesday 17th, the children have just descried another vessel which we think must certainly be the *Ravai.* 2 weeks and 3 days since they left.

Wednesday 18th We are quite disappointed on discovering that the vessel which we took for the *Ravai,* passed by, without so much as giving us a call. But as the wind is very strong in favor of their coming, we shall continue to look for them as long as it continues in that quarter. This evening we all took a walk up and down the beach trying if possible to discover the ship, but all to no purpose. We returned the house. Sister P Lois Louisa, Alma and myself with 7 children, composed of halfbreeds, quadroons, and pure blooded natives. Teofai (the grandmother of Luna Williams) brought us in a watermelon which I divided between 12 of us, it was just sufficient to show us how they tasted, and remind us of home.

Thursday 19th I spent nearly all day in reading a weekly journal called the Brother Jonathan. In the evening attended meeting as usual. *Friday 20th* I washed. A number of the Raivavai people called in the evening and desired to see my (hohoa's) pictures which I suppose some of their Tupuai friends had been telling them of. And as I presumed it would be a great curiosity to them, I accordingly promised to prepare them for their inspection, on the following monday.

Saturday 21st I ironed and reconnoitered my house. Moved my toilet table and chests, just to have something new, and received the approbation of my sister, nieces and son for making my room look materially better.

[An Exhibition of Pictures]

Sunday morning 22nd I arose early (altho I felt quite feeble) and prepared my 4 children for meeting. On account of having visitors they must be dressed in their best apparel today I conducted them to the house of worship in the best order possible, and was much pleased with their obedience, and orderly conduct. Immediately after the forenoon meeting the crowd of natives came round the house expecting the exhibition of pictures. I was somewhat impatient with them, knowing or at least believing, that they could not be mistaken in the day. I told them as plainly as I could in their language, that this was our sabbath or the Lords day, and that it would be very improper for me to exhibit them on this day. Some of them seemed inclined to make sport of what I said, while others appeared perfectly satisfied. I told them that the next day I woud prepare them for their gratification, but as I could talk but very imperfectly in their language I could not tell them the hour I would have them ready. On reflecting a moment I was satisfied as to the cause of their calling that day, on their island they keep the 7th day holy instead of the first, as they have formerly done here. Accordingly *Monday morning 23rd* they commenced coming before I got my breakfast, and I was obliged to send them away again. I made all possible haste and as soon as I could sent for brother Pratt to come down and assist me in tacking them up in the middle room, as they have no frames I sew them on a cloth, and then suspend that to the wall. br P—— came down and said he would stay awhile to keep order among them; They were coming and going all day, and I must give them the credit of conducting themselves tolerably civil. *Tuesday 24th*, the tall livewy brother as I call him called in to farewell to me, was the first of my knowing that they were going today, I had intended writing a long letter to br James, but it had actually sliped my mind untill he came in. I told him I would like to write a few words if he could wait, he said "papai papai" which signifies write write. Accordingly I wrote a short epistle in my own and Alma's name, and they are now making their way to the vessel. Yesterday they had the greatest dance and powwow that I every heard but as they had no intoxicating drink among them we were not in the least afraid of their doing any mischief. Although I was a little startled just as I was going to bed. I had fastened my doors, and the children were all in bed excepting little Luna, I was sitting in my rocking chair with her in my lap, when I observed my window curtain near the head of my bed gently move to one side; at first I thought it was the wind, as the window was open, but the second thought told me the wind was not in that direction. I paid no attention to it untill I had put her in bed. I then walked directly to the window, raised the curtain, and met a man face to face. I confess I was a little surprised and vexed for a moment. I told him to go away, and that he was a bad man, as plain as I could in his own language. He was very soon missing so that I had no need to call for my pistol, which I should have done had he not gone, or explained the cause of his being there. I might as well mention, that this is not the first time we have caught them looking into our windows (or trying to) just as we were going to bed, and have warned them against it.

[An Uninvited Guest]

Wednesday 25th the children (all except the two youngest) went after Goauvers [guavas], which are a very good fruit resembling apples. I was left alone as the little children were both asleep. A native man whom they call Mia came into the middle room, apparently as independant as though he was at home, seated himself on the settee, and finding himself very comfortable, immediately fell asleep, stretched at his full lenght. I did not feel exactly pleased with him, although I was not in reality afraid of him. I however felt a desire to plague him a little, I went over to the meeting house, after having shut both the outside doors and left his room perfectly dark, thought I would ask br P if he was there, to come and talk to him; ask him what he wanted, whether he had no house to sleep in, or whether he came here to steal in the absence of the family. But br P was not at home, I staid awhile and returned found him still sleeping, but the children coming in at the same time, their noise soon aroused him. He arose very deliberately scratched his head and walked off without speaking a word to any one, thinking I suppose that he had paid me quite a compliment. But that is strictly in accordance with their habits, almost as much at home in one house, as another. *Thursday 26th* some rain to day; attended meeting as usual, Teofai brought us a nice melon. After supper took a walk with the children, to Taati's house, to see little Epraim Gruard.

Friday 27th, this evening one of my favorite ducks died, probably from a blow received from some person. It was a present to us from Queen Pitomai, one of the english breed that she brought from Ravavai.

I felt very sorry, but as it died so suddenly we concluded to cut of his head, and dress it, and if on examination we found it died from a blow, we should not hesitate to eat it. *Saturday 28th* I cooked the duck found it very good. Concluded it died from a blow on its back. Sister P came down and ate with us. I also sent some of it to the children. Teofai ~~also~~ brought us another very large melon, which made us quite feast.

This day is what the natives call mahana maa, that is the day they prepare their food for sunday, and the following week. Two of our native children go home to sleep this night. Which leaves Alma and Mysefl alone with br Gruards two children.

Sunday 29th hard wind and rain this morning. I arose early, ~~and prepared~~ for meeting. Quite a general attendance to day several brethren from Mahu. Brother P preached very plain to them in the evening on the subject of rejecting the gospel. Many of them paid the most profound attention. I could not help thinking it would have the desired effect.

Monday March 1st very rainy day Queen Pitomai brought us a fine load of cocoanuts, which we prized very highly as it is very hard work for Alma to get them; besides they are rather scarce at this season. *Tuesday 2nd* We went to wash, took all the children, who gathered Goauvers while I washed. In the evening the queen brought us a chicken and some papi hadi's, very pleasant and light tonight.

Sister P and myself with the children sat on the beach sometime watching the movement of the waters and the beautiful full moon which never looks so spendid to me on land, as when seen shining o'er the mighty deep. I have lost one day this week in consequence of very rainy weather. I find it was *Wednesday* that I washed, and *Tuesday* I spent in reading. *Thursday 4th*, I ironed my clothes, and neglected the prayermeeting, thinking it was Wed——.

Friday 5th considerable rain today. The boys went after (Nohaneha, that is) grass for the floors, which we have to renew quit often, in order to have it fresh, and clean. The weather is now very warm and rainy.

We have had some nice fat turtle brought us this week as well as baked pig. The natives are now very busily engaged in making limejuice for Tahiti market. They work together in large companies, and keep a constant singing, somewhat resembling sailors pulling ropes. *Saturday* we put down our clean grass, previously however we heard the cry of pahi O O, on inquiry found the men at Tuamai had seen a ship passing the motu's, and concluded it was the *Ravai*. But is [it] was impossible for it to come into harbour today in consequence of adverse winds.

[Called to Tahiti]

Sunday morning, 7th day of March, about 3 oclock, I chanced to be awake, ruminating in my mind the changes and chances of this mortal life; untill I was so far from sleep, that I began to think it had entirely departed from me the remainder of the night; and surely so it had for I very soon heard the sound of pahi O—— and then surely sleep departed from my eyes and slumber from my eyelids. I however waited untill I was convinced by their continued shouting that a ship was certainly coming into harbour, and then arose and dressed me. Sis P and girls were soon here, and watching with eagar eyes for the small boat to come off, but after waiting sometime and seeing no stir, concluded they intended waiting till morning light, and so returned home. But they had been gone but five minutes when the boat came on shore. Alma came in and informed me that his father and br Grouard were coming in he had only done speaking, when br G—— and Ellen came in, and informed me that my husband and Frances had staid behind in Tahiti. That the brethren had engaged a job of work building a house and had sent for us to come immediately. I was not a little shocked at the information. But hardly knew whether I was pleased or displeased, and concluded ^at all events^ to make the best of it. They told me quite a flattering story of my husbands earning 3 dollars per day, and that they had taken a 1300 dollar job by which means we were to be taken back to America. They br G and Alexander—— seemed pleased with the plan and brother P—— and Layton approved of it and so I had not a word to say, only that I hope it will be for the best. It will (they say) cost them a 1000 dolls to fit up the *Ravaai*, and then she is so small, that it would be uncomfortable going so far in her.

The *Ravaai* has been 4 weeks coming from Tahiti. Lay 2 weeks at Rurutu, on account of headwinds.

Capt G—— tried to preach there but they wholly rejected him, and even mocked at him. So strongly are they bound up in sectarianism, it almost seems that the english missionaries have bound them over to perdition. Capt G preached this morning and br P—— in the evening and administered the sacrament.

They ordained Raitoro to preside over the church on this island who is a very good man, and quite a preacher. The friends here feel very sorry to have us leave, even threaten to confine br P——, those who do not belong to the church. They say that it is not because they do not believe the gospel, and respect us, that they are not baptised, but that they have been so long kept under restraint by the english Missionaries, and now the law of the french permits them to sing and dance as much as they please, and they wish to enjoy it a little longer, but in addition to that they also wish to have now and then a drunken frolick, as they have today *Monday 8th*. It is a very rainy day, the rain comes down in torrents. This evening I am alone with the children, my heart seems sad indeed, I tried but could not read, and so thought I would write. Ellen returned from her fathers after we were all in bed, and her father and br G accompanied her. Her father proposed that she and I should lodge together, and that br G—— should sleep in the middle room as a Tiai—or <u>watch</u> on account of the drunkards who were carousing about. But we were not all disturbed by them, although I slept but very little during the night. One of the drinkers came in today and wished me to let him have a tumbler said offered me the money for it, said as I was soon going to Tahiti I could get more. I did not like to part with it but to save talking with him in my broken way and get rid of him I let him have it.

[A Quilt for the Queen]

Tuesday 9th very dull cloudy weather. I cut pieces for my new quilt, and kept myself quite busy through the day. Br and sis P and br G spent the evening with us. *Wed—— 10th.* Ellen and Alma washed I spent the day in sewing on my quilt. In the afternoon br G—— brought us a pig and dressed for our supper. We also had fresh fish brought in which served to make us a very plentiful supper. Br P——s were with us in the evening.

Thursday 11th I finished the top of my quilt, and attended prayer-meeting as usual, this evening have been sewing quite late, Br and sis P and G—— with us. *Friday 12th* very warm pleasant day. Ellen ironed. I made the lining of my quilt, finished the skirt of my dress, which br Richmond sent us from Tahiti by G——. Cooked beans for supper. Walked up to br

P——s Was accompanied home by them and Grouard spent the evening in singing and music on the accordion.

Saturday 13th day I finished my dress. Spent the evening alone, Ellen and Alma ran away to her father's. I put the children all in bed and resumed my writing. I now feel in quite a hurry to get my sewing done, all things ready for my voyage to Tahiti which I can but dread when I reflect upon that ever to be abhorred sickness which I suffered in coming here. All I have to comfort me is the hope of its not being as bad nor the voyage so long. It appears to me quite a task to pick up my things and get on board without my husbands help, but I expect Capt G, and br P, will willingly assist me.

Sunday 14th day. Just returned from meeting. br G—— spoke to the people quite lengthy.

Monday evening day 15th Today I have cut and made a pair of pantaloons for Alma, covered my quilt frames, and got my quilt on, all by myself; excepting br Grouard assisted me a little in fastening the corners, and suspending it. I succeeded with it better than I feared I should, feel very tired to night; think I shall surely sleep soundly.

Tuesday 16th Ellen and Alma went to wash, I quilted very steadily all day, sis—— P—— helped me in the afternoon. *Wednesday, 17th* she came down again before breakfast and quilted untill schooltime. Ellen and br G—— also assisted today. *18th* I finished my quilt by staying from prayermeeting. The time begins to seem long, inasmuch as we have to go we feel anxious to get away.

Friday morning March 19th. I arose this morning feeling quite debilitated, having laboured for four days with uncommon diligence, in order to accomplish the several little jobs of work which I had intended to before leaving this Island. But notwithstanding my disagreeable feelings I went (after breakfast) and with Alma's assistance washed our clothes and ironed them the same day, besides doing some sewing. Tomorrow will show me (or at least some future day) how far I have tresspassed against the laws of nature, in going beyond my strength.

Saturday night 20th This morning I felt very lame and tired but it wore away before night, so that I can say that I feel usually well. The day has passed away almost imperceptibly. I finished my new quilt, and sent it to Pitomai vahine by Darius. This evening sister P and myself had a time of bathing in the ocean, we took advantage of the low tide and enjoyed ourselves finely.

[Preparing for the Voyage]

Sunday evening day 21st. Br Grouard preached this morning, a sort of farewell discourse, which we called very good; br P—— spoke this evening. Br

Layton has had a very sick day with the cramp colic. His house has been filled with attendants trying to do all they could for him. I saw him at noon he was very bad, I called again this evening he was easy, among the numerous remidies some of them had eased him.

Monday 22nd I cut my new dress which Queen Pitomai gave me. Remarkbly warm day, in the afternoon I took my sewing over to the meeting house and sewed with sis P. she makes that her sitting room. In the evening Br G——s little Ephraim had quite a sick turn, Sis P was here and also br G they sent for her to come home. He soon got better, and she returned.

Br G—— was reading Combe's treatise on nature[29] which was very interesting to us and the time passed away almost imperceptibly untill br P arose after having been in bed near two hours and came down to enquire into the cause of her staying so late, of which fact, we were entirely unconscious untill reminded by him.

Tuesday 23rd. Ellen washed I did the housework and sewed some on my new dress, have been afflicted all day with distress in my stomach. Br G—— killed a pig for supper.

Wednesday 24th have enjoyed my health well to day, Sewed very steadily. Spent the afternoon in the meetinghouse with Sis P—— went over and took supper there, while Lois and Ephraim ate here with Ellen. Br Grouard stays with us since his return principally. I had a long conversation with Sister this evening upon some of the principals of the church. *Thursday 25th* quite rainy today. Attend prayer meeting as usual, The first time I have attempted to speak to them in their native tongue. I felt it quite a cross. I however succeeded better than I had anticipated. *Friday 26th* been sewing quite steadily. Called this evening br and sis P—— br Grouard and Tali.

Saturday 27th. Today I finished the new dress which was presented me by the Queen, and made me and apron. Some rain today. Called this evening Revitoro vahine and her daughter, br Elexander, wife, and Tu, Br G—— has been reading to us from Combs writings.

Sunday 28th of March Quite rainy and unpleasant I spent the interval between the meetings in reading Combes writings on the organic laws of nature. Have been reading again this evening. I admire them much. *Monday 29th* Very rainy. I have cut a dress for Luna today spent the evening reading Combs. *Tuesday 30th* Some rain today. I spent the afternoon in the meeting house. Sister here this evening, br G—— and herself got their combativeness quite excited upon the subject of the native character.

Wednesday 31st I arose very early for me this morning, felt quite well for sometime, but before breakfast was ready I began to feel unwell, I had intended to wash today but felt so miserable after breakfast that I gave it over for awhile and sat down to sewing, but after resting awhile I felt so much revived that I concluded to try my washing however late. Accordingly I went with Alma Darius Luna and little Benjamin F Gruard. I had quite a cool time for washing. The boys made a native oven and baked quite a lot of Gooffers. I felt very week all day I however accomplished my washing in tolerably good season, returned home assisted Ellen in getting supper, and finished a dress for Luna, Br and sis Pratt and br G—— spent the evening with us.

April 1st. Very pleasant. Ellen washed and ironed. In the afternoon we attended our female prayer meeting as we now expect for the last time I felt quite affected with the idea of its being the last of our assembling with them, some of them also seemed to regret our leaving them very much. After they had all ceased speaking and praying we (sister, P, Ellen, and myself), went to each separately, laid our hands upon their heads and blessed them in the name of the Lord. The good spirit accompanied us, our meeting continued quite late. Returned home spent the evening listing to and reading Combe.

Friday 2nd, today, I have made a hat for B F G, jun. We have a beautiful pleasant moon this evening.

Saturday 3rd I commenced packing my chests and trunks, I worked very busily all, was very tired at night. *Sunday 4th* Br Gruard preached his farewell discourse which was very excellent. Br P administered the sacrament this evening. After meetings were over we visited sick man by the name of Taati, he is near his end with consumption he is a very good man, his wife and family are also worthy members of the church.

Monday evening 5th. Washed today, and ironed this evening, have been on my feet nearly all day, feel very much fatigued. Br G—— has commenced loading the vessel, thinks some of sailing tomorrow.

[Farewell to Tubuai]

Tuesday 6th of Apr about 4 oclock we sailed from Tupuai. The natives almost universally called to say ia orana, and bring some little present. I knew not the day before whether we should have sufficient food brought to last us to Tahiti but when the day for our departure arrived the food was brought in so bountifully that Br G—— said I had plenty to go to California with. I had the good fortune to get every thing that I wished to bring, that is there was nothing forgotten. I was truly affected with the kindness and attention of the brethren and sisters, and the regret seemed to experince at our leaving them. Some were very anxious indeed to accompany us. And the only way we could console them was by telling them we would use our influence in favor of having a vessel sent for them. We got on board in season to get through the pass before dark, the wind being in our favor our little craft moved on through the smooth waters with much quietness. The evening was remarkably pleasant, we could distinctly hear them from the shore (after we got well under way) shouting ia orana outou, which is "peace be with you" I have no doubt, but that the dear creatures felt very lonely and will continue to feel so for sometime there is now only one white man on the island, he is an old gentleman by the name of Rogers who expects to die there and that soon.

Soon after getting on board I thought I would go below and reconnoiter my berth, before I began to be sick. I suceded in regulating my bed and returned on deck, but by that time was so sick and faint that I concluded to go without my supper, to prevent vomiting. I had rather a miserable night of it, and arose the next morning very faint, having eaten nothing for 24 hours. Sister P was also nearly in the same condition only she ate supper the night previous and threw it up again. We had our couches made on deck where we received every attention from the capt and friends but got very little relief for several days. The weather continued very pleasant, very little wind, which made it more comfortable for us sick ones, but notwithstanding we felt very anxious to get through our journey. The 4th day we were followed some distance by a shark, the water was very clear and still and we could see it very plain, the water seemed to magnify the sise of its appearance and gave it a silvery hue, it was truly a splendid sight to me having never seen any thing of the kind before. Our men had just been killing a pig the innards of which served for bait, they threw it over and he immediately seized it and was hauled on board with perfect ease, such a shouting and flying about I never saw. We were all anxious to see and yet fearful of going near it, one child was knocked down by its flouncing. The natives dressed and ate it, but I understand the meat is not very palatable.

Sunday morning day the 11th of Apr we hove in sight of Tahiti. My head and eyes being weak I did not try to extend my sight so far as to see it, having little or no wind we did not come near enough for me to discover it untill *monday the 12th*, when behold ~~when~~ going on deck in the morning ^I perceived^ we were very near it, and all hands admiring its curious appearance, resembling a pile of mountains heaped one upon another in every shape and of every size, some so small and high that they appeared like one high rock spiriring up to the skies. *Tuesday 13th* we came along side, so near we could distinctly see a number of cascades falling ~~a number of~~ some hundred feet, and forming a beautiful appearnce from the vessel. And immediately two men in a canoe were seen coming to us. They came along side and brought us a basket of oranges, Our Capt then sent of a boat for fresh water, as ours was very brackish. They soon returned with a quantity of good water which was [*illegible crossout*] quaffed off by greedy lips.

[Reunion at Tahiti]

We had the whole length of the island to sail, and as there was little or no wind it took us untill afternoon *Tuesday* to get into harbour. As soon as the vessel anchored the boat went off and on returning brought Mr Crosby and Frances. They were quite overjoyed to see us—having waited so long beyond their expectations. They were however perfectly satisfied with our apologies. An awning was raised over the deck where we staid untill towards evening, when Mr Crosby returned to the ship and escorted us to his dwelling. We found them very comfortably situated in a small framed house with br Whitaker and family, consisting—3 rooms, 1 tolerable sized room and 2 bedrooms. A very nice little yard in front of the house shaded with breadfruit, burau, bananna and other trees, and beautifully variegated with flowers of almost every hue; among which is the red rose, all in perfect bloom. Tahiti is most assuredly the most delightful place for fruit, flowers, and shadetrees, that I ever beheld. The only deficiency I have yet discovered is good society, and in that respect it is sadly deficient. Br P—— and family all took supper with us, br and sis staid over night, while the girls returned to the vessel in co with Grouard, Layton, and Elexander, and families. The brethren fortunately found a house on the beach large enough to accommodate 3 families, which they rented for 20 dolls per month. My husband and Whitaker pay 8 dolls pr month for their house. Mr Crosby had 100 dolls saved when we arrived. *Sunday April 18th* Br P and girls called up to drink a little wine and eat a few sweet cakes and cheese; Towards evening we took a walk on the broome, which is a very pleasant street, but so crowded with people on that day, and especially riders on horseback that our excursion was not so agreeable as we could have wished. We walked a mile to a large substantial bridge built over a small stream, the railing of which is covered with zinc and painted white. We also passed through the artificial breastwork built by the french in their war with the natives, which is something of a curiosity to those who have never seen anything of the kind. We picked and ate a few goauvers on our way. On our return home we were met by numerous pleasure parties, among which were 3 sisters of charity, with their novices, or pupils; consisting of white children, halfbreeds, and pure natives. They appeared very decent and orderly. We arrived at our dwelling quite fatigued and dusty. *Sunday 25th.* Br Whitaker and family gone to a native meeting, consisting of brethren from Ana. This evening we called down to br Ps took supper and returned by moonlight. While there we took a walk on the broome, in co with br and sis—— P. Louisa and the little children. We were much delighted with the fragrance and luxuriance of the scenery on all sides, but especially the government garden excited our curiosity, and the soldiers barracks. We walked a mile perhaps, and returned sooner than we should have done, on account of rain. Br Grouard and Pratts, expect now to go to California and leave the remainder of the brethren behind; to finish the job, and come after them as soon as convenient. G—— has an opportunity of going as first mate, and they all get passage at 50 dolls apiece. And in consequence of the vessels all being loaded with oranges at this season, we find it difficult for us all to get passage in one. Although it would be much more agreeable for the com to continue together, yet we consider it wisdom, to get away as the [*word missing*] opens. I expect to be left here without any white female friend or associate which makes it rather disagreeable on account of understanding the Tahitian dialect so imperfectly. They the <u>brethren </u>have made me the offer of going, or staying as I choose, but I think it most proper for me to stay with my husband, and son, and share their fates, be they what they may.

[The Pratts' Departure]

Thursday 29th I went down to assist Sister P—— and girls in sewing. They expect now to go in one week. The vessel is now gone around the island for oranges. Sister Grouard has given up the idea of going to Cali, and intends sailing for Ana tomorrow. *Friday 30th* She went on board the vessel bound for that island. They sailed about 2 miles, and were becalmed near shore. She finally repented of her undertaking and left the vessel, stop at a camping place of a number of brethren from that island, and sent down after her oldest little son to come and see her; his father however would not let him go. I presume her intention is to go to Cal.[30]

    Sat May 1st Sister P—— spent the day with me, she is quite troubled about Frances' ill health, she has been unwell ever since she has been in Tahiti, probably owing to change of climate and diet.[31] Quite rainy to day.

    Sunday May 2nd, br P—— and Whit—— gone to native meeting. The weather is extremely warm.

    Tuesday 4th The French government made a great display of the fruits, and other productions of the island, together with boat racing, horse racing, and other feats such as climbing greasy poles &C In the evening they exhibited splendid fireworks Throwing up rockets and other exhibitions of powder and fire. After which several pieces were acted on a stage and the whole concluded by dancing. We were led into it unintentionally; not understanding the order of the evening, we thought we would walk to Br P——s and see what we could learn of it. just before we reached their place we met them coming out on the same errand We therefore joined company and commenced walking. We intended going to some retired place at a humble distance from the main body of the people, where we could see a little of what was acting. But to our surprise when we got into the street which led to the place of action, we were accosted by a french officer in splendid uniform and invited to follow him. We knew that to decline would be impolite and therefore suffered ourselves to be led on. My husband had neglected to wear his coat, and was requested by him to return home and get it. We were led to the most conspicuous place, and seated among gentlemen and ladies who were dressed in very costly apparel, while we were in our sunbonnets. We felt a little chagrined to be so distinguished among them, however we were treated with much politeness, and upon the whole were much interested with the entertainment.

Sunday 9th I attended the catholic church for the first time in my life. They have a small house, but neatly finished, and an organ. They chanted nearly all their prayers, which are in the latin language. The sermon was in the Tahitian.

Monday 10th The ship *Callio [Callao]* returned with her load of oranges bound for California.

Tuesday 11th Sister P—— sent for me to come and spend the day with them, as they expected soon to leave. I went after breakfast, and staid untill bedtime I assisted in sewing through the day. In the evening Mr Crosby and Ellen, played the violin, and accordian. We also had a little dancing on the occasion. *Wednesday 12th* they expected to sail, but some difficulty between the capt and crew prevented them. *Thursday 13th* They got all their things on board, and came to our house near night, staid untill *Friday* evening, when they all went on board, I accompanied them; found the vessel very dirty, and in great disorder. Br Grouard and Pratt however soon succeeded in reconnoitering things so as to render their little cabin quite pleasant, and comfortable. I waited untill after sunset, some expecting sister would return with me to sleep, but after getting her birth prepared she concluded to stay and occupy it, the girls also being unwilling to have her leave. Br P came home with me, and returned immediatly to the ship. The next morning we all went off to the vessel to say goodbye for the last time (at least for the present). Found them very comfortably situated and in good spirits. They were pleased to see us coming especially the children, they shouted and laughed, little Benjamin F Grouard said "Aunt Caroline here's me." We staid only a few minutes and returned. We watched the vessel for sometime, untill at length she was not to be seen. She sailed on *Friday May 14th 1852*, a few minutes before 12 oclock A M. When my husband and br Whitaker returned from their work in the evening they brought me a line Which on examining I found was from sister P, sent back by the pilot, a frenchman who took them out of the harbour, stating that she was in good spirits, and better than she had been for sometime, she requested our prayers, and bade us goodbye again. *Sunday 16th* passed off rather dull. In the evening my husband

and I took a short walk on the broom road, just to get a little fresh air, but it was so remarkably warm and still that we found ourselves very little refreshed by the exercise.

[Passing Time in Papaete]

Sunday 23rd Another week has passed away, nothing worth recording having transpired. Plenty of business has prevented my being lonesome. Papiete is so full of noise and confusion that I frequently think I should prefer the quiet scenes of Tupuai. And also when I reflect upon the abominable licentiousness of the people of this place, I am led to abhor it. It appears to me that this people cannot long continue in this awful state of degradation, in which they are kept, by vicious white men, who come among them, and who instead of trying to improve their morals are continually sinking them deeper and deeper in the vo[r]tex of wickedness. Methinks the punishment of such men should be severe, when we reflect that they have been born and reared in a christian land, will not the sins of this dark and benighted people be visited sooner or later upon their heads I am sure any reasonable mind will answer in the affirmative. To see so beautiful a land as this, so defiled by its inhabitants, is really distressing to a virtuous mind.

Sunday 30th This week Capt Johnson arrived, ten days from Tupuaui; bringing letters from there, and from br James Brown at Raivavai. Whose letters quite excited our compassion for him. His situation is really a disagreeable one at present; being confined to the island and yet forbidden to hold publick meetings, and threatened with mobbing in all its hideous forms, and afflicted with sickness besides. But says the Lord has raised him up a few faithful friends—members of the church, about 20 in number, who are remarkbly kind to him, and are unwilling that he should leave untill they can go with him. The king of this land returned from here, short time before the arrival of Jonson. Brother Pratt sent letter by him to James, but it got lost. and all he could tell was that we were all here, waiting for an opportunity to sail to America. Which intelligence undoubtedly increased his anxiety to know what remained for him to do.

However, his mind will probably be relieved soon, as the brethren have sent by Rutliff to bring him to this place. The american consul has offered to take him into his care untill we can all get ready to sail together for California.

Friday a vessel sailed, and carried Mr Evans by whom I sent letter to sister P——. Quite rainy for several days. *Sunday* afternoon it being cloudy and cool, my husband and I took a walk of about a mile to a pleasant stream of water, followed up its banks a short distance untill we came to a retired spot where we had a fine bathe, and returned home much refreshed. *June 1st Tuesday*, last night an american schooner the *Golden rule* by name, was wrecked on the reef about two miles from here, at a passage called Tanoa, she was loaded with oranges and other productions of the islands, and bound for California.

Friday 4th a large vessel arrived from Sidney, bound for California with some 60 passengers. This day Mr Colly moved into his new store which our brethren have been erecting for him, he is highly pleased with it; he has a large quantity of valuable goods. He seems somewhat inquiring into our religion and inclined to be favorable. My husband gave him the voice of warning, and the Evidences of the book of Mormon.[32]

Sunday 6th, the streets have been full of people from the ship, walking to and fro, to recreate themselves. We also desired a little recreation, and took a pleasant walk with Alma, and Alfred [Layton],[33] on the wall of the city; which is built of turf, and beautifully over-grown with grass, with a nice little path on the top where we can walk in indian file, with perfect ease. We ascended the embankment near the broome road, and traced it clear to the beach. We then took the road which led us on to the peninsula where we saw the machinery for hauling up ships out of the ocean. It is called the Patent slip.

We returned home by the beach which we found so crowded with natives and frenchmen that we could scarcely get along. We were however much pleased with our excursion. *Wednesday 9th June* Capt Henry died of the third apoplectic fit. His death occasioned quite an excitement, and his history perhaps might be interesting in some respects, but I am almost wholly ignorant of it. I learned from his daughter Mrs Pool that he was the first white child born on this island. That his father was the eldest missionary here, who by the by is now gone either to Sidney or England. He was 50 years old when he died. His wife died near a year ago. They have left a large family of children, several of them quite young. I understand they mourned very bitterly for him. Intemperance was probably the cause of his death. I called on them the sunday evening previous to brother P——s leaving in co with himself and family. Mr Henry treated us with much politeness and familiarity. He urged us untill we could do no less than sit down to the tea table and drink a cup with them. He then invited us into his sitting room, where wine was set before us. Mrs Pool led us about from one room to another to show us their different apartments, which were very nicely furnished. She gave us an account of her mothers death, which occured while she was in San Francisco. Her father also spoke several times of her death and appeared very much affected, even to tears, which we attributed to partial intoxication. He was however no doubt a hearty mourner for her. She has the name of having been a very judicious house wife, and an tender mother.

Their children are very delicate in appearance.

Mr Pool returned from a voyage of several months to Sidney, a few days previous to the death of his fatherinlaw. Report says he has brought a thousand pounds worth of silks, and satin goods.

Sat—— 12th, Capt Jonson sailed for Tupuai.

[Saying Goodby to Luna]

My little girl which I have kept so long, and taken unwearied pains to instruct, came with her grandmother to see me for the last time, to say goodby. Her friends were unwilling that we should take her home with us, consequently I was obliged to give her up. She accompanied us from Tupuai with her grandmother, to this place, to visit friends which they have living here. I felt it a great pity for her to go back again into heathenism, after being so far instructed in the english language, and habits of civilised living. And as her friends do not belong to our church, I shall have no hopes of her being gathered with us at present, if ever.[34]

[A Change of Governors]

Monday 14th the new governor arrived, A large man of war came into the harbor, towed by a steamer at 10 oclock. Several canons were fired, and a great gathering accompanied his arrival. At two oclock he came on shore, when the firing was renewed, the natives running again from every quarter. He was conducted to the government house accompanied by a large concourse of people, and two Catholic priests.

Tuesday 15th all the first sett[l]ers of the place assembled, as I suppose to receive, and acknowledge, him as their lawful sovereign. *Wednesday 16th* he came on shore in his regimentals, which was attended with cannonading and a gathering of the people. The exgovernor at the same time, left the island, and went on board the man-of-war, bound for france. We understand that the new governor is quite a religious man, that he disapproves of the drunkenness and licentiousness of the people *Thursday 17th* another white man, (a carpenter) died, left a native wife and several children.

His extreme licentiousness was undoubtedly the cause of his death. I wrote a letter to br Hank at the Pamutus in great haste expecting the vessel would sail immediately, but did not, untill the next day. We have invited brother Hanks to return home with us if he chooses, and can get here in season.

[A Penalty of Death]

Friday 18th, another death occured, of a frenchman on board a manofwar, while suffering the penaties of their law, for using insulting language, to the exgovernor. It was occasioned in the following manner, as I understood it They attached a weight to his feet, tied ropes to his arms, and raised him upon the yardarms, then let him drop suddenly into the water, the distance of some 60 feet. After stangling him sometime they raised him up again, the blood was gushing from his mouth and nose. They let him fall the second time, and on raising him, found him dead. They then took him outside the reef, and buried him in the broad ocean. Very little was said about it, ~~the~~ neither the natives nor anyone else, daring to speak a word openly, against the government department.

Sunday 20th towards night I took a walk with my husband, to a retired bathing place, where we had a good bathe; and I felt much refreshed by it. We returned home in the cool of the evening. We had a shower of rain a short time before which rendered the air, together with the fragrance of the orange trees, very exhilerating to our spirits.

Monday Tuesday and Wed—— remarkbly rainy, accompanied with strong winds. *Saturday 26th*, a large vessel arrived from California bound to Sidney *Friday 25th*, the exgovernor sailed for France; being as I understand ordered away, (by the new one,) Quite a number of sailors and passengers were put into the calabouse last night for improper conduct. *Sunday 27th* remarkably rainy accompanied with high winds. *Monday Tues and Wed* rain. Another vessel arrived from California this week the *Agate* by name, Capt Jonson master. Br Whitaker has been talking with him about taking us passengers, but he wants all the money we have a little more, so that he came away quite discouraged.

[Engaging the *Agate*]

*Thursday ^ July 1st^* he saw him again and engaged our passage Mr Crosby and myself take cabin passage. ^for 175 dolls^ Alma goes with the rest of the co, in the steerage, at 50 dolls aper and find themselves, besides they have to build themselves berths. We consider it a hard bargain, but accept of it rather than wait for a better chance.

Friday ~~July 1st~~ 2nd he br Wh concluded to go around with the capt after oranges, br Alexander accompanies him also as steward.

*Saturday ^morning 3rd^* the *Agate* left very early, but having no wind is still in sight of the harbor. I understand the new governor is so very sick, that his life is despaired of. *Sunday ~~3rd~~ 4th.* We are now left alone in the house. it seems very lonely since Br W's left us, but it proves to me the truth of the old adage "that there is no loss without some gain" We now have a good chance to pick up, and pack our things, and no natives to stand around in the way, as sister W being a native herself always has a crowd around her.

Monday 5th, two british men of war came into the harbor accompanied by a steamer, or at least one was towed in by her, and the other the french pilot instead of bringing it in, landed it up on the reef, where it staid untill morning; the steamer has now gone after her, we understand it is somewhat injured. The french made a great display of their military powers, on their arrival, the cannons roared both from sea and land, for some time.

The british have a very splendid band on board We were highly pleased with their music last night. The second manofwar has just come in, The french again renewed their firing.

Whether there are hostile feeling between them or not, I am not able to say. Report says the two governments are at variance. I am informed that there is an admiral on board one of the ships. Last night I was taken very unwell, more so than I have been before since I came to the islands. I think I must have taken a sudden cold by sitting in the wind. I was in great pain the forepart of the night, throughout my whole system. I am unable to work today.

[Reflections of Past and Future]

Tuesday 6th Alma has gone with sister Layton and family to get oranges for our journey; which has left me quite alone; nothing to prevent me from reflecting upon the past, and looking forward to the future, The latter of which my organ of cautiousness induces me to do with dread. In consideration of the past trials and privations we have been led to endure for these eighteen years, and judging the future by the past. And as we are now about to enter upon another very important task, that of crossing the great Pacific Ocean, and entering anew upon the stage of action; to provide ourselves a home and the necessaries comforts of life, with nothing but our constitutions, (and as regards my own a wornout one) to depend upon. Were it not that we have long since learned to trust in the Lord, we should be of all creatures the most miserable. But I consider that it woud be ingratitude in the highest degree for us now to distrust His guardian care, after His having led us thus far by His hand of mercy. And as He is the only source from whence we can derive any permanent hope, it would be foolishness in the extreme, not to "lay hold upon that which is both sure and steadfast, and which entereth into that within the vale."

Friday 9th Queen Pomare went on board the british man of war. She was dressed in her royal apparel, and made a very spendid appearance Both the french and british ships, poured forth an effusion of powder just as she steped into the boat. She was accompanied by a number of the quality of the island. The band I presume did their best to entertain them. They returned after dark, another explosion of powder was the result.

Saturday 10th I completed the last job of sewing and repairing, which has kept me busily employed for 12 weeks. I have made in the time, 7 prs pantaloons, 7 shirts, 5 dresses, 6 Shimeis, 2 skirts, 1 Bedtick, and 2 coats. Idleness has been a perfect stranger to me. I have had a little halfbreed native boy to teach, besides assisting my own son in his studies. Preaching the gospel in Papeete has been entirely out of the question. Br Whitaker had given them a thorough trial, previous to our coming here. My husband has laboured incessantly for 5 months to earn means to take us home to our native country, and has just merely saved a sufficiency, to accomplish that object. So that contrary to scripture I am sure that we have been on a warfare at our own expense. But we have enlisted for life, and have said that we were willing to spend, and be spent in the cause And the Lord has thus far taken us at our word.

[Awaiting the *Agate*]

Saturday night Br Alexander returned from Papara in co with the second mate, having walked 30 miles in 5 hours, merely to learn the truth of the reports that were in circulation in that place. Viz that an American man of war had come into the harbor here, and was at war with the french. He informed us that the vessel would not be here in less time than one week. My husband expects to be out of work in two or three days and feels anxious to be on his way to California. *Sunday 11th* nothing worth relating. *Monday* I commenced reconnoitering and packing my trunks. *Tuesday 12th* the English ships of war went out, with little or no ceremony. I did a large washing with Alma's help on *Wednesday*, and *Thursday* begin to look for our vessel, *Friday* heard again that it will not here before *Sunday 18th*. We took a walk to our former bathing place, and had a fine bathe. This day several native brethren came with their bibles, to get instruction concerning certain passages of scripture.

Monday 19th A ship in sight we hope it is ours, as my husband is now out of employment and very little means to subsist upon, and dare not infringe upon our passage money.

Tuesday 20th another vessel from California, but no *Agate* comes yet, We feel sometimes almost in dispair, but desire to "let patience have her perfect work". This evening took a little walk with my husband, called at the American consul house to return a musical instrument which he had been repairing. It was a guitar belonging to an american lady who has recently come here for the improvement of her health. Her husband I understand is a partner in the *Agate*. ^Adams by name^ I expect we shall have their co to California. We returned home by the broome. The evening was cool, and pleasant, I enjoyed the walk finely. *Wednesday 21st* I took a short walk this evening, with Alma, and Alfred, on the embankment, which we found very pleasant.

Thursday, 22nd Kelly and Gray's Schooner just returned from San Francisco by the way of the Sandwich islands. *Saturday 24th,* received a line from br Whitaker. He informs us that we may expect them on Sunday night, and exhorts us to have all things in readiness, to take our departure from this "damnable place" as he calls it. But we have waited untill we have got almost over our hurry. My husband had the good fortune today to sell 5 canes, or walking sticks, for 10 dollars, and 1 last night for 4 dolls. Besides he now has the offer of work untill we go, or untill the ship returns.

Sunday 25th No arrivals to day

Monday 26th morning, Report says the *Agate* is in sight. Great joy among the children, and also with myself. Between 1 and 2 Pm the ship came to anchor. We immediately commenced taking our things on board, and just as the sun was setting we came on ourselves. We found the deck somewhat in disorder, the capt being on shore, and the crew soon left, telling us we must keep ship for the night. Accordingly My husband, Alma, and Myself, were Capt, passengers, and crew, untill near bedtime. We had an opportunity to look about the ship as much as we pleased. We found every thing very convenient, and to even more than answer, our expectations.

I will just observe that I had few tears to shed on leaving Tahiti. Our good friend and br Mohana or Pohe, was very faithful to us, called on us very frequently in the absence of the vessel, brought us a little food, lime juice, &C, and we in return made him quite a number of presents; we should have been extremely pleased to have had him accompany us, but it was not convenient. I formed no acquaintances with any white person in Tahiti, excepting a partial one with a Mrs Stevens, a catholic woman, who is a dressmaker, and keeps a small store. I called on her in co with sister Pratt and Lois, the day they left, she was very polite and friendly. On my observing that I expected to stay, and my sister to leave, she invited me to call on her and form an acquaintance, which I intended to have done, but our circumstances were such as to deprive me of the privilege of trading but very little, consequently I had no particular business with her, and as I had previously understood that she was opposed to our faith, and did not call on me, I felt myself justified in remaing a stranger to her.

Br Whitaker and Alexander returned to the ship in the course of the evening, and we had quite a sociable time hearing them relate the particulars of their voyage around to Papara. They speak in high terms of the capt, and crew. We retired to our berths at a late hour, found it so remarkbly warm that I slept very little through the night; was obliged to keep my fan in almost constant operation.

[Setting Sail for California]

Tuesday morning 27th, the capt and mates returned the ship, accompaied by a capt Hughs who we expect for a fellow passenger. Capt Johnson (who is master of this ship) treated us with much kindness, made us welcome, told us to consider ourselves at home and make free with anything we wanted. He is a middling sized, dark complexioned, man, easy and agreeable in his manners. *Wed—— morn 28th* The capt and crew were on board at an early hour, accompanied by another passenger, viz Gibson the merchant of Tahiti, who is a scotchman by birth, and is now on his way home to visit his friends in scotland. has a native wife and children in Tahiti. Several other gentlemen unknown to me came on board with the french pilot and accompanied out the harbor and then left us.

We sailed near 12 oclock, had quite a strong breeze, the vessel soon commenced her violent motions, which brought with them that awful seasickness which I had so long dreaded, and which rendered me almost insensible to surrounding objects for nearly one week. The Capt and passengers manifested a good deal of sympathy for me, but all their sympaties were of no avail. Mr Gibson presented me with a nice bottle of Cologne water, as an expression of his benevolence. In about eight days we had a partial calm in which time I so far recoverd my health as to be able to sit up a little, and also sit to the table. But the next rainy weather that came I was nearly as bad as ever. The winds in the meantime have been taking us towards the sandwich islands. *Sunday Aug 8th.* The weather tolerably calm my health a little improved, but my head and stomach miserably weak. About the *10th* the weather again stormy, my sickness returned so that I kept my bed one day. A calm however succeeding brought me up again.

Thursday 12th We hove in sight of the sandwich islands, where we have been becalmed ^or nearly so^ for 3 days. *Saturday 14th* we have now a fine prospect of the islands, which have a very beautiful appearance. I would like to know how br Lewis and the friends are getting along, but I dont expect we shall give them a call this time.

Sat evening the weather being remarkbly pleasant and the water smooth, our vessel moved along like an ocean bird, and every thing seemed to wear an air of cheerfulness. Br Whitaker played his violin Br Alexander and the second mate are trying to keep time with their feet, while myself and husband took a walk on the upper deck, where we had a fine prospect of the various islands which compose the groups of Sandwich islands. We had been then 17 days at sea, and it was the first time I had enjoyed anything like health or happiness. But from that time to this *Aug 27th* my health has been improving; and really I can hardly believe my senses when I reflect upon my comparatively comfortable state. The winds have been unfavorable for us untill within one week past and we are now going on our course with a sea almost as smooth as glass. I can scarcely percieve any motion at all of the ship. We hope in one week more to arrive at our destined port.

Sunday Sept 5th Just arrived in sight of the harbor. Since my last date I have had another severe turn of seasickness which lasted me for 3 days, caused by a rough sea. We have all hands been cleaning up and preparing to take our departure from the vessel into the golden city. I belive our hearts are all under a little excitement being exercised with many hopes and fears ^with respect to our success in getting homes and business here^ Our capt in a special manner, he is expecting to meet his family, a wife and 3 children whom he has been absent from 3 years. 5 minutes to 2 oclock they are now casting anchor Several gentlemen from the city have already been on board, to get the news.

PART THREE

Upper California

Mission San Jose and San Francisco
September 1852–November 1855

CHAPTER NINE

Mission San Jose, California

Journal, 6 September 1852 to 20 January 1854

[Arrival in San Francisco, September 6, 1852]

Monday Sept 6th. Still on board the *Agate*,

Soon after we cast anchor, my husband and Br Whitaker, went on shore; found sister Pratt and Louisa [Ann Louise], and Ellen, living in San Francisco; Br P Frances and Lois, with Br Grouard and family, are at St Jose Mission.[1] I also understand that Capt Johnson found his family all alive and well. But his brother who went back after their family lost his oldest daughter 16 years of age, on the passage and had brought her body preserved in salt, I think from Panama?

Monday Morn our capt returned to the ship. I congratulated him upon his success in meeting his family in safety, he replied that he was truly thankful for the blessing; he took breakfast with us and immediately returned to his friends on shore my husband and the other brethren also accompanied him; but they soon returned. In the evening the vessel was taken to the wharf, we immediately went on shore and commenced our walk, the sun was set before we left the vessel, but we had a clear sky, and the streets were so illuminated that we scarcly missed its light.

We landed on long wharf. I can hardly describe my sensations in passing the splendid brick buildings whose windows were adorned with every variety of merchandize, and illuminated with globes of every hue. Having been so long shut out as it were from the world, and accustomed only to seeing low cabins, of heathenish construction, I felt that a new era had certainly dawned upon my life which ~~certainly~~ would never be erased from my memory. I found my limbs very weak, but it was getting late and we walked on as fast as we could untill at length we arrived at the dwelling occupied by sister Pratt She had been looking for us sometime. I found her very comfortably situated, with plenty of employment, I commenced

167

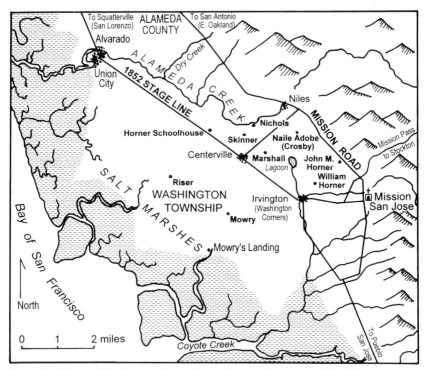

Upper California: Washington Township, Alameda County, 1852–1853.
Washington Township (present-day Fremont and environs) was originally part of
the land grant of Mission San José in East San Francisco Bay.

sewing with her; the next day, Brother and sister Mora [Barton and Ruth
Mowry][2] called to see us and offered us a room in their chamber free
of expense, We were truly thankful, I began to realize the answer to my
prayers while crossing the mighty deep; I could plainly see that the hand
of the Lord was with us. We staid one week with sister Pratt, or at least ate
and drank with her, but slept in father Mourey's chamber.

Sept 12th we came to live with them; The old gentleman gave my
husband a job of work, and I assisted in cooking.

Mon 13th We attended a ball or party at brother [Quartus S.] Sparks,[3]
which was got up by some of the young brethren, on account (as I understood) of the return of the missionaries from the islands of the pacific
We had a very pleasant ride from the plaza in the Omnibus, There were
3 loads of us. Br Sparks had every thing prepared in good style, we had 3
fiddlers, and a very agreeable time, returned at one oclock.

Our religious meetings were held at the house of a brother
[Theodore] Thorp. A welchman by the name [Thomas] Morris[4] was the
president of the branch. Br Sparks was their chief preacher. We staid 3
weeks in San Francisco.

In the meantime my husband received an invitation from a brother Neil [John Naile, Naegle], of Sanhosa to come and live with him.⁵ He offered him 100 dolls per month and to board his family. The brethren thought it a very good offer, as business was rather dull in the city, and house rent very high. Accordingly he concluded to visit the place, to see how he liked the situation, and location of br Neils residence. *Tuesday Sept 21st* he crossed the bay in co with brother Mowrey upon his launch.⁶ Alma and I staid with sister M. Sister [Fanny] Corwin visited us, and spent one night in their absence. We enjoyed ourselves remarkbly well. Sister Pratt and a sister Hollinbeck also visited ~~made us a visit~~ us. They returned *Saturday the 25th.*

[Moving to Mission San Jose]

Mr Crosby was very well pleased with the proposals of br Neil, and had engaged to proced forthwith on the following monday, to San hosa. I shook hands and bid the sisters, and friends, goodbye on sunday, and *Monday morn Sept 28th* we put our baggage on board Mowrey's launch. Sister P, accompanied us to the wharf, We concluded to take Alfred Layton our former little charge, agreeable to the wishes of his parents.

We had a little perplexity in getting down to the wharf. Alma and Alfred ran into a cake shop to get a few cakes for their boat ride, and the clerk not being quite ready to attend them, they were detaind untill we had got out of their sight. We were constantly looking back for them, and in the meantime hurrying on as we had heard that the capt was waiting for us. We finally arrived at br [Henry] Christy's establishment, he met us at the door, we told him our predicament, and asked him to go in search of the boys, which he readily agreed to. Mr Crosby at the same time had gone to inform the capt of our difficulty. Br Christy very soon returned to us with them. They said when they returned from the shop to the street they could see nothing of us, and concluded we had taken another street, they looked about, and accidentally saw the drayman with our baggage, and knew it. They therefore determined to pursue it, believing it would them to us. Br Christy said he knew them by Alfreds white pantaloons recollecting the Tahiti fashion of black coat and white pants and knowing that we were late from there. We finally all arrived in safety to the boat, accompanied by sis P and br C I bade them farewell and descended into my little cabin, where I staid but a few minutes, and returned on deck, took my seat on a heap of sails and enjoyed the scenery of the ships, for an hour or two. The air was very pleasant and exhilerating, our little boat glided along with great composure, untill we got out of sight of the harbour when the breese freshened and became so cool that I concluded to descend. My husband made me a couch and as I did not rest very well the night previous, I slept the greatest part of the day. We had hoped to get across before dark sister Mowrey had encouraged me with the idea of sleeping in her bed that night, said she had a room and bed in her sons chamber at Mowreys landing and that I should be welcome to it. But the wind and tide left us little too soon, proving the truth of the old adage, "time and tide waits for no man" consequently we were left aground for several hours, and we concluded to give up the idea of arriving to our destined port that night. Accordingly made our beds and slept soundly untill daybreak. As soon as I was sufficently aroused to realize my situation, my ears were saluted with the morning orisons of the sweet blackbirds, which swarm in clouds around the cultivated fields, and by which I knew that we were at our harbor. We all arose dressed ourselves, and commenced our walk, at least my husband, Alfred, and myself, leaving Alma to take care of the baggage, and give information to br Neil if he should chance to come for us in our absence. I was much delighted with the walk, although it seemed longer than I had expected, being about a mile and a half. I was obliged to stop once to rest, which was at a store house, where I saw the greatest quantity of onions, and the largest ones, that I had ever seen in my life. Every thing in nature looked pleasant and cheerful to me, the music of the birds, the sweet serenity of the air, and the sight of distant husbandmen gathering their harvest all conspired to cheer and animate and invigorate my body and mind. We arrived at br Harley Morey's residence just as they were sitting down to their breakfast. We met a very cordial reception, altho we had never had a personal acquaintance with them, yet the fact that they were saints late from Salt Lake city was sufficient to recommend them to our best feeling Our walk had naturally prepared our stomachs for a hearty breakfast, which being over my husband returned to the boat, leaving myself and Alfred to finish our visit. We enjoyed it finely, untill 12 oclock, when br Neil arrived with his team, took us back to the landing. When we arrived there we found Mr C had got impatient through waiting, and had bent his way towards br N's residence. I was obliged to call on the boatmen to assist in loading the waggon as br N had a broken finger, besides being quite unwell. They readily assisted, and we soon found ourselves crossing the extended prairies moving on at a slow rate, in consequence of a heavy load.

[Moving into the Naile Adobe]

It was quite a curiosity to me to observe the various heaps of white sacks filled with grain, which ornamented their harvest fields. When we arrived within half a mile of our new home, we met Mr C, he had been to br N's, took dinner, and returned to br Skinner's,[7] to await our arrival. We arrived about 2 oclock. I found every thing quite as agreeable as I had expected. *Tues Sept 29th* The house is in a very unfinished state, altho the lower part is quite comfortable. The masons are now at work on the second story. We have a pleasant room at the north end of the house with a large window fronting the east, over which is a verander running the whole length of the house. My husband is now employed painting the outside. Br N's workmen are mostly spanish and portugeese. So that we understand very little of their conversation. In the evening after our arrival, Alma and Alfred went over to brother Skinner's after Frances. She came home with them, and spent the evening, is highly pleased with her situation, but thinks she should like to come and live here with us.

Sunday, Oct 3rd 1852 Br Skinner, and family made us a call in their carriage. It is a beautiful pleasant morning, all nature seems to wear an air of cheerfulness. My heart also seems to respond to a spirit of thankfulness, to the great Author of all good, for His preserving care which has been over us in our going out and coming in. And through all the changing scenes of life that we have been called to pass.

Sunday at 2 oclock we attended meeting at the new schoolhouse.[8] Mr Crosby spoke to them upon the subject of entering in at the strait gate. After meeting we went around by br Nicols,[9] stoped and took supper. We had a very agreeable time, returned home after dark. *4th Monday* I cut and made pants for Alma. *5th Tuesday* Frances came to visit us staid 2 or 3 hours. In the evening I wrote a line to sister Pratt. *Wednesday 6th,* br Neil went to San Francisco. I washed and made myself nearly sick. Wed—— night I have a very bad cold. Br Neil returned in the evening, did not go to S F in consequence of the boat being gone. *Thursday 7th* I ironed, and went to br Skinners in the afternoon. In the evening we all went out to the schoolhouse to prayer meeting. Sis Tomkins having spent the afternoon with us, accompanied to meeting. My husband ~~having~~ had a bad cold did not attend. ~~the meeting~~. When I returned found him, waiting for me at br Skinners. It was quite late when we got home. The next day I was attacked with a violent headache, so that I was obliged to take my bed. *Friday 8th night* I suffered very much with my head and throat. *Saturday 9th* was some better but not able to work. Friday morn br Neil set off again for San F. *Sunday 10th* beautiful pleasant day find my health much improved. Frances and Amanda Tom[kins] called on us at an early hour, before I was up. Afternoon Mr C gone out to meeting. *Thursday 15th* Br Neil returned having staid several days longer than we expected, he bought a quantity of new furniture with which I was highly pleased, as we had neither of us any before. Br N—— brought me a line from sis—— Pratt, in answer to one I sent by him, I spoke highly of my new home, and the pleasures of a country life, but could not persuade her to believe she could be happy to live so retired. She however thinks that perhaps she shall try it this winter. She informs me that Br Cristy has had late communication from the spirit rappers which were very satisfactory and interesting to him, that she intends going to see what she can learn from our friends soon.

[The Spirit Rappers]

I have neglected to state the little of my own experience in regard to the spirit rappers, as I believe they are called. One evening while we were staying at Father Mowreys, the principle operator, a young man by the name of Brunelle accidentally called in. He appeared very friendly and familliar with the family, having formerly been a boarder with them. The old gentleman told him that we were entire strangers to the new system, or science, or whatever it might be denominated of conversing with departed spirits, and would like to see a specimen of it, if he was willing to gratify us. He said he should be pleased to do so, but had an appointment at 7 oclock, and had but very few minutes to spare. He however sat down to the table with the old man, and laid his hands upon it, after a few minutes asked if there were any spirits in the room who wished or were willing to converse with us that evening, and if so requested them to tip the table, After making the request the second or third time, the table began to move forward at one end, intimating to them to lay their hands upon the leaf, instead of the end. They accordingly turned the table around with the leaf towards them Mr B at the same time took his leave, saying that he must go to his appointment, assigning that as the cause why the spirits seemed unwilling to communicate to him. Just as he was leaving Sylvester Mowry came in, sat down to the table with his father, and mother, and commenced calling on the spirits for communications. The table immediately commenced responding to various questions concerning the spirit world, the most of which were in accordance with our faith, and quite satisfactory to us. They would also answer questions concerning our living friends, who were separated from us. Questions which those who were the mediums, or who operated upon the table, know nothing about. *Sun 17th* We attended church, Br. Sparks from San Fran—— preached to us. Sis Corwin and sis [Hannah] Evans[10] were also here on a visit. We had a good meeting, several strangers were in, who paid great attention to the discourse. I met br [John] Carter and wife [Mary], who were our travelling companions from Salt lake to Sacramento. They look very miserable, having been sick a great deal of the time since they came here. They informed me of the death of Sister [Elysabet] Arnold who also came through with us. There has been a large number of deaths in that company. But our lives have been spared through many changing scenes of trouble and joy; and we are still the living to praise the Lord. *Sunday Oct 24th* Elder [John M.] Horner[11] spoke upon the parable of the talents Sister Carter was baptized, and had hands laid upon her, for the recovery

of her health. And she told me the next sabbath, that she received immediate releif.

Wednesday Oct 27th Sister Tomkins came up to make us a farewell
visit. She took dinner with me, I accompanied her to br Riser's,[12] spent
the afternoon and evening.

Sunday 31st We took a ride to br Tomkins to say farewell again
expecting they were going the middle of the week, but they have concluded to wait another week.

Monday Nov 1st I felt quite unwell. *Tuesd——* washed. *Wed*, very
high winds. Great fire at Sacramento, nearly ~~report says~~ the whole city
destroyed. *Thursday* also high winds *Friday* morning Sister Skinner and
Frances made us a call. I was just preparing to go to br Nicol's, they made
but a short stay. I accompanied them home in their carriage, and from
there walked over to br N——s where I met a sister Wheeler late from
Salt Lake city. Her husband had called on us several times, gave us intelligence concerning many of our friends in that place. After dinner Sister
S—— and Frances came over, and we had a very sociable time. *Sat——*
Making dress for sis N. *Sun morn. Oct [Nov] 7* Sister Layton, Alfreds
mother, came to see us, accompanied by Isaiah and Tomkins girls. She
was much pleased to see her son, said he had grown fleshy, she spent
the forenoon and returned. Alfred cried when she talked of leaving,
she told him his father was coming to see him soon, and he shortly
became reconciled. We went out to meeting, heard Elder [Harvey]
Green upon the first principles of the gospel.[13] Met sister Mourey from
San F—— has come up to spend the winter with her son on the farm.
Sunday evening br Skinner called in. A gentleman by the name of
Carpenter staid over night, had quite a controversy with br Neil upon
the subject of religion. He has formerly resided here, and worked for
br N. *Monday* heard the Spanish woman who had formerly resided
here was coming back. I was quite astonished at the report, but on
enquiring of br N found it was false. My husband has nearly decided
in his mind to take br N[aile]s farm, the coming year. Which is quite
a task for him, as he has been so long unaccustomed to the business.
Tuesday 9th Rain today. Just finished a letter to sister Lois Thompson.
Frances called in this afternoon, said she was going San F on the following day, I gave her my letter, but she afterward concluded to wait 2
days longer. *Friday* she went accompanied by sister Nicols, and brother
[Alfonzo] Farnsworth. I washed in the forenoon, received a visit from
sister Riser in the afternoon. *Saturday* night hard rain. *Sunday 14th*,
windy and damp. We went out to meeting accompanied by the spanish woman who has lived here formerly. We had no services, as none
came, except br Skinner and ourselves. *Monday 15th* I made pantaloons.
In the evening br N told me he intended going the city on the follow-

ing day. Accordingly, I resorted immediately to my pen and paper, in compliance with F——s request to write. *Tuesday 16th.* Br N set off; left orders for Alma to meet him next Saturday at Union City with the wagon *Wed 17th.* I washed. A capt of a sloop staid with us over night. He is a Sweed by birth. Br N employes him to carry his produce from Union City to Francisco. *Thur 18th* cold rain. A polish pedlar staid with us over night. *Friday 19th* Tomkins, Carter, Goodwin, Fuller, and some others set off for San Bernardino by land. Hyram Clark came here, staid 2 nights. *Sat 20th* Alma went accompanied by H C to Union city to meet Mr N and Frances. Returned between 3 and 4 oclock. F was very glad to get back into the country again, she does not seem to like the city much Br N traded a good deal, told me he spent 1500 dollars; Bought wire for fences. One thousand dollars worth.

Sunday Nov 21st remarkbly cold rainy day, no meeting. We spent the evening in singing with the violin. Sang all our old mormon hymns, and some songs.

Mon 22nd Br—— N—— paid off several of his workmen. Some of them have been with him some length of time. It gives me a feeling of sadness to see persons turned out upon the world, to seek a new home, and friends, in a land of strangers. But such is the case with thousands in this country they have no continuing city. But the most of them come here to obtain a purse, intending to return to their friends again. Some by diligence and good management obtain the object their ambition, while others draw blanks.

[Thanksgiving Day, 1852]

Thursday Nov 25th Was thanksgiving day. Br N took us down to br Mowreys Sister Riser accompanied us. We had a very pleasant ride and visit. Just 6 oclock when we arrived at home. The moon shone clear and bright, and we went over to br Horners to meeting, had a very good one. Br Horner spoke at some length upon the blessings of living in this free country, and gave many important hints to us to live godly righteous and sober lives, as the ancient prophets had forewarned us that no people would be permitted to prosper long upon this land unless they kept the commandments of God. He exhorted us to pray for our rulers that they might execute judgment and justice. Mr Crosby seconded what had been said, and spoke of the second coming of Christ. Frances staid over nigth. The next day *Nov 26th* our cook <u>Wm</u>, left us, and went to br H's; he felt very bad to part from us, shed tears on the occasion. Said he did not expect to find another place where he should feel so much at home. *Friday* Frances and I got dinner for the first time. We cleaned and brushed up the dining room and kitchen and commenced our services in the cooking line. I felt very tired this first night but hope I shall be able to hold out faithful to the end. In the evening had spelling and writing school.

Saturday I ironed, and made mince pies, kept very busy. In the evening had an arithemtic school, together with music and waltzing by Jonah, the spanish boy. *Sunday 28th* very rainy, and unpleasant. No meeting. Hervey Green called, said there was a wedding last night at Mr Horners, his brother and his wifes sister were joined in holy wedlock. *Mon 29th* rain. *Tues 30th* washed *Wednesday Dec 1st* rain again. I ironed. Frances made pies. *Thursday* also very rainy. Spelling in the evening. *Friday* quite pleasant teamsters all went to the Barkederer [embarcadero]. *Sat 4th* rain in the forenoon quite pleasant in the afternoon. A gentleman called to see Mr N——; wished to get work, and information concerning the country; appeared to be a stranger.

A Russian pedlar also called towards evening. Said he had just come to the country. I thought his goods were quite reasonable. Tolerable pleasant this evening; all of us writing.

Sunday Dec 5th. Tolerably pleasant but very muddy. H Green came and escorted Frances up to Mr Horners. Br Naile has also gone on an excursion which leaves us quite alone.

Br [Isaac] Harrison called. Heard Brs Pratt and Whitaker are going to Francisco tomorrow, and intend leaving for the lower country soon.

Our old cook Portugeese Wm, came over to see us. Sunday evening, had quite a sociable chat by the kitchen fire. *Mon 6th* I washed. Quite pleasant. Mr Crosby plastering the chamber. Br Naile and teamsters gone to the Landing with produce. Father [Hervey] Green called to see if we wished to send to his school said he was going to commence tomorrow. But the schoolhouse is far off and roads so muddy, that it is not possible for our little Tahitian boy [Alfred Layton] to walk; and Alma has a plenty of business to attend to at home. I intend to try and teach them evenings.

Tuesday 7th Mr N—— killed a fat hog, he sent a team for Mrs Riser. She came and spent the evening with her husband. We had music on the violin, and songs in the evening. *Wednesday 8* I ironed, The spanish boys left. It really seemed lonesome, especially when Jona came to take off his things. Although he could not speak much english, yet there was something so pleasant and sociable in his manner, that it rendered his company very agreeable. We also discovered that br N looked and seemed rather desolate, after they left. They have lived with him sometime. I presume the spanish people seem near to him, having resided among them for several years, and generally been treated with kindness. He speaks their language quite fluently.

Friday 10th. Rainy and unpleasant. In the evening Mr Morrison came after Frances to go and watch with his brothers wife, who he said was very sick. She went accompanied by Mrs Riser. Returned next morning after breakfast said she was a very distressed person and could not live long. They said she mourned very much the absence of her friends, and thought her husband did not feel for her as he ought. He has also been sick nearly all the time for one year.

Sat 11th. Tolerably pleasant day.

Sunday 12th We heard the death of Mrs M[orrison]. Mr Naile and Frances gone to Union City for a ride. They had not got far from home when a spanish boy came in and told me that one of his five matched horses had fallen down before the wagon and was dead. I could hardly credit the tale at first but the return of one of the hired men, soon confirmed the report. Mr N returned to the house, got another horse and then proceded on his ride, intending to return in season to attend meeting at two oclock. But being detained so long with his horse, and finding the roads very muddy, he was too late. We attended meeting for the first time in several weeks, in consequence of rain our meetings have been neglected. We had a very good time today. Br Morris was up from San F. We also found our old acquaintance Henry Jacobs, whom we had not seen for several years.[14] He has been 3 or 4 years in Cal—— has passed through a variety of fortunes, and has at last been burned out by the great fire at Sacramento. His wife has I understand also left him. He seems to have got his mind quite awakened again to the subject of the gospel, made quite an exciting speech in our meeting. Appeared highly pleased to see us, and acknowledged for the public his old friends, and acquaintances br and sister Crosby. Said it did his heart good to see them. The next day *Monday 13th* was quite pleasant Father Maurie [Mowry] called to see us. We sent letters by him to Francisco. *Tuesday 14th* I washed, while Frances prepared for a spanish fandango, which came off in the evening, It was Almas birthday [his 16th], although we none of us thought of it at the time. It was attended with very good order and upon the whole was quite an agreeable party. The co generally staid over night althou they only danced untill 12 oclock. *Wed 15th* I finished my washing. On going to bed I found I had taken cold. I[n] the course of the night I had a severe chill which was accompanied with violent headache.

Thurs 16th I kept my bed, took a sweat and physic.

Frid 17th I was able to be up again, but felt quite feeble. *Sat 18th* and *Sun 19* rain every day since Mon.

Mon 20th. Tolerably pleasant in the forenoon, In the afternoon rain again. *Tuesday 21st* rain. *Wednesday 22nd* rain part of the day. A pedlar called and took dinner. Frances had a very sick turn which lasted the afternoon and night, she was however better in the morning. *Thurs 23rd* night a br by the name of Branden from Salt Lake staid with us. *Friday* Frances baked and prepared a little for Christmas. I made a star and elevated it on the east side of the front room.

Sat Chrismas day tolerably pleasant in the forenoon. Br Naile went to the mission. Br Henry Jacobs staid with us overnight, with whom we had a very agreeable visit. We talked over olden times, he spoke of his trials in the gospel, and seemed rather to murmur at his fortune. He said I reminded him so much of Zina [Huntington Young] his first wife that it revived all his past trials on her account. A young man by the name of Carpenter also staid with us, late from the northern part of Vermont; he knew several names of my acquaintance. It seemed amost like seeing, or rather hearing, from old acquaintances.

Sunday 26th very pleasant sky, but so muddy that we have not tried to get out with the wagon.

Mon 27th tolerable pleasant day. The spanish people had a dance in the evening. Mr Naile went and took Fr. Br Jacobs called again to see us, brought his violin. He and Mr Crosby had fine times playing together. He staid over night, and the next day *Tuesday* being rainy he staid all day, and all night again. Mr Riser moved into their new habitation. In the evening we had quite a time of dancing. We danced Cotillions, Country dances, and Waltzes. The hired men with their thick boots made rather an awkward appearance, but upon the whole we enjoyed ourselves very well. *Wed 29th* remarkbly rainy day, Br Jacobs stills stays, and keeps the viol ringing. *Thurs 30th* the clouds broke away, which seemed to cheer up our hearts and we concluded we would have a new years party, and commence the evening previous. Accordingly Br Naile, and Jacobs, set off to invite the guests. Frances went to cooking, I ironed, mended cleaned up the house, and made sundry preparations for the coming event.

Friday evening 31st the party commenced at early candlelight. The most of them were strangers to me, and many more attended than we expected. Br H B Jacobs, John Cheny, and Mr Crosby, played the violin. A young man by the name of James Foxall called the cotillions, and it all passed off in good order and harmony. Some of the party staid untill after sunrise.

[Mission San Jose, 1853]

Sat January 1st, beautiful pleasant day, after having so much rain and bad weather it truly cheers and revives my heart see the sunshine once more. *Sun 2nd* tolerably pleasant. Afternoon all of us went to meeting, quite a general attendance. Elder Green spoke to the people. *Mon 3rd* I washed and cleaned up the house. Towards evening br Henry Jacobs called on us, and informed us of his intentions of marrying the widow Clawson. And requested us to prepare an entertainment for the occasion, which we all declined, as we had just got cleaned up after the other, and for one I did-not feel able or willing to prepare for another so soon. *Tues 4th* Mr Crosby commenced his farming for the season. Started two teams at ploughing.

[Belated News of Mother's Death]

Wednesday 5th Today I am 46 years old. this evening I received letters which informed me of the death of my mother, who died nearly a year ago.[15] The letter had been to Tahiti and was brought back by br Richmond, who delivered it to Ellen in San Francisco, and she sent it to us by Henry Greene. Thus I have had an opportunity of proving the fallacy of the spir-itual telegraph system. I was informed by that science that my mother was as still living, whereas she had been dead near one year. *Jan 10th* There were two couples married in our chamber. Mr John M Horner officiated. H B Jacobs to Mary Clawson, and Horatio Stanley to Edna Stuart. The party passed off in very good style.

 Tues 11th Br Naile left for San Francisco. *Wed* I washed. *Thursday* I cleaned house. Frances got quite lonesome, went and took a horseback ride. While she was gone br Nathan Tanner arrived, direct from Salt Lake city, on a mission to the Sandwich islands. He informed us that a large co of elders were at SF on their way to Australia and other places. *Saturday* br [William] Hyde arrived. *Sun 16th* Ellen came up from SF to make us a visit arrived just as we were taking breakfast. Afternoon we attended meet-ing at the schoolhouse. Br Hyde and Tanner spoke to the people. We felt cheered and comforted to hear of the prosperity of the church. *Mon 17th* received a visit from br and sister Skinner and sister Nicols. Br Hyde and Tanner also spent the day with us. *Tuesday* evening We visited br Jacobs, had quite a pleasant time. *Wed* had a church meeting in the schoolroom over head. Br Naile returned while the meeting was in session. *Thurs* eve-ning we had a dancing party on Ellens account. *Sat eve 22nd* Visited at br Skinners, had dancing and a agreeable time. *Sun 23rd* baptising in the morning, some 13 persons rebaptised. *Monday 24th* Ellen returned to the city. Br Naile took her to Union City, had some trouble got mired, had to get a buggy, got the shaffs broke &C.

 Tues 25th I ironed some. *Wed. 26th* finished, wrote a letter to Emeline Wells. *Thurs 27th* looks like rain. Light showers in the night. *Fri 28* toler-ably pleasant. In the evening another party came off in our chamber. It was made by James Foxall and Horatio Stanley. There were upwards of 40 gentlemen and only about 12 ladies. We had an excellent treat, and notwithstanding we were mostly strangers to each other, we enjoyed our-selves very well.

Mission San Jose. The earliest known daguerreotype of any California mission, this image was taken by a traveling artist in 1852, when the Crosbys arrived from Tahiti. The stage road in the foreground went from the mission to Union City and was declared "a public highway" this same year. Courtesy of Santa Barbara Mission Archive-Library.

Sunday 30th attended meeting at the schoolhouse. Preaching by br Horner, had quite a full house, and good attention paid. The sacrament was administered [communion], and a good spirit attended us. After meeting my husband rebaptised a capt who lives at br Horners. *Mon 31st* I cleaned the house. F—— baked and prepared to commence attending school.

Tuesday February 1st I washed F went to school. In the evening received a visit from br and sister Jacobs, br and sister Riser. Had a little dancing on the occasion. *Wed 2nd* I ironed.

Thurs 3rd I finished ironing, and assisted about the housework. ^A young man named Greene called and wished to stay over night late from the gold mines, recently from Hartford Conn—— my husband gave him a short job chopping wood.^ In the evening I was called on to attend the birth of br Wheelers child, (which) was born at 1 oclock *Friday morning 4th.* We all retired to rest about 3 oclock, had quite a comfortable sleep. I arose about 7 ate breakfast with sister Jacobs, and soon after set off on foot for home, the wind was remarkbly high, and cold. I was considerably chilled when I arrived home about 9 oclock. In the afternoon We

F—— and myself visited at br Riser's in comp—— with Mrs Tison and two of her sisters, the miss Morisons. We had a very lively agreeable time.

Sat 5th I finished pants for Enos Nicols. Br A Farnsworth called in the evening. We had a very sociable time, sang songs &C. *Sun 6th* attended church saw two of our old acquaintances. Alexander Badlam[16] who lives at or near Sacramento and Chapman Duncan, late from Salt Lake city, on his way to China on a mission. We were highly pleased to see him. He accompanied us home, staid untill after supper, when br Naile escorted him over to br Horners on horseback. Previous to leaving he informed us conserning the science of Astrology, which he says has been revived lately, and which he considers to be a very correct science. We were highly interested with his conversation, and felt sorry to have him leave so soon.

[A Wedding Party]

Mon evening Feb 7th another wedding party (or rather an infair, as the marriage ceremony was celebrated at the mission by a catholic priest) was held in our chamber. It was conducted in purly spanish-style. A short time before sunset they all arrived on horseback, two on a horse generally. They all came in a crowd direct from the mission with considerable whooping and shouting, which reminded me of a company of Indians. They however received a check from one of their leaders previous to arriving at the house, which silenced them very suddenly. A large co repaired to the chamber, while another portion of them seated themselves on the verander and commenced gambling. Tables were spread and a variety of liquors served out in profusion. They danced all night, and many of them staid untill ten oclock the next day. Several spaniards got drunk and tried to fight, but were prevented by others. Two americans got to fighting in the ballroom, and both fell on the floor. I retired to my bed at 11 oclock but slept none untill 3. When their dancing subsided a little, and I slept 3 or 4 hours.

February 10th Br Naile and Frances went to San Francisco were gone 3 days returned saturday. I had all F's work and my own to do, which made it rather hard for me, however I got along very well, but was glad to see her return, She said she had a very good visit. She brought several letter from her mother, from San Bernerdino.[17] She seems highly pleased with the country, and is happy in the society of the saints. They returned Sat—— evening in fine spirits.

Sun 13th Several young men called in. In the afternoon we went to church F staide at home to prepare supper. Quite a cold wind, I got considerably chilled in coming home.

Mond 14th some signs of rain, in the evening it rained very little. Brs John Chene [Cheney] and Alphonzo Farnsworth called. We had quite a sociable time, mixed with music on the violin and flute. T*ues 15th* I washed.

Wedn 16th Frances helped sister Riser, which left me alone again with the work. ^In the evening Mr Barnes and a Mr Willis called to engage the chamber for another dance, which is to come off the 22nd, Washingtons birthday.^ *Thurs 17th* I did a large ironing, which made me 3 very hard days works. In the afternoon br H B Jacobs and wife, with Mrs Edmunds, (a sister of Jacobs) and her daughter, a girl 12 years of age, visited at br Risers. In the evening they came in to see us. I was very much fatigued with my days work, so much so that I could hardly feel sociable. Br N had the teethache and retired to his room. I like Mrs Edmunds quite well. She appears to be a woman of excellent principles. They live in the gold mines on deer creek.

Friday 18th Feb We prepared ourselves F—— and myself to make a little visit at Morrissons, but were prevented by com calling, untill evening, we got Mr Crosby and bro N started out, had a very pleasant walk. It was almost as light as day. Mrs M—— is a very pleasant woman, her two sisters also appear well.

Sat 19th I felt quite miserable John Chene called in the evening, played the violin, had a sociable time. *Sun 20th* Mr Crosby and Frances Alfred and myself took a walk upon the mountains. We admired the scenery below us very much, we had a splendid prospect of this beautiful valley, We gathered a variety of flowers, and returned highly pleased with the excursion. In the evening, Mr Barnes and Willis called again to make farther arrangments for their ball. Wm Morison and another young man I do not know were also in. We had very lively times, Jokes very free between Mr C and Morrison.

Mon 21st Frances was rather unwell. A pedlar called. I bought cloth, cut and made a coat for Alfred. *Tues 22nd* made some few preparations for the evening. The company commenced assembling before sunset, and continued untill 9 oclock. The hall above was crowded to overflowing, so that they proposed dividing the party, which was carried into effect. A portion of them came below and danced a short time. At 12 oclock several persons left, which made it more comfortable for the remainder. They then all repaired to the hall and dan[c]ed untill 3 in the morning, when they dispersed in very good order. The managers returned the next morning and paid us 25 dolls for the trouble of the house. We soon got it cleaned again, and were quite well satisfied.

Thursday 24th I washed, rain in the evening.

Friday and *Sat* also rainy. Sat evening *26th* it faired off the sun shone again very pleasantly.

[A Ride in the Foothills; An Enraged Bull]

Sunday 27th We, Br Naile, Mr Crosby, Frances and myself, took the most pleasant horseback ride I ever enjoyed. We set off at 10 oclock, ascended the mountains near home, continued rising one after another for several miles, untill we arrived at a spanish settlement, which is located in a sort of vally in the mountains. It is the most beautiful and picturesque scenery I ever beheld. The hills were covered with a soft green verdure, well calculated to satify the appetites of the numerous herds of cattle which adorn their lofty summits and in many places beautifully variegated with flowers of almost every hue. My heart was truly cheered and enlivened with admiration and delight. I observed to the party that I was almost tempted to envy the aborigines of this country their extreme happiness in being permitted to range free and uncontrolled, exempt from those cares which continually disturb the minds of those enjoying civilisation. We feasted our eyes with the bounties of nature, We made a short pause at the spanish settlement, they came out and wished us a good morning, gave us a little refreshment, consisting of bread and new cheese, with pure cold spring water. They keep a sort of dary. I counted 13 nice young calves, in a corrall. We arrived home near 1 oclock, and being somewhat fatigued with our lengthy ride Frances and I concluded to spend the afternoon at home, while the men rode on to meeting. Sunday towards evening we had quite an excitement raised by the men trying to kill a beef. It was one of their wild california bulls. Br Riser shot and wounded him, but not so as to cripple him in the least. Br Naile caught him with the lasso, but by some means he lost his hold of the rope. The bull became enraged and turned upon his horse and he was obliged to flee from him. In the meantime Frances and Alfred had been taking a walk upon the hills gathering flowers. They were making their way to the house entirely ignorant of the danger they were in when the creture saw them and made towards them in great haste. We all stood on the verander watching their movement, the men shouting to her to make her escape to the road, the other side of the fence, and br N—— on his horse with a large white wolf skin was trying to frighten him and turn his course, which he finally succeeded in doing. Fr—— was some distance from the house, and none of the men dared venture into the field on foot to warn her of their danger; finally a portugee boy jumped on his horse and rode out to her, but it was with much persuasion that they could make her believe she was in much danger, but finally to satisfy their feelings she ran to fence and got through into the road. While the bull made his escape to the mountains. ^In the evening we attended prayermeeting Horner', very good attendance^

Mon 28th I washed. *Tues March 1st* We received a visit from H Jacobs, his wife and sister Mrs Edmunds. Mrs Riser, was in. We had a very agreeable time, they decided on spending the evening. Accordingly br Naile invited in a few of the nearest neighbors to spend the evening with us. And the consequence was dancing. We had 3 violin players, who took turns at dancing. We danced untill 12 oclock, when the company left with good feelings. *Wed 2nd* I cleaned house, and ironed. In the evening two gentlemen from the mission called, and left us tickets to attend a ball at the Mission hotell on friday March 4th. *Thur 3rd* I ironed nearly all day. Prayer meeting in evening, in our chamber. We injoyed it well, the speakers all manifested a good degree of the Holy Spirit.

Brother John M Horner is the president of the branch, he is a very devoted christian and a good man. We have prayer meetings at his house on sunday evenings, and on thurs evenings at our house.

Friday evening March 4th br N—— and F—— attended the ball at the mission hotel. I had no desire to go myself, and my husband was of the same mind; accordingly we staid at home. They returned the next morning at day break.

Sat 5th I did the housework and F sewed. In the afternoon she and br N visited at br Nicols's. I wrote to sister P. H Greene called told me he was going next day, to leave for San Bernardino.

Sun morn 6th I finished the letter. carried them out to meeting, and delivered them to him as he passed. Br Horner spoke to the people upon the subject of revelation, and was succeeded by Father Greene. Br and sister Harrison came along and rode out with us to meeting. This evening prayermeeting at br Horner's. All gone but myself and children.

Mon March 7th Frances went to live with Sister Riser. I had all the housework on my hands. It seemed rather hard for a few days, but I soon became accustomed to it, so that I performed it with comparative ease, and did some sewing besides. *Tuesday* we had rain. *Wednesday* I washed. *Thurs, 10th*, several brethren came to meeting but were late and president not attending it was adjourned. *Friday* ironed, *Saturday* evening we visited at br Harrisons, a number of brethren and sisters were in and the consequence was dancing. We had 3 violins, which filled their small house with music. We returned home at twelve oclock, much pleased with our entertainment. *Sunday 13th* took a little walk on the mountains in company with br Naile A [Ammon] Greene Mr Crosby Frances Alma and Alfred, we gathered a lot of flowers of various kinds. In the afternoon I attended meeting with my husband Frances staid at home. I saw sister Morey, she informed me that she expected sister Woodberry [Elvira Stevens Woodbury] to come and live with them.[18]

Sun—— evening Mr Crosby and Naile attended meeting at br Horners. *Mon 14th* br Naile set off for San Francisco but finding no boat going he returned. *Tues——* set off again and returned. *Wed* I washed. Just as I was finishing sister Woodbury came, direct from br Horners. I believed it was her the moment I saw her, she had come up from San Fran the day before on a launch. I had not seen her in 3 years. I thought she had grown considerable taller and looked better than formerly. She staid one night and returned to br H——'s to await the arrival of Moreys for her.

Thursday evening we had quite a good meeting here. Br Naile left for San Francisco towards evening.

Friday I was attacked with a very bad cold.

Saturday it was still worse, I feared I should be obliged to give up work. I however succeeded in keeping about, drank freely of ginger tea. I have neglected to mention a br Sheffer who arrived here on Wed the 16th direct from San Bernardino and brought us a few lines from Sister Pratt, the news was rather stale as he has been 5 weeks in coming. He staid with us untill Saturday, when he found employment at br Horners. He is a young member of the church, left Indiana 2 years ago for Oregon, came to Council bluffs where he called to visit some cousin he had residing there, and becoming acquainted with our people, he believed the gospel and united himself to the church, he staid there one year, and then emigrated to Salt lake city where he staid long enough to locate his wife and one child, and then left for the lower country.

Sunday 20th day This morning he called in co with Hiram Clark and Ammon Greene, informed us of his success in getting business. It is a beautiful day. F took a little ride on horseback returned in season to let Jon—— have the horse to ride to church. We neither of us attended to day on account of colds. Towards evening Mary Clawson called. She looked very sad, said she had been weeping gave us an account of her late husband Henry B Jacobs leaving her in consequence of his old wife coming and claiming her previous right. In the evening Mr Crosby attended prayermeeting at br Horners. Br Naile returned from the City of San Francisco just as we were going to bed.

[John Naile's Departure]

Mon 21st beautiful pleasant day. I made mince pies. Br Naile brought us home a quantity of flour and other provisions to last us in his absence. He informed us that he intended leaving for Indiana in one week, that he expected to have the co of several of his acquaintances to N Y—— which seemed to cheer and encourage him. Several capts of vessels having made their fortunes in this country are about returning to their native land. *Tues—— 22nd*

Wed—— 23rd I washed; in the afternoon br and sister Skinner made us a call. It was rather windy and unpleasant, they made a short stay and returned

Thurs——— 24th, a pedlar staid with us last night I traded with him a very little. ~~Friday 25th I ironed~~ Thursday eve we had a prayermeeting at our house, we enjoyed the good spirit and had a good meeting. 3 new members were confirmed into the church.

Friday 25th I ironed did some sewing. In the evening we had quite a sociable chat with br N concerning his journey, and traced out his course on the map

Sat——— 26th, baked bread and pies, felt very unwell untill near night, when I became much better. The spaniard Jonah and his wife were in. Mr Crosby commenced playing the violin. The result was a little waltzing.

Sunday 27th very rainy. Br N. looked and seemed very gloomy, this morning, said he did not feel well. I exhorted him to keep a light heart and a good one, and keep on a cheerful countenance although he might feel sad; for by so doing, he would cast a cheerful influence around him, and would eventually partake of it himself. Father Greene and Ammon spent the greater part of the with us. A capt Mayo successor of Capt Oscar Hedberg called in a short time. Sun——— evening the rain still continues. Tomorrow br N——— expects to leave. It seems to be a great task for him. *Mon 28th* The weather was calm and pleasant. Br Neal was in good spirits; he arranged all his affairs in true order; drew writings with his tenants, and set off about 10 oclock for Union City, having bid us all an affectionate farewell and received our blessings and good wishes in return. It really seemed lonesome after he was gone. The idea of the long journey he had before him caused us to feel much concern for his welfare. But we trust as his motives were those of duty to his parents, that he will be blessed and prospered and be returned to us again in peace and safety.

Tues 29th I was called on at an early hour to witness the birth of sister Riser's little son. It was born at nine oclock AM, I spent the day with her.

Wed 30th I washed. *Thurs 31st* br and sis Skinner and sis Nicols visited us.

Frid——— April 1st This day the vessel is to sail that carries our friends to N Y. We heard several canon in the morning, which we supposed were signals for their departure. *Sat 2nd* the spanish man Jonah went down to the harbor and brought home the articles that br N had sent us.

Sunday the 3rd of Apr A young man from Salt lake City by the name of Thomas Gates, has been staying at br Risers 2 or 3 days, talks of going to the Australian gold mines, and wishes Charles Allen to accompany him.

Frank Silver [Silva] is here, afflicted with poison. Wishes us to board him a week, or untill he is able to work. I intended to have gone to church this afternoon, but felt so very unwell that I went to bed instead thereof.

Mon 4th day Frances and myself washed for Mrs Riser

Tues——— 5th I cleaned house baked pies &C

Wednes——— 6th of Apr 23 years today since the church of Jesus Christ of Latterday saint was organized with 6 members. It is now spread to almost every nation under heaven, and to many of the islands of the sea.

Just as we were finishing our dinners br Farnsworth drove up to the house with Ellen P, direct from San Francisco. We had expected her up to conference and were pleased to see her.

In the evening Jonah and his wife were in, and the girls proposed to dancing. Alma and Frank Rose joined them and they had quite lively time. *Thurs 7th* E and F rode down to br Skinners, and returned just before night. In the evening the brethren convened for prayermeeting Sister Evans and sister King came up with Ellen to attend conference, came to meeting with br Skinner and staid over night. I enjoyed their visit very much. *Friday 8th* We took a pleasant excursion up on the bluffs. The sisters from the city were highly pleased with the place and their walk. said they dreaded the idea going back to the city again. Sister King had two beautiful little girls with her Lizzy and Harriet. Sister Evans had 1, little Janette, a fine little girl 4 years old. Toward noon Alma came to inform us that br Farnsworth was waiting at the house with his carriage to convey them to br Nicols's. I concluded to accompany them. Accordingly we arrived there near 12 oclock, had a very agreeable time with sister N——— she prepared a good dinner for us; while we were partaking of it br Loyd came after sis Nicols to go to visit his wife as she was quite sick, she felt sorry to leave us; but thought it her duty to go. We all felt that she ought to go and were willing to dispense with her company. She therefore left us to set things in order after dinner, and went, she found her in much pain, but after administering some mild herbs which she carried with her for that purpose, she left her much better than she found her. In the meantime we repaired to br Skinners, where we took supper. In the evening the brethren and sisters met in compliance with an invitation, to that effect to have a little dance. The party was conducted according to the order of the church, being opened by prayer and singing. Br Morris from San Francisco was present, and came home with us. He staid with us two nights. *Sat——— the 9th* our conference commenced, business principally occupied the time from ten untill two oclock. H B Jacobs and Eliza Ira were disfellowshiped in consequence of unlawful conduct in regard to matrimony. *Sunday 10th* meeting convened at ten, the congregation was quite numerous. Br Horner spoke quite lengthy, showed the difference between the original sin and the actual transgressions of men, and disclosed the atonement for both, in plain scriptural terms. In the afternoon, the sacrament was administered, several church officers ordained, and a short address by elder Greene. We returned home at 5 oclock. Ammon Greene took supper with us. Br J Cheny, A Farnsworth, H Clark, spent the evening. We had quite a variety of music on the occasion. Cheny played the violin, Mr Crosby the flute, and Ellen the accordion. We had a very interesting time. *Monday the 11th* It was rainy. Br Morris came over from br Horners, staid untill after dinner, when Mr C carried him and Ellen out to br Loyds, to take the stage leading to Union city. Mon night Mr C returned, said he was too late for the stage; consequently was under the necessity of going down to the city. They arrived about 20 minutes previous to the sailing of the *Union*, as such is the name of the Steamer.

Tues 12th the weather continues rainy. *Wed 13th* A man called near noon to get work, My husband needing a hand engaged him. He proved to be a gentleman from the state of N H by the name of Little, and brotherinlaw to Dr Richardson of Salt lake city. My husband engaged him for the season, for 65 dolls pr month. He is 47 years old, and a farmer by occupation has a wife and 8 children in the town of Lyman N H.

Thurs—— 14th Frances washed. Quite rainy in the afternoon. Just as we were finishing our supper, James Foxall called, informed us that Tomas Burns from the mines had arrived in the valley, that his wife being very sick desired to see the elders of the church, and requested Mr Crosby to accompany him to the house of Mr Allen, who was br in law to said Burns. He also went for br Horner and Greene They found her in the last stages of consumption, very weak and occasionly deranged, withall afflicted with a violent cough. They said they could not get faith to bless her with health, but merely prayed that she might have patience, and the holy Spirit, comfort and strengthen her in her last hours. I have not heard from her since. *Frid—— 15th* I ironed, and assisted some about house work. *Sat—— 16th* F—— and myself visited sis Harrison. We made arrangements with Alma to commence getting supper previous to our ~~gathering~~ returning home. We set off at 2 oclock, had a very pleasant walk through flowers of almost every hue, which perfumed the air with their fragrance, rendering it extremly exhilarating. Called a few moments at sister Wheelers, invited her to accompany us, but found her too busily employed to leave home. Sister H was much pleased to see us, we spent the afternoon very agreeably, A br from Salt lake city is boarding there who has been quite sick latly with something resembling the smallpox, but which I believe to have been the Eyresipitis. His name is Abby, is now recovering. We arrived home at 6 oclock found the fire burning and the teakettle on. We soon had the supper in readiness, while we were eating it commenced raining, it rained quite steady during the night.

[The *Jenny Lind* Disaster]

Sun Apr—— 17th remarkably rainy time, no going or coming, which renders the day long and lonesome. A part of it however was spent very agreeably in singing Psalms and hymns with the violin and flute, accompanied by our newly hired man from N H, who is a good scientific singer. John Cheny spent the evening with us, Mr Crosby read the account of the *Jenny Lynd* disaster, which was shocking in the extreme. Our San Francisco friends happened to be on the *Union* that went to her relief.[19] They were on their return from conference, and proved a blessing to the poor sufferers.

    Mon 18th Tolerably pleasant, I washed. Capt Mayhue [Joseph A. Mayhew] called. He appears like a friendly intelligent man.

    Tues——— 19th Frank Silver is here again complaining of poison; wishes us to board him until he recovers. Very rainy, This morning there was quite an excitement raised by our spanish man getting his team into an old well that had been dug in the field, and the water used for irrigation. They however succeeded in getting them out without injury.

    Wed 20th Tolerably pleasant, I trust the rain is over for the present. This evening Frances attended a ball at mission hotel accompanied by John Cheny.

    Thurs——— morning 21st they returned after breakfast, Br [Thomas] Morris also arrived about the same time, quite rainy. I set the table and made them some fresh coffee. After eating Alma went with br Morris to Union city to get his things as he has come up to stay with us a while, and is making us a garden; He is a gardener by trade, a welchman by birth, is afflicted with lameness, has a fever sore on his leg, which troubles him occasionally.

    Friday 22nd very pleasant day. After dinner F——— A——— and myself went up stairs to making sacks. Soon after we saw two ladies with 4 children coming. I immediatly came down and made preparations to receive them. They proved to be sisters Harrison and Wheeler. We enjoyed the afternoon very agreeably with them. Sister Riser was in, spent the afternoon for the first time since the birth of her son. *Sat 23rd* We received a visit from Father Mory, his wife, and Harley's wife and children. We had long been expecting them, and were highly pleased at their arrival. Harley's family expect soon to leave for San Bernardino. They left at 5 oclock. Soon after James Foxall called in, requested the privilege of bringing a small company here to dance this evening, to which we objected. I told him I thought that we had, had our share of the parties, and as the nights had become short, and the men were weary, and did not like to be disturbed, I should rather be excused. And further more we had been censured some by scrupulous observers, in consequence of having so much dancing at our house. He sat and conversed awhile, expressed a great deal of dissatisfaction with the church, both in regard to principle, and practice. We, my husband and self exhorted him to read the scriptures and try to get his faith renewed, and then repent and do his first work. He complained of being neglected by the brethren, and went away apparently quite dissatisfied. We spent evening in singing Psalms with Mr Lyttle. Sang all the old fugues, and went to bed with grateful hearts.

Sunday 24th, a company consisting of John Cheny T Burns, Mary Clawson, and a young lady by the name of Pack came along on horseback, and wanted Frances to accompany them on a ride. But it was not convenient for her to go. In the afternoon we attended church. Mr Crosby spoke to the people, was followed by elder Greene. We went to the evening meeting also at br Horners.

Mon 25th Frances washed. I spent my time principally about the house. Am—— Greene called in the evening Said he had just recd—— a letter from his sister in Salt lake city. *Tues*—— *26th* We, Mr C, Fr—— and myself went down to br Mowrey's on a visiting excursion as Harley, M——, and family were soon expecting to leave for San Bernardino. We thought we would make them a farewell visit. We set off at half past nine, had some little difficulty in finding the road as none of us had been there this season, and much of the land is now under cutivation which last year was waste. We however arrived there at 11 oclock, I was very much chilled with the cold wind, and felt quite unwell while there. Notwithstanding I enjoyed the visit very well. We left at half past 5 oclock, reached home a few minutes after sunset. On our return we fell in company with Mr Barnes, he said he had been absent sometime on business, at Stockton and San Francisco. On reaching home we found Br Morris presiding over the kitchen, he had got their dinners and making preparations for supper, but we soon released him from his station. *Wed*—— *27th* very cold wind. I felt very lame, had a bad cold went to bed 2 or 3 hours in the middle of the day. *Thurs 28th* Very dull cloudy weather. *Friday 29th* quite rainy I made sacks. Frances very unwell, said she did not sleep much last night.

Sat—— *30th*, and last day of *Apr.* More pleasant than it has been for several days past. I baked light bread in the forenoon. Afternoon visited br Skinner. A miss Johnson called spent the afternoon with us. Was doing sewing for sister S. She seems like a very fine girl, is keeping house for her brother. They are late from Boston Mass.

I called at Mr Tisons, found her quite unwell. On my return home, called in with miss Johnson found her very pleasantly situated.

Sunday morn—— *May 1st* beautiful pleasant day. Frances quite unwell. Called John Cheny, and Mary Clawson Soon after Henry Webster and Margaret Emily. Wished F—— to ride with them, but she was unwilling and unable to go out. Mr W and Miss E took dinner with us. Br Morris Mr C and myelf attended meeting in afternoon Br Horner spoke first upon the subject of the saints inheriting the earth, was followed by Mr C upon the apostacy of the church. Cyrus Ira came home with us from church, took supper, sang some, talked of his trouble with his wife, and of trying to get a divorce.[20] Br Skinner called after supper. I read a letter from sister Pratt to F and myself.

Monday May 2nd Mr C and Alfred left for San Francisco. The spanish man carried them to Union city, where they took the steamer *Union* at 7 oclock and arrived in SF before 12. I arose at 5 oclock, did a 2 weeks washing, in the course of the day; found myself quite fatigued at night.

Tues 3rd Quite an excitement raised by one of Mr Riser's hired men whipping a horse belonging to Mr Naile, in an unmerciful manner. *Wed 4th* a few minutes after 12 Mr C returned in great haste. The boat had arrived at 11 oclock and not finding Alma there with the team, he feared some accident had befallen him and came up in the stage. ^We had mistaken the time of the boats arrival^ Ellen Pratt also came as far as br Loyds, while Alfred and the newly hired man stoped at the landing until Alma and his father returned with the waggon for them and the baggage. We F—— and I rode along with them to br Skinners, where we met br and sister Morey and Harley's wife, we had a very agreeable visit. Mr C and Ellen arrived at 5 oclock, just as we were taking tea. We had a very livly time. Mary Clawson took supper with, she lives with the br Cheny's. We returned home a little before sunset, spent the evening very cheerfully music of various kinds, vocal and instrumental.

Thurs 5th Received a visit from Mrs Tison, her sister and cousin, a young man who has been very sick and just recovering. Mrs Clawson and Riser also spent the afternoon with us. Called two pedlars.

Friday 6th I finished ironing; felt very unwell, Did some mending. *Sat 7th*, made light bread, washed some. Ellen also washed. Towards evening took a walk to see the garden, in compliance with an invitation from father Morris, our Gardner.

Sunday the 8th The girls were expecting to ride but were disappointed in getting saddles. John Cheny and Mary Clawson called. All went to meeting in the afternoon.

Mon 9th somewhat cloudy. The girls went to visit sister Wheeler.

Tuesday 10th they were intending to visit at Mr Horners but were prevented by rain

Wed 11th I washed. The girls went with Mrs Jonah on a horseback ride over the mountains, to her fathers. Returned a little after noon. Capt Mayhue called.

Thursday 12th very rainy. Mr Crosby went to Union city to get a letter. Myslef and the girls had a visit appointed at Mr Lloyds and notwithstanding the rain we accompanied him that far. Found sis L washing. She said br Mowry had just left in the stage for San Francisco. We spent the afternoon very agreeably, returned home a little after sunset. Father Morris had made the fire, and had the teakettle boiling when we arrived. The evening was spent with music, by Mr Crosby and Ellen on the violin and accordion.

Friday 13th the girls assisted at br Horners, I felt very unwell in the afternoon. Music again in the evening. I went to bed early.

Sat——— 17th I arose at 5 oclock, Baked bread and cooked the Dinner, while Frances washed for Mrs Riser. Ironed in the afternoon.

Sunday 15th Lucretia Horner and a young man (who is probably her intended husband) visited here. Also Ornaldo Morey and Elvira Woodbury came in a carriage, took dinner with us. I rode to meeting with them. Sister Woodbury brought a lot of letters. One from sister Lois Thompson, one from sister Pratt, and two from her husband on the Sandwich islands. Br Horner preached the coming forth of the book of Mormon, was followed by br Greene. The sacrament was administered. Br Skinner and family and br Farnsworth asked for a letter of recommendation as they were about to leave this branch and remove to San Bernardino. Br H Wilkins and A Greene, called in the evening. Br W sang beautifully both welch and English. We had plenty of music, both instrumental and vocal.

Mon 16th Mr C carried the girls down to Union city, Ellen intended taking the steamer *Union*, but they were one hour too late, and returned to await her next trip. Soon after they turned back, they met br Skinners folks who were also going to the city for the same purpose, and were much disappointed at mistaking the hour of the boats leaving. I was glad to see Ellen return not that I wished her disapointed, but I had not said all I wished to her, and had likewise forgotten to give her the letter I had written to her mother. Br Skinner called in the afternoon, said he was going down to San Francisco on a launch that evening with his goods, and requested Mr C to bring his wife and children down to the steamer with Ellen on thursday morning. *Tuesday 19th* I was very unwell with a cold, and pain in my bones, rheumatism vs.

Wed 18th Mr C went to br Nicols with the wagon and brought Sister Skinner to our house.

In the afternoon sister Nicols and Mrs Scot visited us, sister Riser was in, we had a very pleasant party, but my health was so bad I could not enjoy anything much.

Thurs 19th I arose at 4 oclock. We had an early breakfast and they left for the steamer at half past 5 oclock.

I felt much better in the morning, so that I concluded to wash, and with Frances help got through by 12 oclock but I was then so exhausted I was obliged to go to bed.

[Finishing the House]

Frid 20th I endeavored to assist my husband in papering the house, but was really so unwell that I was under the necessity of going to bed before night.

Sat 21st I felt some better, worked very busy all day at papering the middle room. Br [Bechias] Dustin came to work for us. He was from Salt lake city last year, has been sick 8 months in the goldmines, is an old man of 55 years. We finished the room in good style, got through just before sunset. *Sunday 22nd.* Beautiful pleasant day, all nature wears an air of loveliness and gayety. But I was so unwell that I did not attend church. Frances was also quite ailing with a cold, and staid at home. In the afternoon we walked to the garden, which is some little distance from the house. Mr Crosby attended prayer meeting at br Horners in the evening. *Mon 23rd* Frances washed I baked light bread and assisted other ways about the house. Mr Crosby ceiled my bedroom overhead. *Tuesday 24th* finished the woodwork and prepared the ceiling for the other room.

Wed 25th I washed Mr C ceiled the other bedroom.

Thurs—— 26th papered my room, *Friday 27th* papered F——s room[21]

Saturday 28th I ironed finished a letter to br Lockwoods——

Sun 29th sent my letter to the office. Father Morris returned from a visit to San francisco. Frances went on a horseback ride, in co with Jones Dire,[22] John Cheny, and Mary Clawson. They returned about one oclock. At two we went to church, Mr Horner spoke remarkably well. There was a funeral appointed at 9 oclock; it looked like rain and we did not stay. A Mr Hoyt died with consumption.

Mon—— 30th I cut a coat for Alma, and a coat, and pants, for Alfred. *Tues 31st and last of May.* I made pants—

Wed the first of June I washed F—— assisted, got through by 11 oclock. Mr C—— commenced painting the house. I commenced Alfreds coat. Fr—— took a walk to the canion with Alma for the cow, brought home a lot of flowers. I got the supper, found myself very much fatigued at nigth.

Thurs 2nd Capt Mahue called, spent an hour or more in conversation, we think him quite pleasant man.

Friday 3rd I ironed, finished coat for Alfred, commenced Alma's

Sat—— 4th Mr C—— still painting. Remarkably warm day, br Dustin very unwell, gave up work, went to the mission, bought medicine. I finished Alma's coat

Sun—— 5th I took a walk, in company with Fr,—— Alma and Alfred. We went up into a beautiful canion variegated with flowers, and shady trees, whose foliage perfumed the air rendering it extremely exhilarating. We found a few blackberries, which were the first that I have seen growing since we left the states. We returned perfectly satisfied with our walk. The sun had become extremely warm, we had been under the necessity of satisfying our thirst several times from a cool rivulet that murmured along down its rocky bed, and finally lost itself in the sand.

We returned in season to prepare dinner, rest ourselves, and then went to church. Mrs Riser accompanied us for the first time since the birth of her little son.

Br Horner and Mr C—— were the speakers for the day. The sacrament was administered. Br O—— Morey and sis Woodbury came home with us, made a short stay and took Fr—— home with them, br M promised to bring her back the next day.

Mon—— *6th* Extremly warm weather. I had all the cooking and other work on my hands, but luckily for me our former cook, portugee Wm, was here on a visit, and was so kind as to lend me a helping hand.

About 5 oclock Fr returned according to my expectation. She was well pleased with her visit. I believe she thinks young Mory a fine ~~you~~ man. She saw an exhibition of the spiritual rapping system, which was something new to her. Oregin Morey, the eldest of the two brothers who live together, is what is termed ^by the spiritual rappers^ a perfect medium. A young man and his wife from the mines staid with us.

Tues—— *7th* I went out some distance to accompany Alfred on his way to school, he as usual was very unwilling to go alone, I then left him crying and returned to the house. Soon after Fr came in said he had come back to the gate and set down. Mr C—— went and chastised him, sent him on again, altho at a late hour. In the evening called br Greene and his son Ammon, who was very unwell.

Wed—— *8th* We Fr—— and I took a walk with br Morris to the garden, found it flourishing very well, gathered raddishes and lettuce.

Thurs—— *9th* washed in the morning. In the evening called Mary Clawson, and brought letter to Fr from her father mother, and Lois. Good news from the lower country.

Friday 10th I accompanied Alfred on his way to school as far as br Nicols, I spent the morning very pleasantly with her. In the afternoon she came with me to Mr Morrison's and Tison's, to visit a sick woman sister of Mrs Tison, late from the mines.

Mrs Coons was there, to whom I had an introduction for the first. We spent an hour of two there, sister N——, then returned home. I called at Br Cheny's, staid a few minutes, and came home, it was near 6 oclock. Mr C had finished painting while I was away, and got the things partially regulated.

Sat 11th I ironed, churned, and assisted otherways about house.

Sun 12th Beautiful pleasant day. Alma and Alfred have gone to the creek to wash themselves. Frances gone riding on horseback. At two oclock we Mr Crosby br Morris Alma Alfred and myself went to church. Mrs Riser accompanied us as far as Tisons, to await our return, intending to ride home with us. We called for her when we returned, but she had gone to br Cheny's. In the evening Mary Clauson came with her to help her home with the children.

Mon the 13th remarkably warm day. I commenced bonnets for sister Nicols.

Tues 14th We washed got through before noon.

[Eben Dyer's Arrival]

Wed 15th entremely warm, some of the men nearly gave up through extreme perspiration. In the evening, just as we had got through supper, a young man a stranger called at the door and enquired if we knew Jones Dire, said he had been in search of him all day, had just arrived in Cal had been shipwrecked on the *Courier Pigeon* 70 miles below San Francisco. That said Dire was a brother of his. I told him that we were his particullar friends, were well acquainted with him. We invited him take supper and tarry with us untill morning, when his brother would be here, as he was teaming by here every day. He seemed very thankful for the offer, as he was very warm, and much fatigued. Our portugee sailor boy received him very cordially, and was full of interrogations concerning his passage, and the Boston shipping department. The next morning *Thurs 16th* the brothers met here, they had not seen each other for 6 years, yet recollected one another perfectly well.[23]

Frid 17th I ironed. Mr Blithe, the pedlar called, had not been along before for sometime, in consequence of a fall, by his carriage capsizing, which broke the collar bone of his neck. We traded some 12 dolls with him. I bought a shawl, table cloth, and towels. He engaged a home here whenever he came to this vicinity, on a trading expedition.

Sat 18th, not quite as warm; another pedlar called. Mr Crosby finishing the verander. Frances went to br Nicols in the morning of an errand, and returned soon. In the meantime I churned, and performed sundry services, about house.

Sund 19th quite pleasant, and not so excessively warm. After breakfast we took a walk to the garden, found things in quite a fluorishing state. I sent a letter to the office to sister Levina Baker and husband.

After dinner br O Morey and sis—— Woodbury called. Sis W brought letters that she had red from her br and sis Carlos and Amelia Stevens, who are now in Bristol Kendall Co. Ill Brother Carlos seems apparently to possess a spirit of apostacy made some hard expressions concerning the church. and expressed much dissatisfaction at the nonfulfilment of the pr[o]p[h]esies. After meeting they returned with us. Sister W read the answer that she had written to his letter which was very lengthy, containing 4 sheets of paper. Amelia writes quite affectionatly and with a much milder spirit. She talks of coming to live with sister Lois Toms. in Nauvoo. While we were eating supper two pedlars called, and requesting supper and lodging.

In the evening Brother Doroty came in, one of our travelling companions from the states to Salt Lake valley,[24] accompanied by Am Greene. We had neither seen him or heard from him in 3 years. I scarcely knew him at first sight, but soon recollected his countenance. He seemed very much depressed in spirit. I enquired after his family, he said he did not know whether he had any, that he had been separated from them two years. His wife had refused to be with him &C.

I was quite surprised at the relation, and wonder what could have been the cause. Our pity was considerably excited for him, but conclude to suspend our judgement untill we understand both sides of the subject.

Mon June 20th, he called again, wished me to write a line to his wife. Whom I have highly respected ever since I knew her. I hesitated a little, fearing she might think me intrusive, but finally consented to write at all events.

Tues 21st We Mrs Riser Frances and myself went on a little visiting excursion to Mr Nicols, and Capt Scots. Br Riser was so kind as to take us down in the wagon in the morning, and came for us again at night.

We spent the forepart of the day at Nicols, had an excellent dinner of green peas and new potatoes, Shortly after dinner Mrs Hanion called in with the intention of staying a while, but finding us about to leave, very politely withdrew, after inviting us to call on her which we partially promised to do. She is very sociable and in my estimation quite agreeable.

At 3 oclock we went over to Capt Scots, Mrs N—— accompanied us. It was the first time we had been there, found them very pleasantly situated. The capt was not at home, his wife is apparently a very fine woman, rather plain looking, but quite ladylike in her manners.

She told me she had sailed with her husband 11 years that the first five, she was seasick continually. They have now been farming in Cal—— 2 years, and are apparently settled for life. They have two children, a daughter of 10 and a son of 4 years.

The sun was set before we arrived at home. We found Mr Morris and Crosby doing something about supper, but we soon relieved them, and brought things around in good order.

Wed 22nd nothing transpired worth relating.

Towards night the reapers came with their machinery, and commenced on the barley. They worked a few hours, and broke their machine, were under the necessity of going to the blacksmiths.

Thurs 23rd Mr Hamer our hired man from Tahiti left us, being tired of farming. He was of irish descent but had been brought up in england, was apparently a well educated man, 34 years of age, sandy complexion and withal quite agreeable in his manners. He expressed much regret at leaving, but said it was too monotonous a life for him, having been so long accostomed to change, and been master of several large vessels, been called Capt Hamer, the idea of going out to service as a farmer was rather humilitating to him.

Accordingly Mr C paid him his wages, and sent Alma with a team to carry him to Union city, where he intended taking the steamer for

San Fran and from there was going to Tahiti, where he has a native wife, whom he professes to esteem very highly. The boys returned at two oclock. Said they were sorry to part with him, he bought lemonade crackers and rasins, and treated them finely. Previous to leaving he presented me with his accordion, Said I had been a mother to him and that he felt himself under obligations to me.

I washed in the forenoon Fr in the afternoon. The reapers staid overnight, two of them came in to the sitting room, desiring apparently to converse with us. ^one^ Said he came from Ill, where he had been brought up had lived in Cass co. And to crown the whole, that he was present at Carthage when "Ol' Jo Smith" as he called him was shot. My mind was instantly caught away to scenes awful in the extreme. Oh what a train of solemnities rush upon the mind, at the idea of that awful tragedy. Little did the unthinking fellow know the feelings his careless relation of circumstances fraught with such lasting events, ran in our minds.

Friday June 24th Daughety came here to work he said on account of the streams being very high between here and the mines he had concluded to wait a while, untill they should fall.

Sat 25th The reapers came again and finished their job. I ironed. Father Greene staid here the previous night took breakfast, talks of taking up a school again.

Sun 26th we attended meeting, Elder Greene spoke upon the different dispensations that have been delivered to man, from Adam down to the dispensation of the fullness of times. It was very interesting and was heard apparently with a good degree of interest by the whole congregation.

Mon 27th, 9 years today, since the death of Joseph, and Hiram Smith. That awful tragedy was acted June 27th 1844.

Tues—— 28th, last night two pedlars staid with us, had a horse and carriage. The owner of the goods was a german who had been two years in America, and nine months in Cal. He appeared to be a fine fellow, said he and two brothers, owned a store in Puebla [San Jose Pueblo].

I traded some, bought an oilcloth for the table, a piece of curtain calico &C. The before named young Dire who was shipwrecked on the *courier Pigeon*, came to live with us. I rcd a letter from sis P dated May 1st.

Wed 29th We washed, Another pedlar put up with us A polander by the name of Isaac Bennet. I bought a bolt of bleach muslin.

Elder Greene brought me a letter from sister Lois Thompson. It had been detained a long time in San Jose Puebla. The letter was dated Jan 28th A D 1853.

I ironed in the fornoon. Afternoon we went to br Wheelers. Mrs Riser accompanied us. Alfred went with his little cart to haul the children. We enjoyed the time very agreeably. Edna Stewart was there. Mrs Harrison came in with her children, and spent the evening. We had green peas for supper, which was quite a rarity. Arrived home just before sunset. And found a br Sheffer here, a before named gentleman formerly from the state of Ia. He was in pursuit of employment, and Mr Cr, engaged him to work awhile for him.

Friday July 1st I did some ironing, churned, swept the chamber and verander, finished a shirt for Alma. Wm Stately a cook from Tisons called, told us that Mrs T—— had sent two of her sisters who were deranged to the insane asylum at Stocton. Music in the evening.

[Harvest Time]

Sat 2nd I finished pants for Alma. The reapers here, expect they will stay over sunday. Mr Barnes called in the evening; house full of men. he made but a short stay, wanted to get a job of threshing.

Sunday 3rd Br Sheffer went to San Jose Puebla, to get letters, Mr C, Alma and Alfred accompanied by br Wheeler ^went to church^. F—— and I staid at home. Father Morris gone to San Fran. Sun—— evening We sang with the violin. Fr received many compliments from the gentlemen on her musical talents. I had a conversation with br Doughety concerning his trials, of being separated from his family, and the probable cause of it. He said it was shown to him in a vision, years ago.

Monday July 4th 1853 This is the 77th anniversary of the independance of the United States. Great celebration at Union City.

A great dinner and ball at Mr Ralphs hotel. Our men none of them attended. We thought we would try to give them a little pleasure at home, accordingly we exerted ourselves a little more than usually, and set the two tables in the best room, so that we could all eat togather, and succeeded in getting quite a variety. Mr Wm Morrison called with his little nephew just before dinner, in his new carriage. We invited him to stay and dine with us, to which he readily consented, and paid us many compliments on our nice variety.

Tues—— 5th We have now 11 hired men; which makes 16 in the family. Washed this forenoon. Judson Stodard called and took dinner with us; lately from Salt Lake city.

Wed 6th br Greene called, was very unwell, we made him a cup of tea, which he said, cheered and revived him very much. The reapers left, after dinner.

Thurs—— 7th I ironed in the forenoon, and Fr in the afternoon. Francisco Rose lamed his arm, loading potatoes. I bathed his arm and shoulder with camphor but he was unable to use it for 2 or 3 days.

Friday 8th repaired shirts, and did other sewing. Two pedlars called. Fr traded some. Mr Crosby hauling potatoes to the Barkederers.

Sat 9th Shelling peas for dinner. Mr C had trouble with his team, was obliged to change them for another, carried only one load. Potatoes very low, somewhat discouraging to farmers.[25]

Sun 10th Mr C—— writing letters to his sister Lois Thom none of us attended meeting, excepting br Daughety. Sunday evening called br Jones Dire.

Mon 11th Welain [*spelling unclear*] called, asked for dinner; we made her a cup of tea, &C. ^Two pedlars staid over night.^ After eating she smoaked her pipe, and observed to Frances that I was very saintlike, having no bad habits of that kind. She was particular to thank us for her dinner, and said she was coming to stay all day with us soon.

Tues 12th We all went to the garden, gathered peas, cucumbers, turnips &C. ^Tues night another pedlar.^ *Wed 13th* washed, got through soon after dinner. Mary Clawson came to visit sister Riser. Br Riser gone to San Francisco. John Cheny came in the evening. Commenced playing the violin, which soon aroused the ideas of the young people, and set them to dancing. Mr Joseph J Bagley was in, a cousin of Mrs Riser, who is boarding with her.

Thurs 14th Another pedlar called, goods very cheap.

Lost his pistol by the door, also his yard measure. Alfred found them. We F—— and myself, bought oilcloth for 50 cts per yard. Frances accompanied Mrs Clausen to Allens and Wheelers. Staid a short time, took dinner and returned. Two more pedlars.

Friday 15th I ironed churned, and assisted otherwise about house. Mr Royer and Sheffer called in the evening.

Saturday 16th Shelling peas for dinner. Received a visit in the afternoon from Miss Catherine Kenny, and Miny Scott. In the evening we had a little old fashioned music. A few old fugees. Mr Little sang bass, I sang the air with the violin. It passed with considerable spirit.

Sun 17th Frances and Alma, accompanied by br J Dire went to the mission to buy pears. They got a fine lot and brought home. Brother D—— paid 14 dolls for them, and refused to take any remuneration. About 12 oclock Mr Morey and sister Woodbury called, spent the afternoon. Our wagon was gone so that we did not go to church. Mr C and Daughety walked. Mr Morey took us out to ride, had quite an agreeable time. When Mr C returned from church he brought a stranger with him, a brother in the gospil by the name of Nash, a welchman by birth. He brought us letters from sister P and Ellen.

Br N sang very beautifully in the evening, several new hymns, some of them his own composition. Hyram Clark spent the afternoon and evening with us, had not been here for some time, we had very agreeable visit with him. Br Nash staid over night, took breakfast.

Mon 18th Mr Crosby engaged him to work, he promised to come in one week. Made sacks in the afternoon. Another pedlar put up with us.

Tues——— 19th I washed, visited with Mrs Scott and Nicols at Mr Risers. In the evening Crosby and Riser had a conference concerning the harvesting and farming affairs. Tried to settle some unpleasant feelings which have existed between them.

Wed——— 20th I ironed, Feel quite unwell with the headache. Cut me a gingham dress. Brother J Dire called in the evening.

Thurs 21st Mr Crosby went to the mission. ^Saw Br Horner who offered to assist him in borrowing money.^ Heard Mr Naile had arrived at San Francisco. We all feel very anxious to see him return. Very high winds in the afternoon.

The evening passed off in conversation with Mr C and Frances concerning his company business, which I believe is always attended with perplexities of various kinds.

Frid 22nd Nothing worth noticing. I made a fine sack. Times quite dull, nothing seems very encouraging.

[Arrival of Australian Saints]

Sat 23rd No Mr Naile arrives yet. The boys picking peas, all of us shelling in the afternoon. I made one dozen sacks. Mr Greene called direct from San Fran. brought a line from John Layton, informing us that his wife has had the measles, and been quite sick, that he thought of sending her back to the islands, when Capt Richmond arrived. Elder Greene also informed us that, Elder [Charles W.] Wandall [Wandell] had returned from Australia with a com——— of brethren,[26] and gone to San Bernardino. In the evening called Mr Lad, Royer and Sheffer. Mr C——— played the violin.

Sun 24th Elder Morris returned, has been much afflicted while to the city, with sickness, and lameness, both of his legs now sore. I wrote a line to sister Daughety, one of our travelling [companions] to Salt Lake city. Her husband wished me to write and ask <u>her</u> for <u>him</u> if she was willing (as they had separated) to let him take part of the children to the church in San Bernardino. At two oclock attended church. Br Wandall preached; or rather gave us a history of his mission to Australia; which was very interesting to me. The sacrament was administered, and a good spirit prevailed. Elder Greene and Ammon came home with us and took supper. Henry Webster and Margeret Emily called at the door ^in a carriage,^ asked F to ride with them, she readily consented, but rode only a short distance. After supper the conversation turned to br Daughety, and his trials; occasioned by his wife leaving him.

Monday July 25th 1853 We have now 12 in family, besides 9 Spaniards. There are 15 men engaged in reaping, and binding wheat. Mr C choose to have his wheat reaped by hand, as he thought he could save more than to have it cut by the machine.

We have a great deal of cooking to do, 21 persons to eat. Mr Blithe is here with a very large load of goods. I dislike to see him coming, for I am owing him and have not the money. He came in and very politly invited us to trade with him. I told him that I had not yet used the others I bought, and if he was not willing to wait any longer he might have them again. He said he was very willing to wait on, and rather than take them again, he would choose to leave as many more with me.

After dinner Mr Morris returned from Mr Horner's with a horse and cart, took all his things over there. Said Br Horner wished him to come and attend his nursery.

It seemed quite lonely to see him going off. But taking all things into consideration, we concluded it would be best for him to go. He expressed much regret leaving, said we had been very kind, that I had kept him clean and comfortable. Said he should call often to visit us.

Tues 26th I churned, made a few sacks, and assisted about cooking. Br Jones Dire called in the evening, quite sociable time. Br Riser gone to San Francisco. A young miss [Delina] Cheny from Salt Lake City arrived at her br today.

Wed 27th ✝ 3 more Sapiards came to reap, who with the men we had before make 23 in family. I washed in the forenoon. Frances baked, got dinner, and washed in the afternoon. While I baked. We began to think it was coming rather hard on us, talked some of calling in one of the hired men who had been cook on a vessel to assist us, providing we should fail. We spoke to Mr Crosby and soon perceived that it would not meet his mind, as he said Frank was one of his best reapers. We accordingly talked it over and concluded that we would try to get along with Alma and Alfreds help, awhile longer.

Thurs 28th I felt very lame and tired. One of the men was sick, gave up work. After dinner I laid down slept quite a while, had very unpleasant dreams. Mr Riser returned from San Francisco, at sunset, brought a little money to Mr C. I believe he is a little encouraged concerning his crops. Wheat 5 cents pr pound but potatoes very low, only 1 1/2 cts pr pound.

Frid 29th 1 year today since we left Tahiti. It seemed to me then like starting anew into life, and so it has proved with us, our trials are of a different nature from any we ever met with before. Thousands of cares we never experienced before, and business for every moment.

Sat 30th Churning, baking, cooking, by the wholesale. Visitors in the afternoon, the Miss Morrisons came and took tea with us. Mrs Riser was in. We enjoyed ourselves finly. Br J Dire called in the evening, brought us two letters, one from John Layton, and one from John Hamer, a man that worked for us awhile.

[Missionaries to China]

Sun July 31st This morning called a br Wade an elder on a mission to China. Staid last night at br Risers in co with Cyrus Camfield. He seemed to know us very well but I did not recollect him; he gave us a great deal of information concerning the Great Salt Lake City. Frances went to the mission with br Jones Dire, brought home some pears.

At 2 oclock Mrs Riser and myself went to church with a waggon full of men. The two missionaries were present, we had a very good time. Br Greene, Morris, and Wade took supper.

Mon Aug 1st Baking, cooking of allmost every description. Plenty of news from Salt Lake

Tues—— 2nd I washed. Mr C hired another man, I believe from Valparaiso; he speaks the Spanish.

Camfield, and Wade, were in the afternoon, told us many things concerning the church.

Wed 3rd Ironing, churning, cleaning house, and a little sewing in the afternoon.

Thurs 4th I did a little more washing, sewing in the afternoon.

Frid 5th, Ironing. Considerable conversation with br Wade. He told me the trials and great cross it was to him to go on this mission. The idea of leaving a young helpless family to be gone 3 or 4 years from them, was almost like death. And then to go among a strange people, and be under the necessity of acquiring a knowledge of the language, he said he was obliged to summon all the fortitude and resolution that he was master of to his aid. And when once he had made a resolve to go in the strength of the Lord if it cost him his life, the burden left him, and his heart was as light as usually.

Sat 6th The hired men mostly took a ride to union city and spent the afternoon. Mr Horner brought his wife and sister King to visit us. Sister King came up last Thurs, on a visit to his valley, her husband called while we were taking tea. We had a very agreeable time with them. Mr H called for them again at sunset.

Sun 7th Frances and I both went to church.

The wagon was full. We had a very good meeting. Quite a number of new members from Salt Lake city Mr C administered the sacrament. Sis—— Loyd was the only female excepting us. Arrived home at 5 oclock.

Mary Clawson was visiting Mrs Riser and called a few minutes.

Mon 8th remarkbly pleasant morning. Frances took a horse back ride. Took dinner at Tisons, and called awhile at Nicols's. I cooked the dinner for the men, and family; 14 in number. Made some tomatoe preserves, and performed sundry other extras in the housekeeping line.

F—— returned in time to get supper, was much pleased with her excursion, and visit. She saw Mrs Z[acheus] Cheny[27] at br Nicols, who promised to visit us on Wednesday.

Tues—— *9th* Our labor in the cooking line is considerably reduced only one table of men, besides the two boys and ourselves. Received a visit from Mr[s] Z Cheny, from San Francisco. Her husband called towards night, and Frances accompanied them home to their brothers, who live about half a mile from us. There are 3 brothers, and 1 sister living together.

Wed 10th Washed. In the afternoon made a few sacks.

Thurs 11th I ironed in the fornoon; in the afternoon made sacks Elders Camfield and Wade pursued their way on the their place of destination.

Friday 12th I made sacks. Frances made mince pies. Afternoon received a visit from Miss Margaret Emily and H Davis. We enjoyed their visit well. Our men finished reaping.

Sat 13th I washed the floors and windows in the morning, made sacks the remainder of the day.

Sun 14th Br Riser brought in a letter from J C Naile. Dated 14th of June, informing us of his safe arrival at his fathers, their healths, and intentions of leaving for this place the 20th of the month. He also stated that he had started two wagons a carriage, 16 horses, and 20 cows, which we understood were coming by land. We are now looking for him daily.

Frances and br J Dire took a carriage ride to Puebla [Pueblo San Jose]. I had quite a severe turn of colic. Took painkiller, bathed my feet in warm water, went to bed; got into a perspiration, and soon got easy so that I arose and assisted the boys in getting dinner. I had intended going to church, but did not feel able, consequently the men concluded to walk.

About 4 oclock arrived Maj Russel, his wife and 3 children. They live 18 miles from us in Amadors valley. They came to visit br Riser's, but finding them absent from home, came in and spent the afternoon with us. I also had 2 or 3 other visitors, gents which with own men made quite a company to get supper for. Frances did not return untill near dark.

I set two tables at the same time, and then was under the necessity of setting one the second time. Mary Clawson called in the evening. Frances was much pleased with her ride, admired the city of Puebla much.

Mon 15th br Riser's and Russel's took a ride to the mission, invited me to accompany them, but I declined in consequence of a bad cold, and sore throat. Mon night two pedlars staid with us.

Tues 16th this morning there were a number in to trade they had their goods spread all over the floor. The pedlars said they were hollanders, both short men one quite thickset with red hair, the other small and dark complexion.

Wed 17th Washed this forenoon, felt very unwell when I began but after getting warmed up to the business I felt better; got through before noon. After dinner scrubed the diningroom floor,

Thur 18th I ironed, cut undergarments. Mr C went with one load of potatoes to market, very low 1 ½ pr pound, wont pay the expense of digging.

Friday 19th Mr C went with another load. Frances and Alma went to br Horners on a visit. They set off at 9 oclock. I expected them to return before sunset. But I was disappointed. Alma came home alone after supper. Told me ~~that~~ that Frances was going to stop overnight.

Sat 20th I had plenty of business, baking and cooking of allmost all descriptions. It was a very warm day, I had a great deal of exercise through the day. Frances returned after sunset accompanied by Margarett and Henry Webster. She was highly pleased with her visit, said she had been to Union city in the stage took dinner at the public house, returned went to the Mission ^had a feast of pears^ got the promise of a feast of peaches on Wednesday next

Sun 21st Mr C set 3 of his hired hands at liberty untill the threshers come. Accordingly 2 of them went on a visit to San Francisco. At 2 oclock we went to church. Mrs Riser Fran and myself. Elder Greene preached his farewell discourse being about to leave for San Bernardino and Salt Lake city. The meeting passed off with considerable spirit. The sacrament was administered. A gentleman and his wife from Santa Clara attended our meeting, appeared to be enquiring into our faith, Br Horner offered to let them have books, and give them all the information they wished.

Mon 22nd Nothing transpired worth noticing. We Frances and myself talked of going to visit Mrs Scott ^who we heard was very sick^. But about noon I had a very bad turn of feeling unwell, and gave up the idea.

Tues 23rd Mr C was going to the landing with a load, and concluded to ride along as far as br Nicols, and go to see Mr[s] Scott. I arrived between 9 and 10 oclock, sister N went over with me. I intended to have staid through the day, with her but as she had other attendance for that day, I left, promising to come the next. I returned with sis N; her husband was gone to the redwoods, expecting to be absent 3 or 4 days, she had a young man by the name of Adams from San Francisco staying with her. She invited me to stay with her through the day, which I did, and as I had no work of my own, sewed for her. Mrs Simms called and brought me a little sewing. I passed the afternoon very agreeably, returned home just after sunset.

Wed 24th about 8 oclock Capt Scott sent his carriage for me. I went, found a Dr Ober there from San Fran And a lady by the name of Kelsey who had been with her since the previous morning. Mrs S I could see was decidedly better, altho very weak, and could scarcely speak above her breath. Mss K soon left and I took her place. At noon br and sis Lloyd called. sis L was very unwell. Capt S went with the Dr to the landing as he wished to return home. A Mrs Treefry, niece of Mrs Scott, also left, she had been with Mrs S a week I did what I could for her. Sis Nicols came over a few minutes. About 5 oclock the capt returned and brought a Mrs Cornell from Union city, which relieved me. I was much pleased with her appearance, although an entire stranger she really appeared so familiar that I thought I must have seen her somewhere before. She is about my own size but 10 years younger. Said her native place was the city of Brooklin NY. That her maiden name was Hauly. She appeared much inclined to be sociable, invited me to visit her, which I should be much pleased to do. The Capt sent his carriage with me home at night thanked me much for my attentions through the day. I told if I was needed again I would willingly come.

Thurs——— 25th I washed kept on my feet nearly all day.

Frid 26th Ironed and assisted about house. Just before supper Frank Rose returned from SF brought a cousin of his with him wanted to get him in to work. Brought cloth, oranges, and a letter, from Layton. The thrashers came on today with their machinery, which brings 5 or 6 more men into the family.

Sat 27th cooking and washing dishes was the order of the day. I sewed a little in the afternoon.

Sun——— 28th I arose earlyer than usual. One of the threshers was sick, has the chills and fever. After breakfast Margarett Emily and Henry Webster called over to accompany Frances and J Dire on a ride through the mountains. At two oclock we attended church. Mrs Riser and myself, Mrs Horner and Mrs Lloyd were all the females present. Br Wandall preached from the 6th chap of Math, was succeeded by br Horner. Meeting closed by Mr Crosby. After which there was an anatomical lecture delivered by a young physician. Said he intended continuing them for several sundays. I considered it rather interesting than otherwise. Br Wandell and Ornaldo M[owry] accompanied us home, spent the evening, had quite an agreeable time with them. They informed us that missionaries to China had returned without accomplishing their desired object, probably in consequence of commotions in the government of that country.

Mon 29th cooking again in abundance, 14 men, besides the boys. ^Br Nicols with his wife and children made us a call.^ Dr [J. M.] Selfredge [Selfridge] called to see Mr Preston the sick man, said he was threatned with a billious fever. I feel to pity him as he is apparently a very modest young man, and destitute of any near friends in this country. Received a call from Blithe, ^the pedlar^

Tues——— 30th Frances went on a visit to br Nicols, left me with 14 men to cook dinner and supper for did not return untill after sunset.

Wed——— 31st Washing day. Mr Preston is some better I finished pantaloons for Alfred, Mr Riser was in this evening. The threshers getting along very well. One of the chilanians gave out and left. Mr C sent Alma over to Capt Scotts and got 2 or 3 new hands.

Thurs Sept 1st. A beautiful pleasant morning. I arose between 5 and 6 oclock, fed the chickens, hung up my clothes, set the second table, made gruel for the sick man, &C In the evening commenced a little job of sewing for Mrs Simms. I am considerably troubled with weak eyes.

Frid 2nd They finished threshing wheat. Mr Bagley (a young man who has been given up by the physicians as a victim of consumption,) has become quite smart, and sewed sacks two days, very steadily. I heard that a company from this valley leave today for the Great Salt Lake City.

Sat 3rd Mr Preston had a turn of fever, seems somewhat disheartend.

Sunday 4th morning, very pleasant. Mr C been quite restless through the night; feels troubled in mind about raising more to pay his hands; has not yet had a chance to turn anything in the produce line, and still has to pay out money, which he is obliged to raise on the credit of the crops. We both feel burthened in mind; but we know from Whom is our help, and to Whom to apply in every time of need. Mr C went to br Nicols, for assistance, but got none, his excuse was that he was about to invest his money in land, at a hundred dolls pr acre. He returned rather heavy hearted. I felt much depressed in spirit all day. I was however considerably comforted at meeting. Heard the two missionaries speak; late from China. They gave an account of their journey, to and reception in China, the manners habits and religious faith, also government affairs of the country, which are now in great commotions, being rocked with civil wars. A great prophet has arisen among them who professes to be dictated by the holy spirit. He compells all to bow to his mandates.

[End of the Wheat Harvest]

Sunday evening Just as we were sitting up the supper called Capt Mayhew and brought Mr C a hundred and thirty nine dolls, which afforded him temporary relief, by enabling him to pay some of his workmen who were wishing to leave, I considered it quite providential.

Mon 5th Mr C got kicked by a mule which came near injuring him seriously. The threshers complaining very much of hard work, and rust. Mr C wanted two more hands, just as they were sitting down to supper two travellers called, wishing for work, he accordingly hired them.

Tues 6th ~~br C Duncan came to see us staid over night~~

Wed 7th I washed in the forenoon Frances in the Pm. Mrs Simms sent for some sewing I had been doing for her

Thurs 8th Mrs Nicols and Corwin (a lady from San Francisco) called, they had been riding on horse back for pleasure, were accompanied by br Harrison. In the evening called br Duncan staid overnight.

Friday 9th he went to Chenys, and Nicols. Returned again at night— slept here.

Sat 10th he left went to Horners. Frances is quite unwell, a great deal of cooking to be done.

Sund 11th very pleasant. At two attended church Br Horner spoke to the people on repentance and baptism. was succeeded by Tho Williams.[28] Mr C closed the meeting.

Mon 12th Nothing worth noticing. Frances health rather poor. She is much afflicted with dispepsie.

Tues 13th they finished threshing. I really was rejoiced and was glad for them, that they had got through so dirty and disagreeable a task. In the PM they went Risers.

Wed 14th Washed between breakfast and Dinner. Mr C paid off several of his workmen. Some of them expressed an unwillingness to leave, requested the privilege of making this house their home, while they stay in this part of the country.

Thurs 15th Frances continues quite poorly. I persuaded her to give up the work and try to do something for her health. She has a great aversion to taking medicine, or employing a physician. I proposed to her to take Davises painkiller, to which she consented. Mr C went to the Mission, bought several kinds of medicine. Quite a quantity of rain fell this morning. About 10 oclock it faired off, and br Dougherty set off to the mining regions to visit his family. I took charge of the kitchen. Frances retired to her room commenced making herself a dress; blue english merino. She seemed unwilling to leave the housework; said she felt much better when stiring about, than when sitting. I told her to make her dress, and recommended her to go to the city and try to get something for her health. She told me somethings concerning herself on my questioning her closely that excited my fears and I was resolved that she should spare no pains, in doing what she could any longer.

Friday 16th She complained of her bowels paining her, looked very bad. Afternoon Delina Cheney came to visit us, for the first time since her arrival in Cal. We had a very good visit, John came in the evening, brought a young man with him. [William] McGary who is also a fiddler.[29] Joseph J Bagley and Charles Allen was in. We had very good music and a little dancing. They retired at half past 10 ocl——.

Sat 17th F—— still very unwell seemed to have some fever, thought it was occasioned by the painkiller. In the afternoon I sent Alma to Dr Selfridge for an emetic, the Dr was absent and he got none. In the evening Frank went found him at home, and got one, I bathed her feet in warm water made mustard seed drafts for them, and gave her the emetic. I was up with her untill ten oclock. The emetic had a very good operation.

Sun—— 18th I arose at 5 oclock got the break out of the way in season for meeting, which convened at 9 oclock. A sort of conference meeting, appointed some new officers in the branch, administered the sacrament. The presiding elder br Horner choose two counselors, Viz br Dustin, and Mr Crosby. Rinaldo Mory was appointed clerk. Two children blest. Several persons here to dinner. I could not well get ready in season to attend the afternoon meeting. sister Wheeler, Woodbury, and br Morey spent the afternoon with us, the family mostly went to church. Received letters from sister P—— also from sister Lockwood, last week. Sister L's arrived Thurs—— 15th sept sister P'——s on sat following.

Mon 19th Frances took rhubarb, which made her very sick untill Tuesday afternoon I prevailed on her to lie down and keep still, Sister Riser brought in some medicine which checked effects of rhubarb she was some better, but still had some fever and headache. Sister Corwin called in a little while monday, said she would come again tuesday or wed and spend the day with us. When Mr C returned from the landing on tuesday he brought with him John Layton. He found Alfred quite unwell and afflicted with a boile. They were much pleased to see each other. L said he wanted A to go down to see his mother as she talked of going back to the islands.

Wed 21st Alma went with the team and carried them to Union city. They went off in good spirits. and I hoped and prayed they might both feel better for their visit. I felt very lonely after they were gone but, had no time to brood over melancholy, my hands full of work. They had not been gone long, when sister C—— came according to promise.

I was pleased to see her; but could not spend as much time with her, as I wished, on account of having so many men to cook for; and no one to assist me except Alma. I however got along very well. Made a custard and sweet cake, for dinner; which with a cup of tea, and several other little articles, passed off very well. Sister Nicols came up in the afternoon. Sister Riser came in and we had very sociable time. Sis Ri and I put our mights together for tea and made quite a variety. Two pedlars staid overnight with us.

Thur 22nd I washed. About 11 oclock br Daugherty returned from his excursion to the mining regions. did not bring his children as he intended when he left found them attending school, and so well provided for that he could [not] conscientiously separate them. He said his wife sent her respects to me, said she received my letter and intended to answer it.

Friday 23rd I baked, bread and mince pies, felt very much fatigued at night, Daugherty went after Dr Seffridge for Mr Lyttle.

Sat 24th Ironing, cleaning house, cooking, is the business of this day. Br D—— left again for Santa Cruz

Sun 25th I had the headache, didnot go to church, wrote a long letter to sis Pratt. Mr Crosby walked out to meeting Alma went to the mission and bought some grapes. When Mr C returned from church brought br Duncan with him he staid overnight. We had a very sociable visit with him. I sent my letter by him to br Horner. Heard he br H is not going to the San Bernardino conference, as he intended, but has got br Wandell to go in his stead.

Mon 26th I finished my letter, br D—— took it off. Very pleasant morning, no one about the house, excepting Alma and myself. Little Catherine Riser comes occasionally to disturb my reflections.

Tues, 27th I baked bread. I spent several hours reading. Got some papers from Cincinnatti, sent to br Naile. Probably he ordered them sent before he left for home.

[Gloomy Future Prospects]

Wed 28th I washed, felt very miserable. Alma helped me some. After dinner I cleaned the floors, kept on my feet nearly all day. I get so fatigued the moment I sit down I drop to sleep, unless some one is by me to converse with. Just one year today since we arrived here to this house. Where another year from this will find us, I know not. It seems to me that instead of becoming easier it is a greater burden to me to <u>move</u>, than formerly. Our prospects for the future look gloomy; if we come out clear of debt we shall I trust, be thankful. Produce is at the lowest price.

Thurs 29th This morning Mr C carried off a load of fowls, Dr Selfridge called to see Mr Little, but he had gone out and he left his medicine with me. I boiled beef and vegetables for dinner. Put the old black hen to setting &C

Frid 30th and last day of Sept. I had a very restless night last. It seems that some power superior to our own is striving against us, and trying if possible to make us unhappy. Notwithstanding all our faith and hope, and desires to trust ^to the contrary^ in God. It is a beautiful day abroad, only within our own hearts sorrow, disappointment and care reigns undisturbed. O God the Eternal Father. I ask the[e] in the name of Jesus Christ to remove this burden from our minds, if it is Thy will. But if not, O give us grace patience and meekness to bear up under every difficulty, and O may we sometime learn to trust in Thee, and say Thy will be done.

Sat Oct 1st Time rolls steadily on. I have been writing a letter to sister Dolly Lockwood who lives in Newton Ohio. Ironed and baked to day, cleaned floors &C—— My health is unusually good. God grant it may continue

Sun 2nd Received another letter from sis Pratt. Friends all well, and the saints prospering, laying out cities, building house, and enlarging their borders. Went to church, sister Riser and myself, Mr C Alma. Had what I considered an unusualy good meeting. Mr C spoke from the book of Mormon, and was succeeded by br Lewis. After which br Horner administered the sacrament. Singing went off quite lively. I thought rather better than usually.

Mon 3rd Very warm. I felt very lonesome, went in and sat with sis R awhile in the forenoon, in the afternoon she came in ~~here~~ and sat with me. Mr Bagley also in. Eben Dyer left. He is a fine young man, we all respected him much and was sorry to have him leave. He made me a present of a little box before he left, and said he would come and see us once in a while.

Tues 4th the weather is remarkbly warm for the season. Sister Harrison came up and us a visit. She intended to make two of it but Sis Riser insisted upon having her stay there; accordingly I went in and spent a part of the afternoon. I was baking bread and could not stay long. We enjoyed the visit finly.

Wed 5th I washed. Just after I got through Jones came with his shirts I put them in soak and washed them next day.

Thurs 6th Blithe called with a very large load of goods, begged of us to take something to lighten it. I took a pair gaiters and a bolt of calico, at 10 cents per yard. It had been wet with salt water, and he sold it at a reduced price. Afternoon I baked pies.

Frid 7th This morning a gentleman called to get subscribers for the Pacific news, a weekly published at San Francisco He looked and talked like W W Phelps. Said he was a native of Boston had lived there and at Lowell all his days untill within three years past, he had been in Cal and prefered this climate to any he was ever in. Just before supper a four horse carriage was driven up to the house, I thought it was the stage probably come to bring Frances home, or pedlars. But it proved to be and old gentleman by the name of Patten from Salt Lake city, on his way to San Bernardino, he had met br Sheffer at Sacramento and persuaded him to accompany him to the lower country. He is nearly 70 years, and is smart and lively as a young man.[30] They staid over night with us. The old gent said he had lately received a letter from his wife stating that the people of Utah Territory were having trouble with the indians. That they were constantly committing depredations upon the inhabitants, stealing their horses, killing their cattle, and had killed and wounded several persons. I wrote a few lines by them to sis Pratt.

Sat 8th Just sent 2 letters to the office, one to sis Lockwood in Ohio, and another to Carlos Stevens Ill. I am looking for Fr to day.

Sun 9th It is a beautiful morning, a sort of holy calmness seems to preside over my mind, altho I had very unpleasant dreams last night, but

I think it was in consequence of being very tired when I went to bed. I dreamed of seeing br Pratt in great trouble on a very boisterous ocean, or bay, I thought he was in an open boat which was drawn by a cow, thought she was struggling and plunging with all her might to get to shore through the waves; while br P sat in the boat covered with water. I thought I also saw a great storm of wind coming, dust flying waves rolling &C. While I myself was in a very dangerous situation, being upon the brink of falling down a precipice. I stood sometime in hopes some one would come to my relief, called aloud to my husband, who was near by, but too busy to hear, or come. When suddenly a little child caught me around my waist, and down we went together and found ourselves standing upon our feet, and no harm done us at all. Just as I commenced writing this dream, came Sister Woodbury Rinaldo Morey and br Lewis. Sis W brought a letter from sis Lewis, who is at the Sandwich islands. We learned from her letter that she is tired of staying there and wishes our counsel about her coming to Cal. Sis W said she had already written to her to come, and if she could not get along without she would help her to pay her passage.[31]

After dinner we all went to church. Sis Riser myself and Woodbury rode in Moreys carriage, br L rode with Mr C in the wagon. We had a very good meeting. Mr Lewis spoke to us upon the plan of salvation. This morning *Mon 10th* he sets off for his home in Utah Territory. Br Dougherty returned last night, a little before sunset. Quite a hard rain this morning, which somewhat surprised us. But has now faired away, and the sun shines very pleasantly. Yesterday morning John Cheny brought me a letter from Frances stating, that the longer she staid the better she liked, and requested me to send her some articles of clothing, but said nothing with regard to her health. I wrote her a few lines and cautioned to try to do something without fail.

Tuesday 11th quite cloudy and looked like rain this morning. Mr C went to Barkedera with a load. This is my oldest sister's birthday. She is now 58 years old. 18 years since I saw her. I was then 29 years, or in my 29th year, and she was 40.

Wed 12th Mr C paid another of his workmen, and he left for San Francisco We have now ~~olny~~ only two workmen, and one boarder. I washed. Baked veal for dinner. This evening Jones Dyer came in, and said he had heard that Frances had come home, that someone had seen her come off the boat at Union city. I thought perhaps it might have been the case, and she was staying at br Horners; but I now think it a mistake.

Thurs 13th This morning our boarder br Dougherty left. Mr C took his trunk on his load as he went to the landing, and carried it to Alviso, or near there, where he expects to work one month. Br Dustin called and took dinner with us. Showed me a letter from his wife, dated Aug 28th. It gave an account of the death of her youngest son a boy 12 years old, he was killed by a flash of lightning while driving cattle into the yard, An ox was also killed at the same time. Br D seemed very much affected at the reading of the letter, wished himself in Salt lake valley, but said he had made arrangements to stay another year. His wife importuned with him to come home; even offered to sell their place and send him means, if he could not come without. She seemed almost inconsolable at the loss of her son.

Friday 14th I ironed, sewed some on my dress. Had quite a restless night, but felt much better this morning than I expected to, had quite comfortable day. *Sat 15th* Oct is half gone. Time flies on with lightning speed. And will soon waft us o'er this lifes tempestuous sea.

Sunday 16th I arose at 7—breakfast at half past. Frank Silver took breakfast with us, After which he and Frank Rose took a ride to Squatterville [San Lorenzo] to visit some of their countrymen. Alma went to the mission. Got a letter for Mr Little and a paper for br Naile. Attended church at 2 oclock. Sister Riser and her children, Mr Little, Mr C——, Alma, and myself. Mr Horner spoke to the congregation upon the literal fulfillment of prophecy. Administered the sacrament. Conference appointed next Sunday, to be held at our house in the forenoon and at the schoolhouse in the afternoon.

Sister Lloyd informed me that she intended going to San Francisco tomorrow, and would carry a line to Frances.

Mon 17th I enjoyed a very still quiet day wrote a letter to Frances, and one to Alfred, did some jobs of mending. In the evening the men killed a beef. Mr Little went this morning to seek himself another home, and work, was quite successful, found a job at Lloyds, returned at noon. Intends leaving tomorrow for his new place of abode. It is a beautiful moonlight evening.

No clouds do arise, to darken the skies.

Or hide for a moment, the moon from our eyes.

The heart must be sad indeed that cannot rejoice when all nature smiles around.

Tues——— 18th Mr C commenced hauling his wheat, took two loads to Mr Horners mill, but finding no chance to store it, concluded to take no more there, untill he could see br H himself, and make further arrangements. Afternoon went to Capt Mayhew's with two loads. Br Riser prefers having him haul it to the latter place. Mr Little went off with them this morning. He requested the privilege however of calling this house his home for the present or at least while he should stay about here.

Wednesday 19th Oct 1853 Here I am alone in the house, lonesome as a church mouse. I step into sister Risers occasionly. Baked mince and pumpkin pies to day. This has been my washing day for sometime. I hardly know why I neglected it today. Br Dustin called just as we got through supper asked Alma if we would keep a pedlar Said he was [*illegible crossout*] ~~was~~ very tired and almost sick, Alma told him he could stay. Accordingly I prepared him a place at table. he said he had been sleeping on the ground, and eating a negroes cooking for sometime, and felt glad to get home once more. He had been making fence for br Horner.

Thurs 20th I washed, and regulated the chamber. Heard br Farnsworth had come from San Bernardino. Br Dustin called again to night to stay with us.

Frid 21st Very warm day. Br Farnsworth called and took dinner with us. Brought me a letter from sister P, told us concerning their conference, said he would call again before he left and take a letter back, informed me that a number were coming up from San Francisco to attend conference. Heard the brs Cheny's and their sister have gone to the city. I felt very sorry that I did not know they were going, as the letter I sent to Sister Lloyd was returned to me in consequence of her not going as she expected. She got on board the steamer, but the water being very low they could not get out of the creek. She got tired of waiting and came back. Br Wheeler called this evening just at dark, said he was going to move tomorrow up into the mountains, where he and br Harrison had a claim.

Sat 22nd I baked bread and sweetcakes, made window curtains in the dining. Just before supper came brs Dustin and Doroty, to stay over night and be here to attend meeting

[Conference at the Crosbys, Fall 1853]

Sun 23rd I arose at half past 6 oclock got breakfast as early as possible and regulated the house in order for meeting at ten. At ten the meeting convened according to appointment. Quite a number of elders present among whom was br Wandall missionary from Australia, br C[hapman] Duncan late from China br Sparks from San Bern a br Meeks from Union City Tho Williams from Salt Lake City A br [Isaac] Nash and wife from Union City, beside those who belong to the branch. Br Horner was chosen president of the conference C Duncan chosen clerk protem in consequence of br Morey who declined in Br Wandell made his report from the San Bernardino conference And requested our united efforts to assist the church at ~~San Bernardino~~ that place in clearing their land from debt. Br Sparks spoke quite lengthly, was succeeded by br Horner, who administered the sacrament, meeting closed by br Duncan. Sister Evans and Lincoln were up from San Fran—— A good spirit prevailed and the meeting passed of[f] with a good deal of animation. Adjourned untill halfpast two at the schoolhouse. I gave the brethren a bite of pie and cake, those of them that staid, and went with us to meeting. I rode out with Morey and sis Woodbury.

Br Wandell accompanied us, and told me a little of his troubles concerning his family. Said it was now six years since he left them in New Orleans and came to Cal——, that his wife had gone back to NY and from there to Savannah, that his death had been published in the NY papers which he thought had been done by some designing man to deceive her. That serious difficulties had occured between them sometime ago, which probably would never be settled, or removed. He is now striving to get means to remove them to Cal—— as soon as possible, requests a little assistance from the brethren in this place in order to accomplish his desired object. I feel to sympathize with him and would willingly assist him if I had the ability to do so. He br W returned with us from meeting took supper and went with Mr C and Doughety to evening meeting at Mr Horners. Alma and I stay alone this evening.

Mon 24th Mr C and Frank commenced hauling wheat to Mr H. Alma and I were alone all day or at least untill 4 oclock.

Sis Riser went to br Nicols, invited me to accompany her but I did not feel in a visiting spirit, besides I wished to write letter to sis P to send by br Farnsworth. Accordingly she set off alone with her two children in the wagon. I wrote a lengthy letter to sister Pratt.

[Frances's Surprise Visit]

Tues 25th Alma and I were alone again. Mr C returned at half past three, sister Riser was in occasionally, and I was several times in there. Br Riser spent evening with us. Conversation turned upon the different public speakers in the church. Their names were called up one after another. Br J Smith S Rigdon, O Hide, O Pratt G J Adams, and Sparks. The next question was whether young Joseph Smith would eventually succeed his father as president of this church. Br R went home at 9 oclock and we retired to rest. I had just got into bed and laid my head upon my pillow when I discovered a light in the sitting room by our door being a little way open, I observed to Mr C that there was a light in other room, he said perhaps we had left a candle burning. I told him I did not. He opened the door looked out and said there was a light there, and the next moment, closed it saying there was a woman in the room, and I had better get up and see who it was, I confess I was quite surprised, who it should be that had come at that time of night, and got into the house without us hearing any noise. I could not imagine. However I thought I would not be afraid of her at all events, but find out who she was if possible. I arose and opened the door, and who should meet me but Frances, I did not recognize her the first moment but thought it was an english girl of my acquaintance from Salt lake. The surprise was so great that it set me into a sort of tremor which lasted for sometime. However I was much pleased to see her, and after talking a few minutes we went to bed, as it was then ten oclock. Sister Evans told me on sunday that she F intended to stay a week or ten days longer, which was the reason of my being so surprised on seeing her so soon.

Wed 26th It is 19 years today since we were married. Little did I think then that I should be such a traveller, having never been more than half a dozen times out of town, and never out of the province since we arrived there.

Fr arose early as usually. I think she is perhaps some better but far from being well. She brought a little medicine with her said the Dr counseled her to come home and practice riding a little every day, and in ten days she must come back to see him. After breakfast Alma got up the horses and they rode off a mile or two, and returned, she had a light chill in the morning, said she also had one the morning previous to her leaving Frisco complained considerably through the day of cramp in her stomach.

Thurs 27th It was a beautiful day. I washed in the morning. I had a headache nearly all day. Aternoon sister R had company Mr Brazee called to make her a visit. Meeting appointed here but no one came excepting br Harrison, B Horner at the city. Br Harrison proposed laying our hands on the table as an experiment to see whether we were any of us mediums. Accordingly we gathered around it seven of us, kept our hand on it half an hour before we perceived any motion. At length it commenced tipping and answering any question that we asked, either in the negative or affirmative just as we willed it. None of us believed there were any spirits about it, only those who were engaged in operating or looking at it. It made upon the whole a good deal of sport for us.

Friday 28th I ironed, sewed some. F rode to the garden. After she returned I got on the horse and rode a short distance, which was the first time I had been on horseback in six months.

Sat 29th Very warm day. I baked and boiled salt meat and vegetables for dinner. Frank had trouble with his team. The mules took fright and pulled a post out of the shed, to which they were tied, and ran off with it into the mustard. F got some hurt, but not seriously. They got them back, and they got away the second time. They However succeeded in securing them safely in harness. In the evening we had quite a time burning straw and mustard, the house was almost surrounded with fire, but no injury done to anything.

Sun Oct 30th Parley Evans came up to see Alma. They concluded to take a ride to the mission and get some grapes. Mr and Mrs Riser and Frank also went in the wagon. Sister R invited me to accompany them, but I declined in consequence of having the toothache. J Dier and H Clark called. Br Morris also came along and rode out with us to meeting. Br Harrison called took dinner and accompanied us to meeting. Br Horner was at San F. no one came excepting us, we sang a hymn and came home. In the evening C Allen and J Foxall were in. Charles was very sociable, but James was very sober, scarcely spoke only as he was interrogated upon some subject.

Mon 31st. F rode out to br Nicol's. Mr C finished hauling his wheat. Frank brought home a new accordion, which he purchased at Union city for 8 dolls. Br Farnsworth called, took supper with us. he took our bundle of letters; he seemed to have a deal of trouble in disposing of several animals which they left here last summer. Said he intended to dispose of them that night at all events.

[Burning the Fields]

Tues Nov 1st 1853. Last night we had the greatest fire I ever saw. The men set fire to the straw and mustard, and burned over a large wheat field. It was very still, yet the fire roared several times resembling thunder. Whirlwinds would occasionally get into it , and carry the blaze to a great height. We all went on the upper verandah where we could see it plainly.

F and Alma intended taking a ride to Morey's today, but Mr C concluding to go to the city tomorrow, discouraged them,. F Frances had some preparations to make in order to accompany him. The men commenced digging late potatoes this 1st of Nov.

Br and sister Riser were in this evening a few minutes.

Wed 2nd This morning we arose early. Alma went down to Cheny's to tell Parley Evans to be ready to accompany her, F to the city, as his mother wished him to return with her. He came over and told her that the boys wished him to stay untill friday when John was going down, and he would accompany him.

After breakfast they set off. Alma went with them to bring the team and wagon back. I expect to be very lonesome in their absence. A returned at 12 oclock. Said the steamer had not arrived when he left. That his father and Frances went into Mr Denis to await its arrival.

Only three of us to eat dinner. The boys have gone to their work and I am alone in the house. This evening I read untill 9 oclock, chemistry

Thurs 3rd We arose rather later than usually. I hastened to get the breakfast, and went to washing. Alma brought the principal part of the water. I cleaned the floors, after I finished the washing. It kept me very busy all day. Evening came I some expected br Horner would have a meeting here but no one came, except br Harrison who merely called a moment on business. I amused myself by reading singing and playing the accordian. Frank played his upstairs with Alma, and Jonah's help.

Friday 4th Frank arose earlier than usually, made the fire and called us. I arose at half past 5 oclock, got breakfast near six. Alma made preparations to go to meet his father and F at Union city, but the men did not bring up there so that he could leave untill near 9 oclock. After he was gone I baked meat, made 8 mince pies, and 4 loaves of bread. It kept me very busy, through the day. Just as Fr[ank] and I were sitting down to dinner Eben Dyer called in, said he was very unwell and unable to work, thought he would call around to see his friends. I invited him to eat dinner with us, gave him a cup of tea, and a piece of pie, which was all he wished.

[Alfred's Return to his Parents]

About 2 oclock Mr C and Alma arrived with neither F nor Alfred. I was considerably disappointed to see neither of them. Mr C said F was obliged to stay in order to see her physician, as he was so busy, that she could not get him to come to see her while he was there; and that br Layton was going to the San Bernardino and had concluded to take Alfred with him.

I must confess that I felt quite sad for a while to think of giving him up entirely. But when I reflected that he was in the care of his parents who undoubtedly had still more tender feelings for him than I had, I tried to reconcile my mind by reflecting that they were all happy in each other society, and I would give mysefl no further uneasiness on his account. Mr C brought home several articles of provision sugar, butter, ham &C Br Riser was in this evening, I read some in the pacific. Retired at 9, was very tired, slept soundly untill 5 in the morning. Breakfasted beteween 6 and 7 oclock. After which I churned, and Ironed, moped the diningroom, and various other little jobs such as making preserves &C About 3 oclock Capt Scot drove up with his carriage, and two ladies, one of which I soon discovered to be Frances, and the other on being introduced proved to be a miss Scot—— a niece of the Captains, late from the eastern states. The capt had found F ~~there~~ at Union city and offered to bring her home, accordingly took her up to his house to see his niece, and then brought them both over here. I fancied the appearance of the young lady much.

Br Dustin called, said he had been making fence on disputed land, for a Mr Scribner, and that one of the squatters had threatned his life if he did not desist, and leave. Said he was going to Union city, and intended to have him brought to trial.

Sunday 6th Alma went to br Cheny's to see Parley Evans, and invited him over here, he came and staid only a short time. I wished to know when he was going home, and engaged him to carry Alfreds clothes to him. He said he intended to go the next day, and would take them along. Accordingly I put them in a bundle, wrote him quite a lengthy letter, and after meeting Alma carried them down. Father Morris called in and rode out with us to meeting. Frances and Alma went on horseback, sis Riser and myself rode in the wagon with the men.

Soon after our arrival at the house of worship, we discovered a company of men bringing a corpse to the burying ground Mr Horner invited us all to go out to the grave. I did not learn the mans name, but understood that it was an old gentleman who had been cook for Blaco.

After the burying, we all returned to the house. Mr C spoke to the people on the subject of testimony, And endeavored to show what testimony the Lord required us to believe, whenever he established or ushered in a new dispensation The sacrament was administered by Mr Horner, meeting closed by br Duncan. I felt well pleased with the meeting, felt that the good spirit was with us. Br Morris, and Dougherty came home with us, br D took supper. John Cheny was here in the evening, had music on the violin flute and accordian.

[Frances's 19th Birthday]

Monday 7th This is Frances birthday. She washed her own cloths cleaned her room; and kept herself very busy all day. I think she appears much smarter now than she did before she went to the city the last time. She got a new recruit of medicine which probably helps her. Monday evening Mr C is mending my accordian. Frank is playing his up chamber. Time passes off rather lively than otherwise. Br Duncan called this afternoon. Mr C was not in. I had some conversation with him. He said he was going to br Lloyds to stay overnight, as he had never made them a visit, and *Tuesday the 8th* intended going to San Francisco. Frances is Ironing to day, Nothing transpired worth relating.

 Wednesday 9th I washed in the forenoon, got dinner, cleaned floors &C F took a walk over to br Harrison's. Said sister H would visit us next day.

 Thurs 10th Sister Pratts birthday. I ironed. We expected sister H but she did not come. H Davis and Margaret Emily called to see Frances, The young man is out of health.

 Friday 121th quite cloudy, some rain last night. I worked out in the morning cleaning the dooryard and round the hen house, feeding chickens &C, untill I felt quite fatigued. Baked bread and pies, boiled beef, pork and vegetables, for dinner. About noon Sister Nicols called, said she had been to visit a sick child of Mr Allens one of our neighbours. She staid a short time, took dinner with us, and returned. Towards evening I had the headache, probably took a little cold working without my bonnet.

 Br Riser his wife Frances and myself had quite a time trying to drive the hens from the shed to the henhouse. This evening Sister Riser called in with a Spanish woman a Mrs Baker, whom she had been making a silk dress for, came in to see how we liked the fit, and fashion. Mrs B wished F to make a dress of white muslin for a little child belonging to a friend of hers, which child she said, she intended to baptise the next sabbath and wished to make it a present of a suit of clothes. It is a practice among the catholics in California, for the God parents of a child to baptise it, and also to assist its parents in supporting it if necessary. It seemed a great curiosity to me, and a very strange idea, that any people conversant with the bible, and professing to believe its teachings, should so far stray from the written words of God, as to suffer females, holding no authority whatever, to baptise.

Sat 12th Quite cloudy and dull through the day. Evening came. Frank brought down his accordion. Mr C played the violin, Alma the flute, and we had some singing which passed of the evening quite merrily. C Allen was in a while.

Sunday morning 13th day Frances and Alma gone to Mr Horners. Mr Little and a Mr Jones (who came to the country with Mr L) called and spent 2 or 3 hours. Alma left F and went to the mission, got the Cincinnatti papers, and returned precisely at 12 oclock. At half past one we set off for the afternoon meeting, accompanied by Sister Riser and the children. F came from br Horners with Margaret on horseback. Br Horner spoke upon the Sabbath, and showed that it was typical of the great sabbath of rest, when Christ should reign with his saints on earth a thousand years. We returned home a little before sunset, got supper and prepared to go to evening meeting, got the horses harnassed and after consulting sometime upon the expediency of trying the muddy road in the evening with a lot of ladies, Mr C concluded we had better stay at home. Accordingly he went on foot and alone. Returned at 9 oclock said no one attended but the family, excepting himself. Frank Rose, Frances, Alma and myself, spent the evening in reading, singing, playing the accordion, and conversing. Time passed off quite agreeably.

Mon 14th I arose at 6 oclock, felt very dull and lame. After breakfast Blithe called. I bought stockings, and a vest for Mr C. About 10 oclock it commenced raining, and continued untill near night. Mr C made two traps for catching rats. Br R was in, and took one of them into his apartment. We understand that there has been a decision made by the court with regard to the land titles in Cal. And that the most of the spanish claims are valid. But it is thought that Beard and Horner will not hold theirs, or at least not all of it.[32] Music this evening on the violin

Tuesday 15th Rain in the forenoon. I cut two vests, and made one, for Alma, Mr Riser was in this evening, said he had secured two qr sections of land that day, one for himself and one for Naile.

Wednesday 16th quite dull weather. I made another vest. Mr C and Alma went to Union city to get themelves boots. Got me a pair of shoes. Came home in the rain. Charles Allen was in this evening. We had music on the violin and accordion, had some singing.

Frances had a very strange turn of feeling dizzy headed, and nearly lost the use of her limbs, she made no complaint for sometime, untill I noticed that she did not appear natural, and questioned her with regard to her feelings. She thought it was the effects of her taking blue pills, she had taken one for four nights in succession said they affected her in the same manner once when she was at the city. Mr C was just going to bed. I spoke to him to make a fire, and warm water to bathe her feet. I was some alarmed hardly knew what course to pursue. In the first place I bathed her head, face, and hands, with camphor, and gave her a dose of pain-killer. I then bathed her feet in warm water made mustard drafts and put on them, and gave her summer savory tea. By this time she said she felt usualy well went to bed, I put a warm iron to her feet, in hopes of [*illegible crossout*] causing perspiration if possible. At half past ten I went to being very tired I soon droped to sleep. At twelve I awoke, got up and went into her room, she said she had slept soundly untill then, that she felt well. Accordingly I retired to my bed, but my nerves had become a little excited, and sleep had departed from me. I was very restless the remainder of the night.

Thursday 17th I washed. F, was about, smart as usualy, but had some fever, and slight headache. In the evening Henry Webster, and Margaret Emily called, spent an hour or two very agreeably to us at least. They said they had been taking an excursion on horseback, and concluded to call here and wait for the moon to rise.

Friday 18th dull rainy weather. I spent the day cooking baking had some of my clothes to wash over, in consequence of the horses.

Saturday 19th some rainy in the morning, faired off towards noon. I cooked beef and vegetables for dinner. Made pies &C. Afternoon sister Nicols called on us, staid two or three hours. We made her a cup of tea, and had a very sociable time. I finished my ironing while she was here.

Sunday 20th quite pleasant. F took a walk up to the mountains brought back bushes and flowers. Toward noon we recd a call from Mr Wm Morrison, and two of his sisters, Mrs Tison, and Mrs Shuck. At two oclock went to church, Mr Crosby Alma Mrs Riser and myself, had quite a full house. Brother Horner spoke upon the order of the gospel administered the sacrament, and gave an invitation to any one to come and be baptised. A gentleman and his wife from Santa clara came forward candidates. Accordingly we all repaired to br Chenys where the ordinance was administered with due solemnity. The sun was set before we arrived home. Frances wondered where we had been staying so long.

Mr Little was here, took supper with us.

[Addison Pratt's Mission]

Monday 21st I felt very dull and lame in consequence of taking a little cold the day before, Cooked dinner of salt meat and vegetables. Br Harrison called at night, said he thought his wife would visit us the next day. F got supper. Just as we had through Alma steped to the door and who should he meet but his uncle Pratt from San Bernardino. He turned around to F and said here is your father. We looked and it was him with his dog and gun, We were much surprised at seeing him. He informed us that he was again on his way to the islands he and br Grouard had been sent to try to cheer and gladden the hearts of the poor islanders, who are groaning under bondage. But he also informed us that they felt somewhat disheartened with regard to their mission having seen brethren from that country at San Francisco, and they counseled them not to go, as they thought it be the means of their having the chains bound still closer.

He told us many things about San Bernar. Said he was somewhat fatigued having walked from Br Morey's. We made him a fresh cup of tea, got him some supper.

Frances was quite overjoyed at seeing him. He brought letters from Ellen to her. Said br Grouards wife had left him and gone back to Tahiti.

Tues 22nd he took his dog and gun went out and shot two geese. We cooked them or one of them for supper. Sister Harrison came, as we expected. We had a fine visit. Bro H was at work for br Riser, he came in and took supper with us, and spent the evening.

Wed 23rd I washed, had a fine day. Bro Pratt went out again, but said it was so clear, that he could not get near enough to reach them. I got my washing out before noon. F got dinner, after which she and her father took a walk to br Nicols. I cleaned the floors, tended the chickens and kept myself busy untill about 3 oclock, when I changed my clothes and sat down to write a few lines in my journal.

Br P and F did not return at night as we expected. We spent the evening in playing a little on the accordion, Alma and myself. Mr C taught Frank to spell, he seems quite anxious to learn.

Thursday 24th Just as I had got dinner nearly ready, F came with two ducks, her father had been out and shot them in the lagoon. I had a goose baked for dinner. Just before we sat down Miss D A Morrison came in and took dinner with us. She and her sister Mrs Tison were at br Risers on a visit. After dinner we were invited in to visit with them, we went enjoyed the time remarkably well. Mrs T informed us that she had heard by a man who had been towards Oregon, that Mr Naile was on his way home, and had a wife with him.[33] We also learned from br P that a large co was coming through by the south pass, with large herds of sheep and cattle, and we think it more than probable that br N is in the co. It was thanksgiving day. One year ago we, sis R, F and I, were at Moreys, in co with br N[aile] on a visit. ^This evening Mr Jones Dire brough us a letter from sister Lois Thomson^ About 8 oclock in the evening br Grouard arrived. Mr C had gone to bed, and we were not expecting to see any one from a distance at that time of night. But he arose, and sat up an hour or two.

Friday 25th it was very rainy. Br G staid 'till after dinner. The conversation ran principally upon the philosephy of A J Davis, in whose writings br G. seems highly interested, had one of his books with him. In the afternoon he went to Moreys to see br Pratt, left his book here for us to read in his absence. I like it very well as it seems to be founded on reason.[34]

Saturday 26th Very rainy. I mended and repaired shirts and stockings in the forenoon. Mr C and Alma got in potatoes. Towards noon it rained so hard that the men were obliged to come in. Just before supper br Pratt and Grouard arrived from Moreys. We had very sociable times the forepart of the evening. Br G—— was full of philosophy, and A J Davis. At half past 8 he proposed that we should unite in laying our hands on the table to see whether we had any influence accordingly we took it into the stoveroom, and seated ourselves around it seven of us in number, but after sitting about 40 minutes and perceiving no motion we gave it up, and concluded we had no power.

Sunday 27th Quite rainy in the morning. Br Morris came over and brought us letters. Br Horner ~yet~ being absent and it being very rainy and bad roads they concluded to stay at home, instead of going out to the schoolhouse. Hiram Clark[35] called. Conversation ran upon philosophy and religion.

Sunday evening John Cheny was in. Mr Little staid over night with us. John played the violin. Mr C—— the flute, and Frank the accordion, quite a little band.

Mon 28th Very pleasant day. After breakfast br P and G left for Moreys. Br G—— bade us goodbye as he intends going to the mining regions before he returns. F and I washed. Towards night br P returned with his bundle of dirty clothes. Heard br Horner had come home from SF—— and as he and br G wished to see him he concluded that he would go back to Moreys for him. Accordingly he arose very early *Tuesday 29th* and went to Moreys, got G—— and came up to br H'——s but he had gone again, so they did not see him. Br P arrived here about 10 oclock, said he was mad. After dinner he and F went off on a hunting and fishing excursion to the creek about a mile from here, returned just at dark, with one duck and 3 fish. I have been writing to sister Lois Th. Re'cd a letter from her a few days since, Also re'd one from sis P last sunday, written since her husb left.

[Sociable Occasions]

Wed 30th and last day of Nov 1853. We had a baked goose for dinner I ironed in the forenoon. Afternoon F—— and I went to visit sister Harrison. We prepared everything in order for supper, left br P to preside, and make the tea; after supper he and Mr C—— and Frances came over to spend the evening with us. Frances and I left home a little past two oclock, took a straight course through the fields, found it rather rough and tiresome walking, but soon arrived at our destined place, when on knocking at the door discovered there was no one at home, we were quite disappointed. I was very tired, and did not feel willing to leave the house untill I had rested myself a while. Accordingly we opened the door went in and set down. There was a very savage looking dog lying at the door, the first sight of which made me hesitate some about going in, but as he made no objections to our entering we felt quite safe. We then concluded to go over to Christopher Knoler's and endeavor to ascertain where Harrison's people were. On arriving there Mrs Brazee the houseke[eper] told us they had all gone to br Nicols, went early in the morning. She invited us to stay with her untill evening, when br Ha—— people would undoubtedly be at home. Accordingly we staid and spent the afternoon very agreeably. Charles Allen was there and a young man by the name of Samuel Mires [Myers] one of the morm battallion boys, late from the gold mines, he appears like a very civil wellbred young man. After supper we invited Mrs B to accompany us to br Harisons, to which she readily consented, just as we were about to leave our gentlemen called for us. C Allen had informed them at the door, that we were there. We found br H. and family at supper.

Sister H said she was quite sorry that she happened to be absent, and hoped we would take the trouble to come again. The gents proposed that br H—— should try his gift at tipping the table, as he professes to be a medium. Mr C, Pratt, and myself, sat down with him, untill we got the table charged. We found that we could spell any name that we chose to unite our mind upon. We made quite a laughable affair of it, convinced ourselves that it was the minds or spirits of the living instead of the dead that operated upon the table. It was ten oclock when we got home. F—— looked much fatigued and said she felt weak. She however seemed usually well the next day, and *Thurs Dec 1st* it being very pleasant, we (accompanied by sis Riser) went to Mr Tisons, on a visit. We enjoyed the time very agreeably. F and I returned at sunset, sis R spent the evening, with her husband.

Frid—— 2nd, very pleasant. br P is helping Mr C about his potatoes; expects to finish them today. I ironed 7 shirts this forenoon for br P. This evening br Dougherty came soon after we ate supper. And as he had not been to supper, I made him a cup of tea. We had a very sociable time conversing upon philosophy, ~~and~~ astronomy, and theology. Br D—— staid over night, said he was making preparations to commence farming operations next monday, in co with J Dire and J A Bagley.

Sat 3rd br P went early on a hunting and fishing excursion was gone all day. F—— and I baked bread and cakes, and prepared for sunday. I finished my letter to Sister Lois. Br P did not return untill after supper, said he was led some distance into the mountains by a man who was hunting deer, but found none, he brought home 3 birds and a duck, besides a few small fishes. The duck was a remarkably handsome one, he skined the head, dried and stuffed it. The birds were also very pretty. One was a quail, one a yellow hammer, and the other a California blue Jay. Mr C finished hauling in potatoes this afternoon and dismissed Frank Rose his last hired man. F—— said he could not refrain from shedding tears when he thought of leaving us, that he never expected to find a place where he should feel himself as much at home, as he did here. He asked me and Frances to bring forward our bills against him as we had done some washing and mending for him, and he wished to satisfy us for it. We told him we had no demands against him, but on the contrary I told him I intended to make him a present of a pair of shirts as soon as I could make them, he seemed very thankful and said he should try to make me some present.

Sunday morning Dec 4th 1853 It is a beautiful pleasant day. The mountains and valley are becoming quite green and fresh. Alma went the mission with my letter to Nauvoo. Got one for Mr Little. Br J Dyer called a few moments. Towards noon came br Morris. At two oclock we went to church, accompanied by br P, br Morris, C Allen, Bagley, and sis Riser. Fr and Alma rode on horseback. Br Horner did not arrive untill after the meeting was opened. Mr C opened the meeting by singing reading, and prayer, after which br P. spoke upon the subject of his mission to the islands, and was succeeded by br H and Mr C——. Thier counsel was that they should wait untill they could get further intelligence from the islands respecting the state of political affairs.[36] Sister Brazee came along and accompanied us to church.

Mon 5th Mr C and Alma got wood. Frank and br P washed. At night we made up our minds to go to br Moreys the next day.

Tues. 6th br P went very early on a hunting excursion, did not return untill after breakfast, when he came with two geese. About ten oclock we set off for br Moureys, left Alma to keep house and dress the fowls. Arrived at M's about 12 oclock, found all well. The old gent was making a chimney. We staid untill about 4 oclock, when Mr C and myself left and went on business to Beards landing, called at Capt Mayhue's, but did not get out of the wagon. The capt was not at home, but his agent was there. It was a beautiful moonlight night. We arrived home at 7 oclock, but F—— and her father staid intending to go to San francisco in a day or two as br P was very anxious that she should see Dr Winslow.

Wed 7th I washed. Baked a goose for dinner. Mr C commenced work on the house. I kept myself very busy through the day.

Thurs 8th I ironed, towards night made mince pies. Baked them in the evening. I felt quite fatigued when I got my work done, and concluded

I would go to rest earlier than usually. Accordingly we retired a little after 8 oclock. We had not been in bed long before some one knocked at the. Mr C asked who was there, and was answered a "friend" when I discovered that it was br Grouard. He had just come from the city in search of br P. intending to take Moreys boat, and as he was not here, he said he would go to M's that night. Accordingly he left about 9 oclock.

Friday 9th just as we were sitting down to dinner, arrived br P, Grouard, Frances, and Sis Morey. Br P—— and F had given up the idea of going to the city at present. After dinner sister Morey proposed that we should take a ride over to br Harrisons and make a short visit. Br G agreed to accompany us, as escort. We left about two oclock, had a very pleasant ride and visit, found them well and washing. But the tubs were soon put out of the way and we had a very pleasant time. Conversation turned upon spirit rappings, and the philosophy of A J Davis. We took tea by candlelight, and returned soon after. In the evening sis M and I went in to see Sister Riser. We slept together. It was a very rainy night and the wind blew exceedingly. Sis M was rather restless.

Sat 10th we visited at br Horners, set off at ten oclock with Alma for teamster, sis R with both her children sis M and myself. We had not proceeded far when on crossing a wheatfield the horses became balky and refused to go. Our com soon got frightened, and we sent Alma back to get a man to come to our assistance. Charles Allen chanced to be on hand and br P sent him, he had some difficulty in getting them started, and off the stubble ground, but as soon as they got into the road they went very well. Sister M however said she dared not trust Alma to drive them, accordingly he went back. We had a long cold muddy ride, arrived at twelve oclock.

We had a good visit, was highly entertained, took tea twice, took a little walk in the garden, and returned home. It was quite showery all day, but nothing to hurt us. On arriving home found Frances had 8 men here to supper. Br Riser and his hired man <u>Frank</u> in consequence of sis R's absence, had taken dinner and supper with us, also a strange gent from Capt M's took dinner here. After supper it faired off, and br G concluded it best for them to return to Moreys. She said if they were willing she would like to return that night.

At 7 oclock the moon shone bright and they set off.

Sun 11th It was quite fair. Mr Little was here, staid ^the last^ last night. Alma went to the P—— O. Got two papers, and a letter for Mr L. We attended meeting at two oclock. Br H—— was absent, went to Santaclara to hold church.

Mr C conducted the meeting. Br Morris spoke to the people. And spoke well, After which Mr C made a short address, Br M closed the meeting. J Cheny J. Dier and Charles Allen were in the evening.

Mon 12th rather cloudy and unpleasant. We received a visit from Mrs Edmunds, and Mrs Brazee, they spent the afternoon and evening. Br and sis Riser took supper with us, also S Miers and C Allen. We had the large table full. The evening passed off quite agreeably, but the co were under the necessity of going home in the rain. We invited them to stay over night, which they declined.

Tues 13th Quite pleasant, I washed. F cooked dinner, Br Wheeler called and ate with us.

Wed 14th [*illegible crossout*] Very hard frost last night. This was Alma's birthday. He is now 17 years of age. I cleaned floors and did a little sewing. Two pedlars called.

Thurs—— 15th I ironed in the forenoon, in the afternoon we Frances and I visited at br Nicols. We found them all in a state of confusion, fixing their house. Br N has been building an addition, is now finishing it. I think it will look very nice, and be quite comfortable, when he finishes it. Mr C called in just before night, they invited us to stay and spend the evening. We staid a short time after supper, untill the moon got up so as to give us light, and then came home, which we reached at 7 oclock. The moon shone beautifully, and we had a very pleasant walk. ~~Thur~~ *Friday 16th* Quite cold and frosty. I cleaned house, got much fatigued. Towards evening, br and sis Harrison came, took supper with us, and spent the evening. We had a very good visit with them. Frances and br H are talking of a picknick party, which is to come off between Chrismas and newyear, at our house.

[A Young Lady's Illness]

Sat—— 17th Very pleasant weather. F went to visit a young lady, who is very sick at Capt Scots, a niece of theirs, set up with her all night. Says she is very low, but seemed a little better when she left. Came home this morning quite early. *Sun 18th* Very pleasant day. Frank went to Squatterville. We had no co in the forenoon. Went to church Mr C, Sis Riser and myself. Returning home met capt Scot, inquired after the young lady, he said he thought she was a little better, I offered to go and sit up with her, said he would be obliged to me, would send his carriage for me if I would come. A little before sunset came Sister Woodbury and br Morey. Took supper with us and staid untill the moon rose. Soon after supper the carriage came for me to go.

I found the young lady very low indeed, her eyes were stationary her throat and jaws so badly swollen that she could ~~not~~ open her mouth but very little, just sufficent to admit a teaspoon between her teeth, and it distressed her very much to swallow. They were under the necessity of keeping some one sitting by her continually, as she could not speak loud enough to be heard any distance. I watched her from ten untill five in the morning, without sleeping a wink. She seemed to revive a little in the course of the night. Said she could see better, seemed to be more reasonable, and spoke plainer. Her unkle and aunt are remarkably kind to her. They treated me with much politeness. The Capt sat up untill twelve oclock, when he retired, and one of his men took his place to keep fires. I had hot tea twice in the night. At 5 in the morning Mrs Scot arose and took my place. She insisted on my lying down and taking a sleep before I came home, which I did, and slept 3 hours. When I arose, she prepared me a warm breakfast, after which I was brought home in the carriage. It was a very cold night for this country; And the house being cold I felt much inconvenience from it. Dr Selfridge called twice while I was there, he seems very faithful, and attentive to her.

Monday 19th It was near ten when I reached home. I was very lame all day, and in the night I could scarcely turn myself in bed. I took a cold which was probably the cause. I bathed my back with Davises painkiller, put an old plaster on it, and it soon got better. Br Riser was in this evening. I retired at an early hour.

Tues 20th Mr C went to the embarkedera with barly and fowls. We had very little rain. It has been remarkbly dry this month as yet. I cut pantaloons for Alma. In the evening had a little spelling school. F made candy. Mr C read uncle Toms Cabin.

Wednesday 21st Very cold and windy. About 11 oclock I was sent for to go and assist in laying out Miss Scot. The messenger said she had just breathed her last breath as he left. I was considerably shocked at hearing of her death as we had understood that she was thought to be some better. I was assisted by two ladies who live at Mr Barnes's, an elderly woman by the name of Goodale, and her niece by the name of Mack. We found it a very unpleasant task as she was much mortified and scented very bad. But it was the last we could do for her, and we did it with goodwill.

The family felt very much afflicted at the loss of her society. I staid with them untill evening, when the man brought me home on horseback, as their carriage was gone to Union city. My nerves had become a little excited and I slept but very little through the night.

Thurs—— 22nd It is a beautiful pleasant day. I would have attended the funeral, but the men were busy with the teams, and none of them thought it their duty to go.

Accordingly F and I washed. I got through before dinner. Received a letter from br Dougherty. He seems to wish to excite our sympathies for his trials and afflictions, for some reason or an other. For one I certainly feel to compassionate his case, but have no means or power to afford him any relief. Having never heard the opposite side of his story I am not competent to judge between them. Mr P Morrison called this evening said he intended going with his sisters to San Fran to spend Chrismas.

Friday 23rd Ironed, Two pedlars called. F, sis R, and myself, bought calico dresses. Mr Foxall called to see about making preparations for the Chrismas party. Brought letter from br P to F. Spelling this evening.

[John Naile's Return]

Saturday 24th very pleasant in the afternoon, but a little rainy in the morning. I finished pantaloons for Alma. About 3 oclock Sis Riser came in and told us she expected Mr N would be here this evening. Br R had been to the landing and Capt Mayhew told him that he saw Mr Naile at the city the day previous.

We were all highly pleased at the intelligence, and began to tell it from one to the other. F and I began to set the house in order to the best of our abilities, and prepared supper, which was nearly ready, when he arrived. He looked just as natural as though we had seen him every day; seemed much pleased to get home, said the two preceeding nights had seemed a week long, in consequence of his impatience. He thought we had finished his house, ^and made it look^ much better than he expected we would. Told us concerning his journey, of the losses and misfortunes he had experienced. In consequence of starting the journey too late, his stock died for want of feed, that part that lived, he left in Salt lake valley with his parents, who accompanied him that far, and stoped with their oldest son. He had made all possible speed from there, left his team and wagon at Sanbernardino, and came up by water, his brother a young man of 22 or 3 came with him, intending to stay and carry on the place while he goes back to Salt lake in the spring. Says he intends going again in Feb. He arrived on Chrismas eve, left his br at Oakland, to come up in the stage next morning. Himself feeling anxious to get home that night hired a horse of an acquaintance, and came on horseback.

Sun 25th Very pleasant day. F and A went to Moreys with the wagon. I thought of going to church on horseback. But when the time came I concluded to stay at home, and Mr C rode. F and A returned at meeting time.

Sun afternoon while they were all away but myself George H[enry] Naile arrived. I knew him from his resembling his br. He came in and inquired if this was Mr Nailes house. I told him it was and asked if he was his brother, he replyed in the affirmative, and wished to know where he was said he expected to have met him at the schoolhouse where the stage left him. I told him that he had gone out for that purpose, but had probably missed him by some means. John Cheny called in the evening to see him, br N.

Mon 26th I washed. F cooked, weather continues pleasant. Br N brought me a line from Sis Pratt. Evening we had music, both instrumental and vocal.

Tues 27th I ironed F cooking again, and preparing for the party which is to come off on Wednesday evening. I made new white curtains for the windows. A pedlar staid with us over night. I bought pink ribbon of him to tie my curtains back. Music again and a little dancing among the young people.

Wed 28th some what cloudy and an appearance of rain. After breakfast Mr Harrison came with his wagon, and brought Mrs Brazee with a load of good things for the occasion. About 4 oclock the party assembled. We had the tables set before they arrived and tolerably well laden with the Harrisons liberal share. The most of them brought an abundance. Capt Band united with us and appeared highly pleased with the entertainment. About 12 oclock we had tea and coffee, with bread and butter cheese cakes and pies, and plenty of wines, and candies.

We danced untill four oclock in the morning, when the most of them left, but a few staid over night, among whom was br Wandell and sis Lincoln from San F. ^*Thurs 29th*^ We breakfasted at 8; after which they left, Sister Woodbury staid untill towards noon and Alma went home with her.

Afternoon Mr C and N had a settlement.

Br N seems to feel quite poor in consequence of his unsuccessful journey in attempting to bring stock across the plains, which together with the dull sale of crops has brought him under embarressments with regard to moneyd affairs. And Mr C finds himself in possession of almost a solemn nothing after himself and family have laboured hard a whole year. But these are only a common occurrence in human life, and it would not be wise for us to give way to dejection, or suffer ourselves to be cast down on the account. We have had quite a struggle in refraining from it, and for myself I think I have nearly overcome it. What the Lord has in store for us I know not; but I pray Him to give us strength to endure all things. We expect now to be under the necessity of seeking a new home. Where another year will find us I know not.

Friday 30th we had quite a task at cleaning house. Toward noon a musician called with a hand organ, and played very beautifully, we invited him to stop and take dinner. I felt very heavy hearted all day and music had little or no charms for me. At night my nervous system had become so excited that I slept very little.

Sat 31st and last day of 1853. I felt rather gloomy and disconsolate. Towards night F set off while I was in the kitchen without letting me know where she was going, or that she intended bringing any company home with her. After supper she returned with the Chenies and Delilah A Morrison and informed me that she had started up another party. J. Cheny left his first load and went over to Allens Harrisons and Edmunds after another. Br R Morey and Sis Woodbury also happened to come on a visit, and the room was well filled. 4 of the gents were fiddlers, so that they all had the privilege of dancing occasionaly.

We had tea with cakes pie and cheese between toward eleven. They all retired shortly after twelve, apparently much pleased with the entertainment. Delilah A M staid over night.

[1854: The Necessity of Moving]

Sun morning Jan 1st 1854 I found I had taken a very severe cold, my head and lungs were very much oppressed and upon the whole I was quite indisposed, so much so that I did not attend meeting. Mr C walked out. F and the two Mr. N——s rode on horse back. Br Morris called on his return from meeting, took supper with us. Mr Little staid with us saturday night. Br Morris brought us letters from the friends at San Bernardino. Mr Bagley was in, this evening. My cold was very oppressive, Mr C also has a bad cold.

Mon 2nd I felt some better, arose at the usual time. Mr C went early to Mr Horners, took breakfast there. Received an invitation to attend a party on tuesday evening. After breakfast I washed, but felt very unwell. F cooked dinner. After which she did her own washing. I spent an hour or two in writing.

Tuesday 3rd Shortly after breakfast Mr C came in and informed us that we were under the necessity of moving into Mr Risers apartment as they wished to come into to the large house to commence farming operations for the year. Accordingly we commenced gathering up our affairs, myself at work in one part of the house while F regulated the kitchen I cleared my bedroom, and then went into assist Sis Riser in picking up her things. We had quite a hard days work. But got through about four oclock, got supper and prepared ourselves for our evening's visit at br Horners. It was rather late when we got started, arrived just as they were taking supper, had rather a long cold ride. We had an excellent supper and very good dance, the party adjourned at 12 oclock. Frances staid over night. I came home rather heavy hearted, not knowing where our location would be for another year. Bro H gave Mr C no encouragement of work or situation, said he was not building any in the city at present. The house seemed rather dark and lonely the first night.

The next day *Wed—— 4th* I ironed and tried to regulate the house to my mind My cold was very bad. Towards evening Henry N[aile] went after Frances, he made a short stay and returned in the forepart of the evening. Mr Bagley called in, talks of buying Mr C's potatoes, went out with his gun, shot two geese, made me a present of one of them.

Thurs 5th Mr C set off at an early hour in the day intending to go to San Francisco, Alma went with a wagon and carried him to Capt Mayhew's landing where he expected to take a launch bound for the city; took along a fat hog for sale, but on arriving at the landing he found no boat ready to sail and concluded to return and wait untill another day rather than pay 3 dolls to go on the steamer, as money was rather scarce with him. In the evening the young men from the other house were in H N and Frank Rose, cards were brought forward for diversion, F and her unkle were playing when they came and they readily joined. This was my birthday 47 years old.

Friday 6th I whitewashed the house, felt very much fatigued and unwell all day. ^Very high winds all day^ Mrs Brazee called and took supper with us, she complimented us very much upon the improvement we had made in the house. H N and F R were in, again, we had reading and spelling writing and arithemetick. J C N came in and joined with us in spelling and arithmetick.

Saturday 7th I whitewashed again, made it look much better the second time. After I got through we put up pictures and other curiosities in the ornamental line and found our room wore altogether another aspect. It was much admired by our evening visitors, who examined the curiosities and made many complimentary remarks upon the internal improvements of our habitation. We had music on the violin, and a few songs with many cheerful remarks by Mr Bagley and others. Eben Dyer called and staid over night.

Sun the 8th Very pleasant warm weather I arose with my mind quite composed with regard to our future situation. I desire to trust in the Lord and do good, and I believe we shall verily be fed, as the scripture declares. I find there is nothing so important in a saint as humility. I am also convinced that those who possess the most property are not always the most happy. And I believe it quite possible for persons even in poverty to be measurably happy. This morning Frances went to the Mission with Henry Naile. It was the first time she had attended the catholic church, and thought it a great curiosity.

From thence they went to Mr Horners, stoped, took dinner, and went to our meeting. Mr C Alma myself went in the wagon. Br Morris came along and rode with us. On arriving at the schoolhouse found there had been a funeral there, it was just closing as we arrived, and the people were coming out with the corpse, whom we understood to have been a young man by the name Smith, had been sick some 5 years had probably come to Cal—— for his health, and was now dead. His funeral was attended by a methodist preacher, we all accompanied them to the grave, and saw him restored back to his mother earth. It served to solemnize my mind and prepare it to listen with renewed diligence to the words of eternal life as set forth by br Horner at the afternoon church; his discourse was principally an enhortation to saints to persevere in the ways of well doing, and try to keep up with the church, lest peradventure we might find ourselves far in the rear, and our minds become so darkened that we should not be able to judge between truth and error, and our religion appear quite a different thing from what we thought it to be when we first espoused it. He administered the sacrament meeting closed by Mr C. In the evening called Mr O[rigin] Morey and Miss D[elina] Cheny, on an evenings excursion. We had a very lively sociable time, the moon shone very beautifully. They left at about 8 oclock.

[Looking for Work]

Mon 9th Mr C set off intending to go to San Francisco but was a little too late for the boat, and consequently returned after going to capt Mayhew's and finding no launch going. He was quite fatigued and rather depressed in spirit on returning, as he could hear of no chance for work or a situation for us. Soon after he left in the morning, Frances went to Mr Cheny's. In the course of the day Jo[hn] Cheny called and left an invitation for the boys to come down in evening as they intended dancing a little.

Afternoon Sister Nicols called up a little while with 3 children, made a short stay. When she left I accompanied her almost to Tison's. She wanted F to come and stay with her a week, to assist her in quilting. I told her I thought she would visit her the next day, as she intended doing so when she left. We Mr C and myself spent the evening alone as Alma went with the boys to Cheny's.

Tues 10th Mr C went to Union city, to see what discoveries he could make in that place, called on br [Isaac] Nash took dinner, But found no opening, or encouragement, from that quarter. He saw Capt Mayhew and proposed going on to his ranch. Cap told him he had only a small house on it at present, but that he intended moving the one he then lived in at the landing on to the ranch, and that if he expected to stop there himself he should be highly pleased with the idea. While he was gone I washed, felt very gloomy and dejected all day. Mr J C N went to San Francisco, this morning. In the evening Henry N. and Frank were in, had quite a sociable time with them.

Henry N seems to be of a very frank lively turn of mind, quite different from his brother. I had a very restless night; scarcly slept an hour, for some cause or an other I hardly knew what. My heart was apparently as heavy as lead, Gloomy forebodings of trouble distressed my mind, and caused sleep (the great soother of every woe) to depart from me.

Wed the 11th we arose at an early hour. I prepared breakfast for Mr C as he intended leaving for San F. He set off between 7 and 8 expecting to reach the boat and sail at ten. I baked pies and ironed, after he left. Frances and Miss Cheny came along, going to Mr Allens, and called for me, but I felt so unwell that I could not consistently go, and declined the invitation. After I got through ironing I lay down and took quite a sleep. When I awoke it was dark. I heard the men with their teams, and thought it was morning, and that I had slept all night. But arose and found I was mistaken. Alma had let the fire all die away, and it took some time to start it. We however got it to burning, and I got out the accordion to endeavor by some means to while away the gloomy hours of evening.

A took the instrument and commenced playing, when soon came Frank, with his. I got the flute for A, as the accordions would not cord, and we had considerable music. I sang two or three tunes with them, and found my spirits quite revived.

In the course of the evening called F Silver and smoked a cigar with F Rose. As soon as they left I resumed writing.

Thurs 12th Last night I slept very well; although it seemed rather lonely with no one in the house, but Alma and myself. I arose rather late. After breakfast finished a dress for myself. Br Harrison called. I had quite a sociable time with him.

Mr N returned from San F just after sunset, said he didnot see Mr C, but heard he had arrived previous to his leaving. Alma and myself spent the evening alone. He played the violin and I sang a little, and read some, and the time passed away.

Friday 13th I was awakened by feeling the cold rain dropping down upon my bed, my shoulders were quite wet, and the clothes were wet through to the tick. I found it was earlier than I choose to rise, accordingly placed the washing tub on my bed to catch the water and laid down again. I laid untill Alma got the fire started, which took him some time, as the wind was wrong for the stove to draw, and the house was filled with smoke. Br Riser came in to assist him in starting the fire, the rain came in upon us in several places, and there was quite a quantity in the stove.

He finally succeeded in getting it to burning, and I arose and got our breakfasts. I then had quite a task to dry the bedding. F's bed and mine were both very wet. I got the clothes dry made the beds and set down to sewing finished a shirt for Alma. Afternoon I went in and sat awhile with sis Riser. The sun shone out, and it became quite pleasant again. Little Kit R[iser] followed me home, staid and eat supper with us, her father called for her and found her asleep and on the bed. In the course of the evening the wind arose and blew the smoke into the house at a great rate. We were under the necessity of opening the door, and discontinuing our fire, which made the house cold and unpleasant. Alma spent the evening in reading. I in writing.

My heart by some means or another, has become disburthened of a load, which it has carried about for several days.

Sat 14th Last night was a very rainy and unpleasant. The wind blew so hard that we could not keep a fire in the stove in consequence of smoke, I put my shawl around me, sat and read awhile, and then went to bed. It was not long before it commenced raining, and I was obliged to get up and set a pail on my bed to catch the rain. I was very restless the forepart of the night, but at last I fell asleep, and slept very late in the morning. It was ten oclock before we ate our breakfast. It was a cold rainy day, I could hardly keep fire enough to be comfortable. About 4 oclock Mr C returned from San F—— and informed us that he had engaged a house on Horners new purchase, and intended moving down next week.[37] I was well pleased with his prospects, and thankful that he had been so fortunate as to get so good an offer. Br Horner told him he believed it would be a first rate chance for him, to use his own words. In the evening Fr—— and Henry were in a little while.

Sun 15th toward noon Frances came with John and Delina Cheny. They staid and spent the afternoon with us. We went into Mr Risers awhile, after which Mr Naile came in to our apartment and took supper with us. We had a very agreeable time with them. Mr C went to br Lloyds for a trunk and other articles which he left there the day before, returned just before supper.

Sun evening Frank Rose came in to get Alma to play the violin in com with himself who played the accordian. J C N who played the guitar, his br played some clappers.

[Leaving the San Jose Valley]

Mon 16th Very rainy and unpleasant. Frances and I washed as we expect to stay only two days longer. We all feel sorry to leave this valley, we think it the most pleasant place we ever lived in. This evening we expected br Naile in to have a settlement before we left, but he did not come in consequence of having the teethache.

Tues 17th It was rather pleasant. I ironed my clothes and Frances, while she packed her trunks and did some baking. Mr C went to capt Mayhew's; returned about noon.

Mr Little called in the afternoon, staid and took supper with us. He is a man that we all admire very much, for his upright and honorable conduct. He also seems to think something of us. Made us several presents of articles that he did not wish to move, as he intended going to Shasta to his nephews residing there. In the evening br N came in and we had our affairs settled in an amiable manner. He staid sometime and was very sociable. Frances spent the evening in with Mrs Riser.

Wed 18th We commenced packing our things, kept very busy all day, got every thing in good shape.

In the course of the afternoon br N came in and invited us to come to a party at his house this evening. Said he had made one particularly on our account as we expected to leave so soon. I thanked him for his politeness, and told him I supposed it would be the last we should enjoy in this place. Fr went in and assisted Sis R in making cakes and pies. Toward evening it commenced raining and proved to be a very dark rainy night, and the party did not convene. Henry N came in and expressed much disappointment. Soon after sis R came and invited us to come and bring the violin in there. But I told her I did not think we should be likely to go tomorrow, and they could have party tomorrow evening. They however insisted upon our going in, and accordingly we all went. They soon organized a sort of a band. Mr C played the violin Mr N the guitar Alma the accordian, Frank used a tin pan for a tamborin Henry Naile kept time with bone clappers, which made more sport than music. We finally all repaired to the large room, and the most of them commenced waltzing and dancing french fours and they kept it up untill ten oclock. They had cherry brandy with cakes and pies nuts and &C. After dancing as long as they wished H and J C N—— and C Noler sang duch [German, *deutsch*] songs for an hour or more. They all enjoyed themselves apparently well. The rain ceased before bedtime.

Thurs 19th We arose early and prepared to take our departure. It was quite a pleasant sky, but very cold and the ground frozen hard. Frances and I wished to call on sister Nicols and concluded we would start on ahead of the load, and give her a call. We accordingly set off, we found the walking muddy, as it had began to thaw. The wind seemed to increase, and we knew it would be very uncomfortable riding on the load to Union city. We therefore determined in our own minds to invite br Nicols to take us with his wagon. We met him at the door and I made known to him our desires he seemed to hesitate a little said he was just going to ploughing. I told him I would give him his price, for his services but he said the money would be no object, if he went it would be merely to accommodate us. I felt sorry to trouble him, but could not well avoid it. We had a very sociable time with Sis N. she made us a cup of tea, which warmed, and prepared us to proceed on our way. At twelve oclock he had his team in readiness, and we set off. We found the road somewhat muddy, and the wind extremely cold. I think I was never more chilled in my life. Frances also complained very much. We arrived at br Nashes at two oclock. Neither of us knew his house, consequently br N enquired at the hotel and was directed to the one next above the ball alley. They have a new house, two stories high. The lower part is occupied for a wagon and blacksmith shops. Br N—— was not in when we arrived. Sister Nash was very little acquainted with us, having never seen Frances or br Nicols. And me but once, she however recollected me, and treated us with much kindness and politeness. We sat sometime by the stove when br Nash came in. He welcomed us to his dwelling, and treated us with brotherly kindness. For which May the Lord bless him and his.

We had been there near an hour, when Mr Naile Crosby and Alma arrived. They started sometime before we did, but we had missed of them somewhere.

The steamer came in just as they arrived, accordingly they put the goods immediately on board, and came up to br N[ash]'s. They complained very bitterly of the cold. Mr C and Alma had walked nearly all the way, and had not suffered as much as the teamsters.

Mr Naile and Nicols, left us and returned about 4 oclo. We spent the evening very agreeably. Mr Little called in and took his things that we brought him. He made me a present of 3 linen towels, wished us much success and left Sister Nash parted her bed. Br N. Crosby, and Alma slept together. Sister, Frances, and myself. It was a severe cold night, but we slept very well, and late in the morning.

Friday 20th, the weather was still very cold, many of the old sett[l]ers said they had never known it so cold in Cal. The ground froze hard and continued so all day. We were expecting the steamer to leave at 7 oclock AM but it was delayed as I afterwards learned waiting for Mrs Horner, untill the evening tide. At 5 oclock she gave her signal for leaving; accordingly we took leave of our friends, and went on board. But after a fruitless attempt in consequence of low water, they gave it up for the night. We were issued into the cabin where we found ourselves very comfortably situated. The Capts wife was on board going to San Francisco. We had seen her before and had some acquaintance with her, and were therefore glad of her company. After supper Frances requested her uncle to conduct her to see a friend of hers nearby. They were gone an hour or two. I was very sleepy and dull untill they returned. Br Cheny spent a part of the evening with us. The capt and Clerk also. The name of the former is Allen Treefry [Trefry] and the latter Whipple.

CHAPTER TEN

San Francisco, Horner's Addition

Journal, 21 January 1854 to 21 June 1855

[Docking in San Francisco]

Saturday 21st I was awakened at an early hour, by the sailors preparing the steamer and trying to get her off, or out of the creek. About 6 oclock she sailed. At 7 we breakfasted. I had a very good appetite, and felt very well all the way, untill we arrived in sight of San F, where the waves caused the boat to rock considerably. And I found that my head was quite affected by it. As soon as the boat tied up, we left, and went up to Mowrey's We arrived about 12 oclock. Sister M had not washed her breakfast dishes. She seemed pleased to see us, and very soon had an inviting meal before us, of which we all partook freely, and felt much refreshed. Mr C went in search of br [Chapman] Duncan, found him and learned that we could not have the house we were expecting, in consequence of its being still occupied. But told him of another, and a better one, which he thought he could get on reasonable terms. In the evening br Duncan called, and we had quite sociable times. Sister Picket came down to see me. I had not seen for a number of years ^and should not have known her^ yet she knew me. I admired her appearance much, she invited me up to her room. I accepted the invitation, called on her toward evening, spent an hour or two. We talked over the scenes through which we had passed with the church spoke of Mother Smith, and many others of our acquaintances.[1]

    Sunday 22nd quite rainy and disagreeable. I assisted Sis M about her work. Mr C went to see br Grouard in accordance with an invitation received from him the previous evening. I went up again to see Sis Picket, one of her little twins had the chills. Herself and daughter have been quite out of health. Mr [William] P[ickett] works in the printing office. While I was sitting there br Duncan came up and invited us to come down

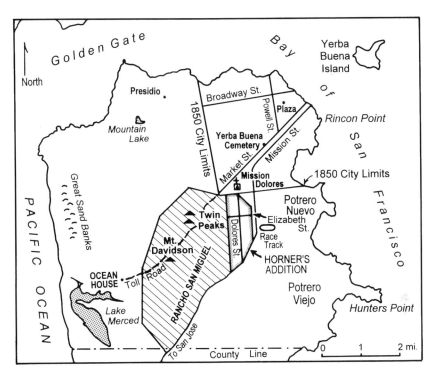

Horner's Addition could be reached by a pair of plank roads connecting the main part of San Francisco to the old Mission settlement two miles out in the country. Several streets were laid out, including John, M, and Horner. Elizabeth and Jersey Streets still retain their names, intersected today by Dolores St.

to meeting. Said there had a few brethren and sisters come in and wished to have a meeting there, sis P said she could not have on account of her boy being sick. I went down. Br Duncan and Everly took the lead of the meeting, and it passed off tolerably lively. Closed by Mr C. Sister Evans invited us to come to her house, which we did that evening, and called on Amanda Cheny.

Monday 23rd it rained. Mr C went to see about engaging a house. Got one for 20 dolls pr month near the old Mission house. Went out with a load of goods, came across a man who told him the building was not fit to live in, and offered him another and better one free of rent for one month. He accordingly took his things to it, or at least one load and came back to Mourey's, staid untill

Tuesday 24th when he left to take out the remainder of our things, agreed with br D[uncan] to escort us, Fr and I at night. It was a very rainy day, and br D thought it unproper for us to go that night, and counseled us to wait untill the next morning. He spent the evening in conversation.

Lithograph by Charles B. Gifford of Mission Dolores, San Francisco, 1860. The view is looking west from the Potrero Nuevo across the Noe Valley, site of John M. Horner's land purchase. Courtesy of the Bancroft Library, University of California, Berkeley.

Mr Mowrey on the priesthood, which Mr M seems inclined to deny. I sewed for Sis M. Sister Corwin called to see us awhile.

[A Temporary Dwelling]

Wed——— 25th, we F and I arose at an early hour, made a fire and got us a little breakfast. Br D arose soon after, but would not eat with us, said it was too early for him to eat. We set out ten minutes before 8 oclock, came down to the plazza where we found an omnibus ready to carry us direct to the mission Dolores[2] We waited a few minutes for the driver to speak to some one, and then proceeded. The sun arose and shone pleasantly. There were no passengers in the carriage but us three, untill we got nearly out of the city. When a young lady came out with a book in her hand, the stage stoped, and br D observed that she was a school teacher, who taught at the mission. The road was very wet, and br Duncan requested the driver to go a little beyond his usual stopping place, to a pair of bars, where we alighted and walked a few rods to our new dwelling ~~where~~. We found Mr C and Alma cooking their breakfast in very comfortable style. The place looked quite as well as I expected to see it, as also the little furniture answered my expectations. Br D took breakfast with them, and left to go to his office. We then set about regulating the house, and by night had things in tolerably good order. Br Pratt came up to see us at night, and commenced boarding with us.

Thurs 26th We baked bread and pies. Mr C went to the city, bought fresh fish, and vegetables; got wood &C.

Friday 27th We washed, and cleaned the dining room floor Mr C made a table.

Saturday 28th After breakfast Alma and I went to the store and market. I bought a large wooden bowl, chopping knife, bread knife, a half dozen tumblers, beef and cabbage. Returned home, prepared dinner, boiled the beef and made a dozen mince pies; finished baking them in the evening. Frances making herself a dress, scotch plaid. She and her father expect to leave for San B——— in one week.

[Horner's Addition]

Sun 29th A beautiful pleasant morning. I arose at 7 oclock F and her father took a walk over to the milk establishment. I prepared breakfast, and ate between 8 and 9. After which br P and Mr C went to San F, to visit the brethren A[masa] Lyman and [Quartus] Sparks, late from San B. Alma Frances and myself took a walk over the hills, to take a view of br Horners new purchase, and to get a peep at the Spanish house where we expect reside, after a few weeks. We admired the scenery very much; and think in short time it will be a great place. We walked from bluff to bluff untill we arrived at the top of a high one nearly in front of the dobie house where the spaniard resides of whom Mr H bought the land. We then sat down to admire the prospect. And we came to the conclusion that altho it was now quite retired, yet it was a most beautiful and romantic place. F—— got tired and came home a little before us, but A—— and I concluded to ascend one more bluff, in order to have a fairer prospect of our future residence and the valley in which it is located. We found that the prospect was much improved by changing our position, and after gazing with great admiration as long as we chose we came home. Our little dog kept close by us through the whole of our walk and frequently excited our mirth by the little pranks and manners he was constantly acting out. We had a fair prospect of the bay, and gave a longing look towards the beautiful valley we had lately left, and which ^in all probablility^ we shall never behold ^or at least visit^ again. It was half past twelve when we arrived at the house. Frances went about making some fried cakes or doenuts.

We made us a cup of tea. I spent an hour or two writing, and reading the Deseret news; untill I found myself in the arms of Morpheus, sweetly resting myself after our walk.

The afternoon seemed rather long. No one came to the house, and the men did not return untill after dark. It was near 6 oclock when they arrived. Said they had come direct from meeting. Br A Lyman preached to them quite lengthy. They brought home fresh fish, which we fried, and had a very good supper. Mr C said br Lyman was coming out here the last of the week.

Mon 30th It is a beautiful day. The valleys bluffs and mountains are becoming quite green; the sun shines clear and bright, as summer. My heart is as light as if it never knew sorrow or sadness. Thank the Lord, were it not for occasional calms, I am sure my vessel would have been discarded as unseaworthy long before this. Mr C went this morning to see a spaniard about a job of painting, returned without seeing him. Concluded to go to the city, to see a Mr Grouard a painter. While he was gone he came out here in company with a Mr Sebley to see him, and missed of each other on the way. Mr C bought me some cotton batting for comfortables [comforters]. Frances seemed quite unwell today. We had two new boarders commence at dinner, both from Salt Lake. One a young man by the name of Higgins the other by the name of Conover. Cyrus Ira passed this morning, gave me a call said he wanted us to board three or four men. I told him I could not well take more than three or 4 untill we get into the other house. Alma gave us a specimen of his mechanism by building a round house. It made us a deal of sport. Afternoon I commenced my comfortables. Mr Little called today, spent an hour or more with us.

Tuesday the last day of January 1854. It has been a very warm day, not a cloud to be seen. I washed some and worked some at my comfortables. Mr C painting the fence around the park. This evening he is writing to br [Thomas W.] Whitaker in answer to two communications lately recd from him.

Wednesday the 1st of February 1854. Another pleasant day has passed away. I finished washing, also my comfortable. Cyrus Ira called at the door and talked a few minutes. Mr Grouard came out from the city, took dinner with us said he expected to leave for the lower country, next week. Frances is I think rather more unwell than usual, complains very much of a weak stomach. I am anxious that she should see Dr Winslow.

Thurs 2nd Very pleasant in the morning. I ironed, cooked beans for dinner. Alma went to the store, and market. This evening br P entertained us with a history of some of his sea voyages when a young man. The wind arose from the east toward night, and brought with it a mist or spray, which made the air very damp and cold, our house being open rendered it unpleasant for us.

Friday 3rd rather cloudy, and an appearance of rain. I cooked dinner for the men, and sent A—— with it to them. Afternoon I made another comfortable, for F's bed. She cooked the supper. Alma made a woodbox. We had quite a sociable time at supper. Conversation turned upon the different nations of the earth, their strength, power and dominions, their wars and contentions with one another. Br P read some in a newspaper. Mr C fixed a parasol for Frances.

Sat—— 4th cloudy and damp all day; I finished my comfortable cooked dinner and sent to 5 men. Made a lot of mince pies, baked some in the evening. Made buiscuits for supper. After supper Cyrus Ira called in. Showed us several plays, requested F to read with him, one of them. She declined, saying she was unaccostomed to reading plays. Frances been preparing her things, to go into the city tomorrow, will probably stay a few days to see Dr Winslow.

Sunday 5th a remarkbly rainy day. Br P gave up the idea of going to the city, he and Mr C both intended going, but the rain prevented them. Toward noon Cy—— Ira came in and spent a few hours with us. I read one of his plays. A tragedy. We ate supper between 4 and 5 oclock. It has been a very unpleasant rainy day, and this evening the wind blows cold, with frequent showers of rain.

Mon 6th This is Ellen P's birthday [her 22nd]. Toward night it faired off, Br P got quite anxious to know when the brethren at San Francisco intended sailing, and invited Mr C and Alma to accompany him to the city. After supper they set off. F and I were alone. I wrote a letter to Sister Pratt. They returned at ten oclock. Br P said he saw no one to get any information from. I had quite a restless night, slept none untill after 12.

Tues 7th I washed. F and A got the dinner for the men. This morning I was on the verandah, as two men passed, both strangers to me. One spoke to me from the road saying "good morning sis, why dont you come over and see us. I live just over there, pointing in the direction of his house,) my wife would have been over to see you before now, but she has been very busy latly as our cook is gone." I thanked him; told him I was a stranger in the place and knew no one, but would like to become acquainted with the neighbors, and should be pleased to have his wife call. He observed that he thought she would. Afternoon we, myself, Alma, and Frances, took a walk down about the mission, called at the stores, but found them rather destitute. Returned quite fatigued.

I made buiscuits for supper. In the evening wrote a letter to sis Skinner.

Wed. 8th Very pleasant day. I felt much fatigued all day. Finished my letters, hunted up some little present for the girls. About noon br Horner came in his carriage with his wife and Sister Cheny, he left the ladies, and went away to be gone two hours. Br Duncan was with him. They were gone 3 hours. We had a very good time with the ladies, they took dinner with us. Just before we sat down to dinner a gentleman called enquiring for br Pratt, and brought a letter to F Said he had just come from San Bernardino.

He appeared very gentlemanlike, ^said his name was Leach^ and on conversing with him I found I had once been acquainted with a br of his but so long ago that it was sometime before I could recollect him. He offered to pay for his dinner, but I told him he had paid in bringing a letter. He thanked me and went over to see br P. Soon after br Horner's left br Grouard and Christy came in, staid and took supper with us. We had very sociable times. They left between 7 and 8. Br P fixing up his things and preparing to leave on the morrow, I went to bed at ten. F and her father sat up untill near twelve.

[Addison and Frances's Departure for San Bernardino]

Thurs 9th I arose between 5 and 6 oclock, prepared breakfast and ate near seven. Between 7 and 8 br Pratt and Frances left. Alma accompanied them to the Hotel where F intended taking the omnibus, but br P wished to make calls on the way, and chose to walk. They some expect to sail next Saturday, have some business in the city before leaving. F said she should not say goodby now, as she intended coming back sat morning, to see me once more, and to say goodby. It was quite a task for me to keep a light heart when they went off, for in despite of what little philosophy I was mistress of a deep drawn sigh would occasionly escape from my heart.

And when I went into her room the sad vacancy would stare me in the face, and cause me to exclaim. Oh Frances! <u>Gone</u>.

I was obliged to keep very busy all the morning, making pies, cooking dinner and regulating the house. About one oclock br Duncan called, said he had not been to the office to eat with the men, and would take some dinner with me, if convenient. I then set dinner for him and Alma, he left soon after. I took the old accordien to try if possible to divert my mind from a threatning gloom to which it seemed inclined, and being overcome by weariness I soon found myself in the arms of morpheus, from which I was aroused by A playing the violin. One of our boarders concluded to take lodgings with us in consequence of rain. I retired to rest early, as I slept little the night previous.

Friday 10th Arose at 6 oclock, breakfasted at 7. Ironed in the forenoon. Afternoon as I was busy putting away my clothes I heard a knocking at the door and on opening it who should I see but sister E[lvira] Woodbury. I was quite surprised to see her. She said she had been travelling about to find me for sometime, not understanding the direction given her by Frances. Said she came down yesterday with R[hanaldo] Mowry on the *Union*, and saw F there at Frisco and feeling anxious to see us had come out in the stage for that purpose. She brought a bundle of letters, 2 from her husband in the Sandwich islands, one from her sister Lewis, and one from her sister Amelia in Nauvoo. She read them all to me; staid three hours and went back. ^She brought us an invitation to attend a party at M's that evening, but it was too unpleasant for me to think of going^ I made her a cup of tea, and we had sociable times while she staid. It has been and is now very unpleasant this afternoon and evening. Mr C has gone to the city to see br P and learn whether he intends going or rather sailing tomorrow. ^I wrote a letter to Alfred.^ The rain and wind are very intense, Our house is so open that we can hardly keep a light burning. About 10 oclock Mr C returned. It was raining very hard, and he was wet through.

Saturday the 11th Soon after breakfast br P came with a drayman to get F's trunks. ^Told me she was not coming back to say goodby. The weather had been so bad, she had not been able to go out before and was obliged to do her shopping that forenoon as they expected to sail at 4 oclock^ Br Cristy sent us a couple of nice pigs, which he wishes us to keep on shares. Alma had a pen made ready to receive them. I droped a line to F and told her I was expecting she would slip off that way. I meditated sometime upon it. I have sometimes thought it an unfavorable omen for friends to part in that way. But am not altogether decided upon it. I was full of reflections the remainder of the day. The evening was very cold and windy. Higgins staid here. In the night the wind blew severely, accompanied by rain. We thought and spoke of our friends who we expected were on the water. The Lord preserve them.

Sunday *Feb 12th* It faired off a little this morning and Mr C concluded to go to the city as he had some errands, but the wind arose again about 12 and blew severely. I almost fear for the safety of our friends on the ocean. 2 oclock Mr C not returned yet. Rain and wind very severe. About 4 oclock ~~Mr C~~ he returned. He informed me that the steamer had not sailed yet, but was expecting to at 6 oclock. Said he went on board and saw them all once more. Said F did not get her jewelry the day before as we expected she would, and wished him to make a selection for her. Accordingly he went and got some that pleased her very much, paid 18 dolls for them.

F sent her daugeryotype to us, I had to look at it sometime before I could see that it looked much like her, but after contemplating it for a length of time it began to look very natural, and now it seems like looking at her whenever I look at it. In consequence of ill health her countenance is subject to changes, which I attributed to it's not looking natural at first.

Monday morn 13th. fine pleasant day. It really seemed so agreeable to see the sunshine after such a cold storm that I wished to stay in it, and gaze at the prospect around. The house looked lonly within, and in spite of business I frequently found myself on the verandah looking out for some one, and yet expecting no one.

Near 12 oclock Cyrus Ira called at the door, and told me that he saw the steamer *Southerner* sail at 6 oclock the previous evening. I was then satisfied that they were really gone. And I tried to reconcile my mind to the idea of living alone, with no female companion about the house. I have been accustomed to that way of living for years. But it has now been sometime since, which makes it seem very lonely.

Tuesday 14th Feb Quite pleasant. Alma and myself trying to get along as well as we can without F. But we find her absence leaves a blank in the house which is hard to be overlooked. We concluded to wash, afterwards cleaned the kitchen floor, made pies &C.

In the evening one of our boarders brought home a new treatise on Geology, which he read to us. It is a very interesting science.

Wed 15th Last night I slept very little, which I could scarcely account for, I was quite free from pain, but my mind was restless. Very cold wind today. I have been sewing some, repairing shirts for Mr Higgins. I have a bile [bule, boil] on my face which troubles me some.

Thurs 16th This morning my face is badly swolen and quite painful. I ironed. Afternoon went to bed, slept two hours. Arose at 4 oclock. Two gents called at the door. A gentleman by the name of Kellon wished me to board a workman of his while he guarded a house and lot close by. Said he had had some difficulty with regard to tittle, another man had tryed to dispossess him, had torn away his fence in the night, and caried it off. Said he had used him very treacherously, but he did not intend he should get the advantage of him again. I agreed to board him, accordingly he came in and took supper with us. Said he was a native of Louisaana, had been a soldier in the mexican war, been sometime in Call made his fortune several times and spent it as often. He said he would divert our minds some evening with a sketch of his experience in the war.

Friday 17th The sun shines very clearly, but the wind is very cold. I have had a headache, and been quite unwell today. I think it all proceeds from my face. Baking bread and meat.

Sat 18th Tolerably pleasant day, been poulticing my face, was much troubled with it in the night.

[The Spanish Adobe]

Sund 19th quite fine this morning, rained some last night. After breakfast I took a walk with my husband to see the Spanish house that we expect soon to occupy. I found it answered the description I had previously heard of it, It remind me of some very ancient castle or building we read of in history. I think I shall feel very lonly with a small family in so large a house. We found two boys at home, probably of the ages of ten and fourteen. They were very polite to us, showed us all the different apartments, which we found very dirty, and inconvenient. The fowls were allowed to run nearly all over the house.

I never saw such floors in a dwelling occupied by white people before; but the walls were quite clean. The verandah runs the whole length in front, and across the ends. A wood part extends across the back, which is divided into 4 or 5 rooms, which have been occupied for storerooms graneries &C. A very dull sober looking parrot hung at the front door in a tin cage. I asked the little boy if was sick, he said no, and got some bread that we might see it eat. Said it could speak a few words of Spanish. We then went up the ascent towards the mountain to see some springs, which issue forth in great abundance, watering the valley below. From thence we bent our course to the park,[3] which I admired very much, called and examined our lots, but do not fancy them ~~much~~,

We went into a little office close to the park where we found our two boarders, who sleep there. We then went directly home. Alma had also been taking a walk with his dog, but reached home before us. Said he had been quite over the mountain, where he saw the broad ocean, and also the mountain lake,[4] which is a beautiful pond of fresh water situated near the height of the land. I found myself extremely fatigued on reaching home, so much that I went to bed and lay an hour or more before I could muster ambition sufficient to assist Alma in getting supper.

Mon 20th Tolerably pleasant, but cold wind.

My face was much worse, probably caused by exciting my blood or taking a little cold. I again resorted to poultices, laid in bed a part of the day, had rather a restless night. *Tues 21st* Quite unpleasant morning. Mr C went to his painting, but it soon commenced raining and he returned. I was very unwell all day. Mr Dolon called in co with two other gents who wish to come into this house. Mr C told them we would try to let them have it next week. Our two Salt Lake boys went to the city, returned about 4 oclock.

Wed 22nd Very steady rain all day. My face is some better. Higgins left, went to work for Cyrus Ira. Conover quite unwell did not come to dinner or supper. Our new boarder begins to entertain us with his history. Says his name is Kearney; that he is a nephew of Gen Kearney who led the mormon battallion through to Cal. And that he is one of fifteen heirs to a very great estate lying in the city of N Y. That he has an undisputed tittle to the land upon which Trinity church, and the Creton waterworks, are built. Says it is worth 8000000~~dolls~~ dolls. This evening Mr C and Alma occupied their time on the violin and accordian. I told them they played me to sleep, and then played me awake again.

Thurs 23rd Quite pleasant. I felt very weak and unwell but my face getting better. I sewed some, and assisted A about cooking.

Friday 24th Felt much better, washed with A's help. Baked meat for dinner, warm biscuits for supper. Our boarder Cap Kearney failed to pay his board as he agreed last night, but says he will give us an order on Mr Kellen, and leave, Says Mr K is a wholesale and retail dealer in paints in San Francisco, that he is very pious. Mr C told him that if he had been punctual man he would have come as he agreed and paid his board.

Sat 25th Quite rainy in the morning. Toward noon it became rather fair. Mr C went and bought wood. I sewed in the afternoon. It commenced raining in the evening, and rained nearly all night.

Sun 26th it rained steadily. Our boarders Conover and Higgins went to the city, returned in the rain. We spent the day in reading Gleasons pictoral magazine, which we find to be very interesting, and Mr C has determined to subscribe for it.

Mon 27th Another remarkably rainy day. It really seems gloomy. Our house is so cold that it is very uncomfortable. Mr C is reading a new paper. The illustrated London news.

Tues 28th The rain seems to have subsided, but the wind blows very cold from the NW. Last night when Conover came home to his supper, he brought his brother with him. He spent a night ~~with~~, and returned to the city intending to sail for the States the next day in co with Tho Williams and a Mr More, Who are going to buy goods and carry to Great Salt Lake City. Mr C also brought us br Pratts favorite Spaniel dog, which escaped from us at Union city as we were coming down from San Jose. The little fellow seemed to remember us, altho it is about 5 weeks since we left him. And it was evident that our little dog and it knew each other. It was really diverting to see them play, and rejoice over one another. Made pies. Alma went to the meat market, had fresh beef and warm biscuits for supper.

Wed——— San Francisco March 1st A D 1854. Very fine pleasant day, the first we have had for more than a week. It really seemed too pleasant to stop in the house. I felt a desire to stand in the sunshine and gaze at surrounding objects untill I found my sight ^or my eyes^ were becoming weakend by the extreme brightness of the sun. Mr C and Alma started to go to the city, to get a load of eatables, but as the teamster could not well go today, they returned to wait untill tomorrow. I washed, baked light-bread, cleaned floors &C.

Thurs 2nd We arose rather earlier than usually, as Mr C and A wished to get an early start for the city. Breakfasted by candle light, after which they set off, got a man by the name of Jonson who drives Mr Horners team to go with them ~~to the city~~. Rained some in the morning, but about 10 oclock it cleared away, and the remainder of the day was tolerably fair. They returned at 11 oclock with a very large load of provisions of various kinds. Alma produced as the amount of his loading to schoolbooks viz The history of the united states, and Mitchels intermediate Geography. They are very fine books, and by diligence, he can obtain a great deal information from them. He seems highly interested in them at present. Mr C bought about 70 dolls worth of provision I did two weeks ironing, made a few pies, and sweetcakes.

Friday 3rd cold rainy day. Mr C went over to his work, but it rained so that he spent the time in the office with br Badlam. Afternoon it cleared away, and he pursued his business. I commenced a letter to Frances.

Sat 4th tolerably pleasant, I made sheets for my cot beds Also a night cap. When Mr B returned, told me that the new house was not finished, and he thought it would not be in less than a week. I told him we would try to make the best of it.

Sunday 5th. Br Badlam came up with Mr Conover from the office and took breakfast with us. I observed that he looked as young and smart as he did ten years ago. He was very sociable, is now assistng Mr C in his job of painting. After breakfast they concluded to go to the city, left near eleven oclock, and returned at 5. They brought home a lot of newspapers, and a letter from sis Addison Pratt, conveyed by sis Elb [Elizabeth] Pratt late from Salt lake city. They informed me that there was a company of brethren from the Sandwich islands here who were going to sail for San Bernardino on tuesday next.

Monday 6th Very pleasant, but quite cool. After breakfast I sat down to finish my letter to sister P and Frances. While I was writing came br

[Thomas] Morris, I was much pleased to see him, he staid 3 or 4 hours and left, as he said, to seek some asparagas plants, for Mr Horners garden. Mr C was not at home. Alma and I had a very good visit with him. He took dinner with us, and was very sociable, told us concerning our old neighbors in San Jose valley which interested me very much. This evening A and myself are alone Mr C gone to the city. I wrote a letter to sister Elvira Woodbury.

Soon after br M left, br P's dog was missing, probably followed him. Mr C returned at half past nine.

Tuesday 7th Very pleasant in the morning. I washed. Alma went in search of the dog, went down to the bay, and around the mission, but found nothing of him. Two men called inquiring for work. A Mr Selby and Squares called to see Mr C, went over to the plazza, where he was painting. Afternoon the wind blew cool. Br Badlam came home with Mr C and took supper. Said he thought he would come to board with us before long.

Wed 8th Alma bought beef. I made light bread, did some sewing and some reading. Quite pleasant and warm.

A fire engine company were organizing. We heard the music and saw them parading. They were dressed in uniform all in red shirts, black morocco belts, and glossy caps. Their music sounded very animating to me. A went out to the street, and followed them some distance. Mr Conover is complaining of a very sore eye. I expected br Badlam here to take supper, but did not come I understand he went home with Cyrus Ira.

Thursday 9th Very pleasant. It now begins to look like spring. I feel very anxious to get where we can be making a garden, and other improvements. It seems as though we were only living by the halves, or not more than half living, in the situation we are now in. Br B came up to supper, says he has now commenced boarding with us. Mr C gone to the city.

[Almon Babbitt's Visit]

Friday 10th Conover brought home a Daily Alta Cal, which gave an account of the arrival of the *Galiah*. And further that Mr [Almon] Babbit arrived, or was one of the passengers, on his way to Washington, as Secretary of state for Utah Territory.[5]

Sat 11th Very cold wind, accompanied with some rain. Mr C has got through with painting, and wishes very much to move, but fears we shall be obliged to wait on a while longer as the Spaniards new house is not finished we expected it would have been. He Mr C has gone into the city today to see br Horner about it. He wrote a letter to elder O[rson] Pratt, at Washington City, and sent by br Babbit, requesting br P to send him the Seer a periodical which he is publishing there. He returned before night, said br B appeared very familiar and friendly, and had promised to accompany him home the next day after meeting and stay with us over night. Brought me a letter from sister P. and one from br Whitaker.

Sun 12th Tolerably pleasant. After the men went to meeting I put the house in as good order as possible, reconnoitered my own dress, and made my calculations for supper, with the expectations of having the secretary of the state ^or territory^ of Utah take tea with me. But when the brethren returned they informed me that he had been requested to preach again that evening and on that account declined coming, but thought he would be out the next day if it did not rain.

Mon 13th it rained very steadily all day. The men staid in the house. Br Badlam studying the Chinese, he makes some sport for us, is quite shrewd in many of his remarks.

Tues 14th Another tremenduous rainy day. Neither business or pleasure for anybody that I see. I had the headache in the afternoon and evening. Br Cyrus Ira called in and spent a part of the evening, was very sociable, but complains of being very unhappy and discontented, says he is a "miserable man." Mr C recommended him to go to the church, and get him a wife; he thinks he should be hardly suited with a woman of common talents; he was on his way home from the city, and I noticed that he had been taking or stimulating very highly with brandy.

Wed 15th The rain seems to have subsided a little. Mr C gone to work. This evening br Ira called and took supper with us, we had quite sociable times. He brought me a letter from sister Woodbury.

Thursday 16th Quite pleasant, outwardly, but myself quite unwell both in body and mind. Mr C went up to the spanish house, thought to make a commencement towards cleaning it up, but understood he did not intend moving under a month or six weeks, and came home quite discouraged. It gave me the horrors to see him in such bad spirits, and after he left and went to the city, I gave way to my feelings in a flood of tears, which I have not done before for many years. In the midst of my grief, who should I behold coming toward the house but br Horner, Babbit, and Sparks. I tried to cheer up as well as I could, but I think they must have discerned my feelings in a measure. Br Babbit said he was determined not to go away without seeing me, and altho the steam was up, and the boat near sailing, he ventured to come, and stay a few minutes. I hardly knew what questions to ask him, among the many I wished to ask. He told me somethings that he thought I would like to know Viz: that he had been through Indiana lately heard Dr Knight was alive and well, and yet in the faith of the gospel. His children married and carrying on business for their father. Said his wife Ann was in Kanesville, and that himself was leading a bachelor life. He talked very fast while he staid, but left in a great hurry. After they were gone I felt still more lonely, and gave free vent to my grief, by calling to mind the many places we had met br B in, and the perplexing scenes through which we had been called to pass in the intervening time. He told me that the property or situation we left in Salt Lake Valley had now become very valuable. Asked if I didnot intend going back sometime. I told him I would like to go as soon as convenient, but knew not when that time would come.

Alma and I washed. Mr C returned toward night, said he had not seen br H, but had laid his complaints before br Duncan, who informed him that he br H intended coming himself to live in the Spanish house, and thought probably we should occupy a part of it. Br Badlam lectured us some on the unpropriety of getting impatient, prophesied that we should do well, and prosper, if we were only patient.

[House and Job Secured]

Friday 17th foggy and cold. Mr C went up to the park, staid untill noon waiting to see br H, but he not coming, he returned, and proposed trying to get another house in a few days, nearer to his business. Soon after he returned br H called, in co with Mr Hopkins his br——in-law, we were just taking dinner by ourselves, I invited them to eat said they would willingly, ~~he~~ Br H informed us that the Spaniard had agreed to move in a few days, that he was going to work tomorrow hauling away manure, and cleaning up about the house, and would like to have him join him. Told him he intended reconnoitering the house and making it comfortable and pleasant. That his wife wished us to live in it with her, for company, as the house was very large. We felt somewhat comforted on learning his goodwill towards us, said Mr C would have business as long as he wished to work.

Sat 18th Tolerably pleasant today, I have been ironing and repairing clothes. The gloom and extreme heaviness which has pervaded my mind for a week past, is giving way measurably, and I think I can almost look upon our situation in a somewhat reasonable light. Yet I almost fear to flatter myself with anything cheering, for fear of disappointments.

Sunday 19th rather gloomy, with occasional showers. Mr C did not go to church. I wrote two letters. One to Ruth and Mary E Ki[mball] and one to sister Marial Crosby. Music on the violin and accordion.

Mon 20th I washed. Very pleasant. Mr C worked with br Badlam. Very sociable times at supper.

Tues 21st fine day, baked light bread, wrote two letters, one to John Eagar, and one to br Busby. In the evening wrote another to br and sis Everett.

Wed 22nd, beautiful day. Mr C gone to the spanish house to work. I have been writing a letter to sister Cobb and Eliza Snow.

Thurs 23rd Quite pleasant. Mr C informed me last night that he intended moving to day, and wished me to have the things in readiness by noon. Accordingly I set about picking up and setting things in order, while he and Alma went and cleaned the house. I kept on my feet all day, or at least all the forenoon. They returned at noon, and Mr Truet with them. Said he wanted to eat a few meals with us untill Mr Horner got moved and settled and then he expected to board with them. About 2 oclock the team came for the first load. The wind rose at noon and blew very severely all the evening.

Mr C got very warm by scrubbing and cleaning house, then coming out in the wind he took a severe cold. Br Badlam came with his wagon, and took me and a few light things.

I found the floors very wet, and the rooms looking dark and gloomy, and smelling so much like a stable, that I actually felt, that I had got in one, and tried to console myself with the fact that our Saviour conde-scended to dwell in a stable, or manger, and by that means, set us an example of humility. The gloomyness of the house, added to the already depressed state of my mind, and I will not attempt to describe my feel-ings. But I had no time brood over them, for I was obliged to go to work forthwith, to cook supper for four men. I got my supper in good season and Mr Truet called it good, and ate very heartily.

Frid 24th they cleaned the front room, while I baked light bread, and regulated the kitchen.

Mr C got through white washing, and set up the bed, made a fire in the chimney, we all went in and soon came Mr Truet and Conover. I invited Mr T to sing, which he did. Sung, Home again, and played some on the accordion. Br Horner came in a minute. We spent the evening very pleasantly, retired to rest at ten, slept soundly untill 4 in the morning.

Arose at 5 *Sat 25th.* I ironed. Mrs John M Horner and Wm's wife came in and sat awhile with me. I went in there awhile, afternoon made pies.

This evening the house was quite ful of young men. Mr C selling them some clothing that he bought in a chest, without knowing what was in it. Thinks he can sell enough to get his money back, and keep the most valuable articles, or at least those that he wishes to.

Sunday 26th cool and cloudy. I have written a letter to Sister P, and daughters.[6] No going to church to day.

This evening we had music again. Br Ira and a number of others were in. I sang some, quite lively times.

Mon 27th I washed, got very tired. Br Duncan came out, staid over night. Mr John H and wife went home Br Duncan came in and spent the evening with us and slept here. Mr Truet sang Napoleans grave, a beautiful song, also The Raven which is very pretty. We sung some hymns. Music on the violin and accordion.

Tues 28th Br Duncan left towards noon. Bade us goodbye and advised me or us to come to the valley as soon as convenient, he said so as to be on hand to go to Jackson co with the church, when they went.

When Mr H returned from taking br Duncan to the city he brought Mr and Mrs [Earl] Marshall home with him. Br Zaccheus Cheny came in a minute, said he intended bringing his family out to see us.

Wed 29th I made light bread and pies. Mrs Marshall came in to see me a few minutes. Afternoon Mr and Mrs H went with them to the city, and when they returned brought Henry Webster and wife Mrs H's sister. ^They brought me a letter from my oldest sister and her daughter.^ Br McNeer (on his way home to Michigan) called and staid over night with us. We had quite a sociable time with him. Mr C has a very bad cough.

Thurs 30th I ironed. Mrs Webster came in to see me awhile. Afternoon I went in and sat with them a short time. Frank Silver called on us said he had started for home if he could get his money that he had on interest, he should go on the first boat, he told me concerning our old neighbors in San Jose valley, whom I was much pleased to hear from. He staid over night. Br McNeer also came back from the city, and staid the second night.

Friday 31st and last day of March. Mrs Webster came and bid me good-bye, her husband also called in, previous to leaving. Frank Silver told me that he could not get his money untill the sailing of the next boat, which would probably be two weeks, and asked me to board him for that length of time, to which I consented. He also requested me to keep his money ^that he had^ for him, as he was going into the city, and did not wish to carry it with him. After dinner I had a job of cleaning windows, and sealing [ceiling], in my front room. Mrs H came in a while, told me their cows had come, and that I should bring my pitcher every night and morning for milk for my tea and coffee. I thanked her and offered to pay her, but she said she wanted nothing.

[Keeping Company with Mrs. Horner]

Sat April 1st very pleasant morning. Mrs H and I took a walk up the mountain side, to a spring of beautiful clear water. We admired the scenery very much. The ground was covered with a thick coat of grass, and adorned with a variety of flowers, which perfumed the air and rendered it very pleasant. We also admired the distant view of San Francisco and the bay spotted with numerous vessels. She showed me how her husband intended bringing the water from the spring in lead pipes to the house. She also showed me the plan of their new dining room, and land office, that Mr C is now building.

Sunday 2nd Quite pleasant. Br Horner came in before breakfast, and informed us that we could ride with him to church if we wished to go. Accordingly we made ourselves ready, and at ten, set off. We had a very pleasant ride, reached br Cheny's at eleven. Sister Evans and Delina C, had gone to take a view of the cemetery, thinking there would be no meeting. But as there were quite a number present, the brethren concluded they would have one, which they did, and appointed a conference for next Saturday and Sunday. They also took into consideration the plan of hiring, or building, a house for public worship, knowing that they had for sometime rather intruded upon sister E's good nature, by crowding into her house, every sunday. Br Horner said for one he felt quite condemned, for not trying to make our doctrine more public. And the elders all agreed with him in his determination to place it in a more conspicuous position. Meeting closed between 12 and one. We had a fine ride home. After supper my husband and I took a walk to the park, called on a Mr Willis who live near it; he is a great musician, has a bass viol, violin and guitar. He and Mr C played a number of tunes togather, on the bass viol, and violin, he invited us to call again, and said he would come, and return our calls. It was near sunset when we returned. My husband borrowed a music book of him for Alma to learn, (rules for playing on the violin).

San Francisco April 3rd 1854 AD Mon—— I arose at 6 oclock, breakfasted at 7. After which I washed. Alma assisted his father at Joiner work. Afternoon he is painting the sealing in my front room.

Tuesday 4th Mrs Horner called in asked me if I wished to go to the for a ride, or on business, as the carriage was going. I thanked her and told it would not be convenient for me to leave home.

Wed 5th Mr H and wife went to the city, and on returning brought Sister [Zacheus] Cheny and her children.

Thurs 6th This is the birthday of The Church of Jesus Christ of Latterday Saints, organized A D 1830 with 6 members, and it now numbers many thousands. I visited with sister Cheny. She took dinner with me today. I enjoyed her visit finely.

Friday 7th Mr H went to the city again. Carried br and sis C home. Mr Crosby also went with them, and traded some. purchased himself some clothing, and furniture to the amount 6 Windsor chairs, and a rocking chair, table, looking glass, carpet and a bolt of curtain calico, bleached muslin &C. Alma and myself whitewashed, and cleaned floors preparatory to receiving the new furniture. I was very well pleased with them.

Sat 8th I finished cleaning my sitting room, worked very busily all day. Afternoon came Henry Wilkins, staid over night.

In the evening Mrs H came in and invited Mr Crosby to come in and bring his violin, said brother H wished him to come and play him a tune. Accordingly we went, and had quite a musical time, vocal as well as instrumental. Br H Wilkins sang welch and we all joined in singing hymns and spiritual songs. Alma with Mr H's hired men went to hear one of our neighbors make music.

[Conference in San Francisco, April 1854]

Sunday the 9th This is the appointed for our annual conference, being the sunday following the 6th of April.

Towards meeting time it commenced raining. Just as we were ready to set off it rained quite a shower and Mrs H declined going. We waited one hour longer than usually, when br H told me that he was going, and that I could go if I wished, I told him I was already and would like to go. Accordingly we went, accompanied by Wm [Horner]. We had a good meeting and returned without any rain, Mr C Alma and br Badlam rode home with us, and we had a very sociable time. Soon after we reached home Mr[s] H came in and invited us to come and take supper with them which would save me the trouble of cooking, adding that she presumed I was tired, being at so long meeting. We thanked her, and cheerfully accepted the invitation. Br Badlam accompanied us, and was quite talk-ative at the table. Mrs H replied to some of his sayings in quite a shrewd joke, which rather put br B to the blush. I spent the remainder of the afternoon with her.

Mon 10th Br H and wife went to the city again, brought home sister Delina Cheny. I made my carpet but found it lacked one bredth. In the evening came Mrs H, sis D[elina], and br Badlam. Br [William] McBride was also here, came out with br H.[7] We had music on the violin and accordion, with some singing, enjoyed the eve finely.

Tues 11th Br Mc left; said he was going to visit the neighboring villages for the purpose of preaching to them, if they would hear. Mrs H, Delina, and myself, took some very pleasant walks, up the hills and down to the park, after we returned I made a cup of tea, and invited the ladies in to sup with me.

Mrs H was rather low spirited, being troubled about some little dif-ficulty between her husband and a squatter concerning land. I told her if she would come and take tea with me I would tell her fortune, upon which she came readily. I told her I thought her husband would get along with his land affair with very little trouble, and come off safely in the end. We succeeded in getting her mind lightened of its burthen, in some degree. This evening Mr C went to the city. Delina spent the evening with me. She retired before 9 oclock but I sat up and read untill after 10, as Mr C was late in returning, and I felt in a spirit of reading. I read 3 numbers of The Seer, a periodical published in Washington by elder O[rson] Pratt.

Wed 12th I finished my carpet, took a walk with Mrs H and Delina, to see br Cyrus Ira. Found him at home, studying plays, is preparing himself for acting on the stage. Sis D took supper with us, she spoke often of Frances, and wished she was here. Told me she expected to be married soon, and invited me to attend.

Thurs 13th Towards noon came Mr Origin Mowry. We all suspected his business was to wait on sis D home, and so it proved. About 4 oclock they set off intending to take the Omnibus at the Mission. I commenced my bed curtains. Delina assisted me some, before she left.

Friday 14th, a very warm pleasant day. I finished my curtains put them up. Br Ira was in this evening, read and spoke some of his plays. Mr Truet sang, a song to us on his way to his bedchamber.

Sat 15th Another warm day. br H and wife been in the city nearly all day.

Sunday 16th quite warm and pleasant. Br H invited me to ride out to church with them. We set off at ten, there were 7 of us including the children, which filled the carriage. Br H took a different route from what he had when I been with them before, and I thought it much more pleasant. On arriving at sister [Hannah] Evans, our place of meeting, we found a number collected, ~~for meeting~~ and among them was br [Jefferson] Hunt, the representative from San Bernardino.[8] He spoke to us upon the subject of tithing, and showed to us from scripture that it was for our own interest to pay our tithing punctually. Br Horner read a letter from br A Lyman and C Rich, which appointed him [John Horner] president over all the brethren in U[pper] C[alifornia]. We reached home at 3 oclock. The wind blew very severely all the way, and we were very much chilled. I got our suppers as soon as convenient and went immediately to bed, and slept untill dark.

Mon 17th Cloudy with very little wind. I washed.

Tues 18th Still and cloudy. Mrs H came in and informed me that she had just read the death of Sarah Ann Stevens, a young lady who had formerly lived with her ^or in her family^ as teacher and who went to the Sandwich islands for her health, but died in 5 weeks after reaching the place.

Alma ~~gone~~ went to the city for a letter; returned without it, probably because he did not say it was advertised.

Wed 19th While I was taking breakfast Mrs H called and invited me to go with her to visit Sister Lincoln. I cheerfully accepted the invitation, and about 9 oclock we set off. Br Horner took us in the carriage up broadway to the nearest point from her house, as it is situated on quite high land, and rather difficult getting to it with a team. We had a very good visit, were introduced to several strangers, Mass[achusetts] people. One was a Dr—— Sprout, Another a market man by the name of Folsom who has lately married a lady from Mass, by the name of Crosby. She was stopping with sis L[incoln] while she made preparations for house keeping. We formed some acquaintance with her, and I admired her appearance much. She expressed much pleasure in meeting many of her States people, and forgetting that she had lately changed her name would answer to mine, and then beg to be excused. We were also made acquainted with a Mrs Greene, who resides in the basement story of Sister L's house, she sang to us while sister Lincoln played on the pianoforte. The aforesaid Mrs G, was also late from Mass, is a splendid singer. Sister Lincoln made us a nice dinner; and about 3 oclock she accompanied us to sis King's, where we made a pleasant call, and then returned to sister Evan's to await the arrival of br Horner. While waiting droped in to br Cheny's, spoke with Delina, and Agnes Smith. We also saw a Mrs [Eleanor] McLain, who attends our church and wishes to be baptised, but is prevented by an unbelieving husband.[9] She wished to see br H to ask his counsel with regard to her proceedings in that respect, but he was so late that she said she dared not wait longer as she wished to be at home before her husband.

We reached home a little before sunset, being much chilled with facing the wind.

On arriving found a letter from Cousin Amelia Stevens of Nauvoo, Alma rode out with us in the morning, got the letter from the office and returned on foot.

Thurs 20th Quite rainy. I ironed Mrs Horner called in and sat with me awhile

Friday 21st Br H and family went across the bay to their old home, expecting to be absent 3 or 4 days.

Sat 22nd Quite warm and pleasant. I made some repairs on shirts, and other articles, cleaned house &C. In the evening Mr C, Alma and Mr Truet went to Mr Willis', to hear and help him make music. I spent the evening in reading Miltons paradise lost.

Sund 23rd Beautiful pleasant morning. After breakfast br Ira called, very sociable, singing and speaking pieces. None of us went to church. A br from the Sandwich islands called to find whether he could learn anything from that qr. His name is Gaston, said he had been here one year, left a young wife on the islands, had written several times, and had no returns. Wishes to hear from her previous to sending her money. Alma accompanied some of the hired men, to the catholic church. It was the first time he had ever attended, and thought it great curiosity.

I finished my letter to sister Levina Baker. Mr C writing to Nauvoo.[10] C Ira here again this evening.

Mon 24th Rain last night, quite unpleasant this morning. After breakfast Higgins and Norton the cook went to the city. I sent my letter to the office. We looked for Mr H and family, but they did not return.

Tues 25th fine pleasant day. I washed, got much fatigued, lay down a while. About 5 oclock came Mr H's The wind was blowing, and they were quite chilled. I had a fire in my sitting room, and invited her to come in and sit with me, untill she got one made in hers. She came with her little girl, told me concerning her visit, and meeting, and remarked that she was pleased to reach home again, in consequence of being so tormented with fleas

Wed 26th Mrs Horner went to the city to trade some. Bought herself a bonnet, and also one for me, paid 14 dolls for hers, and ten for mine. On returning brought a letter from Frances to me, which I was pleased to receive. It was dated the 12th of April. It seems that they had not recd the one I sent by Duncan, when she wrote this.

Thurs 27th Quite warm and pleasant. I baked and ironed. Felt rather unwell, in consequence of having a restless night. After I finished ironing, I felt quite fatigued and lay down awhile, had a very sweet sleep of about an hour and a half long. I arose and prepared supper; After which br Morris came in and sat a while with us, brought us two of the Deseret News. Mrs H came in and expressed great concern for her husband in consequence of his staying out later than usually. I proposed to her to let one of the men go in search of him to which she readily consented. Higgins offered his services, and finally two of them set off agreeing to take separate routs, and in consequence of finding him, they were to make it known by shouting. Mrs H took her seat at the window with long-ing eyes and anxious ears to hear the signal. She had not waited many minutes, before she heard the shout from one of the men, and presently the well known voice of her husband saluted her ears, when all her fears were dispelled.

Friday 28th Very cloudy and unpleasant. Afternoon it rained pro-fusely. Br Morris and Alma commenced work in the garden. Sister Lincoln that was, changed her name last night, by marrying a Mr Sargent. Cyrus Ira has been here this PM. speaking and reading plays. He observed to me that it was his birthday, 30 years of his life had passed away. And he frequently regrets very much that he has not pursued a different course of conduct, with regard to improving his mind.

Sat 29th Very windy. Mrs Horner invited me to take a walk with her to the park, to call on a Mrs Carter, late from San Bernardino, who lives in Mr Horners office near the park.

We had quite an agreeable time. I admired Mrs C's manners and appearance much. But was sorry to learn that she was much dissatisfied with the conduct of the leading members of the church at San Ber.

Sun 30th and last of Apr. I had a pleasant ride to church. Mr C, and br Morris walked. Mr C called on br Christy on his return home, and he sent me a present of a bottle of wine. Mr C is a very kind hearted liberal soul; but for some cause or another he has not attended our meetings for several months.

[Delina Cheny's May Day Wedding]

Mon the 1st of May AD 1854 I got through with my work about 9 oclock, came into my sitting room and very soon Mr Ira called with a new play which he read to me. I thought it quite interesting. In the evening we attended the wedding of Origin Mowrey and Delina Cheny. Br Horner performed the ceremony, after which we had a very splendid supper. The bride and her maid were dressed very nearly alike; in plain white muslin, and they looked very beautifully. The rooms were adorned with flowers, and other ornaments, which gave them a very pleasant appearance.

Mr Colwell, (the brides brinlaw) conducted the wedding and the time passed off quite livly; in fact it seemed very short to me. In consequence of br H getting one of his horses feet lamed just as we started, we were obliged to turn back, after we had got some little distance from the house, to change horses, which made us late in getting there. We reached home at 11 oclock. The winds had ceased to blow, which made it quite pleasant riding.

Tues 2nd Very pleasant. I baked light bread. Afternoon felt very sleepy lay down awhile, and took a refreshing sleep. In the evening, ~~evening~~ lectured on the English grammar to Alma and A Higgins.

Wed 3rd Remarkably cold, and windy. I washed but felt very unwell all day. After I got through washing I lay down, and as I was much fatigued soon fell asleep. While asleep br Rinaldo Mowry called to see me. Alma told him I was sleeping and he walked into see Mrs Horner. However I caught the sound of his voice, and immediately arose. He returned shortly and showed me the likeness of Barnard Stevens, a second cousin of mine, and twin br to sister [Elvira] Woodbury. He had sent it from Bristol Ill to his sister in Cal. It was a fine looking picture, and looked very natural. Remarkably cold wind, has lasted for several days.

Thurs 4th I ironed in the forenoon. PM I went in to sit awhile with Mrs Horner. Mr Crosby went to the city, returned in the evening. Br Ira was in awhile reading plays.

Frid 5th rather cold, I finished my ironing, cooked dinner, and retired to my sitting room to write. Mr H came in and sat with me sometime.

Sat 6th Repaired clothes. Quite warm. The cold winds ceased to blow, which is a great relief to us.

Sun 7th Very warm. ~~and~~ In consequence of the carriage being taken to shop for repairing, we Mrs H and myself did not attend church. We therefore took a little walk over the hills to gather flowers. Had a very pleasant time; found a few ripe strawberries.

Mon 8th I arose at 5 oclock; after breakfast I commenced with my quilt. About 10 we received a call from Mrs Picket and Carter, both new neighbors to us, and their first call. They took dinner with Mrs H. Mr Gaston the gent from the Sandwich island also made his appearance, took dinner with us. PM I put my quilt in the frames and quilted a very little. Sister Picket told me that herself, or daughter, would come and assist me, some day in the course of the week.

Tues 9th After breakfast I went to quilting; found it very hard sewing. PM Mrs H came in and assisted me two or three hours. We had a very sociable time. In the evening Mr C finished letters to Sister [Lois] Thompson and Amelia Stevens.

Wed 10th I finished a letter to Sister Woodbury. Felt very unwell in the forenoon. PM I was some better, quilted steadily. Mrs H, was in. Conversation turned upon the sealing ordinances of the church, and the resurrection of the dead.

She seemed very dark upon the subject, and much inclined to unbelief. It proved to me the impropriety of trying to instruct one who rejects the impulses of their own consciences; by refusing to obey the first principles of the gospel.

Thurs 11th Br Horner took his family out for a ride. On returning brought Mrs Picket's daughters, the two miss Smiths [Agnes and Josephine].[11] They assisted me 3 or 4 hours, ^on my quilt^ took dinner, and left at two oclock, Said their mother was very unwell, and requested them to return at that hour. They are very modest amiable girls, I admired their appearances much. The youngest [Josephine] plays the accordion, and is a very good singer.

Friday 12th of May, I wrote a short letter to sister Thompson. Sent two gold dollars to her little boys. PM finished my quilt and took it off the frames about 5 oclock. Father Morris carried the frames to sister Picket.

In the evening I lectured Alma and Higgins on the grammer.

Sat 13th Very cold and windy. I hemmed my new quilt, made light bread. PM I was very unwell went to bed awhile. In the evening br Horner invited his men to go and remove a fence from off his land that had been made by a squatter, and offered to give each of them a lot as a reward, and let them choose for themselves. Accordingly they all set off Alma among the rest, and removed about a hundred posts. They were not absent more than an hour.

After they returned br H and his wife came in and spent an hour or two with us, Mr C played the violin, Alma the accordion. Mr Truit sang several songs. I sang the indian student. It was eleven oclock before I went to bed.

Sun 14th I felt quite unwell insomuch that I did not attend church. Wrote a letter to San Ber. Took pills before supper.

[Addison Pratt's Lost Dog]

Mon 15th I feel much better. Conover found br P's dog, which had been gone two months, he was at a frenchmans near by. The man said he followed him from the city, refused to let Conover take him, but said if the owners would come they might have him.

Accordingly Alma and Higgins went, but he would not let them have him short of their paying two dolls. Alma got the rope around his neck, but the fellow brought out his six shooter, and forbid them taking him short of paying two dolls. They came and left him, but after consulting awhile, Higgins said he would pay for him, and call him his own, untill such times as he could send him to his master, who values him very highly, for his hunting faculties. Alma therefore received the money from Higgins, and went for the dog. The little fellow had been away so long that he seemed to have forgotten us. In the afternoon I heard him making a strange squealing noise, and as he was tied at the door I thought he might be choked. I therefore ran out to his relief, and found him in a fit, very badly cramped and trembling like the ague. I called br Morris who was close by, he came and raised him up, and he soon came out of it, and appeared quite well again. Br M thought they might have poisoned him, but I thought not.

The evening came, Mr C concluded he would go and take him into the city, and see if br Thorp would take him down S B. He set off about sunset, and returned near 11 oclock. Said br T did not like the trouble of it much, but finally concluded to take him. Mr Truet was in a while before bedtime, practising upon his phrenological talents.

Tues 16th It was very warm and pleasant in the morning but afternoon very cold, and the wind blew a gale. Mrs Horner came in and told me that there were two ladies there from San Francisco who had come to buy lots. Mr C playing the violin this evening. Mr Truit Mr Ira, and Conover, were in. I read the account of Dr Willard Richard's death.

Wed 17th Very pleasant morning. I washed, got my clothes out early, and dried before the wind arose. Mrs H—— in awhile. Received letters from Frances and her mother, also one from br Whitaker.

Thurs—— 18th. After breakfast Mrs H, and myself took a walk to the park, called on sister Carter. Staid an hour or so and returned. I felt quite fatigued and had resource to my wine, carried in some to Mrs H, and the little girl.

Towards evening I went in and sat awhile, read Frances letter to Mrs H. She told me that she expected her father and mother Horner that evening. Just before supper they arrived, in co with br and sis Mowrey. Came by land from San Jose Valley. Said they had a very pleasant excursion indeed. Br McBride was with them. Br Mowrey's took supper with us and spent the evening, likewise br Mc. I had a very agreeable time with them.

Frid 19th Quite cold wind. br Mowreys left, and went to the city. I ironed, Cyrus was in; reading to me. He brought a new song to Mr Truit. In the evening I lectured, Alma and Higgins on grammer.

Sat 20th Very cold and unpleasant. I wrote some, read repaired garments, &C. Heard Capt Hunt, and br Thorp, sailed at 4 AM.

[Excursion to Lake Merced]

Sund 21st I arose late. Br Ira breakfasted with us. Complained of feeling unwell. About 10 oclock Mrs H sent me an invitation to ride with them, to the lake house, which I readily accepted.[12] And as they were then in the carriage I merely threw on my shawl and bonnet, and ran out to them. We had a very pleasant time in going, found good roads, adorned on both sides with flowers of every hue, whose sweet odors perfumed the air, and rendered it very exhilerating. We saw very little improvement, after we left the old Sanhosa road. A few Squatters are beginning to do a little towards farming. I admired the situation of the Lakehouse much. Several persons had already arrived (even at that early hour), on an excursion of pleasure.

We did not alight from the carriage, or speak to any one about the premises, with the exception of one man by the name of Jones, who Mr Horner recognized as belonging to San Fran and introduced him to his wife, and she to me. We observed that he appeared rather stupid, and br H concluded that he had been stimulating quite early. Mr, and Mrs Horner senior, accompanied us with their carriage. The children seemed to enjoy the ride finely. We reached home precisely at 12 oclock. I was considerably chilled with the cold wind. Alma made me a fire, by which I became warm shortly, took a bite of dinner, and prepared for church, at two oclock Mrs H came in and invited me to dine with them which I declined. At two we went to church, br H, Cyrus, and myself, the only occupants of the carriage. Mr C having gone in the morning. Met br N[athan] Tanner, late from the Sandwich islands. Said his health was poor, and had been so for sometime. That the climate did not agree with him, and thought he should not return to them again, but should probably go home next fall. I invited him to visit us, to which he assented, and would probably have come home with us, could we have given him an invitation to ride. But as we ourselves were passengers of charity I did not feel it my privilege, to invite him. He looked very feeble and pale, and I felt a degree of sympathy for him.

On returning Mrs Horner informed me that Mr and Mrs Hughs had been out to see me, and regreted very much my being absent. Left word for me to come and make them a visit, forthwith. Evening lectured on grammer again.

Mon 22nd Remarkbly cold and unpleasant. Baked light bread and pies, read, wrote, and talked, with br Cyrus.

Mr and Mrs Horner senior, left this morning early, before I saw them. I felt somewhat disappointed that they did not so much as say good-bye to us. Father Morris also left this PM, for Wm H's intending to be absent two weeks. Br Horner brought home a new cook. A woman from Boston. Singing in the evening with the violin. Mr Truit, Higgins, Alma and myself, sung Lilly Dale, afterwards Truit and I sung Fanny Gray.

Tues 23rd Very cold wind accompanied with rain. Mrs Horners babe quite unwell. I went in after breakfast, sat awhile. She seemed much affected with her childs illness, shed tears, said her husband had gone after a physician. I thought it was afflicted with worms. Mr O Mowrey and wife came, took dinner with Mrs Horner afterwards came in to my apartments. I read Frances letters to Delina. Brother H returned with Dr Ober. Who intimated that he thought the child threatened with dropsy on the brain, which much affected her mother, although he was not positive with regard to it. Jones Dier staid over night with us.

Wednesday 24th After breakfast, I went in to see how the sick child was. Mrs Horner thought she was no worse, and was willing I should go on my visit to the city, as I had been talking of. As I had told her the night previous, that if she was any worse, I would not leave her. Br H set off before nine AM, which gave me very little time to prepare myself for the ride. The wind was blowing a gale when we left, and on arriving at Sister Evan's, I was quite fatigued. The brethren and sisters were already collected to attend to the baptism of sister McLain, Sister Evans, and Sister King. I did not feel like riding any further and therefore staid with sister Cheny, untill they returned. We had quite a good time at the confirming after they returned from the water, sang several hymns, exhortations by Tanner and McBride. About 3 oclock sister Cheny accompanied me to see Mrs Hughs, formerly Mary Parker. We went in co with sister King, called a few minutes at her house, she went to the next corner with us to show us the house, and then returned. Br McBride also accompanied us. On arriving we found Mrs Hughs absent, we waited an hour or more for her return. Br Mc got impatient and left. She returned soon after. And was apparently much pleased to see us. Pursuaded sister C to stay untill night. I had intended to stop with Sister King over night, but feeling quite unwell, I dreaded going out again, and as I had not seen Sister Hughs for a long time concluded to stay and make her at least one good visit. She intends leaving for San Bernardino in a short time, says this climate does not agree with her health. I enjoyed my visit with them remarkbly well. Mr H came in at 9 oclock from his shop; as he keeps the clay street market and is seldom at home earlier, he was very sociable and friendly, invited me to stay a week. I admired him as a gentleman for his politeness, and sociability.

Thursday 25th Next morning Mrs H accompanied me on a shopping excursion, and piloted me to what she considered the best places to trade. I traded about ten dollars, much to my satisfaction. She then accompanied me to Sister Kings, stoped a few minutes and left. I staid an hour or so with sister King, and then she took her children and came with me to sis Evans, where I left her and went to see sister Morewy, found her and husband alone, had a very pleasant time with them, they made me a nice dinner, after which sister M accompanied me to sis Evans again. We had a very lively sociable time there. I waited untill near five oclock before the carriage arrived, and I began to fear least br H had forgotten me and gone home. But very shortly br Cyrus Ira came for me with the carriage and I was soon on the way home, where we arrived near 6 oclock, the wind blowing a gale, all the way from the city. I got supper, ate and went to see how the child was getting along, found her much the same, and her mother somewhat distressed about her.

Friday 26th great eclipse on the sun. The weather very cold. Mrs H thought her little girl worse and sent for the Dr again. I was in several times in the course of the day, could not discover any alteration in her. In the evening Mr Truet was in we had singing, and music on the violin. Mr T trying to learn us some new songs, I sang myself hoarse. Went to bed tired had bad dreams, waked myself shouting for assistance to get out of water.

Sat 27th Arose with a disagreeable feeling in my head, but was relieved by taking snuff for the catarrh.

PM wrote a letter to sis P. Evening went in to br H's to sing with the violin, and Mr Truet. Mr Wm H was there. Returned at nine oclock, finished my letter. Near eleven oclock when I went to bed.

Sun 28th Very pleasant morning. We think the eclipse has changed the air or warmed it; at least the course of the wind seems changed. Br H and wife rode out with the children this morn. Their little girl still continues quite unwell. Dr Ober is tending her, but gives very little medicine. Mrs H is rather dissatisfied with his proceedings. At ten we went to church. Mr C and myself accompanied br H in his carriage. We called for sister Carter, but she had gone on horseback. Reached Mrs Evans's about 11 oclock expected to hear br Rich from San Bernardino, but were disappointed, as he sailed the night previous. We carried letters to send by him, but as he was gone we left them with br Jackson who said he could send every week, and would send them with his. We had a very good meeting The brethren turned it into a sort of conference meeting, all spoke as they were moved upon by the spirit. Sister McLean the newly baptised member expressed her feelings very zealously. Also sis Burton. Meeting closed at one oclock. Sister Carter tied her horse to the carriage, and rode home with us. Towards night she called up to see the sick child. At 5 oclock Mr C and I took a walk to sister Pickets. sis Carter accompanied us. Had very pleasant time. Shortly after we reached there, Mr Truet, Ira and Higgins came in. The consequence was several songs were sung accompanied with the accordion by Miss Josephine Smith. Mr Picket came home just after sunset; and was quite sociable and polite. Reached home at nine oclock. I was much fatigued and faint. Mr C got some wine and reduced it for me. I drank heartily, went to bed and slept soundly.

Mon 29th Another fine morning. I found myself well and more wakeful than usually. I think the sick child better.

Tuesday 30th Very warm and pleasant morning. Afternoon quite cold and windy. I washed and kept busy all day. Evening we had singing by Mr Truit and myself, with music on the violin.

Wed 31st and last day of May 1854. Not so pleasant as yesterday. Finished washing, went in and sat awhile with Mrs H, she felt quite discouraged with regard to her little girl.

Thurs June 1st tolerably pleasant. I ironed. Mrs H went to the Dr's with her little girl. Afternoon made mince pies.

Frid 2nd I staid nearly all day with Mrs H. Her babe seemed worse, had a chill in the morning, and spasms all day.

Sat 3 Again I was with the sick child a great part of the day, and half of the night, she was very bad. Dr Ober brought an assistant, or counsellor with him, they both decided that it was dropsy on the brain. In the night she had a chill, which was followed with fever, and sweating. Sister Pickett was here. My husband and I took dinner or supper in Mrs Horner's room. I staid untill 12 oclock. Came home, went to bed, slept untill 8 oclock.

Sun. 4th I was in Mrs H's again nearly all day The Dr came about 9 oclock. Thought the child's symptoms some better. Sunday night I was up untill 11 oclock, when I retired to my bed feeling very unwell.

Mon 5th arose at 6, got breakfast went in to see the child, found her not so well. Came home and went bed quite sick. Near 12 came sisters Sargent, McLean, and Burton. They came in the omnibus to the Mission and walked from there. Sister Pickets daughter arrived about the same time. They all came in to see me, found me covered up in bed. They offered to do anything they could for me, Mrs H invited me to come and take dinner with them. But I requested to be left alone in bed untill I got well warmed, and soon found myself in a perspiration and free from pain. Sisters McLean, and Sargent left at 4 oclock, Sister Burton and Agnes Smith staid over night. I was in again to see the child in the evening. It had another sinking turn, and we all thought it was dying. I retired at 10 oclock.

[Death of the Horners' Babe]

Tuesday 6th before I got my work done Mary came and told me that the babe was dying, it had had spasms all night, and suffered extremely. It died 10 minutes before 9 oclock AM. ^Wanting 6 days of 20 months.^ She had been badly cramped for several days, was much mortified before she died. We were all thankful to see her released from pain, and even her mother who was nearly broken hearted at losing her darling child, said she felt comforted on seeing her free from pain.

Sister Burton assisted me to wash her, and change her clothes. Mrs Horner and Wm and Mary (the nurse for the children) wept bitterly all the time. Br H also seemed much afflicted, But he endured the trial with saint-like patience, and fortitude, and no murmur escaped his lips. Sister Picket Burton and myself made her grave clothes. Mr Crosby made her coffin.

Br Horner went to the city and brought sister Evans home with him. Sister Burton also concluded to stay several days with me, as they decided on taking the child up to their ranch to bury it by their other friends, and expected to be absent several days.

~~Wednesday 7th~~ PM came Capt Allen Treefry (capt of br H's steamer), and his wife from Union city. They staid over night, Sister Evans also staid.

Wed 7th they set off at 8 oclock to take the 9 oclock boat for Oakland. Accompanied by Capt A and lady. Sister Evans returned with them to the city Mr Truet went over to inform their friends the day previous. Mr Jonson one of the hired men went with the corpse. In the evening Cyrus was in, we had a little singing.

Thurs 8th very warm and pleasant. Sister B[urton] and I took a little walk up the side hill, found a few strawberries, and flowers, had a very sociable time. We returned and went to sewing on my dress, which she sis B, cut the day before. I assisted Catherine Mrs H's housemaid in gathering up every thing pertaining to the child, and removed them to the chamber, where they would be out of sight of the mother.

Friday 9th very warm in the morning. PM I went with Sis B—— to visit sister Picket and family. We had a very pleasant time. Mr C came to escort me home at night. Sis B staid intending to take the coach for the city the next day. We reached home near nine oclock.

Sat 10th rather cold and windy. I was alone again only as I received occasional visits from Catherine, the housemaid, who had a quarrel with the cook, and was full of her complaints.

Sund 11th very cold and blustering, no one went from here to church, but br Morris.

Catherine invited me to go with her to see her fowls which I did, and admired them much. In the course of the PM she had a quarrel with the cook, came in to enter her complaints to me as usual, but as I was on my bed, she laid her grievances before Mr C, who made her rather a short reply, which caused her to leave in quite a rage. Near 7 oclock Mr Truet came in. Told us he had just returned, and that the family had also come. I immediatly went in to see and welcome them home again. They said they had come round the bay by land. Mrs H was very gloomy, and dejected, said also that she felt quite unwell, came in for ginger to make herself some tea. She described to me the burying place of her children, said they removed their little son that was buried some years since at the mission and laid them side by side under a large tree near Henry Webster's.

Mon 12th Very cold wind and some rain. I sat with Mrs H a part of the day, she was also in my apartments sometime. I tried to divert her mind from the gloom and sorrow that pervaded it, but apparently in vain. She said it was impressed upon her mind by a dream or some other way that Joseph was going to be sick as the little girl was.

Tues 13th Very pleasant day. I washed in the morning. Mrs Horner invited me to take a ride with her to pick blackberries, but as I was washing I could not consistently accept the invitation.

PM we took a walk to call on our new neighbor who lives near us, by the name of Loveland. We had never seen the lady, before, accordingly as I was the oldest I introduced Mrs Horner first and afterwards she presented me to Mrs Loveland. We found her a very sociable pleasant lady. Said she was late from N Y. Quite a young woman in appearance, has one child only, it has been sick for several months, and looks very bad. She herself also has the chills, stays alone with her child every day, as her husbands business call him to the city daily. She was very polite to us thanked us for calling, and invited us to come again. We made a very short stay, and returned, Found the wind very boisterous.

Wed 14th, I finished washing but as the wind blew very hard I did not put them out.

~~*Thurs 15th*~~ C—— Ira came in, was very sociable. Said he intended taking a boarding house or grocery, remarked that he had been idle so long that he had lost his appetite, and felt very unwell. I observed to him that I thought active employment, more conducive to health than idleness.

Thurs 15th Very pleasant this morning. Put out my clothes, dried and brought them in before noon.

PM I ironed some. Mrs Horner was in, said she felt very lonly, and unhappy, spoke of her husband's embarrassment in his money affairs; herself and Mary had been doing the work in the kitchen for several days. She mourns the loss of her little girl very much, is almost inconsolable. Last night I dreamed of seeing Frances, I shall be looking for her return in a few days.

Frid 16th Quite pleasant in the morning. Br H and wife went to the city. She came in and invited me to go with them, but I was too busily employed to leave. She said her husband expected to receive several thousand dolls for a piece of land, at ten oclock I finished ironing; made pies. Mr Truett came in and ate ~~some~~ with us. Near 4 oclock Mrs H returned, came in, told me that her husband was disappointed in not getting the money; seemed to feel quite afflicted. She also told me that she missed a valuable diamond ring; thought it was taken from her drawer while she was absent last week, to bury their child. I was very sorry, as I had assisted the house maid in regulating the house, and saw her take the ring, and bestow it some where, I could not tell where. The maid who is an elderly irish woman, swore by everything sacred, and holy, that she was innocent of the crime. Sister Burton was also witness to her taking care of the ring, which was laying in the drawer, when she opened it.

Sat 17th I finished ironing, cut my cape, and finished my dress.

Sun 18th very pleasant morning. We all went to church. Had a very good meeting. Sister McLean invited the sisters to meet at her house on tuesday. I also received an invitation from sister Sargent to visit her the next day in co with Mrs Horner, and Sister Evans, who came home with ~~came us home with us~~ after meeting, and staid over night. We had a very good visit with her. She spent the evening in my room.

Mon 19th Very warm and pleasant. We set off at 9 oclock Br H had business towards the lake house, sister E and myself, and the children, stoped at sister Pickets, untill they returned. We had a fine pleasant ride, arrived at sister Evans at 11 oclock. Br H left us in the centre of the city to walk the balance of the way. We called on an old gent and wife by the name of [Richard and Sarah] Knowles, who are of the Brooklin co. The old lady treated us to gin, bread and butter &C. Was much pleased to see us, took us into her garden, and was very polite. Sister Evans made us a cup of tea for dinner, after which we went to sister Sargent where we had a very pleasant time. Her new husband came home in the course of the afternoon, was very polite and sociable. I admired his appearance much.

Himself and wife accompanied us to sister Evans, where we stoped untill Br H called for us. While waiting I ran into see sister Burton found her very comfortably situated, with plenty of business. It was quite late when Br H called for us, and the sun was set, when we reached home, and the wind blew very cold.

Tues 20th Remarkably cold and windy. Br H didnot take his carriage to the city consequently I was disappointed in going to sis McLaen's. Sister Picket was also expecting to go with us, but it is probably all for the best, that we did not go, as it is a very cold unpleasant day, the air is thick with fog, and the wind very boisterous.

Wed 21st Rather more pleasant. Afternoon I spent a few hours with Mrs Horner.

Thurs 22nd Quite pleasant. I washed. Mrs H went to the city, invited me to accompany her, but it was not convenient for me to leave home. When she returned she brought Josephene Smith with her, she spent the night, with us. We had singing, and music on the violin. Mr Truet came in and sung several songs. And upon the whole we enjoyed the evening pretty well.

Frid 23rd. Very pleasant calm for this place. Mrs Horner invited me to accompany her to Pickets. I cheerfully accepted the invitation. Toward 11 oclock we set off, Josephene went to the city with br H. Mrs H and myself spent the time very agreeably Br H returned between 5 and 6 oclock. When I reached home I found Robert Curtis in the sitting room. I did not know him at first, but upon taking a second look I discovered who he was. We were pleased to see him, as we consider him a worthy young man. He staid over night with us, and we had a very pleasant visit with him.

Sat 24th Very warm and pleasant, the calmest day we have had in two months. Ironed, baked light bread, strange gent from the mines took dinner with us, a friend of Mr Jonson's from Mich—— Robert F—— Curtis left for San F. We took a walk in the garden this evening. Alma and myself were walking by ourselves when we were joined by Catherine, and Mary.

We admired the neatness and order, in which it was arranged. Just as we were going to bed, Mr Truit came in with his new bass viol. Accordingly he played and we sang a few tunes before retiring to rest.

Sund 25th While eating breakfast Mrs Horner came in and informed me that they wished to set off earlier than usual as they desired to pass the cemetery on the way to church.[13] I told her I should be pleased to accompany them and would be ready as soon as possible. I therefore left Alma to regulate the kitchen; and prepared myself with speed. We had a pleasant time, spent near an hour, in walking among the graves.

I observed that the most of the inscriptions, or names, were persons from the eastern cities, and young men.

We reached meeting in good season, had a pleasant interview. Heard br P P Pratt is on his way to San F. Think Frances will perhaps be in the same boat.

Mon 26th Mr Crosby went to the city to do a job of work on Mr Horners Steamer, expects to be gone through the week. I spent a great part of the day with Mrs H. Alma and myself took dinner with them. In the evening Mr Truit was in and played the bass viol, while Alma took his fathers place on the violin. I sang several songs, and time passed off quite agreeably.

Tues 27th Just ten years, since the murder of the prophet, and patriarch, Joseph, and Hiram Smith. My mind has been drawn back to that memorable event, a great part of the day. What scenes of sorrow, and affliction, have we, as well as many others in the church, passed through since then! What the Lord has in store for us, for ten years to come is known only to Himself. But that we may have grace and patience to endure all things, is my prayer.

Wed 28th Mrs H was in, and requested me to spend the day with her again, to which I consented and took dinner with her. She is very lonly since the death of her child, and still feels very unreconciled to it. I made undergarments for brother Morris. This morning sent a letter to br Horace Barnes, of Bristol, Kendell co, Ill.

Thurs 29th Very foggy with high wind. About 9 the fog dispersed measurably, and it became tolerably pleasant. I washed. Toward noon we received a visit from Mrs Loveland, our nearest new neighbor. Her little boy is some better, but still looks pale and feeble. Her own health also is rather poor. We think her a very agreeable person. No *Southerner* arrives yet. We wonder at her delay. Towards evening Mr Loveland called for his wife. Br Horner was late home tonight, Josephene Smith returned with him, from her visit to the city.

He informs us that the *Southerner* arrived this morning with elder P P Pratt on board, but no Frances came. And as yet I have received no letter. I felt somewhat disappointed, although I have never felt very certain that she would come. Br H says there are some 20 elders at San Bernardino bound for the Pacific islands who are expected up the next trip of the *Southerner*, and possibly Frances may be in that company.

Mr H talks of moving his family back to San Jose, which will leave me quite lonely. We some expected to visit at Sister Pells today, if Mrs L had not sent us word yesterday, that she was coming today.

Frid 30th and last day of June. There is quite a cold wind. Alma has gone to pick blackberries. Brought home 2 quarts, which I made into preserves.

Sat July 1st Mrs Horner was in quite early, but complains of being more unwell than usually, brought in a medical work that Mrs Loveland sent her, to see whether I understood the names of the medicines. But it was a Homoepathic work, and entirely new to me. Toward noon she went home, and took her bed. I was in occasionly, untill two oclock. When Mr and Mrs Sargent came with all their family. Mrs H was unable to leave her bed, and I was under the necessity of taking her place, at the dinner table, and waiting upon the table company. I had felt quite unwell myself all the morning, but I found it quite essential to lay aside all gloomines, and try if possible to assume an air of cheerfulness, in order to render their visit as agreeable as possible. Br Horner, Mr Crosby, and all the men, were absent, excepting Mr Smith, so that Mr Sar—— had no one to visit with, but him.

A little before sunset, Mr Horner arrived bringing with him elder P P Pratt, Mr Crosby, br Morris &C. Br P—— looks just as natural as though I had seen him every day, and he observed that he thought I appeared as young, as when I lived at his house, in Kirtland. He said he made no stay at San B——d——no—— and brought no word from our friends.

Sun 2nd Very pleasant morning, but I found I had a very unpleasant headache, and gave over the idea of going to church. After the men went to meeting I went to see how Mrs Horner was, found her lying in bed. I staid with her part of the day. At twelve oclock I laid down, and slept two hours, found myself much refreshed thereby.

At three they returned from church, Br McBride, came with them. Spent the evening with us.

Mon 3rd. Quite pleasant again in the morning. Mr Crosby gone to the city again to work, expects to stay another week. Mrs Braphagle [*spelling unclear*] called to see Mrs Horner. I spent a great part of the day with Mrs H. she is still confined to her bed. In the evening we had music by Mr Truit, and Alma.

[Fourth of July Celebration, 1854]

Tues 4th of July. Great celebration at the city. Canons were fired at 4 oclock, and continued nearly all day. The morning was remarkably warm. After dinner the boys all went to the city, Alma among them. Mrs Horner is confined to her bed. Br H stops at home today. I went in and sat awhile, came back and wrote a letter to San Ber

Wed 5th More airy this morning. I washed some, read, wrote, and sewed. Sat up late, and read Godey's Lady['s] Book. Mr Truet and Alma made music in the kitchen.

Thurs 6th Very warm this morning, no wind untill 11 oclock. Mrs H much better today. C Ira was in. I had quite a lengthy conversation with him, on marriages, early, and late, and also on the various religions of the age. He observed that he intended to get the Koran, and read that; believed he should like it, as well as he did the bible.

PM I went in and sat awhile with Mrs H. A gent from the city called to see br H, about buying land, as he said for a schoolhouse, for boys, or young men, a sort of boarding school.

Music again in the kitchen, both vocal and instrumental.

Frid 7th remarkably warm day. Mrs H is much better. Invited me to take a ride with her to the city, and visit sister Origin Mowrey. We set off between 9 and 10 found the sun very oppressive. On arriving, found the friends all absent, gone to San Jose valley. We concluded to continue our ride to sis Pells, found her at home with her daughters children, and much pleased to see us. She treated us to sweet cakes, nuts, and drink. We spent 2 or 3 hours, quite agreeably, and returned, reached home at 4 oclock feeling much oppressed with heat. The evening was very pleasant. While Mary and I were walking in the yard Mrs H came and told me that br Hiram Blackwell was within, and wished to see me.[14] I therefore went in, and found him there, just from Great Salt lake city. I was much pleased to see him and received intelligence from many of our friends in that place.

Sat 8th Br Blackwell went to Pickets, towards evening returned, and spent several hours with me. Mr C did not reach home untill 8 oclock; the night being very foggy and dark. Mrs Loveland visited Mrs Horner. I was invited in, but was too busy to leave, and did not see her. She left her respects, and a promise to visit me, the next time she came.

Sund 9th Went as usual to church. very few attended. Sister Evans gone to San Jose. Sis Sargent became offended at br Pratt discourse the sunday previous and withdrew from the meeting. Br Blackwell bore testimony to the truth, and we had a very good meeting, after which we went down to the Steamer *Union*, and br H brought home Mr C's tools.

Mon 10th Mr C went to work with Cyrus Ira, building a small house, for some one, on the Puebla road.

I washed. Toward noon came Sister Picket, and her twins. I had a very pleasant time with them. About 3 oclock as we were conversing upon the deaths of br Joseph and Hiram br Morris brought in a young man by the name of Joseph Smith (3rd, son of Hiram [Hyrum] deceased.)[15] who was on his way with 20 other missionaries, to the Sandwich islands. The wind was blowing very cold, and he had no coat with him. I therefore offered him one of Mr C's which fitted him very well. His aunt Agnes Picket was very pleased to see him, and much affected at his sudden appearance; even shed tears, when she reflected upon the great undertaking of an orphan boy, of 15 years But he seemed in good spirits and quite cheerful.

They left at 3 oclock. Mrs H, and children, accompanied br Horner, to the city, and were gone all day.

In the evening came Orson Whitney, and Henry Richards and staid with us over night. Brought me a letter from sister Pratt, but no word from Frances, not much said with regard to her coming. We had a very sociable time with them.

Tuesday 11th Very pleasant morning, the brethren left at 7 oclock. An alarm of fire in the city, we could see the smoke very plainly from here. Br H Blackwell spent the forenoon, and took dinner with us, then left for the city. Br Horner and family, gone across the bay, expecting to be absent 3 or 4 days. This evening O Whitney returned, with his cousin Mills, a young man who came recommended to br Horner, as a carpenter, wishing to obtain employment.

We had music again, on the violin, and bass viol, accompanied with singing. Whitney, and Mills, found a man here by the name of Smith, who they discovered to be a cousin of theirs, and were quite pleased to make his acquaintance.

Wed 12th remarkably warm and still, no wind untill 2 or 3 oclock and then very little, which died away with the sun setting. Joseph Smith came, with Agnes, and Josephine, his cousin. The girls made us a fine visit, but Joseph was sent for to the city to meet br Parley Pratt, on business concerning their mission. Br Blackwell spent the day with us, and escorted the ladies home, at 5 oclock. It was a beautiful still evening. The full moon shone clearly, and the boys all went to the musician's near the park, to gratify their organs of tune and time They were absent untill 12 oclock. I felt much fatigued, and restless, through the night; finished and sealed my letter to sis P. Mr Crosby wrote one to br Whitaker. Retired at ten.

Thurs 13th another warm morning, Br B took breakfast with us, after which he left, intending to sail at 4 Pm.

Br Whitney went to the city intending to cross the bay to visit H[iram] Clark, was too late for the boat. Higgins took sis Picket to the city. On returning brought me two letters. One from sis P——, and another from sis Everett, of Great Salt lake city. Also brought butter, flour, and lard.

Frid 14th Last night about 12 oclock, the men in the chamber imagined they heard someone in the house below. They had just returned from a call at Mr Willis, and had not been asleep. Accordingly they all arose and came down with a loaded gun, prepared to meet a burglar, but after a strict examination of all the lower rooms, they concluded it was the rats having a regular fandango in the parlor, and thought best not to disturb them, and retired.

Very warm day. I cleaned house, did a little washing, made pies, and doughnuts &C. Higgins went after br H and family, but returned without them, said br H came to the city, but left his family at the ranch.

Sat 15th cold and foggy with high winds, Ironing and repairing garments, With an hours sleep kept me busy through the day.

Sun 16th A beautiful morning. The brethren all went to the city, to church, I Alma and I staid at home, as br H was not here to go with the carriage. I spent the day in reading, and playing the accordion. Slept from two untill 4 oclock.

Evening C Ira was in, was nearly intoxicated, raved, and cursed Christianity, to a great degree. Said he was the most miserable man living, that he had neither father, or mother that cared for him, sister or brother, wife or child, that every one despised, and scorned him, that he wished himself dead, and was determined not to live much longer in his present state. Intimated that he would either marry, or put an end to his life. We tried reason with him, but to no use. Mr Crosby invited him to go to bed up stairs, but he refused, and went home.

Mon 17th Cold and damp. ^*Tuesday 18th*^ Higgins went quite early with the carriage, to the steamer, to bring home Mr Horner and family. They reached home before breakfast, very cold and chilled. Said they had been on the boat over night. She was unwell, came in and sat sometime after breakfast with me. I washed, and cleaned up the chamber. Went in and sat a while with Mrs H. Music in the evening, on the bass viol violin and flute.

Wed 19th another cold foggy day with some rain. I dried my clothes, read some, sat awhile with Mrs H, and mended garments.

Thurs 20th This is Mr Crosby's birthday. He is now 47 years.

I looked for br P P Pratt and wife to visit us today, as they sent me word that intended coming one day this week.

Br Horner took his family with him in town, and invited me to accompany them, but I was too busy, and also myself expecting com and therefore declined. I baked, ironed, Br Badlam came took dinner and supper with us.

When Mrs H came home, she brought me a letter from Fran San be——di——no. She writes that her health is somewhat improved, but that she is still weak. But as soon as she feels well, we shall know it, by her sudden appearance among us,

We had a pleasant time with music, in evening.

Friday 21st Very cold stormy day. Mrs Redding Horner was here. I sat with them awhile. PM. Sister Horner IM[16] took her bed, being very unwell.

Sat 22nd Very pleasant morning. Mrs Loveland called in a few minutes. Mrs Redding Horner also came in awhile. Mr Crosby returned late from the city, where he had been employed since friday morn.

Sun 23rd Beautiful pleasant morning. Sis IM H still keeps her bed. I attended church in company with br Horner, Mr Crosby, Mrs R H, Elder P P Pratt spoke to us concerning practical religion, exhorted us to remove the dead branches from our midst, and be more prayerful. He complained of some of the members for having spoken reproachfully of himself and family. Declared himself, and them, innocent of any crime, before God and man. He appointed a day of fasting and prayer for the church. We reached home about 3 oclock PM.

Mon 24th Quite pleasant morning. I washed. Mr Crosby gone to the city to work again. Mary slept. Mrs Redding Horner spent the evening with me. Br Badlam talked some to her upon the principles of the gospel.

Tuesday July 25th AD '54 Very windy and foggy. Mrs R Horner went home, gave me an invitation to visit her, which I promised to do if ever I go to the place.

Mr H brought br Parley and wife home with him. They took supper and spent the most of the evening with me. Br Pratt blessed me, and my family, and said that peace, should dwell in my house. I had a very sociable time with them.

Wed 26th Remarkbly windy. I ironed, and wrote a letter to Frances. Mrs H—— is up again. Sister [Elizabeth] Pratt spent a of the day with me, br P was in in the evening, talked Spanish, related a vision or dream, of one of his family concerning the resurrection.

Thurs 27th Was our fast meeting. We set off at 9 oclock reached the city about ten, meeting in Mowreys chambers which br P, now occupies. He presided. The good spirit was with us, and rejoiced our hearts exceedingly. Sister [Elizabeth] Jones spoke in tongues, br Curtis phrophesied to Sister McLean, that her husband would yet come into the church, but that she would first have great troubles with him, but her prayers would eventually prevail.[17]

After meeting, Sister Horner, and myself, took supper with sister O Mowrey. Mrs S Mowrey was there, also, a Mrs Edgerton, who was one of the Brooklin Co, and formerly, a member of the church. She now lives in Calavarus [Calaveras], and came here on a visit. She inquired of me concerning Grouard Said she was acquainted with his first wife, and blamed him very much for leaving her. Said she was a good woman. Reached home near night. I took supper with Sis H. Orson Whitney and Joseph Peck, staid with us. We had a very sociable visit. Br Badlam was also in, and Higgins.

[A Hanging]

Friday 28th Today, Shepherd was executed, for the murder of Wm C Day. Higgins and Alma went to see him hung, but were too late, they saw him cut down, and heard some one say that he denied being guilty with his last words.

But he had previously left a written confession of the crime, which was published as soon as he was dead. Sister H—— is preparing to go over the bay tomorrow. I sat awhile with her, she seemed quite cheerful, said it was the first time she had felt like singing, since her little girl died. I joined her in singing one hymn. Alma staid with his father in the city, and went to the theatre, expecting to hear Ole Bull the great Violinist perform. but was disappointed by his being sick.

Sat 29th A returned early this morning. Br H—— and family, left immediately after breakfast, expecting to return on Monday. The men all went to the city. Mr Truett and Higgins moved to the office, and commenced housekeeping by themselves.

This evening Badlam, Smith, and Catherine, took supper with me. Mr C returned, just before dark. Cyrus Ira was in. Mr C, and br Morris, had a lengthy conversation, with Mr Smith, on the gospel, and its ordinances

Sun 30th Quite pleasant. Br Badlam proposed taking us into the meeting, as he said he was obliged to go, ^to the city^ to get feed for the horses. We had a good discourse from br Pratt. Several strangers were in.

On our return home, we called at Sister Picket's. Br B was obliged to go near there for feed, ^as he got none at the city^ and said we could call a few moments, if we desired.

The wind was blowing almost a gale, when we returned. We found Orson Whitney, H[enry] Richards, and Robert Curtis here on our return The boys staid over night, and all hands went down to spend the evening with Higgins, and Truett. They returned between 10, and 11 oclock, just as I had lost myself in sleep. I was much fatigued and nervous when I retired rest, occasioned by being out in the wind, I was obliged to get up to get clothes for Alma to make them beds. I then retired again, but was disturbed by their talking for near an hour.

As soon as they ceased I soon found myself in the arms of morpheus again, from which I was suddenly aroused by the return of br Morris from the city. It was then 12 oclock, and my nerves had become so much excited that I could not sleep untill 2. Mr C was going to the city again in the morning consequently I was obliged, *Mon 31st* to arise at 5, to give him his breakfast. He ate, and left about 6. At 7 I prepared breakfast, for myself, Alma, and the three young men, who left shortly after. Badlam went to the steamer, for br H, and family, found him, but his family stoped at Union city, untill the next return of the boat, in consequence of Joseph's ill health. He came out, and staid over night.

Tues Aug 1st AD 1854. Quite cold and unpleasant. I washed for the missionary boys. Their clothes were very dirty, as some of them not been washed since they left home. Which a little surprised me, as they staid some time San B——d——no.

Wed 2nd, Very dull and unpleasant, I slept late, In consequence of being remarkably weary, last night. Breakfasted at 9—— After which I finished my washing cleaned my floor &C. The wind is very severe, and the fog, dense. Mr C returned near 8 PM, said the steamer had not yet arrived, that br H was awaiting its arrival with some anxiety, expecting his family to come on it.

Thurs 3rd very cold and unpleasant. Br H has not yet returned, we fear something has befallen the steamer. I have been ironing today, feel very weary. Slept very little last night, in consequence of fatiguing myself with work, and exciting my nerves.

Mr C—— repairing an accordion for Josephen Smith

Friday 4th, I finished ironing, repaired clothes &C. Toward night br Horner arrived with his family. Wind blowing a gale, and the fog very dense.

Sister H—— came in, and brought a letter from sister Tomkins, which she handed me to read. I was struck with a remark from sister Tomkins concerning Fra[nces]. She observed that her health was very poor, and if she did not get help soon, would not ^in her opinion^ live long.

Sat 5th Last night I dreamed of seeing Frances and her mother. We were in a strange house, the inside of which was being sided up, like the outside, but unfinished, and Frances was reaching over the top of the clapboards to spit up the phlegm, from her stomach, and the amount of it surprised me greatly. I awoke with a heavy heart full of anxiety for her. Mrs H wrote back to sister T—— I sent love.

Baking and cooking of various kinds kept me employed through the day.

Sun 6th Very cold, Br H's, have gone again over, or rather around the bay, by land. His steamer has been detained in consequence of an attachment.

Two brethren staid here last night from Santa Clara. Br Dodge and Barrows. They have gone to the city to meeting, expecting to return here to night.

Mon 7th quite pleasant day. Br Morris returned alone last night. The Santa Clara brethren concluded to stop over night in the city. Br M—— brought me a letter from sis P, which she sent Pres—— [David] Sealy.[18] Orson Whitney called on us, took his clothes which I had been doing up for him. He offered to pay me, but I told him that I would willingly give him that much towards his mission, as I considered myself a fellow missionary with him, that we were both engaged in the same cause.

PM I went over to Mrs Loveland's, to see how she and her sick babe got along. I found them both very unwell. The child looks like a little ghost, is very uneasy, and wearies its mother very much, to take care of him. I staid about two hours and returned. Towards night the Santa C—— brethren returned took supper with us. We had a very agreeable visit with them.

Tues 8th Was a remarkbly warm pleasant day. It was so rare a circumstance for us to have a still day, that it had like to have over come us. The brethren left for home quite early.

PM we received a visit from the two Miss Smiths, Joseph S[mith]——, and M M [W W] Cluff. I made them a good dinner. Mr C and Alma entertained them with music, we sang hymns, and passed off the time very agreeably. Beautiful pleasant night. C Ira was in. Br H came home late, staid over night, said his family would not return untill next week.

Wed 9th plenty of wind again today. I washed. Mr C is laying floor in the verandah. PM I lay down awhile to rest, and slept near two hours. This evening Higgins was in awhile.

Thurs——— 10th Mr Crosby was out of lumber, and was under the necessity, of going to town, to get a load, and also to get provision. Returned about 5 oclock. Said he saw br Sealy set off for San B——d——no. Sent respects to br Pratts, and an apology for not writing.

Friday 11th I ironed. Had a very restless night, in consequence of taking the sits bath, previous to going to bed, which excited my nerves so much, that sleep departed from me, untill near two in the morning. I then slept about 3 hours, but felt quite well through the day.

About 1 oclock PM called brothers [John T.] Caine and [Joseph A.] Peck, two of the young missionaries, to the Sandwich islands.[19] Br Caine had never been here before. I like his appearance much. They spent the PM and night with us.

Sat 12th After breakfast br Badlam invited the elders to take a walk with him to sister Pickets.

It is a beautiful pleasant morning, which is so much of a rarity to us, that I think it worth recording.

I wrote a letter to sister Pratt, repaired clothes &C. Just as supper was ready the two brethren Caine and Peck returned, staid with us over night again. Br Badlam also returned from the city and informed us of the arrival of two elders from the Sandwich islands, Canon [George Q. Cannon], and [James] Hawkins.

Sun 13th Mr C accompanied the brethren to the city to attend church.

C Ira came in just as they were leaving, and invited me to accompany them as far as his house to see a nice picture that a young man by the name of B C Turnbull was drawing.

Accordingly Alma and myself, went with them, and examined the drawing, which we all pronounced very nice, although in an unfinished state. The young man expects to receive 50 dolls for it, from one of the picture galleries in San Fran, when it is completed. C Ira lent us a book, and we returned. Immediately after, Catherine left for the city, and was gone over night. Badlam took supper with us. Mr C——— returned between two and 3 oclock PM.

Mon 14th very pleasant morning. Truit and Higgins came in just as we finished breakfast, I gave them a cup of tea and a piece of sweet cake, which I had been saving for them. I washed, baked light bread, kept myself quite busily employed through the day. I found that I was much fatigued at night; and slept soundly.

Tues——— morning Aug——— 15th. Remarkbly warm and pleasant. I slept later than usualy. Breakfasted at 8. After which I put out my clothes, which were two dosen in number, mostly shirts, belonging to the young missionaries.

We received a visit from a little bird, which staid some time, being unable apparently to find his way out of the house. They are very plenty about the house and garden. The name of their specie is unknown to me. *Wed 16th* ^Another very warm day. I ironed. Br J Dier staid here last night.^ PM brs Peck and Spears [George Spiers] came out to see us. They took dinner, spent the greater part of the PM, and then went to sister Pickets, where they stoped over night. Br Horner came out from the city this morning, took breakfast, and a new recruit of clothes, for himself, and family, and returned. Said he left his wife sick in bed, that she would not probably be able to return, before the middle of next week. Br Badlam accompanied him to the city, and brought out a load of lumber. This evening C Ira was in, brought with him a school prospectus, got up by a young man by the name of Turnbull.

Thurs. 17th This is the third warm day, with neither wind or fog, that we have had in succession. Brs P[eck] and S[piers] left immediately after breakfast, for the city. Br P said he wished to be there to send clothes by the boat, to br Caine, who is at Mowreys Ranch, employed as a cook. PM he returned, in search of a couple of gold pens, which he said he lost from his vest pocket, either where he slept the previous night, or on the way to the city.

He rested himself awhile, and pursued his searching to Sister P[ickett]'s. I spent the PM in repairing shirts and pants. I understand that Sis P is about to remove to the city, to spend the winter, and feel quite sorry to part with them.

Frid 18th This morning we are visited again with the wind and fog, nothing transpired worthy of note.

Sat 19th Rather more pleasant. Bro Dougherty came to see us, on his way to Oregon, for his health, and also to visit a bro of his, residing there. He staid over night, told us concerning his difficulties with his wife, said he had consented to give her a bill of divorcement.

Sun 20th Quite pleasant. Mr C—— Alma, and br Dougherty went to church. Catherine went to the city Toward noon I concluded to call on one of our neighbors, Mrs Loveland, found her alone with her babe. Spent two hours with her. Mr L came home just as I was leaving, they both urged me to stop and dine with them, but I thanked them, and declined the invitation. I felt much fatigued on returning. Mrs L lent me a medical work on the cold water system.

When Mr C returned from church, he informed me that he had heard that br Grouard was near here. Early in the evening, he arrived with his wife, direct from Great Salt lake city. I like her very much, she resembles sister Jane Lewis, so much, that she seems very natural, to me.[20]

Mon 21st very pleasant morning. Near 9 oclock Catherine returned from the city, brought me a present of a piece of wedding cake, a friend of hers had been married, and saved her some of the cake, and she requested her to send me a piece, accordingly she folded a piece of two kind in nice white paper, and tied it with two ribbonds, one white, the other blue. I was much pleased with it. Just as we were sitting down to dinner came br Sparks, from the city, he took dinner, and staid over night, we enjoyed his visit very much. The evening was spent in singing, and music on the violin, and accordion.

[John Horner's Illness]

Tues 22nd I finished and sent a letter to sis P, by br Sparks, who said that he would send it, with one of his own, soon. Cold windy day. I baked pies. About 4 oclock br Sparks left. Sometime after dark br Horner and family arrived, having come by land from San Hosa valley. Br H was quite unwell, with teethache, and sore throat.[21] They brought me a letter from sister Woodbury. Who is now living at Isaac Horner's.

 Wed 23rd br H—— staid at home, and endeavored to doctor his face but it still continued quite painful. ~~Evening came br Mcbride~~

 Thurs 24th Very pleasant. Sister Grouard and myself went to visit sister Picket. We had a fine time going, enjoyed our visit extremely well, but had a high wind, and an abundance of fog to brace against in returning. We left at 4 oclock, sat down once to rest, Reached home at 5, found Alma, and br G, had his mules harnessed, ready to come after us, had we waited a few minutes. Immediatly after we reached home, came Mr and Mrs Forbes. They had never been here before, and Mr Forbes thought if he could get away at an early hour in the morning he would never come again, as he was nearly frightened by the cold wind, common to this place. Br and sister H being absent when they arrived, ~~and~~ Mr Crosby conducted them into my room. Mr F informed me that he saw a shocking sight in coming down, two frenchmen who were hung by a mob at San antoine [San Antonio], for stealing cattle. They were butchers who had for 2 or 3 years practised selling stolen beef, many of them fine american cattle. Some cows. They were hung at 6 in the morning, and were left as a spectacle to others untill 11 oclock.

 Frid 25th Very stormy in the morning, Sis G—— was washing. Br Badlam went to the city brought br McBride home with him. br H still very unwell. Frank Rose came to see us, staid over night.

 Sat 26th Quite pleasant Sister Grouard and myself took a walk over the hills, accompanied by the little boys Wm and Joseph [Horner].

 Sun 27th quite pleasant. Mr Crosby and Grouard went to church. Sister G—— and I went in to see br H awhile. Br Badlam went for the Dr.

I spent part of the day studying the water cure system. Mr C sat up untill 12 oclock with br H—— and then br Badlam took his place.

Mond 28th Very pleasant morning. Mr C—— and Grou went to the city, bought some necessaries. Brought 3 letters to us. One from John Eagar, one from Zina D Young, and another from Frances.

Sister Grouard quite unwell today, they expect to leave tomorrow. I wrote a line to send by them to the friends in S——B——di——no.

Tues 29th Rather stormy and unpleasant. Br G—— and wife left, about 8 oclock, to pursue their journey to S——B——dino by land. Immediately after they left called a Mr Selby desiring to see br G. Mr C went to work on Cy Ira's new house, I washed and cleaned house, was very tired and restless at night.

Wed—— 30th quite pleasant. Mr Wm Horner and wife, Mrs Ralph, and Mrs R H, came to visit br J M in his sickness. Staid over night. Br Riser also came, took supper and staid over night with us, just as we were going to bed, Mc Bride and W—— [Washington] Rogers came, staid over night I had never seen Rogers before, on conversing with him found he was a son of Noah R who went with the first co of missionaries to the islands.

Thurs 31st I baked pies and bread. Br Merrick came and staid over night with us, quite sociable time in the evening. We found br Merrick to be an intelligent, agreeable young man.

Friday Sept 1st AD 1854. Cold and cloudy. Ironed. Br Badlam left for Sacramento.

I have felt much depressed in spirit and body, for several days, owing to indigestion, foul stomach &C—— Br Tanner came out from the city to see us, staid over night. We enjoyed his visit well, believe him to be a good man

Sat 2nd. Br Tanner left after breakfast. Mr C continues his work with Cyrus. Br Horner is getting smart again, has been out in the garden today. Redding Horner, and Wm Emily came to see J M H, staid over night. Cyrus Ira took supper with us.

Sun 3rd rather unpleasant, none of us went to church, but br Morris. About noon came br Riser again, having been to Sacramento, and brought down a child, which he buried there, some 3 years ago. The child was one year old. The fathers intention is to bury it in the burying place near centreville, a new town which John M Horner has laid out, between Union city, and San Jose mission, and which is intended as a gathering place for the saints who wish to settle in this part of the country.[22]

Mon 4th rather pleasant. Br H—— has so far recovered his health as to go to town again today. Br Riser also left this morning. I have just finished a letter to br P[hilip] B Lewis and wife, who are at the Sandwich islands. I intend to send it by the young missionaries, a part of whom, expect to sail on Wednesday. I have been troubled with gloominess for several days, great depression of spirits, I have been reading a medical work, on the water cure system; and have come to the conclusion that I have the nervous dispepsie. I have been trying to get resolution sufficient to commence treatment, but have not yet been able

Teus—— 5th. I washed, cleaned my floor, and did sundry other chores. When Mr C returned at night he brought us two letters, one was from Frances, and the other from Lois Thompson.

Wed 6th I ironed; did not feel well. Went in and sat awhile with Mrs Horner. Cyrus was here in the evening, quite sociable times.

Thurs 7th This is our prayer, and fast day. We all left for meeting about 9 oclock, reached there between 10 and 11, had an excellent meeting, enjoyed a good degree of the spirit, had some interesting instruction from br Pratt. Soon after the meeting closed, came br C West, and F Dewey, just returned from their mission to the Indies. We were much interested with the account of their travels, as it was new to me, not recollecting of having heard, or seen travellers from that country before, relate, or give a description of the place, and people; their manners and costoms, religious faith &C. Br Badlam returned this morning from Sacramento complains of being very unwell.

Friday 8th, remarkably warm pleasant day. We received a visit from Mrs Loveland. Sister Horner is quilting skirts. Mrs L and I went in, and assisted awhile. The ladies all came in and dined with me. Mrs Redding Horner is here yet. We had a very agreeable time. Evening came br C West, staid over night, gave us a further account of his travels.

Sat 9th Cold and windy again. While we were at breakfast came br Dewy, having staid the previous night at br [Ambrose] Moses, at the mission house. They both took breakfast and spent the day with us. I prepared dinner, while we were eating came br J[oseph] Peck and Edw Partridge, two of the young missionaries destined to the Sandwich islands. They also took dinner with us, are stopping with Higgins. Br West spent the evening in br H's, Br Dewy stoped with us untill bedtime. We had music on the violin and accordion. Br D—— is something of a musician.

Sund 10th Mr Crosby and the brethren gone to church. Br H's did not attend in consequence of Wm being somewhat indisposed. I spent the day in reading and writing. In the evening commenced a letter to Lois Thompson. Mr C is also writing.

Mon 11th This morning I felt very unwell. After breakfast I cleaned my kitchen, and tryed to work off my feelings, but found it in vain. At eleven oclock I went to bed, and lay 2, or 3 hours. I was in great pain, and had a high fever. No one knew that I was sick, nor came nigh me, to learn whether I was or not. After a long time Alma came in the room, to see what had become of me, when I asked him to make me a fire, to warm my feet, which he did. I then arose, and after getting my feet thoroughly warmed, I went about getting supper; but found it quite a task. However after getting a warm cup of tea, I felt much better; and in the evening I finished my letter to sister Lois Thompson. Br H brought me 3 letters. Sis P—— El—— and F wrote me.

Tues 12th Sent our letters to the office. Mr C also mailed a pamphlet, to br Horace Barnes, on the subject of polygamy; written by sister Belinda Pratt, in a letter to her sister. Mrs Redding Horner went home this morning.

Sister Horner came in to see me, invited me to bring in my work which I did, took my letters, from E,—— and F, and read them to her. She gave me the one ~~sister~~ sister Tomkins sent her to read, we spent a few hours together very agreeably.

Wed 13th Rather pleasant this morning. Sister Horner invited me to go to the city with her, but I declined in consequence of having some indispensable business at home. I finished an undergarment for br Canon. Washed &C. Lay down and rested about an hour, then arose and prepared supper. Cyrus was in this evening. Conversation turned upon the different religions, extant in the world. Their proprieties and improprieties. Br McNear, also called in the course of the evening. Staid over night with Mr H's.

Thurs 14th, quite pleasant again. I ironed. Mrs H came, and sat awhile with me. Told me concerning her visit yesterday. I finished ironing, got a little dinner, and sat down to write; but was so sleepy I could scarcely see. I sent br Canon's garment to him, by Higgins.

15th Friday I repaired garments, Mrs Horner came in awhile. Informed me that they were going over the bay tomorrow. Br H Wilkins came home with br H, called in to see us. Said he was on his way to the states, to see his friends.

Sat 16th beautiful pleasant morning. Br Horners, left at an early hour. Mr Crosby went to the city, brought home some groceries, by the return of the carriage. We had quite a time of singing, in the evening. Br Wilkins, Badlam, and Cyrus Ira were present. Mr C played the violin, and we sang nearly every hymn in the book, besides some that are not in it.

Sun 17th Another fine day. Alma has gone to church, accompanied by br Morris, and Wilkins. Mr C did not feel like walking so far today, and as br H's were away the carriage did not go consequently there was no chance for me to go. Alma returned after the first meeting. Br Morris came at evening, said they had a good time, and that br Lyman held church at Union City, in co with br Sparks. It has been a remarkably warm day for this place.

Mon 18th Another very warm calm day, I wrote a letter to Zina D Young, yesterday, and one to Bishop Everett, and wife, today. This evening the atmosphere was remarkably warm, which was so uncommon a circumstance, that we feared the consequence might be an earthquake; as I have heard that in countries where earthquakes are frequent, they consider heated as indicative of one.

Tues 19th This morning the wind returned again, acompanied with fog. Br H Wilkins came in and read us a letter from his father.

Wed 20th Quite cool again. I washed today. Felt much fatigued at night, was very restless, slept badly.

Thurs 21st. Ironed. Just after breakfast Higgins called to get the team and carriage ~~and~~ to fetch home br H's family from the city. About 10 oclock they arrived, said they had slept on board the steamer. Mr C was busy putting glass doors in to their sitting room, which made in much disorder. Sister Horner went directly to work at housecleaning, and soon had her new diningroom in ample order. Mr Ralph and family came out at night staid over night. A br [Henry W.] Bigler late from the Sandwich islands staid with us.

Frid 22nd Br Bigler left, and returned to the city, said he thought br Canon would be out to see us that day, but he did not come. After breakfast sister proposed ~~that we~~ taking a walk to Mrs Lovelands, to which we consented and accordingly went accompanied by sister Ralph. We found Mrs L quite smart, and her child much improved.

Sat 23rd Sister Ralph left at an early hour. Br Wilkins went to the city. I sent a line to br Canon, to be conveyed to sister Pratt. Spent a part of the PM with sister Horner, her husband has returned to the other ranch, expecting to be absent untill monday. I spent the evening with her. Mary cut her hand quite badly, came in to my room, to get me to do it up for her, which I did as well as I could. Br [Bechias] Dustin staid over night ^with us we had a very agreeable visit with him.^

Sun 24th very fine morning. Sister H did not go to church and consequently there were nothing said about the carriage being taken untill near noon, when I came to dress Mary's wound, I discovered that it needed something more than we had, to dress it properly, and proposed going, or sending for something to the city. Sister Horner thought br Badlum had better take us in which he did. We arrived just as br Lyman was closing his discourse. At intermition br B took sister Jones home, and she invited me, to accompany her, to see her husband; said he was very weak, having had quite a severe attack of cholera.[23] I accepted the invitation, and found him as she had said, but improving.

While we were there, br and sis [Isaac and Hester] Nash arrived from Union city. Br Nash came over by br Pratts request to preach to the Welsh people of San Francisco. Br Pratt preached to us in the PM. On returning called at a drug store and got some balsam for Mary's hand.

Mon 25th cold and windy as usual. I sewed some. Br Ira was in and took dinner with us, he also called again at night and took supper. Mr C played the violin, br Badlam danced. They also had singing. I spent an hour with sis H.

Tues 26th. I washed, cleaned floors, baked light bread. Br Henry Richards visited us. Sister H also had company. Isaac Horner and wife, and two children came. Br Horner came home late last night.

Wed 27th I wrote a letter to John Eagar. Br Bigler came to see us, staid over night.

Thurs 28th Very foggy this morning. I feel quite unwell, and dejected. I sent a present of dried fruit, by br Bigler, to br Canon ^also 3 letters to him to carry to the valley.^ I ironed, and wrote a letter to Ellen Pratt. Br H——— and wife, and Isaac H's folks went to the city, attend meeting.

Frid 29th More pleasant this morning. I have just written a letter to Frances. Mr Crosby is putting in glass doors in the front part of the house. I had a sleepless ^or rather restless^ night, last, and felt very nervous this morning. I dreamed of seeing a piece of road which I understood that br Morris had made, and graded it with brick. It was built on descending, and sidling ground and was intended to be raised on one side, to make it level. But instead of that, br M——— (in order to revenge himself on the owner of the road,) ^for some miss usage^ had made it to slant with the ground, so that a carriage would be inclined, to run off sideways. I thought that my husband and myself were the first to walk over it, and as we came to the lower end, the bricks became soft like wet clay. I attempted to carry a baking kettle of pudding over it, and the bricks gave way under my feet, and I became much fatigued with my load and gave it to Mr Crosby. I was much surprised that br M should take so much trouble, and make so bad a piece of work for the sake of revenge. I also dreamed of finding large specimens of gold, which I thought we had laid by sometime since, and now as it was a scarce time with us we brought them forth.

[Time Gliding By]

Sat 30th and last of Sept. So glides away one month after another. Time hangs rather heavily upon me. I still feel as it were in a state of banishment. And dont know that I should feel better, in any place. It seems that I am deprived of society in a great degree. And what is life without friends, and compaions in travel, who will readily sympathize with us, and with whom we can "bear each others burdens, and so fullfill the law of Christ."

This morning I sent letters to Ellen, and Frances, by br A Lyman. Spent sometime with two sisters Horners. This evening br H sent in, to invite us to attend a prayer meeting, in his sitting room. We readily accepted the invitation, and repaired to the room, where we found the family, already assembled. We enjoyed the time, for two hours, very well, in singing, praying, and speaking.

Sun Oct 1st Remarkably pleasant morning. But as we were 4 miles from the city, and no money to pay our passage, we could not consistently attend church. Br H and family went. His sister with two children accompanied them. Mary and I took quite a pleasant walk over the hills, called on Mrs Loveland a few moments. We found a number of very pleasant building places in our walk, and admired the picturesque scenery, of the hills, the bay, and the city. Reached home at one oclock, being some fatigued, I lay down a few minutes. After supper sister I Horner came in, with her little girl. She told me concerning the meeting, and their ride up the bay road, in coming home. C Ira was in this evening, very sociable times. Br Morris returned from the city, at 8 oclock.

Mon 2nd. Very warm and still. We think our summer is just commencing. Mr Loveland brought his little boy over this morning, he looks very feeble. Sister Isaac Horner was in this evening. Music on the violin and accordion.

Tues 3rd Another remarkably warm day. I washed, and kept myself in a perspiration nearly all day.

Wed 4th This morning the wind and fog returned again, which rendered the air very damp, and changed the atmosphere materialy.

Thurs 5th Tolerably pleasant. I put out my clothes, and dried them. Mr C gone to work on a small building on the San Hose road, a mile from home. Last night I awoke at twelve oclock, found my head felt very heavy, and painful, but after turning several times I felt relieved in a degree, yet sleep had departed from me, and refused to exercise its soothing influence over my brain, the remainder of the night. About 4 oclock I arose, and seated myself in my armed chair, but fearing I should take cold, concluded to retire to bed again, tho not to sleep. At half past five I arose to prepare breakfast for Mr Crosby, as he wished to leave at six. I expected to feel very bad through the day, but as good luck would have it, I felt no great inconvenience from so sleepless a night. This was our monthly prayer and fast day, but br Horner did not go, and I had no opportunity to attend, altho my heart was sad, and heavy all day in consequence thereof. I frequently feel that we are outcasts from all society, and living almost in hermitage. But the Lord grant that I may endure it patiently, and without murmuring, and in his own due time grant us relief from our seclusion, by restoring us to the bosom of the church, His people.

Frid 6th Quite pleasant. I ironed. Br and sis Horner went to the city. Mr and Mrs Watkins from Santa Clara, came out with them. PM there was a cattle show at the race course, near by us. Alma went down, but on hearing their terms, came home without seeing them, "thought it too much for so little."

Amelia Althea Stevens married Jonathan Crosby in the
Nauvoo Temple in 1846. From Elvira Stevens Barney, *The
Stevens Genealogy*, p. 219. Used by permission, Utah State
Historical Society, all rights reserved.

Sat 7th I arose early, prepared breakfast for Mr C, who left at 6
oclock. Br Horner and family, went to San Jose. After they were gone, I
brushed and cleaned house, gathered new flowers to replenish my flower
pots, and put things ample order. Br Badlam went to the city, brought me
a letter from Mary E Kimball G S L city. I perused it with pleasure, and felt
truly thankful that we were not entirely forgotten by our old friends. As my
retired situation sometimes causes me to feel, as if I was entirely forgotten, by everybody. But at others I feel to bless the Lord, that it is as well
with us as it is.

Truly we have many blessings, which thousands of the saints are
deprived of, and which we ourselves, have many times been denied. But

what are a few of the luxuries of life, in comparison to the society of those we love, and whose faith, and confidence, we prize above all price, truly I feel to say with the poet. Society, friendship, and love, Divinly bestowed upon man. Oh, had I the wings of a dove, How soon would I taste you again, But I believe, upon more mature consideration that this retirement is for my benefit, inasmuch as it teaches me a lesson which I otherwise could not learn, that is, it teaches me to prize the fellowship of friends, and brethren. Which I have many times (undoubtedly) esteemed lightly, in consequence of becoming so familiarized to it.

Sun 8th Beautiful pleasant morning, all nature appeared in its loveliness. My mind has been calm and tranquill today. Mr C and myself staid at home, Alma went to meeting, returned at 4 oclock. Cyrus Ira was in awhile, his mind is again all confused on the subject of religion, has been reading philosophy, and infidelity, untill he knows not what to believe.

Mon 9th We had several showers of rain, which much revived the face of nature, and rejoiced the heart of the gardner.

Tues 10th. Br Horner and family, have just returned from Union city, brought me a letter from Sister Woodbury, with one enclosed from Amelia Stevens, from Nauvoo. Who states that she has united herself to the Icarian society[24] in that place, and seems much pleased with it.

Wed 11th I washed, after which I went in, and assisted sister Horner on her new white dress, which she is making for the ball, at Union city. Cyrus, and Henry were in this evening, livly conversation on various subjects.

Thurs 12th Some rain this morning. After breakfast I went to assist Sister H in preparing for the ball. She left at ten. Br Badlam conducted her to the city, where her husband had gone previously, I asked him to go to sister Evans and get sister Woodbury, which he did, returned about 2 oclock. We had very sociable times reading letters, and conversing upon various subjects. In the evening we had singing, Br Morris, Badlam, and Henry Wilkins were in. Sister Woodbury has improved very much in the art of singing of late.

Frid 13th. Sister Woodbury talked of returning to the city but I would not consent to it. She brought with her the likeness of her sister Amelia A Stevens, which looks very natural. Br Horner and wife, returned late, from their excursion, to Union city.

Sat 14th Quite pleasant, Sis Woodbury returned to the city with br H. Her visit brought many past scenes to our remembrance both merciful and afflictive. Old friends were brought to mind and compared with new ones, and in many of instances, the former were prefered. Mr C went to town this PM, traded some, rode home with br Horner in the evening.

Sun 15th Very pleasant morning. I accompanied my husband, br H, and wife, to church. We set off at an early hour, in order to ride some

about town, had a very pleasant time, reached the meeting place in due time, very few attended. Br H decided on turning it into a prayer meeting. I enjoyed it very well, but was obliged to return as soon as the first meeting closed. We reached home at 3 oclock. Henry W, and the girls were in. We had music both instrumental and vocal.

Mon 16th cold and windy. Mr C making fence. Br Cyrus Ira called about noon. Conversation turned upon the history of Eng the reigns of the different kings and queens, since my remembrance. Sister H came, and invited me, to bring my work in, and sit with her which I did. Her husband returned between 4 and 5 oclock PM. She gave me one of Gleasons pictoral papers, which he brought home. It is a very interesting periodical.

Tues 17th. Very dull and unpleasant. Nothing transpired worth noticing.

Wed 18th. I washed. Tolerably pleasant day.

Thurs 19th. We attended prayer meeting. Br Horner went in to the city, at an early hour, in the omnibus. PM Sister H proposed going into meeting, to which we readily consented. We arrived in due time, found a number of the young missionaries assembled in council concerning their mission. We had a very good time. Saw sister Sparks, just from San B——dino. She informed me that Frances Pratt started intendeding to accompany her, but that on reaching Losangelos, they for some cause, gave up the idea of coming, and that F went back with her mother and sister Hunt, who came with them, but that she went to visit a friend, where she spent a few days, and then concluded to proceed to San Francisco. After meeting we went to the Union depot, in search of br Horner, but he had left, a few minutes previously. On arriving, found him at home, a few minutes before us. Alma whitewashed my rooms while I was absent.

[California Art Union]

Frid 20th Quite warm and pleasant. Sister Horner proposed going to the city again for the purpose of visiting Duncan's Chinese Sales room. Or rather the California Art Union. Which includes some of the greatest curiosities my eyes ever beheld. We spent several hours, in examining the articles below and then repaired to the galery above, to see the beautiful paintings. There were visitors, constantly going to an fro, of all classes, and descriptions. Sister H, and myself, became much fatigued, by walking through the long aisles. Br H met us in the lower room, and accompanied us to the fair of the California Farmer, where we saw variety of curiosities. The superintendent was very polite to us, made sister H. and myself a present of a very large pear, and apple, and a cluster of very nice grapes; invited us to call again. It was nearly dark when we reached home. I bought a ticket in Duncans lottery, and Mr C bought two, intending to try our luck, for once.

Sat 21st Very fine warm day. I felt quite unwell, but still succeeded in cleaning my rooms of lime, and PM went in to visit with Mrs Loveland at br H——'s. Br H—— gone to San Jose. I spent the evening with his wife. About half past seven we were visited with a light shock, of an earthquake, which considerably excited Sister Horner.

Sun 22nd Quite rainy and unpleasant. We did not attend church. Higgins, and a young man by the name of James, took breakfast with us. Cyrus Ira spent the evening with us.

Mon 23rd It still continues rainy, and unpleasant. We had thunder, and hail.

Tues 24th More pleasant. I washed, but felt very unwell all the morning. Br Ira came in as usual, to free his mind, and release it from study. We had music in the evening, both instrumental and vocal.

Wed 25th Some rain this morning, PM more pleasant. I ironed, also made grape jelly. Evening br Morris and the children, ~~including~~ with the hired girls, and young men were in, to hear the violin. Some singing on the occasion. Br Ira was present, staid untill after 9 oclock. He went home, and just as the clock struck 12 he returned in a great hurry, spoke to br Horner, told him he thought he had something in one of his ears, and wished him to arise and examine it to see what he could discover Which he did, but made no discovery, and he finally concluded it was merely imagination, and so went to bed in <u>there</u>, and slept the remainder of the night.

Thurs 26th This is the anniversary of our wedding. 20 years ago we were joined in marriage. And Oh what a variety of scenes have we passed through, since then, both mercifull and afflictive. Travels by sea and land Sometimes in adversity, and at others in prosperity, but more frequently the former. But we have been led to see the hand of God in it all, and to acknowledge his mercy and goodness.

Friday 27th, tolerably pleasant, Mrs Loveland called a few minutes.

Sat 28th I went to the city with br and sis Horner, Br H left us at the plaza. We went shopping about, I traded ~~near~~ 11 dolls. We called at Mr Carringtons, found br, and sis Knowls there. They were just sitting down to dinner, and insisted upon our eating with them. They had a baked pig, and what they called an old fashioned, english pudding, tea and wine were offered us, but we prefered water, as a beverage.

After dinner we went to sis Evan's, saw sister Sparks, and Hollenbeck. I went over to Mowreys, found them making a comfortable. It was quite late when we reached home. Cyrus took supper with us, after which he staid untill near 9 oclock.

Sun 29th fine pleasant day. Went to church. Br Pratt preached, had two meetings. Br P left us, gone to Santa clara.

Br Morris presided again. Reached home after dark. Br Naile came home with Mr C, staid over night. Also br Dustin staid with us.

Mon 30th. Fine day, br Naile, and Dustin left after breakfast. I spent the day on my feet, baking, cooking dinner. Cyrus dined with us. Evening came br, and sis. Sparks, Sister Evans, and her little girl, staid over night.

[Frances's Return]

Tues—— 31st, fine morning, we all took a walk to the mission, and visited sister [Lydia Ensign] Moses and her daughter, Mrs Valanche [Ann Frances Valencia].[25] Soon after we reached there sister Sparks was taken quite sick, and went to bed, where she remained all day, being unable to sit up. About 1 oclock, an omnibus came in, and who should alight from it but Frances Pratt, direct from San B——dino, She was accompanied by Mrs Swesy [Sweasey], formerly Mrs Eagar. They had accidently met in the omnibus. I was quite surprised to see F as I had lately given up all hope of her coming. We spent the afternoon very agreeably, ~~with~~ had a fine supper, after which Frances and I came home, Sister Horner waited for her husband to come with the carriage. We had a pleasant walk, and sociable times, coming up the hill. ^Mr C and Alma were as much surprised to see F as I was, but all much rejoiced^

Wed Nov 1st AD 1854 Very fine day. Frances had a great deal to tell us, of the S——B——d——ns. I think her health is much improved. Br Jones Dire staid with us last night. Cyrus was in, this evening. His conversation ran upon the resurrection of the body, his mind is still in doubt with regard to it.

Thurs—— 2nd. Beautiful weather now. The cold west wind which has troubled us all summer, is now dying away, gradually. Fr—— and I washed. PM the cold wind returned upon us.

Frid 3rd, another fine day. Frances gone to the city in co with br and sister Sparks, who came home with br N last night. I have just finished a letter to M[ary] E Kimball. Sent two to the office this morning. One to br Joseph Barnes, another to sister N Hide of G—— S—— L—— City.

Sat 4th Very fine day, Mr C—— went to the city, returned about ~~near~~ noon. PM. we all took a walk over the mountains, to see the broad ocean. We found it quite a task to ascend them but felt very well paid for our trouble, in admiring the majesty of the scenery, being refreshed by the sweet air of evening, we returned well satisfied with our excursion.

Sun 5th Fine day Mr C went to the city to attend church. Br J M Horner over the bay, Sister H proposed going to Catholic church, accordingly we set off accompanied by Mrs Redding H, Catherine, the housekeeper, Mary and the children.

It was rather late when we reached the church, but we staid as long as we desired to, being unable to understand much of the services. (We reached home about 12 oclock. The sun shone very warm, I felt much fatigued, and laid down awhile) We admired the order, and apparent devotion of the worshipers. Although I knew they were in darkness and superstition, yet believe we can profit by some of their examples. Cyrus Ira was in awhile this evening. Mr R Horner called in, in search of his wife, who has been here at J M H's a week.

Mon 6th I washed, Br and sister Sparks came out with br H, spent the evening with us.

Tues 7th, rather cloudy, and unpleasant. Br Z Cheny and wife, sister O Mowrey, and her Niece D. Cheny's daughter came out from the city, and made us a visit. We enjoyed it much. Evening Frances went home with them, to attend an evening party. Sister Sparks spent the evening with me. About 9 oclock, came br S, and Caine,

Wed 8th. Sister Horner is much afflicted with teethache, her face badly swollen. Br H Blackwell, and Partridge, came out, and made us a visit. Br B brought us letters from sister P, and Ellen. Alma also received a letter from Ann L.

Thurs 9th I washed for br Caine. Had a very sleepless night last, in consequence of drinking strong tea. Fran returned at night.

Frid 10th I ironed. Mr C butchered two hogs, one for himself, and one for Mr H. Evening I wrote Sis Pratt. Cyrus came to board with us yesterday, gave us his cooking stove, and various articles of crockery.

Sat 11th, fine day. Mr C gone to the city. Br H's gone over the bay. F—— making mince pies. Evening br and sis H, returned, did not cross the bay.

Sun 12th, morning foggy, and unpleasant. At ten, fog disappeared, and the sun shone brightly. F—— and I accompanied br and sister H to church. Meeting was held in a new place, which we have rented of br Cheny for 15 dolls pr month. Br Curtis presided F—— staid over night, went to Pickets, The wind blew very hard as we came home. I was quite chilled.

Mon 13th Making sausages. About noon F—— returned. Said she had been to the dentists, had a tooth extracted and one filled, that she was going in again, in the course of the week, to have some new ones put in.

This evening br Sixtus Jonson [Johnson] came out from the city with br Horner, took supper and spent the evening with us, He complained of a sick headache, and went to bed early. Cyrus gone for lumber to finish his house, returned late.

Tues 14th. Making sausages again. Br and sis H—— gone over the bay. F slept in their room with the children.

[Caroline's Bad Cold]

Wed 15th I have a cold, but still conclude to wash. F—— and myself have a hard days work, washing, scrubbing, making sweet cakes, and doughnuts.

This evening, Edward Partridge came home with br B, spent the evening with us, also br Jonson, br Morris and Badlam, were in. The brethren made themselves a deal of sport concerning their tickets in the Art Union. My cold is quite bad. However I slept well, and arose *Thurs 16th,* much refreshed. Frances received a letter last night from Ellen. They seem to regret her leaving them so abruptly. All alone to day. F——, and Alma gone to the city. Mr C—— at work on C, Ira's house. I ironed.

Frid 17th last night my cold increased to that degree that I think I never suffered more a night in my life, untill 3 or 4 oclock in the morning, when I fell asleep, and slept 2 or 3 hours very quietly. My husband had no rest untill 2 oclock, but was up every few minutes all night, trying to do what he could to alleviate my distress. I was near strangling for breath, several times, and was obliged to sit up in bed a great part of the night. Mr C—— got the breakfast, and went to his work as usual. Alma washed the dishes. About 7 oclock I arose, and went into the kitchen, made me a bowl of ginger tea, which I drank, and again retired to my bed. Sister H came in to try what she could do for me, made a poultice of fried onions, and laid on my neck and breast, which I think afforded me almost immediate relief. She also gave me lard and molasses, simered together to loosen my cough. And towards night I felt much better. F returned a little before dark, and prepared supper. I rested well through the night, and feel thankful that I am improving.

Sat 18th I was still better, but not entirely well. I kept about house, but did not accomplish much. F assisted sis H on Mary's dresses. I went in awhile, and took my sewing. We F, and I dined with sister H.

Sun 19th F and I both stoped at home, I did not think it prudent for me to go out on account of my cold, and she did not feel in the spirit of going. Br H's people went, and on returning brought sister P B Lewis [Jane Stevens] with them, who has just returned from the sandwich islands. I was quite surprised to see her, as I did not think she would come, without her husband. I discovered that she had sufferd with disease, and grown old. We had a very social visit.

Mon 20th, Sister Lewis returned to the city, having made us rather a short visit, but feeling anxious to find a home, where she could have employment at needle work, she felt unwilling to stay longer at present. F—— sewed for Sis H. Br Blackwell spent the evening with us, also John Cheny. Br, and sis H—— were in. Mr C, and J Cheny, played the violins together, and the evening passed off very agreeably.

Tues 21st. Very pleasant morning. J C took breakfast with us and left soon after. Br Blackwell went to work for br H. I felt quite miserable, but tried to sew some on my dress. F and I got dinner, had an oister soup, Sister Horner came and dined with us. Toward evening I was attacked with a pain in my stomach, and bowels, which lasted me untill near 9 oclock.

The brethren had a prayer meeting in br H——s sitting room, I was too unwell to attend. After the meeting closed, I invited them to lay hands on me, which they did, and I had no pain (scarcely) afterwards. I retired to rest at 9 oclock, after anointing myself with oil, had a good sleep.

Wed 22nd. I arose at 7 oclock, sat up awhile, took salts, and then went to bed, and slept the greatest part of the forenoon. Afternoon much better, sewed some. Mr C went to the city came home sick.

San Francisco Nov 23rd AD 1854 [*added later*: ^1854^]

Thurs 23rd[26] Very foggy and unpleasant. Sister Horner went to the city, and invited F, and me, to accompany her, but I was quite unwell, and F did not feel in the spirit of going. It was the day appointed by the Gov, for prayer, and thanksgiving. And as it was also our weekly prayer meeting day, br Morris went in, and held a meeting. They returned quite late. Mr C—— Alma, and myself are complaining of a billious disease. Evening passed very agreeably. Br Ira lecturing on phrenology. I read some in Moore's poems. Br B——c——k——well and Jonson spent evening with us. Mr C and br Morris read several anecdotes from newspapers &C.

Frid 24th foggy again. Sister H called in, said she was going to Union city, that Wm Horners child was very sick, and also Mrs Forbes.

Isaac Horner has lately buried a child, about 20 months old. She informed us that sister Woodbury came down yesterday, and went to sister Sargent's to work, Near 9 oclock the sun shines very clear and bright. My health is much improved. Read Shakespeare. This evening Alma is complaining of his bowels.

Sat 25th Quite pleasant. Br Horner, and Wm went over the bay. Br Blackwell went to the city. F—— sent letter to Lois. I finished my dress, aired my clothes, &C.

Sun 26th Very pleasant day. None of us went to church. F, and myself took a walk, over to neighbor Lovlands. Carried her a boquet of flowers, found her bathing. Her babe is much better, than it has been. We had a pleasant time. She took a short walk with us, promised to visit us in the course of the week. I felt very unwell, and lay down awhile after we reached home. Evening I read Moore and Biron. Found it injured my eyes, they pained me considerably, untill 12 oclock. It was near one before I slept any.

Mon 27th Also pleasant. F and I washed. I felt quite as well as usual. Higgins boarding with us, Mr Thair called in the evening.

Tues 28th We dried the clothes. Br Horner came home, said his wife would come in the course of the week, that the sick ones were better. Br Jonson left for the islands this morning. Br Caine came out and took his clothes, expecting to sail in a day or two.

Wed 29th Br Blackwell went to the city, brought a letter from Ellen to Frances.

Thurs 30th and last of Nov. Rather cloudy, with frequent appearances of rain. PM we rcd. a visit from br Cristy. He arrived between one, and two oclock, and left at 8 in the evening. We enjoyed his visit much, and consider him a worthy man, and kind friend.

Friday the 1st of Dec, was a beautiful pleasant day, after breakfast Frances went over to Mrs Lovelands, according to promise last sun, and helped Mrs L to bring her babe over here. I put things in the best order, and prepared to receive them. They came near noon. We enjoyed ourselves extremely well; her childs health is much improved. In the course of the PM br Cristy called again, with two little orphan boys, from the asylum. He is their guardian, and took them out for exercise, and pleasure. We admired their appearance very much. The eldest being a fine healthy looking fellow. But the youngest is consumptive, has a hectic cough. Their ages are 10 and 12 years. About sunset Mr L called, on his way from the city. We persuaded him to take tea with Mr C, and Ira. After supper they left, giving us a pressing invitation to visit them in return. Br Horner came home this evening, said his family would not return untill next week. He informed us that his br Wm's child was still indisposed, but he thought it might recover if it was not injured by medicine. He brought me a letter from sister Eliza R Snow, of Great Salt Lake city. She sent it by Mrs Anna Granger. It was dated last Aug. I was much pleased to receive a line from her, as I ever esteemed her very highly, in love, for her work's sake.

Sat 2nd cloudy in the morning, but cleared away toward noon. F—— washed some. I commenced a letter to Sister Pratt.

Sun 3rd, rainy, and unpleasant, but we persevered, and went to church. Br Morris and Blackwell accompanied us, called at Pickets, and were introduced to a br and sister Mount late from Great Salt Lake city. The lady was formerly Sarah Lawrence, a step daughter of Josiah Butterfield.

Josephene went with us to meeting. Br P P Pratt was present and gave us a very good discourse. We all felt edified, and encouraged. An evening meeting was appointed. Morning service closed at two, we reached home at 3 oclock. Quite pleasant in the evening. Br P—— appointed a conference at Santa clara, to come off on the 30th, and 31st, of this month. Evening Alma, and br Blackwell went to meeting. I had a sleepless night. Mr C troubled with a cold, and bad cough.

Mon 4th rather unpleasant, I felt much better than my fears anticipated, last night. Spent my time in the kitchen, ~~mostly~~ I made pies. About 4 oclock br and sis Horner with the children arrived. Joseph commenced halloing as soon as he came in sight of the house. I went and opened the gate for him, he was much pleased to get home again, as were the rest, apparently. At supper Mr C had a very spirited conversation with C Iery on the authorities of the church. Evening Alma playing on the violin. Br Blackwell left for Stocton this morning to visit a brother.

Tues——— *5th* very fogy and cold, br Horner left very early, intending to go to Oakland, to vote for the county seat. Returned late.

Wed———. *6th.* Quite pleasant morning. I washed, took my time, and endured it well. Sister Horner was in several times, and told me concerning her stay over the other side. This evening came br Bechias Dustin, looked very miserable, and said he had been sick, and suffered very much from being disappointed of going home this fall, to Salt lake. I really felt a simpathy for him, I could hardly describe. After supper he requested the brethren belonging to the house to collect in our room, and have a meeting, for prayer, and conversation. To which they all consented, and we enjoyed a couple of hours very agreeably. Meeting closed with, When shall we all meet again, Which seemed quite appropriate, as the old gentleman talks of leaving for San B——d——no.

Thurs——— *7th* This is our monthly fast and prayer meeting day. I staid at home to leave room in the carriage for F——— and Sister Lewis; should they both, or either of them, wish to come out, as I expected they would. I was quite alone through the day, papered a box for Ellens accordion, Br H's returned without either of the ladies, but brought br P P Pratt. I wrote to Ellen. In the evening came Jones Dire, staid over night. Received letters from Amelia A Stevens. She writes that she is married to a frenchman, and has joined the Icarian society.[27]

Frid 8th. br J Dire left about 9 oclock, took E's flutina to the city, to send down by Sparks. Br P came in awhile but also left for the city with br H. I went in to see sister H. She said she felt in quite an ill humor, on account of being disappointed of going to the theatre, the night previous.

Sat 9th Sister H——— came in soon after breakfast, and asked me to accompany her to the city, to visit sis Morey. I was pleased to accept the invitation, and as br H——— was in somewhat of a hurry, she offered to help me about my work, and wiped the dishes for me. But before we reached the city we changed our minds, and concluded to go to Mr Pickets. We rode about the protraro, sometime before we proceeded towards the city.[28] Br H wished to show some gents, some lots of land. We spent the afternoon very agreeably. Sister H———, Josephene, and myself went out a shopping, after dinner, had a pleasant walk, traded some. Picket came in and was very sociable, but spoke very hard of the authorities of the church and finally condemned nearly all the authorities of the priesthood, enmasse. Frances was there, and accompanied us home. Agnes also came with us, to spend a few days. We had a pleasant ride home, where we arrived a little after dark.

Sun 10th fine pleasant morning. I accompanied br, and sis H——, to church. F—— and Agnes staid at home. Sister Lewis wished to come with us, but the carraige was too full, I was sorry, for she looked very unwell and disconsolate. We had a good discourse from br Curtis, several strangers were in, he spoke upon the first principles of the gospel. We rode over to Rinconpoint,[29] to get the Irish woman, who works for sis H. Reached home at half past two. Br and sis Horner were in this evening. I sang the Indian Student, also the Indian hunter. After which we sung a number of hymns, and Mr C played the violin.

Mon 11th quite pleasant. Sister Horner and myself decided on visiting sister Mowrey on the following day. Evening came sister Lewis. The air being quite cold, she was considerably chilled. We had a very sociable time, however.

Tues—— 12th, Beautiful morning. We set off about 9 oclock, took quite an excursion over the protraro, in co with a couple of gentlemen who wished to purchase a situation. We arrived at Moreys at half past ten, made a short call, and went to sister Evans. Promised sis M—— that we would return and spend the afternoon with her. From sis Evs, we went to sis Sargents. We understood that sis Baldin (the doctress) was there, and sis H wished to consult her, with regard to her health. We found the ladies all in good health, and spirits. In the course of our conversation, we accidently touched upon polygamy. Myself on one side, and the three sisters were all engaged against me, and very warmly too. We returned to Sis M' s at two oclock, where we spent the PM, very agreeably. Mr Morey left, and went over the bay to their ranch, while we were there. Rinaldo was there and spent the PM with us, also sister Evans. I assisted sister Morey in preparing dinner, and sister Horner washed the dishes. Sister Morey seemed depressed in spirits, and told me that her husband had been talking very unkindly to her, concerning her faith in the gospel. She asked me to stay over night, but I declined on account of not having considered it sufficiently.

We reached home after dark, found them all lively, and in good health. Frances had been working for sister Lewis. Br and sister H—— were in awhile. We had singing with the violin. Cyrus and myself sung a song on the death of general Wolf, which was composed by Thomas Paine. And contained in his age of reason.

Wed 13th, fine day. I commenced washing, but Agnes and F took the business out of my hands. About ten oclock came Mrs Hoskins, and her husband's br, on a horseback excursion. They made us a very genteel call, and expressed a great deal of pleasure, in our situation, admired the location of this place very much. We treated them to pie, and wine, gave ~~them~~ her a nice booquet. She invited us to visit her, which we all promised to do. The evening passed away very agreeably, we took supper in sister H's, and had a nice treat, and a sociable visit.

Thurs 14th This is Alma's birthday, he is now 18 years of age. The girls ironed. Mr C—— is making chimney. Br Badlam returned from Sacramento. The evening was spent in reading, and conversation, with Mr C, br B——, Irey, and sister Lewis.

Frid 15th Beautiful day, took a walk with Agnes and Frances to where Pickets used to live, and examined the ruins of their house, which had been burned latly. Returned by br Irey's new house. He saw us, and came over from the grocery, close by, unlocked the doors, and let us in. We admired the situation, and construction of his house, and think when finished, it will be very pleasant. We had an up hill walk home, and found it not so easy as going down, besides the sun was very warm upon us. Evening we had music, and br Badlam danced.

Sat 16th This morning Agnes went home, and F—— accompanied her. Mrs Loveland also came over, and went to the city. I kept myself very busy about house, also cut shirts for br Morris. Sister Lewis took supper with sister H. Badlam ate with us. The evening passed away quite cheerfully, as br Irey was very sportive. Sister L, and myself, got our spirits much revived. We all had a time of washing ourselves, before going to bed.

Sun 17th Beautiful day. I some expected to go to meeting, but as there was only room in the carriage for one of us, I willingly gave way for sis Lewis, as she had business in. I will try to improve my time as agreeably as possible, to atone if I can for the disappointment. Sunday evening F—— returned and Josephine Smith came with her.

Mon 18th weather fine. Sister Lewis returned, br Hawkins came with her, took supper with brother Horner, but spent the evening with us.

Tues 19th rather cold and cloudy, I sewed on br Morris's shirts, fitted sack for myself, br Blackwell returned from Stocton. The evening passed away very agreeably, br B—— read some in the Book of Mormon. C Irey sportive as usual.

Wed 20th I washed. Sister Lewis making herself a dress for the conference. Evening came brs Whitit and Farrar [William Farrer] to make us a visit, and stop over night.

Thurs 21st, brs Whitit and Farrar returned to the city. Sis Horner accompanied her husband to the city, called on Sister Jones, and then went to the prayer meeting. I made me a sack.

Frid 22nd I ironed. Evening, came Joseph Pugmire, with his violin. Accordingly we got together in the large room, and danced a few cotillions. J M H—— danced for the first time in his life. We enjoyed a few hours very agreeably, and closed our interview with a prayer by br Blackwell.

Sat 23rd, Br Badlam went home to Sacramento. Josephine also left us, and sister Lewis returned to the city. Br J M went to Union city, and his wife came back with the carriage.

Sun 24th Quite foggy. Mr Crosby Alma, Mrs Horner and myself went in the carriage to meeting. Sis H—— and I went to sis Sarg to see sis Baldin, but found her absent on her profession. Just as we were leaving sister Mclain passed us crying said her oldest son had got his face burned very badly, by flashing powder, and she feared he had injured his eyes, she requested our prayers for him.

[A Christmas Party]

Br Curtis spoke to us awhile, and was succeeded by br Sparks. Several strangers were in, and a good spirit was manifested. After meeting we decided on having a party at sister Horners on Crismas day in the evening. I called in to see sister Burton, found her sick in bed. I also called on sis Mowrey. Called at Pickets, and brought Agnes home with us, sent to sister Jones's girls to be ready to come out with Josephine on the morrow. Cold wind coming home. Evening spent a few hours with sis Horner and br Blackwell, conversation turned upon the subject of the gospel. Sister H expressed a great deal of doubt and unbelief respecting it.

Mon 25th Crismas day. Some rainy in the morning. Catherine went to the city. When the carriage returned, it brought Josephine Smith, and Sarah Jones, also J Pugmire the fiddler. Frances made cakes and pies, Cyrus Irey went to town, and bought wine, and our party assembled in the dancing room about 6 oclock PM. We had not been long together when we received the addition of Capt [Jefferson] Hunt, and Mrs Evans. Mr Caldwell, and his lady. The time passed away very agreeably. Capt H was remarkably cheerful, and danced with much spirit. Br Horner seemed to enjoy it finely, he and Mr C being the first to open the exercises of the evening. We danced untill about 12 when the entertainment closed with prayer by Capt Hunt.

Br Horner sent his carriage with Caldwell, and the Capt, and their ladies, but the remainder stoped over night.

Tues 26th Very warm and pleasant. The Miss Smiths, Miss Jones, and br Mory took breakfast with us, and at 9 oclock left for home. I felt very dull the remainder of the day, retired early to rest, slept soundly, arose at 7 oclock in the morning.

Wed 27th Cold wind. I washed a large quantity of clothes, felt very lively. Br Irey came in near night, told me he had thrown away his tobacco, and intended to refrain from it, and spirituous liquors from hence forth. I congratulated him on his good resolution and hoped he would be able to keep it sacred. Father Morris was in, in the evening, and seemed quite anxious that we should go to conference, offered to let me have five dolls to assist me in going.

Thurs 28th. Some frost last night, but sun shone very clearly this morning. Ironed in the AM. PM Br Morris gave me 5 dolls, said I might wash some for him, which I agreed to do. Toward evening he set off for conference

Frid 29th I washed again. Br H. and wife went to the city. Returned late. Br Cristy visited us, and spent the evening. We enjoyed his visit well, and esteem him highly, as a sincere friend. Beautiful evening.

Sat 30th. Br Horner, and family left for Union city. I ironed clothes for br Morris. Evening I read Shakespear. Cyrus went to the city, returned at ten oclock brought me a nice pie. Heard sister Lewis gone to conference.

Sun 31st Very cloudy, and some rain. Br Irey quite sick, and vomiting. Blackwell gone to the city, returned toward night, bought books for Ellen P, evening he wrote her a letter, and gave it to me, with the books, to send whenever I had an opportunity. Great storm of wind and rain ^which did some injury to the fence^

[San Francisco, 1855]

Mon Newyears day 1st, 1855 AD. Quite rainy, and unpleasant. I finished a shirt for father Morris, had a restless night, in consequence of being disturbed, or suddenly awakened, by C Iray, who came in late. ^Br Dustin staid here.^

Tues 2nd. Pleasant day. I washed, and felt quite well, notwithstanding my sleepless night. Mr C went to the city, returned after dark, brought a letter from Lois Thomp. Br J M H and family returned about sunset. Say they did not go to the conference, in consequence of its being rainy.

Wed 3rd Very rainy a great part of the day. Mr C at work on a bureau. I ironed. Toward noon, a gent by the name of Willis called on Mr C, wishing him to repair the damages the storm had done his buildings. PM went to work on them. Frances writing to her mother. Br J M H—— and several of his men planting cabbages. The evening was spent quite agreeably around the kitchen fire; reading news papers, and other interesting matter.

Thurs 4th Some rain. Mr C worked on Willis' fence. Frances took dinner with Sis H. I spent an hour or more with her PM.

Frid 5th My birthday, altho I did not think of it untill it was past. Evening came br J Dire, staid over night.

Sat 6th very hard frost last night. But sunshines finely this morning. Cyrus gone to Union city. Br D left after breakfast. Evening Frances went to the city in br H's carriage, with the intention of spending a week among her friends. Mr Wm Horner, and wife, with a Miss MacCoy came out to visit their friends. Cyrus returned without accomplishing his journey to Union city.

Sun 7th very rainy and unpleasant. I wrote to sister Lockwood and Lois T. Blackwell went to the city to church, when he returned br Sparks came with him, took supper with us. The Mrs H's called in to see me a few minutes, invited me to come in and spend the evening with them. After supper we went in, and enjoyed an hour or more in lively conversation. Br Sparks told us the particulars of the conference, which were very interesting.

Mon 8th rainy and unpleasant, Mr C——— at work for Willis.

Tues 9th I washed, cleaned house, and kept myself very busy. Mrs Horner came in a few moments.

Wed 10th finished my letter to sister Dolly Lockwood.

Thurs 11th I ironed, wrote a letter to Lois Thompson.

Frid 12th br Sparks is staying out here, was in several times.

~~*Sat 13th*~~ finished, and sent my letters to the office, also wrote to Ellen, and sent to br Thorp, Alma went to the city to draw his prize, got an engraving, worth two bits.

Sat 13th very fine pleasant morning. Sis Horner came in and invited me, to accompany her to the city, Said her husband wished her to go, but she did not feel like going without me. I scarcely knew how to leave home, as it was Saturday, and I had business laid off for the day, to make preparations for the Sabbath.

However, as I had not been to the city for 3 weeks, I could not well deny myself the pleasure. I had also been wishing to go for sometime in order to do some little shopping.

I accordingly left all, and made myself ready as soon as possible. We had a pleasant ride, did my shopping, and reached Sister Mowreys, near 12 oclock, found sis Mo sick in bed, and Frances there waiting on her. She seemed quite cheered, and revived on seeing us. I combed her hair and she sat up the remainder of the PM. Sister Corwin called in a few minutes, we had a very good visit. Br P P Pratt came, and took supper with us, also br Horner Br P related a vision, which had been seen by a woman sometime since, in Cal, which seemed quite remarkable to us all, but it was too lengthy to mention here.

We reached home, a short time after sunset.

Sun. 14 another fine day, I attended church, in co with br and sis Horner, br Sparks, and the little boys. Br Pratt was present, and preached an excellent discourse on the subject of the Godhead. We had a crowded house, and they all seemed pleased, and satisfied with his explanation. We all truly saw the necessity of our having a larger room for our meetings.

After meeting, took an excursion to the south park. Reached home near 4 oclock.

Monday 15th I baked pies, and cookies, sent some to Mrs H——, as she was doing her own work that day, in the kitchen, her maid being gone to the city on a visit.

Tues 16th I washed. Quite a pleasant day. Mr C—— at work on a bureau

Wed 17th He went to the city, traded some, rode in, and out, with br Horner. This morning br Henry Wilkins, and a Mr [John] Binley, were rebaptised. Cyrus Irey came home very much intoxicated, commenced cursing, and using profane language at the table. ~~Which~~ Mr C—— forbid him using such language in his house, but as he persisted in it, he finally asked him to leave, which he accordingly did, took his bed and walked to his new house,

Thurs 18th I ironed. Cyrus came back a while after breakfast. I asked him to eat, told him I had kept the tea warm for him, ~~and~~ he said he would take some tea, but did not wish to eat. Spoke of his being drunk the night previous, and appeared feel sorry that he had made himself appear so very disagreeable.

The boys all went to the city to attend meeting. Brs Morris Blackwell, Wilkins, Binley, Charles Baker, and Alma, Jones Dire called out, ~~and~~ took supper, and returned to the city, intending to cross over to Oakland, on the 8 oclock boat. The boys arrived after dark. Cyrus was in again Said he intended to reform, had drinked nothing today.

Frid 19th Tolerably pleasant. Mr Crosby went and took down an old house for Mr Horner. Brs Sparks and Blackwell spent the evening with us, br S told us of his travels in preaching the gospel, and debate with Mr O Bachelor.

Sat 20th, Mrs Loveland visited sister Horner, I spent the PM with them, very agreeably. Br Sparks left, with the intention of sailing for S——n B——dino, in the evening. I had letter written to send by him, but neglected to hand it to him, and so missed of sending by him.

Sun 21st, beautiful day. I attended meeting in co—— with br H's. Br Pratt spoke upon the covenant the Lord made with Abraham, and his posterity, and showed from scripture that the "saints were to inherit the earth, and dwell therein forever."

After meeting called by Pickets, brought home Frances and Agnes.

Mon 22nd, very fine weather. Frances, and Agnes made a dress for Catherine, Mrs H's hired woman. Br Morris, and Bl——k——ll were in. Br Bl——k——ll informed me that Sparks had returned; having only been to Monterey.

Tues 23rd I washed, the girls made another dress for Cath——. Sister Horner went to the city, and brought Sis—— Mowrey home with her.

Wed 24th Remarkably warm pleasant day. Commenced a dress for myself. Sister Mowrey, and Horner took dinner, and spent the PM with us, We had very sociable times. In the evening had prayer meeting in br J M. H's sittingroom, enjoyed a good degree of the holy Spirit. Mr Wm Horner was present.

Thurs 25 Very warm. Sister Mowrey went home. Sister H accompanied her. When she returned in the evening, she came in my room and informed us that a man by the name of McLain, (whose wife is a member of our church) had (without her knowledge or consent) sent their children, three in number, home to the eastern states to their friends, and that on informing her she had nearly gone distracted. She further stated that her husband and brother had engaged to help her off in the next steamer, to follow them. What their object could have been in sending them off in that way, I have not yet learned.

Frid 26th Another very warm day for Jan. Vegetables are growing finely in the garden. I ironed, sewed some on my dress. Frances washed, and ironed. Sister H. had company. Mr Ralph, and family came, and staid over night. Very beautiful evening, the moon shines clearly, and the face of nature appears like june in many parts of America. I have been writing to sister Pratt.

Sat 27th Mr R, and family left, The girls took a walk on the hills, I sewed on my dress. PM spent with sis H. Agnes finished my dress. When br J M H. returned from the city, he brought papers which gave an account of a steamboat explosion at Sacramento in which some 40 lives were lost, mostly Chinese. Another addition to the enormous catalogue of accidents.

Sun 28th attended church. B Parley spoke to us, very much to our edification. Several strangers were present. Had a pleasant ride home. Sun evening we had a very agreeable time in singing hymns. Br H Wilkins, and Blackwell were in, and united their voices with ours. Mr C—— and Alma played the instrumental part.

Mon 29th, Somewhat cloudy again. The girls and Mr C accompanied br H to the city. Mr C—— bought a bottle of Dr Guy Scotts extract of yellow dock, and sarsaparilla for Frances, also Lyons Rathairen for the hair. Brought me a bottle of the latter, which I admire very much. Some rain this evening.

Tues 30th Mr C—— commenced work again for br J M H. Rain again today. I baked bread, read some in the medical almanac, Town talk &C.

Wed 31st Quite rainy, and unpleasant. This eve—— br Dustin came and requested us to board him awhile. Prayer meeting in br H——s sitting room, quite a lively meeting. Br Hawkins came out from the city. Mary returned.

Thurs Feb—— 1st More rain, I finished a shirt for br Morris.

Frid—— 2nd. Very pleasant. I washed, cleaned floors &C; felt much fatigued tonight; slept very soundly.

Sat 3rd. Another pleasant day. I ironed, baked light bread, and kept myself very actively employed through the day. This evening read letters of br Dustin's, from his wife. I admired the poetry she sent him, which she composed on the death of her little son, that was killed by lightning, in great Salt Lake valley, in the summer of '53.

Sun 4th Very warm and pleasant. Went to church in the carriage with br J M H. and wife. Set off rather earlier than usualy. Went over to Southpark, which is owned by a man by the name of Gordon, who is building a long row of large elegant buildings, and adorning it with beautiful walks, shrubbery, flowers &C.

I enjoyed the meeting well. Br Horner was the principal speaker. Mr Crosby rode home with us. We saw br [David] Sealy from San Bernardino. He informed me that our friends in that place were well, and prospering. Evening, My husband, and I took a walk over to Mr Lovelands, made a short call, and returned. Shortly after Sister H came in, and informed us that the little german boy, that lived at Lovelands had been thrown from his horse, on returning from the city, where he had been to visit his father, and was badly injured by 3 carriages running over him. The intelligence created quite an excitement, and we all felt very sorry, as he was a poor orphan.

Mon 5th, After breakfast I walked over to see the child, found him as badly injured as their fears had imagined.

Br Dustin returned toward night, informed us that he intended leaving for San B——d——o, and so on to Salt Lake valley next Sat—— Cyrus was in this evening, Mr C, and Alma making music on viols.

Tues 6th Very warm, and pleasant in the morning, but towards noon it became cloudy, and cool. Mr C—— at work on the bureau.

Wed 7th cool and cloudy. I spent a part of the day with sister Horner. When br J M H—— returned at night from the city, he brought with him br, and sis Jones; also br B F Jonson, and Caron [Karren] two elders directly from the Sandwich Islands. It was our weekly prayer meeting evening, and we were pleased to see them, and much more to hear them relate the dealings of the Lord with them, and the success of the gospel, on the islands of the sea. I had a cold coming on me, and was unwell, and restless a great part of the night.

Thurs 8th Sister Jones came in, and took breakfast with me. She complained of feeling quite unwell. We had a very sociable time together. After breakfast brs Jonson and Couran came in, and were introduced to br Irey, they had some talk with him, and called him a "queer genius". I went to br H's toward noon. Soon after they left, for the city, to attend the weekly meeting there. Sister Jones seemed rather distressed in spirit, said her husband had been out of employment for a month past, and they had no means of support, only as they, herself and girls) got a little occasionally. I felt a sympathy for her, as I do for all the poor saints. Br Morris made them a present of a few vegetables.

My husband went to city, and attended meeting, called at Mr Pickets saw Frances, said she was coming home next sunday. That P's expected to leave on Sat, as we had understood previously. He also informed me that Sister McLane expected to leave on Frid 9th. Br Morris, and H—— Wilkins attended a meeting this evening at br Jones of Welch people, br Henry [Wilkins] spoke to them upon the subject of the gospel in their native language.

Friday the 9th Some rain this morning, but pleasant this PM. Mr C still at work on the bureau. Father Horner, and wife are here. Came last night with J M.

Sat 10th quite cloudy, and unpleasant. Father H—— and wife left quite early. Mary Haly accompanied them home to her fathers. Sister Horner having come to the conclusion that she did not want her any longer. My cold is very bad. I went in and sat awhile with sister H——. Retired to rest at an early hour, but slept very little through the night.

[A Spell of Sickness]

Sun 11th Beautiful morning, I arose at 8 oclock, felt very miserable having slept very poorly, in consequence of bad cold, and nervous debility. Br H—— sent Wm in, to see if I wished to go to church. I told him I was unable to go. After breakfast sister Horner came in to see me, and invited me to accompany them. But I told her I could neither enjoy it myself nor let others in consequence of coughing, and therefore thought I had better stay at home. I requested her to call and let Frances come home with them if she wished to come. Accordingly on their return they brought her and sister E—— Woodbury with them. The evening passed very agreeably with brs Dustin, Wilkins, and Binley, Frances, and Elvira. They sang a few hymns to the accompaniment of the violins. Mr C attended meeting in co with Father Dustin, afterwards called to bid Sister Picket and family goodbye. They informed him that they intended waiting untill the next Wed—— and take a schooner, instead of the steamer. Sister P sent much love to me and wished she could see me again before they left. I thought I would write her a few lines, if I did not get able to visit her, merely to wish her much peace, and happiness.

Mon 12th Last night I was restless again as usual, slept none until 12 oclock very pleasant this morning. Br J M H. went across the bay, and was absent that night. Frances went to the city to see a lady who wished to hire a housemaid. Sister Woodbury and I spent a part of the PM in sister Horners apartment. Just as I was going to bed I took a chill, which was succeeded by a violent fever, and I had a very sick night. Sister W——d——b——y slept with me, and I was obliged to call her up, to get me drink, and a wet cloth for my head, and back. My fever passed off, and I got some rest toward morning.

Tues 13th, I was under the necessity of rising to prepare breakfast, as Frances was away, and sister E W was very unwell, and had come out to spend a few days, and recruit her health. I managed with the assistance of my husband to get us a little breakfast, and then went to bed again. Sis W washed the dishes, fixed me a small pill of opium, and then she lay down with me. Sister Horner came in, and found us both sick together.

I felt very easy after taking the opium. About noon, Sis E W arose and made me a dish of arrowroot gruel, which I ate, and felt somewhat refreshed. A while after noon Frances returned. Said she had given over the idea of going to live with the stranger, altho she admired her, and her habitation very much. But felt herself unable to undertake the task.

Toward evening came br Lawson, direct from the Sandwich islands, where he had been on a mission nearly two years. We enjoyed a good visit with him. ^My husband and he laid their hands on me, and prayed, and I felt quite relieved^ He read us letters from Great Salt Lake city, one from John Smith patriarch, and several from his wife, Sister Thompson, as he called her. I admired them much. Mr Crosby also received a letter from Evan M Green, with the Goveners message enclosed. It was very interesting to us, and rejoiced our hearts much. Br Greene was an old acquaintance in the church, and the first preacher of our faith that my husband ever heard.

Wed 14th This morning I felt some better. I rejoiced in the power of the priesthood. After breakfast I wrote a letter to Sister Picket, merely to say goodbye, and wish her prosperity in her new home. Frances washed. Evening came br Curtis, and attended our meeting. I thought it passed off very well, but br Curtis said he felt that there was a spirit of darkness prevailing.

Thurs 15th it was a fine pleasant morning. Br Blackwell set off for Stocton and Sacramento, intending to hold meetings, and proclaim the gospel to the people of those places, if they would consent to hear him. ^Sister Woodbury returned to the city.^

Friday 16th The sun shines with unusual brightness, and the face of nature is clad in a coat of beautiful green. Br Dustin has set out again for the city and has hopes of obtaining his money today, and of leaving for San Bernardino tomorrow. His health is very poor, and in all probability will not live very long, which is the cause of his great anxiety to get home.

Br Caran staid at br Horners last night, came into see us this morning. He has also gone with br D—— and expects to leave on the morrow.

PM I went in to see sis H; found her in bed, and quite unwell.

Sat 17th Still quite pleasant. My health improves slowly. I commenced taking Dr Guy Sotts improved extract of yellow dock, and sarsaparilla; intend to follow it, untill I prove its efficacy. I recommended it to sister Horner, and she sent for a bottle of it. Cyrus was in this evening. We had music on the violins, and Frances sang several songs.

Sun 18th Fine morning, but I did not feel able to attend church. Frances went in the carriage. Mr C—— and Alma walked. They stoped to a second meeting which was appointed to take into consideration the propriety of building a house for a printing office meetings &C. Father Mowrey offered to rent them a piece of land on broadway. The wind was very boisterous when they returned. Mr Crosby brought home a letter from br Dougherty, who is now in Astoria Oregon, went there last fall for his health, thinks it is somewhat improved. They also informed me that Sister Picket and family, with B F Jonson and Caran, sailed on the steamer *America* for San Pardro [San Pedro] yesterday. Frances received a letter from br H K Gay, one of our travelling companions from Great Salt lake city, in 1850.

[A New Meeting House]

Mon 19th Quite a cold wind. Mr C went to the city to examine the house that Father Mowrey offered the brethren to hold meetings in. He found it in rather an unpleasant condition, but concluded to repair it, and make it sufficiently respectable to answer for the present necessity. When he returned he brought me a letter from my youngest brother Joseph Barnes. It was the first I had ever received from him, and it gave me great joy. He informs me that he is still a single man, has his niece a daughter of br Cyprians, living with him, enjoys himself as well as his circumstances will admit. Gave me some intelligence concerning our old neighbors, and friend, said our relations were all well. And that he talked of coming to Cal. Br Jones Dyre came out, and stoped over night with us. We had quite a sociable time with him. He brought an invitation to Frances to accompany him to a ball at Haywoods hotel, Squatterville. She had had a previous invitation to attend a party at Z Cheny's, San Jose plains, and he concluded to accompany her to the latter place.

Tues 20th Very pleasant morning. F—— scarcely knew what to do with regard to going. She had some cold, and I felt that she would be exposing herself. And on my account she was loathe to leave, as I had been unwell for two weeks past. Her desire to go however prevailed, and they set off at 9 oclock, intending to take the omnibus at the mission, and reach the city in season to go up on the ~~union~~ steamer *Union*.

After she was gone I went to washing, washed two dozen pieces, and endured it very well. Cyrus Irey was in, and invited us to attend a party at his house on the 22nd; urged me very hard to promise to attend, but I considered my poor health a reasonable apology for declining the invitation.

Mr C writing to Evan M Greene. Br Morris was in this evening.

Wed 21st Mr Crosby went to the city in co with br Morris to work on that house which the church talk of renting for a place of worship.

I ironed. Sister Horner sat with me awhile. Mr C returned at night. Said father Mowrey talked of hiring him, and if he did, we would move to the city. This evening Mr Crosby wrote a letter to Evan M Greene.

Thurs 22nd Great celebrations of Washingtons birthday. We all had an invitation to a ball at Cyrus house, but declined in consequence of ill health. Mr C went to the city again to work. I have just finished a letter to br Joseph Barnes. Br Horner came out from the city quite late. Mr Crosby rode home with him. Cyrus and Frank were in again and urged us very hard to attend, but could not get us into the spirit of it.

Frid 23rd Mr C went to the city again to work. Soon after breakfast came Frances, and br Dyer. F had a bad cold, and was quite hoarse, but said she had had a fine time, and enjoyed herself well. Afternoon Sister Horner went to the city, and invited me to accompany her, but I did not feel able.

[A Robbery at the Horners']

Sat 24th Sister H—— came in quite early this morning, and inquired if anyone disturbed us the night previous, said she heard some person about the house and thought she had a glimpse of someone through the window, but feared to awaken her husband lest he should endanger himself by going out, and that on examination they had discovered that Wm Horner who slept in the large room, had been robed of all the money he had about him, and his knife, that she missed two shawls, which she wore home the night previous, and left them on the centre table in the sitting room. We had all lived very carelessly, without bolts, or locks, but considered it a warning to us to be more on our guard, and Mr C went the same day and secured the doors.

Sun 25th Very pleasant morning. I attended meeting in company with br and sis Horner. Had a new place of worship, altho very humble, it seemed quite comfortable to the most of us, yet some thought it rather too much so, for a place of public worship. Br Pratt declined attending, but gave as his reason, the ill health of his wife. The brethren however were not very well satisfied with his apology. Br Horner spoke first, after which br Morris (our president) made a few appropriate remarks, and was succeeded by br Hawkins. The pres—— then called on Mr Crosby to make some remarks, which he did, after which we sang a hymn, and the meeting was closed by br Horner. After meeting br and sis H called at sis Evans. I went in with sis Mowrey. Sis Corwin called in also. I had a pleasant time in conversation with them. The evening was very calm; and pleasant.

We reached home about 4 oclock. Mr Crosby bought another bottle of Dr Guysotts improved extract, of yellow dock and sarsaparilla, for me, and a bottle of Dr Wistons balsam of wild cherry for Frances.

Mon 26th Very rainy, and unpleasant. Mr C doing some small jobs in the shop. Br Horner told him this morning, that he would pay him for his labor here, before he left for Salt lake, which was certainly a better promise than we had expected.

Tues 27th Quite cloudy this morning, but I thought I would wash notwithstanding. I got my clothes out, when it commenced raining, and continued so that Mr C thought best to take them down and put them in the tub again.

[Working for Parley P. Pratt]

Wed 28th, and last day of feb. It rained very steadily untill near night when it slacked up a little. Br Farrar came out with a message to Mr Crosby, from br Pratt; Who requested him to come into the city, and do a job of joiner work, on a house which he (br P) had hired for a bookstore. Br Farar staid over night with us, we had our weekly prayer meeting in br Horners, as usually. The weather being very unpleasant, none of us seemed to be in very good spirits. I proposed to father Morris not to continue the meeting, but merely consider it as family prayers, accompanied with singing, and a short exhortation from our president. We spent an hour and a half, very agreeably. Br Henry Wilkins lead the singing. Mr Crosby made the first prayer, after which brs Horner, and Morris prayed. Br Binley said a few words also C Irey, br H closed.

Thurs March 1st, some rain in the morning, but cleared away toward 9 oclock. Mr C accompanied br J M H to the city, expecting to be absent several days. I put out my clothes. My health quite poor today. Think I am troubled with the jaundice. Frances sewing for Catherine. This evening br Hawkins came out. Brought a pair of shoes for Frances that her unkle sent her, took supper with us, and stoped over night. We sung several hymns, and had quite a lively visit with him.

Frid 2nd This morning I felt very unwell, had considerable fever and felt my old nervous affection very sensibly.

I assisted some in the morning work, and about ten oclock I laid down, and did not arise untill near 12. I then arose made me a cup of sage tea, bathed my head and face with camphor, and felt much better. I then ironed the starched clothes, and Frances ironed the others. Toward evening I felt much better. Sister Horner came in and sat awhile with me. I repaired garments, shirts &C. Frances and I were in with sis Horner when her husband returned from the city. Alma is playing the viol this evening.

Sat 3rd finished shirts for Alma, wrote a letter to sister Pratt. Mr C returned late from the city, said he expected to do several days work more next week.

Sun 4th quite pleasant, but none of us went to church. Br J M H has stoped running his carriage, which deprives us the privilege of going as often as usually. Mr C——, F—— and I, took a walk over the hills, which was very pleasant, we gathered a lot of wild flowers, of which there is now quite an abundance. I had a bad headache after I returned, and laid me down awhile. Br Dustin came out after church, to stop with us awhile, or untill he gets his money from br J M H.

Mon 5th It is very rainy and unpleasant. Mr C waited untill towards noon before he went to the city, to resume his labours again for br P.

Mrs Horner brought me a Spiritual telegraph paper to read, which I found rather interesting, as I had heard nothing of their progress for sometime. Afterwards Cyrus brought me the daily Chronicle, which told the dark side of the story concerning the new gold mines.

Tues 6th another very rainy day. Br Morris came home from the city, where he had been stopping since sun, brought me my book of mormon. He also brought a letter from Wandell to sister H requesting the privilege of having a dancing and conversation party at their house next Sat—— night. I worked very steadily on a dress for myself, spent the evening knitting. C Irey was in, requested the privilege of sleeping upstairs over night as it was very dark and raining.

Wed 7th another rainy dull day. I finished my dress. Br Hawkins came out. Br Morris felt rather undecided with regard to having a meeting, but concluded to have a short one. We all repaired to br H' s dining room where we found the family assembled, br H—— among them. We had quite a lively time, and instead of a short meeting it continued untill after 9 oclock.

Thurs 8th Still rainy. I wrote to br Dougherty. Sent it to the office by father Morris.

Frid 9th Quite pleasant, we concluded to wash, as it was the first pleasant day we had had through the week. Br Morris went to the city brought out a sister Goodfellow, whom he intends marrying, would have had the ceremonies performed that evening had not elder Pratt counseled them otherwise. He had previously informed us of his intention with regard to his marrying, and we as well as himself expected it would come off that evening, consequently we were all a little disappointed.

Sister Horner came and invited me in to talk with her, Sis G——df—— said she could think of nothing to say. I went in and conversed with her awhile, and invited her, with her little grandaughters to come in and hear the violin awhile. They came and stoped about half an hour.

Sat 10th Very pleasant. Mr C went to the city and brought home his tools. Frances and I ironed. Sister Goodfellow came in and took dinner with me, after which we came into the sitting room. Sis G—— observed that she wished me to pray with her which I willingly did, and she also prayed. She wished me to counsel her with regard to the step she was about to take with father Morris. But I did not consider it my prerogative. Br Badlam returned from Sacramento. Br Blackwell from that place also. Br McBride came out from the city, took supper with us. Showed us a number of letters, one from his daughter at G—— S—— Lake, one from Chancy West, Mormon Island, and one from Chapman Duncan, Great S—— Lake City. Father Dustin spent the evening with us, or untill 8 oclock, when he and Mr Crosby went in to br Horners.

Sun the 11th day. It is very pleasant this morning. Br M[orris] took his lady and her little grandaughters in the carriage to the Mission where he intended taking the omnibus for the city, and the carriage returned, for Frances and Catherine. Henry and Frank accompanied them. Frances expects to accompany sis Evans to Sacramento before she returns. On a pleasure excursion, Capt Hunt invited them to come, and br J Dire was to escort them. Received two letters from S—— B——d.

12th Mon very unpleasant again today. Mr C—— worked over his bench, made it smaller, and put it in the backroom, made some picture frames for me, quilt frames for sister Horner. Evening br Dustin and Badlam spent with us.

Tue 13th Still rainy. I felt very gloomy, and unhappy all day. Toward night I went in, and sat awhile with sis H. She had just got off her quilt. We had a social chat, for an hour or more. She told me what she had heard of Mrs Marshal, that she was very insane, and even raving, so that they were obliged to confine her, by tieing her hands and feet. That she frequently said she was possessed of a devil, and had more devils than Mary Magdalene. Had requested them to baptise her, in clear water, and wished br J M Horner to officiate. We spent the evening in the kitchen Father Morris sat with us an hour or two. I wrote in my back journal.

Wed 14th We had several hard showers. Mr C finishing picture frames. Also making a small workbox. I have been knitting for the first I have done in Cal——.

Thurs 15th Very fine pleasant day. I washed. The wind became high and cold toward noon. Baked light bread. Sister H—— came in, and informed me of the death of one of our neighbors, a lady by the name of Scott, she died the night previous, in childbed. The evening was spent in co with Brs Morris, Badlam, and Dustin.

Friday 16th Another fine day. The brethren all went to the city.

Br Dustin expected to get money from br J M H to help himself off on the morow, but came home disappointed again. Intends to leave soon at all events. Mr Crosby made him a present of a coat and spenser [spencer: short jacket] to carry to one of his sons, which pleased him very much.

Sat 17th continues pleasant. I felt rather depressed in spirit, and thought I would call on Mrs Loveland a few moments. I set out about half past two. It had been several weeks since I had been as far from the house and the face of nature appeared unusually delightful. I marveled with myself how man could be unhappy while every thing smiled around him.

I had a pleasant time conversing with Mrs L an hour or two, I have for sometime been thinking that I would introduce the subject of the gospel to her, and find out if possible what her feelings were on upon it that subject. But as yet have said very little to her, as she never seems inclined to speak upon the subject of religion.

Sun 18th Another beautiful Sabbath. Br Dustin invited us, (myself and husband) to ride to meeting in his carriage. Said Sister Horner declined going in consequence of the ill health of Joseph, their youngest son. We very readily accepted the invitation, and to save the expense of the toll gates went around over the hills, found the roads ruff and sandy, but got along very well. Came out into pleasant valley on Dupont st, and continued, untill we came to Parleys bookstore, where we called and took br P and wife in with us. We were quite early, and sis P and myself went in to see sis King a little while; found them living in one of br Che[ney's] houses, where we have formerly held our meetings. Br P—— was very interesting in his remarks, and spoke quite lenghty. Meeting closed we called into sister Mowrey's, Sis Corwin, Pratt, Pell, and her niece, sister Jones, and her two daughters. Sister Mowrey invited me to stay several days, but I could not well do so, as Frances was away from home. We reached home in good time, had a pleasant trip of it. Br Henry Wilkins was driver. Brs Dustin and Badlam spent the evening with us, Mr C and Alma entertained them on their violins.

Monday Morn March 19th. Br Dustin having received a span of horses, and a carrige of br Horner set off about 8 oclock for Santaclara intending to join a family in that vicinity for S—— B——d——o. I had time to drop a few lines to sister Lewis, and sent them after him, while he waited. I went into deliver a message to sister H from sis Jones, and found her in tears, in a room by herself. She tryed to conceal them however, by washing her face, and combing her hair, putting on an air of cheerfulness &C. She expressed much concern for Joseph's health, which I thought was illfounded.

The men cheered br D after he was fairly off, and I presume rejoiced for him. But br J M H looked very thoughtful.

Immediately after he was gone I went into the chamber to make beds, and found that he had left his blankets, through a mistake. Br

Horner let him a pair just as he was starting off, so that I suppose he will try to dispense with them.

Tues 20th Very pleasant. I washed a large quantity of clothes. Some for br Morris. I was much fatigued at night and felt rather restless.

Wed 21st Sister H came in and asked me if I wished to accompany her to the city, said she was going in the omnibus, and intended returning soon. But as I had no particular business, I declined. Mr Crosby went in, and bought a few articles for finishing a workbox which he was making for Frances, called at Parleys bookstore, got a number of new books, and returned in due time. Sister H came back in the heat of the day, much fatigued and disappointed at not finding br Parleys book establishment. I took in my work and sewed with her awhile. Mr Crosby spent the evening reading the Biographical sketches of Mother Smith, or Joseph Smith the Prophet.[30]

Thurs 22nd Very warm. Mrs Loveland was at Mrs Horners. I spent a few hours with them, took dinner with them. Mrs L came into see my new bureau, and admired it much. I spoke to her on the subject of Mormonism. She observed that she liked the mormon people, but knew very little of their doctrine. Said her husband was partially acquainted with it, And liked all but the plurality of wives. I advocated the system some to her, and tryed to show her that it was purely scriptural. She contended that this was an age of improvement, and that we ought not to patron- ize the dark ages. I spent the evening reading Joseph S the prophet, and found it very interesting. Cyrus came in took the book from me and read a few moments, but soon arose and swore that it made him mad when he thought of his being killed, and regreted his not having a better set of men around him. We made no reply to his wild unqualified expressions, I proceeded with the perusal of my book.

Frid 23rd One year today, since we came into this house. It is much warmer and more pleasant than it was a year ago.

I have practiced washing myself all over in cold water for several mornings past, and think I feel much more lively. Ironed today.

About two oclock br Thorp came out from the city, called awhile at br Horners, and then came in to see us, he admired Mr C's work very much found him at work at the little box. We took him in to see the new bureau, which he thought quite a curiosity. Mr C talked some to him con- cerning his assisting us to San B——dino. He gave him encouragement. Said he was going to the lakehouse, and would perhaps call when he came back. I gave him a lunch of pie and cheese, and he set off. He informed us that sister Evans and Frances had returned from their excursion to Sacramento, and were highly pleased with it. In a few hours he returned, called a few moments and went home to the city.

Sat 24th I reconnoitered my dressers, assisted Mr C—— in finishing off his writing desk; and now dressing my work box. Father Morris went to the city intending to go over the other side of the bay in a day or two.

    Sun 25th fine pleasant morning. Mr C—— and I started off for meeting. I intended taking the omnibus at the Mission hotel. When we reached there, I thought as it was very pleasant walking I would walk a while untill the stage overtook me, and then get in, but it did not arrive untill we had accomplished more than onehalf the length of the road, and I concluded to keep my money untill the next time, and finish out my walk.

[The Meeting Hall]

We reached father Mowry's just after they had gone to church. I took drink of water, and proceeded to the place of worship. It is a very pleasant hall on Powel street, a short distance from Broadway. It is situated between two large churches, the one a catholic, and the other the Episcopal or church of England. Our meeting was held in an upper room, we had two pairs of stairs to ascend found father Morris stationed outside to direct us in entering the hall. Br P—— had a goodly number who paid the strictest attention, while he spoke upon the first principles of the gospel. Meeting closed, I repaired with sister Corwin to Mowrys. Sister M in the mean time had been sent for by Silvester Mowry's wife, who was very sick. However we felt ourselves quite welcome to sit there untill afternoon service. Sister Corwin proposed to my husband to go out to the bakery and get us something to eat, which he readily consented to, and brought in two pies, and a number of nice cakes. We had a fine lunch. Br Hawkins came in with his singing books and we sang a number of hymns, preparatory to the afternoon service. I learned from sis Jones that Frances was at her house, and somewhat afflicted with poisen, which she got by walking about the mines, getting flowers, and eating Seagoes [sego lilies]. I therefore decided on going home with them after the evening service, to see how she was. I found her with a bad cold, and her eyes red and swollen with poison, but still cheerful and happy as usualy. I had partially promised sis Mowrey to come and stay over night with her, but Sis Jones would not consent to my leaving. I therefore concluded to stop with them. She had calls from several persons in the course of the evening; among whom was a Mr Dunham who crossed the plains to San Berdino with a wheelbarrow, and came from Salt lake in co—— with them. He brought with him a Mr Clark printer. They both seemed very inquiring on the subject of the gospel as declared by the Latterday saints, had attended br Pratts lectures, and seemed well entertained. We sat up late, and slept very little after going to bed. Sister Jones had a chill and complained bitterly.

    Mon 26th I felt very lame and tired, but still enjoyed a good visit with Mother J—— and her daughters. Frances went to see Mary Hughs, and engaged to come and work for her by the month.

Afternoon we (F and I) went to Mrs Hoskins store, found her nearly sold out. I traded some with her. I bought a wreath and pair of gloves. F—— traded several dolls. We returned to Sister Evan's where we took tea. After supper sister Evans and I went to see sister Sargent, who had had a pair of twin girls born the night previous. We thought them very fine looking little girls. Their mother was highly pleased with them, thought them the greatest blessing she ever received.

Returned to sister King's stoped an hour or more, and sis K went with me to br Mowry's where I staid over night. F—— went to the theatre with J Dire. I had a very agreeable visit with br and sis M. Br Alred was also there. Rinaldo M—— was quite unwell with a bad cold, and br A was sweating him. His mother was also quite feeble consequently I offered to assist in carrying necessaries upstairs and waiting upon him. We soon got him into a perspiration and he felt much better. I lodged with a Mrs Comstock, formerly from Yorkstate, who has lately parted with her husband, has left him in Stockton, and come to the city to get employment. She gave me a brief history of her trials with her husband, and I truly felt a sympathy for her. Between 4 and 5 in the morning we were awakened by the fire bells ringing, and men gathering to the place where the fire was raging. We looked out of the window and discovered the light which proceeded from it very distinctly.

Tues 27th After breakfast F—— and I accompanied by br Alred came to the plaza, where we found an omnibus waiting for passengers, and steped in. There were two Spanish ladies sitting within when we took our seats, one of them however left before we came out of the city, the other came through to the mission with us.

[In Search of Employment]

Wed 28th This morning Frances went back to the city to live with M Hughs. Her unkle accompanied her, and went to several cabinet and joiner shops, in search of employment, as br J M H—— had ceased his operations in the building line, and consequently he was thrown out of business. He spent a considerable time in making enquiries, called on br Carrington or who had formerly been called a br, but came home rather discouraged. Said business seemed to be almost at a stand. Several shops closed and nothing doing. He finally came to the conclusion to busy himself with some small jobs at home, untill br Pratt got his printing press in operation, and then try to do something in it. Evening br Hawkins came out and staid over night with us, We had a very good time in singing. Brs Alred Badlam Hawkins, and Mr Crosby, together with myself and the violin made considerable music. B H—— closed the interview with prayer.

Thurs 29th rather cold and unpleasant. Brs A—— and H—— breakfasted with br J M H, after which they came in and sat awhile, and left for the city I washed. Mr C and Alma killed a fat hog. Evening we had br Bad's company again. He delivered quite a lecture to <u>me</u>, for not seeming to like him, as well as he wished me to. I made very little reply to his preambles, merely observing that I indulged no ill will to any one, but did not always feel in the mood to receive the company of gentlemen. That I was naturally fond of retirement, but at times was also as fond of <u>co</u> as <u>any</u> one.

Friday 30th Another very rainy day. Mr C making canes, or walking sticks, of his island wood, thinks of sending one as a present to br Young pres

Sat 31st and last day of March. We cut sausage meat. I made mince pies.

Sun April the 1st 1855. rather more pleasant, but showery. Mr Crosby gone to church. I put out my clothes to dry as they had laid in the tub three days. I spent a great part of the day in writing up my back journal. My husband returned late from meeting. Said there was quite a large congregation in the PM. And that the conference was appointed to be here next friday and saturday.

Mon 2nd quite pleasant We finished our sausages. sent a couple of sacks to sis Horner.

Tues 3rd I washed, felt very tired and sleepy, laid down and slept 2 hours, I slept very little the night previous, thought I should be very sure to sleep that night, but was quite disappointed. Slept only 2 hours.

I arose *Wed 4th* at 6 oclock. Ironed in the forenoon. PM went in and sat awhile with sister H—— and a Miss Clementine McCoy, a young lady who is staying with sis Hor ~~awhile~~ on a visit. While there Mrs Underdink called. I felt tired and unprepared to meet strange co and therefore left. Br Badlam spent the evening with us, said he intended leaving on the morrow for sacramento.

Thurs 5th Very warm pleasant day. This is our monthly fast meeting day. Mr C attended meeting. I could not conveniently go, and as I felt rather lonely thought I would call on Mrs Loveland, as she was also alone, I took a little present along to her, and the little boy; a sack of sausage, and a piece of pie. She seemed very thankful, and pleased with it, said she knew not how she could repay me, but thought perhaps it might come in her way sometime. She observed that her husband was not doing any thing in the way of making money, and that they were obliged to deprive themselves of many of the luxuries of life. I spent an hour or two, and returned. Mrs Horner said I could send Alma over with a basket of vegetables, I called him, and told him to gather every variety that the garden afforded; and I also sent her a bowl of yeast.

[April Conference, 1855]

Toward evening the brethren from Santa clara and San John [San Juan Bautista] began to arrive to be in readiness for the conference. The first company was a sister and her children, by the name of Brimhall. I was on the verandah with sis Hor when she came up, I asked her if she was travelling, not knowing how to introduce myself to her, as she was an entire stranger to us both. She said she had come with her husband to attend conference, and that there were a number more on the way, and would probably arrive before dark. Mr C returned from meeting just before sunset.

Evening sister H—— invited me into see the newly arrived company. I went in and found the wife of John P Greene, now the widow Bruce, and was highly pleased to meet her. She had come in co with her daughter, a sister Warren, and Whipple. She also seemed highly pleased to meet us here. I conversed sometime with her, and then invited her into my room, to see a letter that we had lately received from her stepson, Evan M Greene. We spent a few hours in very agreeable conversation, refered each other back to Nauvoo, and even to Kirtland and Yorkstate. A brother by the name of Twitchel also spent the evening with us and took up lodgings for the night.

Friday the 6th of April. This is the 25th anniversary of the birth or organization of the church of Jesus Christ of Latterday Saints. Which was then organized with 6 members, and now we have 7 times that number at our little conference here in California. The conference convened at 11 oclock. Br P preached long, and strong to us, after having got through with business affairs had an interval of an hour, and then came together again, when the travelling elders reported themselves, and the people with whom they had been labouring. It was quite interesting.

After the afternoon meeting, br Horner gave them the privilege of having a dancing party in the evening, if they wished, some felt much pleased with the idea, but for one I was not very much in favor of it, as I was ~~very~~ much fatigued, and wished to retire early. The meeting held late and it was 8 oclock before I got my work done. Br P addressed the company on the subject of dancing. Showed us the propriety of the Saints enjoying themselves in innocent amusements, after which we had singing and prayer. We danced an hour or more when we again sang a number of hymns, to the accompaniment of the violins. We continued untill half past 11 oclock when we closed by singing and prayer. Br Gates took a company to the city and the remainder staid over night. Brs Alred Merrick and MacBride slept in our part, and br H's had their beds full. Some of the co brought their beds with them. Near sunset or after br and sister

Wallace, br Dodge, and sister Lewis, arrived. The meeting was adjourned to br Mowrey's corner of Broadway and Powel streets.

Sat 7th very warm. The co all left at 9 oclock and repaired to the city. Br Blackwell returned this morning.

Sister Bruce asked us to change a five dollar piece but we told her we had no money, whereupon she applied to another br then gave me a dollar, saying that if I had no money I should have that. I disliked the idea of taking it, as it was money which she had laboured for at br Dodges. However as she insisted on my taking it I did so.

Mr Crosby and Alma, and all the men except Frank, went to meeting. I went and sat a while with sis Horner, and Miss McCoy. Alma returned about 5 oclock; but his father did not arrive untill 2 in the morning; when he informed me that they had another dancing party at Mowrey's, and that he went down after Frances, and took her up; that they danced untill 12 oclock, and broke up.

Sun 8th Very warm. Mr C set off at 9 oclock. Said he would go on early, and wait for me at the plazza, as I intended to take the omnibus at the Mission Dolorus. I set off at half past 9, found an omnibus in waiting at the Mission, and steped into it. There was one gent in when I took my seat, and before we got to the city the seats were all filled, ^with gents and ladies^ and a number of gents on the top. I found my husband in waiting for me, and we walked up to the meeting. I was much fatigued, as it was ascending all the way. We had quite a large meeting, and very good attention.

Old Mr Marshall, who is an apostate Mormon, and was much the worse for liquor, tried to make some disturbance, by muttering and grumbling a reply, to some of br P's sayings. But I believe the doorkeeper ordered him out or silenced him some way. At intermition sister Mowrey invited me home with her. I went, with sisters Bruce, Jones, Lewis, Woodbury, Brimhall, and Miss Whipple. There were also as many brethren, they had two tables set together, and everything nice. At three the afternoon service commenced. The Sacrament was administered, some very appropriate remarks made by brs Pratt and Hunt, and the conference adjourned untill the 6th of Oct, next. ^Sister Horner came to the PM meeting. told me she intended stoping over night, and going to the dentist next day.^ After meeting I came down with my husband to the plazza, where I found a buss in waiting, and steped in. Mr C walked on, and we did not overtake him untill he reached the second gate. He overtook me soon after I passed the mission burying ground. The wind was high, and I found it quite tedious in climbing the hill. The sun was near setting when we reached home. I got supper as soon as possible. Just as we got through in came Henry Wilkins, and 3 brethren by the name of Twitchel. One an old man, his son, and nephew.

They sat and chatted awhile, and left at half past 8. I retired early but for some cause which I could not discover, I did not sleep untill after 12. My husband was also very restless.

Mon 9th We arose at 6 oclock. I had promised Catherine the night previous that I would give the brethren their breakfast, if she would relieve me of them that night, for I was so tired I could scarcely walk.

After breakfast they set off, The young men shook hands with us and invited us to visit them if it was ever convenient.

Miss Clementine McCoy went to the city. It was a cold windy day. Toward night sister Horner returned with her teeth all out, had been to the dentist to have a new set put in, but found she must wait awhile for her mouth to heal.

Tues 10th I washed, altho the weather was unpleasant and rainy. Toward evening came br Brimhall and his family in the rain. They came in and spent the evening with us. He played some on the violin.

Wed 11th Today would have been sister Lois's birth day, had she been living. ^Br Gay called and spent several hours, took dinner, and went to see Frances.^ Br Brimhall, set off quite early intending to reach home that night. This evening came Brs McBride, and H Bigler, Sister Lewis, and Sis Whipple Sister Lewis came to stay a week with us, but the remainder of the com intended moving on the next day. They all put up with us. We had a very sociable evening visit with them. We had singing, br Bigler prayed Br Horner came in rather late, sat and talked awhile.

Thurs 12th It being very rainy br McB concluded to wait another day, in hopes of having fair weather. Accordingly we had sociable lively times the sisters spent the day with me, but the brethren breakfasted at br Horn Toward evening I felt quite indisposed from a bad cold. ^Mr C went to the city, brought me two letters, one from sis Pratt, and one from sis Pickett.^ Br Blackwell came in, and said that sister Horner requested us to come in, and dance awhile, they all concluded to go, but myself, I begged to be excused, as I could not rally ambition sufficient, I therefore spent the evening alone. Read Orson Spenser on the Patriarchal order or plurality of wives. I enjoyed myself well, could hear them dancing very plainly.

Friday 13th it still continues rainy. We all arose early to prepare breakfast After which they set off. They had not proceeded before it commenced raining again, and continued rainy all day. I felt quite unwell and put off ironing untill the next day. Mr C went to see br Pratt, and engaged to take a quantity of his books ^and try to sell them in the city and its vicinity.^

Sat 14th I ironed in the forenoon. I got very warm, and in quite a perspiration, probably took some more cold, which occasioned me a very sick night. I felt the chills runing over me for an hour or two, after which my fever was high, and cough severe.

Sun 15 This morning I did not feel able to get up or do anything. Sister Lewis assisted Mr C in getting the breakfast, I arose between 7 and 8, washed myself all over in cold water, but found I had no appetite for my breakfast. I assisted sis L—— in doing up the dishes and soon after went to bed, where I lay nearly all day Toward evening I arose went into the kitchen, and prepared supper. Mr C went to meeting and did not return untill near dark.

[A License to Preach]

Mon 16th Raining again. I felt some better this morning. Mr C and Sis L prepared the breakfast again. I washed in cold water, and felt much revived, ate arrowroot gruel for my breakfast. Sister Jane L—— is washing. I laid in bed a part of the AM. Toward evening I arose and prepared supper for the family but ate gruel myself. My husband returned from the city, showed us his licence ^which he had received from elder Pratt to preach in S—— F, and vicinity.^

Tuesday 17th Mr C started off to commence his mission among the inhabitants of San Francisco. It rained some in the morning still he persevered, got his books from br P's, spent his time untill near sunset, and then returned. Said he had been laboring with the people of St Anns valley, between this and the city, Said they all treated him with the utmost politeness and respect, but cared very little for his books, Some would like to read, but were unable to buy. He lent some, gave away a few tracts, conversed with several persons, Some promised to attend our meetings the next Sabbath. My health some better today, had no fever last night, but a great deal the two previous

Wed 18th It is a beautiful day. My husband arose at an early hour made me a fire to wash by, as I have practised washing me all over in cold water for several mornings, and think it an advantage to me in breaking my cold. After breakfast he set off again on his rather singu[lar] mission. He was quite fatigued last night. Said he would rather do a good days work at home, than walk to the city and back again. However was determined to persevere, and perform his duty to the best of his ability. My health very poor, laid in bed a great part of the day. Mr C returned late, said he sold 6 or 7 dolls worth of books. But he seemed very tired and looked pale.

Thurs 19th He set off again at his preaching tour; visited the inhabitants of Southpark, found one man who listened with some attention for an hour or more. And promised to look into the subject more attentively. ^Saw br Whipple and said he sent word by him to sis Lewis that he would take her to San B——dno free of cost if she wished to go^ He performed some business for Foster Curtis, in purchasing a reaper attended the thurs prayer meeting, and returned. Informed me that Sister Woodbury was going to take Frances place, and she was coming home. I had not expected F to stay long, and was not disappointed. This evening br J M H paid him ten dolls, which came in good time.

Frid 20th fine pleasant morning. Sister J—— Lewis went in town, when Mr C went again on his fourth expedition. I felt very gloomy and unwell, laid in bed nearly all the PM. When Mr C returned at night he brought me another bottle of Guysotts Yellow dock and Sarsaparilla.

Sat 21st My husband spent the day at home; expected to have had a chimney to build, but br J M did not get the materials ready consequently he spent the day in the house, or rather in his shop, making accordian keys.

Sun 22nd This morning he and Alma accompanied H Wilkins to church. Shortly after they left Frances came home accompanied by Frank Silver, who she accidently fell in co with in the stage, and he brought her carpetbag up the hill for her. He wished much to see Mr C—— felt some troubled about his money which br J M H was owing him, wanted Mr C to take his note and offered to give him upward of 20 dolls to collect it for him.

He staid awhile, took a little dinner and left, said he thought he would come back the next morning, when Mr C and br H were at home, and get his note renewed. Alma returned after the morning service, but his father staid untill after the PM meeting, did not reach home untill night.

Mon 23rd quite cloudy and unpleasant. Mr C went to work for br Horner, putting up a partition in his large room, to make a bedroom. I did not feel very well; and Frances had a bad cold and cough.

Tues 24th. It is rather more pleasant today. I washed. Fr—— coughed quite hard in the night. I got up, got the cherry balsam, and persuaded her to take some.

Wed 25th I ironed, and prepared my skirt for quilting. F——'s cough continues hard. It distresses me to hear her.

Thurs 26th Very fine morning. I went in and sat awhile with sister Horner. After which I wrote two letters, one to sister Picket, and one to Ellen Pratt. This evening I read a novel called The Little wife.

[Departures for San Bernardino]

Frid 27th Mr C went to the city, carried letters to sis Lewis to take down to San B. Br and sis Dodge staid at br H's last night. Sister Dodge came in the morning with her little girl who has been very sick, and is still quite feeble. They are now on their way to San B, are going down by water, and intend taking their carriage and horses.

Sat 28th. When Mr C returned yesterday he brought letters from Ellen and Lois, to F—— and me. Fran wrote an answer back last night. I got my skirt on yes——, and intend to get it off today. It is very fine this morning. Father Morris returned last night. He seems to feel quite discomposed in his mind, and rather mourns his disappointment in not getting off to the church this spring according to his expectations.

He told me that br Horner thought he could dispense with his services here, and advised him to go over the bay, and stop with Wm Emily. I sent letters and garden seeds to San B——d——o by Sister Lewis. Also wrote a few lines to Sis L——, and sis Jones. This afternoon finished quilting my skirt.

Sun 29th Mr C—— went to meeting alone, no one I believe went from the house. PM afternoon came br J Dire, and staid overnight. I wrote a letter to sis Lockwood, and family. Sister Horner was in awhile. I read some in the evening. *Mon 30th* Very fine morning. Mr C is making a signboard for our meetinghouse. Frances and I washed. Alma went with miss McCoy to get signers for a school; she succeeded in getting one dozen.

Teusday the 1st day of May, after breakfast I proposed to F to take a walk over to Mr Lovelands, as we had neither of us seen her for 3 weeks. Accordingly F selected a nice boquet, and we went over, found her rather unwell and in melancholy spirits having latly heard the death of her eldest brother who died in Lima N Yorkstate, she wept as she told us the particulars of his death. We made a tolerable lengthy call, and returned. As we were passing Mr Thairs strawberry garden, he observed us, and called to me to come and see his strawberries. We could not slight the invitation and turned back to the gate, he escorted us through different avenues, and showed us the different kinds, and explained to us their peculiarities, in regard to the male and female kinds, had them placed in rows side by side. I never before discovered the difference in their appearance, but could easily distinguish it on seeing them contrasted. He gave us each a handful, and we thanked for his politeness, and left.

Wed 2nd, quite fine today. I ironed, became much fatigued, and afternoon lay down to rest. Mr C built a chimney yesterday and today.

Thurs 3rd This is our monthly fast day. Mr C went to the city and attended meeting. I prepared some dress skirts to make me a quilted skirt. About 6 oclock my husband returned, faint and weary.

Frid 4th very warm and pleasant for this climate. Mr C varnishing furniture. PM I put on my quilt and worked very steadily untill night, found myself much fatigued. Br Morris came in and told me that he had withdrawn his engagements with sister Goodfellow in consequence of her confined to br Taylors children, and that he had decided on going to Salt lake with br J M Horner, and intended to start inside of 3 weeks. Said they would join the may co at San B.

Sat 4th Remarkably fine weather. I finished my skirt, in the AM Br Morris left to go over the other side the bay.

I spent the PM in writing my back journal. Some of my reflections became so painful I could scarce refrain from tears. In recording the circumstances of leaving my fathers house for a foreign land, the great grief of my mother and sisters.[31]

Sun 6th quite windy and unpleasant. Frances proposed going to the city, but for some cause I did not feel in the humor of going. And she set off alone with her unkle, and took the omnibus at the Mission. I spent the day in reading, became very sleepy and drowsed Some time, Mr Crosby returned late, faint and weary. Said br Pratt had returned from his excursion to San John. And that he preached an excellent discourse. Henry Wilkins spent the evening with us. Miss McCoy also sat awhile with us. I felt some unwell today and was restless last night.

Mon 7th More calm and pleasant this morning. Miss McCoy commenced her school in br H——'s office. Mr C gone to the city with a load of cabbages. Sister Horner came in awhile, and I went home with her, and took a cup of tea for dinner. Mrs Loveland called with her husband and son. They had been taking a ride to the Mission.

Tues 8th I cleaned my floors, and reconnoitred my rooms. Some expected Frances home, wrote some in the PM. Spent the eve in reading the Deseret News. Mr C brought home a letter from Evan M Green, yest. He writes us good news from headquarters. Said he showed Mr C letter to Joseph and Brigham Young. Br Joseph sent word to him to come home this season if he could conveniently.

Wed 9th Quite cloudy and unpleasant. I washed. This evening Mr Thair called in a while. Informed us that he intended selling out his improvements. My husband made him an offer for them. He was very sociable, and invited Alma to go home with him, and said he would make him a present of strawberries. We thanked him for his liberality, told him they would be very acceptable but that we did not wish to take them from him without paying for them. He said we were welcome to a bowl of them. Accordingly he bade us good evening, Alma accompanied him home, and soon returned with a fine lot of them. They really looked very tempting, but we found them quite sour. I therefore decided on making them into preserves. I told Alma that he should take the gent a pie the next day, ^in return for his berries^

Thurs 10th very windy and unpleasant, with some rain. I finished a letter to sister Lockwood and Amelia Danforth.

Frid 11th, it was also rainy and unpleasant in the morning, but toward evening it became quite pleasant. I put out my clothes.

Spent the evening reading. Mr C and A played their violins.

Sat 12th Quite a fine day. Mr C went to the city to mail letters. One to sis Lock. and another to sis Thompson. While he was gone Frances came out with br J Dire made a very short stay, came to get some clothes, and returned with the intention of accompaning sis Evans over the other side of the bay, the next day. We had several little showers while they were here. F—— said she had entirely recovered from her cold, had had no cough since she left home. Said she attended the Bacchus Minstrels the night previous and was going to the theatre that night. I cautioned her against being out in the night air, and advised her to be regular in her habits, and especially in retiring to bed.

Sun 13th Tolerably pleasant, some light showers. I had thought some of going to church this morning, but my ambition failed me; as I had breakfast to get, and the work to do up after it; then myself to dress, and walk half a mile to the omnibus; the grass I expected would be wet between this and the mission. And then I thought of coming up the hill after meeting; and so summing it all up, I concluded to stay at home another week. Mrs Horner, Miss McCoy, and the irish woman, went to the Catholic church. I felt dissatisfied and discontented to stay at home so much, being deprived the privilege of attending public worship. How can I be contented to live in perfect seclusion from the world, as well as from the saints, neither doing any good or receiving any. I feel to exclaim How long O Lord shall thy people suffer with poverty, and be in bondage. O that thou wouldst open the way before us, in thine own time, and in thine own way. And may we not murmur or repine, but see thy hand in all our ways, and be satisfied.

While I sat at my table writing the ladies who had been to the catholic church returned; it rained quite a hard shower while they were coming home, which came near spoiling their clothes, and obliged them to run. I was very glad that I did not accompany them, as I had half a mind to ask them to wait for me when I saw them going.

At night when Mr C came home, he brought a br by the name of Alfred Bibee [Bybee], formerly from Indiana, we were partially acquainted with him there. It rained quite hard when they came, so that I was again glad that I did not go out from home while the weather was so unsetled.

Br Bibee had been sent on a mission to Oregon, from San B——dino. He was quite anxious that Mr C should go with them. There were 3 of them in co. We had a very sociable visit with him, conversed on upon old times, some 14 or 15 years ago; and the scenes we had passed through since then.

Mon 14th It still continued raining, and we invited br B to stay and spend the day with us, but he said his companions were expecting him back to the city, and intended going to Sacramento that day, and he did not like to disappoint them. He therefore borrowed our umbrella and set off in the rain. It continued rainy all day.

Tues 15th About 3 oclock this morning we were awakened by Mr Loveland who called up one of the boys to go for the Dr for his wife, who was about to be confined. Shortly afterwards sis H—— came to my door, and told me she expected we should soon be sent for, and thought we had better be getting ready, accordingly I arose and prepared myself, but as no one came for us, I concluded to get my breakfast, and before I finished it, Frank returned, and informed us that we were all too late; the business was all concluded before the Dr arrived. The grass being very wet we could not well go over untill after noon, we took a walk about 2 oclock found it very pleasant, and dry. Mrs L was very smart and comfortable had a nice daughter to present to us. She had a lady from the city staying with her, with two little girls. We had a very agreeable time, took a walk on the hills to see if we could find some strawberries, but found none and returned home. Cyrus Irey was here when we reached home.

Wed 16th I washed, it was a very pleasant day. Mr Crosby is talking of buying Mr Thayres strawberry garden. I baked light bread.

Thurs 17th rather windy and unpleasant. I ironed.

[Assisting in Childbirth]

Frid 18th Sis Horner came in before breakfast and informed me that Anna was quite unwell. After breakfast I went in to see her, she said she had been sick all night. I was in several times in the course of the day. Mr Crosby went to the city, and carried a letter to sis Pratt to send by brs Hunt and Thorp. He returned about 4 oclock with br Parley P Pratt, who came out with his horses and carriage, desiring his horses pastured here, untill he gets ready to leave for Salt lake valley. And wishes Mr C to fix, and cover his wagon for him.

I was in with Mrs H—— but came in home, made a fire for br Pratt—— and then went to preparing supper. He ~~Br Pratt~~ was very sociable and interesting. After supper I went in again to stop with Mrs Horner. Dr Bourne was there. I felt very unwell several times thought I should be obliged to leave and retire to my bed. Brs Horner and Binley spent the evening in my room. Cyrus and some others were in.

After they left I came in and got me some camphor and water to take for my stomach, got my feet warm by the fire, and finally requested my husband and br Pratt, to lay hands on me; for I really felt so bad that I could scarcely hold up my head. They administered to me, and br P said I should have strength to do my duty, and continue my assistance. He also prayed for the sick woman, that she might be carried safely through her troubles. I then returned to them, went in the kitchen and drank a cup of coffee, felt much revived, and continued my services untill one oclock, when the child was born. At two I returned home and went to bed, but slept very little in consequence of being much fatigued and nervous.

Sat 19th I arose at 7 oclock. Mr C went in search of br P's horses. He took breakfast with us, and went away in the rain. I wrote a letter to Frances, and put her up a sack of clothes, ready to send the first opportunity. Evening again I was in to see Mrs H—— and child. Found them doing well.

Sunday 20th Mr Crosby intended going with br Pratts horses and wagon, but the rain prevented, and he went off on foot as usual. I went in and helped Mrs H to bathe, combed her hair &C. Br J M H set out for meeting, but returned in consequence of the rain. I spent the day in reading. Cyrus took supper with us.

Mr C returned late, said the meeting was very small. ^H Wilkins and C Baker spent the evening with us^

Monday 21st We arose at an early hour; prepared breakfast. And Mr C ate; in order to be ready to accompany Cyrus to the lake house, where they expected to find a job of work. He waited untill 7 oclock, and as Cy did not come, concluded that he had taken another course, and so set off alone. He had not been gone many minutes when C came. Said he had not been to breakfast, and sat down and ate with Alma and me.

My husband was not certain of finding employment, but as Irey gave him encouragement he concluded to go and try for a chance. I some expected he would return at noon, but as he did not, I judged he had succeeded. Toward noon came brs Hawkins and Rinaldo Mowrey, who brought each of them a horse out for br Horner to pasture for them. They called on me, and took a lunch. I had a very sociable chat with them. Sister H—— came in to see them awhile. They both said they expected to go with br Pratt in July and wished we were going to accompany them. I ~~also~~ seconded the wish, but had very little hope of receiving my desire in so short a time.

Evening, Alma and I alone. He playing the viol, and I writing.

Tues 22nd Fine day, I washed. The wind rose very high toward noon, and I did not put out my clothes. PM I baked, read, and sewed. Evening I also read in the Book of Mormon. Retired at 10 oclock.

Wed 23rd Very windy morning. I put out my clothes. Called into see Mrs H. Charles Baker went away. I sent Frances clothes by him.

Spent the evening in writing my back journal, wrote untill near 11 oclock.

Thurs 24th Very warm this morning. Wind westward, very little rain. After breakfast I called over to see Mrs Loveland; found her sitting by the kitchen fire, in very comfortable circumstances. Mrs Roberts is still with her. I carried her a boquet of nice flowers. They invited me to stop and lunch with them. But I was not needing anything. I sat an hour and half with them, and returned. Took a new route, kept near the brow of the hill, which brought me out to the west road, which leads over the hills. I felt quite fatigued after reaching home, and laid down, and slept an hour and half.

Frid 25th Ironed in the morning. Spent PM in writing in my journal.

Sat 26th Beautiful day. I made doughnuts. Frank bought me a fresh Salmon. Wrote some in the PM. Some expected Mr C home to supper but they did not come untill after 8 oclock. And then he seemed very much fatigued. Said he had worked very hard, and came near giving over, several times. And I thought his looks betokened it, very much. He had been at work at haying; something he had not done before, for a number of years.

I warmed some water for him to wash, and shave himself. After he had washed, I took some consecrated oil and anoint his back and shoulders. He had sweat so profusely that they were nearly blistered. His face and neck were sunburnt, and upon the whole it gave me very disagreeable feelings to see him brought to such hard labor, at his time of life. I felt that I could weep for him, if it would be of any use, but knowing it would not, I did what I could to cheer, and comfort him. And I told him I had prayed for him that his strength failed not; he had a sore hand when he left home which I feared would trouble him, but he said it had not much. He soon seemed to forget his trials, in a measure, and told me we would have our likenesses taken, when he got through with that job. I really sometimes wonder <u>why</u> it is that some persons seem <u>destined</u> to get their livelihood, by the sweat of their <u>brow</u>, in very <u>deed</u>, while others apparently glide through this life in comparative ease, and comfort.

Sun 27th Quite windy this morning. Mr C—— so much fatigued that he could not go to church. PM Alma and H Wilkins went, intending after meeting to stay, and attend the American theatre.

Cy—— Irey came up and took supper with us. About 6 oclock Mr C set off back to his work, to be there in season, to commence operations in the morn. I felt very sad, and lonely, to see him leave his home, and go off 3 or 4 miles on foot. Alma was away, and I was entirely alone. I took the accordion and tried to excite my musical faculties, but all in vain, my heart strings were too much relaxed, and I gave it up, and took my pen to commit my feelings to my journal. At ten retired to rest. Alma and H W—— came in between 2 and 3.

Mon 28th Washed. Alma said he did not understand much of the comedy which was performed last night, in consequence of being too far from the actors.

Tuesday the 29th Pleasant morning. I sat awhile with sister Horner. Mr Crosby came home just at supper time, very much fatigued. Catherine Galleger called in to see a few moments. Staid over night at Br Horner's.

[A Visit to Parley Pratt's]

Wed 30th Beautiful day. Mr C going to the city to help br Pratt move, and I thought it a good time to go in and make a little visit. Accordingly I got my breakfast as soon as possible, dressed myself and the carriage being in readiness we set off, accompanied by H Wilkins, John Ohair, and Mrs Galliger. We went over the sand hills, to shun the toll gates. Our team being rather balky, the ride was rather an unpleasant one. We got through safely, and arrived at elder Pratts just as they finished their breakfast. They were much pleased to see us, asked us to eat breakfast to which invitation I complied, as I ate very little before leaving. Shortly after, sister Goodfellow came in, with her little granddaughter. When she left she invited me to walk home with her, which I did, and sat sometime, we had a very sociable time together.

I returned to br Pratts about noon, sat a few moments, and then went to sis Kings. Found her washing. She soon got through and I had a very agreeable visit with her. As the wagon was not coming back that night, I was under the necessity of staying untill the next day, when br and sis Pratt said they would come home with me. Sis King invited me to stay with her, which I did. ~~I had a very pleasant visit~~. Mr K—— came home at night, and was very sociable, and I consider him an agreeable man.

Thurs 31st. Very warm day. Br Pratt moved into sis Evans house. About one oclock we left the city, came over the sand hills a part of the way, as br P said he had no money to spare for toll. We had a very warm, tedious time of it. He was almost exhausted with walking, and over exertion. But he soon got rested. Rinaldo Mowrey came soon after us, with a span of mules to get pastured. I prepared supper, and we all ate very heartily. Rinaldo went home. Br P—— and wife staid. My husband was absent, gone to the lake house to work. Br and sis H—— were also absent, gone over the bay. *Frid June 1st.* Mr C returned home. Said he had got through there, and expected to get a job of [Samuel] Branan, making fence. After breakfast br P—— left for the city, but sis Elizabeth staid. Mr C went to see Branan, but was too late to get the job. He however got a promise of a few days work from the man who took it.

June Sat 2nd High winds. Sister Elizabeth entertained me, with a little history of her travels, and trials, since she came into the church.

[A Portent of Murder]

Sun 3rd. Fine morning. I awoke about 5 oclock, much troubled in mind concerning a dream. It appeared to me that a murder had been committed, and that my husband had been suspected, or at least we heard he had, and that his life was threatned. But he feeling perfectly innocent, was going to see the dead man when the murderer came along and walked with him. I was troubled, and went into a strange house to avoid seeing what I feared would be the case that one or the other would be shot by the friends of the murdered man. I thought I heard my husband call to them, telling them to put up their pistols as they were coming to them unarmed. But the next I heard was the groans and cries of the man who was considered the murderer, and was going with my husband to see the dead man. I was in an unfinished chamber, and saw no one about the house and as I came to the stairs, a large Shaggy dog met me at the top of the stairs, and appeared very friendly, walked down before me. I still heard the loud breathing of the man who had just been shot, when I awoke. I told my dream to my husband, but he paid no attention to it. At half past 9 oclock we set off in br P's wagon to meeting, accompanied by sis P——. Meeting was held in sis Evans house, which was very well filled. Br Parley spoke unusually well to us, we thought. He spoke about 2 hours, appointed baptism at sunset, and a special conference the 16th of this month. Mr Cr—— and myself came home alone. Sis P—— said she would perhaps come out with us next Sunday. We called at Mowreys. Origen and his wife were there. Delina thought they would be out to see us in the course of the week. We reached home at 4 oclock. Found the people all in an excitement concerning a murder that had just been committed over west of us. The man was carried by in a wagon just as we got home. My husband went down to the road to see him as he passed, saw him lying in the bottom of the wagon, but did not speak to them. We learned by the family here that he was shot by a couple of young men, who have been stoping in one of one br H's houses, or rather a house built by a squatter on br H's land. He was not dead when my husband saw him, but we soon heard that he died before he reached his home. I felt sorrowful, and thought of my dream. The names of the young men were Marion and Brace. They had frequently called at br H's and spent an evening in their kitchen. Marion had been suspected, and captured for Stealing, once before this spring, but as nothing was proved against him he was released. Henry Wilkins and John Binley, 2 of br H's men, went in search of stolen property. Returned just before dark, with each of their arms full.

Mon 4th The excitement still continues. We understand there are 2000 dolls reward offered for the capture of the murderers. Today the boys went again in search of property, found quite a quantity of articles cashed [cached], or buried. Brought them home with them. 2 good saddles, which they found owners for. Shirts, coats, soldiers uniforms, and I know not what. PM Frank and Henry gone to attend the inquest upon the body of the murdered man, who (we hear) had a wife and 5 children.

Tues 5th Mr Crosby gone to work on fence for Brannan. Br H and wife returned last night. Brought no news in particular. This evening we have the intelligence of the death of John Marion. He was closly pursued by the people, and officers in the vicinity of Oakland, and rather than be taken alive, shot himself. Brace we learn is not yet captured. Report says that Marion was courting Mrs H's hired girl.

Wed 6th Washed, cleaned my floors. Alma whitewashed the stairway, I washed off the stairs, afterwards cut undergarments for Mr Crosby. He came home feeling very much fatigued, and low in spirits. Evening John Binley came in, told us concerning his family being broken up. His wife left him, and took a man by the name of Swartout. Said he had a child 7 years old, and that the law would allow him to take her any time, when he could raise means sufficient to proceed lawfully. Wished me to take her, and keep her for him, asked me if 3 dolls a week would pay me for keeping her, and making her clothes. I told him it would. And offered to teach her besides. He said his domestick troubles had nearly ruined him, and been the cause of his drinking too freely, and spending a great deal of money.

Thurs 7th I arose at 6 oclock, prepared breakfast for Mr C——, he ate and went to his work. At 7 Alma and I ate. Ironed in the forenoon.

PM Mr Binley came in and commenced talking of his wife and child, told us he had married and that his wife had left him, and taken his child, which was a girl now 7 years. Said he intended to get her soon and wished to hire me to keep her for him. Said he would pay me 3 dolls pr week for keeping her, would find the material if I would make her clothes. Which I agreed to do. Her mother is now living with a man by the name of Swartout, now at San Juan [Bautista]. He (Binley) had been drinking and I had not much confidence in his story. Mr C finished work for Branan. Evening I went in to borrow a paper for ~~Mr C~~ him; got a Chronicle, saw the news of Beckwiths death, (of San Juan.) He was shot by a man whose name was Saffrons and his friends pursued the murderer and shot him, as he refused to be taken. They quarreled concerning some hogs that they owned in co——.

Friday 8th very warm and still. I picked green peas. About 10 oclock Binley came and asked me to make him some pea soup, said he was sick. I did so, and Mr C carried upstairs to him, found him lying of the bed, with a bottle of liquor by his side. Spent a part of the PM with the two Mrs Horners.

Sat 9th Mr C and Alma gone to the city. I sent sis King a few green peas. I also sent a letter to Frances. While they were absent sister Corwin called on us, in company with a young Mr Gordon who she introduced as her nephew from N York. I took them into the garden to gather flowers. She wished to carry some to her grandchildren, said she had 4 of them.

I asked her if she was not going in to see sister Horner, she observed that she did not know what to do about it, said she did not think sis H wished to see her, as she always turned her back in her face, whenever they met. But concluded she would not be so <u>low minded</u> as she termed it, to notice such conduct, as she had never laid a <u>straw</u> in her way. I offered to go with her, ~~which I did~~ found sis H—— in quite good spirits, and tolerably polite. Sister C informed me that there had been a late arrival from the islands; that Joseph Peck had returned, in consequence of ill health.

She insisted on my visiting her, gave me her address, I promised to do so as soon as convenient. Alma returned with a new coat, went to work in the water with Henry W, got his feet wet, and felt quite sick. I bathed ~~the feet~~ them in warm water, and after getting warm he was some better, but complained of the headache all the next day, and was troubled with a bowel complaint.

Sun 10th Mr C went to meeting. Sis H—— called to see if I was going to church and if so requested me to bring Elizabeth Pratt out with us, said she had a job of dressmaking for her.

When Mr C returned from church he brought Joseph Peck with him. I thought he looked very thin in flesh. Mr Thair also called a few moments. C Ira dined with us.

Mon the 11th Br Peck staid with us last night. Binley and Henry were in awhile in the evening, music by Alma on the violin. This morning cold and windy Rinaldo M came out for his wagon Mr C and Peck rode to town with him. We received letter from sister L B P. Boat arrived last night. She writes me quite a sympathizing letter, in answer to a low spirited epistle from myself. No news of moment. I spent the evening with sister H; her husband absent; the little boys complaining of feeling unwell.

Tues 12th Very warm and pleasant, no wind of any account. I cut shirts for A. Sister Horner in a while. Mr C—— making workboxes

Wed 13th Winds rather high. I washed; finished a shirt for Alma. Br Ho—— returned toward evening.

Thurs 14th Beautiful morning. Picked peas. Ironed.

Frid 15th quite pleasant in the morning. I felt a sort of heaviness of heart coming over me, and thought I would strive to drive it of by running over to Mrs Lovelands awhile. I took my sewing along with me, and as she was anxious that I should stop untill afternoon I did so, and enjoyed a good lunch with her, had a very sociable time, reached home about 4 oclock. Mrs L read me a letter from her sisterinlaw, brothers widow, whose husband had recently died very suddenly, with the cholera, in Lima Yorkstate. The letter was highly interesting to me, and had the appearance of having been indited by a very intelligent and spiritual minded person.

[A Special Conference]

Sat 16th This is the day set apart by br Pratt for a special conference of the church in this vicinity. Mr C—— and br Horner went.

Sun 17th fine morning, I resolved on going to meeting, and accordingly set off with my husband and Al—— at half past nine, found the omnibuss in readiness, and steped in. As I waited several minutes Mr C and Alma reached the city before we over took them, and gained the Plaza nearly as soon as I did, so that we all went to meeting in company. Had a very good time, Several members of this conference were disfellowshiped, among whom was br Sparks from San B.[32]

Br Pratt gave him the privilege of speaking in his own defense, and replying to the complaints that were brought against him, which he did at considerable length.

He denied the charges that were brought against him in one sense, and in another confessed them, and finally left the subject in the same light that he found it. Br Pratt then offered to rescind the note that was taken against him Sat—— if any one would make the motion, but no one felt disposed to do so.

[Jonathan Ordained to the Conference Presidency]

Mr C was ordained to the presidency of this conference in br Pratts stead untill another should be sent to take his place. Rinaldo Mowrey was ordained to the office of an elder. Several letters of recommendations were given to those going to Great Salt Lake city. The sacrament was administered by Mr Crosby, and the Good Spirit was with us, and comforted our hearts. Br H came in with his carriage and gave us a ride home, came over the sand hill, to shun the toll gates.

Mon 18th Mr C—— arose early to go to the city, to do a job of work in co with br Hawkins for Hollenbeck. I expected Frances home at two oclock, but the wind was so boisterous that she stoped in the city with sister King, untill the next morn.

^*June*^ *Tues 19th* Quite calm and pleasant. Near 9 oclock Frances arrived, said she had only two hours to stay, came for her trunk, wanted Alma to take it down to the mission for her. She was very communicative while she stayed. Sister Horner and I went with her almost to the mission. Had a pleasant walk. Frank Silver called on us, staid two or three hours. I was sewing for Catherine Doniphan. Mrs H——s irish womman. Rinaldo, and Hawkins came out after their teams, intending to start on the morrow, They fatigued themselves very much by running after them, as they had no horse up, to <u>ride</u>, came in, in a great perspiration, I gave them a little brandy sling, with bread and cakes which seemed to refresh them. They concluded to wait untill br H came home with his horse, and then caught them with ease. Mr Crosby came Wed 20 home late, seemed quite fatigued, having walked all the way from the city, after doing a days work. I wrote a short letter to sister E Pratt.

Wed 20th He arose at 5 oclock, and left for the city again. I sent a letter to the office for John Eagar. Hawkins came out for br P——s horses, said Elizabeth [Pratt] went to Sacramento yesterday, I had a conversation with father M[orris], about his going to the valley, he wished me to do a little washing to help him off.

Thursday 21st, very warm and calm. I washed, PM sewed for Catherine Don[iphan].

CHAPTER ELEVEN

San Francisco, the City

Journal, 22 June to 16 November 1855

[Another Move—Into the City]

Fri 22nd The wind rather high today, I ironed. PM I sat awhile with sister Horner. Br Morris returned, from the east side of the bay. Said he had secured his team, and sent it by land to Sacramento, and that he was going by water Intended to hitch teams with Sister Bruce. He informed me that he saw my husband in the city, and that he spoke of moving in to be nearer his business. The information affected my nerves so that I did not sleep untill 2 oclock AM

Sat 23rd Dull and foggy, Br M bade us an affectionate farewell, and left at 10 AM. Sis H—— and children gone over the bay, expecting to be absent several days. I finished a job of sewing for Catherine Doniphan. Alma accompanied H Wilkins to the city, and attended the theatre. Mr C arrived quite late, was undecided in regard to moving, however thought he should, if Mr Hollenbeck continued to give him employment. Wished me to come in the first part of the week, and see if I could find a tenement that would please me, that we could afford to hire.

Sun 24th This morning I felt very feeble and unwell. None of us attended church. Mr C—— was much fatigued from his weeks labor, and did not feel able to go.

[George Q. Cannon's Arrival in San Francisco]

Toward noon came a br Bull, direct from Salt Lake city. Informed us that br George Canan [Cannon] had arrived, with his wife, and two or three assistant printers, to assist br Pratt in the printing business here, and was quite disappointed to find him gone and on his way home. They immediately dispatched one of their number to see my husband, while br Canan went over to San Jose to see br Pratt, as he was expecting to hold his last meeting there that day, and take his leave on monday.[1]

Br Bull gave us much information concerning the people and place. Staid over night.

Mon 25th Mr Crosby arose at 5 oclock and accompanied by br P, went to the city. I arose immediatly after, prepared breakfast for myself and Alma, after which I went and picked a mess of peas. A assisted me in shelling them, I also gathered a fine boquet, to carry to sis King and her children. Dr Bourne called out, to see the Mrs Horners. Just as I was setting off, I discovered him also selecting flowers, and asked him if he was going direct to the city, he answered in the affirmative, and said if I was going he would ^be happy to^ be my company. I thanked him and accepted it. We found an omnibus in readiness and took seats, reached the city near 12. I went direct to sister King's, found them well and pleased to see me, and also highly pleased with the peas and boquet.

Sis K made me a cup of tea and got a good dinner, while we were eating Mr Chivers called and ate with us. After dinner I went to Mowreys, and spent the PM. I was introduced to sister [Elizabeth] Canan, found her quite agreeable. She is a very tall person, more than 6 feet high. Sister Elvira Woodbury came soon after me, said she had left sister Hughs at Santa Clara, where she had been staying and returned to seek a home in the city again. Br Whipple also called and I had an introduction to him, and br Wilkie, one of the printers who came with br Canan. ^Mowrey and wife went with me to see the house they had offered to rent us.^ Sis M much afflited with toothache. At sunset Mr Crosby called for me, and I accompaned him to Mr Hollenbecks where I spent the night. Had a good visit. Mr H is apparently a very familiar pleasant man, has been once baptised into the church, but now says he does not consider himself a member of any society, political or religious. Sister H took me into her flower garden which I admired much, thought I never saw a finer collection of flowers, or those more thrifty and luxuriant. She gave me the privilege of selecting a specimen of each kind, which I brought home with me.

Tues 26th I came up to sis K's at 11 oclock, stoped awhile took a lunch and came to Mowreys, called to see how she was. Saw Mrs Harker there, found sis M better. Came to the 12 oclock buss, took a seat and shortly after found myself climbing the hills this side of the Mission Dolorus, against the wind, which was blowing a perfect gale, reached home near 1 oclock, much fatigued, I laid down and slept an hour or two, Br J M H and family returned shortly after me.

Wed 27th I washed and baked, and made some little preparations for moving. Mr C finished his jobs about Mr Hollenbecks house, and came home.

Thurs 28th I ironed and commenced packing my chests and drawers. Mr C brought one load to the city, after he returned, killed a pig.

Frid 29th We came with two loads. I came on the first, reached my new habitation about noon. The weather was remarkably warm, so very different from what we had had out to Horners Addition that I found myself almost overcome with the heat. The men also complained very much.

Alma and I regulated the house as well as we could, while his father went back for the last load. I felt very anxious to get the house in order before the sabbath, as our meetings were appointed at our place, and I disliked the idea of having them find the house in disorder.

Sat 30th Alma and I made the best use of our time, while his father went to see Mr Hollenbeck, and bought us some articles of provision.

Sun July the 1st [*added later:* ^1856^ *(incorrect)*] The meeting convened at 11 oclock. The brethren and sisters nearly all attended, and more than filled the front room. Bro Canan was with us, and brought fresh intelligence from the Lake, we were all well pleased with his arrival, and felt our spirits cheered and comforted by that portion of the good spirit which he manifested, and also his assistant bretheren brs Bull and Wilkie. The sister admired my new habitation, and complimented me on the expedition I had used in arranging my houshold affairs, and getting them in so good order. We had two meetings, several persons took dinner with us. One family of strangers, late from the mines, by the name of Potter, who are on the way to San Bernardino. Brs Bull and Wilkie put up with us.

Mon 2nd More cool and comfortable. I baked, did a little sewing. Evening we expected br Hide [Orson Hyde]. Mr Crosby, went with the elders to the wharf to see if he had come, but did not discover him, and returned.

Tues 3rd, about 9 oclock he came in with Mr Mory, had found his way up here enquired for us at Mr Mo's, and so was escorted in. We discovered that he had grown very fleshy, and looked some older than he did the last time we saw him. He stoped and dined with us, afterwards went out to br Horners, stoped overnight. The fire company are out today, their music is quite enchanting.

I wrote a letter to sister Pratt

[Fourth of July Celebration, 1855]

Wed 4th Last night there was an alarm of fire, which proved to be a false ~~alarm~~ one. We were kept awake near half the night by fire crackers, and other confusion. This morning br and sister Mount called on us. They live at Napa city. We are having great celebrations today, in commemoration of the independence of the united States. The music is really enchanting. One company paraded just in front of our house, it was a grand and majestic scene. ^Br Hide and br and sister Canan took supper with us. Br Hide preached in the evening, few were in, he spoke on the gathering, and second coming of Christ^

Thurs 5th Br Rosacrans called. Said he was appointed to superintend the States prison, and thought he should move his family down here. Said his wife was at Sacramento, and sent her respects to Frances and me. PM the fire companies had large celebration. They presented a very splendid appearance. Br Hide left at 3 oclock, having blest us in the name of the Lord.

Frid 6th I sewed very steadily. Sister Woodbury was in a while ^Sister Hollenbeck called to get her flutina mended, was very sorry that she did not hear br Hide, said her husband would not come with her.^ We looked for Frances, and sister Evans, but looked in vain. Br J M Horner called, enquired for br Cannon, sister Jones called.

Sat 7th Remarkably warm day, I sewed for Catherine. She called at noon with Frank Cronkit her intended husband. Brs Canon Bull and Wilkie all dined with us. Mrs Comstock in this PM, said she had got a place, and was going to it this evening, while she sat here fath Morey called her and informed her that they had come for her, she bade me goodbye and left.

Sun 8th More cool. Meeting convened at 11 oclock. Opened by prayer by br Horner, speeches by several of the brethren. Closed by Mr Crosby. Several brethren dined with us. Meeting again at 3 PM.

Br Canan on the press, was succeeded by several others, all seemed anxious to do what they could toward establishing it in this place.

Appointed a meeting on Tuesday evening to take further measures concerning it.

Mon 9th Mr Crosby still at work for the press. Toward noon came Frances with br and sister Cheny and sister Evans. Just before they arrived, sister Dagroot called, and informed me that sister Hollenbeck was quite sick, and had been so for several days. I told her that I had been thinking that was the case as she was absent from meeting on the sabbath. I told her I would go down after dinner and see her. When sis Evans came she said she would accompany me. Sis H had requested br Canan to come, and accordingly he went with us. We found her in bed, looking very bad, had been under the Dr's care since Sat morning. She observed that the devil had been trying to kill her, but had not succeeded yet. Said she had willed us to come to her, and sis Dagroot was the first to understand her situation. She requested br C—— to administer to her in the name of the Lord, by the laying on of hands, which he did, and anointed her with oil. Before we left her she said she felt that she should soon be better.

Br Canan told us that br P P Pratt's work on Theology had arrived from England, and that he was under the necessity of raising 26 dolls to defray the expense of shipping before he could obtain them. Sister H made him a present of several dolls, and told him that when he got them she would buy one of him. A Mrs Hart from Benecia was stopping with her a few days.

I got the privilege of gathering me a nice <u>boquet</u> from her flower garden. We returned, having had a very pleasant walk.

Evening sister Evans and Woodbury were in. Also John Cheny and br Wilkie. Sister Jones and her two daughters called in the PM.

Tues 10th quite windy and cold. Fr and sis E went shopping. I finished dresses for Catherine. Alma went out to br Horners, and brought our cat ~~out~~. I took my sewing into sis E's. While there a man called, late from San B——no by the name of Wicksome [Wixom]. Said he was going back the next day, and would take letters for us. Evening the meeting convened according to previous appointment; The brethren subscribed upwards of 40 dolls towards establishing the press, for printing the book of Mormon in the Hawaian language. Frances complained of headache, and laid down.

Wed 11th Cheny and family returned home. F—— accompanied them. Alma went to with them to the boat. I washed, baked &C. Br Wicksome called near 12 oclock, took our letters, I sold him a hymnbook, for one dollar. Cold wind this PM. Sister Woodbury called. Mr Sargent came in with her, and was introduced to Mr C. I was in to Mowry's a few minutes this evening.

Thurs 12th I dried my clothes. Sis Woodbury spent the PM, and took supper with us. Br Henry Wilkins and Frank Cronket called. Cronket took the dresses I had made for his wife, and paid me 3 dolls. Mr Crosby sent pamphlets to various friends in the states and Canada.

Frid 13th I called up to see sis Cannon and King. Mr Crosby and Alma doing a job for br Cheny, painting and papring a house. I came home and ironed. Sister Mowrey came in awhile. I finished ironing and carried a little present to sis C——.

John Cheny came in this evening and played the violin. I felt much fatigued and retired early.

Sat 14th This morning felt rather ill, but went with sis M, to visit sis Hollenbeck, who is still sick. One week this morning since she was taken. Found her still in bed, but some better. We met Mrs Hart the lady from Benecia who had been staying with her. She observed that she was glad we were going as she, sis H—— would be lonely in her absence, and need company. While we were there sister Dagroot came, and went directly to work assisting Elsa to get dinner. She seemed to make herself much at home, observed that she had been there every day through the week.

Sun 15th Father Mowry came in and informed us that br Amasa Lyman, had arrived in the city. We also understood that br [Joseph] Haywood had come from Great Salt Lake City. Shortly after breakfast br

Lyman came in, and gave me a letter from sis Pratt, and two for Frances. I
had previously received one by br Dodge. Meeting opened by br Curtis. Br
A Lyman spoke at some length. His subject was the kingdom of God. Told
us his business here was to raise means to pay for the ranch, that they had
sent out a large number of elders to travel through the state of Cal—— to
preach the gospel, and if possible obtain means to liquidate the debt, and
redeem the Rancho from the mortgage, which it was under.

PM the sacrament was administered. Several persons spoke. Br
Haywood spoke of old times in Nauvoo, and of our sufferings together in
the war with the mobbers.

Mr Crosby also refered to it. Mr C—— invited br Haywood to put
up with us while he stoped in the city, which he readily acceded to, and
told us that whenever we came to the Lake we must come to his house,
and we should be made welcome[2]

Mon 16th Fine day. Sister Hollenbeck came to see me. The first of
her being out since her sickness. She had been to the Dr's, looked very
feeble. I had a good visit with her. Br Amasa called in and conversed
sometime also a br Norris. Br Haywood quite unwell, and laid down.

This evening Mr C—— brought home a br Fotheringham, late from
Indie, Missionary to that place, from Great Salt Lake city. He requested
permission to make his home with us, while he stoped here, said he had
a fine pet bird that belonged to elder Nath—— Jones, his companion
to Indie, and several other articles which he would like to bring up. We
made him welcome to our accommodations. Br Dodge, and [George]
Moore from S——B——dino also slept here

[Nathaniel V. Jones's Pet Bird]

Tues 17th Br Fotheringham brought his bird, which was a great curiosity
to us all. Speaks very plainly, several persons in to hear and see it. PM he
brought the remainder of his things, which consisted of his bed trunk, a
box of crackers, box of lard—2 earthen jars of ginger preserves, and an
earthen can for water He has told us many circumstances of his mission
to Indie, which are very interesting Among his baggage was the portrait
of elder Nathaniel Jones, taken by a Chinese Artist. Br Lyman, Norris,
Biby, Haywood, and Fatheringham, took supper with us. I washed, baked,
and cooked supper all the men. Evening the conversation turned upon
communications with spirits, and we were up late.

Wed 18th This morning I wrote a letter to sister Pratt, sent by br
Biby, who sails this PM at 4 oclock. Sis King and Canan, came into see
the bird. After dinner br Biby left. Shook hands with me, and said if we
came down by water to send him word and he would meet us there at San
Pardro [Pedro] with his teams and take us up to his place. I thanked him,

and told him we should be much obliged to him, and would endeaver to reward him for his kindness. Wished him a safe and speedy passage.

Shortly after he left, came sister Combs [Olive Coombs], from Napa; with her little girl, and infant baby. I gave them a little dinner, and they left in search of sister Woodbury. Sister C said she had promised to let her little girl go through to the valley, with sister Woodbury. And that she and the remainder of the family intended going to San Bernardino, if possible, this fall.[3] From here they went sis Kings. Mr Sargent called and wished to see the new bird, which he declared to be a great curiosity.

Thurs 19th Ironed in AM. PM called brs Haywood, Lyman Judge [George] Stiles, and then 2 or 3 other gentlemen that were strangers to me, to see the bird. They were highly delighted with it. One of the gents whose name I believe was Thomas requested [*illegible crossout*] the privilege of bringing his wife and little daughter to see it before they sailed for N Y. Said he would not have them go without seeing it on any account. I told him they could call any time. Br Haywood invited them to come to our meeting on Sunday, and he thought he would do so.

Frid 20th Mr Crosby's birthday. 48 years of age. He cut his foot yesterday, which begins to trouble him some, today. Br A Lyman came and took breakfast with us, spent the evening with us last night, in co with br Norris. Br Lyman gave us a sketch of his history, from his early childhood, until he joined the church of Jesus Christ of Latterday Saints. Sister Corwin and Mowry called a while. Sister C quite unwell.

Sat 21st Very wet this morning, fine rain. Br L breakfasted with us, I called on sisters King, and Canan. Fire in the 1st ward last night. Broke out about 9 oclock. It was very light all around us. I thought it near but found it was some distance. Heard a child 4 years old was burned to death I went into sister Mowry's, she was alone. Said her husband had gone to join his circle of Spiritualist. She had been out to the fire; seemed very lonely.

Sun 22nd, I felt very unwell this morning, but had everything to do before meeting time, My head was so distressed that I went to my chamber before the AM meeting closed. ^Br A Lyman preached to us much to our entertainment^ At noon Alma kindled a fire, put on the teakettle, and I made a cup of tea, for sister Hollenbeck, and myself and by raising a little perspiration, my head soon became relieved, and I enjoyed the PM meeting very well. Mr Hollenbeck called with the carriage for her, while she was sitting at dinner, which deprived her of the second meeting. She went away rather reluctantly.

Capt Hunt spoke to us, in his plain shrewd manner. He (with brs Lyman and Badlam) took supper with us. Br Badlam has staid with us two nights past. A number of the brethren spent the evening with us, among whom was a bro Meder [Moses Meader] from Santa cruse [Santa Cruz], one of the Brooklin co—— He talks of helping br A Lyman in paying for the San Berdina rancho.

Mon 23rd cloudy and unpleasant. Some rain in the night, sufficient to wet the planks considerably. Brs Hunt and Lyman, and Badlam took breakfast with us. Sister Combs called in, and sat sometime with me. J Cheny went home, took letters for Frances. I did a job of sewing for colored man. Brs Dodge and Badlam suped with us. Mr Selbey called a few minutes enquired after the friends at San B——d——o. Said he had been to the mines.

Tues 24th This is the 7th anniversary of the Saints arrival in the valley of the mountains. Very dull cloudy day. I washed and baked.

Br Badlam left for Sacramento. Henry Wilkins took dinner with us. Elder A Lyman, Capt Hunt, and Badlam breakfasted with us.

Mr Crosby and Alma papering the Rose Inn. Judge Stiles called today. Evening A playing the violin.

Wed 25th Ironed. Br H Wilkins called again, brought me a nice boquet. Sat and conversed a while, informed me that br J M Horners' family had gone over the bay to their ranch again. Br Nathaniel B [V.] Jones Missionary to the Indies returned from Sacramento, and called on us. I thought I should know him by his portrait, which br Fotheringham had left with us, but I could see little or no resemblance between them. I never had any acquaintance with him, but knew his wife very well. I asked him if he was any connexion of the Jones that married Rebecca Burton. He answered, not much, only happened to be the same one. I was pleased, and told him I knew his wife and her sister.

Thurs 26th this evening came br Sealy direct from San B——d——no, by water. Br A Lyman brought him in, and introduced him to us, and left him to put up with us, for the night. Br Jones went to the hotel to stop with his brother.

Frid 27th fine warm day, been very cloudy and foggy for sometime past. Br Sealy and Jones took supper with us. Just as we were rising from the table br Lyman came in with three young men who have just arrived by land, and who belong to the 50 who have set out on a mission through Cal—— to raise money to liquidate the debt, which is due on the ranch, their names are Holliday Boil and Nelson.[4] I went directly to work to cook supper for them. They said they had been out over night on Capt Wandell's boat, and had a very rough time.

[Room and Board at the Crosbys']

After supper several others came in, among whom was Calvin Reed, one of our neighbors in Great Salt lake city. They all staid over night. Brs Sealy and Jones took the beds, and the others camped on the floor or carpet in the meeting room.

Sat 28th I had 9 men to cook breakfast for. Immediatly after, they all dispered to their various places of destination. Capt Hunt went over the bay to San Jose. PM, brs Lyman Sealy, Norris, Dodge, and Warren, went to Sacramento. And a number of others bent their course towards Petaloma, and Napa. Br [Isaac] Nash came in from Union city. Sarah Jones called to enquire for her brotherinlaw, from San B——d——no. Br Luddington, was also in, came down from Sacr——m——to with sister Jones, and her daughter, who have been absent 2 weeks on a visit with her daughter Markham. Br L—— gave a little history of his travels. Br Nathaniel V Jones moved his effects into a vacant house near Cheny's, but still comes here to get his meals, and keeps his bird here.

Sun 29th Br Nash called, and said he was going directly home, and could not stop to attend meeting, as the boat would go and leave him. I sent a letter to Fr——, which her Unkle found in the office. Meeting convened at the usual hour. Elder N V Jones gave us a brief history of his travels in the Indies We were all much interested in his recital.

Mother Jones gave us an account of her visit to Sacramento, and her interview with Sister Markham, who has left her husband and came with her son to Cal—— very much at varians with the church. She sis Jones and sis Corwin dined with us.

PM Meeting passed off quite lively. A day of fasting and prayer was set apart. Br Jones took supper with us. After supper my husband and I took a walk to Mr Hollenbecks, we enjoyed it finely, had a sociable chat with them returned by moonlight. Mr H—— told Mr C that he had given up the idea of building for the present, in consequence of the wharf being broken away over his waterlot, where he intended building, but said he would hire him to make fence around his lot where he lives. They treated us to nuts and pie.

Mon 30th, very pleasant day. I washed. Sis King came in awhile. Also sis Mowry Origen Mowry came in to see us. Alma and I washed for br Fotheringham, also some for br Jones. PM came in sister Hollenbeck with a load of groceries to br Canons. Who the church here have agreed to provide for, while he prints the Book of Mormon, in Hawaian language. Sis King informed me this morn that they were out of provision, that br J M H—— had disappointed them in sending vegetables and other articles as he had previously promised them. I sent them pork, and potatoes.

Tues 31st This morning br Sealy came from Sacramento. Requested me to do a little working for him, which I did immediatly. After which I ironed.

Sister Goodfellow called, said she had been afflicted with rheumatism, and unable to attend meeting. Also sister Dagroots daughter called, said her mother was sick. Sister Corwin called a short time.

About 6 oclock came in Sisters Jones, and Mowry. Sis Jones informed us that her soninlaw Phillips had an appointment that evening to preach to the welch people, and wished some of the brethren to come. Accordingly they nearly all of them went, and the people concluded that they would prefer a sermon in english; ~~Accordingly~~ therefore, it fell upon br Jones to preach.

Wed Aug 1st, been ironing all day. Ironed 16 shirts, besides many other articles. Br Sealy left this morning, to commence his mission, in the mines and other places. ^he gave me 4 dolls^ Alma went out to br Horners to get potatoes, for br Canon.

Thurs 2nd was our monthly fast and prayermeeting. Very few attended, but still the Good Spirit accompaned us, and we all apparently felt, its influence Sister Corwin came early, and brought me a present of a fine boquet, and small box of tea, a little sugar and cheese. She and sister Jones spent the PM with us, also sis J——'s soninlaw, Phillips. We had a good supper, with the addition of two pies by sis Corwin, which formed quite a variety.

At early candlelight we had a meeting appointed for the Welch people, Only 3 attended. They said many of their people had left the city. Brs H Wilkins and Phillips spoke in their native tongue, ~~while~~ and br Canon spoke in english. They seemed very well pleased with the meeting H Wilkins staid overnight with us. The brethren and sisters stoped sometime after meeting, and we had a very sociable chat. Sister Sargent spoke of going to the Valley of the Great Salt Lake.

Br Canon informed us that he had received a letter, directed to br Pratt, from sis McLane, said she was in St Louis, waiting for the emigration to Great Salt lake. Had left all her children in New orleans with her parents.

Friday 3rd Br [Isaac] Goodwin came from Union City, brought letters from br Fotheringham to br Jones. Said his mission was at Santaclara, and San Juan. He staid over night with us. We had a very sociable evenings chat with him. Alma commenced work in the printing office.

Sat 4th. I felt rather miserable, Baked light bread, and made doughnuts.

Sun 5th we had a very good meeting. Br Jones spoke much to our entertainment. PM the sacrament was administered, several persons bore testimony to the truth. After supper my husband and I went to sister Kings, and spent an hour or more, very agreeably; in company with br Jones and Goodwin. Br G—— came home with us and staid over night.

Mon 6th. I sent a letter by him to Frances. I cleaned out the chamber, cut some garments, sister Mowry came in awhile in the PM. The evening I spent in filling up my back journal.

Tues 7th I washed, sister Hollenbeck called. PM came br Fotheringham from Santacruse. We were all pleased to see him, and especially br Jones, as he had been waiting for him, rather impatiently.

Toward evening Capt Hunt and a young Mr Granger called, capt informed me that Frances was talking of coming home the next day.

Sister Woodbury called a few moments, said she was going to sister Sargents.

Wed 8th Sister Corwin called to get a piece of my bread, Said her daughter and family were away on a visit to San Jose, and the servants made bread that she could not eat. Shortly after she left, came Frances, sister Evans and br Cheny. I felt quite nervous and unwell in consequence of one of our neighbors who live the next door, punishing his daughter, a girl 12 or 13 years. Her cries, and screams, terrified, and alarmed me so, that I did not recover from the effects of the excitement, for several hours. ^Mr Hollenbeck called to let Mr C know that he was ready to set him to work, but he was too late as he was engaged.^

Evening we went up to sis Kings, spent an hour or more.

Thurs 9th ironing. Mr Crosby commenced work for the men who are making patent washing tubs. Br Fotheringham left at 7 oclock AM.

About 12 sister Evans and Cheny left for San Jose. At 1 oclock br Jones set off for Union city, and from there intended pursuing his way to Great Salt l. He spent the PM in getting his provison and trunks on board, and finding the boat was not going out untill 4 in the morning, he concluded to return and stop another night with us. We were quite pleased to see him, and joked him some for coming back to stay the first to save expense. We thought well of br Jones, but never had any previous acquaintance with him. We believe him to be a good man, He observed that he felt himself indebted to us, Mr C told him that perhaps we should need his favor sometime in return, and he thought he should be sure to remember it.

Br Taylor spent the evening with us.

Frid 10th I called into Mrs Stuart's, She was looking very lonely told me that they all felt very bad, at the loss of two very favorite Canaries which the rats had devoured the night previous. I condoled with her by relating similar circumstances of my own losses. I went up stairs, and sat awhile with sister Mowrey. She and her husband told me that I looked and appeared much like sister Meder, of Santacruse.

PM Sister Jones and Sarah called a little while. Frances writing letters to San B. I received letters from sis P, bearing date of July 25th, in which she informed me that sister P B Lewis is very low, that she had gone to the mountain for a change of air, but 3 days after was no better. Ellen P talked of going up to wait on her, she had written to her husband at the Sandwich islands to come home immediatly. Sister observed that she should not be surprised if she did not live to come back.

Sat the 11th I cleaned windows, ironed some, wrote some for Dennis, &C———. Cyrus Irey called; informed me that Dr McClintock was imprisoned for drunkenness, sentenced to 20 days, and could not be redeemed short of 50 dolls. That he wished him to take him out, and let him work for him, untill he was satisfied. But said he had not the means of doing it at present, but intended to try in a few days.

Sun 12th. I arose feeling very unwell, insomuch that I could not attend church, but could hear quite distinctly from my chamber.

Frances made a cup of tea for dinner, which revived me some, and I tryed to attend PM service, but became so faint and sick that I was obliged to retire again. Br Whipple took supper with us. Evening we went to sis Kings. They had a spiritual meeting at Mowry's. Mr Crosby and br Cannon were in awhile, said they could not do much while they were there, but as soon as they left, the table danced over the floor.

Mon 13th Very pleasant day. Took a walk in co with sisters King, Cannon Frances, and the children; went down Powel street, to the north beach. We enjoyed our walk finely, went out on the wharf to get a good seabreeze. Returned to sister Kings, rested awhile, took a little refreshment, and came home.

Evening when Mr C came from the shop, he informed us that he was going to work for Mr Hollenbeck, that they did not keep in employment there, and he did not like to loose his time. Accordingly F—— and I accompanied him down there to inform Mr H—— of his intention to come and do his work. He told him to come, as he was ready for him. We spent the evening very agreeably, with sister H—— and Elsey. Mr H—— went with his little boy to see the circus, as he had previously promised him, and he would not be denied. He told us we must excuse him, and visit with his wife.

Tues 14th Mr C and Alma both went to work at Hollenbeck's. I washed baked, &C. Frances slept with sis K, was quite unwell this morning, did not come home untill 11 oclock. Sis—— Woodbury called on her way to the boat, going to Union City.

This evening Alma and his father playing their violins. F—— gone to stay with sis King. Br Cannon received a present from br Cheny, across the bay, of vegetables.

Wed 15th Warm and pleasant. Pm F—— and I went into sister Mowry's and Mrs Steward's. Evening sister M called and took supper with us.

Thurs 16th Wrote letters to sis P. Br Sealy and Nelson returned from Napa city. Toward noon came Br Nash and wife, and br Jones from Union city. come to buy teams and other necessaries for their journey to the valley. I ironed and F made mince pies. Br and sis Nash, br Jones and sis Cannon and br Sealy spent the PM and took supper with us.

Sister Corwin called a few minutes, sister Mowry called this morning and took a cup of tea with me, brought me a present, some dried apples and a piece of new cheese. Porter Rockwell was in the evening.

Friday 17th. Received a letter from sis P—— San B, informing us of sis Lew—— failing very fast. Ellen was up on the mountain taking care of her. Said her cough was very bad, and she could not sit in a chair one min.

Br Sealy and Nelson left for Sacramento. I sat down and wrote a letter to sister L P in answer to her last. This evening we were in to father M's—— Br and sis Nash were in, Mrs Steward also, conversation quite lively. Br Jones left for Sacramento, in co with P Rockwell.

Sat 18th I made pies. Frances sewing for sis King.

PM br George More left for San B——dino—took our letters.

Sun 19th meeting as usual, very good attendance. Br Nash spoke to us, on the eve of leaving for Salt Lake, was followed by br Cannon. PM we were addressed by brs Curtis and Cannon.

Mon 20th Very warm. We washed, br and sis Nash went home, called and bid us Goodbye. Evening F—— went down to see sis Jones; found her very sick, insomuch that she was unwilling to stay alone with them, and came back for me. I was tired having been on my feet all day, but yet I could not refuse to go, under those circumstances. My husband went with us, we staid untill near twelve, when we returned, but Frances staid over night. My husband and 3 other elders laid hands on her and anointed her with oil in the name of the Lord, and rebuked the disease

Tues 21st. F—— returned quite early, Said sis Jones was still very bad. After breakfast I decided on going to see her, went over to see if sis Mowry was able to accompany me. She thought at first that she was unable but after a little reflection, concluded to try the walk. Origen Mowry and wife came down to their fathers. Delina called on us. Soon after sister E Woodbury came along and went with sis M—— and myself to sis Jones's. We found her very sick, and much distressed. Sometimes I feared she would never be any better, but still had hopes that as this was the 3rd day of her fever she might begin to amend. Sis Mowry proposed a medicine for her a Sort of Balsam, which she sent down, and it seemed to relieve her almost immediately. Sister Wo—— and I staid untill night, and then returned. F staid overnight. Elders Curtis, Cannon, Everloth, and Crosby, met in council.

Wed 22nd Sis Woodbury here writing. Sent money to Bagley to buy teams for her journey to the Salt Lake Valley. Shortly after breakfast came Capt Hunt, Dr Andrews, and N V Jones, direct from Sacramento. Dr A—— quite ill,—with his old complaint, the asthma. Took his bed soon after he came and did not rise untill supper, when I carried him a cup of tea, to his bedroom, His cough was very distressing.

Evening came in br Phillips, Mother Jones's soninlaw. Said <u>she</u> was much better. He took supper with us. Shortly after came Cap Hunt, to enquire after the Dr's health, found him in bed. The conversation turned

upon the state of the world at large, their great indifference to the subject
of religion. Cap H—— said he could not find one in the course of his
travels that had any desire to investigate the subject of the gospel.

Thurs 23rd When sis Woodbury returned from sis Jones, where she
staid last night, she brought us a letter from br Whitaker, San B——d——o,

No news in particular, only br Grouard and a number of other dis-
affected members, are talking of going to Oregon. Says they think the
twelve and first presidency very bad men.[5] Dr Andrews arose about 7
oclock—went to the barbers. Said he did not wish to eat, untill 9 or 10
oclock. Frances spending the day with sis King. Evening sis Mowry was in
awhile. Fr went to stop with Sis—— Jones again.

Frid 24th I felt quite unwell. Frances and Sis Mowry proposed going
to sis Sargent Fr went over and helped sis M to get ready, and came back
to inform me.

When we went in, we found a stranger within, who sis M introduced
as being a missionary late from Australia. I asked his name which he
said was Paul Smith. Said he was an englishman, left Eng in '51 ^with
eld O Pratt for Salt Lake^ (and went to Aus—— in '52, where he had
been untill he sailed again for Amer Said he touched at Tahiti, saw br
Hawkins, and several of the native Saint that he gave br H—— a quantity of papers books &C. Said br Hanks was on another island. He also
informed us that he touched at the Sandwich isl saw some of the elders
there, understood they expected to return, at least some of them, in the
next vessel. Sis Woodbury received a letter from her husband to the same
effect. We invited him to bring his wife to our place, as he said she was still
on board the vessel. In the meantime we took our walk to sis Sargent's,
where we had a fine agreeable visit took dinner and then returned, found
elder Smith had brought his wife to br Cannons, but left his trunks at
Mowrey's.

Sat 25th This morning came br Lyman, from Sacramento. Also br
Norris. Br L took breakfast with us, spent the greater part of the day. This
evening two boats came in from the south.

Sun 26th Quite a full meeting. Two new comers from the Indies,
Br Finly a missionary from Eng—— and br Davis a native of Indie. Elder
Lyman preached in the morning, but was too much indisposed to attend
the afternoon service. Br Finly spoke to us, We all admired his address,
and sentiments, he was followed by br Curtis.

Br Cannon absent, gone over the bay. Meeting closed by br Crosby.
Sisters Cannon and Woodbury lunched with us.

Br Everleth took the Indie brethren home with him to sup——. Br
Lyman stoped with us. Evening I took a walk with my husband to the printing office P O He mailed a letter to Great Salt Lake city. Fr and Al——
also took a walk.

[Jane Lewis's Death]

Mon 27th Frances went direct to the P O—— and brought me a letter from her mother, with one enclosed to sis Woodbury. I was expecting to hear sad news concerning sister Lewis, and according to my expectations the first line ~~told~~ betrayed the sad intelligence of her death. She died Aug—— 11th '55 with the consumption of the lungs, a disease with which she had been afflicted all her life.

Frances went to Sister Sargents to carry the letter to sis Woodbury but she was absent on business. She returned and shortly after sis—— W came in. Seemed quite cheerful, I was out door washing, I dreaded telling her the news and therefore informed her that she had a letter here from Ellen P—— She took it and the first line revealed the sad story. She [*illegible crossout*] burst into tears, and wept aloud. I knew she would, and therefore prefered having her learn it from the letter. She wept so much that she could not finish reading. I took it and read to her. She soon became comforted on learning that she had everything done for her that she desired, and that Ellen staid with her night and day for more than a week previous to her death. We were all deeply affected with her sickness and decease; when we considered the trials and journeyings by sea and land, of which her short life had been composed.

But we did not mourn as those who have no hope, for we verily believe that her reward is sure in heaven. She certainly has accomplished more in a few short years than thousands who are permited to tarry three score and ten.

Elder A Lyman took breakfast with us, complained of feeling very ill, and laid down awhile. Toward noon br Finly returned with the remainder of the Indie brothers, and sisters, viz br Tate and his little son, sis Davis and her daughter and sister. We were much engaged in business, and could not spend much time with them. And as I had been weeping, I feared they would think me very poor company. I however apologised as well as I could, and I believe I satisfied them. We prepared them a dinner, and they all ate quite heartily. bro Davis remained to take care of their goods. Br Lyman entertained as well as he could, by telling them of San Barnerdino, and I believe rather counseled them to go to that place.

Tues 28th Br Lyman breakfasted with us. I ironed. Fr made pies. PM came sis Woodbury, felt quite gloomy, and troubled in mind. Said she was unhappy, and restless. Sister Curtis sent for the strangers from Indie to come and sup with her, also requested Fr—— to come and assist her on a job of sewing, but she being unwell, Sis W offered to go in her place.

PM Mr Sargent called to see br Lyman. Said his wife talked of going to San B——d——o.

Wed 29th Cool and cloudy. F—— gone to br Curtis's. Brs Finly and Davis were in. I told them concerning the intelligence offices. And they said they would go directly to them, to seek employment.

Br and sister Jones, and br Lyman were in. Sis J—— walked up for the first time since her sickness. Said she talked of moving into Mowry's chamber. At 11 oclock called br Norris, and informed me that he intended sailing for San B——d—— at 4 PM, and would take whatever communication I wished to make. I thanked him, told him I should be happy to acknowledge the receipt of Sis P's letter by the last mail.

He requested me to do an errand for him to elder Lyman should he call in a short time Viz to meet him at the Blue Wing at half past 2 oclo I proceeded forthwith to writing, about one oclock br L called and I delivered my letter, and message, gave him a lunch &C. He said he intended sailing to Sacramento this evening. PM Sisters Mowry and Smith called. Evening Husband and I were into father M's, and also went upstairs to see the Indie brethren and sisters. Sat with them sometime.

[Little Johny Tait]

Thurs 30th Brs Finly and Tate called, and informed me that they had got the refusal of a situation at harvesting for 40 dolls per month, 12 miles from Oakland; and that they intended leaving immediately for said place. Br Tate wished me to take care of his little <u>son</u> in his absence Said he would reward me for the same. He seemed very much afflicted at the idea of parting from the child, as he had taken the sole care of him for several months. The thoughts of his having brought him away from his mother, and then being compelled to leave him among strangers in a strange land was very distressing to him, and he wept so that he could scarcly speak. I told him I would do as well as I could by him, and he said I was the only one he knew, that could take him, [*illegible crossout*] ~~well as I could~~ or that he would like to entrust him with.[6] Br Jones Dier was here, and going directly over to Oakland, offered to accompany them, which they were highly pleased with. They prepared their luggage, and set forth immediatly for their destined place, apparently with many hopes and fears. We all felt a sympathy for them. For one I knew how, by experience, having passed through trials of a similar nature many times in the course of my wanderings.

Br Tate gave me the keys of all his trunks, told me that br Davis would bring me the one that contained the little boys clothes.

Soon after they left I went over to br D's, and found the little fellow very willing to come with me. I had observed him on their first arrival and thought him an interesting child. But notwithstanding I considered it quite a responsible task to take upon myself. Yet I could not conscienciously refuse him the favor, as his circumstances were such as required a friend. He had mourned his absence from his wife, untill ~~with~~ a long sea voyage 18 weeks, had very much reduced his system; We all feared he would be unable to endure very long the hard labor of the harvest field. He said he expected his wife was coming untill within a very few minutes of the ships sailing, that he had brought everything on board even to her clothes expecting she would come with br Finly, that just before the vessel set sail br F—— came without her, saying her mother would not let her come. He said there was no alternative for him but to come along without her. He received a letter while in China saying that she would come in the next vessel that left. The child was very happy and quiet, retired early to bed and slept late the next morning.

Frid 31st Capt Hunt called, said he was going to Sacramento that eve admired my little boy very much. I took him out to walk called on Sisters Cannon and King. Sister Davis and her sister were in awhile.

Sat Sept 1st The sisters called again. I made pies, gave them a lunch. The little boy still happy and quiet.

Sun 2nd very warm. We had a crowded house. PM the sacrament was administered I was obliged to retire to the chamber with my little boy as he was frightened at the crowd of people, and disturbed the meeting with his cries. Evening br Davis came in with his violin to play with Mr Cro

Mon 3rd I had Dennis the blackman to wash for me. This evening also br Davis, wife and sister came over to sing with us; we had quite an agreeable time.

Tues 4th Frances and I went to Mr Hollenbecks, and made quite a pleasant visit. Mrs Marsh, eldest daughter of Mr H was at her fathers on a visit, and informed us that she had left her husband and, got a new home, was living with a Mrs Avery. Her mother had previously informed me of a dissatisfaction between them.

Wed 5th I ironed, had 13 shirts, to do up, felt much fatigued at night. Br and sis Jones, br Phillips, and br [Theodore] Turley[7] called awhile in the evening. Sister Jones informed me that she had moved into sis Sargents house. We had not seen br Turly since we left Salt lake city. I discovered that he had become quite gray in the cause of truth.

Thurs 6th was our monthly fast, brs Turley and Frisby attended, We had a very good meeting, enjoyed a good share of the holy spirit Evening sis Woodbury and Anna Jones were in. Mr C—— and Alma attended an auction store.

Frid 7th remarkably warm day br Turley called. I did some repairing of clothes. *Sat 8th* warm and pleasant. I took a walk with the little boy. Called on sisters King, Cannon, Mowrey, Davis, and Mrs Steward. Mr Crosby was at home, and attended market. Bought flour, cheese, Smoked herring, &C.

Sun 9th We had quite a full meeting. Br Turly was chief speaker, and spoke much to the edification of his audience.

Sister Corwin brought me a paper of tea, accordingly I made her a cup at intermition, and we had quite an agreeable time with her and sis Jones Several persons spoke in the PM, and we had a very lively ~~time~~ meeting. Br Turley took tea with us. Elder Frisby called awhile. Evening took a walk with Mr C—— and Frances, to call on sis Goodfellow, found her quite comfortable with her little grandaughters. She informed us that br Taylor ^her soninlaw^ was in Placerville, employed at mechanical business for 5 dolls pr day; did not know when he would return. We reached home a few minutes before 9 oclock. It was very pleasant walking the shops and fruit stands presented a very interesting appearance.

Mon 10th I arose early performed a large washing; much fatigued at night felt that I had taken some cold. Frances went shopping with sis King.

Tues 11th, I felt very lame this morning. Arose at 6 oclock, prepared breakf after which put out my large washing. Had the headache. Toward noon took a walk with little Johny on Stockton street, bought two pair of shoes took the little boy to see the toy shops, saw the little nimer bird that elder Fotheringham brought from the Indies. It was sick and would not speak to me. Sister Hollenbeck called, and Fr went home with her.

Wed 12th I cleaned up the chambers, took up carpets, &C. Frances ironed in the AM, and I in the PM. We also baked light bread, and made doughnuts. Sister Davis in a while, her husband gone over the bay to harvesting with brs Tate and Finly. *Thurs 13th* this is a great day with the Jews. I understand it is their newyears day. They assembled in their synnagogue, at an early hour, and again at evevening. Our people had a meeting at br Jones's, sister Sargents house the same eve——. Br Turley spoke to us upon the order and blessings of the priesthood. And showed that it was the only true source through which God conveys intelligence to man, so as to make them wise unto Salvation; and brings them into His celestial kingdom.

We were all highly edified with his remarks, and received a testimony, that he spoke by the Holy Spirit. Received letters from S——n——d——o

Frid ~~15~~14th Very pleasant morning. We took a walk to sister Sargents and Jones. Afterwards Sister Cannon came along and we went to visit sister Goodfellow. We had a pleasant walk, and fine visit. Had an introduction to a Mrs Hayden, who resides in the same house, she informed us that she came through Great Salt Lake City, 2 years ago, Stoped two weeks, and formed some very agreeable acquaintances, was very happily disappointed in them. Admired the place very much, expressed a wish to spend her days in the place, but could not fellowship all their principles.

Said husband was an artist, also a dealer in oils and paints. My little Johny was much fatigued after we reached there, and slept sometime. Frances, and sis Cannon came away and left me to take my time with the little fellow. We walked slowly, reached home at 6 ¼ oc

Sat 15th I felt very unwell. Walked up to sister Kings, her husband reached home the day previous, but was gone out so that I did not see him. I also called on sis Cannon, her husband gone over to the redwoods to preach the next day. Called at Mowrys, Mrs Eagar was there, took Anna, sis Davises sister home with her, with a promise to learn her to work, and give her clothes &C.

Sun 16th Our meeting was rather small. Mr Crosby spoke first and was followed by br Curtis, who threw out some insinuations, which sister Woodbury thought applicable to herself, and accordingly replied to them. Mr Crosby then qualified some of his sayings and was succeeded by br Turley, who bore testimony that he believed they had spoken by the spirit of God.

Sisters Corwin and Jones took dinner with us. Frances quite unwell did not attend meeting. PM br Everleth spoke to the people, and very much to the purpose. Several persons were in, Strangers.

[Saints from Foreign Lands]

Mon 17th Last night immediately after the meeting closed, came several elders from the Sandwich islands. Sister Woodbury br Turly, and Keilah took supper with us. Br K—— late from the islands, slept here.

This evening came other vessels, and brought brs Woodbury and Frost with a company from Aus——. Alma went with br Woodbury to br Everleth where his wife was staying. F—— and I washed, and baked light bread.

Tues 18th I felt very unwell; went to the market for materials for making mince pies. We ironed in the Am, Pm we made the pies, a dozen or more. Br and Sis Woodbury br Turly, and Nelson took supper with us.

Br Frost called. In the evening another company arrived from Calcutta A br Johnson one of their principle members called in co with a number of the Australian com. We had a great time of introducing and being presented; shaking hands, wishing each other success &C.

Br Sealy and Nelson slept here, and breakfasted with us.

Wed ~~20~~19th bro Rich arrived from S—— B——dino. brought letters from sis P and Ellen. They informed us of a melancholly accident which had lately transpired in there place. 3 men in a fit of drunkenness went to a neighbors house, and got him to go for more liquor; while he was gone they behaved rudely to his wife; on his return she complained to her husband, and he attempted to put them out; and in course of the excitement, he testifies that 2 of them stabed him, and the other held him. They said his wounds at first were considered dangerous, but the present prospect was that he would recover.

The rioters were held to bail in the sum of 3000 dolls.

Thus we see through the influence of liquor, all manner of crimes are committed, by men ^of general good morals^ who have had the advantages of a good education, and examplary parents. Sister Evans and her little daughter slept here, with Fr and me. The houses of all the brethren being full of strangers, saints just arrived from foreign lands, "Flocking like clouds and doves, to their windows" Frances attended the theatre, in co with br Mount, from Napa city. Brs Sealy, and Nelson, stoped with us.

Thurs 20th I traded some with a pedlar. Evening we had a number of unexpected visitors. Brs Sealy, Turley, Nelson, and Woodbury, took supper with us. Afterwards came 3 more, brs D Holiday, H———. Boile and a br Sparks, they said they had not been to supper, I therefore invited them to eat such as we had cooked, as it was too late to cook a fresh supper, besides it was our meeting evening, and they all wished to attend. We had the table to set 3 times. Sis W came in and assisted in setting it the third time. I could not get through in season to go to meeting, so staid at home with Alma, and Johny. I had a host of dishes to wash, and it was near 9 oclock when I got through The front room was filled with lodgers, I was much fatigued, and retired early.

Frid 21st Some of the brethren gone to attend conference at Sacramento. Elds Lyman, Rich, and Cannon. The Australians, and Indie brethren are expecting to sail for San Bernardino tomorrow.

Frances sewing for sis——— Jones. I have felt very heavy hearted today, and quite unwell. Evening Mr C——— and Alma playing their violins.

Sat 22nd Frances came home quite early. Brs Sealy Holiday and Boile breakfasted with us. Afterwards I took a walk with little Johny, called to see the brethren and sisters who were going to San B———dino. Went into Mowrys found them at breakfast. Went into Sis Cannons, and Kings. Sister Evans came home with me. Near 12 oclock br Taite came. Johny and I were sitting in the front room, when his father suddenly opened the door and came in. The little fellow was so much surprised, that he commenced crying, and refused to speak with him. The poor man was sadly afflicted with a felon [acute tissue inflammation] on one of his thumbs, said he had not slept any for a week.

We all discovered that he had pined very much, and truly felt a sympathy for him. I kindled a fire and warmed some water to dress it, I truly thought I never saw a worse looking sore. It pained him quite badly that night, and the next day.

Sun 23rd. Beautiful morning. We had a very good meeting. Sisters Corwin and Goodfellow spent the intermition with us. PM a stranger called, invited Mr Crosby outside to speak with him and asked permission to attend our meeting, said his intention were honest, and to get a knowledge of our principles. My husband informed him that our meetings were public on the sabbath day and that we were always pleased to have strangers come in, and ready to impart unto them all the information we were capable of.

Evening we went into br Cannons a short time. While we were there came sis Mowry and Smith. Sis M said her husband had his spiritual friends there, said she was so tired of those spirits that she knew not what to do with herself. Sis Smith said they had haunted her so that she had left the room above, and come down stairs.

Mon 24th Frances sis Evans, and Cannon went to visit Sis Moses, at the Mission Dolorus. Br Taites hand much better. Frank Silver called Also H Wilkins, and left his trunk. Lawyer Brunk the gent who attended our meeting on the Sabbath, and to whom Mr C lent books, called to return them. I conversed with him awhile, he told me some of his trials, and past experience; and declared his great objection to our faith, which is at present the great stumbling to this generation; Viz Poligamy. I gave him 2 other books. Joseph Smith, the propet, and the Pearl of great price. I told him when he had read them we would furnish him with treatises on poligamy. He said he wished to converse with my husband on the subject, and appointed tuesday evening to visit him. When my husband returned I informed him of the promise I had made, to give him discourses on that subject, and as we had none in the house he went to br Cannon, and got some for him.

Tues 25th Very warm day. H Wilkins brought his things here, preparatory to his leaving for San B——. Left his trunk to be sent down by water, but he himself was going by land. Shortly after returned and took his trunk to carry by land. Toward evening came lawyer B—— again, returned the books which he appeared very well pleased with; but said there many things in The Pearl of Great price, that he could not understand with out further instruction. Said he was unexpectedly called away and regreted that he was deprived the pleasure of investigating it further for the present

Wed 26th. Very warm day. Sister Evans Frances and myself visited at Mr Carringtons. Had a very agreeable time. Mrs C made us a nice supper, and treated us with much politeness and respect.

Thurs 27th. I performed a large ironing in the AM. PM I accompanied sister Evans to sister Jones' s to spend the evening. Sis Sargent visited with us. Sis Dagroot was in a few moments. Evening was our weekly prayer meeting. There were a number of visiters in, besides some of the travelling elders, which made it quite pleasant and lively. Br Wilkie opened the meeting by reading a hymn, and praying, but br Hunt seemed to be the leading <u>star</u> of the <u>evening</u>. After supper sis E and myself went into sis Sargents to see the babes, thought they looked very delicate, as though they had hardly a sufficiency to eat to satisfy their natures.

PM while I was absent came br Finley from his employment at harvesting. Frances kept house in my absence, baked light bread and cooked the supper for the men, evening they all came up to meeting except Mr C he was much fatigued, and as lawyer Brunk called to converse with him on the subject of poligamy, he staid at home, and spent the time untill 10 oclock in conversation with him.

It was a most beautiful evening. Past 10 when we returned. Br Finly came and slept here.

Frid 28th Another very warm day. Br Lyman called and took some shirts belonging to himself and br Norris. Said he came down late last night from Sacramento.

PM Br Finly came in and said he intended going to San B——d——no on the next boat, and requested br Taite to accompany him, which he br T also decided on doing if possible. I told him I thought he would wish before he got through that he had waited untill his sores were healed. Besides he would have his little boy to care for. But he thought br Finly would willingly assist him, in all his cares.

We expected the steamer would leave on Sat. I therefore commenced straightway to reconnoitre Johny's clothes, and put them in perfect order for the journey, laying each kind in seperate places. The little fellow was pleased with the idea of <u>going</u> like all children, but said he would come back again to see me. I truly feel that we shall be lonely without him, and that he will lose a good friend in leaving me. Yet I commend his father for wishing to keep him with himself.

Br J Dire came this eve—— and took Frances to the theatre.

9 oclock br F—— came in, said the boat was not going untill monday.

Sat 29th I had a very busy day. Two breakfasts to get, washed a few clothes for Johny, made a large pan of fried cakes. Sister Evans came in awhile Br J Dire was here, brought in a bottle of brandy peaches. Sarah Jones and her little niece were in, and all had quite a time of eating, and drinking. PM I starched and ironed for Dennis, also repaired shirts which kept me very busy all day. Fr—— assisted in getting supper, and then went again to the theatre. I had the work to do up, and br Taites sores to dress. At the same time Johny commenced crying for a share of my attention, and I felt that I needed more than two hands to accomplish all at once. However by preserving composure, and a good degree of patience, I managed to bring everything into its proper shape in due time.

Br Henry Jackson put up with us. Br and sis Jones came in after 9 oclock, said they were going to a shoe shop. I retired to rest near 10 oclock, feeling much fatigued, and somewhat nervous. Besides Johny seemed unwell, and restless. I droped off to sleep after sometime, but was soon awakened by Johny crying, and got up to regulate his bed. I then slept no more untill 2 in the morning. Frances came in about 1——— I arose in the morning near 6 oclock

Sept 30th feeling very miserable, but after breakfast I felt much better. I had steady employment untill almost 11 oclock, when I took my seat in the meeting room, but soon found it to warm and crowded to keep my seat, and gave way to others and went to the kitchen.

Our lower rooms were crowded, and many standing around the door. Elder A Lyman <u>held</u> <u>forth</u>, much to the <u>edification</u> of the audience. Sisters Corwin and Hollenbeck spent the recess with us. Br Rich spoke to us in the PM, and was followed by Lyman, who said they did not expect to be with us at conference, and therefore called a vote of the church to know whether they received br Cannon as president of the church in all this upper country, and said it was their wish that he should do so; He was universally received.

Henry Jackson M Wheeler and a one leged man by the name of Wm Richmond took supper with us. The latter was one of the Mormon battallion who had his foot hurt in the service, and lost his leg in consequence of it. Said he was seeking for a pension from the <u>government</u>, and expected to obtain it.

[Little Johnny's Departure]

Mon Oct 1st fine morning. I felt weak and nervous, but had a large washing on hand, and the colored man having disappointed me, we had it all to do ourselves. Br Taite and Finly were to leave in the PM, and I did not like to have them carry away dirty clothes and therefore we washed, starched and ironed them for them. Johny kept in good spirits, but I could not refrain from tears when I reflected upon his being separated from a second mother, to whom he was as much attached as almost any child to a mother. I believe his father was almost tempted to leave him with me, but though[t] if his mother should come from Indie that she would feel bad to find he had left him among strangers, and therefore concluded to keep him with him, feeling assured that he would find friends in San B——d———no. Br Taite expressed many thanks for my kindness, and said he would never <u>forget</u> <u>us</u>, in <u>time</u>, nor, <u>eternity</u>. I kissed John and they shook hands all around, and left about 3 oclock for the steamer. Sister Mowry came in to bid goodbye. The little fellows situation excited much sympathy, from us all. To be turned upon the world in a land of strangers without a mother, at his tender age was truly a pitiable condition. But I believe the Lord will protect and defend him.

Br T's sores were mending fast when he left, but still were very troublesome. He was wholly dependent on br Finly's care, for himself and Johny, And he could not have had a <u>better</u> or more <u>faithful</u> person to lean upon. I therefore felt reconciled to see them go on their way, to their place of <u>destination</u>. Br F—— stoped a few moments to wait for their <u>shirts</u> that we were hurrying to finish. He also expressed many thank for our kindness to them, promised to write to <u>me</u> and <u>Frances</u>. Evening br Lyman took supper with us. Br Wheeler and Richmond spent the evening. Fr—— went again to the theatre.

Tues Oct 2nd I felt very lame and weary, but still kept about my work, finished ironing. Fr—— went to the P O—— but found no letters. Came back and made pies I cut garments for br Barrows. Sister Mowrey came in, also a pedlar called, of whom I purchased <u>linen</u>.

I prepared supper and sent Alma for brs Rich and Lyman. While we were eating, Mother Jones and Sarah came in. S—— sat down and ate with us. Before they left, br Woodbury came, and as he had not been to supper I invited him to eat. While he was eating came sister Mowry. She was very sociable, staid an hour or more, and asked me to go to sis <u>Kings</u> to see sis Evans a few minutes, as she was going to leave the next morning. It was then almost 9 oclock, however we had a sociable little chat, and returned before ten. Mr Crosby went to the auction sales, bought two nice money purses which he presented to me and Frances.

Wed 3rd. Frank Silver called. Told me his friends had heard that he [was] dead, by being shipwrecked. Also informed me that Frank Rose was married. He gave me a gold watch and ring which he wished me to send to Mrs David Cheny and her daughter Rachel. While he was here sister Evans came in, on her way to San Jose and he delivered them to her. Said he was going to the mines.

Br and sis Woodbury came in, said they talked of leaving on the schooner for San B——d——o, tomorrow, were going out to buy a wagon, to take with them. Delinina Mowry called and sat awhile with us.

Thurs 4th This is our monthly fast day; I wrote a letter to sister Pratt and Ellen; ^Eld Woodbury called and bade us goodbye. Sold me a pully bed^ before meeting time, expecting the people to assemble as usually at 11 oclock, but to our disappointment only 3 or 4 persons came; the breth all being so full of business, that it was not expedient for them to attend. And therefore the meeting was defered untill evening, we met at br Jones, and had a very good meeting. Wm McGary staid over night with us.

Henry Wilkins also returned from the other side of the bay, with the intention of going down with brs Lyman and Rich. McGary said he was also going.

Frid 5th I spent a great part of the day in reading the Mormon, a paper published in N Y—— by elder John Taylor.[8] PM I repaired shirts.

Sis D—— Mowry was in again with her babe. Toward evening I cooked some, and prepared for the semiannual conference which convenes tomorrow

[More Departures for San Bernardino]

Sat 6th The conference convened at 11 oclock, called to order by elder Crosby prayer by br Canon. Who was chosen to preside at the present conference. Short address by eld Crosby, was followed by Cannon, who warned us against speaking evil of those in office in the church, or presiding over us before he closed br A Lyman came in, and made a very excellent speech to us, for our profit and learning. He was followed by eld Rich who also spoke well. They were both just ready to set sail for San Bernardino, And therefore the conference was adjourned untill tomorrow.

Frances and I sent letters by br Rich. They blessed us in the name of the Lord. Eld Lyman said he did not know that he should be here again under a year from this time. Shortly after the close of the meeting, they passed by on their way to the boat. I was up stairs, looked out of my window and bade them good bye. There was elds Lyman, Rich, Brig—— Gen—— Hunt, brs Warren, Dodge, H Wilkins Wm McGary, and I know not who beside, that were bound for San Br. It seems to leave quite a blank in our society, but it will probably soon be filled by others, as this seems to be only a resting place; or rather a place for preparing to go further.

Evening came br Dire and his br Eben. The young folks proposed going to the theatre, and Alma and Dire went after Sister Jones daughter, Sarah came, but Anna was otherwise engaged. Frances and Sarah went with Alma and Jones Dire. In the meantime br Barrows came in to invite Fr—— to accompany him, but finding her engaged, he insisted on my husband and I going with him, and offered to pay our fare or bill. I did not altogether feel in the mood of going but please the men I consented to go, for the first time in my life. I found it tolerably interesting. But felt no particular inclination to repeat my visit again soon. *Sun 7th* we had quite a full meeting, and a good one. The conference closed, and adjourned untill next April.

Evening Fr—— and Dire went again to the theatre with Origin Mowrey and wife. Mr Crosby and I went into Mr Mowrys awhile. Delina left her babe, which cried and was quite troublesome.

Mon 8th I washed in the AM, got through by 12 oclock. PM, I repaired shirts, and other garments.

Tues 9th I baked and ironed. Evening went into M's to grind coffee. Joseph Cheny and B Evans put up the mill, and ground it for me. About 10 oclock PM some one knocked at the door. I arose went the window to ask who was there, and was answered "Badlam" I then called up Alma to let him in, and gave him lodgings.

[A Visit to Samuel Brannan's Home]

Wed 10th fine morning. I went into Mowry's, asked the old lady to take a walk with me to see sis Goodfellow, but she informed me that she had a previous engagement to sister Corwin, and requested me to accompany her, to which I consented, and returned home to make preparations to that effect. Shortly after I reached home I received a call from Mrs Galliger an irish lady which detained me untill Sis—— M came in. We then hurried off, took the stage at the corner of Broadway and Stockton and for 12 ½ cents each soon found ourselves at the residence of S Branan Esq. on mission street.[9] On ringing the bell, and enquiring for Mrs Corwin, we were escorted by the steward (a colored man) into the parlor, and soon joined by sister C——, and invited to her private apartment up stairs, where we enjoyed a very pleasant visit with herself, and grandchildren, who made frequent calls to her room, while we were there. We had lunch at one About 4 oclock we were invited to dinner, where everything bore the appearance of wealth and plenty. The room was adorned with beautiful drawings, and pictures of various kinds. Which with the abundance of silver ware with which the table was supplied presented a very splendid appearance. As we ate by ourselves, we took our leisure, and enjoyed it finely. While sitting at the table we heard Mrs Branan playing the piano in her parlor, and on rising sis C invited us in to hear her more distinctly, but to our disappointment found she had retired to her chamber, and was engaged in looking after her children, her eldest daughter being somewhat indisposed.

Mr Branan and his eldest son Samuel left for Sacramento while we were there. The little master was very polite to us, on leaving came in to bid his grandmother good bye, and we shared with her in his kisses, and good byes. I thought him a very pleasant child. His grandmother told me that he was 3 months old when they left N Y—— in '46.

They have two daughters of the ages of 6 and 4, and another son of 2 years, which is the number of their family.

At half past 5, sister C accompanied us to the stage, at the corner of Miss[ion] and second street, where we waited a few minutes. She was so kind and careful as to give directions to the driver where to leave us, probably discovering that we neglected to do so, before taking seats. We reached home in due time feeling well pleased with our visit.

Thurs 11th of Oct This is sister Lavina Bakers birthday. 60 years old. I feel almost astonished when I reflect how old we are all becoming. Istead of our parents it is now our older brothers, and sisters, who are hastening on towards 3 score years and ten. And very soon it will be said of <u>them,</u> as well as <u>us</u>, that they are gone the way of all the earth.

But so runs our race. And since our days must fly; well keep their end in sight.

We'll spend them all in wisdoms ways, and let them speed their flight.

I made a call on sister Goodfellow on Tailor and Broadway. Where she has latly moved, with her two grandchildren, and her soninlaw's wife their stepmother. She seemed quite unhappy in consequence of the choice he had made, in selecting a mother for his children, having chosen one, or rather been chosen by one, who is diametrically opposed to himself in religious principles, and even curses the church of which he is a member. She was absent so that I did not see her. I lunched with the old lady, and her little granddaughters, and spent an hour or two very agreeably. Margaret the eldest accompanied me home, and stoped an hour or more, by the consent of her G——Mother.

Evening we attended meeting at br Jones's Very few attended. Yet the good Spirit was with us, reached home at ten, found br Badlam here with Alma.

Frid 12th Br B—— breakfasted with us; intending to go to Sacramento at 4 oclock, in co with a br by the name of Paul Smith, an elder late from Aus——, who with his wife is on his way to Great Salt lake. At 12 oclock br S—— and wife called to say goodbye, said the boat was to leave at 1——. Evening came brs Badlam and Falk, who was an entire stranger to us, but said he had been sometime in the church lived in Kirtland, Nauvoo and had been at Salt lake. Had been burned out latly, and lost a considerable property. He seemed quite an intelligent man. They both took supper with us and stoped over night. Frances went to see Mary Hughs, returned at 6 oclock. Br J Dire took her to the theatre.

Sat 13th Very pleasant morning. Toward noon I went in to sis Mowrey's, they invited me to stop and take dinner with them, and as I saw they had a fine lot of tomatoes I concluded to do so Br J D spent the evening here. I felt very sleepy, and retired early

Sun 14th Beautiful day. Br and sis Cannon gone over the bay. Our meeting was rather small, but quite good. We all seemed to enjoy a good degree of the Spirit. Br Badlam spoke to us in the AM and was followed by Curtis. PM we had a testifying meeting. The brethren and sisters spoke all around, and bore their testimony to the truth of the gospel. After meeting Frances went home with sister Moses who lives at ex mission Dolorus. Sister Mowrey came in awhile in the evening. Said she suffered much from the opposing spirit of her husband, who is a rank Spiritualist. Said the Spiritualists had a meeting at Mr Stewarts that evening.

Mon 15th The colored man washed for me. F—— came home at 10 oclock

[Phillip B. Lewis]

Tues 16th Yesterday the mail steamer *Golden Gate* arrived from Panama— bringing over a thousand passengers. Just heard at 4 oclock PM that eld P B Lewis has arrived from the Sandwich islands.[10]

Wed 17th When Mr Crosby returned from work I informed him of br L' s arrival, and he said he would go in search of him. Accordingly he went and found him at eld—— Cannon's, and invited him home with him to supper, he also invited br C—— and his comrads but sister King had made ready for them, and therefore they declined. Br L, came in with Mr Crosby, and spoke in the same composed manner that he would if we had seen each other quite lately. I thought he had grown old, and thin since I last saw him.

On conversing with him he confessed that his sight and hearing had failed him very much, and that he was greatly debilitated, from living in a warm climate. When I spoke of his wife's death he remarked that he was not sorry that she was dead; that she had suffered enough. Said if she was alive he should still wish her to live, in hopes that she might recover, but since she was gone he was satisfied that she was at rest. He talks of going to San B—— My husband told him to bring his things, and stop with us while he staid in San F——. Which he did this morning, *Thurs 18th* brought 3 trunks and a high basket. Frances has been sewing for Sister D—— Mowrey I have done a large ironing, starched shirts, and various other things. I invited br Cannon, and his coadjutors, Bull, and Wilkie, to come and take supper with us to night, as their housekeeper is absent this week. F—— came home in season to get the supper for them, and told me to retire to my chamber and rest untill the supper was ready, which I willingly did.

Frid 19th Frances helping Delina. Zacheus Cheny and wife came from across the bay. J Dire and Wm Baker called. Br Dier took supper with us. *Sat 20th.* Frances, Amanda Cheny and D Mowrey went to the mission Dolorus to visit sister Moses. PM I felt very unwell, went to sister Mowrey's, found her sick, and taking a warm bath.

When F returned she brought Clarisa Moses with her who staid over night, and went to the theatre with Fr and Dier.

I retired to bed in good season, but had a very restless night, slept none untill after 2 oclock in the morning.

Sun 21st I arose feeling far better than I had anticipated. We had a very good meeting, Br P B Lewis gave us a history of his mission on the islands, but seemed not to have the spirit of preaching. Said he was not a preacher, but rather a laborer &C.

About 11 oclock br and sis Cheny left and Fr accompaned them, intending to stay a week. Evening br Lewis went home with br Everleth.

Mrs Eagar attended PM meeting, stoped and took supper with us. She was very sociable, spoke of her troubles while in the church, and thought the Brooklin co misused her. Wished me to give her the address of her son John, which I did in writing.[11] She invited me to visit her, and left to go into Mr Stuarts, wished to get a communication from the Spirits, expected to find a meeting of Spiritualists there. Beautiful pleasant night. Mr Crosby asked me to take a walk as it was too pleasant to stay in the house. We started out, and he proposed going to the Turn Werein [Turnverein] Hall, on bush street. We found a very fine band of musicians, and a songstress among them, and altho it was german music, yet it was quite diverting. We reached home a little after 11. Alma came in a few minutes after, been to the Union theatre. *Mon 22nd* I performed good days work; washed and made light bread. I was tired and restless, it was late before I slept much.

Tues 23rd very warm day. I took a walk with br Lewis to see sis Hollenbeck. Made a short stay, and called on sis Jones. She was quite out of health. We sat awhile with her, and then went in to see the Sargent's twins. Sis Corwin called on sis J while I was there. I intended calling on sis Armstrong, went to her door and knocked, but no one opened unto me and I left and came home.

Wed 24th baked and ironed. Eben Dier boarding with us.

Thurs 25th Sister King came in a few minutes in the morning. PM I went to her house, and stoped an hour or more. Lizzie gone to dancing school

Friday 26th very warm in the AM. Sis K brought a letter from the P, O for Fr. She also got one herself from Great Salt Lake City from Sis Burton, (that was) but now sis Gates. She informed her that she was married, was highly pleased with the place and people; was happily disappointed. Said she had heard that sister McLane was on the way to the valley, in Dr Blair's co———. Would be in soon. I went in to sis K's toward evening with sister Hollenbeck, who called on me awhile. While we were in Sister Corwin came, and we had a sociable time. The conversation turned upon Wm Smith, our prophets bro, we all wondered where he could be, as we had none of seen or heard from him in a great while. Sis C——— spoke of his conduct in N Y. several years ago. Said she once requested him to refrain from coming to her house, as his conduct was not in accordance with her ideas of propriety.[12] 5 oclock I went to market, bought meat and tomatoes. Br Lewis out this evening. Alma playing the violin. 21 years today since we were married. ^Various have been the scenes both merciful and afflictive through which we have been called to pass.^

Sat 27th Dull cloudy day. Eben Dier and Wm Baker called. I baked pies and light bread. Delina M—— came in with her babe, and took a cup of tea with me. Said her mother had gone over the bay to visit Mrs Eagar.

Sun Oct 28th very cool morning. Our meeting was very small, but a good degree of the Spirit was manifested both AM and PM. The subject of the gathering was the prevailing topic. I believe they all felt the importance of it very sensibly.

At recess br Wandall called in, said his clothes were dirty, and not decent to attend meeting in. Which he plead as an apology for his nonattendance. Evening Alma went to the theatre. Br Lewis took a walk. We retired early. I did not hear br L when he returned At 12 Alma came, and found himself locked out. But as I was awake he was soon let in. I became restless the latter part of the night, and slept no more untill after 3 oclock.

Mon 29th Very cold and cloudy. Br Lewis going tomorrow. Cy Iray called, bragged that he was making money. Said in 3 years he would be worth 50,000$. Eben Dier came back, said he had been to Sacramento. At 1 oclock Frances came with br and sis Cannon. Evening went to the theatre.

Teus—— 30th. Dennis washed for me. Fr—— did some for herself.

Wed 31st She commenced sewing for a Mrs Jenkings milliner, On the corner of Dupont and Broadway. Sister Jones and Sarah called. Br Lewis, Flanders, and Salter, left for San B——

Evening J Dier invited me to go to the theatre, and as Fr did not wish to go, I accompanied him, and Alma. The performances were anything but interesting to me. I felt quite disgusted with their shallow plays. And the dancing of Mdm Monplaisir was in my estimation a perfect outrage ~~against~~ upon the feelings of any modest lady.

We reached home about 11 oclock.

Thurs—— Nov 1st, our monthly fast day. The brethren all so much engaged that only one attended, Br Cannon was there to preside. 9 women and two children composed the meeting. We enjoyed a good degree of the Spirit

Nearly all spoke and prayed, and felt well satisfied with our meeting.

Frid 2nd I ironed, and baked, and prepared supper for 3 or 4 men.

At night found myself much fatigued. Fr went to the theatre with Al and J D

Sat 3rd I made pies cleaned house mended garments &C. Eben and Jones Dier both boarding with us.

Sun 4th Very good meeting. PM the sacrament was administered. A stranger called at intermission and asked if the latterday Saints met here, he was answered in the affirmative, accordingly he came in to the meeting, and we soon discovered, that he felt himself much at home as he sung with us, kneeled in praying, and observed the strictest order. ^After the close we found he was a Scotch br who came with Br Wilkie from Eng——^ Just before the close an other stranger called. He was a colored man, I should think a halfbreed, He asked permission to speak, but as it was so late the brethren thought proper to refuse him. After the services were closed, he informed them that he had once belonged to the church. Sarah Jones stoped and took supper with us. After sup—— Fr went home with her to stay overnight.

[Time to Leave]

Mon 5th Very cool morning. Mr C and Alma went to their labor as usually. I got a second breakfast for the two Diers, and just as we were sitting down to the table they both returned with a large load of tools on their shoulders. I was a little surprised, but soon learned from them that Mr Hollenbeck had discharged them, before the job was finished; and from what we could glean of circumstances we concluded that some difficulty had occurred in the family, and that he Mr H—— thought his wife was making a confident of Mr Crosby. He would not acknowledge that he had anything against him, but said did not want any more work done at present.

Accordingly we understood that our time had come to go to San Bernardino and decided on making preparations to that effect. I was sure that the hand of the Lord was over us, and believed that all would be right.

The two brothers were here in waiting for a boat, and were pleased with the prospect of having our company.

Frances and I washed, we thought perhaps for the last time in San F.

Tues 6th we ironed. I tried to get through in season to go and have our daguereotypes taken, but it was too late, and we concluded to wait untill tomorrow. Sister Cannon came in and sat awhile, took a cup of tea with me, had heard from Mowreys that we expected to leave soon, and was quite surprised. Delina M was also in a few minutes Evening the young folks gone to the theatre.

Wed 7th This is Frances birthday. She is 21 years.

We all went and had our Daguerotypes taken, first in a family group and after in separate cases. Fr living with us, had hers in the grou[p.] I was not quite satisfied with mine, as it had the appearance of my being excited. From the Daguerian gallery we went shopping. I bought a china

Frances Stevens Pratt, San Francisco, 1855, from print of daguerreotype with shattered glass cover. Courtesy of Special Collections and Archives, Utah State University Libraries.

shawl, dress and breast pin. My shawl was 15 dolls black silk 1.37¢ pr yard, which he gave me for 1.25. Breast pin 8 dolls. We also bought a bolt of bleached muslin, at 11 cts pr yard, which nearly exhausted our purse. We then came home without half the articles that we felt we needed. My husband sent a note to br John M Horner to let him know our determination to leave, and solicit a little assistance from him if possible.

Thurs 8th Rather dull and cloudy. Frances complaining some, has a bad cold. Went to a party last night, with Mrs Stewart, at Mr Langs staid over night, slept with Mrs Comstock an acquaintance of ours.

Evening myself and husband attended prayer meeting at bro Jones's.

Frid 9th fine warm day. Our vessel not yet arrived. Mr C gone to work with O Mowrey.

Sat 10th beautiful day. Yesterday PM I called on sister Goodfellow Found her in very good spirits, spent an hour or more very agreeably with her. Returned just before sunset. The young Diers proposed going to the American theatre, to see the Ravel Troupe, a new set of actors lately come to the city. Frances and I told them we would go for the last time while we stayid in this place. Accordingly we went, and were well entertained.

This PM I went to Mrs Jenkings shop, to engage me a bonnet. Took my braid that queen Pitomai gave me, and she promised to make me a bonnet of it. Sarah Jones in this evening; also an Aus—— brother. Frances and J D—— playing cards. The long looked for vessel arrived last evening.

Sun 11th rather cold and unpleasant. Meeting convened as usual. Elder Wandell was present, asked for a letter of recommendation to the church at San Bernardino, some discussion upon the subject, in consequence of his having neglected meetings, and omitted other duties; also some feelings which were known to exist between him and elder P P Pratt and his wife Elizabeth. He confessed his faults, and asked forgiveness. The brethren all spoke around, and he arose several times, and plead for mercy; tried to extenuate his conduct, by relating to us the unfavorable circumstances in which he had been placed, and finally obtained a note in his favor.

Mon 12th Washed our clothes probably for the last time in San Francisco. Evening came a Mr Ball from San Bernardino; brought letters from sister Pratt, and E Woodbury. He spoke rather discouragingly of our going there at present. Said they would all or nearly all lose their improvements, in consequence of the land being under a mortgage. And said the men possessing the mortgage were particular acquaintances of his, and had assured him that they intended to foreclose the same in a short time. Shortly after him came a sister Mount from Napa city in co with a Mr Day from the same place. We had a very sociable time.

Tues 13th rainy day. I ironed, finished a letter to sister Lois Thompson John Robinson one of the Aus—— brethren boarding with us.

Evening Mr C and Alma out shopping. I packed up my clothing.

Wed 14th Understand the vessel leaves on Sat; Mrs Mount called again took dinner with me. Frances went shopping with her Br and sis Horner called, also br and sis Hopkins.

Br H informed Mr C that he could do nothing for him in regard to money, but said he would see him again before we left. Mrs Carrington called on me and sat a short time Sister Mount and Mr Day came up and took supper with us Fr went to theatre with them. After they were gone came Mr Ball and spent the evening with us. We enjoyed his visit much and found him a very pleasant young man.

Thurs 15th We took our things on board the vessel, or a part of them. I went shopping. Sister Goodfellow called I called on sis King found her very sick. Sis Mount was in again. Evening attended meeting at br

Cannons Had a very good time. Great time shaking hands, and wishing us a pleasant passage, also blessing one another and requesting prayers.

Friday 16th sent the remainder of our luggage on board and went over to Mowreys, saw sis Corwin and Jones there. Toward evening Delina and I went shopping. Came back took supper. My husband—self and Fr slept there. Had a fine visit.

PART FOUR

Southern California

The San Bernardino Years
November 1855 to December 1857

Chapter Twelve
San Bernardino, A New Home
Journal, November 1855 to December 1856

[Sailing Down the California Coast]

Sat 17th arose at 6 got a cup of tea, bade all adieu, and went on board the schooner *Laura Bevans*, found it crowed with freight and passengers, cabin very small. Mate seemed polite and kind.

1/2 past 8 we were under weigh, moving very pleasantly. I felt much better than I expected to. Sat down to write. Told them I would write the history of our passage while I was able to do so. Capt Moreton soon came into the cabin and commenced conversation. We found him a very agreeable pleasant gentleman.

Our vessel glided along very smoothly, so that we could scarcely perceive that it moved. I did not feel much sick but had no inclination to stir about.

Sun 18th we were still moving on at a rapid rate. I kept my bed untill near noon, when I arose and went on deck, but found myself in the wrong place, and soon came to my berth. Sun evening I suffered considerably with sea sickness. We were beset with a calm which detained us about 24 hours. The vessel also commenced rolling, and myself and Alma were quite indisposed. I suffered considerably before I could manage to throw up, but felt much relieved thereby.

Mon 19th Still becalmed, gents playing cards in the cabin. Mr C—— and Capt Moreton talking on mormonism on deck. Got a light breeze.

Tues 20th tolerable good wind. I felt much better, arose at 7—— took breakfast and felt quite natural. Afterwards went on deck to look at the land, only a short distance from Santa Barberry [Barbara]

At 12 we anchored in the harbor, and the men went ashore. Jones and Eben [Dyer] brought us grapes and nuts. We were much diverted at

Coastal California route from San
Francisco to San Bernardino, 1855.

seeing them catch fish, of which the harbor was full. The birds also came
around us in flocks and the men amused themselves in shooting at them.
I staid on deck untill I became quite fatigued, came into the cabin and
resumed writing. Capt said we could go on shore in the morning if we
wished.

Beautiful pleasant evening. Moon shone clearly. All hands fishing.
Frances and the gents playing cards. I staid on deck untill I found it too
cold for comfort. Came below and took my berth.

Wed 21st fine morning, all hands going on shore. I wanted to go, but
Frances declined, and we gave it up. Mr Crosby went off. Capt discharg-
ing cargo. Several passengers left here. All seemed well disposed towards
us. One man with a roman nose thought the United States government
ought to take the mormons in hand for practicing polygamy and clear
them all out of Utah. Mr C told him that they could not do it constitu-
tionally. He asked why then they imprisoned men in some of the states for
having two wives. Mr C told him that it was contrary to the laws of some

of the states, but not to the laws of <u>this</u> the state of Cal and that it was practised here with impunity.[1] The gent was obliged to acknowledge the fact, but thought it was not right. The supper being ready conversation closed.

Santa Barbary is rather a gloomy looking place, nothing looks like improvement, very few nice houses, mostly Spanish cabins. The old mission house stands about two miles from the landing on a pleasant eminance. We thought some of going on shore to take a walk Fr—— and myself; but as there was not much to be seen, and some trouble in getting off the schooner, we gave up the idea. The men brought us grapes and nuts from shore. Cologne &C.

About 4 oclock they took in their anchor, hoisted sails and directed their course toward San Pedro, where we arrived at 11 oclock *thurs evening 22nd.* We had some rough weather during the day and evening, and I had a bad turn of seasickness accompanied with a dreadful headache. In the course of the evening I threw up a great quantity of billious matter, which relieved my head and stomach very materially.

At supper the gents brought up the subject of Mormonism, commencing with poligamy, as it usually does. They Mr Wallace of the Los Angles Star, and capt Emerson of Los A——g——s, proposed to Mr Crosby the subject, and requested his evidence from scripture. But as soon as he commenced speaking they began to ridicule the scriptures and altho they had previouly confessed that the bible was the best book, and contained the best code of laws and rules for our faith and practice that the world afforded yet they both declared themselves unbelievers in it, and their unbelief in Jesus Christ being the Savior of the world

Frances was very unwell, and laid in bed almost all day.

[Disembarking at San Pedro]

Frid morning 23rd we were all brought on shore. It had rained almost all night, and the bank was very slippery, so that we had hard work in ascending it. Got our shoes very much loaded with clay. But on reaching the <u>house</u> found it quite as comfortable as we had anticipated. It is an old Spanish structure perhaps a hundred years old The roof is covered with raw hides. some parts of <u>it</u> much decayed. They are now repairing some of the rooms, and making them quite agreeable. The steward conducted us through a long diningroom, where was a table set large enough to accommodate 20 persons, and turned us into a room where were 5 beds and a table covered with books and papers. I sat down and finished a letter I had commenced to sis Mowrey, and put in the office. We had not been there long when a young man came in and beged our

Ann Louise Pratt, ca. 1855. Courtesy of Special Collections and Archives, Utah State University Libraries.

pardon for intruding and told us <u>that</u> was his office. After dinner the steward came, and showed us to another apartment, where were only two beds. The fleas troubled us so bad, that I did not sleep any through the night.

Evening came a br Wm Johnson direct from San B[ernardino] on his way to F—— [San Francisco], brought us letters, and spent the night with us. We had very social times. *Sat—— 24th*, rather rainy and unpleasant. The remainder of our goods were brought on shore. PM we, F and myself, and the two Diers, took the stage and came to Los Angles, arrived at sis P——s [Pickett] about 7 pm found her nearly recovered from her sickness, with which she had been afflicted for several weeks. Herself and girls were pleased to see us. and we had a very agreeable evenings visit.

Sun 25th Beautiful day. I felt somewhat cheered and comforted by the remarkably pure air. Br Gruard called to see us. Spoke very disparagingly of San B——. Said he would see if there were teams here from Said place that would go to San Pedro for our goods, went out and found two just ready to leave for home, but said they were unwilling to go, having been already sometime from home. Pm called a young man of this place by the name of Hunter, and I asked him to enquire for teams going to San B——, he said he would do so.

Jones called to see how we were getting along. I wrote a few lines to Mr Crosby by way of consolation; knowing that he would think the time long if he waited for teams. Recommended him to come to Los An. Sun evening we sang a number of hymns, among them were Come come ye Saints, which had the effect to calm and console my mind.

Mon 26th slept well last night, beautiful day, sent my letter to the Bell[a] Union [*a prominent Los Angeles hotel*] to go to San Pedro. Br Dier called, said he intended to purchase team at the auction sale of horses today.

Sewed some for sis Picket, had a lengthy conversation with her on some principles in the church. PM Henry Wilkins called on his way back to San F. Said br Wandell reached San B—— Sat the day he left. Shortly after came H Jackson and br Daily. Said there were teams on the way out here. Evening came Harvey Green. On his way to the upper country.

Tues 27th Still stopping at Los Angles, at sis P's, took a walk with her Called on Smith's, Anderson's, and Pine's, like the place very well. Br Mecum called, and said we could ride out to San B—— with him. Br Swartout came, and I engaged him to go down for Mr Crosby, and our goods; he said he would go this PM. Mr and Mrs Pine called over to see us toward evening. I admire them much, had a very sociable chat with them. While at Andersens we saw br and sis Sloane just from Salt lake, on their way to Sacramento to visit their daughter, Mrs Warner. Several gents called in the evening. A Mr Rodes, Mr Wallace, who came down with us on the schooner, and a Mr Williams from San B——. had very sociable times, with singing, and music on the accordion. Br Swartout set off by moonlight to San P—— for Mr Crosby. I sent a line by him. Br Mecum called and informed us that he would be ready to leave at 12 oclock on Wed——.

Wed 28th fine day, girls washing. ~~Br Mecum set~~

Br and sis Sloane came to see sis Pickett. Soon after came Ellen and Ann Louise in the stage, came out to meet us. They came with the intention of staying a few days but as we were nearly ready to come back they concluded to return with us. Accordingly at 2 oclock br Mecum came for us in an open carriage, but said he would put up a temporary cover when we reached the Monti [El Monte]. We took leave of our friends and came on toward San B—— reached the Monti about sunset and passed on to a br Thompsons who keep a public house a little this side. On arriving found they were the ones I once knew in Iowa, Bentonsport. They informed me that they had been after Strang, and proved his system false, and then went with the Brewsterites, and became dissatisfied with them, and at length had returned to their first faith.[2] They treated us with much kindness and familiarity. A large number of travellers put up with them. and we were all invited into the upper room, where we found a nice hall and two fiddlers, and the young people proposed dancing, several cotillions were danced. Sis T—— parted her beds for the girls, and I slept with her. Br Mecum proposed to us to rise at 4 oclock, and set off by moonlight, in order to get through before dark.

At 4 *Thurs 29th* he came and knocked at the door and informed us that he would soon be ready. We arose and prepared ourselves for our ride; found the air very cool, but pleasant and agreeable.

[Arrival in San Bernardino]

At 10 we reached the Coco Mungo [Cucamonga] ranch. stoped at a Spanish house, where we stoped and ate breakfast. Br Mecum made a fire, and fried some beef and pork, made some coffee or tea, spread a piece of a bedquilt on the ground, and we borrowed a few dishes of the spanish people. We had nice light bread, and the negro cook, gave us a piece of warm cornbread which he was making, and we made quite a hearty meal.

We then came on to another Spanish house, where Ellen bought a few grapes; reached br P's [Pratt] after sunset, he was out hunting. Sister and Lois came out to meet us, said they did not expect us untill next week. Sis looked very old and had lost several teethe since I saw her. Louise had also grown so large that she did not look natural. Evening the girls all except E went to a party. She felt very unwell and thought it was on account of her eating grapes and drinking sour wine.

Friday 30th San Bernardino. Sis P—— and I took a walk before breakfast, called on br John Phillips, he offered to rent us his house for 12 dolls pr month half money, and half labor.

It is a two story building, only one room below, and one above. Sis Jane Steward called, and offered to sell us her house. Afterwards invited us to a quilting the next day. PM took a walk called on Grouard's, Laytons, Hills.[3]

Sat ~~Nov~~Dec 1st took a walk to br Lymans, went on the roof of his new house, to see the city, had a very pleasant view of the valley. Returned to br Stewards, where the married ladies had been quilting sometime before us. We enjoyed a very sociable visit, had a plentiful supper, and came home well pleased with the party. Evening Capt. Hunt and family called at br Pratts and we had dancing on the occasion. Mr C arrived at ten oclock. ^Alma and the teamster came at 11. We had been absent from each other one week.^

Sun 2nd, Went to meeting in a schoolhouse. Br Rich spoke to the people, I was highly edified with his discourse.

Br Tomkins and family stoped after meeting and took supper. Several young men in in the evening, had music by Mr C Ellen and Alma.

Mon 3rd Took a walk with sis P—— went to the P O—— called on sis Hunt and [Mrs. William] Crosby.[4] Mr C commenced making a house, of a frame that had been put up by Hill and Layton for a machine shop, took it down to make it smaller.

Tues 4th Br Newel left his horse for sis P—— and myself to take a ride. We went to see sis Patten, formerly sister Repsher. Found her living in a poor little house, in a very retired place, had been very sick, but was recovering. Her husband was gone from home. She was highly pleased to see us, and considered it a God send to her, and she felt much better when we left, than when we came. She invited me to stay overnight but I declined on account of wishing to wash next day.

We returned to Chapmans, where we left our horse, and walked across the field. Called in a few minutes while he got our horse ready.

Wed 5th I washed, took my clothes over to br Laytons to wash. Took dinner with her. Evening came in br and sister Cox.[5] We had a very sociable chat with them. The girls all gone to a wedding. Albert Stodard married Ellen Niece, and had a very large party.

Thurs 6th I ironed, repaired garments, Mr C and Alma worked on the new house. Evening went in to br [Thomas] Whitaker, he was absent, had a very pleasant little call. Mr C called on br Lewis.

Frid 7th I ironed at sister L[ayton]'s, took dinner with her and sis Whitaker. Evening the girls went to capt Hunts to a sewing party, making clothes for a family who are sick.

Sat 8th I spent my time in working a collar. Went over to the new house, staid sometime. Mr Crosby got a fall from the roof of the house, which hurt and lamed him some. Evening Wm McGary was in, also Harriet Hunt. Sis Pratt read in the Illustrated Manners book.

Sun 9th Attended church. Br Turley spoke to the people, and was followed by br Rich. They both spoke very much to our edification. Br [Ebenezer] Hanks came home with sis P—— and Ellen, spent the PM and took supper; after which myself and sis P took a walk to Woodburys, found her alone, her husband gone to the coast after our furniture. Evening we went to prayer meeting, had a very lively one. Frances went home with Tomkins girls.

Mon 10th Sewed for sis P—— made a sack [*sleeved, loose garment*] for Ann Louise. Evening br Woodbury returned with the goods. Mr Bishop was in. Sis P read the water cure book.

Tues 11th Ann L went to sis Hopkins to work. I made a sack for sis P.

[The New House]

Wed 12th Mr C laid the floor, set up the stove and bedstead, and moved in a part of our things. The boards were very green, and I felt doubtful as to the propriety of sleeping here, untill they had become dry, but we finally concluded to try it, as we had already staid to br P's long enough to make them a good visit. Sister reasoned with me against the idea of my sleeping here, but I asked the Lord in the name of Jesus to protect us, and preserve us from harm, which he did, and altho the first night was a severe cold one, yet none of us took the least injury from the open house and damp floor.

Thurs 13th I commenced to paste up the cracks in the walls. Sister Pratt had a visit appointed at br [Daniel] Starks, and insisted on me going with her. Frances came and took my place, and I went.

We had a fine pleasant visit. Sis [Mary Hamilton] Sparks was also there, and told us concerning her troubles with her husband [Quartus S. Sparks]. I truly felt to sympathise with her. Mother Jones called on me this Am, and was also there this Pm Sister Starks has poor health. Sis P—— and I sewed for her while we were there. I bought some house paper of her to line my new house, and promised to sew for her, On our return home called at Sparks' new house. Had an introduction to Dr Sinclaire. Sis Sparks took me around the different rooms, I wished her much joy, and told her I was glad to see her so comfortably situated, and did not envy her or anyone any thing they enjoyed. Reached home about 5 oclock. Mr C and Alma ate supper at br Pratts. Evening br and sis P were in here, also John Robinson Mr C made some cloth windows, which answer a very good purpose.

Friday 14th Alma's birth day. 19 years old. Mr Crosby went to see br Carter to try if he would let him have a small hog, for meat. Found him killing a large quantity of them for market, but did not like to trust, but his wife interceding for him, he finally consented to sell him a pig at 15 cts pr lb. and, take his labor for part pay. Evening Ellen was in, and invited Alma to go over with his violin. I went with them, he played a few tunes and the string broke. I commenced papering my house today.

Sat 15th beautiful day. I resumed my labor at papering, had to send for four rolls more I worked late, or untill 9 oclock before I got through ~~papering~~.

Sun 16th I felt quite lame and weary, did not attend meeting. Evening br Tate and his little son called and took tea with us.

Br T—— requested me to take his boy again, to which I consented; he said he would bring him the next day. We went to meeting, enjoyed it well.

[Little Johnny Tait's Welcome Return]

Mon 17th I washed. F—— spent the day at her fathers. PM br Tate came with the little boy. He stole away from us that he might not hear him cry, he only cried a few minutes, and soon became quite happy. The night was quite cold, and as he slept alone did not keep very warm. Toward morning he called for his father, I arose and took him into my bed, and he soon fell asleep.

Tues 18th put out and dried the remainder of my clothes, put down my carpet, kept myself very busy all day. Toward night took a walk with sis P——, called at several places, took little Johny with us, returned before dark. Br Robinson spent the evening with us. Eben Dire called awhile.

Wed 19th fine day, sun[n]ed my bedding, regulated my house, &C. Evening attended prayer meeting at James Stewarts, had a good meeting.

Thurs 20th. Baked and ironed. Frances gone. Mr Crosby commenced labor for br [Charles] Crisman, in co with br Layton. Br and sis Woodbury took supper with us, after which sis—— Woodbury went to sister Stewarts. Br W spent the evening, also J Robinson. Sis P and br P were in, invited us over there, to see br and sis Jackson, but I declined as we had company of our own.

Frid 21st quite cloudy. Alma and br Wo—— went after wood. I went with sis P—— to a quilting party, at br Crandells. Set off at ten oclock, called for sister Morse, who accompanied us.

We had a very agreeable time. The ladies present were sis Morse, Barton, Wicksome, a sister Smith, daughter of br Crandells, sis Pratt, and myself. We had a sociable visit, and an excellent entertainment. Reached home before dark, found Frances had had company. Miss Harriet Hunt, Lois P and Wm McGary.

Evening br Tate was in. Br W—— and Alma got in late, Jones Dire called. Conversation turned upon Spiritualism. Br T related what he had seen of it, and expressed his faith concerning its origin; Viz that he believed it to be the works of darkness.

Sat 22nd Fr—— and Ellen went and slept at bishop Crosby's,[6] last night. I repaired clothes, baked light bread, cooked supper &C.

The girls returned in the PM. Alma assisted br P—— in killing a hog. J—— Dier was in. Ellen took supper with us. Was making herself a sack for Cristmas. I cut and made a sack for myself.

Sun 23rd We had a light shower this morning. We went to church. Br Cox spoke to the people, and was followed by eld Rich. They both spoke well, and much to our gratification.

After meeting we went to br Riches in co with sister Pratt Had a very pleasant call. We admired his situation and house much. We first went into Mary Phelps apartment, as br Rich and his wife Harriet Sargent were out on a walk, but they soon returned. We sat awhile with br R—— and then went into sister H's where we had a very sociable chat with her.[7]

They invited us to come again, and make them a visit. Said they would also come to see us. Returned before dark, called at sis P's awhile, found br Wandell there and a number of young men. Came home found br and sis Whitaker here he was playing the violin. They stoped only a short time. Mr Crosby gone to evening meeting.

Mon 24th Remarkably cold and windy Frances and I washed. I felt very gloomy and sad all day. Sis P came over and took dinner with us, invited me to a party at her house in the evening. The young people had a candy pull. I did not feel in the mood of going, and therefore stoped at home. Jones Dier took supper with us. My heart was heavy and sad, and on being left alone I had recourse to prayer, from which I was much relieved.

Br P came over and invited us over the second time. Mr C went awhile, but I declined, and went to bed.

[Christmas Day, 1855]

Tues 25th Dec Christmas day. I baked pies, pudding &C. Br Taite brought us a present of a pair of fowls, for the occasion.

Evening went over and took supper with sis P.

The girls all gone to a grand ball at Ed Dailys.[8]

I assisted sister in preparing supper for her company.

Br and sis Cox and sister Morse were with us. Dr [Ira] Burrows [Burrus] called awhile, also a stranger from Los Angeles. We had a good supper, and a sociable visit. Toward nine oclock the girls came in from the party and insisted on our going over a few minutes to see the company, accordingly Mr Crosby went over with sis Morse Pratt and myself. We found the house full, and staid but a very few minutes. Pres Rich was present with his wife Harriet. *Wed 26th* very pleasant. I ironed. Took my sewing over to sis Grouards, went in to see Charles Hill who I found looking very bad, had been having the fever and ague; seemed quite discouraged, said he wanted some rice, but could not find any at the stores. I told him I could accomodate him with some, and he sent his little girl with me to get it.

Sis P and myself received a letter from br Joseph Barnes.

Thurs 27th Dull and cloudy this morning. Mr C went to his work as usual, but returned in consequence of rain. PM finished a table for Woodbury's. We received two numbers of the Mormon. Also recd a letter from br Joseph Barnes, of Dunham, Canada east.

Frid 28th quite muddy and unpleasant, in consequence of yester-days rain. Dier was in this evening. Said he talked of buying a house of br Phillips and Jones. Party this evening at Rollins's.

Sat 29th fine day. I accompanied sis P—— and Fr—— to br Simeon Andrews on a visit. Called at Stark's, got a little job of sewing of her to help pay for some house paper I bought of her. Had a fine visit with sis And[rews] ^Saw a letter from her sister Sarah Dell, formerly Milikin, she lives in St Lewis.^ Mother Jones called just before we left. Said she was going on monday to return to San F——. Was buying eggs to take up with her.

Evening attended a candy pulling at br Pratts, where they had a little dancing. We staid untill 9 oclock and came home.

Sun 30th cold wind. I staid at home. Wrote 3 letters, 1 to Joseph Young, Addison Everett, and sister Eliza R Snow. Understand the mail leaves on Wed, for Salt lake.

Br Sealy came home with Mr Crosby from meeting, and made us quite an agreeable call, invited us to call on them. Br H Boile [Henry G. Boyle] also called on us, and invited us to return the compliment. Sis Whitaker and Dennis were in. Evening Mr C—— went to prayer meeting, I finished my letters. Frances writing to San F.

Mon 31st and last day of 1855. I washed, baked &C. Evening Frances gone to another party. Br Elexander called, I closed, and directed my let-ters to Great Salt lake city.

[New Year's Day, 1856]

Tues morning January the first AD 1856.

Beautiful morning, but quite cold. Br Elxd——r called to borrow tumblers for his party. I ironed after breakfast. Frances took her sewing over to her fathers, but soon left it and went to Edward Daily's and assisted in washing dishes. They also danced there a part of the day. Br Woodbury called down and invited my husband and self to come and partake of a New years supper with them.

Sister Pratt came in to inform me that she was going to the hall with br Layton, and wished me to cook supper for br P——, and the children, also sister Layton and her children. Said she had a nice fowl in cooking,

Lois Barnes Pratt Hunt, ca. 1855. Courtesy of Special Collections and Archives, Utah State University Libraries.

that she would send over to me, with other things. But I declined on account of being previously engaged.

At 4 oclock I went to sis Wood——b——s, Alma went with me to carry John T., as the wind was high, and he seemed unwell.

On reaching there found she had other company. Br P B Lewis, br and sister Combs, and sis Steward. Evening came a br and sister Lee. We had an excellent supper, composed of quite a variety for the place. My husband did [not] return from his labors untill after sunset, and I left word for him to come as soon as he returned. He reached there about 6 oclock, and consequently supped by himself.

We then enjoyed a social visit, untill near 9 oclock. The wind died out and we came home, feeling very well satisfied with the interviews. Alma returned between one and two oclock.

Wed 2nd I arose at 6 oclock, prepared breakfast in haste, as Mr C—— wished to get off earlier than usually. Alma informed me that Frances was unwell the previous night, and went to <u>bed</u>; though[t] she would stay several days at br Tomkins's.

At 12 noon I went into br Pratts. Saw a young man by the name of Campbell, a person we met or rather fell in with at the Monti, as we were coming in from Los Angeles. I did not recognize him immediatly but knew I had seen him somewhere. Evening came Frances, and br Dire. F quite unwell.

Thurs 3rd quite pleasant. Sister Pratt and myself went to Mowreys. Had some trouble in finding them, went first to the old place where they formerly lived. Found br Davids lived there. Sis D—— told us where they lived, and soon we found our way to the house. Sis Stodard lives in the house with them. We had a very agreeable time altho short. Were treated to a nice supper, and returned before dark.

Frid 4th day, I received an invitation to spend the day at sis P's, in co with Sisters Sealy, Spark and sister Morse. Had a fine vis—— and good supper, after which they all came over with me to see my location. Ellen spent the evening with us. Mr Crosby returned from work with his leg badly swollen, from a small cut on his shin bone. Said he intended resting a day or two, to nurse it.

Sat 5th of Jan. <u>My birthday.</u> <u>49</u> years of my short life is past.

What a life of wandering for 21 years; but previous to that time I lived in the one town, scarcely knowing a change. I scarcely know which was the most agreeable, for the Lord has comforted me in my travels, and I have realized his guardianship in thousands of instances.

Sister Grouard took supper with us. Mr C staid at home and repaired an accordion for Josephine Smith

Sun 6th [*added later:* ^*1856*^] fine warm day. Mr Crosby's leg still swollen, and inflamed. Concluded to stop at home today also,

Frances, Alma, and I went to church, heard good preaching. Old eld Hughs just returned from the north, or Washington Territory. He gave us an account of his travels and mission, which was quite interesting to us all.

After meeting br A Farnsworth called on us. Also bishop Crosby made us a very agreeable call. Evening I went to prayer meeting; had a very good time.

Mon 7th quite warm. I washed. Sister Hill called. Mr Crosby still at home, his leg ~~still~~ swollen and inflamed, but think he shall go to his work tomorrow, if it is no worse, Br Layton in this evening, told us he had sold his house to Wm McGary, for 250 dolls; He intended going to the islands in the spring. J Dier also in a few minutes.

Tues 8th Very warm. Frances gone to Hopkins. Sister P—— called and asked me to go down with her in the PM, but my business was such that I could not leave home. Baking bread and pies. Br P B Lewis made me a visit. Said he had been to Tomkins, & bought veal for nine cents pr pound.

Alma commenced his studies. Mr C—— went to his work as usually. Returned at night, said his leg was doing very well.

This I record in answer to prayer, as I had asked the Lord to heal him of that affliction, realizing the peculiaraty of our circumstance and the great inconvenience it would subject us to were he too long laid up with lameness.

[Lois Pratt Injured in Fall from Horse]

Wed 9th This morning directly after breakfast Alma came and informed me that a sad accident occured last night to Lois Pratt; as she was returning from a party with Miran [Myron] Tanner. Their horse threw them off, and hurt her very much, nearly broke her underjaw, and striped her of all, or nearly all of her clothes. That they wraped her in shawls and blankets, got a buggy and brought her home. The horse ran untill he finally killed himself. I went over and found her in bed, the Dr was there dressing her wound, her face badly swollen.

Thurs 10th of Jan Some appearance of rain. We have had very little as yet this winter. Br Robinson spent the evening with us last night. J Dier was also in. My husband and self called over to see Lois, found her in bed, sleeping soundly, her face still swollen badly. Dr Sinclaire was present. We stoped but a short time. This morn I called over again, found her sitting in the rocking chair reading, apparently very comfortable.

Ellen had just received a present of oranges from the mission San Gabriel, and presented me one of them, which seemed quite a rarity at this season of the year. Sis P and I called on sis Grouard, her babe quite sick with whooping cough.

Evening called Foster Curtis and Boid Stewart; we enjoyed a few hours very agreeably with them.

Frid 11th Sis P called, and invited me to accompany her to a quilting. Said sister George Clark had sent for us to come and help her that day. I consented to go, and made myself ready at 11 oclock. called a moment to see sis Grouard's child. Found it very sick, They had it packed in a wet sheet.

We reached sis Clarks near 12 Am. Found the widow of Hiram Clark there. Also two sister Crismans, sister Stark, Dodge, and after-

An early sketch of the two-room, two-story adobe Council House, which served as a court house and for weekly worship services during the Crosbys' years in San Bernardino. Courtesy of California Room, San Bernardino Library.

ward came sis Hunt and Harriet, her daughter. We got the quilt off in good season, Sister C made us a splendid supper, and we enjoyed a fine visit.

On our return home called on sis Sparks and her mother, a few minutes. We also called at the house where br P B Lewis stops, but he was absent. His house looked lonely and desolate. We reached home a few minutes after sunset. Br Robinson spent the evening with us. Mr C read the Deseret News.

Sat 12th Br Goodwin made me a present of a goose. Evening came brethren Alexander, Taite, Isaac Goodwin, and Eben Dier. Alma went to mill.

Sun 13th. Rather boisterous. I had quite an unpleasant night, much troubled with nervousness. Felt better after breakfast. Attended church, heard br Turley, also br Rich.

After church cooked the goose. Br Taite took supper with us. Frances came in and ate with us. She is still stopping with her mother in Lois's place. Evening went to prayermeeting. Had a good time. I wrote a letter to sister Picket.

Mon 14th Fine morning. Mr C—— at work for br Pratt. PM took a walk with sis P—— went to the store, bought dried fruit, and spices, found them reasonable in regard to prices. Br Robinson spent the evening.

[Sister Patten's Burdens]

Tues 15th, washing. Toward noon came in sis Pratt, and with her sister Patten, I bade her welcome to my house, and invited her to stay, and spend the day, or at least the remainder of it with me, but she rather declined in consequence of my being so much engaged in business. I however insisted on her staying, as I had previously heard that her husband had forbid her his house, and advertised her, forbidding any one to harbor, or trust her on his account. I discovered that she felt very much afflicted, and burdened in mind, as well as body, and told to stay with me, and she should be welcome, untill she could do better. I truly felt a sympathy for her, and a willingness to assist her what I could, and strove to alleviate her distress as much as possible. Knowing that she had suffered much for the gospels sake, and that she still remained firm in the faith. She related to us her difficuties with her husband, and attributed his abuse, to a jealousy which he for a long time had cultivated toward her, on account of her religion.

Evening we went to the council house to a prayer meeting, where we enjoyed a good degree of the holy spirit. She came home with us and staid over night.

Wed 16th She conversed with us untill 12 oclock, upon her trials and suffering in the gospel. The next morning ^Wed 16th^ she arose before me, and informed me, that she felt very unwell. Being of a nervous billious temperament, and quite overcome with sorrows, she was compelled to take her bed, and I commenced waiting on her. She was exercised with a tremendous pain in her head, accompanied with vomiting. She requested the elders to be sent for, which I did immediatly. Brs Pratt, Woodbury and Mr Crosby came in, and anointed her with oil, laid their hands on her, and rebuked the pain and disease with which she was afflicted, and shortly after she began to feel better.

PM sister Pratt came in, and took tea with us, and she became quite revived. She however kept her bed a great part of the day.

Evening previous she sent a line to Mr Sparks, attorney and counsellor at law. Requesting him to visit her, and give her counsel how to proceed with regard to obtaining something of her husband for her support. Alma was the bearer of her note, and brought word back that he would see her the next day. She then requested some of us to go with her to her husband, to be witnesses that she had offered to come back to him, and do her best to please him, if he would lay aside his anger, and promise to use her well. Accordingly br Pratt and myself offered to go. She told us, and others that that was the 8th time she had been to him, and tried to make a reconciliation with him.

But all her efforts proved in vain, he still remained inexorable. Told her in our presence, that he did not want her about him, that he could do his own work, accused her of trying to injure him in respect to character and property, talked very severely to her and appeared very angry. I tried to converse some with. Told him I recollected his staying over night with us once when he was on his way to this place, while we lived at br Nailes ranch, and invited him to call again. But he declined, saying that he had no inclination to visit, and lived a miserable life at home. She repeated her offers to come and do for him as she had done, but he positively refused to receive her again on any conditions, or to give her anything for her support. But told her she might have her clothes, and what little she brought there from Great Salt lake.

Sister Knight happening along at the time, was also witness to the conversation that passed between them. Quite in dispair she returned with me, and as before stated went to the evening meeting.

Thurs 17th We had some rain last night. This morning I had an invitation to a quilting, at Phineas Daily's, but feeling quite unwell I declined going Sister Patten did not feel in the humor of going and so we concluded to stay away. But toward noon she had a call from a sis Parks, requesting her professional services, as midwife. She had previously engaged herself to her, and therefore went immediately. I was left alone again, and felt very unwell the remainder of the day.

[A Caged Lion]

In the course of the Pm I heard a child crying very bitterly, and thought it was sister Laytons little girl, but shortly after she came over with her, and informed me that br P Daily's little child, just across the street from her, had got badly injured by a pet California lion, which they had in a cage near the house. As the child was passing near the cage, he reached him through the grates, and tore his arm badly. Shortly after they sent to me for beeswax to wax a thread, as he (the messenger) said to sew up the wound. He told me it was not as bad as they had anticipated. They had dancing there, after the quilting, notwithstanding. Their floor being very bare we heard the noise very distinctly.

Frid 18th. Quite windy. I commenced ironing, and shortly after sis Patten returned. Said she was quite fatigued, and would like a little refreshment. Accordingly I made her a cup of coffee, and prepared a hasty meal for her, after which she assisted me in ironing. We spent the evening very agreeably togather. We conversed of Kirtland, Nauvoo, Great Salt lake, and every place where the saints have been located. Sis Patten spoke of the death of Judge James Adams, of Springfield, who died in

Nauvoo in the summer of '43. Rehearsed the particulars concerning his visions, His being forewarned of his death, and her visions respecting it, all of which was very interesting to me, as well as my husband.

Sat 19th Frances returned, and offered her assistance, I set her to making pies. Sis P—— also offered to assist me in sewing, and I gave her a pair of linen undergarments to make for Mr Crosby. We all became very busy.

About 10 oclock came sister Tomkins and sis Pratt who had been up to visit in her sis T——'s neighborhood, for two days and nights.

We enjoyed an excellent visit togather, Br Tate was in a few moments, and conversed with us upon the things of the kingdom of God. Evening Sis Pratt myself and husband accompanied sis Patten to br Riches.

Sun 20th Somewhat cloudy. Sister Patten accompaned us to church. We heard an excellent discourse from br Rich. After meeting sis P——t——n went to visit a patient. evening attended prayermeeting at the meeting house, was much edified.

Mon 21st Some what rainy and unpleasant. All of us sewing. Sister Stark sent me shirts to make. Evening F—— attended circus.

Tues 22nd Washed. Sis P—— went to see her husband and got a few of her things. Evening Fr—— gone to circus again.

Wed 23rd quite stormy. Mr Crosby stoped at home in consequence of rain. Evening dark, and cheerless. Br Taite brought us the Mormon from the P O.

Thurs 24th more pleasant. My husband gone again to his work. Sister Patten gone out on a visit, with sis Pratt. Returned after dark. Sis Pratt spent the evening with us. We had some conversation of spiritualism.

Friday 25th Sewing for sis Starks, Sis Patten still with us.

Sat 26th quite pleasant. Sis P—— making arrangements for housekeeping. Went at evening to visit her husband, found him relenting a little. He gave her a fowl to bring us.

Sun 27th fine morning. But I felt quite indisposed. Yet I attended church, and felt relieved thereby. Evening I wrote letters to bro and sis Cannon, brs Bull and Wilkie. Also sis Mowrey and Corwin, and sister Goodfellow. Sis Patten went again to visit her husband ^and staid overnight.^

Mon 28th Alma helping br Pratt. I washed. PM Alma burnt brush and prepared the lots for plowing. Sister Patten returned and told me that she had at last effected a reconciliation with the old man. That he had become very humble, but was quite sick, and confined to his bed. She went to the store to get necessaries for him. She blessed us in the name of the Lord for our kindness to her gave me one dollar in money, brought me a bottle of milk, and said I should have more. Evening br Robinson was in.

[Little Emma Grinnell]

Dancing at Laytons. Sis Pratt requested me to come and spend the evening with her. Little Emma Grinnell[9] was quite sick with the whooping cough, and the girls were all gone to a party. I was much fatigued, had been washing, and did not feel able to go untill near 9 oclock. I then went over a short time.

Mr Crosby and br Pratt gone to the Seventies meeting.

Tues 29th I ironed Mr C—— and Alma ploughed the garden, and sowed barley. PM Ellen P—— came in with two Miss Smiths a family of the *Brooklin* company,[10] who have lately moved into this place. When they left I accompanied them to P Dailys to see the California Lion that tore their little childs arm. They had sold it, and expected the owner to take it the next day. I thought it quite a curiosity. Its head had the appearance of a large cat, its fur like the Maltee race.

Evening we attended a lecture delivered by elder Rich before the Library association, found it very interesting.

Wed 30th I accompanied Sis P—— and Frances on a visit to sister Skinner. Called on br Smiths, were very cordially received. Called again at old br Kades [Jonathan and Susannah Cade]. The old gent quite feeble, but both wishing very much to go to Great Salt lake city; talk of going with br Rich in the spring. We had a very pleasant visit at br Skinners. On our return called at Calvin Reeds. Reached home after sunset.

Evening sis P requested us to call over, as the girls were all gone again, and the little child still very sick. After supper we went and staid untill 9 oclock.

Thurs 31st Quite a foggy morning. Mr Crosby gone to work on br J Dires house. Alma bought flour. Paid 8 dolls pr 100 wt. Been planting potatoes. Evening came br and sis Davis, and took supper with us. Had a very agreeable time with them. Sis Patten, and a young english man, called to get some of her things that she left here.

Frid February 1st After breakfast I took a walk to sister Pattens. Found the road longer than I had anticipated. Turned in by br Chapmans. Sis C came to the door and invited me into her house But I declined being in haste. She then walked with me to the creek and saw me safely over, invited me to visit her &C.

Sister Patten gave me a little variety of garden seeds. I stoped a few moments to rest mysefl, and then returned. She came out to the main road with me, to put me in the direct way.

I had a very pleasant walk, but found myself some fatigued . Br Taite called shortly after I reached home.

PM I went in to br P's to see the little girl She requested me to hold her awhile which I did.

Evening came br and sis Grouard, and spent a few hours with us. Br
J Robinson, in awhile.

Sat 2nd of Feb Mr C gone again to br Diers. Alma planting potatoes
I mended stockings. PM went over to sis P's again. Think the child better Lois gone riding with Wm McGary. I returned and called in to sis
Grouards. Frances cooked supper. Ellen here, ~~took supper~~ and ate with
us. Spent the evening, played the accordion with the violin.

Sun 3rd We all went to church. After meeting br Tomkins and family called on us, also br and sis Woodbury, and br Whitaker. br and sis
W—— took supper with us.

Sister Andrews called, and brought her sisters likeness, or daguerio-
type which she had just received from St Louis Her name formerly was
Sarah Miliken, but now Dell. Toward evening we went over to br Pratts,
spent an hour or more. Little Emma still very low.

Evening went to prayer meeting, enjoyed it very well.

Mon 4th After breakfast sister called at the door, and informed me that
the little girl was changing very fast, and requested me to come over, which
I did and found her much changed. We could not prevail on her to speak
more than one word at once. I was sensible she could not continue long.

Dr Burroughs was called in, but gave us very little encouragement
left a small dose of Dovers powder to quiet her nerves. Said he would call
again, and if she could bear it would give her an emetic. He also ordered
her put in a warm bath After the powder and bath she fell into a deep
sleep, from which she never awoke. She died at half past one oclock Pm
She had been sick only 10 days. The whooping cough was probably the
cause of her death. Thus ended her short life.

Sister Pratt and Ellen mourned heartily for her. Sis Grouard and
myself laid her out. Sis P—— said she would come home with me, and
spend the evening, as she felt very sad. Accordingly we came over, and
Frances advised her mother to stop over night; thought she would sleep
better here than there. I prepared her a bed by herself, and she retired
early But notwithstanding she had been disturbed so long, she could not
sleep, but a few moments, but became very nervous and wished me to
come and sleep with her, which I could not do on account if its being a
cott. I however arose and lighted the lamp, which she kept burning for an
hour or two. Near one oclock she fell asleep, and slept untill near 5——.

Tues 5th at 2 oclock we went to the grave, and committed her remains
to the dust. We had quite a smart shower on the way, but the sun shone
brightly while we were in the burial ground, and we walked about and
oberved the graves, and especially sis Jane Lewis's, and her little childs
who lay by the side of the new grave into which the little charge of sis P's
was now laid.[11]

Wed 6th This is Ellens birthday. She is now 24 years of age. F—— and I washed. Made pies. Evening came br Lewis and Flanders Stoped untill 9 oclock. We had a very sociable visit with them.

Thurs 7th I hung my clothes out. And then took a walk with sister Pratt. Called on the sister Lymans, and sis Davis. Came back to br Orin Smiths. They invited us to stay and take dinner, and as I felt quite unwell and fatigued with my walk, we thought proper to accept the invitation. Had a fine dinner, and an agreeable time. Were much pleased with the family. The circus company all boarding there.

I returned from my walk feeling much better than when I went out. Found the house alone. Frances gone out for a ride with Mr [Daniel] Rathburn [Rathbun]. We spent the evening principally alone. Mr C—— and Alma played on the violin and flute.

Frid 8th Ironed, sis P—— called. While she was here, Sis Stark ~~called~~ sent her little girls to inform ~~sister Pratt~~ her that herself and sis Skinner were coming to visit her that pm if agreeable. We told them we should be pleased to see them, and sis P went home to make preparations Shortly after came sister Hunt, and said she sent me word by sis P—— that she was coming to make me a visit that pm, but she forgot to do the errand. Accordingly she took me by surprise.

I made her a cup of tea, and gave her a little dinner, and she staid untill about 3 oclock, we then both went over and visited with sis P's co, which consisted of Sis Skinner Stark and Hamilton. We enjoyed a very agreeable time; had an excellent supper, and evening we all went to the councilhouse to prayermeeting.

[Death of the Hill Child]

On my return home met B Hill who was going in great haste after the Dr for his little child, which he said he believed was dying. He requested me to go down, said his wife was alone, with the child. I asked my husband to go with me, and we found the child in spasms, and thought it was surely dying, but it survived untill 12 oclock The Dr left at 11 and I came home at the same time, thinking the child much easier.

Sat 9th Frances came over before breakfast, and informed me that the child was dead. I was some surprised, as I thought it might live on sometime when I left. We went down to see if they required our service and while there Ellen came in. She and F—— made the shroud.

Br Grouard in this morning. Said his family were well, and liked their new habitation in the country very much. Evening Alma gone to the circus

Sunday Feb 10th Beautiful day. I went into Mr Hills to see who were going with them to bury their child. Found quite a company collected.

I did not expect to go, but as there were 3 wagons going, and a good chance I pleasureably accepted the invitation, and accompanied them. We had a pleasant ride. It is about 2½ miles from the city. A place where brs Grouard Hill and Kip have selected themselves a home. Before the coffin was put in the ground, br Grouard made an address to the company, on the subject of death, and the spirits of our departed friends. But said nothing of the resurrection of the body from the grave. I believe the Spiritualist do not believe in the resurrecton of the body. After the burial we all went into br G——'s house, which is a mere shanty, put up to serve them for the present, or untill he finishes an addobie which he has commenced.

We reached home at 3 oclock. I felt much fatigued and laid down and droped to sleep a short time, untill br Layton sent over to ask me to make him a dish of gruel, as he had been several days sick. Br Whipple called to get subscribers for br Cannons paper.[12] ^He informed me that his daughter at Salt lake, was married to Henry Bigler.^

Br Tait also came in and took supper with us. Informed us that there was a prospect of his going to Salt lake city soon.

Mr Crosby went with him to evening prayermeeting.

Mon 11th Alma went to work on the irrigation ditch.[13] Mr C working on br Pratts house. I washed. Frances at Tomkins's. Sis P—— over in PM.

Tues 12th. Very warm day. Alma gone again to work on ditch.

Mr C went again to work for Crisman. I baked bread and pies.

Toward night Frances returned from Tomkins, going to another party. Sister Pratt and myself took a walk to sis Pattens. I got milk and butter.

Wed 13th Received a visits from sis Skinner, Read, Patten, sis Pratt and Ellen.

Br Tait called and informed me that he intended leaving for G—— S—— L C—— on friday next. He seemed quite affected at the idea of leaving his little son. We enjoyed a very social time, my lady visitors and myself.

Thurs 14th Sister Pratt and I visited sister Hunt. Her daughters Harriet and sis Daily came over and spent the PM with us.

On our way home we called on sis George Clark. She has a young child about 2 week old. She spoke of the one she had lost, and wept bitterly.[14]

[Departure of William Tait]

Frid 15th This morning I went over to br Skinners to get pink roots, Called at br Jo Matthews to see br Taite, but he was absent.

Came home and found him here. He bade us goodbye and left, in co with John Robinson. He wished to leave his little son with us, which we consented to, but expected he would leave some article of value that we could dispose of for the benefit of the child, but on examining the trunk, found he had left nothing.

I felt disappointed, and thought I would go and see him again. Accordingly I went and left word at the Blacksmith shop, where he was expected in soon, to tell him to call again and see me, before he left, which he did immediatly. He told me his situation and how he had been obliged to dispose of everything to help himself away. But said he would send me something for John the first opportunity He took dinner with us and left.

In my morning walk I accidently met br Lewis who bade me a fare-well, and said he expected to leave in the course of the Pm, in the same company with br Taite.

Sister Woodbury called a few moments, and invited me to visit her the next day. I worked in the garden with Alma toward night. Br Woodbury took supper with us.

Sat 16th After breakfast I went to work again in the garden. Ellen came in with some flower roots for me.

PM went to sis Woodbury's, took Johny with me. Had a fine visit She came home with me, and staid untill dark.

Mr Crosby returned late from his work. Went to Skinners and bought flower of br Farnsworth for 7½ dolls pr hundred wt. Louise was in awhile. Alma went over to do a job for Ellen setting up bedstead.

Sun 17th I had a sore throat and was so much indisposed that I did not attend church. After meeting br Woodbury called and invited me to accompany them, himself wife and Mr Crosby to the burying ground, to put stones to sister Lewis and her childs graves.

It looked like rain, and I at first thought I could not go, but after reflecting awhile concluded to go, and set off with my husband to meet them at the house latly occupied by br Lewis, where the stones were laying. Passing br Pratts we invited some of them to accompany us and Frances came out and we all went into br Whitaker to await their arrival. It shortly commenced raining so that they did not come, and we came home.

After the rain was over, br W—— came along and called for Mr C and Alma, who went with him and put them up.

Mon 18th My cold very bad. Sister P—— was in a part of the day. Evening she and girls all came over with Wm McGary, to have a time of music making. We had quite a band. Two violins, a flute and an accor-dion.

Tues 19th Ellen and Frances went to Los angeles, with br Freman Tanner. E—— was going to San Gabriel to visit an old friend, and Frances intended visiting sis Pickets. I went over to see them off and finally spent a greater part of the day.

Wed 20th my cold some better. Sis P—— spent the day with me. Alma went to work on the water ditch, but the rain drove them home. *Thurs 21st* Quite pleasant. I washed. PM sis P—— called. While she was here came sis Patten. She had been to the store. Seemed pleased to find us together, and invited us to visit her next week. I bought ten peach trees for one doll, of a Spaniard

Evening called br Farnsworth, and spent an hour or more with us. Br Pratt was also in awhile. Mr C read in the Mormon, from an extract of the history of Joseph Smith, concerning the pretended prophet Matthias, who visited him in Kirtland. Br Farnsworth wished me to do some sewing for him.

[Rainy Days]

Friday 22nd Pleasant in the morning, but rain toward noon. I ironed, baked light bread, &C. Alma set out peach trees, grapes vines &C.

Sat 23rd. I had intended going to br Tomkins today, but storms prevented me. Snow and hail fell today, but melted nearly as fast as it fell. Sister P sent for me to come over and sit awhile with her. Saying the girls were all gone and she left alone. I went over a few minutes. She told me that Lois had gone to nurse sister Grundy, who has lately been confined with an heir.[15]

Sun 24th Looked very much like rain. I did not attend church Br and sis Whitaker came in awhile PM.

Mon 25th Some rainy. Sister spent the greatest part of the day with me. Mr C— went to his labor as usually, but returned about 2 oclock, Said their lumber had failed and the workmen dismissed untill next monday. Accordingly he polished canes for br Woodbury[16]

Tues 26th Quite rainy. Mr C went back to the mill and got the privilege of making sash, from some remnants of lumber that was remaining there.

Sister Pratt was with me in the AM. We had a visit appointed at sister Patten's, and thought we would go if the weather would admit. PM it became more pleasant and we set off. Found her alone and pleased to see us. She was putting on a quilt. I rendered her what assistance I could. The old gent was in a fine agreeable humor. Shook hands with us, and apparently tried to make himself quite agreeable. It rained some while we were on our way coming home, which made it unpleasant walking. We however got home in safety.

Wed 27th Another cloudy day with some rain. Alma went with br Pratt after grapevines. Sister P—— was with me again in the AM

Thurs 28th rather pleasant, but the wind rose toward noon. Sister Pratt called, in the morning, and informed me that sister Cox was quite sick, and asked me to visit her, which I promised to do, And accordingly went over a little after 12 AM.

I found sisters Blackburn, Pratt, and Harriet Hunt, with her, all doing what they could. She said she had taken cold, and by over exertion had brought on a weakness to which she had been before subject. I staid an hour or more with her, and then accompanied the sisters to sister Grundy's, who has a young babe. Lois P was with her. All doing well. We made a short call, and sis P—— and myself returned.

Frid 29th and last of feb. Wind very severe. Just before 12 came sisters Pratt and Blackburn to spend the Pm with me. We enjoyed it finely, Sis Blackburn read some in Nichols Journal, concerning Spiritualism. I discovered that she and sis P were inclined to believe considerably in the system, but I had very little to say on the subject.[17]

Toward night sister Cox sent for sister Blackburn, and said she was not as well as she had been, which we were sorry to hear.

Br Whitaker called, and invited us to attend a meeting at the council house. Evening I went with my husband to the meeting.

Sat March 1st cold and windy again. Sister Pratt spent a part of the Pm with me, and invited me to come over in the evening with my husband, which I partially consented to, but br Woodbury called and we were thereby prevented.

Sun the 2nd. Very hard frost last night. Ice froze quite thick. We fear the peaches may be injured, if not killed.

I intended going to church, but got belated with my work, and Johny was unwilling to stay at br Pratts, and upon conclusion I staid at home.

Evening attended meeting in co with my husband, and sister Pratt. PM called br Whitaker and wife. Sister Pr——tt and C[harles] Burk. Also Alphonse Farnsworth and brought me some sewing.

[Sociable Visits]

Mon 3rd Very pleasant and warm. I washed, Alma went on the ditch. Mr C at Crismans as usualy. Sister Pratt over toward eve. Br Grouard called in the early evening, Said he was intending to lecture before the library association that evening, at the school house. Made some brief remarks in favor of Spiritualism while here.

Tues 4th Spent the PM at sis P——s, made a shirt for A Farnsw evening br Davis spent with us. We had a very sociable time with him.

Wed 5th Another warm day. Alma planted potatoes, and onion seed. I ironed baked and attended to my little chickens.

Thurs 6th was invited to sister Pratts to supper in co with sis E Daily ~~and~~ Harriet Hunt, and Wm MacGary. It was Lois's and Wm's birthdays. Sis P made a chicken pie, and a nice cake.

Evening we were invited to spend with them. Mr Patten and wife called to see us, and as we wished to go we invited them to accompany us, which they very readily consented to. We enjoyed a few hours very agreeably, had a little dancing on the occasion.

Friday 7th Sis Pratt and I went to Tomkins, found it rather a long walk. After dinner took a walk over to br Dires, thought it a very pleasant place, admired it much.[18] The boys moving into their new house while we were there. We enjoyed a fine visit. Amanda [Tompkins] accompanied us some distance on our way home, to show us a nearer route. Reached home in good time.

Sat 8th I was full of business. Baking, ironing and the like. PM called sisters Patten and Pratt. Alma went to carry flour for sis P——t——n. Br Pratt in a while, also Alfphonso Farnsworth.

Sun 9th cool and cloudy. Attended church, felt remarkably dull and drowsy. Saw br and sis Paul Smith, late from Sacramento, reached here last night. Returning home met a young br by the name of Anderson, just arrived from San Francisco. I called in to see sister Cox, found her on the bed, but much better than when I last saw her. PM sister Morse and Pratt and Wm McGary were in awhile. I went with them to br Pratts.

Evening Mr C gone to meeting. Alma at br P's. I find myself alone Writing reading playing the accordion seems to be the order of the evening; together with serious reflections upon the present and past. The many trying and changing scenes through which we have been called to pass.

Mon 10th Was very rainy and unpleasant. Br Woodbury went with Alma after wood, returned at night very wet and cold.

Alma went to sis P——t——ns for milk, found her very sick, and wished Sister Pratt and myself to visit her the next day.

Tues 11th We went up soon after breakfast, found her much better. Br Thompsons daughter, from the Monti was staying with her.

She was highly pleased to see us, and insisted upon our staying untill after dinner, which was contrary to our previous intentions. However,we consented, and I went to work to help her prepare it. Made nice cake, and buiscuits, cooked rice &C. Two gents there, came to see Miss Thompson, with a message from a former suitor. A man by the name of Maxy, whom her parents were much opposed to her corresponding with, and had brought her here, for the purpose of keeping her from seeing him. But he followed her to the place, and was trying to gain an interview. And altho she had previously dismissed him, in the presence of her mother, yet he was not satisfied, but wished her to tell him in the absence of her parents what the true state of her mind <u>was</u>, concerning him. She accordingly wrote him a note in the presence of witnesses and confirmed what she had before stated.

But we discovered that she felt very deeply on the subject, by the occasional sighs which escaped from her bosom.

We reached home near two oclock. I spent the PM in the garden.

Wed 12th Sister Stark sent to inform me that she intended visiting me in the PM if agreeable, and it did not rain. About 2 oclock she arrived. Sister Pratt was also with us and we enjoyed a fine visit together. Alma at work for sis P——t——n, making a milk cupboard.

Thurs 13th Very steady rain all day, which we were all pleased to see. No one in untill evening, when br Phin—— Daily came, and requested the privilege of looking in a dictionary. After studying as long as he wished he commenced conversation, and finally gave us quite a detailed account of his experience in Mormonism, and also that of his father and family, which was rather interesting to us.

Friday 14th Quite pleasant this morning, and I concluded to wash. Shortly after I commenced, came sister P—— and complained of feeling rather dull. She said as it was near 12, and I was washing she would make us a cup of tea, and a little dinner, with which I was much pleased. PM was dull and rainy. Sister staid untill near dark, was piecing a quilt.

Sat 15th. Arose early and prepared for the conference, which convened at 11 oclock. Few persons attended in consequence of bad roads. I set out with my husband on foot, but a br Harris, one of our neighbors, overtook us and invited us to ride. I readily accepted the offer, and he gave me his seat. Mr C choose to walk as the distance was short. We had a very good meeting, heard an excellent discourse from elder Rich.

Sun 16th This is my sister Lockwoods birthday. She is 57 years old. It surprises me to think how fast we are all hastening to our alloted time of life. We all went to church at half past 9 oclock. Br Rich preached us an excellent discourse. Closed at 12, and adjourned untill 2 Pm.

[Elders Called to Missions]

PM the elders were called to go on missions. Br A Pratt, and Ambrose Alexander were appointed to go to the Society islands Br C Wandell, and H Boile down the Pacific coast, with several others. Evening I spent with sister Pratt. Ephraim quite unwell. ^Charles Burk paid us a visit. I had [not] seen him since our expulsion from Nauvoo^ Mr C—— and Alma attended prayermeeting.

Mon 17th Sister Pratt went to spin stocking yarn, and left Eph with me, he was quite unwell. Evening we all went to br Woodburys. She was absent; gone to br Whipples. P Daily and wife were there. We staid a short time and returned. Br Dennis was quite noisy, had been drinking rather freely. Woodburys live in his house with him.

Tues 18th I washed. Alma went to milk for old man Patten, his wife absent. Sister Pratt and Eph—— staid with us almost all day.

Sister Morse and her little daughter were in awhile. Brought an accordion to get repaired. Br Whitaker also called in the eve. Br Woodbury also.

Wed 19th. Sister Pratt gone again to spin. Ephraim staying here. Sister Woodbury called, said she was just returning from br Whipples, that they had a very sick child. She also informed me that sis sister Combs children were quite sick and that she was going to see them. I offered to accompany her, sister P Daily came in and went with us. Found them quite indisposed, but all about. Had quite a pleasant walk. Very warm day.

Sister Combs called here in the course of the PM, had been after medicine for her children.

About 5 pm came sister Davis, and her sister Anna, with the little girl Fanny. Sister Morse was also in with her little daughter 8 years of age, who plays the accordion very skillfully.

Evening came br Davis, and made us a very pleasant visit.

Thurs 20th. Quite warm. I spent the PM at br Pratts, girls all gone, Sis P said she looked for Ell——n and Fr——c——s home at night. About 8 oclock in the evening Frances came and knocked at our door, said she had just arrived, and found the house at her fathers alone, all gone out to make calls. She informed us Wm McGary had returned with them, having met with the man he was going to San F—— to see, which had saved him the trouble and expense of the journey. Br Chase's son had come and brought Wm's money, so that he could now pay br Layton for his house, and by that means help him to accomplish his desires of returning with his family to the islands.

She also gave us a little sketch of her visit at Los Angles. Sister Picket's health quite poor.

Frid 21st Very warm. After breakfast sis P came in and invited me to accompany them to sister Hunts on a visit. But as Alma was absent, and John quite unwell, I could not consistently go. Br Hill dined with us, and preached his doctrine of Spiritualism, and Freeloveism. Evening Sis P—— and Ellen were in awhile.

Sat 22nd remarkably warm day. It quite astonished us to see the hot weather come upon so suddenly. PM came sis P, Ellen, and Frances, My house was very warm, but we had the stove removed the night previous, which made it much more pleasant. I made a dish of tea, sent over for br Pratt, who came and supped with us.

After sunset took a walk with sis P—— and Frances to the store. Took my little boy along, and bought him a tin cup. Had a pleasant walk.

Sun 23rd. Very warm, all went to church but myself and Johny. I stoped at home in the AM, and Alma in PM, while I went to church. We had two excellent discourses from brs Rich and Turley.

Several persons sent on missions. The house was crowded so that it was very unpleasant, and I could not enjoy myself at all,[19] Sister Tomkins came home with me, and took a clock that my husband had been fixing for them. Evening I took a walk with sis P——— and called on a sister Mills, whose husband had deserted her, and refuses to live with or provide for her. She told us of her lonely distressed condition, we felt to sympathize with her.

I went home with sister, and met br Orin Smith and wife, had quite a sociable chat with them. They intend leaving for Salt lake in a short time. Wm McGary and Ellen came home with me, and stoped a few minutes.

Mon 24th More cool and pleasant. Ellen, Frances and Miss Harriet Hunt spent a great portion of the day with me. Sister Capt Hunt came over and brought a clock to Mr Crosby to repair. Minerva Morse came in with her.

Tues 25th I worked in the garden, planted a variety of seeds. Sister Pratt came in and read to me from Nicols' journal. Chastina McMurtry came in at noon, from school. I did not know her and asked her whose child she was. She answered "Mr MacMurtry's." She sat sometime, and I gave her some dinner. Sister Pratt was here, and we sent word to her mother that we would visit her in the course of the week.

Evening I took a walk with sister P, called on sis G——— Clark. Spoke with sis Sparks, as she was milking. On our return called at bishop Collins[20] to ask for garden seeds.

Wed 26th Came Mr Patten and ploughed for us. He brought his wife along with him. I was washing, but notwithstanding we had a very good visit together. Sister P——— came in with sis Starks and we agreed to take a walk to Tomkins on the morrow.

Thurs morning 27th at 8 oclock we set off. Our company consisted of sisters Starks, Pratt, Ellen, Frances, myself and little John Tate We called a few minutes at br McKnights, where we found sister Smith, and a sister Evans, both from Aus———[21]

We then called at br Walkers, and from thence proceeded to br Tomkins, where we left sisters Starks and Pratt, but myself Ellen and Fr went on to McMurtry's, where we spent the PM very agreeably. We called at br Diers both ways, to rest ourselves.

After dinner sisters P, S——— and Tomkins came over to br MC's and spent the PM with us. They had a large bible there which contained the apochraphy,[22] and I was invited to read for their edification. I read a number of chapters, some interesting stories which some of the co———

had never before heard. We found it quite a long fatiguing walk, and on returning to br Tomkins, she proposed taking us home in the carriage, which certainly was welcome news to me as my little boy walked so slowly that I feared it would be dark before we reached home. Br A Elexander made ready the horses and carriage, and sister Tomkins drove them, and brought us home in good style. ^Br and sister Whitaker spent the evening with us, said he expected to leave soon for Salt lake^

Frid 28th I felt quite as well as usually. But sis P came in and complained of feeling very lame and tired. PM the wind blew very severely, and cold. I was out some, and probably took some cold, which brought on the sick headache, so that before night I was very much indisposed, and went to bed without my supper, feeling very miserable. I had a fever and had dreams all night. But <u>sleep</u>, the great soother of <u>pain</u>, so far restored my usual health that I arose the next morning apparently well. ^Great rain during the night. The most we have at one time this season. It cheered us much.^

Sat 29th. I finished a little washing, which I commenced before my walk. Ironed clothes &C. PM took a walk with sister Pratt to see sis Woodbury, whom we found in bed, and quite unwell. Helen Combs was with her. Sister <u>Dennis</u>, who lives in an adjoining room, was reading a book of mormon published by br Cannon in the Hawaian language. It was the first I had seen of that kind, and we were pleased with its appearance, and style.

Sun 30th. Mr C went to church. I staid at home to write letters to G S L city. Wrote one to br Taite. Br J Dire took supper with us. Alphonse Farnsworth called to get Mr Crosby to go and administer to br Skinners child.

Evening we were invited to a singing party, at br Cox'es. Br Ladd was there from San Diego. Sunday night we had hard rain.

Mon 31st rain still continues, which revives the drooping spirits of the Saints and sinners in San B——d——no.

Tues Apr 1st quite pleasant. Frances sewing for me. Alma gone for wood. I have a sore finger, caused by sticking the point of sharp scissors into it near the joint. Been writing letters, one to R R Rogers and one to sister Marial Crosby.

[The Woodburys' Departure]

PM Ellen and Frances gone to sis Woodburys. A co expects to leave for G—— S—— L—— City tomorrow.

Wed 2nd I went up to see sister W——, and carried two letters to send by her, one to Marial Crosby, and one to br Busbee. I also sent two by br Whitaker, in the same company. One to R Rogers, and one to br Taite.

I found sister Wo—— full of business, and concluded to stop and help her. I sewed on her wagon cover, untill we finished it. We had a sociable time. She told me some things which made me feel sad, and caused me to marvel. Frances staid here while I was gone.

Alma went again after wood. Evening he and Frances went to a party, at Wm MacGarys, Br and sister Woodbury came down and took supper with us. Stoped untill 9 oclock. ^We bade them farewell for the last time, expecting they would leave early the next morning.^

Thurs——— 3rd She sent Mary Denis for her notebook, Mr C had been writing tunes for her. After breakfast I went over to sis Pratts. She had gone to Woodbury's, returned toward noon said they had not gone when she left. I spent a great part of the PM there. Evening sis Combs called, and said they had just left, and gone a few miles to camp with the rest of the company.

Frid 4th, I washed. Frances sewing for me, making clothes for Laytons children. Sister P came over and took dinner with us. She cut cloths for Alfred, staid and read Nicols journal, the Mormon, and Western Standard, untill sunset. Evening br Pratt came in, and read untill near 11 oclock.

Sat 5th very warm and pleasant. I ironed. Sister Pratt staid with me the greatest part of the day, and helped me on Alfreds clothes. Pm we all went into see sister Morse, and sat awhile. Toward night a sister Mills called on me. Her husband has left her, and she live alone only a short distance from us, has one very pretty little child, a girl of 15 months.

I spent an hour or more watering the garden. Evening Mr C—— polishing workboxes for birth day presents to Lois, and Ann L Pratt. The colored man here, playing the violin.[23]

Sunday morn April 6th '56 Fine morning. My husband and self, with John Taite, attended church. Meeting held outside, in the Bowery. Elder Rich preached well to us. It was the annual conference. Meeting adjourned from 12, untill two.

Evening br Wandell came with his songbook, to get Mr Crosby to assist him in teaming them songs for a May day party. We took the violin and played the air, while br W—— sang the Bass. They were very pretty interesting songs.

Mon 7th I finished several garments for br Laytons children. PM— came sisters Tomkins and McMurtry, and spent a couple of hours very agreeably, to myself at least. Br Mac—— came along early, and took them off before supper.

Tue 8th I washed in the forenoon, PM went over and sewed for sister P—— on br P's pants. She was fitting him up for the islands.

Evening went with sis P—— to see a new babe, belonging to capt Hunt. His wife Matilda had a fine boy, weighing 11 lbs.

Br Wandell was up again, learning songs.

Wed 9th ironed. Sister Patten called, went to the P O. Returned just as my dinner was ready. I sent over for sister P to come and dine with us. She came directly, and afterwards we sent for br Pratt, who also came and ate with us.

Frances came in just as my dinner was ready, and brought some butter, that she had been buying for us.

We had a very pleasant time together. Br P—— spoke of his mission. Evening F—— and I took a walk to jude [Alden A. M.] Jacksons, for the purpose of getting garden seeds, but found them quite destitute. She gave me (however) a few of what she had, treated us to a cup of tea, showed us her garden, which consists principally of shrubbery, fruits, and flowers, and was remarkably sociable and pleasant.[24] It was near 9 oclock when we reached home.

Thurs 10th Rather cool and cloudy. Preparations being made at br Wm MacGary's for an oister party this evening. We all were invited, but declined, as it was intended wholly for the young people. Evening Alma went, br Dire here, and also attended. Mr C—— and myself spent an hour or two at br Pratts. Returning home, sister Morse invited us into the party, but the house was quite crowded and we came home.

Frid 11th this was sister Lois birth day. She has been gone 21 years. Quite cool, and some appearance of rain. Frances came in and told me that sister Hunt and her daughter, sister [Nancy] Daily, with her mother, sister Pratt) were going to visit sister Jane Morse, who lived a mile or more from here, and that I had an invitation to go with them. I did not feel much in the humor of going out but F—— urged me on untill I prepared myself, and went. There were five ladies of us in all, and 3 children.

We found the roads quite new and rough, the team was also balky, and we were obliged to get out at one place.

We also got a little sprinkled with rain, and while there had quite a smart shower. We were all pleased to see rain, atlho it was some little detriment to us in regard to our visit, as we found sister M—— in an open shanty, with one side exposed to the weather. The rain came on her stove, so that we all took hold and moved it. The two sister Daily's assisted her in preparing dinner, and we enjoyed a fine meal together. We admired the location of the place very much. Sister M's husband had left a short time previous, for upper California. She has 3 sons and a daughter with her. Her eldest (Frank) gave each of us a few strawberry plants, and came home with us to drive the team, as our teamster was a boy, and could not manage them. We reached home in good season. Evening the rain commenced.

Sat 12th Ellen came in and invited me to come and partake of a fat turkey gobbler which they had slain for the purpose of enjoying it with their father before he left. He then expected to leave the next morning for his island mission. Accordingly at the time of supper I went, Found sis Whitaker there. The turkey was very nice and fat. Mr C—— and Alma also came and partook of it, and still there was an abundance left.

Evening the rain poured down in torrents. The hearts of all were revived as many had been propesying a famine for the <u>want</u> of <u>rain</u>.

Sun 13th. It still continued, and no one attempted to go out. No meetings were held.

[Addison Pratt's Departure for Island Mission]

Mon 14th Tolerably pleasant. After breakfast I went over to bid br P—— goodbye. Br Layton was there, and treated us all around for the sake of having us wish them a pleasant and speedy passage to their place of destination. I told him I was not in the habit of drinking spirituous liquors, but would make the motions, for the sake of drinking their healths, and prosperity.[25]

Br Layton set off, and I came home to write a few lines to sister Mowrey by br Pratt. But before I finished I saw br Dire taking him off. Ellen and F accompanied him some distance. After they were gone, sister and Lois and Ann L came over and spent the day with me, said the house looked so lonely they could not feel happy to stay there. We had a very sociable day of it, and evening coming we all went over there and spent an hour or more with them. Ellen returned before night, but Frances staid at Tomkins.

Tues ̶1̶6̶ 15th, this was fathers birthday. Had he lived until now he would have been 89 years old. But he has been gone I think 8 years.

Sister P—— sent for me to come over, and after I finished washing I went, and took tea. Br John Hunt was there, and suped with us. Sister Cox came in the Am, and brought me some sewing, and the butter to pay for it. I was much pleased with the butter, as we were nearly out, and needed it.

Evening we had quite a music party, 3 violins, 1 flute and an accordion. Brs John McDonald, Wm McGary, and Alma, played the violins, while Mr C—— blew the flute, and Ellen played the accordion. The company consisted of sisters Pratt Hunt, Cox, Morse, Lois, and Ann L——, and brs Newel, and John Hunt.

We enjoyed a couple of hours finely, and the party broke up in ̶f̶i̶n̶e̶ pleasant spirits.

Wed ̶1̶7̶ 16th Very pleasant and warm. Sister Patten called, a few minutes. I made mince pies. Sister Tomkins called, and brought Frances home to get some clean clothes, and she went home with her again to finish a dress that she had commenced.

Thurs ̶1̶8̶ 17th I took up my carpet, aired my bedding, and kept myself very busily employed all day. Received a call from sister Knight, an Australian lady. I find her a very pleasant agreeable person. Ellen came in awhile in the PM. Evening Frances came home with br Jones Dire, who spent the evening with us.

Frid 18th We cleaned house and prepared for a little tea party. I took supper at sister Pratts with sister Grouard.

Beautiful evening, spent an hour or two at br P's—Br J McDonald was there and entertained us with ~~some~~ heavenly music, both vocal, and instrumental. After we went to bed they came and serenaded us. I was asleep, but was aroused by hearing them sing "Do they miss me at home——."

Sat 19th quite a comfortable day. F—— assisted me in preparing for my lady visitors, who arrived between 2 and 3 oclock.

Sisters Pratt, Ellen, Grouard, and Morse, came first, and after came Sisters Hunt and Daily. Previous to their arrival Frances had set off on a horseback excursion in co—— with br Dire, Garner, and Amanda Tomkins, toward the Cahoon [Cajon] pass.

I enjoyed a fine time with my visitors, sister Hunt told our fortunes and we had considerable sport. Just as we arose from the table came br Grouard, who also sat down and ate ~~with us~~. with Alma,

Evening Alma went home with br Dire, and staid over night,

Sun 20th I arose feeling very unwell. I had anticipated ~~feeling~~ going to church, but was unable. Mr C went. Alma did not return untill Monday morning. Evening called br T[ruman] Swartout in co—— with Wm McGary. Ellen and Frances took a walk with them. Mr Crosby went to the P O—— and brought me a letter from my br Joseph Barnes. I was quite astonished at the short and abrupt manner in which he wrote. He merely answered the questions I asked him concerning our fathers and mothers deaths and wondered at my being so curious to know. He said that our father Willard Barnes Died Dec 30th 1849, and mother Dolly B died Feb——y 1st 1851.[26] Our youngest sister, Catherine, died Aug. 23rd 1838.

Br Wandell came up to sing awhile with us, and invited us to meet him the next evening,

Mon 21st at sister Pratts to practice a little more on his Mayday songs. We went and were much intertained with the music. Sisters Smith and McNight called on us.

[The Dyer Brothers' Move to Upper California]

Tues 22nd Frances went to assist in cooking bread and &C for the Dires, who intended starting next day for the upper Cal Jones came after her before breakfast.

Sister Pratt came over and spent the PM with me. Evening I went over and sat awhile with her. Girls all gone up to br Dires.

Wed 23rd I felt miserably bad in the morning, got breakfast for the family, and then I went to bed again, and slept an hour or more, felt better, got up and made me a cup of tea. Afterwards I went over to br Cox's,

to see her about some sewing I was doing for her. Got butter. Came home, prepared and went with sister Pratt to br Hopkins. Met Mother Crandel there, had an excellent visit with them. Sis P, and I sewed for sister H——
on a carriage cover. It rained some when we came home.

Thurs 24th I washed. Alma worked on the irrigation stream. Mr C——
staid at home part of the day. PM, the wind was high

Evening it blew quite a gale from the northwest. Very cold. Truman Swartout called with Ann L P. Frances sewing for Sister Hopkins.

Frid 25th Very cold wind from the north. I ironed. High wind all day. Sister Morse called. While she was in br Owen came, and inquired for Mr C, who was absent, I asked his name, ~~and~~ He told me that he was the Owen that went on a mission to Indie. He had seen Mr Crosby, at br Dennis's, and he invited him to call. I had some conversation with him concerning his mission. He told me that he expected his wife had left him in his absence, and taken some one whom she loved better; and added that it was all right. I discovered by his conversation that he was rather wise in his own estimation, he took the liberty to criticise some of elder O Pratts doctrines writings in the Seer. However I thought him quite agreeable, and invited him to call again, when my husband was at home.

Sat 26th rather more pleasant. I finished a job of sewing for sis Cox, and took it over to her.

Sun 27th fine day. I attended church. Br Rich gave us good instruction. Frances staid at home. PM she took a carriage ride with Daniel Rathburn. Toward night I took a walk with johny. Called at Gilbert Rolf's. Introduced myself, and begged cabbage plants. Br R—— said he knew us perfectly well but my husband had passed him a number of times in the streets, and did not seem to know him. I had quite an interesting conversation with Sister R, I was once well acquainted with her parents, br and sister Mansfield.

Mon 28th Very rainy day Mr C spent the day at home, made repairs in the furniture. Frances sewing for her sisters, and preparing for May day.

Tues 29th Pleasant again. I washed. Mr C gone to his work on the mill. Alma hoeing for sister Pratt. Evening they sent for us to come a take tea with them. After dark Ellen came over and invited us over to spend the evening. Alma and I went, but Mr C attended a caucas meeting. Br Wandell, and Joseph Hunt were at sis P's.

Wed 30th and last day of Apr 1856. I ironed. Frances baked for the party.

[A May Day Celebration, 1856]

Thurs May 1st We all prepared for the party, at an early hour. But our escort br Cox did not get ready untill after 10 oclock. We had a pleasant ride, found quite a company assembled. We had several interesting speeches.

One from br Wandell, the Superintendent of the party, 1 by Selas [Sela] Matthews, one of the maids of honor to the queen, 1 from Joseph Hunt a gent of honor. Another from the May queen, Lois Pratt. Elder Rich gave us a very fine discourse, br Skinner spoke well on the subject learning and the sciences. The children sang melodiously. Sister Jackson played on a seraphine and sang to the accompaniment. At 1 oclock we all retired to different portions of the party ground in little groups, where we enjoyed our rural repasts with cheerfulness and pleasure. We had a very nice variety of food, some wine &C.

After our repasts were over, we all assembled again on the dancing ground, where the children enjoyed that pleasant exercise ~~of dancing~~ for about 2 hours. We then returned home well pleased with the diversions of the day.

Evening there was a wedding. Wm Barnet married Ellen Sarine [Sirrine]. After which a ball at bishop Crosbys closed the diversions of the day. Capt Hunt arrived from Sacramento

Frid 2nd quite pleasant. Frances stopping with sister Cox, as she is quite sick, and confined to her bed. I called in a short time.

Sat 3rd cold windy day. PM some rain. Sis P—— and Morse called. Sis P wrote a letter for sis M to send to her parents in Great Salt lake city. Evening I spent in reading the Western Standard. Received a letter from sister E R Snow, G—— S L—— City, which cheered and comforted my heart greatly.[27] ^Also wrote a letter to sisters Haskal and Pomeroy.^

Sun 4th May. Tolerably pleasant, but remarkably <u>cold</u> for the season. I staid at home from meeting, did not feel very well. Pm sis P sent to us to come and accompany her in a call to John Holidays, to see br and sister Hamand [Francis A. Hammond] late from the Sandwich islands. We went and found sis H—— with 3 little boys, her husband had gone to meeting. We enjoyed a very social chat with her, sister Jo Mathews, and Holiday. Mr C went to meeting.

Returned home, received a call from sisters Grouard, Hill, Kipp Denis, and children. Evening Mr C gone to a caucas meeting held by the Harmonialists, in opposition to the church. Many of the brethren attend to discover if possible their object in so doing.

Mond th5 I cut a garment and robes, for myself and husband.[28]

[A Letter from Eliza R. Snow]

Tues 6th Sister Pratt called at an early hour and informed me that we were to have visitors that Pm, and wished me to assist in making preparations, which I engaged to do. Accordingly I prepared what I could conveniently, and at 12—— oclock sister Hunt called over to see a letter I had lately red from sister E R Snow. I read it to her, and then she assisted me in taking over the articles I had prepared. I found sisters Crandell, Sherwood,

Morse, Hunt, and a sister McIntire late from Sacramento, assembled, enjoying each others society with cheerful countenances. By the request of sis H—— I took my letter along with me, and read it to them all. They pronounced it an interesting one, and thought it quite a pleasure to hear from our beloved poetess.

In the course of the pm br Freeman Tanner and Foster Curtis called on sis P—— requesting the privilege of having a small dancing party at her house that evening, as he intended leaving for G—— S—— L—— City, the next morning. She rather reluctantly gave her consent, and told them they must not stay late. Myself and family attended the party, which was conducted with much civility and peace. The gents made eggnogg, and passed [*word missing*] which was quite delicious. At 12 they dispersed.

Wed 7th I arose feeling rather unpleasantly in consequence of a bad taste in my mouth. I intended to have washed after breakfast, but when that time arrived I felt so very unwell that I defered it, and after taking a walk in the garden and finding things looking backward and cold I retired to my bed, having first blistered my hand in loosening the baked dirt around the stinted vegetables. I became very nervous and altho too drowsy to read I could not sleep quietly. I at last decided on praying earnestly to the Lord to remove the cloud of darkness from my mind, and distress from my body. After interceding Him with tears I became quite relieved, and reading a sermon from br Young in the D——s——t News restored me to my usual peace of mind.

Thurs 8th Mr C—— brought home his tools from Crismans, got br Pratts bench, and commenced work in the blacksmith shop.

Frid 9th received a visit from br Eldridge, late from the Australian mission; I had not seen him in 6 years, thought he had changed some. We had a very agreeable time with him, he took dinner with us, and gave us a ~~very~~ minute account of his journeyings and shipwreck on his passage home. It was a very exciting story.[29]

Evening we spent with him at sis—— Pratts, where he related it again. We had music, staid untill 11 oclock.

Sat 10th warm and pleasant. I dressed over my bonnet. Got Ellen to assist me in trimming it again.

Sund 11th. I attended church. Bros Graham and Eldridge spoke and gave us an account of their mission in Aus—— and shipwreck on their return. It was quite an exciting history.

Sun evening had company, br Eldridge, sis Pratt and girls, and Wm McGary, had music, vocal and instrumental.

Mon 12th I washed. Mr C at work on a writing desk for Ellen P——

Tues 13th I ironed. PM went over to sister Pratt awhile. brs Graham and Eldridge were there. The former appointed the next evening to come and converse with us, on the principals of the church.

Wed 14th Sis Pratt came in after breakfast, and requested me to take a walk with herself and Frances, who was quite unwell and wished to call on the dentist. She observed that she thought it would do me good thought I staid at home too much.

Said she would call awhile on sister Stark and then go to see Sister Skinner with her new boy. I readily consented and went, made several interesting calls, took dinner with Sister Stark, after which we went to the Library. Called on sister John Lewis, went to sister Skinners, made a short call.

On our return home Frances and I came by Dr Burrows while sister Stark and Pratt took another course, by the library.

Thurs 15th I cut spent the morning in baking pies &C. PM took my sewing over to sister P's, and spent the remainder of the day. Frances is quite out of health, been taking medicine.

Frid 16th I did several jobs of mending. Sister P—— came over and wished me to come and stop awhile, said she and Frances were alone. Ellen had gone with br Daily's, on a fishing excursion.

Evening She had a sort of a bee to get her corn shelled, and intended sending some of it to G S L—— city. Her house was well filled with shellers who disposed of it in a short time. After which some of the company danced, but my husband and I came home with little Johny.

Sat 17th Br Eldridge called, said he wanted a trunk or box of some kind to take his clothes in to Salt lake. Mr C—— offered him one, and I emptied it forthwith. He appeared very thankful, and said he would remember the favor. Said he expected to leave on monday.

Sun 18th. I arose late, and found I had not time to prepare for church, and so stoped at home. Frances went last night to a br Garners Stoped over night, and this morning went in the stage with a Miss Garner, to Los Angles to stop with sister Pickets daughters while their mother came up to our place on a visit.

After meeting br and sister Tomkins called and invited us to go home with them on a visit, and as I had previously promised to go I willingly consented and went. We had a very pleasant time, Sister Tomkins came away with us on our return, to visit a sick neighbor, I think a sister Gregory. Bro T—— gave us a bucket of new potatoes, which we found very nice.

Mon 19th cool and cloudy. I worked in the garden untill 12 oclock. Alma worked on the irrigation ditch. PM Mr Patten and wife called and stoped an hour or two. I assisted her on a new dress. While they were here came br Hughs and Barton to see about the water which Mr C—— had been using to water his garden. They informed him that it belonged exclusively to their ward.[30] I did not altogether like the spirit that br Hughs manifested, but perhaps the fault was in myself.

Tues 20th It rained last night. I am making soap.

PM took a walk with sister Pratt, called at bishop Crosby's and br Lymans, sis P, wanted lime to whitewash with. We went to Glaziers store, and from there to Jacksons,[31] where I bought a piece of Calico for a sunbonnet.

Evening I went over and spent the time with sister Pratt, she was alone. I staid untill near eleven oclock, cut my bonnet, and talked, we both improved the time to the best advantage.

I found it very cold coming home. Sister Pratt complaining of a bad cold, My husband and son also.

Wed 21st cool and pleasant. I sewed on my bonnet.

Evening Mr Crosby went to the P O—— received a letter from br Taite. He has stoped in Cedar City and employed in teaching a military school. Thinks he shall return here this fall. Sister Pratt spent the PM with me; expect sis Picket tomorrow.

Thurs 22nd. I sewed very steadily on my bonnet. Evening had the headache; retired early. ^Sister P—— informed me that F—— had written back to say sis P could not come at present, was going to the coast to see a whale that had been washed on shore.^

Friday 23rd I made clothes for John T—— PM Ellen came in, found me very busy with my sewing, and offered to assist in getting supper, to which I consented while we were eating sis Pratt came in, and invited me to go with her to spend the evening with sister Hopkins, but I declined, it being so late. I went over to her house, and stoped an hour or so, and then returned.

Sat 24th Great time with chickens 3 or 4 hens hatching. Mr C—— making workbox for Ellen.

Sun 25th Fine day. Sister Patten called, and I accompanied her to church. Br Turley preached first, and was followed by br Rich. Both their discourses were very interesting. Sis P returned with me and took dinner. Bro and sister Smith called on us. Toward evening, I took a walk, went home with sister Patten, had a very agreeable chat with her returned with Johny in the cool of the evening.

That evening sister Pratt came in and told me that Wm McGary and Ellen were thinking of being married that night, and intended coming to Mr Crosby to perform the ceremony. But said it depended on bro Eldridge's return from bro Rich's, as he had gone there to spend the evening, and thought probably br R would insist on his stopping over night, and if so they would defer it untill the next.

[A Wedding: Ellen Pratt and William McGary]

Mon 26th Sis P sent for me to come and assist her in making a wedding cake. Accordingly I went over and stoped 2 or 3 hours, untill the cake was done and then brought it home with me. About ten oclock PM, the party arrived, consisting of the bridegroom bride, bro Eldridge sis P, Lois, Ann L and Alma who waited on the bridegroom and bride. Sister Eleanor Morse had been in an hour or more when they arrived. I seated the company. Mr C—— appointed bro Eldridge clerk. And also asked him to pray, which he did very fervently. The ceremony being over, the cake and wine was disposed of with good cheer, accompanied with many good wishes and blessings on the new married couple. We all regreted Frances absence, and were somewhat fearful that she would have some misgivings on the account of their not waiting for return. Accordingly we all agreed to keep it secret untill came, and a suitable party was made for the occasion. After the refreshment we danced one french four, and one cotillion. We then escorted the bridegroom and bride home.[32]

Tues 27th Sister came over before we were out of bed, and invited us over to breakfast. Br Eld—— was there also, and bade us farewell, as he was about leaving in the course of the day. He took the minutes of the marriage to Salt lake to be published in the Deseret News. Mr C—— also decided on sending them to the Western Standard for publication.

Wed 28th Very warm day. I washed. Sister Morse came in a few minutes in the evening.

Thurs 29th received an invitation to spend the PM at sister Morses with sis—— and Ellen. Had an agreeable time eating green peas and potatoes.

Friday 30th Ironed. McGary and Ellen were in, brought a musicbox belonging to Mr Hopkins, to Mr Crosby to be repaired.

Sat 31st. I wrote 3 letters, one to bro Horner, one to bro Cannon, and another to sister Wm Jones. Sister Pratt was in awhile in the Pm. Evening Mr C—— gone to the office with letters.

Sunday June 1st I did not go to church. Sister sent for me to come there, as she was alone. I went, and took dinner with her. She informed me that the marriage had been disclosed, and that several young men had insisted on Wm making a party immediatly for them, and that the next night was appointed. Br Morse had offered to manage it for him. Evening I took a walk with my husband and sis P——, called on br Hammond's had a very agreeable time.

Mon 2nd Very warm. After dinner went in and sat awhile with sis Morse. Sister P—— was also there. Wm invited myself and family to attend the party. I declined coming, as it was intended wholly for the young people, but told him I would tell Alma to come.

Tues 3rd I washed; felt very well; got my clothes out in good season. Sister P—— came in and took dinner with me, and spent the PM. Evening I took a walk with her to br Chapmans to look at his cows, she talks of buying one of him.

[Quartus S. Sparks vs. Mary Hamilton Sparks]

Wed 4th I ironed. Shortly after 10 oclock AM I was summoned to appear at the district court which was held in one of the schoolhouses, at two oclock, as a witness in the case of Sparks and wife.[33]

Accordingly at two sister and I set off, made our appearance in due form, but was told by lawyer Cliff to repair to some house near, and he would call us when our testimony should be wanted. We therefore went into br Lymans, where we waited 3 hours, and then walked over to bishop Crosbys and sat an hour longer. Had a very pleasant chat with sisters C—— and McIntire.

Br Hanks came in awhile, informed us that the stage had arrived, and Frances had not come. We were some disappointed, at the intelligence. We finally concluded to again make our appearance and get dismissed, which we did, and found our testimony would not be called for that day. Reached home near 6 oclock. Made pies, Sister P—— came over and brought letters from John Young, Henry Richards, and Julius Pratt, all of which she read to us.

Evening A—— went to the office and brought us the Western Standard. Mr C—— read of murders, and hangings in San Francisco. Death of James King of W[illia]m who was assassinated by Cas[e]y. The citizens arose, while the funeral services were being performed, and took Casy, and another murderer by the name of Cora, from the city prison, and hung them by a sort of vigilance, or Lynch law. The papers say it was a very exciting affair indeed.

Thurs 5. I finished my ironing, baked some, &C. Cut shirts and pants for Johny

Friday 6th the heat very intense. Sister Patten sent by Alma for sis Pratt and myself to come and see her as she was unwell. Just before we were ready to go, came Judge Jackson, and informed us that he thought we should undoubtedly be called on to give in our affidavits the next day. Said he was going then to F—— Deweys to take her deposition, and if we chose they would also call on us, but that he prefered having us attend court, as he thought it would have a better influence on the jury.

I told him I prefered giving my affidavit at home, but sister said she was willing to attend court, and therefore I consented to go with her. We took our walk to sister Pattens. Found her tolerably well, but quite gloomy and unhappy, said her husband had been very cross and much offend with her of late; lamented her situation and marveled why it was that she had been called to suffer in that way so long. There is a gentleman stopping with them by the name of Lancaster, a Deist by profession, and quite an enemy to our people, but still he treated us with politeness. The old gent was also in good humor. Sis P—— came a little distance with us when we left, and thanked us much for our visit or call.

Sat 7th Remarkably warm. Am I assisted Alma in irrigating the garden. Pm I went and set awhile with sister Morse.

Sun 8th Sister Patten called on her way to church, stopped a few moments, and went to sister Pratts. But finally concluded to go to br Huntingtons, as she did not feel able to attend church in consequence of headache. I accompanied my husband, sis P——, and Lois. Br Rich spoke well to us. Sister Patten called awhile after meeting, brought information from Wm Huntington, concerning his visit to Great Salt Lake city.

Evening took a little walk with my husband, and sister Pratt.

Mon 9th I intended washing, but did not feel quite sufficient for the task and so defered it. Went over and sat awhile with sister. Came home and went to sister Coxes for butter. On returning with the butter, fell in with Judge Jackson, who informed me that he was in search of sis P—— and myself and wished us to attend court as witnesses in the case of sister Sparks and her husband. It was very warm, and I had eaten no dinner, was coming directly home with my butter, intending to make me a cup of tea, but was informed by br Jackson that they could not possibly wait to take depositions, but wished us to be there in a half hour. Accordingly, I came home and prepared myself in haste, and set off with sis P——. We both felt very bad about going, as it had been represented to us, to be a place unfit for the appearance of ladies. But we met Judge Jackson a little this side of the courtroom, who conducted us in very politely, and we felt better than we had anticipated. We were treated very civilly by the Judge and Lawyer. ^Were sworn by br Hopkins,^ had very few questions to answer, and dismissed. On returning called at Epraims store and bought a primer for Johny. Charles Hill took supper with us, was very sociable.

Evening called br Wandell, and Judge Scott from Los Angeles, who is sister Sparks lawyer. He wished to question me some further with regard to what I knew concerning sister S——s visit to San Francisco in the fall of 54. I refered to my journal and told him all I had recorded and several circumstances from memory. He was very talkative, and inquired concerning our place of nativity, asked my fathers name place of residence, inquired our ages, told us he was 66 years old, and never used glasses, or spectacles. We thought him a very plain honest sort of man. He is very large, weighing nearly 300 pounds. He complimented me on looking so young, thought my sister Mrs Pratt looked 15 years older than I did.

Tues 10th I washed, felt very well. Evening went into sis Pratts. Ellen and sister came home with me. Alma went to br Hopkin's for butter. Mr Crosby attended court.

Wed 11th Alma gone with Mr Patten for wood. Mr C, gone to court again. I put out my clothes, watered plants &C.

Thurs 12th I ironed in the forenoon. Pm received an invitation to visit at sis Pratts with sister Thomas, enjoyed the visit well.

Br Tomkins came in, and told us concerning the decision of the jury Viz, that sister Sparks had got the case, nothing having been proved against her. The judge had given her a bill, and half the property. Br Thomas came up to supper. Mr Crosby also came in.

After tea they all came home with me called to see Ellens residence, which at present is occupied by br Morse's family.

Frid 13th Mr Crosby at work for Tomkins yesterday and today. I quilted for sister Morse a part of the PM, afterward went to sis P's and visited with sister Hopkins. I have made a mistake in the day I saw sister Thomas at sis P's, it being Wed instead of Thurs.

Sat 14th Quite cool and comfortable. Mr C—— gone again to work at Tomkins, repairing threshing machine. Sister Patten called on her way to the store, and left me a little butter. I quilted again for sister M.

Sun 15th I did not attend church, very warm weather, and the house so crowded there is very little comfort to be taken. ^Took a walk to br Riches with my husband in the evening. Mr C brought home a clock to repair for Mary.^ Evening called sister Pratt, with Wm and Ellen McG. They played several tunes with Alma. Sister and I walked out by moon-light. ^*Mon 16th*^ Alma watered the garden this morning. I also assisted him, while in the midst of the work, came sister Pratt and McIntire, to make me a visit. Sister took hold and assisted me some, and sis Mc—— said it was work that she should like were she selted, and had a garden of her own. Mr C finished a job of repairing machinery for Tomkins, and then went to the mill to work for br Hanks.[34] I dressed a chicken and made a very good dinner for the sisters. PM came sister Eleanor Morse. Sisters Mc and Pratt sewed some for me. They left about 5 oclock. I went over to sis P's with them. Got onion sets at Ed—— Daily's garden, and set out in ours, with Alma's assistance.

Tues 17th I cut straw to make a hat for John Tate. Sophronia and Ben were up.[35] I went to sister P's awhile. We recd an invitation to attend a sewing party at bro Hopkins the next day.

Wed 18th I accompanied sister to br Hopkins, where several sisters were already assembled. We had a very sociable pleasant time, and an excellent dinner. Ellen McG—— came in the PM. We returned home a little before sunset.

Thurs 19th Sister El Morse invited us to come and sew for her. At ten oclock I went, and sewed steadily untill 6. Sister P came and brought from the office, two letters, one from sister L Baker, Can and another from

Lois Thomson. Nauvoo. Also the Western Standard. We were all pleased
to hear from our friends. We heard by sister Thomson that Mother Smith
was still living. Evening we had a little dancing at sis Morses, mostly old
people, two or three young couple. Broke up at twelve.

Frid 20th The weather very comfortably cool. I washed. Evening read
the Western Standard.

Sat 21st Quite warm. I put out my clothes. went over to sister P's
awhile. Braiding a straw hat for Johny. Came home, and ironed. Sister
came with me. Read to me in Nicols Journal. Evening Mr C went to br
Riches, carried a clock that he had been repairing for Mary, and brought
back another to repair for Harriet.

[A Letter from Elvira Stevens]

Sun 22nd Remarkably warm. I spent the day at home, laid nearly all day in
bed, or on the bed, with my head and face wraped in a wet towel. About
4 oclock it began to cool off a little. I then arose and got supper. Sister P
came in. Mr C—— brought letters, and papers from the office, one from
bro Wm Taite, and one from Emily M Crosby, bro David C——s daughter.
Sister P—— got a letter from sis Alvira Woodbury, or rather Stevens. She
wrote that she had been to bro Young and got released from her husband, that she and br Lewis were living togather.[36] After supper, I went
into sis Morses found her in bed, quite unwell. Matilda Lyman was there.
Said she had been quite unwell for sometime. While I was there bro and
sister Hammond came to see us. I immediately came home to welcome
them. We enjoyed a few hours in social chat very agreeably. Bro H bought
a chair of us, and agreed to make me a pair of shoes.

Mon 23rd another very warm day. I took up my carpet, and washed
the floor, found it a hard task. Sister Pratt came over and thought it a
great improvement, invited me over to sew with her. Said she was making
herself a new dress for the 4th of July, and thought had better make one.
Accordingly I took the muslin pattern that bro Taite gave me in San F——
went over and sewed untill 6 oclock. I came home got supper, and then
went back to stay with sister, as she and Ephraim were alone. The girls
all absent. Ellen stopping with sister Delynn [Delin], Ann L with sister
Hopkins. Lois gone on a fishing excursion to the Calhoon [Cajon], with
the Hunts, Marsh and John, and several ladies. I had a sleepless night
untill two oclock in the morn, being annoyed by vermin, or rather bedbugs.

Tues 24th, rather more comfortable. Alma mowing barley. Mr C still
at work on the mill. After breakfast I went to the store and bought hickory
[a strong cotton twilled fabric] for Alma shirts, returned and went to bro

Harris, to pay them for butter and milk. Came home took my sewing to sis P's, again. Sewed untill 5 oclock. Came home and prepared supper.

Evening came sis Morse said her husband had been gone all day, that Charlotte was away on a visit, and that she was alone and very lonely. I went home with her and sat a few minutes. The house entirely desolate, 9 oclock and no husband come yet, thought she would go and get sister Pratt to come and sleep with her. I came back and resumed my writing. 10 oclock and all is well. Husband, son and little charge all in bed, safe and sound.

Wed 25th Quite comfortably cool. I washed. Bro Harris mowed barley. Evening Sister Morse in awhile. Said her husband came home the previous night, just as she was going out to sister Pratts, and she discovered that he was somewhat intoxicated, and therefore did not speak to him; but went over and slept with Ann L—— and left him entirely to his own reflections.

Thurs 26th, another cool pleasant day. I ironed, and sewed on Almas shirts. Cooked chicken for supper. Mr Crosby brought home cloth A——s pants, received some money of bro Hanks for work on mill.

Friday 27th Sister Pratt came over and requested me to go to Sister Lymans to a sewing party with her, and the girls, said they were making flags, and banners, for the celebration of the 4th of July. I had sewing of my own that I wished to finish, and declined her invitation. Finished A———'s shirts, and wrote a letter to sister Lovina B——. Also wrote to Sister Pickett, Frances and the girls.

[A Letter to Eliza R. Snow]

Sat 28th Fine cool day. I baked light bread and cakes, puddings &C. Wrote a letter to sister E R Snow. As follows.

San Bernardino June 28th AD 1856
Dear sister Snow. Your communication of March 30th is now before me, and my heart seems inclined to reply to it. Altho I have perhaps nothing of interest to you, to write. But I can assure you that your letter has been many times perused with pleasure not only to myself, but to many of the sisters, who like myself feel it a blessing to receive a word of consolation, and counsel, from one of Zions daughters whose experience, and faith, command our sincrest respect, and esteem. Shortly after I received it I attended a visiting party at my sisters, where were sisters Hunt, Sherwood, Crandell, Morse and a sis—— McIntire, wife of Dr [William L.] McIntire. They understood that I had a late communication from you, and wished

me to read it to them, which I did much to their edification. They all wished to be rememberd to you, or all who know you. I have also read it to sis Patten, formerly sister Repsher. She earnestly requested me to remember her love to you, and ask you to pray for her. She is a very unhappy woman. Her husband is very cross and unkind to her at times, and has lately taken a part with the dissenting party. He turned her out of his house last winter and she came and staid two weeks with me. I believe she tries to be as patient as she can, but she sighs to be relieved from her bondage.

Sister Sherwood has left her husband [Henry G.] and lives with her children. I have understood that the old gent is relaxing his temper a little, and shows symptoms of reconciliation towards the church.

They have had quite an exciting time here this spring. The dissenters accuse our missionaries of exercising an evil influence with the indians. They seem determined to exert all their powers against us, but they are not much heeded as their numbers, as yet, are comparatively small.

Several of our particular friends expect to leave soon for Salt lake. I do not exactly see yet why we are kept here, or why our way has been so long closed, altho I do not give myself much uneasiness about it. Our one desire has been and still is to do the Lords will and trust him for His grace. I believe all will eventually work together for our good.

I hear many complain that they cannot, or do not, enjoy as much of the Spirit of God here as they did at headquarter, but where the fault lies is difficult to determine. Perhaps it is reasonable that we should not, as we are certainly deprived of many privileges which are there enjoyed. But if I am capable of judging there are many good kind people here, who apparently enjoy the Holy Spirit.

It is a very busy time here now. The saints are making preparations to celebrate the 4th of July. The sisters have been, and still are at work making flags and banners for the occasion.

Sister Pratt sends love to you, and begs to be remembered in your prayers. Her husband has gone again to the islands. Ellen is married to Wm McGary. Frances is stopping with sister Pickett in Los Angeles.

Sister P—— takes in sewing, and sometimes has considerable business. She has not been here yet. I believe her husband rather objects to their coming. We expect the girls here on the 4th.

Now sister S—— please excuse this short letter, and if you deem it worthy of a response, write me again. I wish to hear from all my old friends in the faith. But I presume many of them are more burdened with domestick cares than you are, and have not the advantages of writing. Where is sister Cable, please give love to her, Zina, and many others too numerous to mention.

My husband desires you to remember us at the throne of grace. We pray for you, and all pertaining to you, and remain yours in sincerity and truth.

Jonathan and Caroline B—— Crosby.

Sun 29th The weather still very comfortably cool. We all attended church. Bro Rich read the second section in the book of Doctrine and covenants, and spoke well to us. The good spirit prevailed. The order of the ceremonies for the 4th were read. After meeting, sister Hopkins came to sis P——'s, and sent for me to come over there. I went, spent an hour or two very agreeably. Sister Sparks came in awhile, told us some of her troubles with her late husband, from whom she has been divorced. Sis H wished me to do some sewing for her, which I engaged to do.

Mon 30th I washed. Alma dug a well, close to the corner of the house. I assisted him in raising some of the last of the dirt and water, with a rope and pully, which was very hard work. But we succeeded in getting good clear water, a foot and half deep.

Tues July 1st Ironed untill 11 oclock. Charles Baker called to see us. He is an english boy, who lived at br Horners when we were there. Said he was going to G S L city with the next mail. Br Harris called at the door to see if we wanted the water for our garden. Said we could have it for an hour or more, or until the owners turned it off. I was anxious that it should be made the best use of, and went out and helped Alma, untill near one. I then came in got dinner, and went to sewing on Ada Hopkins sunbonnet, sewed very steady untill sunset. But before I got through I felt very sick, with back and headache.

Mr C brought home a new box of tea. I drank some and went immediately to bed, feeling much fatigued, and sick with all.

Wed 2nd Arose feeling bad, finished Ada H's bonnet after breakfast. Then went to sewing on my dress. Felt quite disheartened about finishing it. Made me a cup of tea for dinner. Sophronia G was here and ate with us. PM I felt much better. Ellen came over and found me asleep in my chair. Staid with me until night. Took supper with us. We expect Fr— and sisters Smiths.

Thurs 3rd Remarkably warm day. I had a great deal of work on hand. Baked light bread, two sweetcakes, 8 pies, killed a fowl, stuffed and baked. Also finished my dress, sister P came over, and sewed for me awhile. I was much fatigued at night, but did not retire untill near 11 oclock.

[A Fourth of July Celebration, 1856]

Friday, July 4th we were awakened by the guns. Grand celebration at the bowery. Cannons were repeatedly discharged. I prepared my offering, and my husband and son carried it with the dishes to bowery, and delivered it to the bishop or teachers. At nine we all repaired to the tabernacle or bowery.

Sister Patten came along, and went with us. I cannot attempt a description of the performance. It was very splendid, and in good order. The tables were adorned with a good variety of food, Several nice boquets also appeared on them. The Strangers were first seated, and then the ladies, afterwards the San Bernardino Rangers, and the people generally. Everything passed off in good order, and harmony prevailed throughout the entire company.

I became weary and left about 4 oclock. The assembly were dismissed at 5 with the blessings of our president bro Rich upon them. Evening there were 3 houses opened for dancing. Bros Lymans, bishop Crosbys, and Ed Daily's. We attended at the bishops. They were mostly strangers to me, yet I enjoyed it very well. Sister Pratt wished me to accompany her to see the co, at br Lymans, which I did, found the house crowded, but good order prevailed.

The stage from Los Angeles arrived about ten Am. Frances and Aga [Agnes Smith] found us all absent; left their trunks here, and went into sis Morse's. She being unwell did not attend the celebration. She made the girls a cup of coffee, and resting themselves awhile they came to the bowery. The dinner was all over, and they were just preparing to dance, when they came. Sis Patten called on her way home, and took tea with us.

Sat 5th It was a remarkably warm day. I accompanied Agnes to visit her relative, sister Andrews. We set off at ten, found them rather unwell. Br A—— was complaining of neuralgia, and jaundice; his skin was very yellow. However he was quite social, and apparently happy.

We took a walk in their garden, which is very beautiful. Sister A made us a good dinner, and about 4 oclock F—— came for us, and we went to br Wm Matthews with her. She and her mother had been there sometime expecting to meet us, according to agreement. We made a short pleasant visit at br M——'s, took supper, walked in the garden. b—— M gave sis P—— and me some onions. On our way home we called on sis Hunt, found her alone and looking rather sad. John had just left with the mail for Salt Lake, and I missed sending my letter to sis Snow. I felt sorry, but thought of her text, which is to acknowledge the hand of God in all things. I ever find it a comfort to me, to do so.

Sun 6th Staid at home. Sis—— Patten came along and went to church. PM came sister Hammond, to get a box of jewelry that Mr Crosby had been repairing for her. I accompanied her to sis P——'s, Spent an hour or more. came home and watered flowers, onions &C.

Mon 7th Frances very unwell, anxious to get back to Pueblo [El Pueblo de Nuestra Senora de Los Angeles], to get the cool sea breeze again. Br Mathews told them he would send his son to take them home tuesday. Several young ladies took dinner with me. Agnes, S—— Amanda Tomkins, Louisa Ann Pratt &C.

Frances had quite a sick turn, and her mother went to the Dr's for her. He was absent. Sis Morse gave her opium which relieved her.

[End of Frances's Visit]

Tues 8th Agnes breakfasted with me. They waited for the wagon a long time, untill their patience began to be a little weary. But shortly bro M, and son arrived, with a comfortable vehickle, and they took leave of their friends, Frances for a short time, but Aga probably untill another year. F—— thought she should return in a week or two, but I think she will stay untill the heat of summer is over.

I washed. Sister P—— spent the day with us, cut and sewed on pants for Alma.

Wed—— 9th I put out the clothes, washed floor. Ellen came over, and invited me to her mothers, to see sis Sherwood, but I was too busy to leave, and sent to them to come here. About 11 oclock they came. Half past 1 I had dinner. Ellen assisted to do up dishes, and we all went over to her mothers, and spent the Pm. Had a fine visit with sis S——. Alma gone to work for br Ridley.

Thurs—— 10th A—— gone again. I ironed, sis P in awhile. Pm I am alone with John and the chickens.

Frid 11th Remarkably warm; toward noon called Mr Patten, on his way to Browns place and informed me that his wife was quite unwell, and wished me to come to her that Pm if convenient. I told him I would go toward night, but thought it too warm to go in the middle of the day I sent over and invited Sis Pratt to accompany me and about 5 oc we went, found sis P—— very poorly, but better than she had been. She had two colored women with her. And a boy came to do her chores, and stop with her through the night. She was highly pleased to see us, and before we left said she felt much better, became very sociable, talked over Nauvoo, and many other places. And when we left came with us to the street. We had a pleasant walk by moonlight, reached home at 9 oclock.

Sat 12th Very comfortable day. Chastina McMurtry came, and spent the Am with us. I made a cup of tea for us, and we enjoyed it finely togather.

Sun 13th attended church. Capt Hunt preached. Showed us the state of the government affairs in the United States. The weakness and inefficiency of our officers to maintain the laws. Was succeeded by bro Rich.

Mon 14th Bro Tomkins came, and threshed ours, and sis P's barley. I dressed chicken for dinner. Sis P—— and Ellen came over and ate with us—also bro Sullivan, who was one of the laborers. Pm sewed a straw hat for John Taite.

Tues 15th Washed. Sis P—— in awhile. Complained of the threshers for having damaged her garden, fence, &C. Alma at work for Ed Daily.

Wed 16th I ironed. Baked light bread, sister Morse in awhile. About 4 oclock I went over to sis P's—— found Mr Grinnell there, the father of little Emma who died last winter. He had just arrived from the upper country. Sis P went with me to bro Hammonds, where we had a very agreeable time. Took tea with them, got our feet measured for shoes, &C. Returned by moonlight, found bro Wandell here, with Mr C—— learning new songs for the 24th to teach his school. Mr Crosby played the air while he sang the bass. Bros Mills and Orr called awhile. I treated them to a ripe Muskmelon, the first we have had. Sister Morse and Charlotte, came in and partook of it, with us. In the forepart of the evening one of bro Riches little boys came in crying and inquired for his mother Harriet Rich, said she left him at bro [Harley] Mowry's, to stay over night, and went away, but that he got sick of staying, and started to follow her home, but could not overtake her, and was afraid to go alone, wanted Alma to go with him, which he did, untill within sight of the house.

Thurs 17th Quite warm. I felt unusually fatigued and sleepy this morning. After breakfast felt worse, thought of going to bed, but concluded to wash myself in cold water, and try a cup of tea, and afterwards felt some better. Sat down to write, but my eyes refused to perform their proper functions, and I was compelled to lay by my pen. Made a bed on the floor, where I lay several hours with wet cloths, on my head and face. Toward night I felt some better, but not well. Went to bed early.

Frid 18th Sister Pratt staid with me all the Am. Made a pair of pants for Johny. We had green corn for dinner. Pm Ellen came in and sat an hour or two.

[A Letter from J. M. Horner]

Sat 19th I looked for sister Patten, but she did not come. I have neglected to mention that we rcd a letter from bro J M Horner ^by the last mail^ in answer to the three that we have written him.

He acknowledged the receipt of them all, and said he had no excuse to make, only he had no news to communicate. Thought perhaps he might be able to send us a small sum of money the coming month, but could not tell certain. Said he had "been laboring the most of the past year for his own support, but could pay no debts from that source, must get the means from the property" &C.[37]

We considered it rather a cold comfortless letter, quite devoid of sympathy. He will not probably be troubled with another communication from us. I[t] seems that he does not feel willing to do even as well as he has been done by. ~~And thinks his labor dearer to him, than that of an older and more needy man~~. But I should cease to murmur. Time will bring all things around right, if we trust in God, and are patient. I only desire to acknowledge his hand in all things.

Sun 20th very warm. Mr C Alma and Johny went to church I staid at home, heat very intense. When my husband returned from church he informed me that he had recd—— an invitation to come to bishop Crosby's that Pm, to a singing or rather music party. and wished me to accompany him. I did not feel much in the mood of it, but concluded to comply with his request, and went. We called at sis—— P's for Ellen. Sister Jackson requested Mr Crosby to do so, but she was absent, and her mother busy preparing dinner, so that we went alone, found br Wandell and a Mr Smith sing with sis Jackson, while she played the accompaniment on the melodion or seraphine[38]

Mr C joined them with the flute, but as I had no invitation to sing, I listened awhile, and sister Crosby and McIntire invited me into the diningroom While they prepared supper, I had a very agreeable time with them. Sister Mc—— is quite an interesting woman in conversation. She told me several peculiarities respecting the death of her son, Wm who was killed by being thrown from a horse. She read me several pieces of poetry that had been composed ^to his memory^ by friends of the family. One by David Steward which I thought very pretty, and appropriate. We enjoyed a hearty supper with the bishop, and family, he being very jolly and jacose, time passed off quickly, and the sun was set before we left. Sister C—— said we must come again, and excuse her if she did not return our visits, as she was much confined at home, in consequence keeping public house, and being unable to hire help, on account of not having sufficient custom to warrant them in so doing.

Mon 21st tolerably pleasant. Made light bread. Mr C worked in the shop.

Tues 22nd I washed. Pm came in bro Wandell, enquired if we had melons ripe. Alma went out to see, and found 4 nice ones. We had a famous feast. Ellen, Lois, sis Morse, Ann and Charlotte all came in and enjoyed it with us. Evening I went into sis P's awhile. Wm came home from harvesting, and said he was going this morn with Tomkins to the lower country, with the threshing machine.

Wed 23rd Mr C—— gone to work again for bro Crisman. Alma helping Mr Patten to move his house. Johny and I alone.

[24th of July Parade]

Thurs 24th today the S—— B——dino Dragoons parade. And evening they
have a picnic, and ball at bishop Crosby's. Sis Pratt and all the girls are
going, but as we belong neither to the pioneers nor rangers we have no
part or lot in it.[39] Alma is at work again for Mr Patten Ephraim came over
and staid all night. Sister Morse and Charlotte came in and ate melons
with us.

    Frid 25th I ironed. Sister Patten sent by A for me to come up and see
her new place. Accordingly about two oclock I went with John and Alma.
Lois came in and told me that Mr and Mrs Grouard had come and asked
me to come and see them, but I told her I had promised to go another
way. Ephraim also came and requested me to come and bring a melon. I
sent a melon by him to his mother with an apology for not comng. Went
to sis Pattens, found living under a shade tree, with not more than half a
house altho very pleasant Sister Hawes was there with her children. I took
Johny with me, which made quite party of us. I found myself feeling very
much fatigued when I got there, and could hardly be sociable, but after
resting and getting a cup of <u>tea,</u> I became revived We reached home just
as the sun was setting. Sister Morse Ann Charlotte and sis Adaline Daily
were in. We had melons again.

    Sat 26th sis Pratt came over to consult me with regard to a letter
that Frances had written, asking our counsel respecting her going to San
Francisco for her health. We understand her health is very bad since she
was here. But not from herself. We both counseled her not to go, but to
come home, and go on the mountains, we wrote her a lengthy letter, and
gave her all encouragement we could to come back.

    I went over to sis P's invited sis Grouard and all of them over to tea.
Came back and helped Alma put up boards on the loft got dinner and all
cleared away when they came. Br Grouard also came, in time to eat supper. We had quite a social chat and parted in peace. Evening went into sis
P's, sang a few tunes, while Mr Crosby played the violin.

    Sun 27th very pleasant day. I intended going to church, but just as I
got last chore done, I was taken with pain and weakness in my back and
hips which took away all my ambition, and I went to bed where I laid all
the morning. When my husband came home he informed me that bro
Hanks and wife, and G P Dikes and wife had arrived in the stage, from the
upper country.

    After supper we took a walk to bro David Holidays, found them
absent from home, and went to see bro Davis's. Found them very comfortable; heard him read a letter from br H Findlay. Had a pleasant time

and returned. Met bro Hanks and shook hands with him. Evening Mr C repairing music box.

Mon 28th Mr C gone to his work at bro Crismans. Alma at home, I washed. Sister Morse came over and invited me to come and take tea with her, said she had company. Mother Walker—and her daughters—Henry Rollins wives.[40] After dinner I went over. Found them all enjoying themselves finely. Spent the Pm very agreeably. Mother Walker concluded to stay overnight.

Tues 29th I invited her with sisters Morse and Pratt to visit me, which they did; took dinner, staid two or three hours and then we all went to sis—— Pratts to spend the Pm.

Old sister Walker is 76 years of age, and quite smart and healthy. Evening Mr Grinnell was in and ate melon with us. We received all the back numbers of the Mormon, by the last mail. Bro Pratts family received a letter from him.

Wed 30th Very warm day, some sprinklings of rain, accompanied with thunder. I felt very much oppressed with the heat. Sister Morse and Charlotte sat awhile with me. afterwards came sis Pratt, and told me concerning the letter from her husband. Said she was quite <u>astonished</u> to receive so <u>strange</u> a letter from him. Said it was directed to Ellen and Frances.

Thurs 31st of July Alma went again to help Mr Patten. I sewed the lining for my house. Heard Frances gone to the upper country. Sister Pratt sent for me to come over and see Sister Blackburn and daughterinlaw. I was too busy to leave.

Sister Morse and Charlotte in again. Evening they came and ate melons. Also a br Mills and a strange gent with him. Mr Grinnell came in and ate same. I went over and wrote some for sis Morse. Dancing party at Ed Daily's.

Fri <u>Aug. 1st 1856</u> Mr Patten came early to work for Alma hauling rock to wall the well. Br Graham called borrowed a yd measure of me. Talked some time, concerning his mission to Aus——.

[A Feast of Melons]

Sewing on the house lining. Got dinner for Al and Mr Patten. Sis M in this PM. Expressed a great desire to go to Salt lake. Evening called bro [Richard R.] Hopkins and family, sister Grouard, sis P—— and Ellen with a number of children, to eat melons. Alma had just brought in upwards of a dosen, and they feasted untill all were satisfied, and left an abundance. Our melons are really a great rarity to us, as we never raised any of any importance before.

Our friends have many of them feasted upon them with us. Our saleratus garden, that we were so doubtful of the first part of the season, is likely to disappoint us for the better.

Sat 2nd I finished the house lining. Took a walk to br Riches in eve ^also called at Hopkins^

Sun 3rd It was a very warm day. Mr C—— did not attend church but in consequence of being very much engaged in work, he put the cloth up over head. I assisted some and got the head ache badly. Pm, went over to sis P's. Mr C—— and Ellen went to bishop Crosby's to a music party. Sis came home with me. After sunset took a walk with husband, and Johny.

Mon 4th I washed, dried, brought in, and sprinkled my clothes. Evening Ellen called and informed me that we had received an invitation to attend a quilting at bro Wicksomes the next day. I told her I did not feel it my duty to go from home to work such warm weather; besides my own business demanded my attention.

Tues 5th She called again, and told me that herself and mother were going, and wanted my co——, and if I would go she would assist me to iron in the evening. Said Lois would bake me some bread, and cook my fresh meat. Accordingly I concluded to accompany them, and we set out about 10 oclock. Sis Morse ~~accompanied~~ was with us. We had a long and very warm time in going, found two quilts on the frames, and a lot of sewing besides the house was well filled with the sisters, who got off both the quilts, and hemmed them. They made us a good dinner, had quite a variety. We had a very social time. Toward evening sister Folks invited some of us to walk home with her to see her new situation. Sisters Pratt Morse and myself went. She treated us to melons. Her house is new and unfinished, but very pleasantly situated. We stoped sometime with her, and in the meantime came Ellen McGary and Mrs Crandell daughter of bro Wicksome. We reached home about sunset, found ourselves much fatigued.

Wed 6th I arose at the usual hour, prepared breakfast for my husband, but felt very unwell, and after he went to his work I went to bed, and laid untill 9 or 10 oclock, when Alma made me a cup of tea, and after partaking of it I felt much refreshed, and pursued my usual occupations. In perusing this page I find I am one day in advance of the time. Tues Mother Crandell and sis Hopkins came to visit me. bro H called and took supper with us, we had a fine visit with them. Wed—— we went to the quilting, and

Thurs 7th I kept my bed nearly all the Am. Pm I wrote letters to Salt lake. Finished one to sister E R Snow, and wrote to Emily M Crosby and Wm Taite of Cedar city.

Frid 8th I ironed, in the morning. Alma scrubed the floor for me. Sister Sparks called a few minutes, asked for a melon. Al gave her a nice muskmelon. Sis P got a letter from Frances from San Francisco After supper I went over to hear it read, found she reached there in safety, and felt better in health. Intended making her home with sister Mowry. I also heard a letter from sister Evans to Frances half past 10 oclock when I reached home. I was very tired. Slept soundly, was awakened in morning by a distressing dream.

Sat 9th Thought I heard the cries of a child 4 or 5 years of age which sounded like my own childs voice when he was of that age. Thought he was in the hands of men, who seemed to be enemies to <u>him</u>, or <u>us</u>, who were tormenting him. I was out of sight of <u>them</u>, in an upper room, where I could not consistently get to them. My distress became so great that I awoke with groans, and my husband enquired the cause. I listened and heard the young cocks crowing, and their noise so much resembled the crying of a child that it realy continued my distress of mind sometime longer. I finally asked the Lord to relieve my mind from that dreadful sadness which my dream had produced. After I got my work done went with Johny to bro Dennis, got a few tin dishes. Bro D—— was very sociable. Enquired of br Pratts letter, what news he wrote &C. Said he would never come home again, offered to bet a large ball and splendid supper that he would never return to this place.[41]

Sun 10th I attended church. Remarkably warm day. Bishop Crosby spoke from the pulpit, and was followed by bro Rich. I returned with headache and went to bed. Mr C—— staid at home. Evening came Ann Morse and Lois Pratt to eat melons. The evening was very pleasant, moon shone brightly.

[Social Visits]

Mon 11th My head felt rather light. Still I thought I would wash. Mr Grinnell walled the well for us. Pm Alma and I laid a floor over it, hung a trap door, &C. Negro Phill called in the evening. Told us many anecdotes of the southern states, and the slaves.

Tues 12th I put out my clothes today. Sis P came over, said she was writing to Frances, requested Alma to go to the P O. Asked me to come and dine with her, which I did. She told me of her visit to bro Grouard. Sister Sparks sent to tell me that herself and Sis Stark would visit me the next day.

Wed 13th I arranged my household affairs in the best possible manner preparatory to receiving my co[mpan]y. At one oclock they came. Sister Pratt and Ellen McG——y also. At two came sisters Morse and Clark, wife of George Clark. We had a very pleasant visit. Sister Morse and Ellen assisted me in preparing supper, and they seemed to enjoy it finely. We parted in good cheer, and warm friendship. I received many invitations to return their visits, which I shall be apt to accept, and comply with. Ellen stoped, and washed the dishes. Beautiful moonlight evening. Alma was engaged in irrigating the garden. Mr C—— was examining two [*word missing*] which bro Henry Jackson brought him to repair <u>if</u> he <u>could</u>.

Thurs 14th. I felt wearied and dull all day. Sis Pratt came over and spent the PM with me again. Cut coat for Johny.

Went this morning to see the new Dagurean, who takes likeness on an improved plan. Called Ambrotype and Photographick, admired his pictures. Lois P—— had her likeness taken. Sister and I think of having ours taken <u>togather</u>, to send our friends. Evening I was in to sis M's. She was keeping sister Phin Daily's little boy while <u>she</u> went to a dance.

Frid 15th. Mr P——t——n hauled wood. I helped sis P put on a quilt.

Sat 16th I assisted sis P—— again on her quilt. Felt very unwell in the morning, laid down awhile, had a sort of fever, which lasted an hour or two. Lois made a cup of tea for her mother and me, which revived me very much, brought on a perspiration, which removed ~~which removed~~ the fever.

Evening we had a small melon party. A bro Mills, T—— Swartout, Lois and Ann L, sis Pratt and Morse. We ate about a half dozen. Mistake, it was friday night. Sat night we took a walk to bro Sealy with sis Pratt. Bro Sealy gone to the mountain, had a social chat with her. She treated us to melons, took us to the peach orchard, but they were not ripe. We accepted an invitation to go again when they were ripe.

Sun 17th I staid at home and rested from all my labors. Took a little walk by twilight, called at bro Kipp's. Had a social chat with them.

Mon 18th Went over and quilted for sister Pratt, in co with sisters Morse and Daily. Evening some of the friends were in to eat melons.

Tues 19th washed, baked, and cut undergarments. Mr Wandell called in the evening, Said he was going to leave for San Francisco on his mission to the upper country, in a few days. Offered to carry letters or do business for us.

Wed 20th I ironed, made mince pies. Sister came over and ate dinner with me. Said they had recd another letter from bro Pratt, but it was directed to Ellen, and not a word to herself. Toward evening went in to see sister Cox, found her in bed quite unwell. Staid an hour or two and returned.

Promised to go tomorrow with sister, to have our Ambrotype likenesses taken, to send to our friends, in Canada.

[A Disappointing Ambrotype]

Thurs 21st I arose early, arranged my domestick affairs in good season, and at 8 oclock set out for the Ambrotype chamber, in Dr Burrows new building. Called to wait for sis P. I had previously felt quite unwell, and rather dreaded the task of preparing myself. Accordingly got Ellen to dress my head. She did it after her own taste, and was some time about it, which added to my already weary feeling, and by the time I was prepared to sit I looked like a person of 60 years. I did not feel pleased with it, but did not know that it could be mended. Returned to sisters. Saw bro Wandell who had called to say farewell, as he was ready to leave on his mission to the upper country. He left his blessing with us, and we gave ours to him. Sent letter to Frances by him. I came home, and feeling much fatigued, ~~and~~ laid me down to rest. Alma made a fire, boiled the tea kettle for me, and after taking a cup of tea I felt much refreshed. But still felt billious, and had a dull headache. Ann L took tea with us. Had a restless night. Sister Patten called, and brought me some butter for which I gave her flour.

Frid 22nd Mr C got his own breakfast, and went to his work before I arose. Past seven when I got up, and took a little breakfast. Sister Patten called again. Said she would try to give me something for my health. Ann L Pratt came in, and offered to sew for me awhile. Pm her mother came over Said A[nn] might help me, to pay Alma for assisting her so frequently, proposed her getting dinner, and have Lois, and Ellen come over and eat with us. Which she did. Ellen invited Alma to go to a party (with her,) made by the San Berdino dragoons. Just as he was going a number of young gents called in. Bro Mills brought in a couple, one a man by the name of Jewel, who came down on the boat with us last fall. The other said he was an old acquaintance, and schoolmate, of bro Rich. Said he called to see him, but found he was absent. His name was Scott. Bro Davis was also in. We treated them to melons, and had a very social time with them. Jewel and Scott were in search of stock.

Sat 23rd I still felt very unwell. Ann L came and sewed some for me. Sister, Ellen and Lois were also in. Just at sunset I was taken with a very severe pain in my left eye, and thought I had surely got something in it, bathed it in cold water, got sister Pratt to look into it, but nothing could be discovered [*ink smear obliterates one or more words*] afflicted, and went to bed with it bound up in a wet cloth. I felt tolerably well, ~~and s~~

Sunday 24th it felt a very little relieved, but still pained me some. I asked the Lord repeatedly in the name of his Son Jesus Christ to remove from me all pain, and distress, and heal me of all my infirmities. I was left alone during the meeting hours, so that I had a good chance to exercise my mind. I kept my bed a good part of the day, but toward night arose feeling much better, prepared supper with Almas assistance, and while we were eating came in sisters Pratt and Sealy.

They invited me to walk with them on leaving, but I apologised on account of my eye. However after the sunset I walked over to sisters and sat awhile, came home and learned that my husband had invited bro and sis Kipp, and Hill to eat melons with us. We had some fine ones, but none came ~~but~~ excepting sis K, and Hills little daughter.

Mon 25th I arose feeling quite well, at least my eye was almost entirely well. Altho I discovered that my billious affiction was not wholly removed yet I felt to give God the glory, and thank Him for His mercy in restoring me thus far to health and happiness.

Tuesday 26th I felt much better, and washed. Sisters Pratt and Morse called on me awhile in the PM. They thought me quite presumptious in trying to wash when I was so unwell, but I told them I felt better than when I began. Large party at sister Sparks. Alma went with Lois Pratt.

Wed 27th I went again with sister P—— and Ann L, to the Ambrotype chamber, asked the artist to let us sit again, but he was unwilling to try to better our likeness, saying that he feared it would be worse instead of better. Several persons present looked at them, and pronounced them good, and so we gave up the contest.

Mr Dee Lee [Dalee] however offered to let <u>me</u> sit again and give me the picture if I would pay him one doll—— for the case, which was quite a small one. He had previously been troubled with a lady and two children, and got his mind rather disconcerted, and when he came to mine he appear quite confused. I sat 3 times before he got one that satisfied himself, and that was far from satisfying me. However we left, and went to bishop Crosby's. It was near dinnertime they invited us to dine with them, and after the gents were through or at least the harvest hands, we went in and ate at the second table with the clerks and Daguerian. Sister Dan—— Thomas was there on a visit. We had a very agreeable time with her and sis McIntire. Sister C was much engaged in cooking, and serving, and had little time to spend with us. Returned home quite fatigued. Sister Morse called to see my new picture. Mr C—— came home at 4 oclock having finished a certain job of work. My sister came over with her sewing, seemed much troubled with Ephraim in consequence of his inclination to play the truant.

Evening she was alone, and sent for us to come over to eat melons, said she expected bro and sis Hanks. We went but they did not come.

Thurs 28th I ironed. Lois came in and invited me to come and spend the Pm with them. Said they expected Franklin Dewey's wife and her sister Shepperd. It was quite late in the Pm before I felt able to go. I enjoyed a few hours very agreeably. They are the daughters of bro B[art] Smithson.

Frid 29th I took a walk in co with sister and her daughters Ellen and Lois, to sister Pattens. On arriving found them both absent. Ellen and myself went in pursuit of them, as far as bro Hawes, where we learned that she was out on her professional service as midwife. We called a few minutes at bro [Gashum] Cases, he is a cooper, was making churns, which he said he sold for 3 dolls ~~and a half~~. We had a pleasant call at sister Hawes. Saw a great curiosity, a California lions skin Stuffed; it was a large one, and being crowded full it made a frightful appearance. She said that her husband and a young man who lived with them killed it. She treated us to melons and after resting awhile, we returned. Ellen and Lois commenced getting dinner, and before it was quite ready we saw Mr Patten and wife coming. They were much pleased to see us, made us welcome, and expressed themselves sorry that we found them absent. We had a good dinner, and good appetites to enjoy it. Sister Patten was very sociable, and the old gent remarkably good humored. Returned just as the sun was down I brought home milk and butter, in exchange for tea and flower which we carried them. On reaching home found the Deseret news and a letter from bro Taite, who has reached G—— S—— L city.

Sat 30th I finished several jobs of sewing. Sister P—— came over in the Pm, took dinner with me. We had sociable times, as usualy.

Sun 31st. This morning I had a sore throat, did not arise in season to get ready for church; therefore staid at home, and wrote a letter to sister Pickett. Evening came in Wm and Ellen McGary, and took supper with us After supper sister came in, and invited us over to spend the evening with her. I went, and Mr C came shortly after. The young people prepared to go to singing school, but met company, and returned. Bro and sister Hanks, and sister McIntire came. Tailor Crosby and Harriet Hunt were also in. We were treated to melons, had music on the violin and flutina. It was the first opportunity I ever had to become much acquainted with sister Hanks. Think her an agreeable person.

[Bringing Home a Cow]

San Bernardino, California

Mon Sept. 1st AD 1856. Fine day. I rose earlier than usually, prepared breakfast for Mr C—— and after he was gone, I finished a letter to sister Pickett, and took it over to sisters for them to give to the Stage driver as he passed. Returned and washed. Alma built a correll preparatory to receiving a cow, which we expected Mr Crosby would bring home with him from bro Dewey's. About sunset A—— went to Crismans to meet his father, and assist him in driving her home, but both returned without her, as his cows did not come home untill near bedtime. I was somewhat disappointed, but said nothing. Husband said they would go again early in the morning, and they would be sure to find her.

Tues 2nd they went at an early hour and soon brought her. Johny and myself ran out to see the new cow and calf, and were highly pleased with them. J—— called the calf his, and I of course claimed the cow. He spent 2 or 3 days in feeding, and watering them, and seemed unwilling to leave them a moment, boasted to the neighbors that <u>our</u> <u>cow</u> <u>gave</u> <u>good</u> <u>sweet</u> <u>milk</u>. Evening Mary Dickson called, and invited me to a quilting the next day. Mr Mills came and ate melons with us.

Wed 3rd I ironed. Sisters Pratt, Lois, and sis Grouard, came along, and called for me, but I declined going, as I had plenty of business at home, and had promised sister Patten the next day to help her quilt.

Thurs 4th I did not feel quite well, however sister P—— came along at ten oclock; and I accompanied her to the quilting.

We had a pleasant walk; found quite a small company, consisting of sisters Hughs, Haws and Eames. Sister Patten had a colored woman to assist her in cooking. She made us a nice dinner and supper. A young man called by the name of Anson Vanluven, who brought us home.

Alma and I spent the evening with sister Pratt. Daniel Rathbone [Rathbun] married Sally Ann Garner this Pm. The girls all gone to the wedding. About 8 oclock the co came to E D—— Daily's to dance and the girls came in to change dresses.

Frid 5th Very warm day. I baked pies. Sister Pratt called and wished me to come over and stop awhile with her. Said she was alone, girls gone to a quilting to Wm Matthews.

Ellen and Wm commence housekeeping yesterday.

Evening came Ann L and a miss Button, and invited Alma to go with them to a party at Wm Matthews, and requested him to take his violin with him. Accordingly he went and assisted Wm McGary for which he gave him 1 doll.

Sat 6th I churned 1 lb. and 3/4 of butter for the first from our new cow. Pm Sister was in awhile, brought letter from Frances.

Sund—— 7th I stoped at home.[42] Wrote a letter to bro Taite.

Evening took a walk to bro Davises. Saw their new babe, a fine boy. Bro D—— and his sister Anna came home with us, and ate melons, and we gave them a large one to carry home with them.

Mon 8th I went to bro Cases to buy a churn, he was gone and had none on hand. Came back and took dinner at sister Pattens.

She and her husband were going to a funeral. Bro Gilbert buried a babe 10 days old, died with irresipilis.[43] Johny and I rode home with them as they went. Sis P—— lent me a small churn.

PM I copied a letter for my husband to br J M Horner in answer to one from him.

Tues 9th I washed. Sister P—— in again. Wanted me to walk with her. I declined on account of business. Churned. Mr C—— went to bro Riches and carried the letters, intending to send by him, when he goes to San F.

Evening Sister in again. Said she had been looking at a cow, and thought of buying her. Girls all gone to a party; Wanted me to go over with her and stop awhile. I went and staid an hour or more. She seemed sad and lonely. The girls gone almost every night, and she alone ^with nothing to do but reflect.^

Sept Wed 10th Had an invitation to br Haikes's to a quilting, but could not go. Had promised sister Patten the next day, and did not feel able to go two successive days. I ironed Louisa Ann came in and sewed for me awhile, got dinner and washed the dishes. I cut 4 shirts for John Taite.

Thurs 11th. We went at half past ten oclock to sister Pattens, found quite a collection of sisters both old and young. We worked on 3 different quilts, one had been in the frames a week. we finished that, and nearly finished another, and got the third on the frames, besides we sewed some on a dress for herself. She got two good meals for us, had 14 different sorts on her tables. Evening several gents came in, and we danced a few cotillions. We reached home before 10 oclock. Beautiful moonlight night.

Frid 12th Very warm day. I baked light bread, churned, and performed sundry other services. Evening went into Sisters a few minutes.

Sat 13th Rather more comfortable. I went in and sat awhile with Ellen.

Sun 14th I atttended church, felt quite unwell, prayed to the Lord to remove all pain and distress from my body, and in a short time I was quite easy. But before the meeting closed Johny began to be very fretful, and wished me to come home with him. Accordingly I left and came home, about 12 oclock. The meeting continued near 4 hours. Evening took a walk with my husband and sis L P, went to bro Hammond's. They have a very sick child, a little boy they brought from the islands, has the typhus fever. A bro Green and Snider board there. The two sister Hunts came in awhile. The little boy very weak, I promised to send them a chicken for him.

Mon 15th Very warm. Alma went over with the fowl, the child no better. Evening called at Jacksons store, bought 6 yds of calico for Elizabeth Falks. From thence I went in co—— with sister L P—— to bro Sealy's. Mr C—— came in after us, and we had a fine feast of peaches and melons. Brought home a few peaches. Beautiful evening, had a pleasant walk.

Tues 16th. I washed. Alma went for wood with Mr Patten. Afterwards went to the mill, and brought home a load of flour. Bro Kipp sold out to the city his house, for a prison, or jail, put his goods in our Shop, for a short time.

Evening had an invitation to bro Hunts to a singing or music party, but did not feel able to attend. Alma went with Wm and Ellen.

Wed 17th Extremely warm day. I baked bread pies &C.

[Some Very Good Parties]

Thurs 18th Am I went to br Denis's for tinware. Pm Alma went to Santo [*illegible*] to a party, and ride. A 4 horse team came from there and took the musicians, Wm McGary, and Henry Jacksen with their wives, and Alma and Lois. Sister P—— had co—— sisters Stark and Delinn. I went over and spent the Pm with them. Sister Patten called a few minutes. Evening I was over again, Sister was alone, with the exception of Eph— and Charley Bills. I staid with her untill 10 oc.

Fri 19th remarkably warm. The co—— returned between 11 and 12 oclock perfectly covered with dust. A's eyes were very bad. I think he was very well pleased with the party. Pm I was over again a short time. We had high winds accompanied with a little rain, hardly sufficient to lay the dust, which is now very deep. The thunder cooled the air some, which made it rather more agreeable.

Sat 20th quite cloudy in the Am, near 12 the sun shone out again, warm. I baked puddings and pies, churned, and performed sundries.

Helen Combs called, said they had heard that we had moved away over toward the burying ground. wanted a watermelon for her mother. I have just been rereading a letter from sister Lockwood. They talk of leaving Ohio and going to Ill, where several of their children are already gone.

Sun 21st Very pleasant morning, not as warm as previously. I attended church in company with Mr C—— and Johny. Heard bro Farnham give a history of his travels in Aus) ~~they~~ Was succeeded by bro Rich, and Flemming. Meeting very lengthy. Evening I went into Ellens awhile. Mr C—— and Wm Mc—— went to hear the newcomers from Aus——, sing. I came home and wrote a short letter to sister Dolly Lockwood. Ellen came over, and wrote to sis—— Evans. We wrote untill ten oclock, when Wm came after her.

Mon 22nd, comfortably cool. I washed. Chastina McMurtry came, and spent several hours with me. She had been to the store. Her father called, and took her home behind him, on horseback. I told him to bring his wife the next day, as he said he was coming again. Party this evening at sister Sparks house, by John Christian. Alma went, and escorted Lois P——. I spent the evening with sister. She read a letter she had been writing to her husband. I think it will soften his heart <u>some</u> if he ever gets it.

Tues 23rd Sister Combs called and spent an hour or two. ^shortly after came sister Patten^ About 12 came sisters MacMurty and Tomkins, also came sis Pratt. I sent for Louisa to come and assist me in cook. She came and lent a helping hand. I dressed chickens, made pies and &C. Ellen, Wm——, and bro MacMurtry came to supper. Lois came also. I had the table twice full. Had a very good party, or visit.

Wed 24th I ironed baked, fixed my cupboard against the ants, and fatigued myself very much. Sis L P in a few minutes.

Evening Alma brought home grapes from bro Smithsons, which his father had bought. They looked beautiful, and nice. We hung them in the chamber to dry.

Thurs 25th he brought another bucket full, which made 34 lbs. I was sick part of the day.

Frid 26th Am regulated my domestic affairs, and Pm went to bro Hammonds, to see the sick child, a little half breed that came from the Sandwich islands with them. Found him very weak and low; with typhus fever. Staid 2 hours or more, and returned.

Bro Skelton called while I was in, and anointed <u>his</u>, the little boys, bowels with consecrated oil, and turpentine, mixed. Sister D Thomas was there, assisting sis H——, and an elderly lady by the name of Westover was staying there. bro Daniel Thomas called, and told me that my husband had been appointed to the office of teacher, in this district. Said they wished him to go around, and take the census, and report at conference, the 6th of Oct. Said the council thought he was getting very worldly, and concluded to try him in Spiritual things, or his faithfulness, in spiritual things.[44]

Sat 27th Sister Grouard called between 12 and 1 oclock. Spent a couple of hours with me. I made a cup of tea, and got her a light dinner. She informed me that her husband intended removing to upper California before many months. thought he would go to Nevada, where he had a brother living. She left between 2 and 3 oclock, to go to the store; thought she should stay overnight with sister Pratt.

Sun 28th I spent at home. Very warm day. Pm came sisters Pratt and Eleanor Morse. Staid short time. Evening we took a walk to bro Hunts, to visit a sick bro, late from Aus——. An old gent by the name of White. Found a bro Skelten at sister Pratts, who walked over with her, and us. He spoke some concerning his mission to Indie Said he had no faith in the Hindoes and did not believe that they were of the seed of Israel.

Mon 29th. I washed sister came in toward noon, staid and spent the Pm, assisted in getting dinner. Ellen came in and took dinner with us. I was much fatigued, and slept very soundly

Tues 30th rose early, and at ten accompanied sis P—— to a quilting to sister Pattens. She invited quite a number, but only 4 came. Sisters Parks, and Tomkins. It was very warm. I worked quite steadyly, had a very good party, and dinner. Rode home with sis Tomkins.

Wed Oct 1st I was very unwell, and after sprinkling clothes, I went to bed, but shortly after came sisters Pratt, and Hopkins and insisted on my rising, and going to sisters to visit with them. I arose, and adjusted my hair and apparel, and went over. Felt very miserable all the Pm. Evening Mr C brought home papers. Deseret news. Western Standard, and Mormon.

Thurs 2nd I ironed, made a cup of tea for dinner, and after eating I felt very sick. Went to bed quite distressed, but toward night got better.

Frid 3rd I had a very sick day. Sent Johny over to ask sister to come and see me, but he failed to do the errand, and consequently she did not come untill evening, when she and Ellen came in awhile. Wm also came and conversed awhile. I was very unwell through the night, toward morning Mr C arose and prepared me some soda powders, which seemed to relieve me immediately, and I went to sleep, and rested well.

Sat 4th I felt much better, but had a very lame back, could scarcely stoop without great caution. I resorted to my new remedy. Cold water; wet a linen towel, and laid it four thicknesses on my back. In a few hours it was almost entirely free from pain. And in the Pm I walked over to sisters. Lois had a quilt on the frames, and Harriet Hunt was there assisting her. I quilted a very little. Louisa agreed to come home with me, to help cook something for sunday, but she was obliged to go to the library,[45] and could not come untill evening, when she came, and made a couple of pies. I felt quite well at night, rested finely.

[A Family Ride to Agua Mansa]

Sun 5th Fine morning. Mr C went church. I stoped at home, was rather poorly. PM sister sent over to me, to make myself ready for a ride with bro Anson Vanleuven, said he was coming to take the ~~fatii atoa~~ ^whole family^ out to a ride. When Mr C returned from church he informed me that bro Amasa Lyman had arrived from G—— S—— L City, and had preached to the people that day. I was rejoiced to hear of his safe arrival, and that he still enjoyed the holy spirit and was ready to administer intelligence to the saints in San B——d——o. At two oclock we set off on our ride. Bro had intended going to Mr Roubideaux, but in consequence of get so late a start he took us to Agua Mansa, another Spanish settlement nearer, where we found a plenty of grapes, but no peaches. We found the people very friendly and polite to us, though living in true California Spanish style. No floors or glass in their windows, and they themselves sitting on the ground, or on sheepskins. However their habitations had an appearance of neatness about them. We passed a small catholic church, with a dwelling house attached where their priest resided. On returning saw the priest walking on the summit of a high bluff just in the rear of the church. We remarked that he looked very priestly with his long black dress. We reached home at a litttle past 8 oclock. Johny and I walked from the corner above us and brought his hat full of grapes to Mr C, and Alma who was in here. I certainly felt much refreshed, and revived after my ride.

We discovered that the Spanish people took a fancy to Johny, and asked several questions concerning him, which I answered to the best of my ability.[46] The Land Lord gave him a large cluster of grapes to bring home.

Mon 6th of Oct our annual conference was adjourned for one week. Mr C gone to court, has been chosen as grand juryman.

Tues 7th I washed. Ann Louisa came and assisted me some. Pm took a walk with Ellen Mc—— to bro Hunts, where we met with sisters Blackburn and Pratt, who went in the Am. We had a pleasant call, reached home before dark, received letters from bro Pratt and Frances. He had arrived in San F.

Wed 8th Ann came again, and sewed for me. Bro Smithson sent us 64 lbs of grapes. Alma digging the foundation of our new house. Evening we went into sister Pratts, and afterwards into bro Coxes where we had a pleasant interview, and were treated to peaches.

[A Dreadful Wind]

Thurs 9th dreadful wind, the air thick with dust; everything covered. I felt sick, pain in my bones, and headache. Evening we were invited to Wm Mc's to a little dance we went over, found bro Blackburn and wife there, also Ed—— Daily who insisted on our going to his house to dance, as his wife was unable to leave home in consequence of ill health. Accordingly we went over. I called at sisters a few minutes and she went in with me. We found a house full of young people, who had been disappointed of a party in another place, and many of them had resorted there, to spend a few hours in dancing.

There were 2 violins and a base drum. We staid a couple of hours, and returned. I stoped a short time with sister, and she came home with me. We heard a rumor of Frances being married to J Dier.[47]

Frid 10th another very windy day. Felt very much afflicted, and took my bed. Ann L staid with us part of the day. Toward evening the wind abated and I had a great time in cleaning the dust from everything in the house. Evening we were invited to bro Rollins to a party, but I did not feel in humor of going. Mr Crosby went at a late hour with Ellen. Alma reading the late Western Standard.

[*added later: 1856*] *Sat Oct 11th* I arose fearing we were to have another blustering day, as the old setlers had informed me that when the wind commenced at this season, it usually blew 3 days before it abated. Last night I besought the Lord to rebuke the wind inasmuch as it was consistent with his will, and to my great joy it continued calm throughout the day. Sister L B's birthday.

Sun 12th was the commencement of our semiannual conference. I attended church. Saw br Lyman for the first since his return from G S L. He spoke to the people with much power and spirit.

Pm singing at Wm McGarys. Evening took a walk to bro Skinners with my husband and sister L P——. Had a pleasant interview. Sister Skinner made me a present of a few peaches.

We were introduced to a young Aus—— sister who lives there, by the name of Elizabeth Guy. I admired her much, told her we had cousins by that name.

Mon 13th the conference continued. I attended in the morning. Pm staid at home. Evening went into sister Pratts. Sister Sherwood was there. Soon came in bro and sis Hunt, sister Jane Morse, Dr McIntire and wife. Said they were going into bro McGary's. Accordingly we accompanied them. Sister Matilda Carter formerly Lyman was there, but soon left. In the course of the evening we danced a few cotillions, which went off with considerable glee. Dr Mc—— was a new beginner and made many apologies, but we finally persuaded him to join us. His great reluctance, and entreaties to be excused, excited much risibility.

Tues 14th I washed. Pm came sister Davis and little daughter. She staid and spent the evening, her husband came up and accompanied her home.

Wed 15th ironed, and baked, made peach preserves. Sister P—— came and invited me to walk with her to bro Andrews, to get grapes. The sun was set before we left, but we had a pleasant walk.

Bro and sis Jones came in. Bro Andrews gave each of us four or five pounds each of grapes. We stoped untill the moon rose, and then returned. There was a party of dancers at Wm McG——ys when we reached home.

Thurs 16th I cleaned house, ironed some, put down my carpet &C. Evening Mr Crosby attend a singing party at Col Jacksons. I spent the evening with sister Pratt, girls gone to a party at bishop Crosby

Frid 17th beautiful day. Toward night took a walk with sister Pratt. Called at bro Warrens, then continued our walk as far as bro Hammonds. Had a pleasant time. He informed us that he was going the next day to Pueblo, or Los Angeles, to purchase materials for shoemaking. We reached home about 8 oclock. Bro Hammond came with us.

Sat 18th I made a large soup, or fresh beaf stew. Sister Pratt and Ephraim were here and dined with us. Just as it was ready came the Kanacka sisters, and their children, sisters Hill and Kipp.[48] They all dined, and seemed to relish it finely.

After they left, <u>we</u>, <u>sister and</u> I, took a walk to sister Pattens. Found her very unwell with a cold; she had a quilt on the frames and nearly finished. We sat down and quilted a few minutes. They had a family in the house with them, whom they called the widow Martin and her children. She informed us that she came from G S—— L city with a bro Wells as his wife, but left him, and married a Mr Dart, with whom she lived less than a year, and parted with him, because he wished her to live on bread and water, when there was a plenty in the house. We reached home before dark.

Sun 19th cool and comfortable day. I attended meeting, and was much interested with a discourse from bro Lyman, also an exhortation from bro Rich. Singing in the evening at Wm Mc's.

Mon 20 rather rainy. Sister Pratt and Ann L—— went to the Monti with bro Button. Intending to be gone a week or two on a visit, to San Gabriel and Los Angeles. PM I visited at Ellens with sisters Morse and Daily. Evening Mr C—— gone to attend a lecture to be delivered before the library association, by elder Lyman.

Tues 21st I arose with a lame back, could scarcely get about. After breakfast concluded to wash. Got my hands warm in the hot water, and my system well warmed by washing, and felt much relieved. Bro Paul Smith called a few minutes. Rain last night. Mr Crosby at home today, making preparations for the mason, whom he expects tomorrow, to commence our house.

[Commencing the New House]

Wed 22nd I also felt very lame. After breakfast came bro Mowrey, and commenced work on the new house.[49] Lois came over and assisted me in getting dinner. Wm and Ellen also took dinner with us.

Pm I accompanied Ellen Mc, and Lois P to sister Morses, where we met sister Denitia Lyman, and her mother, old sister Walker. Two sister Rollins's, and others. Had a very sociable time, though short. Made many inquiries concerning my old associates in G S L city. Reached home just as the sun was setting.

Thurs 23rd rather windy and unpleasant. Bro Mowrey came early to his work, took breakfast with us. Wm came also, and worked with him. Ellen came over and assisted me about dinner. At. 4 Pm she went to bro, or col Jacksons to singing school.

Frid 24th I felt very lame, but was obliged to work very steadily. Had four men to cook for. Ellen came and assisted. Sister Jackson made us a call and dined with us.

Sat 25th I picked tomatoes.

Sun 26th. This is the 22nd anniversary of our wedding day. I felt fatigued and staid at home from church. Evening called over Wm Mc——s, where we met a bro and sister Chase, and daughter, They were formerly from G S L city, came away the same spring that we did, have been living 6 years away from the church, and now concluded to return. We had a very social time with them. In the course of the evening came bros Snider and John T Caine late from the Sandwich island mission.

Mon 27th Beautiful day. The masons are hurrying up the house. PM received a visit from sister Combs. Ellen assisted me and took tea with us.

Tues 28th quite blustering. The masons are trying to finish the house today. Bro John T Caine made us a visit. I admire him very much, as a faithful saint.

Wed 29th Very windy. Pm bro Mowrey came and finished the laying of the addobies.

Thurs 30th Still windy, but quite warm. Mr C—— at work in the shop. Alma wheeling addobies from the ruins of the old house, to make a chimney in the wood part.

Friday 31st, and last day of Oct '56. Fine day. Washed, baked &C. In consequence of having workmen to cook for, was obliged to defer untill today what should have been in the early part of the week. Ellen came over and assisted me, and it passed off tolerably easy.

Received a line from sister L B P from Los Angeles, had reached sister Pickets, and found them well, and very pleasantly situated. They had just removed into town, and had a housefull of sewing.

Sat the first of November, beautiful day. Mr Crosby gone to work on the merchant Jackson's store. Evening carried a dozen and half of chicks to him. Bought me new shoes, and sundry other articles.

Sun the 2nd. Cloudy and cool. Last night I dreamed of seeing Frances and J Dyer, also bro Pratt; thought they came home together. Frances looked very fleshy, and well, but br J, her husband, was sick with fever and ague. Bro P—— seemed very distant, and not inclined to speak at first, but after I gave him my hand, sister P gave hers, and he said he wished us to forget and forgive the past &C.

I went with my husband, Alma and Johny, to the bowery, but found the meeting was removed to the schoolhouses. I, therefore returned with John but Alma and his father went to meeting. Pm the sun shines very pleasantly.

Mon 3rd Sent a letter to sister Pratt. Directed to San Gabriel. Washed, and performed several other important offices. Evening Wm and Ellen were in awhile.

Tues 4th wrought in the door yard the most of the Am. Pm went to a quilting to bro Silas Harris'es. Had a very sociable time. Returned in co—— with sister Wellington Sealy.

Great serenading, and electioneering for representatives, today.[50]

Wed 5th This is bro Cyprians birthday, he is 56 years old. I ironed &C.

Thurs 6th I visited at Ellen Mc'——s with sister Lyman and her daughter sister Carter. Sister L came home with me to see my new house. I showed our specimens of shells and corals which we brought from the islands. She promised to come and make me a visit as soon as sister Pratt came home.

Frid 7th This is Frances birthday. Ellen Mc—— had a quilting. I assisted her. Two letters arrived. One from bro Pratt and Frances, and another from sister Lavina and her daughter Lydia.

Sat 8th I spent in cooking. We received another line from sister P Said she was coming home this week. Wm McG—— quite unwell. Ellen came in to get salts in the morning, and evening she came for herbs to make tea. I gave her cayenne pepper.

Sund 9th I attended church at the schoolhouse. Bro Lyman preached on the subject of charity, told it consisted in something beside merely giving to the poor; read or repeated some of the 13th chap of cor——[inthians] 1st. We were all much edified with his discourse. On returning fell in co with bro and sister Hammond, who invited us to stop and see their new residence, which is in John Holiday's chamber.

After we reached the chamber they insisted on our staying to tea, to which we finally consented. Had a pleasant interview with them.

On returning called at br Cox'es. Found her very low with fever, had been sick 2 or 3 weeks, and I had not heard of it, and had not been into see her. I thought it very strange as we lived so near, felt somewhat chagrined.[51]

Mond 10th. This is sister L P——'s birthday. I washed. Mr C building chimney. Evening we went into see sister Cox. Found her some better. Bro and sister Sullivan were in. We staid a couple of hours.

Tues 11th very warm and pleasant. Mr C—— still at work on the chimney. Evening called sister Morse and Charlotte. I ran in to see sis Cox, Said she did not feel quite as well, feared she had eaten too much. She had just been up had her bed made and was too much exhausted to converse.

Wed 12th I ironed, made light bread. Mr C—— and A worked at Crismans. Evening Mr C brought home 25 lbs of sugar. I had an invitation to a quilting at sister Morses, but was too busy to attend. Evening wrote in my journal.

[Sister Pratt's Return from San Gabriel]

Thurs 13th I went to bro Rollins's, to help sister Morse on her quilt Left home at 1 oclock. Had a pleasant time, worked as long as I could see, came along and called at bro Hammonds. Just as I was coming away, met sister Pratt on the stairs. She had come in on the stage in my absence. A Mrs Burns from San Gabriel came with her. I was pleased to meet her after near 3 weeks absence. We returned home together. And shortly after she came over to go with me to a party at Wm McGary's. We all went and staid untill 9 oclock when we returned, and left the young people to enjoy it by themselves.

Frid 14th I had a tea party. Bro and sis Hammond with their children Sister Hunt, Mrs Burns, Sister Pratt. and Bro and sis McGary, all took supper with us. Sister H left at early candlelight but the remainder of the co spent the evening

Sat 15th Very warm and pleasant for the season. No rains yet. Sister was in again, and took dinner with me. Evening I called upon Ellen and Mrs Burns. Took Mrs B's babe over to sis P's.

Sun 16th I attended church with my husband. Heard bro B[enjamin] Matthews relate the history of his travels in the Southern states. Evening attended a singing party at sis P's.

Mon 17th Washed and baked bread. Evening Mr C putting lock on the front door. Rather dull times. Sisters Hill and Kipp called a short time.

Tues 18th Alma laying addobies in the kitchen. I felt rather gloomy.

Evening Mr C gone to the teachers meeting. Sisters Pratt and Morse called, and invited me over to Ellens. I went and found Hannah Rollins, Harriet Hunt, Mrs Burns, and Lois B P. Spent the time rather agreeably untill 9 oclock, when I returned and found Mr C setting glass for Col Jackson. Sister Phillips called in search of a house to rent or buy.

Wed 19th Very boisterous day. The air was some of the time so thick with dust, that we could look at the sun with as much ease as we gaze on the moon. Mr C and Al—— putting the roof on the new house. Capt Hunt brought a load of lumber for Hill. I had a great time in the evening cleaning the dust from the beds, dishes &C. It makes me feel rather impatient, but I try to bear it as easy as I can. I slept none untill after 1 oclock. This is my mothers birthday.

Thurs 20th it still continues blowing, though not as hard as yesterday. Pm it became calm, and I went with sister L P to see sister Cox.

Frid 21st We had some rain, barely sufficient to lay the dust. Evening we went into bro Wm McGary's. Saw Mr Burns from Mission San Gabriel he had come for his wife. Bro Hanks was in, just returned from the upper Cal—— Informed us that he stoped with Frances and her father several days.

Sat 22nd Still continues to rain by turns. The men still at work on the house. Evening Sisters Pratt and Morse were in. We all went to a candy pulling at bro McGary's.

Sun Nov 23rd Quite rainy. Mr C and Alma putting boards on the new house to prevent it's washing.[52] I staid at home from meeting in consequence of rain. Br A Farnsworth called a few minutes. Alma and his father gone to church. PM I called into Ellens to see Mrs Burns about taking Emily Combs home with her. While I was there, there came up a very profuse shower of rain, but it lasted only a few minutes.

Mon 24th quite pleasant. Mr and Mrs Burns went home in an open carriage. Did not conclude to take the little girl. I washed.

Evening Mr C fixing clock for bro Harris. Father Harris was in awhile.

Tues 25th rather pleasant. Bro Morse brought us shingles, and Mr C—— and Alma commenced laying them. I called in to see sister Phillips late from Aus——. She lives in bro—— Ridley's house. Evening Mr C—— and bro Moses Harris set off in their office as teachers, to visit the members of this district.

Wed 26th fine weather. I ironed, made a good supper, and invited sister Phillips and her family, consisting of a son and daughter, to eat with me, but my invitation was too late as she had hers nearly ready, but said she would come the next evening. Evening I went into see sister Pratt. Found Lois alone, said her mother was into sister Ed Daily's. Accordingly I went over to see her, found sis D—— in bed with a young son. I informed sister P—— that the teachers had called to see her, she therefore left soon and came back with me.

They conversed some, and she invited them to pray, which they did. I returned before 9 oclock, found that Johny T—— had gone away in search of me, and had not returned. I started Alma over to Ellens in search of him, but he staid so long that I went myself, as I could not feel willing to go to bed untill I knew he was safely lodged in his. I found quite a co of young folk collected there, and John asleep on E's bed.

Thurs 27th Fine pleasant day. Mr C and Alma hurrying on the shingles. Pm, came sisters Phillips and her little daughter Elizabeth. Sisters Pratt and McGary. At supper time sent for young Phillips who came over, and we enjoyed a cheerfull meal together.

Evening we went out expecting to find a prayer meeting at the schoolhouse, but was disappointed.

Frid 28th I spent a great portion of the time in reading the Deseret news. Read also in the evening. Find the papers very interesting.

Sat 29th cloudy. Mr C fixing floor over the well. Alma topping out the chimney. Sister Grouard called a few minutes. Evening Mr C gone to teachers meeting.

Sun 30th Tolerably pleasant. Mr C—— and A gone to church. I stoped at home, wrote letter to Lavina Baker.

Evening all gone to meeting. I finished my letter.

Monday Dec 1st '56. This is my bro Lymans birthday, is now 52 ys. Cold wind. I washed, had an invitation to a quilting. PM sis L P—— in awhile. I did not finish my washing. Sister spent the evening. Mr C—— gone to Dennis's.

Tues 2nd I put out my clothes. PM went to quilting at Gilbert Rolf's. Had quite a pleasant time, same ten or dozen sisters present, all very agreeable.

Wed 3rd I ironed. Cooked fresh meat soup, ~~invited~~ Evening Mr Crosby went to a singing party at Col Jacksons. Young Phillips and his sister spent the evening with us.

Thurs 4th Quite pleasant. Sister spent a few hours with me.

We had an invitation to an oister supper at Wm McG——'s, but as it was our weekly prayer meeting night we declined accepting it. Attended meeting, enjoyed a good degree of the holy Spirit.

Friday 5th quite cold and unpleasant.

Sat 6th Helen Combs[53] came up and assisted me in mending.

Evening Mr Crosby gone to the teachers meeting. Alma visiting at sister Phillips's.

Sun 7th Fine day. Attended church. Bro Lyman preached long and strong to us. Proclaimed against the dancing in this place. Called on the home missionaries to be diligent in preaching reform to the saints in S—— B——d——o.[54] I acquiesced heartily in what he said. Evening I attended again, had a lively meeting. Enjoyed a good degree of the Spirit of God.

[A "Working Bee"]

Mon 8th fine day. I washed. Helen came again. I felt bad, all the Am. Pm felt much better.

Beautiful evening. Johny and I took a walk, went home with Helen. Staid a few minutes, and then came home by sister P's, called a short time. Sister making pies and preparing for a bee, or party of brethren whom she had invited to get her wood for winter.

Tues 9th I made pies. Helen stoped with her mother. Evening Elizabeth Phillips was here, very pleasant night.

Wed 10th Alma and I put up tapa[55] in the kitchen. Sister came over after dishes, and invited us all over to supper. I got ready as soon as possible and went. Took hold in the kitchen to help Lois. Set three tables together. Mr C put in a window today in her kitchen. The brethren and sisters gathered in at suppertime, and filled the tables. Seventeen ate at the first table, and ten or twelve at the second. She had a genteel variety, and all seemed well pleased with it. Pres Cox presided, and gave us the privilege of dancing as much as we pleased. We enjoyed it finely, untill 12 oclock, when the co dispersed.

11th Thurs Helen came again, I ironed. Mr C killed two pigs. Tho Phillips assisted. Evening went to prayer meeting. Brethren quite zealous.

12th Frid I was very busy taking care of the pork.

Helen did not come to help me. Sister was over in the Pm. Took supper with us. Evening she invited several of the friends of Minerva Morse to come in to her house to pray for her, as she was at the Mission San Gabriel very sick. Was taken at Mr Stoctons where she was at work, but went to Mr Halls where Ann Louisa Pratt was living. Her mother and Harriet Hunt went down to see her, and had sent back a request to the saints to remember her in their prayers. I went over with Wm and Ellen. Sister Hunt was present, bro Cox came in. we sang a hymn. How firm a foundation.

After which br C, prayed, and was succeeded by sister Pratt. I believe we all felt comforted afterwards. And with regard to myself my faith was strong that she would be healed.

13th Sat. rather cold. I made sausages, mended some. Pm, a lady called with a clock to get repaired. Evening Mr C gone to meeting, to report himself as teacher.

Sun 14th Alma's birthday. 20 years old. We all went to church. Enjoyed a good degree of the holy Spirit. Dudly Chase came over with his carriage, ^and after meeting^ ~~and~~ took us all to his fathers, near the mill, Sister Pratt Ellen Lois and myself, with Ephraim and Johny. We had a pleasant ride and a fine visit. Brother Chase exhibited some pictures in a little machinery called a polyorama. It was quite a curiosity to us. There were thirteen different scenes, besides the night scenes.

Shortly after dark he brought us home. We spent a few hours at sisters on our way home, and were joined by another young Chase, and a Mr Anderson, who lives at bro Chases.

Mon 15th I did not feel very well. Helen came and spent the day with me. Baked bread and pies. Evening Mr C gone to seventies meeting.

Tues 16th Helen came up and informed me that her mother had got an addition of another daughter to her family. Which makes her five in number, and only one son.

I washed Elizabeth Phillips came and assisted me some. After we got through and the supper ready I sent her after her mother to come and eat with us. We had a social time. Bro Goodwin called at the door, also a bro White.

Wed 17th rather cold and windy. I went to see sister Combs. found her quite unwell, thought she had taken cold. Spent an hour or more, and returned, called on sister Moses Harris a few moments. When we reached home, found the house locked, and all gone, went into sister Phillips and sat awhile, had an introduction to a bro Jones from Aus——

Mr C—— and Alma went and were baptised. Evening they went to a confirmation meeting. Rain tonight. They came home quite wet.

Thurs 18th Ironed. Sister in a while. Evening cold wind. I accompanied my husband to the prayermeeting. few attended.

Frid 19th. I worked at papering my kitchen. Evening sewed on my bedquilt. ^Called sisters Grouard and Kipp, also sis Patten.^ Felt quite unwell in the night.

Sat 20th. Still papering, worked myself very tired. Sister Eleanor Morse called. Johny quite afflicted with a bad cold. Night I bathed him

in warm water, put consecrated oil on his throatt and stomach. Gave him
some inwardly with molasses. Heard Minerva Morse no better.

Sun 21st Very warm and pleasant, but Johny so unwell I could not
take him to meeting, and so stoped at home with him. Took a walk to see
sister Combs. Evening I intended going, but was prevented by company.
Sister Phillips with her son and daugh.

[Baptism]

Mon 22nd Another fine day. I felt very unwell. At ten oclock went down
to the baptising. Quite a large collection. Several persons went in before
me. I had been dreading it, and found it even as I anticipated. I believe I
made some noise, but not the only one. After baptism the females went
into sister Raisers to change dress. ^John Holiday officiated.^ She was
very kind, and made us welcome. I felt so much better after coming out
of the water that I desired to praise and bless the Lord. I was wholly free
from pain of any kind.[56]

Called with my husband at the P O—— found a dagurotype of Lois
Thompson, and her infant daughter. Alma worked for Mr Patten.

Evening went to the confirmation meeting, confirmed by elder
Hammond. Bro Hopkins recorder. Bro Lyman lectured us some time
before and after. I was highly edified with his remarks.

Tues 23rd Sister Hammond called early to enquire for a little girl,
went to see one of bro Combs. I washed, baked light bread, churned, and
performed sundry other tasks.

Wed 24th I sent an invitation to bro and sister Hammond and family to take a Chrismas supper with us the next day, also sent to sis Patten
invited sister Pratt, bro and sister McGary. Worked very steadily to prepare for the coming festival. Evening Mr C fixing a clock for bro Whipple.
Alma and I went over to see a star that sis P had made for Crismas eve.

[A Christmas Party at the Crosbys]

Thurs 25th Chrismas day. I baked a fowl made a chicken pie made sweet
cakes arranged my house in the best order possible. Helen Combs came
to help me. About 2 oclock came sister Patten, at 3 sister Hammond and
Pratt, Ellen McGary &C. I also invited sister Phillips and daughter but
they were previously engaged. Bro Hammond and the little boys crowned
the company. I enjoyed the party finely. My supper or rather dinner
answered my expectations, and also those of my guests. I received many
compliments from them. After dinner sister Patten left us, though very
reluctantly. She expressed a strong desire to spend the evening with us,
but circumstances would not permit. At 8 oclock we had singing, and

prayers by br Ham[mond] and soon after he left with his family. Sister P—— and Ellen staid sometime longer, and conversation became quite interesting upon the subject of the spirits, and Spiritualism. Mr Crosby and sister P—— could not see exactly alike upon the subject. Mr C—— as usually denounced it—and thought the saints should have nothing to do with it.

Frid 26th Quite warm and pleasant. Sister came over and cut pants for Alma, sister Cox accompanied her, and made me her first visit. I felt fatigued, and not as cheerful as I wished to. Evening Mr C went to meeting, came home with a bad cold on his lungs.

Sat 27th Sister came and sewed for me again. Evening I finished the pants, wrote some in my journal. Mr C—— gone to the teachers meeting. Came home with bad cough, took a sweat, drank freely of pepper tea, and perspired profusely. He felt some better in the morn but did not attend church. I went, accompanied by Johny and Alma.

Sun 28th On returning, sister invited us to call and take supper with her, which we accepted. Just after sitting down to the table Ann Louise arrived in a carriage with Moses Martin, direct from San Gabriel where she had been stopping for two months past. She brought intelligence from Minerva Morse, they think she is a very little better. Sun evening rain falls profusely, I wanted to attend prayermeeting but neither of the men folks wished to attend me, and therefore all at home.

Mon 29th Very wet and unpleasant. I baked bread for Alma to take to the mountains. He talks of going with bro Moses Harris.

Tues 30th rather more pleasant. I washed. Helen Combs came and assisted me. Evening we had a small visiting party. Sister P—— and her 3 daughters—sister Phillips and one daughter, and Helen C—— composed the party. We had a very social time, enjoyed ourselves finely.

Wed 31st Helen staid with me. We cooked, and sewed some. Evening her mother sent for her home. I finished a quilt I was piecing, sewed untill half past 10 oclock.

Chapter Thirteen

San Bernardino—The Final Year

Journal, January to December 1857

[A Tolerably Pleasant New Year's Day]

Thurs Jan 1st 1857 Quite cloudy, with appearances of rain. Rainbow in the west. Toward noon it faired away, and continued tolerably pleasant. Bro and sister Combs visited us, with two children. Received the Deseret news and a letter from Elvira Stevens, which gave us an account of the death of Jedediah Grant. Evening I spent reading the news. Very rainy night. Dancing at Ed—— Daily's.

Frid 2nd, cloudy and unpleasant. Mr C fixing watch for a bro Penfold. Alma took our calf to bro Tomkins. Evening I felt much afflicted with a cold. My throat became quite sore. Bathed my feet in warm water. About 12 oclock I awoke with a high fever, and was much distressed.

Sat 3rd I felt some better, but toward night found my cold increasing. Had a chill and fever again.

Sun 4th Had quite sick day, laid in bed nearly all day. Sent for Helen Combs, to come and attend to the chores. Mr C—— went to church. PM sister came in to see me. Sunday night had another light chill and fever. drank freely of cold water.

Mon 5th I arose and bathed myself in cold water, felt much better. This is my birthday, 50 years of my short life has passed away. I sometimes wonder how or why I have been spared so long, when thousands have fallen on my right hand and left, much younger than I.

Tues 6th hard rain in the night, quite cool and damp today. Helen Combs staid with me. My cold very bad. Sister in a while. Also Wm and Ellen. All of them been to the burial of bro Henry Jacksons child. Wm quite unwell with cold and cough.

Wed 7th Tolerably fair. Helen and I washed. My health very poor tried to wash. After I got through, went to bed awhile. Sister Combs sent

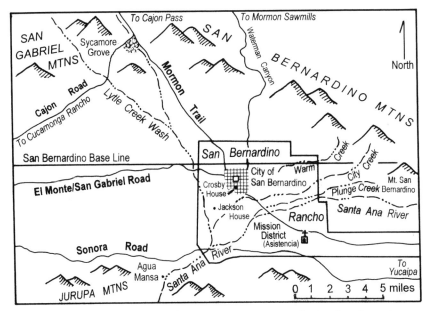

San Bernardino Valley, 1856–1857. Mt. San Bernardino, the landmark used to survey the Southern California base line, is approximately 15 miles further east than shown on the map.

me 4 quails which made a nice soup or stew. I relished them better than anything I had eaten since I took my cold.

   Thurs 8th Quite pleasant. Ann Louise spent a great part of the day with me, made nut cakes, and assisted me in getting dinner.

[The Great Earthquake of 1857]

Frid 9th of Jan—— It was quite fair for the season. At ten minutes or a qr past 8 oclock AM, we were visited with a shock of an earthquake which lasted as near as I could judge about 3 or 4 minutes.

   I arose from the breakfast table and went to the kitchen to take another cake in order to finish my meal, got the cakes in my hand when suddenly I felt a dizzyness in my head, which was succeeded by a sick and nauseous feeling at my stomach. I concluded I had already eaten more than was for my interest and put the cakes in my pocket. I finally began to stagger and reel like a drunken person, and caught hold of a chair and sat down. By this time I discovered that everything was moving around me, my chair jostled forward and back. I put both hands to my head, and exclaimed Lord have mercy upon us. I arose and went to the door, and discovered bro McGary, and family out of the house, meditating upon the wonderful phenomena. As I passed the pool of water, between our houses I discovered it was much agitated. I went over there as I was alone at home. Mr C having just before left to go to Col Jacksons, and Alma had gone for a team to get wood. It was the first earthquake of any importance that I have ever witnessed.

It caused a sensation similar to seasickness, which I found remained with me sometime after the shock passed away. Some minutes after it was over a certain rumbling sound could be distinctly heard in a northerly directing resembling distant canon or like the waves of the seas dashing against a rocky shore.

At a few minutes past 4 in the Pm I discovered another very slight one. Mr Crosby went to doctor a sick ox belonging to sister Pratt. (Brought home fruit trees from Col Jacksons. 5 peachtrees, two apples, one pear, and one plum tree.) The second shock occured while he was gone to see the sick ox, the 1st while he was on his way to col J's.

Evening we retired just before 9 oclock. Alma was sitting by the fire reading, when another slight shock passed over us. I could not feel materially alarmed for some cause or other. I felt assured that the Lord would do all things right, and did not give myself any great deal of uneasiness.[1]

Sat 10th bro and sister Tomkins called and brought a clock to be repaired. Mr C fixed for them while they went to the store. Sister Patten also called. Sister Pratt went out again to Rolands again to see her ox, but found him dead. Sister Grouard spent a part of the evening with us.

Sun 11th fine morning. I did not however feel sufficiently well to go to meeting, therefore wrote a letter to Frances, in answer to one from her by the last mail. We also recd one from Lois Thompson, and a short one from Geo Q Cannon.

Mon 12th Beautiful day. I washed felt quite well, got through in good season. Evening called sister Eleanor Morse and Charlotte her daughter, had a very social chat with them. Sis M said the eathquake made her sick and that she did not seem to recover. I also have several times felt seasick, since frid 9th of Jan——

Tues 13th Very warm and pleasant for the season. Sister L P called, looking very bad, said she had a restless night, and arose with the headache. Seemed much cast down, and troubled with care, and thinking of the earthquake. Some say that the earth has continued being convulsed since frid 9th, by turns, untill now. Some prophesy that the place is going to sink. Say the Spirits have intimated it.

Others have had exciting dreams which have caused many fears for the safety of this place. This PM I spent at bro McGarys. Sister P—— was present, also sis Phillips they expressed great fear, but I told them that I could not feel alarmed, that I was like the boy in a storm at sea, he was asked why he was not more frightened, his answer was "My father is at the helm." I felt confident that the Lord would do all things right.

Sister Phillips in this evening. My husband reasoned with her upon the impropriety of being so much troubled, but she said it was a constitutional weakness, and she could not avoid it.

Wed 14th I spent the Am baking. PM I visited with sisters Stark, Sparks, and Pratt at bro McGary. Sisters St and Sp came over with me to see our new house. Paid me many compliments upon the many improvements we had made since we came here.

Thurs 15th Took a walk with sister Pratt, went to the stores, bought me a dress and pair of shoes. On returning called on sis Hammond. Said she had been much alarmed in consequence of the continued convulsions of the earth, said they had felt a jar every day and every night since frid 9th They live in an upper room where they can discern the least motion.

Reached home between one and two oclock, felt much fatigued. Sister wished me to come back and take tea with her, but I too tired.

Evening I intended going to prayermeeting, it being the first time I had been able to attend meeting for two weeks. Mr C went off to effect a settlement with Geo Crisman. While he was absent old bro Aldridge called and requested him come to his house with bro Cox, to administer to a young woman who was there sick. He invited me also to accompany them, which I did. We had a very sociable and interesting time. My husband anointed both the old lady and young woman, and afterward the three elders laid their hands on them, and blest them with health, and peace. The young lady has lately arrived here from Tennessee, a journey of some 3000 miles by land, was 9 months travelling.

Frid 16th Very warm and pleasant. I feel my health is improving. Finished a coat for John T. commenced a dress for myself.

Sister P—— came in, said she had a very sick night last night, in consequence of a bad cold. While she was in, they sent and informed her that bro Rich had called to see her, and she immediately left. About 5 oclock we had another shock of an earthquake. It was the hardest I had witnessed since the first on friday last. Evening Alma spent at his aunts. Chas—— Cox or Bills came in to get a book that told of earthquakes and many other remarkable events. Mr Crosby read the Deseret News.

Sat 17th I felt about as well as usual, untill 10 oclock <u>am</u> when I was taken very sick with a headache, and was obliged to go to bed. After lying some time in bed I concluded to arise and send for Helen Combs. I wrote a line to sister C—— and sent by Johny. Helen shortly came and assisted in getting supper. My head got better before night. Sister Pratt was here awhile. Evening Mr C was out on visiting excursion with bro Harris, calling on those persons who reside in this ward.

Sunday 18th Very pleasant. I felt much better and concluded to attend church. Helen stoped at home with John. Bro Lyman preached concerning the earths trembling, and explained some of the natural causes. Evening attended prayer meeting.

Mon 19th wind from the north. Helen and I washed. She went home and brought up all her cloths, and concluded to stay with us for the present. Her mother called early, and consented to her staying with us.

PM sister P—— came in and took dinner with us. I baked light bread and prepared for Alma to go to the mountain in co— with bro Harris on the morrow. Evening Mr C gone to seventies meeting.

Tues 20th Fine morning. At 8 oclock came bro Harris, and called for Alma. I put up his provision, and he took his blanket, and set off looking very much like a mountaineer.

Pm we had quite a party of ladies. Sisters Grouard Ellen Mc Lois Pratt, and sister Tomkins. I enjoyed a few hours very agreeably. After dinner felt much better than I did before.

Wed 21st Sister sent for me to come over and go with her to see sister Hammond, but as I was nearly ready to go, sister Paul Smith came in with her sewing. accordingly I gave up the idea of leaving. I enjoyed her company finely, think her a good saint.

Evening sister came and wished me to accompany her on a call to bro Hammonds. We found them well. Bro H was preparing to go to a meeting, Mr C—— called in and accompanied him. Sister and I sewed for sis—— H. Had a very sociable time.

Thurs 22nd We had a visit appointed to sister Stark's. Ironed in the morning. At 1 oclock set off on my visit. Found sister waiting for me. Sisters McGary and Grouard followed us. We found sister Simeon Andrews there. Had a fine visit. On our return home called on a sister Bringhurst late from Las Vagus. Sister Stark came with us to make her first call on the newcomers. Sister B—— is a sister of sis Hammond. On reaching home I felt too much fatigued to attend the prayermeeting at early candlelight. Accordingly sent for sister to come and spend the evening with me. She came, and we spent the evening quite agreeably together.

[A Letter from Brother Tait]

Friday 23rd baked pies. PM Helen went to sister Andrews for pink roots. I finished a calico dress for myself. Evening bro D Savage called and brought us letters from bro Taite, which were the first we had received in 3 or 4 months. Bro S—— said they were teaching a school in Cedar city. They are very anxious to have their little son sent to them.

Sat 24th Very warm day for the season. I made light bread. Evening went with Johny to bro Davises. Carried a letter to him from sister Tait. She told them of her journey in the handcart company, and of burying her little girl in Iowa. Bro Tait told us concerning his going out to meet her, and of the sufferings of the company.[2] Bro Davis and Mr Crosby went to evening meeting. Sister D—— and Anna made me a cup of tea, and we enjoyed the evening finely. We had a pleasant walk home. Bro Davis came half the distance with us, and enlivened the walk with agreeable conversation.

Sun 25th attended church. house crowded with women. The men all took the outside. Bro Lyman spoke long and loud, and was followed by bro Rich. Evening went to prayermeeting. a good spirit prevailed.

Mon 26th Helen and I washed. Bro Tomkins called for his clock, informed me that his wife was quite unwell again with rheumatism. Bro Steward brought a clock to Mr Crosby requesting him to make weights to it, as he had to P—— Dailey's. Evening Mr C gone to seventies meeting.

Tuesday 27th I made mince pies, and light bread for Alma to take on the mountain. Helen went home to help her mother Sister Sherwood and Pratt made me a visit.

Wed 28th immediately after breakfast Alma Helen Johny and myself went up to col Jacksons to get shrubbery for our front yard. We had quite a pleasant walk. Got 3 locust trees, two alanthus, two rosebushes, and several slips. A number of roots of various kinds, made them a short call, and returned. On our way home called at Mowreys a few minutes.

PM Ironed. Toward night set out my plants. Alma left for the mountains in co with br Harris near noon.

Thurs 29th morning finished setting out my plants.

Sister Stark sent to inform me that sisters Andrews, Jones and herself intended visiting me that Pm if agreeable. I was pleased to receive them, they came about 12 oclock. Sisters Pratt and Grouard were also in, and we had an interesting party. Evening I was in sisters awhile, heard some splendid music on a violin, a young man by the name of Watergreen.

Fri 30th accompanied sister on a visit to bro Sealy's After tea called over the ravine to John Lewis's, and Thomas Holidays, returning home called at bro Hunts a moment; called at p o, got a letter from sis Lockwood. They have removed to Delrey Iroquois Co Ill. I was pleased to hear from them again. Their daughter Ellen still has poor health.

Sat 31st finished a bonnet for Helen, also a dress. Very warm for the season.

Sunday morning Feb 1st '57

This morning I felt very feeble and had not sufficient courage to go to church. Accordingly fixed Helen and Mr C—— off, and Johny and I stoped at home. Think of writing to Sister Lois Thompson. Evening, went to prayermeeting. A good Spirit prevailed.

Mon 2nd I felt much better. Washed with Helens assistance. Sister Combs called and took dinner with us. Evening I called on sister Phillips a few minutes. Mr C read Deseret News.

Tues 3rd Appearance of rain, but signs all fail. Sister C. came along and took Helen with her to col Jacksons to get fruit trees and shrubbery. I ironed baked bread and puddings. Evening learned Helen to knit.

Wed 4th Appearances of rain. I cut stockings for H——l——n. ^A—— reached home near 12 oclock from the mountains, been absent one week.^

Evening called into bro McG——s. Bro and sis Grouard were there alone, talk of leaving on frid for the upper country.

[A Rainy Season]

Thurs 5th Very steady rain. Alma went to work for Mr Patten, but the rain prevented him from doing much.

Evening the rain is pouring down. Mr C fixing clock for Haikes.

Frid 6th Sister Ellen McGary's birthday. She was in here awhile I remarked to her that she was half as old as I was. Her mother came in, and offerd to cut a vest for Mr C——, but I had it already done.

Sat 7th baked pies and cakes, and bread. Evening accompanied sister P to the stores, traded some at Clapps and Swartout's. Bought silk gloves—6 bits, gingham for sunbonnet—20 cts pr yd. Returning called on sister Hammond, drank a cup of tea. Reached home, about 7 oclock. Elizabeth Phillips spent the evening

Sun 8th Very pleasant. All went to church except Helen. Bro Lyman preached to us concerning a false report which was in circulation relating to the church being called from here to Great Salt Lake. Prayer meeting in the evening.

Mon 9th Talked of going to see sister Tomkins, but sister sent for me to go with her to bro Hammonds and sew for them that day, and the next day, she would accompany me to see the sick sister Tomkins. Accordingly I went with her, after washing untill 1 oclock. Sewed untill 9 oclock, made a sheet, came home by moonlight.

Tues 10th put out my clothes. Between 10 and 11 we set off, sister, Ellen and myself. Had a pleasant walk. Found sister T——m——ns a little better, altho very feeble. Several persons were in to see her in the course of the day. We sewed very steadily for her. I cut night gowns, and we nearly finished two. Amanda came with the carriage and brought us home. Elizabeth P—— spent the evening again with us.

I went ~~to singing school~~ and staid with sister, while the girls went to singing school. Wm McGary came home from plunge creek, where he had been putting in grain.[3] Had been absent 1 week. Came home for a fresh supply of provisions.

Wed 11th We ironed. Sister Combs called with a watch to get repaired. Said she talked of going on the mountains to cook for Wm Lewis. At 11

oclock came sister Patten, brought her work, and spent the remainder of the day. sis Pratt came and took dinner with us. Brought the Los Angles Star, and read the account of the robbery and murders that have been commited in that vicinity lately. It was really distressing to hear.

Mr Patten called on his way home with some young peachtrees made Mr C—— a present of half a dozen. Evening Helen gone to help sister Pratt pick wool for a bed. Mr C reading Deseret News. Alma studying Astronomy.

Thurs 12th After breakfast Helen went down to help her mother wash. But soon returned saying she was not ready to attend to it. Sister Combs called awhile. I baked light bread and pies.

Wm McGary brought me a letter from the office, which on reading I found to be from my youngest bro Joseph Barnes. I went over to sisters L's, and read it to her. Ellen also recd one from her father. Evening attended prayermeeting.

Frid 13th Remarkably rainy day, and night. Wm Mc came in for milk, said Ellen was quite sick the previous night. Sister Combs came in, said her little child was very bad with dysentery.

Sat 14th rain still continues, very warm weather. Sis C—— in again said her babe was sick with cold. I wrote a letter to bro Tait. Bro Davis came with a watch to get repaired. Evening wrote letter to Ross R Rogers, sent it enclosed in sister Comb's.

Sun 15th Still raining. Mr C gone to church. Returned saying only one woman was there. Alma went to P O, Got 2 Mormons and 2 Standards. Plenty of reading. Helen gone to her mothers to take my letter.

Mon 16th Looked some like fair weather again. Toward noon, rain fell in torrents, and continued untill near night, when it held up. Sister P—— came in and complained of being lonesome, reproved us for not coming in to see her oftener; Evening Mr C—— gone to seventies meeting. rain again. I read in The Mormon, and the American Speaker.

Tues 17th Slept late. Helen had the table set for breakfast when I arose. Mr C repairing clocks and watches. Went with a watch to bro Walker, that he could not make go. Brought home a clock to clean, belonging to an english brother. Alma went in pursuit of our cow, but was too late to find her.

Wed 18th Rains all over for the present. Cold north wind rose in the night. Washed, but on account of the wind did not put out my clothes. Sister Combs in. Lois P called a few minutes. I dreamed of seeing Frances and her father, last night. Evening Alma and Helen over to sisters picking wool.

Thurs 19th Helen went to the store, bought me a dress pattern. Making clothes for Johny. Evening went to prayer meeting spoke to sister Paul Smith about taking him to his father. She said she would readily do so, were they able to get through this spring, but that thier team was insufficient for the journey; and that probably they should not be able to go before next fall.

Frid 20th Helen ironed. I sewed on Johny's clothes, and my dress. Headache all day. Sister Combs called and took dinner with us. Evening Helen gone to pick wool.

Sat 21st I felt much better. Evening went over to sisters and stoped awhile. Mr Crosby gone to teachers meeting. Sis P—— came part way home with me. When I reached home found Elizabeth Phillips here. Alma playing the violin, Helen and Lizzy waltzing.

Sun 22nd Cool wind. Mr C informed me that bro Harris intended going to the mountain the next morning, and in order to have Alma in readiness to accompany him, I should be obliged to bake light bread. Accordingly I set rising a yeast before I went to church. Helen and Johny staid at home. On my return found my yeast nearly ready. Helen and Johny went to her fathers and stoped awhile. Just as we were taking supper we received a call from bro Lyman and his wife Denetia, with sister Pratt. They had been taking dinner with her. We had a few minutes social chat with them. Mr C went with them to the singing school. Evening sister came in and we concluded to go to prayer meeting. I felt very unwell in the time of the meeting. Some of the time passed off rather dull.

Mond 23rd I did not wash as usual being out of soap. Sewed on my dress. Alma went to the mountains. Helen commenced going to school. ^I sent letters to the office to sister Lockwood, and sis Thompson.^

Evening sister was in, and we all took a walk to bro Combs, spent a few hours very agreeably. Mr Crosby gone to seventies meeting.

Tues 24th Appearances of rain. Mr C—— hung a new door in front of the house. I finished my dress. Sister Warren sent me a bonnet pattern by Helen. Cut my bonnet [*illegible crossout*] and sewed some. ~~pm~~

Wed 25th Washed a large washing. Got through at 3 oclock.

Evening went into sis Pratts. Bros Smith Mills, and Coles were there. Had quite an agreeable conversation with bro Mills concerning the Adventists or Millerites, and Spiritualists. Said he heard them debate upon their doctrines.

Thurs 26th Helen went to school, but soon returned, and said she was locked out for coming too late. She cried and seemed quite hurt about it. Evening went to prayermeeting. Sister P—— had another picking wool party, ^but H and I chose the prayer meeting^

Frid 27th Arose at a qr past 6. Milked, made biscuits. Breakfasted at 8. Bro Davis called.

Dull and cloudy with a little rain. Mr C—— making doors to the new house. Near 12 oclock Alma returned from the mountains. Evening I went with Helen and Johny to sister P's, and assisted her in picking wool to stuff a setee or sofa.

Sat 28th Mr C assisted bro Mills in laying a floor in sister's kitchen. Evening I ran over to see it. Sister and Ellen gone to the stores.

Sun <u>*March the 1st AD '57.*</u> [*added later:* ^*1857*^] I felt quite miserable, but still determined on attending church. Felt unwell in time of service, but could not get out in consequence of the crowd. Bro Lyman spoke well. I came home with sick headache, went to bed. Sister Patten called awhile. Spoke of her trials with her unbelieving husband. I spent the evening at home. Mr C and Helen gone to meeting.

Mon 2nd fine day. I felt much better. Finished clothes for Johny. Evening Helen carried eggs to market, got me a box of tea. After sunset we cleaned about the new house, removed old addobics, &C——

I had an invitation to spend the evening at sisters, with sis Patten. Went over and stoped untill ten oclock. Helen and Johny had co in the new house. Alma played the fiddle for them to dance.

Tues 3rd. Washed. Sister P—— had company and invited me over, but I was too much engaged to leave. Sent them an invitation to call on me before they left. Pm baked pies. ^Bro Wm Mathews called on business, and invited me to come and see his wife.^ Evening ran down to sister Combs a few minutes to see her sick children. Found them much better. Helen went to singing school. Mr C to the libra association, expecting to hear a lecture from Dr McIntire, but was disappointed, the Dr being called to attend the sick.

Wed 4th Salt lake mail arrived having been due several days. Report says one of their number has been shot by the indians and lost one of his eyes. We received a letter from bro Whitaker. Pm we were much surprised at bro John C Naile coming in to see us. We had just risen from supper but I soon heated the tea kettle and made him a cup of tea. He spent sometime with us, informed us that the man who got shot was a soninlaw of bro Rich, that he had apostatised and left the church, consequently his wife also.[4]

Evening went into sisters, read a sermon by bro Kimball. Saw John Hunt, and Lewis Newel, mail carriers.

Thurs 5th Very warm day, worked in my flower garden in the morning. Pm took a walk with johny to see sister Smith, found her alone. Bro S—— on the mountain to work. We had a fine visit. She said they were making arrangements to take Johny to his parents when they went. Said when her husband returned from the mountains they would come with their wagon and take us out to ride, thought John would be pleased to take a little excursion, and become gradually acquainted with them. When we returned she accompanied us halfway. Evening called sister Pratt McGary and Morse. Mr Crosby went out with bro Harris, in their official capacity.

Frid 6th was Lois P's birthday. She came and invited me over to dinner, as also her uncle and Alma. Wm and Ellen were present. Mr Bishop

was boarding with them. Just before dinner called a Mrs Thompson from
the Monte, with her little daughter. We had a nice dinner, and enjoyed it
finely. After it was over I invited the married ladies to walk to my house, to
see where we lived. Sister Elzira Dewey was one of the number.

Evening I called over to sisters, expecting to find her alone, supposed the girls would be at singing school, but found they had all had an
invitation to Ed Daily's, with the promise of a treat or entertainment from
a Mr Fordham, as it chanced also to be his birthday. We went over but
did not intend staying but a few minutes, but the young people began to
dance, and it was nine oclock before we left. Sister Pratt Morse and myself
came away before the treat was circulated.

Sat 7th I spent sewing making pies, and so forth. Sister spent the evening with me, Mr C went to meeting.

[Ellen's Fine Daughter]

Sun 8th Staid at home. AM hands gone to meeting. Toward night Sister
called on me to accompany her to Ellen McG's. Said she was unwell. I
went and at 8 oclock PM she was delivered of a fine daughter. We were
all rejoiced that all things moved on so well and prosperous. [*1857, added
later, at bottom of page and again, at top of following page*]

Mon 9th I felt rather unwell, and did not commence washing untill
Helen returned from school. Consequently did not put them out untill
the next morning. Went into sister McGary's awhile.

Tues 10th the wind rose early, and continued to blow untill near
night, when it abated some, and I put out my clothes and dried them.
Evening came sister Patten. Said she had been to see sis McG. Said Mr
Patten had gone to the mountain, and left her alone, that the wind had
injured her house, that she could not keep a fire, and had eaten very little
through the day. Asked me if I had cold coffee or anything to give her
to eat. I immediately got her a lunch, while Mr Crosby read the Deseret
News to her. She spent the time untill 9 oclock. Sister came in, and sat
untill bedtime.

Wed 11th wind continued in the forenoon. I baked pies and prepared for company. PM came sisters Sealy and Stark. I had a fine visit with
them. In the course of the Pm came bro Orson Whitney direct from the
Sandwich islands, on his way to Great Salt lake city. Said he expected to
leave in the morning, and had no time to stay. Evening called bro Davis
went with Mr C to the singing school, to col Jacksons. Alma went down to
inform his wife, so that she need not wonder at his staying.

Thurs 12th I ironed, made light bread, &C. Pm I cut garments for Mr
C—— Lois and Harriet Hunt called awhile. Evening took a walk with my
husband to see sister McIntire, found her sick in bed, with a lameness in

her back. Had a pleasant call. Lois and Harriet were present. H—— staid over night, and L—— came home with us.

Frid 13th sewed on garments for Mr C—— Sister called and took dinner me. After which I went over and sat awhile at Ellens. Sis Hunt was in.

Mail arrived, and brought letters from Canada, also from Bro Pratt and Frances. One from bro Grouard. Sister sent for me to come and read them. Evening I went over.

Sat 14th felt very nervous this morning. Slept badly last night. Arose at 7 oclock, washed my body in cold water, got breakfast and felt much revived. Went into Wm Mc's to ask sister to accompany me to bro Mowrey's. Sis M very sick. Said she would go this Pm. Evening took our walk. Found sis M much better, but not able to sit up only a few minutes. Mrs Caroline Stodard (her sister) was with her. We spent an hour or more, and returned after sunset.

Sun 15th We all attended church. I went and bought a pair of shoes of sister Pratt for Helen. Pm, we had a methodist meeting. A gentleman from Los Angeles preached. Bro Rich requested the congregation to make a general attendence, which they did. And the preacher seemed highly pleased with having so large an audience. He seemed a humble honest hearted man.

Pm went into sis McGary's. Sister Lyman and her daughter Matilda Carter called a few minutes. Sis E Morse was there. Told me that her husband had consented to give her a yoke of oxen to help her to Salt lake city.[5] Attended prayer meeting evening.

Mon 16th Fine morning, churned, washed &C. Evening Mr C—— gone to seventies meeting. Alma playing the violin with Wm McG——. Helen, Elizabeth, and Sophronia dancing.

Tues 17th bro Lee called and enquired for Mr C—— wanted him to assist in putting up shelves and counter in his house, preparatory to his opening a store. Mr C—— absent, but went as soon as he returned. Sisters Smith, and Banks called. The latter to pay for the repairing of a clock. Ironed. Spent the PM at sis McG——s. Evening, there was a party at Ed Daily's Wm McG—— came for Alma to assist him in playing, but he refused to go.

Wed 18th I worked some in the garden. PM sewed for Johny. Evening Dr McIntire called to get his watch regulated again. Said it had taken another fall. Sat awhile and conversed, was going to see a sick child at bro Davids. He complained of being unwell. Said he was all the time trying to save others, but expected he should die and go to <u>hell himself</u>, at last. I told him he was joking.

Thurs 19th Mr C still at bro Lee's, in company with br Charles Burk. AM I worked in garden. Transplanted tomatoes, beats &C. PM baked light bread. Dr McIntire called for his watch.

Frid 20th I spent the morning in the garden. PM took a walk with sister Pratt, called on sister Sparks that was, now Hamilton. Enjoyed a few hours very agreeably, went into see Mother Boothe and her sister and daughterinlaw. Conversed with them upon their native country, and customs; think them very agreeable people. Returned quite late.

Sat 21st felt rather poorly. Took a bath, felt much better. Concluded to visit sister McIntire. Sister Pratt accompanied me. Found sis in bed, but she soon got up. Sister Westover was there, staid and Spent the Pm. Had a fine visit. Mrs Elizabeth Guy lives with them. Sister Hopkins called into see us a few minutes. After tea we called at bro Hopkins to see their new house. Found them living in fine style. Near 7 oclock we reached home. Helen had been over to Silas Harrises, but reached home before me. Mr C—— gone to teachers meeting. Br Davis took dinner with us, spoke some of his experience as teacher, thought it rather a hard task to restore peace in families and neighborhoods sometimes. Evening knit lace.

[The Coombs Family Troubles]

Sun 22nd I heard that sister Combs talked of leaving her husband and seeking a new home. I felt quite unreconciled to it, and after breakfast went down and talked with her upon the impropriety of such a step. She promised to reconsider the subject, and be guided by proper counsel. I exhorted her to shun certain persons who I thought would be an injury to her, and left her with good feelings. PM took a walk with my husband, made several calls, but found the people mostly absent. We finally called at brother Stark's and found them at home. Staid an hour or more, and returned. Evening attended prayer meeting.

Mon 23rd Helen set off to go to school, went to her fathers and soon returned, saying that her mother was entirely helpless from intemperate drinking, and that her babe was crying, and no one but children to take the charge of it. I immediately left my work, and went with her, Found it even so. She lay prostrate on the bed; her babe crying by her side. The other 3 little girls (the eldest of which was only 10 years old) were standing around, looking very sad and forsaken. Her husband who is an industrious man, had gone to his daily labors. I know not that I ever saw a more pityful sight. We immediately seized the babe and the one next to it and brought them home with us. I told the oldest one, that she must be a good girl, and take care of the little sister, which was 4 or 5 years, and if they wanted for anything to eat, come to me and get something. She said they had bread and butter and a duck which their father shot the day before. I kept the children untill after sunset. She sent the little girl after the baby once, but I know she was not capable of taking care of it, and told her I would keep it awhile longer. Before dark returned them to her.

Tues 24th Morning, ^went with my husband to bro Lees store, traded some^ sister Pratt called and informed me that sister Sherwood had invited us to visit her that Pm, at her sons, Dr Stodards. I accepted the invitation, and at two oclock we went, found sister Hunt present. Had a fine visit. Evening Mr C read Western Standard.

Wed 25th cool and cloudy. Mr Crosby and Smith at work in the shop, making a wheel for the gristmill. I cut a dress for myself. Looks like raining. Evening br Smith took tea with us.

Thurs 26th quite cool and airy. Sister came in with Ellen's babe, expecting her to follow soon, but after waiting awhile concluded she was not coming, and carried the child home. Came back and took tea with me. ^I took a walk with Johny, called at bro Combs. Col Jackson came in, conversed with them upon the subject of a separation, counseled them or <u>her</u>, to wait awhile. I called on the sisters Boothe, also mother Hamilton returned by sister Pratt's, and called a few minutes.^ Evening went to prayer meeting, very few attended. However the Good Spirit was with us, and we enjoyed it finely. Bro Hughs took the lead, and spoke much to the purpose.

Frid 27th Still appearances of rain. Sewed on my dress. Sister in. Evening Helen gone to singing school. I called over to sisters a short time.

Sat 28th Finished my dress, also one for Emily Combs. Evening Mr C went to teachers meeting but returned saying there was none on account of an exhibition of some magic performance at sister Spark's. Said the city counsel, and some other officers were invited.

Sun 29th Last night we had quite a shower of rain which has revived and animated the face of nature very materially. Immediately after breakfast Emily Combs came in with her little sister 2 years of age, said her mother sent her to me to get her breakfast, as they had nothing but bread and water for her. I had previously told her father and mother that I would take the child, and endeavor to do a mothers part by her. They both consented to it. And he thought if they separated, that he should put them all out. The little girl ate heartily, and seemed perfectly contented. Family all gone to church. Sun PM meeting at 4 oclock, instead of evening. I attended.

Mon 30th Sister C—— sent the little girl again. I kept it untill evening, when she came and took her home to lodge, thinking it would be some trouble to me to take care of her through the night. Said her little daughter Arabella was quite sick.

Tues 31st She sent her again, and came after her at night.

[Addison Pratt's Return]

<u>*Wed April 1st*</u> [*added later:* ^*1857*^] She came as usual. Shortly after breakfast sister Pratt came in, and soon came Ephraim saying "father has come."

Addison Pratt and Louisa Barnes Pratt. From Elvira Stevens Barney, *The Stevens Genealogy*, p. 123. Used by permission,

We had been expecting him for several days, and consequently he did not take us by surprise. I was washing, baking, churning, had my little girl to care for, and could not go to speak with him untill near night. I found him looking very hale, and fleshy, said he weighed 200 lbs.

He informed me that Frances expected to come on the next steamer. That himself came on the Laurey Bevans, which was the same that we came on, a year and half ago. Sister told me that we had an invitation to call at bro Haike's, to greet the newly married couple. Collins H——— and Ann Morse were married the sabbath evening previous. Accordingly we accepted the invitation, and went at early candlelight, enjoyed a very pleasant conversation, got a treat to cakes and wine. I saw bro Hawkes and was introduced to him for the first time, inquired after her who we used to call Aunt Ann Brimhall now his wife. He invited me to write to her, which I promised to do. Brought home some of the wedding cake to Alma and the children.

Thurs 2nd Mr Crosby went to the mill to work. I ran down to see the sick child, brought back the little 2 years old one. Several ladies called on me, admired my babe much. Think her rather backward, probably in consequence of her having had the dysinterry for sometime previous. Evening went down again to see the sick one.

Mr Crosby came in and administered to it. She was quite low. We spoke again concerning the little child we had taken. I told them we had better have an understanding concerning it. They both said they were willing, we should have it as our own child.

Frid 3rd Mr C went again to the mill. Alma irrigating the garden. Pm called bro and sis Smith and took Johny out for a ride.

Sat 4th I went to bro Lee's and traded some. Helen went home to help her mother, Two of the children sick. Evening Mr C gone to teachers meeting. Sophronia came in and invited me to come and visit at bro McGary's, with bro and sis Pratt and the girls. It was near nine oclock, yet I went and spent an hour or more.

Sun 5th I arose feeling quite well, but after breakfast the wind blew from the northwest and I began to feel very miserable, and altho I was dressed for meeting I gave up the idea of going and staid at home, went bed and laid almost all the forenoon. Sister Combs wished Helen to bring home the little girl so that the sick one could see her but the wind blew so severely that I objected to it.

At noon the old gent called and he thought she had not better go out. Evening took a walk with sister, went to see the sick children at bro Combs, found one quite low, ate nothing for +2 days.

Mon 6th pleasant morn. I went to conference. The house crowded with ladies, men outside. Bro Rich preached well. Spoke of leaving soon. PM I staid at home, baked light bread. Evening had an invitation to sisters to eat cake and drink egg nogg. It was Ann L's 17th birthday, found her sick with headache. She however arose, and joined in waltzing, while Wm McG—— played the violin. The evening passed off very pleasantly.

Tues 7th Cut coats for Johny. Dr McIntire called said little Arabella was very low, and he felt doubtful of her recovery. Asked me to let Helen go down, and assist her mother in taking care of the sick children. I told her to go immediately. She went and staid untill bedtime.

Wed 8th I washed, or rather Helen. Sister Davis came to visit us. Sister Pratt sent for me to come over and visit with sister McIntire, and Guy. I invited sis D—— to go over, and we had a fine visit. Sister Mc—— came over with me to see my house and garden.

Thurs 9th When the stage came in I understood there were 3 ladies in it, and as we were looking for Frances and had heard that the Miss Smiths were coming I concluded they were the three, without doubt. I immediately ran over to Ellens to welcome them but found that Fr——s was among the missing. For some cause or another she did not come, which caused a general disappointment among the friends. It however soon passed off, and we tried to make ourselves as cheerfull as possible, for the entertainment of the young ladies.

Toward night they all came over to see me, had a social time. Evening we went over to sister Pratts where we met bro and sister Andrews. And a bro Wheeler who came down on the steamer with bro Prattt. We enjoyed the evening very agreeably, had music both instrumental and vocal. Josephine played the guitar, Wm the violin and Ellen the accordion.

Frid 10th Very warm. Some appearances of rain. Evening came bro Hawks and took supper with us. We understood by conversing with him that he was an old member in the church but we never had any acquaintance with him. However being particular friends of his wife Ann Brimhall, we soon made his acquaintance. I promised to write her a line by him.

Sat 11th, Still appearances of rain. PM came sister Patten, took dinner with us. Helen went to the store for her, from here she went to sister's, got her to write a letter for her. The miss Smiths came over and took tea with us. Evening called sisters Hammond and Bringhurst, with sis P. I expected bro and sis Andrews but they disappointed us. Bro and sis Pratt McGary and wife, Lois, Ann L——, and the Smith girls spent the evening with us.

[Leavetaking of Apostles Lyman and Rich]

Sun 12th We attended church, bros Lyman and Rich preached their last discourses for the present, expecting to leave in two or three days. House crowded with ladies, gents outside.

Returning home found sister Paul Smith here, said she had called for Johny, that they expected to leave tomorrow at noon. It struck me very sensibly at the arrival of the time for his departure. How many times he had asked me to sing Do they miss me at home. I got dinner and they ate with us. Johny was very cheerful, and pleased with the idea of going to ride. They did not know whether they would take him with them <u>then,</u> or call for him just before the left on the journey. But Johny says "I want to go quicker" accordingly we concluded to let him accompany them home. He kissed us all around and set off very cheerfully. But left sad hearts behind him.

Evening called a few minutes at sis McG's. Saw bro and sis Sealy. Came home and wrote a letter to aunt Ann Hawkes.

Mon 13th Helen went to school. I cut 4 prs of pants. Evening Johny came back; bro S. said they would not leave for a day or two, and thought I would like to see him again. He told me that he did not want to go so soon. Went over to see sis Phillips. Evening Helen washed. Alma went to writing school.

Tues 14th I finished the washing. Dr McIntire called, and informed me that he had been to visit a sick child, and found the mother in a state of intoxication, requested me to let Helen go and stay awhile with it. She had gone to school, but when she came home at night I immediately sent her. ^Bro and sister Smith called—took Johny out to ride, ate dinner with me, when they got ready to go Johny was willing to accompany them and went off cheerfully.^

Evening took a walk with sister. Called on the sick child also at bro Riches to bid them all goodbye, had their wagons all ready. On returning found a company at Wm McGary's and was invited to stop; found sister McIntire and her son James late from the upper cal. They had a little dancing on the occasion. I felt remarkably gloomy and sad, more like praying, and weeping, than seeing dancing. Staid only a short time, and left with sister. Came home and found Alma engaged in writing, had the table spread with books copies &C.

Wed 15th Bro Smith passed on his way to bro Riches. I asked how Johny was enjoying himself, he said they had sent him to bro Shepherd's to play with their little girl, to keep him quiet and divert his mind, untill they were ready to leave. I told him if they did not leave that day I would like to see him again. PM came Sisters Eleanor Morse, and Ellen McG—— Made me a very pleasant visit. Sister M—— ready to start on the morrow. Evening Alma went to writing school.

Thurs April 16th '57. This morning bro Riches teams or wagons rooled out toward the Tehon [Cajon] pass. It is my fathers birthday. We always remembered and spoke of it, while I lived at home.

I went into to sisters to see whether she had done anything, or made an effort, to get a hat for Johny, as she thought she would. Sister Morse was there, just ready to leave. Wm said he would ask Truman Swartout to give him one, if he had any in his <u>store</u>, that would fit. Sister and I went to bid sis Hammond goodbye; her wagon all ready, she sweeping out her house, took hold and helped her. Said she felt bad to part with us, wished one another many good wishes, and parted. Helen and Sophronia went to bid Johny goodbye, found they were gone, and another family in the house. Sis Jones said they left yesterday at ten oclock

Sister Patten called and took a bite of dinner with us, seemed to think there was a sort of coolness manifested by us toward her, also by sister Pratt, and said finally that everyone seemed to feel cool toward her. I told it was her mistake, that we had the same feelings for her that we ever had, but that we had many others to sympathize with besides herself, whereas she had few associates, and none more ready to feel for her than ourselves. That we <u>had</u> sometimes <u>thought</u>, and <u>said</u>, that were we in her place we would not complain as much as she does of her husband, but as long as she lived with him as his wife, should try to make him appear as respectable as possible. She thanked me for my counsel and promised to make good use of it. She then left an invitation for the miss Smiths to visit her tomorrow.

Frid 17th rained very lightly. Mr C went to Crismans. I made pants, &C

Sat 18th Still rainy. I cut clothes for the little girl. Dr McIntire called, left his watch to be fixed. Conversed some time with me. Complained of ill health. Said his son would not take his counsel and come here or go to G S L cit. That his wife was not willing to go without him, but that it would not do for him to stay back on their account. He seemed quite troubled, and I felt a sympathy for him.

Sister came and invited me to take a walk with her to bro Hanks, they have just moved into bro Riches house. Pres Lyman and Rich left with an escort of about 50 of the dragoons to join the camp in the Cahoon pass.[6]

Evening I went over to accompany her sis P—— but she was gone. I then went to sis Combs to see how they got along, found them improving. returned before sunset. Charles Hill called, and asked to stay overnight with us. Made him welcome. Alma went to writing school.

Sun 19th dull, cloudy day. I did not feel quite well. Had pain in back and head. Mr C—— and Helen went to meeting.

PM bro and sis Pratt came over and took tea with us. At 4 oclock Mr Crosby went to the teachers meeting.

Mon 20th Still cloudy. I washed. Sister called and informed me that the miss Smiths were going home in the stage, and if I wished to speak with them I must come over immediately. I therefore left my tub and ran over, took a couple of shells as a present to their mother, whom they had heard was sick and wished them to return home. They were in the stage when I reached there. I merely said goodbye, and sent love to their mother.

Pm we had thunder, and a few sprinkling showers. However I dried my clothes, and ironed some of them. Evening A went to writing school. I felt remarkably tired, went to bed at half past 8 oclock.

Tues 21st Alternately clear and cloudy. I finished ironing. Mr C—— at work for bro Crisman. Alma transplanting beets.

Wed 22nd I sent for sister to come and cut coat for bro Cro, She came and spent the greatest part of the day.

Thurs 23rd She came again, and nearly finished it. I cut dress for sister Combs. Mr Crosby went to Crismans, and came back without work. Sister said she expected Dr Macintire and family in awhile that evening, and invited us over. we went found them there, and had a very pleasant interview. The young people danced a few new dances, were instructed by young McIntire, and his companion Robert Brooks who were late from the upper country.

[Brother Pratt's Faithfulness Questioned]

In the course of the evening Dr Mc—— invited my husband to go out with him. Said he wished a little private conversation. He informed him that he had been conversing with bro Pratt and found to his great astonishment that he was not a true believer in the principles of our religion. That he actually denied his faith in some important points and spoke lightly of others. Said he was greatly disappointed in him, as he had been expecting to receive strength and encouragement from him as he was a travelling elder just returned from a mission. But said he did not wish to cultivate the society of such persons.[7]

Frid 24th Sister came over and finished the coat. I finished dress for the little girl.

Sat 25th, pressed coat, and cut white dress for Helen.

Sun 26th I had a bad cold. Very damp and unpleasant. Mr C went to church. Helen went off on a walk, and brought girls home with her, went to swinging in the new house. I reproved them for playing on the sabbath day and advised them to be still; they soon left. I afterward told Helen that as she went every day to school, I wished her to stay at home or go to church on the sabbath day. 4 oclock Mr C attended the bishops and teachers meeting.

Mon 27th Still cloudy and appearances of rain. Mr C went over to Hanks mill. I washed churned baked light bread, &C. Alma went after water, got the privilege of Wm Petit's by watering D. Sealy's garden for him in his absence.[8] Evening he went to writing school.

Tues 28th I ironed, sewed on Helens dress. Felt very gloomy all day. Mr C making sofa for bro Davis. I assisted him in making cushion. Evening Alma went to a party at Dr McIntire.

Wed 29th Dull cloudy weather. Mr C brought home beef from Crismans. Alma at work on the dam. I finished a white dress for Helen, and assisted my husband in covering the sofa. Bro Davis called and took tea with us.

Evening I called into Ellens a few minutes, herself and husband went to writing school. I accompanied her over to her mothers where she left her babe. Stoped there untill 9 oclock, Mr Crosby came in for me. Bro and sis Pratt invited us to go to a picnic, or fishing party up city creek, on <u>mayday</u>. Bro P—— said he was going the day previous, to take what fish he could, preparatory to it. B[art]—— Smithson was also going in advance to kill deer.

Thurs 30th Quite pleasant. Mr C irrigating the garden, quite a profusion of water. I finished skirts for myself, and cut dress for little Ella. Evening Mr C visited the families in his ward.

[A May Day Picnic]

Frid May 1st. About 9 oclock the carriages set off for the picnic.[9] Sister came and asked me to let Ephraim stay with me in their absence. I consented of course, but knew he would not stay many minutes. She left him a sweet cake, which he ate and then left. I felt rather lonely after they were gone, and somewhat inclined to murmur at my poverty, and lack of the enjoyments which many of my brethren and sisters were blessed with.[10] But finally took down a piece of select poetry which I had previously pinned to the wall, and sung it several times over. The text is 'It is all for the best.' I found much consolation from reading it, and my spirits became cheered and enlivened thereby.

I arranged everything in the best possible order, prepared a good supper, but before it was quite ready the company returned. The wind was blowing almost a gale. The air was filled with dust, and I judged from appearances that the ride could be nothing worthy of envy. was quite thankful that I was safely housed secure from dust. I had a very plenty-full and healthfull supper which we enjoyed with grateful hearts. Helen returned from school just as it was ready, and told us the exhibitions of the last day of the yr &C. Evening there was a grand ball at Ed Daily's.

Sat 2nd May. Quite blustering Helen washed skirts for herself and me. I starched and ironed them, and prepared her for her party at her mothers. 3 young ladies came for her with a request from her mother to come home immediately, as the party had commenced assembling. I hastened her off as soon as possible, feeling sensible that her expectations would not half be realized. which I believed proved to be a fact. Evening called in to Ellen's, and from thence to her mothers. Staid a few minutes, and she returned with me. Mr C brought home the Deseret news, read a sermon from bro Young. Alma attended writing school. Helen came home at 12 oclock.

Sun 3rd I attended church for the first since the departure of bros Rich and Lyman. Heard bro [Daniel] Thomas preach, also president [William J.] Cox who exhorted us to consider this our abiding home and work for the interest of the place by building houses, making improvements with the same ambition that we would at Great Salt Lake city.[11] Evening wrote a letter to Lavina Baker. Bro Harris called, and went with Mr Crosby to visit the saints in this ward. When they returned reported that they found bro Pratt Adison, extremely skeptical, and full of vain philosophy.

Mon 4th Washed. Had a conversation with Helen upon the impropriety of her going away on sunday or any other day, without asking my consent or even letting me know that she was going out. After washing she went to her fathers garden and picked a mess of peas. I felt extremely tired, lay down awhile. Evening went into Ellens. Wm expected to go next day, to the upper country. We all attended a lecture delivered by Dr McIntire, before the San Bernardino Libra Association. After the lecture we went into the writing school a few minutes, taught by Mr Wm Worden.

Tues 5th Ironed, baked &C. Evening called over to sisters again with Wm and Ellen. Bro and sis Pratt went out for a walk.

Wed 6th Wm came in at an early hour, and bade us goodbye, ready to depart for his destined place, in San hosa valley, to labor through harvesting, expecting to work for bro Dire, at San Lorenzo. I made bonnet for Ella.

Evening Alma went to writing school, it was the last of the term.

Thurs 7th cold and windy. I sent over and invited sister to go with me to see sis Patten. She sent back to me to come and take dinner with her, and afterward she would go with me. Accordingly I went over. They had green peas. It looked like rain, and did a very little. However we went and found them quite pleased to see us. We had not been in but a few moments when Ephraim came and informed her sis—— that Mrs Hall from San Gabriel had arrived and Ellen wished her to come home immediately. Whereupon she left, but I staid untill after sunset. Enjoyed a good supper with her and the old <u>man</u>. Who was in an unusually good humor. Sis P——ten seemed to feel cast down, and sad, concerning herself, fearing she had deprived herself of the blessings promised to the righteous, by marrying an unbeliever, after she had been sealed by the Priesthood, to a good man. She read in the Seer, the law of the Lord concerning such persons.[12]

Frid 8th I visited at Ellens, with sister Louisa Ann, and Mrs Hall. I felt unwell and with all rather dejected. Liked Mrs H—— very well, invited her to visit me, which they concluded to do next day.

Sat 9th Spent the morning brushing and cleaning house baking puddings cakes &C. About 2 oclock they returned from sis Jacksons' and spent the remainder of the Pm with me. I enjoyed it well. 7 or 8 persons took supper besides our own family. Evening went over to br P's awhile. While there Gen—— [Jefferson] Hunt late from the representative hall at Sacramento called in, having just returned home. He was full of talk, brought a letter from Frances to her father, containing money. We also received letters from her by the mail.

Sun 10th I attended church heard Gen—— Hunt preach Also bishop Crosby. After church sis Patten called and dined with us. Sister sent me an invitation to come and ride with them, herself Ellen and Mrs Hall. We made several calls. The first at Hopkins, from there to bro Clapps, then to bro Dodges who were absent. We however gathered a lot of pinks of which they had thousands. Next and last we called on sister Stark. We then rode as far as bro Hanks, but they being absent also we came home. Mr Crosby attended meeting of the authorities of the church in this place.

Mon 11th Washed. Helen commenced a new yr at school. Pm visited at Ed—— Daily's, with sisters Pratt, McGary, and Mrs Hall.

Tues 12th, I ironed some of the clothes, and Hellen finished. Mrs Hall and Pratt visitted at sister Morse's. They invited me to accompany them, but I declined.

Wed 13th We all went to Dr McIntires. Had a fine visit. After dinner Dr and wife and sis Guy accompanied us to Gen Hunts, where we found a family party assembled. We were treated to cake pie and Champane.

Sister Ed Daily proposed that we all adjourned to her house in the evening which was universally consented to. And accordingly we reassembled there, at early candlelight. Pres—— Cox and wife came in, and as Gen Hunt expressed it, we had quite jollyfication. Mr Wm Worden played the violin and the party danced untill 11 oclock. They all seemed to enjoy it excepting Dr Mc who complained of a severe headache, and I believe laid down. He was ralied considerably by gen Hunt.

Thurs 14th Beautiful day. Mr C making chest for sis Patten. PM I visited at bro Hanks, in co with Mrs Hall, sisters Pratt and McGary.

[Emily Coombs's Return to her Family]

Frid 15th took a ride with Mrs Hall, Pratt and Ann Louisa to see bro Dires house. Previous to our leaving I received a letter from sis Combs, requesting me to let the little girl come home, that her husband had consented to her taking her home again, that they expected to leave soon for the upper country, and wished to take them all along with them. I told Emily that I was going to take her out to ride, but should be back by 10 oclock, and that her mother could come up at that hour and see me about it.

We found bro Dires house and furniture in rather a bad condition. The mice had damaged their things considerably. Sister P brought away the carpet, rocking chair, cag of syrup, matches, and soforth. Frances wrote to me to take the hair matrass, carpet, and bedstead, if my house was finished, and I wanted them. But as it was I did not want them. Among the articles I found a few beans which I concluded to take and account to Jones for them; there were 11 pounds.

Soon after I returned came sis Combs. She appeared much dejected and sad. We conversed plainly with her upon the impropriety of her taking away the children. She said Helen might do as she pleased about staying but the idea of giving away her little one made her very unhappy day and night. She knew she was better here than at home, was sensible we were doing well by her, yet she was very unhappy without her. I counseled her to pray and get the mind of the Lord, upon the subject. She said she had not done it, but had been guided solely by her impulses. She finally went and left her and afternoon sent me another line on the subject, I sent the line back and told Emily that Mr Crosby would see bro Combs and talk with him, and if he said she must come home I would send Helen with her in the morning. Mr Crosby sent to br Combs to come up. Accordingly soon after sunset he came. I inquired how his wife was, he said bad enough.

Helen had informed me previously that her mother sent Emily to the store as soon as she returned from here, and got a bottle of brandy, and that ~~she and Emily~~ they had been drinking it together.[13]

The old man acknowledged that he had told her that she might get the child home again. Said he did it to make reconciliation if possible, that she worried him so that he did not know what course to pursue. Mr Crosby told him that unless he was willing to bind her to us that we did not wish to keep her any longer. He therefore left, saying he would think of it untill morning and let us know.

Sat 16th I sent Helen down to ask what was to be done, her mother told to bring the little girl down after breakfast, but that she could stay untill they left for U Cal.

Mr Crosby told her that unless she concluded to stop with us and let her folks go, she might as well leave now. Accordingly she carried down the remainder of the little girls clothes, and then returned with Emily to get her own.

I gave them both a charge to be kind to their little sisters, and take good care of them when their mother was in her helpless state, and always speak gently to one another. Told them to remember the hymn, "Speak gently." They made no reply, excepting Helen said she would come to see us before she left for the Upper country.

After they were both gone, and their clothes, I moved away their bed, and regulated things to my mind, and finally felt that I was relieved of a great deal of care. I actually felt free again.[14] Evening my husband attended a methodist meeting at the schoolhouse. I went over to sisters and staid untill he returned.

Sun 17th Fine morning. Attended church, heard eld Hughs. Pm methodist preaching at 3 oclock. Attended, The gent preached against polygamy. Tried to convince us from scripture that it was wrong. Capt Hunt made a short reply. 3 ministers present, one left an appointment to preach in 4 weeks. Called at sisters with Dr McIntire and wife, Mrs Guy, &C. Sister Pratt, Hall, E Mc, and Ann L. ~~They had not~~ set out for a ride together ~~from~~ intending going to bro Andrews. But had not proceeded far when they discovered the tire was off of one of the carriage wheels, and the wheel badly injured, so that they could proceed no farther, but came back, feeling quite disappointed, as Mrs Hall expected to leave next day for her home. Mr Crosby went immediately in search of a wagon shop, found bro Stowe, and engaged him to repair it.

Evening he was out with bro Harris, officiating in his office as teacher.

Mon 18th quite cloudy. Helen called for her books. I washed. Sister Pratt and Mrs Hall came and took dinner with us. Ellen also came and with Gregoria ate at the second table. It rained a little. Mrs H lamented very much that they could not have gone home that day it was so cool, and comfortabe riding.

I sent Sophronia to sis Pattens for butter. Evening Mr C out again with bro H——. Felt remarkably tired, retired early to rest.

Tues 19th cool and cloudy again. Mrs H—— and Ellen intend going today, but Mr C—— saw the wagon mender who said they would be obliged to wait another day.

I put out my clothes. Mr C—— gone to bro Davises, to see some work which he expects to do for him. Also to carry home bro Dodges clock which he has been cleaning.

About 1 oclock Mrs H's Spanish girl came, and informed me that their horse was ready, and they were about leaving, wished me to come over and see them off, and say goodbye. I went just in season. Mrs Hall invited me to come and visit her, which I promised to do if I came that way. I admired her very much for a stranger. She is very social and agreeable, seemed pleased with everything she saw here. Bro Raiser drove the horse for them. We thought they had a very heavy load, and feared the carriage would not hold out. But bro R—— said we must not prophesy evil concerning Israel, for if we did, it should not come to pass.

I moved my curtains back, turned my bed, bureau &C. Sophronia came to stay with us.

Wed May 20th I arose early, picked peas, baked pudding, cake, &C. Expecting Dr McIntire and family. A few minutes past 12 oclock they came. The Dr and wife both quite unwell. Sister Elizabeth Guy accompanied them. I made them a cup of tea for lunch, afterward sis Mc laid down and slept a few minutes. The Dr could not stay then, but promised to return at 4 pm. Sis G went into see sis Phillips a few minutes.

At 3 oclock I went over for sis P—— and girls, sent for sis Cox. There were 12 of us took supper together. We enjoyed it finely, excepting the Dr, who complained greatly of feeling unwell.

Evening Mr Crosby and br Harris went into talk with bro Cox, concerning some cases of unbelief which they found in the ward in the course of their official duties. I was very tired retired early.

Thurs 21st beautifull day sister P—— came over awhile. wished me to come over there in the Pm. I went found her alone.

Fri 22nd Mr Wm Worden took dinner with us. Evening he came with his violin, and some nice specimens of paintings. We had music on two violins, and a flute. Lois and Ann Louisa sung one song, and the entertainment ended with the music box being wound up.

Sat 23rd Cool and pleasant. I wrote a billet to sis Combs concerning some things that Helen took from Frances trunk, and sent it by Sophronia. Pm took a walk with Lois P, to Cachners [Kartchners], ^proved by the girls that Hellen had worn Frances beeds to school.^

Sun 24th Very warm day. I did not go to meeting. Staid at home all day. Charles Hill called, also his little daughter Hue. Evening went into bro Pratts with Mr C——.

[The Picketts' Visit]

Mon 25th rather cool and foggy. I washed. The Miss Smiths arrived in the stage. Sis Pratt came in with Agnes a[nd] Don Carlos.

    Tues 26th I ironed. Agnes, Don C——, and sister Pratt took dinner with us. Evening bro Davis called, took tea.

    Wed 27th Sister came over and insisted my going home with her, Said she was alone. The girls all gone to sis Hunts. I went and staid untill 4 oclock. Mr Crosby worked at bro Davis, making windmill. When he returned at night informed me that bro A Farnsworth and sister E Guy were married.

    Thurs 28th I spent alone. Pm called a moment into sisters. Starched and ironed. Made apron for Sophronia.

    Frid 29th received an invitation to a quilting at Geo Clarks. Had a previous invitation to visit at bro Davis'es. Mr C—— making windmill. About 11 oclock called sis Tomkins and [George] Lord. Also bro Alexander, been to the store. Soon as they left I went to bro D's. Had a fine visit. Staid 'till sunset. Bro D—— came home with us, to assist Mr C with his tools. Evening went into sisters. Sis Tomkins came to bring home the girls, Lois P, and the miss Smiths. Had a social time.

    Sat 30th Invited the sisters Smiths, and bro Pickett, to eat breakfast with us. They all came. Pm I went into bro Pratts and sat awhile with them. Sister was out. I invited the girls to come home with me and take supper. They all came, and we had quite lively times, Ann Louise assisted me. I had quite a nice supper. Afterward she and Josephine washed the dishes.

    Sun 31st cool and cloudy. Attended church. Heard bro Turley and gen Hunt. Alma irrigating the garden. Evening went into sisters. She informed me that she intended going to San Gabriel in the stage the following day.

    Mon the 1st of June '57. Heavy fog, almost amounting to rain. After breakfast I went to see if sister had gone, and met her coming over to see me. We both went into P Daily's to see her young babe. Alma washed for me. Near 11 oclock when the Stage left. Sister thought she should return with the stage on Thurs—— if Ellen was ready to come.

    Pm I ironed. Sophronia washed her clothes. Aga Smith and Don C Pickett took supper with us. Evening Mr C read Desert news

    Tues 2nd Mr C—— making windmill for bro Warren. Dr McIntire called, told us that he was getting up his apparatus for taking daguereotypes. Offered to learn Mr C— if he had a mind to undertake it. My husband proposed having Alma learn.

Wed 3rd I washed a little for Sophronia. PM repaired stockings. Mr C and Alma at work in the shop. Bro Mowrey brought lumber for a wagon bed. We rcd a letter from bro Whitaker, G S—— L city. I read Deseret News

Thurs 4th. About 12 oclock Am the stage arrived, and brought Sister Picket and her son Wm. Came out to join the girls and Don C, who came last week.[15]

I immediatly ran over to see her, as she stoped at bro Pratts but found them all absent, gone into bro Dailys to take dinner. I returned and shortly after they all came in, spent the Pm and took supper with us. Sis P—— looked quite well, and seemed in good spirits. We also received a call from bro Thom—— Burdick from San Gabriel. We had not seen him in 11 years, looks very old and feeble, has been teaching school. He talks of purchasing land in Ukipe [Yucaipa] valley. Evening I went with sis P and children over to bro Pratts. Sister absent, bro P—— and girls alone. Bro Thomas called.

Frid 5th Fine morning. Mr C—— gone to put up the mill he has been making for bro Warren. Sis Pickett and family gone to bro Davids.

Sat 6th dull and cloudy, appearances of rain. Evening I went into sis Adaline Daily's to see how Sophronia got along, as she had left me in the morning, and said she was going to stop with her. I enquired after her, and sis D—— knew nothing about her said she called in the morning and enquired if her nurse was gone, found she was not, and left, supposed she came back to me. I then went over to sisters and found she had spent the whole day at Ed—— Dailys. It was Celia's [Daley] birthday, and a party had convened on the occasion. I reproved her some for deceiving me so. Several of the girls came over to get Alma to come and fiddle for them, but that was entirely useless.

Sun 7th Last night we had quite a shower Cool and cloudy today. I attended church. Heard bro Hughs preach. Pm spent in reading the Millenial Star.

Mon 8th Sister Pickett sent to tell she would accompany me to br A Lymans in the Pm. Old bro Thomas Burdick called and ate breakfast with us, said he had always been doubtfull with regard to the truth of Mormonism. Said when he was in the church the brethren used to call him doubting Thomas. Added that he liked the people, and thought them the best people on the earth. But could not subscribe to all their principles. Pm I went with sis Pickett to bro Lymans, had a very agreeable visit. I called on sister Cornelia a few minutes. Don C was very unwell all the Pm.

Tues 9th Alma washed for me. I felt quite miserable. Very warm day. Sis Pick—— and family went to bro Chases. Sister David called.

Wed 10th [*added later: ^June 1857^*] Extremely warm. Accompanied sis P—— and family to bro Wm Matthews, where we spent the Am. Pm we came to bro D——— Thomases, had a fine visit. Called into Wellington Sealy's with sis P———.

Thurs 11th Still very warm. We all went to Dr McIntire's in the Am. Pm came to gen Hunts. Found sis Whipple there. Had a splendid visit. Sis Mc very unwell.

Frid 12th More air today. Alma gone to the mountains with Phineas Daily. Mr C at work on Judge Thomas store. Yesterday received a letter from sis D——— Lockwood and her daughter Ellen. I was feeling quite lonely this Pm, had been expecting sister Pickett, when who should arrive but bro Boothe and wife, mother and aunt. I was a little surprised at first, but they told me that my husband had often invited them to call, when he had been visiting them in the capacity of teacher, and they had now come, but not to make me trouble. I told them I was all prepared for them, and was happy to receive them. Mr C——— came just as my supper was ready, and we enjoyed a few hours very agreeably.

Sat 13th, this day the comet was expected to come to the earth, but there are no signs of it to my knowledge. Last night I heard a rumbling noise resembling distant thunder, which we thought might be the sound of an earthquake, but we felt nothing. It occured between 12 and 1 oclock.

Quite a cool, comfortable day. Sister Patten brought me butter. Sister Pickett called a short time.

Sun 14th cool and cloudy with a few sprinkles of rain. Attended church. Father Hughs preached again. Elder Baitman and wife were present.

Eld——— B is the methodist minister from Los Angeles. He preached at 3 oclock. The counsel met to draft resolutions for the 4th of July.

Mr T Burdick called just as we were going to church. Said he was wating for Dr Cunningham to call for him, as he had engaged him to take him to San Gab[riel], his home, but after waiting here some time concluded to go in pursuit of him, when he found he had gone and left him. The old gent felt much disappointed. Left his things here and went to Mr Noy's. said he was very unwell with a disenterry.

Mon 15th Sister Pickett came and took breakfast with me, bade me goodbye, ready to leave in the stage. The girls also came over before leaving.

Washed with A's help. Evening called in to see the girls. They had rcd a line from their mother at the Monti. Saying she was very homesick, and unhappy. Sorry she had not come home with sis P. Mrs Hall and Burns both sick.

Tues 16th Remarkably warm day. Pm called Mr Burdick, said he had been very sick since Sunday, and under the Dr's care, was scarcely able to walk. Requested me to board him a few days, untill he could get a chance to go home, had been staying at br Darts. I told him he could stay if he chose to. When my husband came in he asked his price for keeping him a few days, he told him he could stay at his own price. I called into sis Pratts, saw sisters Hunt Harriet and sis Morse. I spoke of loosing my spectacles, when they informed me that they were at bro Clapps store, said they had just seen them and tried them. Said and indian boy brought them there and sold them. Evening I told Mr Crosby, and he went immediatly and got them. I felt rejoiced to get them again. They paid the boy 50 cts for them. He took them from my window, which was left open through the night. The night previous they took 2 fowls from the hen house.

Wed 17th Another extremely warm day. Mr Burdick quite unwell, but walking about. I ironed. Cut white dress for myself.

Thurs 18th Still warm. Last night we were again disturbed by indians taking our fowls, 3 were missing this morning.

Pm the stage arrived, bringing sister Pratt and Ellen. I went over to see them, took tea. They brought word to Mr Burdick that his son was coming after him. The old gent some better but still complaining.

Frid 19th rather more comfortable. Making white dress. Mr B preaching Spiritualism to me. Sister Patten called. Evening Mr C, Alma and Ellen playing on their instruments of music. Lois heard it, and came runing over. Mr B—— thought it very exhilerating. Mr C—— finished his job at bro Thomas's and brought home his tools and bench.

[The Murder of Marion Perkins]

Sat 20th I baked pies and bread. Mr B— heard his son not coming in consequence of his sending him word that it was not best, as he would have chances to go with teamsters next monday.

[*added later:* ^1857^] The old gent walked down in town PM, and when he returned about 4 oclock, he sighed as he sank into his chair. Saying he had just witnessed the most awful scene his eyes ever beheld. Said two men were fighting, and one stabbed the other, with a large knife, three times, when the ~~one~~ stabbed man fell lifeless to the ground. His name was Marion Perkins. His murderer was Wm McDonald. Perkins was intoxicated, and commenced on McD. when Mc—— went home, and got his knife, apparently with the intention of killing him. McDonald was immediately arrested, and confined.[16]

Pm I called over to sisters, and set out to go with the girls, to the American hotel, to see the corpse; but met the sexton taking him to a house used as a jail. We then turned back, called a few minutes to speak with sister Cox. She said she was acquainted with Perkins, that she spoke with that Am. Also the day before, he told her that he was preparing to go to Salt lake soon, and intended staying with bro Riches family while he went on his mission to Europe. Evening bro Harris called on Mr C, to get a coffin made. Said it was his business to see the corpse decently buried.

Sun 21st At 4 Am Alma was called up to relieve the guard at the jail, where he staid 3 or 4 hours. Mr C and C Burk made the coffin. Immediately after dinner Mr Burdick left for home in co with bro Davids. He had been with us five days. Before leaving he made me a present of 2 doll[ar]s, and invited us to come and see them. He observed to me that he would like to talk with my husband an hour or 2 before he left, but that it was not convenient, as he had been very busy ever since he had been here. Thought perhaps he would write him a letter sometime, merely to let him know his mind concerning some articles of doctrine in the Mormon church. After meeting bro and sis Tomkins called. I made them a dinner, had a social chat.

Mon morning June the 22nd AD 1857 [*added later:* ^1857^] I went to the P O, with my likeness which I sent to my sister D Lockwood. Traded 6 dolls with bro Lee. Sister Cox was at the store, and we bought us lawn dresses alike. Returned and sewed on a shirt for Mr C—— Evening had company. Ellen, Lois, Ann L, and Sister Ann Haikes. Charles Burk was in. We had quite a band of music. E played the accordion, Mr C the flute, Alma the violin and Burk the picata. Time passed off lively, and pleasantly.

Tues 23rd Mr C—— gone to bro Davis's. Alma and I washed. Evening called at sisters. She informed me that she expected a wedding to take place at her house, soon, probably on the 4th of july.

Wed 24th I ironed, sister Boothe and her sister called, and got beets.

Thurs 25th I took a walk to sister Pattens, got a little butter. Had a very good visit. Wm McDonald had his trial for killing Marion Perkins. Was found guilty of manslaughter and put under 3000 doll bonds to appear at the supreme [superior] court. Many thought him guilty of wilful and premeditated murder.

Frid 26th I wrote in my back journal. Sewed on sacks, &C.

Sat 27th Baked light bread. Sister Pratt came over and ate dinner with us.

Sun 28th Stoped at home, assisted Alma in irrigating. Worked myself almost sick. Came in in a great perspiration, bathed myself in cold water, laid down awhile, untill I was a little rested, then made me a cup of tea, and felt much refreshed. PM came bro and sis Pratt. Dr McIntire and wife. Sister E Guy, Ellen, Lois and Ann Louisa. We sang a tehitian hymn, also a few english tunes. Had a very agreeable interview. Evening I called into Ellens. While there came John and Harriet Hunt, Truman Swartout and Lois. Mr C followed, and sat a few minutes.

Mon 29th I washed. Mr C making pump for sister Whipple. Alma making adobies. Pm sewed on my white dress. Ellen and Lois called over, and took a cup of tea with me. L—— making her wedding dress.

Tues 30th AM picked peas. PM sewed on my dress. Widow Martin called with a clock to get repaired. I was taking tea, and she partook with me.

Wed ~~31st and last day of June~~ July 1st Very cool and cloudy. I ironed. Sister came along, going to sis Pattens. asked me to accompany her but I was too busy. PM I finished my white dress. Evening sister called on her return from sister Pattens. Bro P was also in, had been looking for Ephraim. Said he had gone away, he knew not where. He seemed quite impatient with him, requested sis to let someone take him that could make him more obedient than she could. She objected, and some unpleasant language passed between them.[17] Salt lake mail arrived. We received two letters. One from sister E R Snow, and another from bro T Whitaker. I was highly delighted with sis Snows letter. She also enclosed one in mine to sister Cornelia Lyman, which she requested me to forward to her. Said she lacked wrappers and was under the necessity of sending the two in one.

Thurs ~~July 1st~~ 2nd directly after breakfast I went to the store, and called on sister Cornelia L. and handed her the letter from her aunt. She was quilting. Sis Denetia was with her. I made a short stay, and went to bro Lees store. Traded some 4 or 5 dolls. Evening called awhile on sister. Girls all gone to the independence ball.

[Preparing For Independence Day]

Frid 3rd Called at bro Pratts, found him very unwell with pleurisy. Said he had had a very bad night. Sister seemed full of care. Said they were lacking material for the coming independence feast, and bro P—— was too unwell to go to mill or store. would be obliged to borrow flour. Came home with me, and got some. Bro Lee's children brought down their offering, and I cooked it, as their mother had taken in a sick woman's babe, to nurse, and having a babe of her own to care for, could not prepare it for them. I spent nearly all the day in cooking. Made 8 pies, two cakes, two puddings, and baked two chickens, which were a donation from bro Lee. At night found myself remarkably fatigued, retired early.

Sat the 4th I was awakened at 3 oclock Am with the morning Salute. It was not very agreeable to me to be aroused so early after so hard a days labor; however I made the best of it. I arose early and put up my offering for the feast, and at 8 oclock Mr C—— and Alma carried it to the rallying point, the new bowery, where tables were previously arranged for that purpose. Mr C being one of the feeding committee stoped to set the tables while A came back to accompany me. I reached in season to see the procession marh from the schoolhouses to the bowery. 24 young ladies all dressed in white, were preceeded by two young men bearing their banner, with this inscription, "The pride of our country." Then followed 24 young men, with a banner, on which was inscribed, "The strength of the nation." Every thing was conducted in peace and order. The tables were loaded with the bounties of nature, and all partook, apparently, with grateful hearts. The dinner was succeeded by toasts and dancing. The dust being very annoying to my eyes I did not stop to see them dance long. On my return called on sister Lee I understood that her children did not find our ward table, and did not get much to eat. I felt sorry for we had and abundance for them. I told her that I looked about and enquired for them, but could not find them. The oldest girl said she ate at another table. Reached home at 2 oclock. Lois called to inform us that the wedding was coming off before dark. Wished Alma to bring over chairs, and help in arranging seats. Ammon Greens wife came in with her.

[Lois Pratt's Marriage to John Hunt]

The house was crowded with guests. The bride and groom, brides maid, and grooms man, were dressed very respectably, and all passed in order except that Ann L did not get into the room untill the performance was all over, which caused some very disagreeable feelings on her part, as well as on ours. Immediately after the ceremony was over, which was performed by president Cox, bro Pratt was attacked with the pleurisy in his side which threw him into great pain, and he was obliged to take his bed.

He called the elders who administered to him, but as he was not relieved he sent for Dr McIntire. The main part of the co repaired to bro Daily's where a splendid supper was prepared and dancing was the order of the evening. My husband and I waited awhile for sister, but as bro P continued in pain she could not leave him. Accordingly we went and left her. The Dr came, and after applying mustard plasters and bathing his feet in warm water, he got so far relieved that she came over a short time. At 12 the party broke up. A co of seranaders called in the course of the evening, with them was the city marshal John Holiday, who I presume came with them to keep order. They were treated with politeness, and spent the remainder of the evening with us. Our clock struck 12 soon after we reached home. Alma staid up all night, to irrigate bro P's, and Ellens gardens. His eyes were quite bad this morning.

Sun 5th in consequence of having to attend to irrigating our lots Mr C did not attend church, one of my eyes being sore I also stoped at home. Sister and Ellen were in. Said bro P much better. That the wedding party were not going to church. I slept a great part of the Am. At 2 Pm arose and made tea. Mr C—— went to a counsel meeting. I wrote in my journal. Wrote a letter to Frances. Evening Lois and John called, and brought home chairs.

Mon 6th Mr Crosby repairing windmill for bro Davis. Alma looking for the cow. I finished my letter, and carried over to Ellen. She put hers in with it, and sent Sophronia to the office. Bro P—— came over, said his side much better. I washed. Sister came in, said she had nearly exhausted herself by planting corn in the garden. Weather very warm. Alma went to Tomkins and got seed corn.

Tues 7th Ironed. Made light bread. Commenced my lawn dress. Evening Ann L came over and said her mother wished me and uncle J—— to come up to bro Dodges, to accompany her home. That she had gone to Dr McIntire's to spend the day, and would meet us at bro D's in co with the Dr's folks.

Accordingly we went immediately after supper. Reached bro D's before them. They soon arrived however, and we had a feast of melons. They were the first I had seen this year with the exception of a few at the celebration of the 4th. Bro D, was as usualy full of sport, and raised many a hearty laugh in the course of the evening. Sister finally concluded to return with the D's and stop over night. Complained of sore eyes. Dr said he would prepare her some eyewater. On our return [*illegible crossout*] ~~and~~ sister Guy came with us, as far as father Kades, where she had been staying a few days, with the old people [Jonathan and Susanna Cade], who are both very feeble. Ten oclock when we reached home. Found A playing the violin.

Wed 8th Very warm. Took up the carpet. Mr C—— painting. Alma planted corn. Pm sewed on my dress. Evening wrote in my journal. Alma playing violin.

[News of Parley P. Pratt's Death]

Thurs 9th Sister came and invited me to accompany her to sister Hunts, said Lois was staying there, and wished us all to come. I did not like to refuse the invitation, but did not feel willing to leave home, as Mr C—— was setting glass and needed me to wash it. He also cut out a window in the north end of the house, and required my assistance. PM she came and told me that Lois had come home, and said we had better wait untill tomorrow, that the gen was preparing to leave for San F, and the next day they would be alo. She brought in Ellens babe, and a new periodical which she had just received from NY, published by a socialist. Read some in it. The gents idea of morality.

Heard elder P P Pratt was killed by McLain. We hardly credited the report at first, but toward 12 Mr C—— went to the P O—— and they assured him of the fact.[18] Bro Pratt took dinner with us.

Frid 10th I put down my carpet, kept myself very busy untill near two oclock, when I accompanied Ellen to sis Hunts. Sister, Lois, and Ann L were there before us, all seeming to enjoy themselves remarkably well.

Sister Hunt sent to the office and got the Mormon, and we read the account of eld P's assassination. Very few particullers were recorded. It is really shocking to reflect on. Ann L and I came home together, sisters Hunt and Pratt went over to Sheldon Stodards and staid over night, with sis Sherwood. Br P—— and Ellen went to bro Sealy's to eat peaches.

On our way home we (Ann L and myself) overtook sis Guy who said she was coming to my house to see Mr C—— about doing a little job for Mother Kade. She sat a few minutes and went to call on sister Farrall, who has just moved into Ridley's house, where sister Phillips formerly lived.

Sat 11th Mr C painting in the new house. I sewed on my dress. Pm he laid a floor in the chamber, moved up Alma's bed, trunk, sister Pattens chest &C. Evening I called into Ellens, sister was present. While there, sis Nancy Daily and Minerva Morse came in dressed in mens clothes, and quite deceived us. It made a deal of sport for the girls and children, but for one I did not feel like laughing very heartily. Alma irrigated for bro Pratt, and Ellen.

Sund 12th Mr C stoped at home to irrigate. Alma attended church. I did [not] go in consequence of weak eyes. After church called sister Patten, Spent the Pm with us. A Farnsworth and his wife called on us.

Mon 13th I washed, made light bread. Mr C went to the mill to work for br Hanks. Alma stacked barley. Bro Pratt assisted him awhile, but had a pain in his side, and got a boy to take his place.

Tues 14th Made pies, Ironed, and performed sundries. PM went into Ellens, finished my dark lawn dress. E gave me some trimming for it. Evening sister and Ellen into our house. Alma irrigated again for bro Pratt, was up untill 3 AM

[A Succession of Quiltings]

Wed 15th I cut shirts for Mr C—— PM went in co with sis P—— and assisted sis Cox on a quilt, which she had had on for 3 weeks. Staid a couple of hours.

Thurs 16th Alma went to sis Pattens and got quilting frames, and I put on a quilt. Charles Burk took dinner with us. Pm sister Cox sent and invited me to a quilting the next day. Said she would assist me again in return.

Frid 17th immediately after breakfast I went. Called at Ellens and took her babe along. Sis Pratt accompanied me. Sister Cox made us a splendid dinner. I left at 6 oclock.

Evening Al playing violin. After we had been in bed about an hour, some one knocked at the door. Mr C—— asked who was there, and a faint voice replied "sister Patten". I instantly arose, and lighting a lamp let her in. She said she wished to put some articles into a chest which Mr C had made for her, and which was in our new chamber. And that she took the advantage of the night and her husbands absence as she did not wish it known that she had things secreted.

Sat 18th Remarkably warm. After breakfast sis Pratt called in and invited me to accompany to in a walk to Lois's residence to which I cheerfully responded. We called a few minutes at bro Moses Harris'es. Found Lois alone in her house, and we thought she looked rather sad. Her father was building a henhouse for her. We spoke cheeringly to her concerning the place, and just as we were coming away her husband returned. He appeared very pleasant and cheerfully invited us to stop longer, and come again, &C. Sister returned with me. I made a cup of tea for dinner, and she spent the Pm, and assisted me on my quilt.

Sun 19th. I attended church. Bro Carter spoke to the congregation. PM the weather was remarkably warm. Sister Evans called on me. Toward night I commenced a letter to Lois Thompson. Evening called in co with my husband on sister Farrall. Think her a very agreeable woman.

Mon 20th. Washed, finished my letter to Lois. Mr C—— assisting Dr McIntire to prepare a daguerean gallery or hall. This was his [McIntire's] birthday 50 years old. I felt much fatigued after washing and found I had a lame back.

Tues 21st I quilted very steadily in the Am. Pm ironed.

Wed 22nd. Had an invitation to sister Stark's quilting but did not feel able to go. Sis P—— and Ellen went. Toward night Lois came in and quilted for me an hour. Her husband called for her.

Thurs 23rd My back very lame and painful. Quilted some. Ellen came and helped me awhile. Sister Homes called for some beets. She and E took supper with us. Mr C—— gave her the bengal locker that bro Fotheringham gave us. Or rather sent it to her sister Mother Boothe, as she had asked him for it. Sister McIntire came, and stoped overnight with sister Pratt.

Frid 24th I had a hard days work, expected the threshers the next day, but toward noon a man called to say they were not coming untill monday. Pm came sisters McIntire Guy, Pratt, McG. The Dr also came and took tea with us. After supper we had a feast of melons. Sent for bro Pratt who also came and enjoyed them with us. The sisters quilted some for me.

Sat 25th I felt very miserable all day. Bathed 2 or 3 times, &C. Sister L P came over awhile, and assisted in getting off my quilt. Pm I bound it, and put it on the bed.

Evening had a severe turn of backache. Bro Tomkins came with the thresher, placed it ready to commence operations early on mon. I went to bed early after bathing, but slept very little through the night, as Alma was irrigating, and disturbed my slumbers by going and coming several times.

Sun 26th A irrigating again. Mr C—— gone to church. My back pained me rather badly. Evening came two of the threshers.

Mon 27th They all came on "bright and early". I arose quite early and commenced about breakfast. Brs Tomkins Burk, and an englishman took breakfast with us. Ellen came and assisted me in getting dinner. We had 6 men to dine with us. At one they finished the threshing, ate dinner and left.

Tues 28th The men getting in barley. I fixed my pink dress.

Wed 29th Alma washed for me. Evening I sent for John and Lois, sis Pratt, Ann L, and Ellen, to come and eat melons. They all came and brought Truman S——w—— out with them.

Thurs 30th came sister Davies with her two children. She saw I felt unwell, and kindly offered to assist me, which assistance I very readily accepted. We got dinner together, and enjoyed it finely.

After school came bro D——, took supper with us, feasted on melons, went to bro Carters, brought smoked pork, roselle plant for jellies, tarts, &C, divided it with me. We enjoyed their visit finely, esteem them highly as friends and Saints. The salt lake mail arrived. Mr C brought in Deseret news.

Frid 31st I ironed, picked tomatoes, put some out to dry. Evening sister and Ann came in to eat melons.

Bro Pratt returned from a hunting excursion, with 3 antelopes.

Sat Aug the 1st 1857. Very pleasant day. I arose at 6 oclock. Breakfasted at 7. Bro P—— sent us a quarter of venison. I baked some, made soup, pie, gave to sister Farrall &C. Alma finishing henhouse. Mr C making a counter for bro Lee's store.

Sun 2nd I stoped at home. Thought I would write to Sister Snow. Got my paper and ink ready to commence, when directly came in sister Louisa P——, and soon after sister Patten, on her way to church. I commenced reading Deseret news, and they became so interested, that they declined going to meeting, and listened very attentively. I read 3 or 4 sermons from bro Young and some of the twelve apostles. Ellen went to church, and returned sick. Evening I went into see her. She had high fever, had been bathing, took pack sheet &C.

Sister Patten stoped and took dinner with us. I commenced a letter to sis E R Snow, after all left.

Mon 3rd Called over to see Ellen, and found her mother very sick with the same complaint, cold and fever, with pain in her head, and back.

[A Little Melon Feast]

Tues 4th A——— and I washed. Sister Jackson called, had been stoping over night with sister Stark, who had been having fits, or paralytic shocks. Said she was better.

Evening went over to see sister, found her quite bad, with fever. Ellen, Louisa and their father came in to eat melons.

Wed 5th After regulating my affairs, went to bro Lee's store, traded 7 or 8 dolls. Got 40 yds bleached muslin, thread, soap. When I reached home found Dr McIntire here, eating melons with Mr C———. We invited him to bring his wife in the evening, to a little melon feast. Mr C——— also invited bro and sis Moses Harris. Sister Mc came before dark, found bro and sis Harris here, and joined them in eating and lively conversation. At candlelight came Lois, with bro Frank Dewey, and wife, Harriet Hunt, and Edna Ladd. They all ate melons to their hearts content, thanked us for the entertainment, and gave us many invitations to return their call.

Thurs 6th ran over to see sister, found her much better, but complaining of great weakness.

Frid 7th I wrote a letter to sister Elizabeth Pratt, finished Sis Snows, and wrote one for Mr C———, to bro Whitaker. Evening went into sisters, found sister Hunt there. I read to them from the Western Standard, more concerning bro Parleys death. Bro Davis called and ate dinner, and melons with us.

Sat 8th Heard the mail was not going untill noon, and wrote a short letter to bro and sis Taite, and Johny. Sent it to bro Daily's, to go by private conveyance, as I supposed the mail was closed. I went into Ellen's, read a letter from Jones Dire and Frances, to bro Pratt. Fr——— said they will not be down, untill another Spring. PM——— Sister Pratt, and Ellen, irrigating.

Evening extremely warm. I think it has been the warmest day of the year. Thunder with rain on the mountains.

Sun 9th remarkably warm, and still, not a leaf stirs. Mr C——— irrigating this morning. I felt very weak and faint. Wanted to go to church, but could not get ready in season. Mr C——— and A——— gone ~~to church~~. Sister sent for me to come, and stay with her, while Ann L went on a ride, to San Bernardino. I went, and took tea with her. She complained of being very unwell. I read to her, in the Western Standard.

Mon 10th extremely warm. ^Rain last night, quite a shower.^ I made pants for Alma. Sister P. came in awhile. Brought Ellens babe. Dr McIntire came to the shop to get his carriage repaired. Came in, and talked with us, a short time. Evening Mr Crosby invited bro and sister Cox to come and eat melons. Sister Pratt, Ellen, Louisa, and Edna Ladd, ^also sister Farrell^ accompanied them. We had some very nice melons, and a lively chat. Lois, and Harriet Hunt, with Jane Stodard's little daughter, were in before sunset, and ate some melons. I showed them our shells, and corals which they admired much.

Tues 11th Quite pleasant. Last night it rained another hard shower. Alma assisted me in washing. Mr C—— at work for John Stewart.

Wed 12th Mr C—— gone again to work for Stewart. I ironed. Alma plastering the kitchen. I some expected sis Hunt, but heard she is coming tomorrow. Bro Pratt Ad—— returned from the mountain, where he has been several days. Said the rain did an amount of damage to the mill.

Thurs 13th Mr Crosby and Alma went to work for bishop Collins, building a storehouse, or grainary for the tithing grain. And also to pay up their tithing.

PM came sisters Hunt, Morse, Pratt, McGary, and Ann L. Sophronia and Epraim naturally followed in the rear. We enjoyed the visit finely. The sisters related dreams visions &C. While I read to them, sister Snows letter, and the Salt lake catechism.

Evening I ran into Ellens, and shortly after came in bro and sis Pratt. E—— told us she thought her cow was sick, and we all out to the yard to examine her, concluded she had the hernail [hernia?].

Frid 14th more cool and pleasant. Mr C——, and A——, gone again, to bro Colllins. I feel feverish, and some what fear I am going to be attacked with the general epidemick, which is a bad cold, accompanied with fever.

Sat 15th feel much better. My cold seems to have passed away. Mr C—— and Alma gone again to bro Collins, worked untill 12 oclock, and then came home. Mr C—— went to a mass meeting. Alma irrigating garden for Ellen.

Evening sister called, and invited us to come over, and eat grapes. My husband and self accompanied her home, spent the evening, in eating grapes; bro Pratt also had whisky, which he and Mr C partook of.

[Death of George Clark's Child]

San Bernardino
Sunday morning Aug 16th AD 1857
This morning before breakfast called bros Pratt, and John G[h]een. The latter informed us, that bro George Clarks' little child, a year and half old, was dead. That it died Saturday night, having been sick only one day, and wished Mr Crosby to make a coffin for it. He consented to do so, and went with bro Geen to see the child. Soon returned with the lumber. He and Al worked quite steadily untill afternoon to finish it.

About 11 oclock I went with sister Pratt, to bro C's. Found a number of persons present. Lois, and Harriet Hunt, were (with another lady) employed in making its graveclothes. Sister Clark conversed with us respecting her child's death. Said it apparently suffered no pain, was sick with diarhea only one day, walked across the house, about a half hour, before it died, Said it had a little spasm, and then commenced breathing shorter and shorter, untill it died, without a struggle, or groan.

Bro Geen was residing there, and he informed my husband, that sister Clark had the spirit of prophesy, come up[on] her, after her child died; and told her husband, that unless they repented and lived their religion, that in 3 weeks, she should be in her grave, and he would be left alone. She alluded to his late reckless way of living, having given himself to drinking, and intoxication. He said that he asked her the next morning, whether she remembered what she said the night previous, or whether she was not a little delirious, but she said she remembered perfectly well, and that it would be even so.

Sister and I stoped a short time, and returned as far as sister Hamiltons, found them complaining with colds. They urged us to stay. And sister Mary Hamilton, formerly Sparks, put on the tea kettle, and made us a nice dinner.

After the coffin was carried by, we went in again. Bros Cox and Thomas came in, the latter gave a short exhortation, and prayed. They then went to the grave. In the course of the day, two others, called on Mr C, for coffins, but he refered them to other mechanics.

PM he attended a counsel meeting. Evening called sister Farrrall and her eldest son, Robert. They made us a pleasant call.

Mon 17th Very warm again. Mr C——, and A——, at work for bro Collins. Pm we had thunder, and appearances of rain. Bro P came in, to grind coffee, said he was going on another hunting excursion, in pursuit of antelope.

Tues 18th rather more cool. I washed. Sister Pratt sent for me, to come, and visit, with her, and sis Thomas. After washing and regulating everything about house, I went over. It was after 3 oclock, when I got ready to leave. I found sisters Thomas and Cox there. Ellen and Ann L had gone to sis McIntires. I enjoyed a few hours very well. Toward night invited the sisters home with me, to eat melons. Had some nice ones. Gave sis Thom—— one, to carry to her husband, she said he was unwell. Dr McIntire brought the girls home, in his carriage. Said he was going to see sister Rolfe, who was sick. Sister and I proposed accompanying him, and got in the carriage. We had a pleasant ride, found sis R some better. She has had an attack of fever, or the epidemick which is passing through the country. Evening A—— playing violin.

19th Wed quite pleasant and cool. Drying tomatoes. Made duff [thick flour pudding] for dinner, carried over some to Ellen.

Thurs 20th I ironed, mended shirts. Wrote some in my journal. PM went into sister Dewels, to see a sick woman, by the name of Webb, wife of

Edwin Webb. She said she had been sick for 8 months. Sister D—— took her home with her that day, to nurse, and doctor her, and if possible, try to cure her. Said she had had a pair of twin children, 3 months old, that the little girl died last sunday. She had the appearance of having the dropsy, Was very much swollen. She was also distressed for breath, and had a cough. I thought her situation a very precarious one.

[Brother Joseph Barnes's Likeness]

Frid 21st. Read some, went into Ellens. The stage came in, but no papers. Alma brought in a likeness, and laid on the stand. I said it was sister Dolly's or bro Joseph's. Opened it and found a letter from the latter, but the minature I should not have known. However I was much pleased with it, and ran over to show it to Louisa. She could not see Joseph in it, but our older bro Horace, and Alma thought it resembled me.

At 9 oclock I went into stay a few hours with the sick sister. She said she felt much better, and slept some, and rested considerably through the day. I stoped with her untill 12 oclock and then my husband came to accompany me home.

Sat 22nd performed sundry duties. After breakfast I sat down with br Joseph's likeness, to try if I could possibly recognize him in it. I talked to it, said, O bro Joe! if I could only see you smile, and hear you speak, I should then think it was you. But neither words nor smiles came from it. Sister came in to look at it again, thought it resembled Horace. PM I ran in again to see sis Webb. Sister Pratt was with me. She thought she felt better. Sis P—— and Ellen went in the evening to wacth but the sick woman thought it unnecessary, and they returned. Alma worked for bro Smithson, threshing wheat.

Sun 23rd Cool and comfortable. I attended meeting, heard a bro Baxter, a scotchman, lately returned from Aus—— mission. He was followed by bro, or pres—— Cox, who warned us against breaking the Sabbath day, said he feared some of our young men, and boys, had gone to a horse race. Exhorted the young sisters, to hold at arms length, those young gents, who spent their Sabbaths, around grog shops, or going to races; "for (said he) they will not make you good husbands."

Pm Mr Crosby invited sister Farrall to come over with her children, to eat melons. Accordingly she came and brought them all with her. I felt quite miserable. Pm was very tired and overcome with heat.

Mon 24th Alma went again to work for bro Smithson. I went in and sat awhile with sister. Just before sunset we took a walk to see sister Frances Clark. Found them just returned from bro Hopkins, where they had been staying since the burial of their little child. Sister Booth was sitting with them. Sis C was talking of her lost child and weeping freely, when we went in. It is quite distressing to hear her lament. We made a short stay, and then went to see sis Webb. She was sitting up, her husband was bathing her limbs, which were bloated to an amazing size. We staid a short time, and returned.

[A Death from Dropsy]

Tues 25th I washed. Mr C—— and Alma making bathing room. Sister Pratt came in with E's babe. About 6 oclock bro Webb Sent his little son for us, in a great haste, said they thought their mother was dying. We went directly, found she had failed very much. She requested the elders to come in and lay hands on her, and I went immediately for my husband, and bro Harris. They anointed her with oil and blest her with ease, rebuked all her pains, and commended her to the Spirit of God, told her she should die in peace, and go to rest from all her cares, and sorrows. Shortly after I asked her if she felt any pain. She said no, excepting a coldness, about her neck, and shoulders, which proved to be the grasp of death. For in about half an hour, she breathed her last, without a struggle or groan, told them she was going then, and closed her eyes in peace.

I assisted in laying her out, Came home about 11 oclock. But by this time my nerves had become so excited, that there was no sleep for me, untill 3 oclock Am. I then fell asleep and slept untill 6.

Wed 26th I ironed, made light bread &C. Mr Crosby and Alma made the coffin. I assisted in lining it; felt quite miserable, all day. PM I went down with sister, and helped to prepare her, to be laid in the coffin. I talked some of going with them to the grave but it was so near night, and the carriages were nearly full without me, I therefore declined. Sister Patten called a few minutes. I had another sleepless night, slept none untill after twelve oclock.

Thurs 27th Mr C still at work on the bathroom.[19] Alma making a partition in my kitchen for a pantry and store room.

I dresssed and cooked a chicken. Sister and Ellen came in and ate dinner with us. And afterward bro P and Ann L. Bro Pratt complimented me on my good dinner, and thanked me for inviting him to partake of it with us. Evening sister Hopkins and children, came to sisters. I went over a moment, to speak with her. She told me she had been out of health for four weeks past. Near 12 when I droped to sleep. Notwithstanding I took nervine.

Frid 28th Very warm day. I felt my system quite relaxed. Sister Hopkins came in, and staid a couple of hours, ate dinner with us, after which I accompanied her to Ellens, where we spent the PM, with sisters Daily, and Clark. Dr McIntire called for sis H—— and children. I invited them to come home with me, to see my new pattentwright bathing establishment. The Dr, and sis D, came, and admired it much. Evening Mr C went out to visit the ward in his office of teacher. I felt lonely, and went into sisters, they were all absent, had gone into bro Cox's. I followed them. Bro C—— had just reached home, had been out on a 2 or 3 days hunting excursion; killed one deer, and caught a few fish.

Sat 29th We had thunder and appearances of rain. Alma finished my pantry. I regulated it, and made duff for dinner. PM went with sister P—— to Lois's. We had a severe storm of wind, with some rain. Had a pleasant visit. John H—— just returned from Los Angles. I slept well at night.

Sun 30th, quite pleasant and cool. I attended church. Bishop Crosby spoke to us, much to the purpose. Also pres—— Cox. PM commenced a letter to bro Joseph. Mr C—— attended the counsel meeting. After he returned we took a walk to Dr Mc's. They were all gone, accordingly we walked to bro Simeon Andrews, where we were treated to grapes and peaches. Visited with bro and sister Sealy, also bro and sis Jones. Had a very agreeable time.

Mon 31st I expected the mail would leave early, and my letter was not ready, which was some unpleasant for me. However toward night Ellen informed me that it was not going untill the next day. Evening I finished, and sent it, together with Alma's likeness, to bro Joseph Barnes.

Mr C—— gone to hear Moses Martin lecture, on Black republicanism. Alma reading in the united states speaker.

Tues Sept 1st I washed in the Am. Pm papered the kitchen and pantry. Sisters Patten and Pratt called a few minutes.

Wed 2nd I slept very late. Bro and sis McMurtry called. He had been to the P O—— got letters from their daughter, and sister, of Great Salt lake city. His sister stated that she was in great trouble, concerning her son, John P Al[l]red. She had heard that he was imprisoned in Cal—— for seven years. She had not seen him in 5 years, requested her bro to make inquiry concerning him, and let her know the worst of it. Bro Mc went in pursuit of a bro Birch, in hopes to gain some intelligence of him, but did not find him. Sister Mc—— wished me to come to her house, and write a letter for them, as they neither of them could write very well. I promised to go if they would come for me, with a carriage.

PM came sister Davis, and her sis Anna, with the children. They took supper with us, afterwards had a feast of melons. Alma played the violin to them, and finally escorted them home. Beautifull moonlight evening. The seranaders of the election were out, making the city ring, with their songs and cheering.

Thurs 3rd, ironed. Ellen sent her babe over to stay with me, while she went out shopping. Evening went with br and sis Pratt, to bro Sealy's, to eat peaches. Had a very agreeable time, ate our fill of very delicious fruit. They also gave us some to bring home.

Frid 4th Mother Dewel called to get a little job done in the shop. Last night I had a rather singular dream. I thought I saw bro and sis Pratt led out, her to be beheaded, and him to be shot. I turned my back upon the scene, and would not see it, put my fingers in my ears, that I could not hear their groans. However I thought they were both to live again eventually. The connexion I could not recollect.

This evening we went to a singing party to br Thomas's. Were entertained by a bro by the name of Hosking, late from Salt lake, on his way to Eng—— on a mission. He sang a number of new songs. Some of them rather comical. Enough so to excite our risible organs, quite freely.

Sat 5th I received a visit from Sister Crandle. She said she had been talking of coming to see me for some time, and as they were expecting to move a half mile farther from us, thought she would come before they went.

I was highly pleased to see her, enjoyed her company much. Sent for sister Pratt, who came and dined with us. We talked of past days, when the Church of Christ was small and could all assemble under one roof, to hear the words of eternal life, from the mouth of the prophet of the Lord. And our hearts burned within us, as we conversed upon the great work of the last days. I read sister Snows letter to her, and she requested me to remember her when I wrote again. Toward night I accompanied her to sisters, where we met sister McIntire. The Dr also called while we were there. Evening br Hosking called and ate supper with us, after which we accompanied him to sisters, where was another singing party, and bro H—— sang his new songs.

Sunday 6th directly after breakfast called bro and sister McMurtry, to get me to write a couple of letters for them, to their friends in Utah. I wrote one to their bro Levi Allred, of Pleasant grove, Utah, before meeting, and after we returned, I wrote another, to Alexander Brown, and wife, who is their daughter. Directed to Ogden city.

Pm called sister Patten a few minutes. I felt very weak, and unwell. Evening took a walk with my husband to John Hunts. He and Lois were absent. We found Harriet there alone. Mr Moses Morse called in, and we sat awhile, and enjoyed an hour or more quite agreeably. Harriet was very polite, and did her best to entertain us, by showing us pictures, and likenesses.

Mon 7th I still feel very weak, and feeble. Took a shower bath, which revived me some. Alma assisted me in washing.

Evening we were invited again to John Hunts. Went with sister and Ann L. Alma waited for Ellen and her father. There was quite a company of us. John treated us to egg nogg. We had songs, and music on the violin and accordion. At ten we came up to Ellens, where the young folks danced untill 12. My husband and self came home at ten.

Tues 8th John H—— started with the mail for Gr—— S—— L City. I cut garments. Pm accompanied sister, Ellen and Ann L to bro Thomas's.

Had a fine visit, were treated to fruit, had a good supper, traded some. Got a box of tea, and pair of shoes. Toward night ran into sister Hunts a few minutes. Sis Thomas accompanied us.

Wed 9th Ironed, cleaned my bedstead. Bro Hosking came to stop with us. Evening sister Farrell and her children came in to sing with us. Bro H—— tried to learn us some of his new songs. Bro P came in, but his folks were gone to a quilting, to bro Grundy's.

Thurs 10th Baked light bread, cleaned the chamber, papered some in the kitchen.

Frid 11th Bro Harris called in the morning, and informed Mr C that he would accompany him on their visiting tour the next evening. After breakfast bro Hosking went out to bro George Day's. Ellen brought me a little satchel that she bought for me.

[An Indian Boy]

Sat 12th I had an indian boy picking tomatoes for me. He also cut some, and put them to dry, appeared quite willing to work. I made him a number of presents, and at night sent him away to his home. But he shortly returned saying he had neither father or mother, or home. Spoke very good Spanish. Said had "no aie padre, no aie madre, no ae casa." I then took him to the shop, and he made him a bed in the shavings, and laid himself down for the night.

Sun 13th fine cool morning. I attended meeting. Bro Hughs spoke to the people with a good deal of interest, was followed by bro Hosking.

After meeting I called over to sisters. Sister Denitia Lyman was there. Sister and I took a walk around the lots. She told me some of her trials, with her husband, his hard Speeches, and the disunion that existed between them. I felt sorry, to know their great unhappiness.

Evening a company of us took a walk to Col Jacksons, to a singing party. Had a fine time.

Mon 14th Bro Harris called and invited us to his house that evening to eat peaches. My indian boy called again for pan [*bread, Sp.*], said he was mucho hungry. I gave him bread and meat.

I churned, washed, made light bread. Bro Hosking came again, took dinner with us, went to bro Mowry's, and stoped over night.

Evening we all went to bro H's, had a fine interview, and a plenty of peaches. Bro Har gave us some to bring home.

Tues 15th Bro Hosking returned after breakfast. We also received a call from bro Baxter, late returned missionary from Aus——. They both took dinner with us, and we had very social times with them.

Wed 16th Sister called early and invited me to come over and visit with sisters Stark, and Sealy. After dinner I went and found them enjoying themselves finely, and sister Guy was also with them. After tea they walked home with me, to see my bathroom. All admired it much.

Thurs 17th I was invited to a quilting to bro Sullivans. Got on the way, and met sister Thomas coming to visit me. I told her that I was glad she had come, for I did not care about going. She said she had an invitation also to a quilting, but did not feel able to quilt. I enjoyed her society exceedingly. She also seemed highly pleased with her visit. I accompanied her as far as sisters, on her way home.

Evening the young people had a party at Ellen's. Alma went.

[A Pleasure Excursion to Lytle Creek]

Frid 18th Bro Cox sent us word, that they were going for a pleasure ride to bro George Day's,[20] and invited us to accompany them. We readily accepted the invitation, and made ourselves ready. At ten oclock they called for us with a spring carriage. Edna Ladd, and their little adopted daughter, were with them. Charlie Bills stoped with Alma.

We were hailed by bro [Isaac] Goodwin,[21] and invited to stop there. Bro Cox told us as we were on a pleasure excursion we might as well stop awhile. I had never been there before, but had been many times invited. We enjoyed ourselves highly. Were treated to fruit of various kinds. Sis Goodwin also made us a cup of tea, and gave us a nice lunch, of peach pie doughnuts preserves bread and butter &C. Upon the whole we had a very jolly time of it, and went on our way rejoicing. We passed bro Dires house, and bro George Garners. Reached bro D[ay]'s in good time, enjoyed a pleasant interview with him, were treated to grapes and figs, wine and melon whiskey. He invited us into his dairy house, gave us bread, butter, and cheese, all of his own make.

We found him very familliar and agreeable. I should judge him to be between 25 and 30 years of age, has a nice vineyard and peach orchard, is a single man, with only one hired laborer, a bro Baldwin, who works his distillery.

We passed many merry jokes, on his getting a wife, and agreed to speak favorably of him, to the young ladies in the city. He made us a present of a bucket of grapes to bring home. Invited us to come again, and teated us remarkably friendly.

On returning bro Cox took a different rout, that we might have an opportunity to see more of the country.

We saw many pleasant locations, admired their large fields of corn, and substantial live fence, which makes quite an imposing appearance. We reached home just before the sunset. Found Alma and Charles had spent the day very agreeably together. Evening went into Ellens. Sister Blackburn was there. Sister P—— invited me to come and spend the evening with them, said sis B—— was going to stop over night with her. But I was rather tired, and did not go over.

~~F~~— *Sat 19th.* I went over to assist sister Sullivan on her quilt but found her house closed. Went into sister Coxes, heard they were all down to her father, Jo Matthew's. Who had a sick child. It died that morning, and Mr Crosby made the coffin, in the Pm I went with sister to John Hunts. Lois and Harriett were alone. We took dinner with them. I commenced piecing me a basket quilt.

Sun 20th I stoped at home. Wrote in my journal. Mr C—— gone to church. Evening I went a few minutes into Sis Farrall's. While there Ann L Pratt came and invited us over to their house to a singing party. Went and found quite a collection. Dr Mc and wife and bro Hosking, Sister Jackson and her stepson Clarence; Harriet Hunt, and shortly after came bro and sister Sullivan, and sis Daily. We sang songs, and hymns, intermingled. Comic, sentimental and religious.

Mon 21st I washed. Sister and Ellen came in, and ate dinner with us. Evening took a walk with my husband, to bro Jone's, to buy some peaches. ^She was alone with her boy.^ Her husband had gone to the mountain. Said she had none to sell, but gave us all we could eat.[22]

Tues 22nd, after breakfast, I went again to sis Sullivan, but she was absent, gone out to invite quilters.

I returned, and sewed for sister Pratt, made dress for El's babe. Sister expected Dr McIntire to call and take her with his wife to sis—— Blackburn's. They did not come untill evening, when they came and took her home with them, intending to go the next morning.

Wed 23rd, Sister Sullivan sent for me to come to a quilting. Accordingly I went in the Pm, found quite a party of young ladies. Evening I sewed on my quilt lining.

Thur 24th. Mr C finished laying the chamber floor. Pm I put my quilt up there on the frames and commenced quilting. Evening took a walk with sister, in pursuit of her shears, which had been stolen by an indian boy.

Went as far as G Rolfe's. Called on sis Dewel, sister Harris, Ellis Eame's, &C. Sis engaged Rolfes' children to hunt the indian and try to get them for her. Evening went into E's and sewed awhile. Bro Sealy brought the remainder of lumber for the floor.

Frid 25th I made bread and pies. PM sis Patten called. I quilted a little toward night.

Sat 26th quilted again. Mr C laying the lower floor. Evening went into Ellens, she and her mother piecing a quilt.

Sun 27th I felt very poorly, but went to meeting, in hopes of getting revived. Sermon by bro Baxter. Before he closed the north wind commenced blowing, and it became so uncomfortable that the president dismissed the congregation, without administering the sacrament.

PM remarkably warm. Evening the wind ceased, and my husband and self went out for a walk, Went as far as Dr McIntire's, they being absent we continued our walk to bro Thomas, where I traded some. Bought me a pair of shoes, and green calico. Had a very pleasant chat with bro and sis Thomas, who we found sitting alone in their dooryard, enjoying the cool evening air, after the warm windy day.

Mon 28th Still very warm. I quilted, quite steadily. Mr C went early over to bro Hanks mill, and did a job of joiner work. Alma preparing to go again with bro Harris to the mountain to work. Went to market, bought sugar. Evening Ellen got on her quilt.

Tues 29th I arose early, prepared breakfast, and Alma set off to the mountain. After he was gone, I washed. Mr C laying the lower floor. Pm I went into Ellen's, Several of the sisters helping her on her quilt, sisters Cox, Sherwood, Sullivan, Stark, Guy and Farrall.

They all came over to see our new house, and quilt, which they admired much. Evening we were alone. Alma gone. It truly seems lonely to see his place vacant, ~~at the table~~ as well at the reading table, as at the evening meal.

Mr C reading general Lee's oration on the death of Washington. I wrote in my journal.

[Emigrants Killed at Mountain Meadows]

Wed 30th I ironed, made light bread. Pm went into E's and assisted a few minutes, on her quilt. Evening bro Pratt called a short time, informed us that bro Wm Matthews had reached home, and brought the melancholly intelligence of a large party of emigrants from Missouri, to Cal—— being killed by indians. Said they excited their rage, by poisoning a dead ox, which the indians ate, and several of them died immediatly. That they then pursued the party a[nd] killed all, save a few little children, and they were taken to Filmore city, and left with the Saints.[23]

Thurs Oct 1st I brought my quilt out of the chamber, as the weather was so extremely warm, put it in the new lower room, and found it much more comfortable. Mr C—— cleaned the clock. Ann L P came in, to bathe.

Evening called bro David Seely. Talked of giving Mr C—— a job of house building, for his bro in law —— [Edwin] Petit. Bro Pratt was also in. We had a very social chat together.

Frid 2nd Mr C—— went to work for bro Seely. I called on sis Harris, and invited her to come and quilt with me a little while in the Pm. I made tomatoe preserves. Sis Har—— came in, and we had quite a sociable time together.

Evening called bro Hanks and handed me a letter from bro Thom Whitaker, from which we learned, that there was considerable excitement among the Saints in that place, in regard to the new Gov.[24] Evening Mr C—— brought home Deseret news, and read several sermons.

Sat 3rd he went again to bro Seely's. Sophronia brought me a letter from sister Tait, which she sent by bro Tanner. It was the first intelligence I had received from Johny since he left, and I was highly gratified with it.

Sun 4th Our semiannual conference commenced. We all attended. Enjoyed the meeting finely. It continued all day.

Mon 5th Bro and sister McMurtry called early, had been to the store, brought all their children. I rode with them to meeting. At noon they came home with us, and took dinner. PM we all went again, had a good time. Our pres told us to come again the next day, as he was reserving the best preachers untill the last. Evening bro Pratt came and assisted Mr C, and Alma in killing a hog. Quite late when they got through.

Tues 6th went again to meeting. Bros [William] Matthews, [Sidney] Tanner and [William] Hide[25] related the circumstances of their journey to Salt lake city, and return. And gave an account of the masacre of a large number of emigrants to Cal—— by the indians. It was quite an exciting affair. It rained last night which made it quite damp, in the bowery.

Wed 7th Alma and I washed, made light bread, mince pies fried cakes, &C. Sister McIntire Pratt and Lois came in, and quilted awhile for me. Lois assisted me in getting supper.

Mail came in from the upper country. Brought me a letter from Frances, and one from sister D B—— Lockwood, and my nephew Charles Barnes, Son of bro Cyprian Barnes. Sister informed me of the death of Barnard Stevens. And also that sister Lois Thompson had buried a little boy 6 years old. Sister Mc spent part of the evening with us, and as the Dr did not come for her, went to sis P's and stoped over night.

Thurs 8th It rained very hard last night, which is quite uncommon at this season of the year. While I was preparing breakfast who should make his appearance but Wm McGary, just from San Jose valley, where he had been at work through harvest. It rained a great deal through the day. I made pies, doughnuts &C.

Frid 9th I ironed. PM came sister, Lois and Ann L—— and quilted for me.

Sat 10th performed sundry duties. ^I made jam of roselle plant, which A—— got of sis Jackson.^ Pm quilted. Evening went into Ellens a was made acquainted with a bro Miles, and Knolton, two young men from Salt lake, who had been sent to the Sandwich islands, but recalled home with all the upper country brethren.[26]

Sun 11th attended meeting, heard bro Rainy preach, was much interested. Saw sister Sargent, just from San Francisco, on her way to the valley.

PM with my husband, called on sister Canan, at bro Buttons. Evening came bros Miles, Knolton, and Baxter. Bro and sis McGary, and all of bro Pratts family, with Harriet Hunt and Lewis Newel. Also sis Farrell. We had lively conversation together with vocal and instrumental music. ^Bro Hanks, and a bro St John called, to see Mr C—— about getting work done on the mill.^

Mon 12th Alma left home in co with bro Harris, for the mountains. I washed, sister Farrell came in to help me quilt, but said she did not like to work alone, and would assist me untill I was ready to go in with her. Took hold of the washing, and we soon had it done with.

I prepared dinner, and just as it was nearly ready, came sister Cannon. We had a nice dinner, and fine visit with her. She also quilted some. At sunset, called her bros, Lucas Hoagland, and David Cannon, to help her home with the babe. Evening I was quite afflicted with sore eyes. Had an invitation to spend the evening with the young elders aforesaid, at bro Pratts. Went over, but could not enjoy it much on account of my eyes.

Tues 13th My eyes some better. Wrote in my journal, which I found in a neglected state. Beautiful weather now. Evening I accompanied my husband to father Aldridge's. Found the old folks alone, they were pleased to see us. thanked us for calling, and invited us to come again.

Wed 14th Mr C—— making sash. I ironed. Little Johny Hayborn staid with me to do chores. Sister called and invited me to come over and visit with sisters Sargent and Stark.

Pm I went over. After supper or rather dinner, I invited the sister to come and see where I lived. They accompanied me home. Sis Sar—— admired the place much, thought she could be satisfied to stay in San B——, if it was the right place for the saints. Sis—— Farrell informed me that a ships comp of Saints had arrived at the coast from Aus——

Thurs 15th Mr C—— gone to the mill to work. I am left alone. But bless the Lord his Spirit is with me, and my heart is light. I feel to trust in Him at all times, and believe He cares for us. Pm came sister Tomkins. I was alone, and was much pleased to see her. She had been to the store. We enjoyed the time finely. I got her a good dinner, and just as it was ready came Mr C from the mill. Evening I went into sis Far[rell's] and carried her a little milk.

Frid 16th I went to Lee's store with eggs. Traded 2 dolls ½. Got hickory for Alma shirts, box tea, coarse comb, first reader for Johny &C. Sister Dewel called for Mr C—— to go and administer to bro Webb's sick child. Evening we were alone.

Sat 17th Very warm. Sister P—— called, told some particulars of the terrible insurrection in India.

Toward night I went in to Sister Dewel's to see a sick child of E——
D. Webb's, found it very low. Dr McIntire called thought it a doubtful
case. When I reached home found Alma returned from the mountain.
Came home for more provision.

[Arrival of Australian Emigrants]

Sun 18th Attended meeting, heard elders Daudle and Hall, late returned missionaries from Aus——. They represented 73 new members from Aus——.[27]
Who were received into the fellowship of the church in this place.

The pres—— made an appointment for Mr Bateman the method-
ist minister to preach at 3 oclock. At the close of the meeting Mr B shook
hands with us, said he had come to live among us. Invited us to call on
them. Said he did not believe in so much powder and bullets, but more in
praying. Seemed to insinuate something, as though we were for war. I told
him I had much rather <u>pray</u> than <u>fight</u>. 3 oclock Mr C—— went to meeting.
I stoped at home to cook something for Al——, to carry on the mountain.

Evening, accompanied my husband to bro Dewels, found the child
had died, at 4 oclock. Bro D—— called to get Mr C to make a coffin for it.
Evening went into Ellens a few minutes. While there, came Frank Garner
and Amanda Tomkins.

Mon 19th Alma went at an early hour, with his two sacks of provision, bound for the mountains. Sister Harris brought hers up to him. He
hoped to find <u>teams</u>, before he got far, who would take his load for him.
I washed. Sister Farrell sent her little boy to do chores for me. Pm came
sister and the girls to help me on my quilt. I cooked a chicken and made
them a good dinner. Sister cut pants for Mr C——. ^bro Baxter came in.^
Evening ran into sister F——ll's ^When I returned found bro Davis here,
reading accounts from indie.^

Tues 20th I put out my clothes. Very still and pleasant. Sister came
and sewed all day. Evening I took a walk with my husband to Lees' store.
We got a gallon of oil, and a wooden box for butter. I felt very unwell.
Returned and went directly to bed.

Wed 21st I ironed. Sister came again, took dinner with us. Finished the
pants, and quilted some. Pm came sis F——ll, and with her a sis Hunter,
just from Aus—— She is the mother of sis E—— Guy. We admired her
address, and thought her much like her daughter. Evening I sewed on a
shirt for Alma.

Thurs 22nd Some expected sisters Stark and Sargent. Made pumkin
pies. Johny F——ll worked for me.

Pm Alma returned from the mount——s. Said bro H was unable
to work, and therefore they had come home. Sister F——ll came in and
quilted a few minutes.

Frid 23rd I made catsup, also prickly pear jelly. Evening finished my quilt, and was much rejoiced, had it in the frames 3 weeks.

Circus rode by, performances at 8 oclock in the evening.

Sat 24th rose at near 7 oclock, felt very unwell, took a shower bath some better; think I had a chill last night. Quite unwell through the day. Took bitter herb tea. Binding my quilt. Sister came in with E's babe. I made light bread.

rained last night, several showers through the day. Sis—— informed me that Mr Sargent had arrived.

Mr C—— attended court, was a juryman on a case between C Glasier and his creditors in San F——. received 4 dolls for his fees. Evening Wm McGary called, with a Mr Vanluven who wished to borrow bro C——s flute, to play in the circus. Wm invited me to accompany them, said Maam Pratt was going, and would like my company. But I did not feel able to go. Bro Pratt came in said the mail had arrived. bro Crosby went over, but found nothing for us. Young elders Miles and Nolton called at Wm's. Bros Pratt and Crosby went over to see them, as Wm was absent. Mr C finished the lower floor in the new house.

Sun 25th I took salts. Mr C went to meeting. A—— and I stoped at home. I wrote or commenced a letter to D B Lockwood. PM called bro and sis Guy, and bro Miles—— Orson. I was not expecting anyone, but still was pleased to see them. ^Got them a good supper, and spent the evening very agreeably in singing with flute and violin.^

Mon 26th Beautiful day. Alma and I washed, churned, made pumpkin pies, and performed sundry other duties.

PM called bros Miles and Nolton, asked me to bake them some crackers, for their journey, expect to leave in a few days. I told them I would make them if they would bring me the flour. They said they had no money, but wished to pay in books. I did not understand that they wished me to find flour, but after they were gone, thought that probably they did.

[A Satisfying Dinner Party]

Tues 27th I commenced quite early, to make preparation for my company Baked sweet cake, made doughnuts, dressed a fowl &C.

The company arrived about 12 oclock. Mr and sister Sargent, with their little son George Lincoln, and sister Stark. The former family late from San F——, on their way to Great Salt Lake city. I enjoyed their visit finely, felt well satisfied with my entertainment, and they ap also appeared to feel the same. Promised to visit sis Stark, while the Sargents stay with her. Just as my dinner was ready came another Lincoln boy, and sister Stark's two sons.

Sister Pratt and Ellen were present, which made 11 persons who dined with us. Evening took a walk with my husband to sis Hamiltons, found them complaining of poor health, but strong in the faith of the gospel. Were introduced to a bro and sister Cochran late from Aus——. Liked their appearance very much. The sis informed me that they were converts of John Eldridge's. Returned home, found by Al—— that bro and sis Guy had called in our absence.

Wed 28th Very warm and pleasant. I ironed. Alma brought pickets from bro Harris's. Mr C—— at work in shop. I felt very unwell. Read and wrote some. Pm had an invitation to a quilting at bro Barton's the next day. Evening took a walk with my husband. Called on bro Guy's, and carried them a few vegetables. Returned to Dr McIntires, and spent an hour or more, reached home at 9½

Thurs 29th Sister sent me word that sis Crandle was intending to send a carriage for us to come and visit her that day, and therefore we should have to decline going to the quilting.

At ten oclock the young man arrived with the carriage. Sister, Ellen, and myself, went with him, and enjoyed the ride and visit finely. One of their daughters a sister Smith was there and visited with us. We also saw bros Miles and Nolton there who were making preparations for their journey to Salt lake. We reached home a little after sunset. Evening had an invitation to bro McGary's, to a pleasure party where dancing was to come off, but declined going, telling bro Pratt that bro Cox, our pres had told us not to dance, untill the ranch was paid for. And for one I did not feel a spirit of dancing.

Frid 30th Very warm, Sister came in, and I proposed going to bro Bartons, to assist her with her quilt; but she thought it too warm, to go in the heat of the day, and therefore we waited untill 4 oclock, and then went, and made a call; assisted her a few minutes, took some of the last stitches. She took it off while we were there. We reached home a little before dark. Evening read Deseret News. We got a letter from bro P B Lewis. Quite exciting times in G S L—— city. Gov Young said "troops cannot come in.[28] ^*Sat 31st*^ I made light bread. Evening spent at sisters in co with sisters Stark and Sargent. Bros Rainy, and Hawkins called. The sisters said Mr Sargent quite unwell. Bro Rainy came home with us, stoped overnight, took breakfast.

<u>*Sun 1st*</u> Nov [added later: Nov. 1857] attended meeting. Bros Rainy and Daudle spoke to us. The bishop also spoke well. Sister Patten called, lost her glasses, and came back to search for them, could not find them. Sister sent for me to take a walk to Lois's with her. Sister Patten went with us. Found several persons in. Marsh Hunt & bro Stodard and wife, H Chase, Ellen, Ann L, Wm McG. I felt quite unwell. Returned before dark. Evening bro Hawkins came home with Mr C—— from seventies

meeting. Bro, and sis P—— were in, sister Patten, also bro and sis Daily Ed—— came in. She brought me a letter, from bro Tait, which was sent by a Mr Brown, and handed by <u>him</u> to Daily. We had singing, and the time passed very agreeably. Bro Tait's letter was also quite exciting, and with the sermons in the Deseret news, created sensations in my mind not easily described.

[Called to the Valley of the Mountains]

<u>*Mon 2nd*</u>, [*added later:* ^*Nov. 1857*^] soon after I arose, my husband came in, and told me he had heard from bro Cox, that we were called to leave this place, as soon as possible, for G S L City. That we must prepare with as little noise as we possibly could. Bro Cox told him to warn the brethren in his ward, that they might have timely notice.[29] We went and told bro Harris. Bro Hawkins breakfasted with us. I washed.

Pm called sister Cannon, made a short stay. I gave her a jar of roselle jam, also a little sack of dried tomatoes. ^for her journey^ Alma went with her to bro Whipples where she puts up, and carried her babe for her.

Tues 3rd A—— went with bro Harris to the mountains. I dried my clothes and ironed. Sister Sarah Hayborn called, and asked me to take her daughter Agnes Matilda, she was intending give up housekeeping put out her children, and go out to service. Said sis Daily wanted her. I consented to take her, with my husbands advise.

Mr C—— and Wm McG—— went to see the newly arrived emigrants to inquire if they wished to purchase situations in this place, S—— B——d, but returned without accomplishing their object.

Pm Mr C—— went to a wagon shop to see something about getting a wagon, had the privilege of coming and making one for himself, in Calvin Reeds shop. Evening Mr C writing to bro P B Lewis.

Wed 4th Alma returned from the mountain, with his blankets and axe. Said bro Harris had given up the business. All hands making preparations to leave for Deseret. wrote a letter to Fr.

Thurs 5 We intended going to sister Starks, but she sent us word to come next day. Loren Babbitt called in co with J[erome] Benson and another man, to examine our improvements. Babbitt talked some of purchasing, said he would call again.

Pm I accompanied sister and Ellen to bro Lymans. Visited with Mother Walker, and Denitia, called on the other sister of the family, had a very agreeable time, returned before dark.

Frid—— *6th* just after breakfast a young man by the name of Mansfield Jennings called, and informed my husband that he had an old wagon to sell, which with some repairs could be made very useful, and told him he might pay him when he could conveniently, and if he never got able, he would not exact anything of him. Mr C readily accepted the offer, and went to see it. Said he offered to pay him ten dollars in money, but the young man told him to keep it for his own use, as he would probably need it the most. Offered to let him do a job of work in a wagonshop towards it. Valued the wagon at 75 dolls. Would take some barley. I considered it quite a God send to us. ^I went to Lee's Store with 5 dozens of eggs. Bought pants cloth for A——, bonnet for myself. Alpaca for apron. Print for shirt bosoms &C.^ Pm accompanied sister Ellen and Ann L to bro Starks, had a fine visit, stoped untill 9 oc. ^Assisted Sis Sargent in making her wagon cover.^ Wm and Ellen returned before dark. Bro P came in the evening, and escorted us home. I sent word to my hus—— to come, but he was absent untill he thought it too late. I reached home at half past 9 oclock. Pm.

Sat Nov 7th This Frances S P Dire's birthday. 23 years of age. Last night the north wind commenced blowing, about the time we came out to return home, and continued all night. Mr C and A—— at work on wagons. Wind high.

Evening sister and E came in a few minutes. I accompanied them to E's, and sat a short time. Lois and her husband called.

Sun 8th We all attended church. Preaching by bro Dawdle, and pres Cox, who told the saints that they were now all at liberty to go to Salt lake, if they wished to do so. Gave them good counsel. Viz to pay all their debts, and make themselves as comfortable as they could.

Mon 9th I washed, churned &C. Evening we expected Lois Harriet and John Hunt, but heard they had company. Wm and Ellen commenced school.

Tues 10th Sister P's birthday. I ironed. Sister came over with a young man, who she introuded as Thomas Henderson, one of her Nauvoo neighbors. Uncle to Nancy, the girl that lived with me in Nau— I recollected the name, and that was all I could remember of him. Toward night I went into bro Cox's. Went into their peach orchard and gathered, some pits. It rained while I was there. The leaves had fallen, and covered them so that I could find but few.

Evening came bro and sis P, and young Henderson. We had quite a social chat together. Very hard rain and wind in the night.

Wed 11th Sister Sarah Hayborn called and asked me to make pants for Johny, the little boy who had been staying with us. Said she had fortunatly had a present of money, to buy the cloth, and was in a hurry to get them made. Had the three pair to make. I consented, and went about it, and before bedtime had them done.

Thurs 12th Rain again last night. Spaniards, and other strangers travelling about the place. Sister came and invited me to come into Ellens, I went but she had gone home. I therefore followed her. While there sisters

F Clark, and Agnes Smith called. Said they were going to Lois's. Spoke of the excitment. Sis C thought they should not hurry off very soon, at least untill they could dispose of their property. Agnes said she nor her mother would not go if they had an opportunity, untill they had some means of supporting themselves after they got there. Said they had been there once in a destitute condition, and knew how bad it was.

Frid 13th. Rather cloudy, and unpleasant. I cut pants for Alma. Finished some I had been making for little Johny Hayborn.

Sat 14th Am churned, made pumkin pies, doughnuts &C. Pm received a visit from sister Agnes Smith. Sister Frances Clark called toward night to accompany her home. Mr C—— and A—— making wagon box for Skinner. Evening finished A's pants.

Sund 15th Very pleasant. Attended church, heard brs H Boil and Wm Sherman, late missionaries in Upper Cal—— After our meeting was dismissed Potter christ[30] took the stand, and proclaimed to us awhile. Many laughed, and seemed inclined to ridicule his strange vagueries. I felt that it was wrong to listen to him, and walked away.

PM sister Sarah Hayborn called and bade us goodbye, expecting to leave on the morrow. Spaniards called to look at furniture. Mr C—— —— was gone to teachers meeting. I told them to come again. Evening we had we had company. 2 bros Tanners, H Garner, Wm and Ellen Lois and John, and Ann L. We had quite sociable times, and enjoyed the visit well.

Mon 16th The Spaniards called again. Mr C offered them house and lots for 500 dolls, together with the furniture stove &C. They promised to call again.

[*added later, at bottom of page: Nov 1857*]

San Bernardino

Tues 17th Nov [*added later:* ^1857^] 2 years ago this day we sailed from San Francisco for this place. I little thought then, that we should stop here as long as we have, but circumstances have favored our staying. But now the word of the Lord from the Prophet is to come to the valley of the mountains, as soon as possible, or consistent.

This evening sister Patten called, and asked to stop over night. Said her husband was intoxicated, and used very abusive language that she did not feel safe in his presence.

Wed 18th I washed. Very pleasant day. PM sis Patten called, and informed me that her husband talked of buying out father Aldridge, told me the offer he had made him, which was to give him 2 yoke of oxen and a wagon, I observed to her that I thought Mr C would sell his place for the same, and she said she would speak to her husband about it.[31] Evening went over to sisters awhile. Wm and Ellen came in, also Mr C——

[The Crosbys' Home Sold]

Thurs 19th This is my mothers birthday. I ironed in the Am. Pm called sisters McMurtry and Pratt. Sister Mc took dinner with us. Old Mr Patten called to look at the place, said he thought he would buy it. Evening they both came down, and talked about it.

Frid 20th Mr C—— went up to see the oxen. Old man loathe to let his wagon go, proposed a Spanish cow in place of it, together with pistols, watches &C. Mr C—— returned, said Old gent promised to call again that day, but he passed by without calling, and we thought he had given it up, but we felt quite calm.

Sat 21st Old gent called quite early. Said he was tight the night previous, and his wife went and left him, asked if she was here. We assured him she was not. He took breakfast with us, after which the bargain was completed, and he went directly home, and commenced moving down his goods.[32] Sister Pratt came in, and toward noon sister Hunt came, offered to sew for me awhile. Bro Skinner called. Mr C—— fixing his carriage.

Sisters Hunt, Pratt, and Old man Patten took dinner. Ann L also. Evening came sis P—— almost sick, with fatigue. Yet she seemed thankful that she had found so good a home, for a short season, but did not intend staying very long in it, should the way open for her to go to headquarters.

Sun 22nd I did not attend church. Mr C—— went. Pm went into sisters with Lois, who came over and took dinner with us. I found Dr McIntire and wife there, She said she had sold everything in the line of furniture. Sis Clark Frances came in. Spoke of the great excitement; all complained of feeling troubled. Sister came home with me, spent a part of the evening. Sister Patten been out on her practice as midwife.

Mon 23rd rather rainy. Sold my chickens to sister Patten. 40 for ten dollars. She paid me the cash. Finished cover for Sk[inner] carriage. Pm called bro Davis with the deed, which the old gent had made over to Anson Vanluven, in order to prevent his wife from holding it, in case he should be taken away. She objected to the arrangement, in presence of Mr C—— Al—— and bro Davis, and myself. Complaind of the injustice of such proceedings.

Tues 24th I washed. Spanish people came to buy furniture. 3 ladies took tea with us. Sold them the stove 2 chairs. Frenchman bought the cow and calf.

Evening Alma played violin. Mr and Mrs Patten were in. Mr Crosby at work in the shop. I sewed on undergarment.

Wed 25th Cloudy atmosphere. At 11 oclock I went to sisters, sewed an hour or two, and she accompanied me to the store. At Wetergreens traded

4 ½ dolls, 2 pairs of shoes 1 ½ each, 2 balls wicking, 1 bit, 1 ½ dolls worth of needles. Went to Louis Jacob's, bought plaid dress, ^3 dolls 20 cts^ and sack, ^20 cts^ under shirt, 1¼. Returned and took supper with sis Pratt.

Thurs 26th Remarkably rainy day. Am I ironed. Mr C attended auction. Bought boots, shoes, and overcoats. Sperry the blind man took dinner with us. I traded one doll with him. Pm cut garments. Sister Patten put on her quilt. Evening Alma read pictorals.

Frid 27th very pleasant. Sister Caroline Huntington, and her son Heber, called to see sis Patten. Came into my rooms. She admired our situation much, thought it might be some time before we should be placed in as comfortable circumstances again. Evening I spent in sis Pattens room. Alma played the violin to us, and was complimented by the company, for his skill.

Sat 28th sister P—— very sick with nervous headache.

Sun 29th Beautiful day. Sister Patten took a warm bath. I assisted her, and after ward, anointed her with consecrated oil, and in company with my husband laid hands on her. She was greatly relieved, and praised the Lord for His mercy; went about getting her breakfast, feeling like a new creature. Shortly after I began to feel much distressed in my back, and lower limbs. I wet a cloth in cold water, laid it on my back, got my feet warm by the fire, while Alma finish getting the breakfast. I did not realize for some time that I had taken her pains upon myself, untill she spoke of it. My husband told me that it was wrong for me to lay hands on a stronger person than myself. But after breakfast I felt much better, and by degrees my pains wore away.

PM came Wm McGary with his large oxen and wagon, and invited us to take a ride with them to father Chase's. Myself, husband, and sister Patten, went, in company with bro and sis Pratt Lois, Harriet, and a new saint by the name of Scott. We enjoyed the ride very much, found father Chase's people rather broken up, sold all their furniture, and nearly ready to take their departure. On returning we found some old acquaintance of sis Pattens here, waiting her arrival. She introduced them as a Mr and Mrs Sanders formerly of Springfield Ill. There was a Dr [*blank space*] with them, one of their boarders, said they had come to buy them a situation in this place. I admired the lady very much. She said she was a catholic by profession, but was not prejudiced against any denomination.

Mon 30th I accompanied them to Col Jackson's, and introduced them as persons seeking to purchase situations. They were treated with much politeness by the Col—— and his family, sis Jackson showed the place, played and sung to us for sometime. Mrs S—— was much pleased with the place, and said she would willingly give her, the 2000 dolls which they asked for it. But Mr S—— and the Dr—— thought it too much, as others were selling so much below. The lady said she had money of her own and would do as she pleased with it.

Evening sister Pratt McGary and McIntire were in. All seemed to admire the strange lady.

San Bernardino Dec 1st

^*Tues 1st*^ ∔ Washed. Mr and Mrs Sanders went to see bro Carters place and seemed highly pleased with it. ^Sister Dewel called to get me to do a little writing for her in making out her account against Ed Webb for taking care of his wife and children.^

Evening sis Patten and myself went into sister's a few minutes. While there a young man by the name of Harris came for sis Patten to go and visit his sick child. She accordingly set off after ten oclock.

Wed 2nd I ironed, cut sack for myself. Evening sister and the girls were in. Also bro P, and Wm. Deseret mail arrived. Mr C read a sermon by bro Young. Considerable excitement prevailed in the minds of some of the brethren and sisters.

Thurs 3rd Beautiful day. Mr C—— gone to work in the wagon shop. Alma on an expedition for Justus Morse, hauling wheat some 12 miles. Expect he will be out over night. I read Deseret news for an hour or 2.

Frid 4th I finished my sack. Alma returned from hauling wheat. Mrs Sanders went to Carters on a visit. Sister Jackson called to see her, about selling their place. Seemed quite anxious, and careworn. Dr Chamblin who had been stopping with Mrs Sanders, offered to go for her, but was mistaken in the name, and went to Curtis's instead of Carter's. Accordingly sis J—— went away without seeing her. Salt lake Mail arrived, everybody anxious to get the news.

[Rumors of War]

Sat 5th Old man Patten informed me that he had completed the trade with Mr Noyse, and that Mr Crosby could now have the oxen when he pleased. Old gent very cross, cussed his wife, and said she might go to Salt Lake as soon as she pleased. But said if she wished to stay, he would do the best he could by her.

PM a company of wagons arrived from Salt lake valley, which created a great excitement in the place. Old Patten went immediately to the town, to get news, which is quite exciting. Said the Mormons had taken 800 head of cattle from the government troops, and burned their wagons and provisions, with the exception of enough to last them back to the states.[33]

Sun 6th rather cloudy and unpleasant. No church. Mr C worked some in the shop. Lois and Harriett Hunt called. H said the gents from Great Salt lake city had gone to San Francisco, that they spoke well of the saints. Bro Hanks came home. Our enemies report that he has brought a great quantity of arms and ammunition.

Evening came sisters Pratt, McGary, McIntire and Lois Hunt.

Mon 7th Mr Crosby killed hogs, br P—— assisted. Bro Carter and wife came to conclude the trade with Sanders. Sister P and I got dinner together, had 6 men and 4 women to dine.

Evening came Wm and Ellen with their music. Also Lois, and sis Ad—— Daily. They danced one cotillion, and a few waltzes. Sister Patten was taken suddenly ill with a cramp in her side. I wet a cloth in hot water and put sulphur on it, and laid on her side, which soon relieved her. She told me to remember that sulphur would cure the cramp. E and L sang several songs, which pleased the strangers much.

Tues 8th I worked all day, trying out lard, cleaning, and taking care of fresh meat. Cut shirts for Mr C——. Evening felt fatigued and sleepy tried to sew on my hood. Ate a late supper which much distressed my stomach, and prevented my sleeping.

Wed 9th pleasant morning. Mr Sanders and Dr Chamblin set off for their old home, and Mrs S—— here, quite unwell. Mr C—— complained of distress in his stomach, and head. Nearly worked himself sick.

Thurs 10th I washed. Alma went with Mr Patten for wood. Mr C finished ironing his wagon. PM called sister [Mary] Folks with her two youngest children, and wished to leave them with me untill she could get them off to Salt lake, said her husband was intemperate, and very abusive, and was unwilling that she should take them with her. In the course of the pm called bro Huntington, and introduced bros E[zra] T[aft] Benson, and John Scott, late missionaries from Europe, who were on their way home to the valleys of the mountains.

I should not have known them from first appearance, as their beards had grown to be very long. However, I soon recognized bro Benson, but bro Scott I was never acquainted with. They said it was only 2 months since they left Europe. Bro B—— seemed very much excited, and warned us to hurry away from here, thought we should surely have trouble if we did not. I told him our situation, and how hard my husband had worked, and was still exerting himself to the utmost of his abilitty to get away. Bro H—— confirmed my statements, but bro B—— said rather than stay here untill Cristmas he would set off with a bundle in his hands. I observed that that might do for a man but it would not do for me.[34] They made only a short call, said they had to buy teams.

Evening sister Folks sent for her children. Their bro said their father was so enraged at their absence, that his mother was obliged to get them home again. I felt to sympathize with her. She said she would sooner die than live in her present situation.

Frid 11th Ironed and prepared for making sausages. Pm Mr Crosby was taken quite ill, was chilly and faint, had been taking salts for several days, but received no benefit from them. Sent Alma after Dr McIntire, but he was absent, then sent to Dr Dickey for pills, but he had none. Evening called bro Cannon in co with bro Pratt. Wm McGary was making sausages for us. They staid untill ~~12th~~ eleven oclock, laid hands on my husband; the next morning ~~and~~ he arose and went to his work again as usually. I bathed his feet in warm water, and made him sage tea.

Sat 12th Alma went to the mountains with Phin Daily after boards. I looked over my dried grapes. Sophronia staid with us.

I felt miserably in the Am. Sister Patten got water and prepared for me to bathe, after which I felt much better. Sister and Ann L went to the store, and got me two calico dresses.

PM called a young man ^by the name of Pool^ and enquired for sister Patten, requested a private conversation with her. She afterward informed me that his wife was enciente and soon expected to require her services as midwife, that he offered to take her on with them to the valley, for her services. She seemed quite elated with the idea and said the Lord had heard her prayers, and sent a messenger to offer deliverance to her, and that she intended to accept the proposal. Evening Anson Vanluven came to board a week with Mr Patten. Sophronia staid over night with us.

Sun 13th Very rainy, continued untill Pm. About 1 oclock elders O Pratt, Benson, Cannon, and several others passed, on their way to Great salt lake city. Sister Patten and myself went to the gate and bade them goodbye. Bro Benson blest us in the name of the Lord. I dicovered that eld O Pratts beard was almost white with age, which quite surprised me. Dr McIntire and wife called and took tea.

Mon 14th rather pleasant. Alma's birthday. I tried to get some sour milk to make him a birthday cake but could find none.

Late in the evening he returned with one very sore eye. Said they staid at the mill, with a man they call Billy Law, where they had very good fare. A represented him as being a very intelligent sort of a man, but a perfect infidel.

I went early to collect a little money due my husband. Called on bro Cox for 6 ½ dolls. He put his hand in his pocket and handed it me. I then went to Geo Clarks, they were absent. Called on sisters Hamiltons, and got her little daughter to take the account to him. Shortly after she brought me the money.

Tues 15th Mr C—— hurrying his wagon, fear we shall not get off much before Christmas. Alma built smoke house, put in the pork. Cut dress and sack. Heard several persons coming back for grain, on account of the scarcity of feed. This morning at a few minutes before 3 I felt a light earthquake.

Wed 16th I washed. Sister Patten went to Rolph's, got sour and sweet milk, also a cheese for her journey to G S L city. (Old P——tt——n came home tight, and swearing about Mr C's taking down a little awning over the door, which he wanted for a wagon cover. The old man felt so bad about it that husband told him he would put it up again. He soon got over his ill humor and was tolerably pleasant. Evening Mrs Sanders went to store and got herself a new dress pattern. Alma's eyes very bad. Sis P—— made him eye water.

Thurs 17th I ironed. Very warm day. Cut 2 undergarments for husband. Sophronia took dinner with us. Mr Jackson called and bought chickens of sis Patten. Evening I sewed on my demings dress.

Frid 18th Very windy and boisterous. Our meat house took fire, and burnt the meat considerably. Wm Huntington was at work nearby, and ran to it first. I felt very sorry, as we had it prepared to take along with us. Evening Ellen came in, and invited me over to her mothers. I went, and found Dr McIntire and wife there. They all seemed much dissatisfied with the proceedings of the people in this place, in regard to leaving, and sacrificing their property. Mr C—— called for me.

Sat 19th Alma making wagon cover. Mr C—— painting wagon bed. I sewed on my dress. Evening finished it.

[Mr. Crosby Taken Ill]

Sun 20th Quite pleasant. Mr C brought home a barrel of sugar. Paid 22 cts pr pound. Mrs Catts [Katz] called on Mrs Sanders. Came in my room admired the place much. Said my house looked like home to her. Her husband has bought out Pres—— Cox. He is a jew merchant. She seemed a very pleasant lady. Directly after supper Mr Crosby was taken very ill, looked very pale, and finally went to bed. Sis Patten and myself concluded the smell of the oil from painting had sickened him. I put a warm iron to his feet, observed that he felt a little cold.

After sometime he went out, and vomited very freely. Went the second time. I hoped he would feel better after it, but he came to the fireplace about 6 oclock, and looked so bad that we began to feel quite alarmed about him. He seemed very nervous, and wild. Said he could not hear well, presumed we thought him drunk, and said he felt so himself. We assured him that he was mistaken, that we had no such idea. He then explained to us what he thought to be the cause of his illness Said that he went into Henry Rollins store that PM, and tasted a little of the oil of wintergreen; that he was very fond of it, and probably took more than he was aware of, that on throwing up his supper it seemed that his stomach was full of it. He trembled exceedingly, said there was roaring in his head, like the roaring of the sea, which caused him to be deaf.

We immediately sent Alma after Dr McIntire. Mrs Sanders prescribed vinegar to counteract the effect of the oil, which he drank. He again took his bed, and complained of great nervous debility. About 9 oclock A came with the Dr and wife. I was pleased to see them. She said she could not stay alone and so came with them. We enjoyed a couple of hours very agreeably. The Dr seemed to think the oil would not hurt him, did not think it the sole cause of his present illness, was afraid it was an attack of fever, said the roaring in his head was a symptom of typhoid fever. He gave him two powders of calamel. We bathed his feet and put on drafts, and for awhile he seemed much easier. But afterwards complained of great pain in his hips. I was up several times with him, felt quite wornout the next morning.

Mon 21st. Directly after breakfast the Dr called again. Gave him a large dose of Salts, and left two ^of Dovers^ powders. Several persons were in to see him, and expressed much sympathy for him. The Dr thought he would be up again in 3 or 4 days. PM he came again, thought his medicine had not operated very thoroughly, and proposed another portion of salts, which he instantly threw up, with a large amount of bile.

Evening I gave him a warm bath, rubed him throughly with a coarse towel, put drafts on his feet, gave him a Dovers powder, and he rested finely through the night. Old Mr Patten came home drunk and cross, and used very abusive language to his wife, in so much that she left his room, and came and slept by my fire. She felt heartbroken and almost in dispair. Mrs Sanders told him the next morning that if her husband should talk to her as he did to his wife, she would leave his house and never come back again.[35]

Tues 22nd Another boisterous day. Husband seemed much better. Dr called at ten oclock, left quenine. I gave salts and after it quenine. Mr Boldin came in, and ate dinner with us. Had a great deal to say about mormonism. Said the united states troops were sure to take Brigham Youngs head off, that he might hide himself in the earth or climb the highest mountains, and it would all be of no use, they would be sure to follow him. We all felt hurt at his coarse rough voice, and corresponding language, and thought it ungentlemanly in him to talk in that way where the man was sick, and unable to converse. We afterwards concluded that probably he had been stimulating too much. I baked pies. Mr C had some appetite.

Pm, sister Patten was sent for to visit a sick child, of Mr Gilbert and altho nearly sick herself, said she would sooner go, than stay, where she was constantly censured by a cross unfeeling man. Evening bro and sis Pratt came in after we had gone to bed, as we retired early on account of being tired and unwell. They stoped only a few minutes.

Wed 23rd Mr C began to feel a great deal better. I washed. Dr called, left quenine, conseled him to take one powder in a day. Complained of poor health himself. Sister Patten staid another night. Mrs Sanders and myself queried whether she had not gone to the camp of the saints, hoped she had.

Thurs 24th We expected Mr Sanders, but was disappointed. I ironed with Sophronia's help. Mrs S—— made a hickory shirt, for Mr C—— PM I called on sister, found they had sold their place for 600 dolls 400 in cash, 200 in dry goods. They seemed well pleased with their trade. I was introduced to a bro Lanforth late from the upper country, he seemed very talkative, said his family had gone on to the valley with bro Crows people. That he was disappointed in not finding them here, knew not how he should get on. Bro Ladd came in, and told of his troubles, had buried his second daughter Phebe. Edna the eldest had been very sick, as also himself. He looked very feeble. Expressed a desire to go to the gathering place of the saints. Mr C called for me, when I returned sis P—— had gone again to visit the sick child. Returned in the evening, said they did not need her services, as they had other company. I felt unwell, and retired early. Mr C and Alma runing bullets. Guns firing for Christmas eve.

[A Disrupted Christmas Dinner]

Frid 25th Christmas day. Sophronia saluted me with "Christmas [*word unclear, perhaps Tahitian*] aunt Caroline." Directly after breakfast Mr Patten moved Mrs Sanders to her new home, at bro Carters. Sister Patten invited us to dine with her, I told her we would get dinner together. Accordingly I set the table in my room, and put on what I had, while she cooked chicken, custard pie, crulls &C.

Just before dinner Mrs Sanders returned, and shortly after came Sophronia. We were trying to enjoy ourselves, as well as we could, when old Mr P—— came in quite intoxicated. It gave her very unpleasant feelings, notwithstanding she was accostomed to seeing him in that situation, yet on that occasion when we were trying to enjoy each others society, perhaps for the last time, it was doubly mortifying to her, as well as us.

She called him in to dinner, but he gave no heed to it. Accordingly we ate without him, and afterward she set his dinner on his own table, but he was much vexed at having to eat alone cursed, and talked very hard to her. Mrs Sanders took the liberty to talk back to him, in his own style, which calmed or cowered him. She left immediately after, but had not got far when it commenced raining quite hard.

After eating the old man came in our room and sat sometime. Still cursing his wife, and telling how much money he had spent for her. Frequently saying she might go to Salt lake as soon as she pleased, but that he would not give her a cent."

Evening called two young men, to buy chickens of sis P——.

Sat 26th remarkably rainy day. Mr C fixed on the wagon cover. Alma went over to the mill for sis P—— to see if she could get an opportunity to go with a small family to G S—— L city. Heard they were not going untill spring. Evening sis Patten staid in our room, untill near ten oclock.

Sun 27th quite pleasant. Sister P—— had an early call to go on an excursion in her official capacity. A Mr Dodson called for her. Pm sister was in a few moments. Ellen also called. Bro P— brought his wagon to the shop to fix for the journey. Said he was preparing it for his wife and Louisa, but thought he should go another way. I worked some on the wagon, binding the door. Evening I made tea for Mr Pat——n, his wife not returned yet. Emtied the bureau.

Mon 28th Washed, took up carpet, &C. Toward night Old Patten went to see what had become of his wife, said perhaps she had gone to Salt Lake. Returned without her, saying she had a difficult case, that they had sent for a Dr. Sister was in again, expressed much concern, and uneasiness about getting away. Complained that she had no one to lean upon, said her husband was going another way, which left her to lead her family again, without a head. I tried to encourage her to persevere, and not give way to unreal troubles.

[Moving Zionward]

Tues 29th Wm McG—— called, thought they should leave that morning After breakfast I went over to see them start. Wm and Ellen both seemed very sad, could hardly smile. I tried to cheer them, but it seemed in vain. John and Lois set off first, and seemed in better spirits.

Frank Garner called and took E—— in his carriage, a way on the road. I returned home, and afterward ironed, and washed carpet. Mrs Boldin and Whitley called. Toward night sister Pat—— returned home.

Evening called Anson Vanleuven. Sister Patten asked him to buy my lookingglass, to which he consented, and paid me 5 dolls. I then offered him a silk dress pattern, which he also bought, and promised to send me a bolt of bleached domestick, and 22 yds of calico. I was pleased and thankfull for the good success I had in trading with him.

Wed 30th Alma and I made 12 lbs of flour into crackers.

Evening went over to sisters, she and husband were going to Dr Mc's. Alma and I accompanied them, had quite a pleasant time. George Clark and wife were stoping there. Said he was intending to leave the next morning for S L city but she was going to his brs in the upper country. They all expressed great doubt with regard to the propriety of Gov Young's movements. Thought his conduct premature. I contended with them upon the principle of obeying counsel, and having confidence in our leaders. Beautifull moonlight night, reached home after 11 oclock.

Thurs 31st, fine warm day. I went shopping with sister, traded 5 dolls. Bought hat for Johny Taite, looking glass, &C. Evening made doughnuts. Dr McIntire called with sister. Said his wife and sis Clark came with him to sisters, but bro Clark came and took them to a new years eve party at the house formerly occupied by bishop Crosby. He complained of being troubled about the movements of Gov Young in resisting government. Husband and sis Patten entreated him to have full confidence in our leaders.

Frid morning Jan 1st AD 1858 we finished loading our wagon, and set off with our faces zionward. . . .

NOTES

Abbreviations

In citing works in the notes, short titles generally have been used after the initial citation. Works frequently cited have been identified by the following abbreviations:

AP   Ellsworth, S. George, ed. *The Journals of Addison Pratt: Being a Narrative of Yankee Whaling in the Eighteen Twenties, A Mormon Mission to the Society Islands, and of Early California and Utah in the Eighteen Forties and Fifties.* Salt Lake City: University of Utah Press, 1990.

APFP Addison Pratt Family Papers, S. George Ellsworth Collection, Special Collections and Archives, Merrill Library, Utah State University, Logan, Utah.

CBC   Caroline Barnes Crosby Journals.

LBP   Ellsworth, S. George, ed. *The History of Louisa Barnes Pratt, Being the Autobiography of A Mormon Missionary Widow and Pioneer.* Logan: Utah State University Press, 1998.

JC   Crosby, Jonathan. *A Biographical Sketch of The Life of Jonathan Crosby Written by Himself.* Holograph. Jonathan Crosby Papers, Utah State Historical Society. Typescript, bound in with journal-memoir of his wife, Caroline Barnes Crosby, in possession of editors.

JH   *Journal History of the Church of Jesus Christ of Latter-day Saints, 1830–1972.* Historical Department of the Church, Salt Lake City, Utah.

Endnotes to Introduction

1.   John Mack Faragher, *Women and Men on the Overland Trail* (New Haven, Connecticut: Yale University Press, 1979), 1.
2.   Caroline Barnes Crosby Journal, 19 November 1856; 1 May 1857; 29 December 1852.

3. Lillian Schlissel, *Women's Diaries of the Westward Journey* (New York: Shocken Books, 1992), 10-16.
4. CBC, chapter 6, fall 1848.
5. CBC, 6 July 1852.

Chapter 1

1. The Family Register lists Willard Barnes's birthdate as 16 April 1766. His baptismal record shows 16 April 1767, in Marlborough, Worcester County, Massachusetts. References to his birthdate vary in the journal, but Caroline noted that he was already 44 when he moved to Dunham, Quebec, Canada in 1810.
2. Dolly Stevens was born 19 November 1771. See Family Register. See also Elvira Stevens Barney, *The Stevens Genealogy: Embracing Branches of the Family Descended from Puritan Ancestry, New England Families Not Traceable to Puritan Ancestry and Miscellaneous Branches Wherever Found* (Salt Lake City: Skelton Publishing Co., 1907), 247.
3. Jonathan and Lois Barnes Crosby were the parents of Caroline's husband, Jonathan, who was also her first cousin. Lois Barnes Crosby, her father's sister, died in 1818, and Jonathan's father remarried nine years later.
4. The life stories of Caroline's sister Louisa and her husband Addison Pratt are an integral part of Caroline's own life experience. A companion to this volume is S. George Ellsworth, ed. *The Life History of Louisa Barnes Pratt* (Logan: Utah State University Press, 1998), hereafter LBP. For an invaluable perspective of early nineteenth century maritime and western American history, as well as a deeply personal insight into the early Mormon church, see S. George Ellsworth, ed. *The Journals of Addison Pratt: Being a Narrative of Yankee Whaling in the Eighteen Twenties, A Mormon Mission to the Society Islands, and of Early California and Utah in the Eighteen Forties and Fifties* (Salt Lake City: University of Utah Press, 1990), hereafter AP.
5. All Saints Anglican Church opened for service on the 26th of September, 1821. C. Thomas, *Eastern Townships: A Work Containing an Account of the Early Settlement of St. Armand, Dunham, Sutton, Broome, Potton, and Bolton* (Montreal: John Lovell, St. Nicholas Street, 1866), 139, 144.
6. Caroline would have been 15 and a half, and the year 1822 rather than 1821.
7. Jonathan's brother, David Barnes Crosby, was born 21 May 1805 in Wendell, Franklin County, Massachusetts.
8. David Crosby married Marial Thompson 21 September 1834 in Peacham, Caledonia County, Vermont. Eight years later, on 17 June 1842, Lois Barnes Crosby, sister of David and Jonathan, married Marial's brother, Harvey.

Chapter 2

1. Founding prophet Joseph Smith claimed God and Christ appeared to him in answer to his fervent prayers and told him to join none of the erring existing denominations. He was informed he would be the instrument through which the church that Jesus Christ had formerly established would be restored to the earth. A narrative history of the early Mormon church is documented from the prophet's own dictations and other contemporary journals and publications and edited by Brigham H. Roberts in *History of the*

Church of Jesus Christ of Latter-day Saints. 7 vols. (Salt Lake City: Deseret Book Company, 1902–32), reprinted often, hereafter referred to as *Documentary History.*

2. The Church of Jesus Christ of Latter-day Saints functions through lay male members officiating in positions of ecclesiastical leadership, in other denominations usually reserved for paid, professionally-trained clergymen. Written to introduce a non-Mormon audience to the Church of Jesus Christ of Latter-day Saints and the Mormon people is Leonard J. Arrington and Davis Bitton, *The Mormon Experience* (New York: Alfred A. Knopf, 1979). A similar reference with emphasis on institutional developments is James B. Allen and Glen M. Leonard, *The Story of the Latter-day Saints* (Salt Lake City: Deseret Book Company, 1976).

3. Edward Partridge and Isaac Morley were among the most respected local-level leaders of the church then centered at Kirtland, Ohio, with branches in several locations along the western frontiers of Missouri.

4. The early church stressed gathering the "elect" out of the unbelieving world to the sometimes-relocated center of Zion. A place of refuge, this location would afford protection against wars, plagues, and other destructive forces of the last days. As the church began to mature missionaries were called to foreign missions beyond the United States and Canada, most notably England and the Pacific Islands. The practice of gathering the Saints to Zion faded toward the end of the nineteenth century, by which time, through its zealous missionary efforts, the church had established congregations worldwide. Allen and Leonard, *Story of the Latter-day Saints,* 61–62, 454–55.

Chapter 3

1. Many notable acquaintances and friends from the earliest days of the church would reappear in Caroline's journals throughout her life. Youthful proselyte Evan M. Greene, son of John P. Greene and nephew of Brigham Young, introduced Jonathan to the church during one of his several missions in Ohio and New England in the 1830s and would revisit the aged Crosbys in Beaver, Utah. Apostle Parley P. Pratt was among those church leaders whose acquaintance was renewed almost two decades later in San Francisco.

2. The Seventies, one of the offices in the higher, or Melchizedek, priesthood, were introduced into the early church organization by Joseph Smith primarily to be missionaries. For an account of the ecclesiastical structure of the church, see Allen and Leonard, *Story of the Latter-day Saints,* 77–81.

3. It is a common continuing practice among Mormons to receive such a blessing as a guide to one's future life.

4. A detailed description of the temple dedication and spiritual manisfestations can be found in Roberts, *Documentary History,* 2: 410–36.

5. Brigham Young became a believer in the Church of Jesus Christ of Latter-day Saints through reading a *Book of Mormon* in the possession of his brother-in-law, John P. Greene. Lucy Mack Smith, *History of Joseph Smith, by his Mother.* 2nd Utah Edition (Salt Lake City: Sevens & Wallis, Inc., 1945), 169–71, 178, 187–88, as cited in S. George Ellsworth, "A History of Mormon Missions in the United States and Canada, 1830–1860" (Ph.D. diss., University of California, Berkeley, 1951), 70.

6.   Joseph Smith's interest in antiquities and ancient languages led to his purchase of certain Egyptian mummies accompanied by papyri scrolls, which he began translating in 1835, and eventually published in the Pearl of Great Price as The Book of Abraham. Allen and Leonard, *Story of the Latter-day Saints*, 67.

7.   Joseph Smith and his associates engaged noted Hebrew scholar and professor Joshua Seixas from New York to teach them the Hebrew language. Probably the prophet's interest in the language stemmed from a desire to translate at least portions of the Bible from the original Hebrew texts. Likely Jonathan Crosby was taught by some Mormon brethren earlier taught by Seixas. This was an impressive early effort at adult education. Roberts, *Documentary History*, 2: 385, 393–94, 397–98.

8.   Brigham Young's brother Joseph, formerly a Methodist preacher, led the missionary effort in Canada, introducing Mormonism to his former congregations.

9.   Joseph Smith's wife Emma was a compassionate woman whose attempts to allay the suffering of others, i.e. the Crosbys, endeared her to church members. Linda King Newell and Valeen Tippetts Avery, *Mormon Enigma: Emma Hale Smith* (New York: Doubleday, 1986), 56.

10. The naïve creation and direction of the Kirtland bank, formed without a state charter and unable to redeem its notes in gold coin, left many Mormons bewildered, some disillusioned, and others shaken in faith. Allen and Leonard, *Story of the Latter-day Saints*, 110–15.

11. If the losses in apostates and the disillusioned at Kirtland had not been outweighed by "repeated transfusions of fresh [convert] blood," such as the faithful Crosbys, Mormonism might very early have lapsed, as did most other nineteenth-century religious movements, into an insignificant sect. Arrington and Bitton, *The Mormon Experience*, 22.

12. Haun's Mill was the scene of a brutal massacre on 30 October 1838, when 17 Mormons were killed and 15 others wounded by Missouri state militia following Governor Lillburn Boggs's infamous "Order of Extermination" to rid the state of "the enemy." Allen and Leonard, *Story of the Latter-day Saints*, 127–28.

13. Jonathan Crosby, ordained a Seventy, received valuable training at Kirtland and functioned, as was expected of many adult male converts, as a traveling missionary. See Davis Bitton, "Kirtland as a Center of Missionary Activity, 1830–1838," *BYU Studies* 11 (fall 1971): 497–516 for the importance of this church center for missionary ventures.

14. By 1838 Far West, Caldwell County, was the most important settlement of Mormon immigrants seeking a gathering place in Missouri. Allen and Leonard, *Story of the Latter-day Saints*, 107.

15. The building had undoubtedly been more than a print shop, with both leadership and worship services formerly held there. Its destruction was thus certainly a symbolic transition event.

16. Three witnesses claimed an angel of God showed them the golden plates from which Joseph Smith translated the *Book of Mormon*. They were Oliver Cowdry, David Whitmer and Martin Harris, none of whom denied the experience even though each later had differences with Smith.

17. In July 1838, most of the remnant of the Kirtland faithful, between 500 and 600 people, with all their personal goods, had left by wagon from Kirtland to Far West, Missouri, arriving there in October to find the Mormon center

an armed camp in the midst of crisis. At month's end, soon after the Haun's Mill massacre, Joseph Smith and other Mormon leaders surrendered their arms and were betrayed into captivity and imprisonment. Alexander L. Baugh, "A Call to Arms: The 1838 Mormon Defense of Northern Missouri" (Ph.D. diss., Brigham Young University, Provo, Utah, 1996, reprinted 2000), 115–72.

18. Thomas Brannan was 63 when his youngest son, Samuel, was born. An emigrant from Waterford, Ireland, he worked in a whiskey distillery to earn his passage to America in 1775. A widower himself, he married the widow Sarah Knox Emery in 1805 and had five children. Death dates for Thomas and Sarah are unknown, but a great granddaughter thought he lived to be over 100. Will Bagley, ed., *Scoundrel's Tale: The Samuel Brannan Papers,* Kingdom in the West, The Mormons and the American Frontier, vol. 3. (Spokane: The Arthur H. Clark Company, 1999), 23.

19. The Crosbys, by leaving Kirtland for Ripley in June 1838, were not part of the exodus from Kirtland to Far West, Missouri one month later, and by the time they and the Pratts were on the road west, thousands of Saints had been forced out of their homes and expelled from the state. They continued their journey along the National Road (which in the 1840s extended from Cumberland, Maryland 600 miles westward to Vandalia, Illinois) until their wagon wheels became mired in the mud of a January thaw in Putnam County, Indiana.

20. Besides the Bible, Latter-day Saints have historically accepted as scripture certain works stemming from the translations, revelations and narrations of Joseph Smith, sometimes referred to as the "standard works," namely The Book of Mormon, first published in Palmyra, New York, 1830, The Doctrine and Covenants, Kirtland, Ohio, 1835, and The Pearl of Great Price, Liverpool, England, 1851. S. George Ellsworth, *History of Mormon Missions,* 407.

21. Addison Pratt purchased 260 acres of unimproved land covered with timber, and another hundred acres with some log buildings fronting on the National Road four miles outside of Pleasant Garden. He became much attached to the farm, but Louisa found herself "alone in the woods." Here their fourth daughter, Ann Louise, was born, in 1840. LBP, 58.

22. Almon W. Babbitt was a somewhat controversial Latter-day Saint missionary, in charge of the struggling church branch still at Kirtland and later delegate to the U. S. Congress from Utah Territory. Through his proselytizing, a small branch of the church was organized at Pleasant Garden, with Jonathan Crosby as its president. Since the goal of the Saints was to gather to Zion, Indiana's outpost Mormon branches were not intended to develop or grow strong. They were primarily stopping stations for Mormon travelers, as the Crosby home exemplified. However, when the majority of converts left the Midwest for the Rockies in 1846, Mormon branches had been established in at least twenty-four Indiana counties. L. C. Rudolph, *Hoosier Faiths, A History of Indiana Churches and Religious Groups* (Bloomington: Indiana University Press, 1995), 484.

23. One of Jonathan Crosby's first actions as president was to ordain Addison Pratt to the priesthood and recommend him as a preacher.

24. Elder Orson Hyde wrote from Franklin, Ohio for publication in the *Times and Seasons* as follows: "I hope the Saints in Nauvoo will show favor to Bro. Jonathan Crosby and Ross R. Rogers of Pleasant Garden, Ia. [*sic*] for they

have spared no pains to wait upon the traveling elders; and they, of their pecuniary have freely administered to their wants. Therefore let them be had in remembrance." Journal History of the Church of Jesus Christ of Latter-day Saints, 1830–1972. Historical Department of the Church, Salt Lake City, Utah, 7 July 1840, hereinafter JH.

25.   Addison Pratt was much attached to his farm and often remarked that he would ask no better fortune than to finish his days there, were it not for the religion he had embraced. Hoping to make his wife more content on remaining, he sold a piece of land and bought a house and lot in Pleasant Garden, so that she could live near her sister. However, Louisa was firmly set on gathering with the church at Nauvoo, and consequently the farm and village property were rented and the Pratts left in the fall of 1841. LBP, 58–60.

Chapter 4

1.   When Caroline and Jonathan left his sister Lois in Wendell, Massachusetts, she had been forbidden by their father to be baptised as a Mormon. She had stated then that she would wait until she was of age and then "do as she pleased." Lois married Harvey Thompson of Peacham, Caledonia County, Vermont on 17 June 1842, arriving within a month with her new husband in Nauvoo.

2.   In October, following the purchase of a house and lot in Nauvoo, Jonathan accepted a mission to the northern states and Canada. He arrived in Dunham, Quebec, in April 1843, where he found his brother David engaged in settling the estate of their father, who had died four years before. They returned together to Nauvoo. "A Biographical Sketch of the Life of Jonathan Crosby Written by Himself." Holograph. Jonathan Crosby Papers, Utah State Historical Society. Typescript, bound in with journal-memoir of Caroline Barnes Crosby, 16, hereinafter JC.

3.   The Mormon militia was long known as the Nauvoo Legion and their potential independent military capability continued to be an issue of controversy among the growing number of opponents of the church for many years. Glen M. Leonard, *Nauvoo: A Place of Peace, A People of Promise* (Salt Lake City: Deseret Book Company, 2002), 112–13, 283, 471.

4.   Wallace Stegner details this common belief of Mormons seeing an uncanny resemblance to Joseph Smith: "In a miraculous manifestation that hundreds attested, his pudgy body on the platform had assumed the length and beauty of the dead prophet's; his mouth had opened to send abroad not his own voice but the incontrovertible voice of Joseph. After that speech there was no question who would lead the Church . . ." Wallace Stegner, *The Gathering of Zion, The Story of the Mormon Trail* (New York: McGraw-Hill Book Company, 1971), 34. Davis Bitton cites nine Mormon diaries, including Caroline's journal, that mention this "transfiguration" of Brigham Young in his *Guide to Mormon Diaries and Autobiographies* (Provo: Brigham Young University Press, 1977).

5.   Samuel Bent, familiarly known as "Father Bent" because of his benevolence, was born 19 July 1778 in Barre, Worcester Co., Massachusetts. He married David Crosby's widow Marial as one of several plural wives before leaving for Iowa where he presided over the church at Garden Grove until his death in August 1846. "Sealings and Adoptions of the Living; Index 1846–

1857," Family History Library film 0183374, p. 165. The importance of the temporary settlements and the sacrifice of life Samuel Bent made in attempting to provide for the needs of his people during their forced exodus is discussed by Leland H. Gentry in "The Mormon Way Stations: Garden Grove and Mt. Pisgah," *BYU Studies* 21 (fall 1981): 445–61.

6. The Nauvoo Temple Endowment Register, p. 34, indicates the Crosbys received their endowments 19 December 1845. Their marriage was sealed in the temple 21 January 1846 by Heber C. Kimball in the presence of Willard Richards and Phineas Howe Young. FHL film 0183374, p. 209. Washings, anointings and sealings are portions of the LDS temple ordinances, which Joseph Smith taught would give new insight into a believer's relationship with God and eternity and were a step toward restoring ancient truths. Some 5,000 church members participated in such ceremonies at this difficult time. Robert Bruce Flanders, *Nauvoo: Kingdom on the Mississippi* (Urbana: University of Illinois Press, 1965), 335–36. Allen and Leonard, *Story of the Latter-day Saints*, 169–70.

7. For an account of the Samuel Stevens family in Nauvoo, see Barney, *The Stevens Genealogy*, 231–33.

8. As early as 1844 Joseph Smith instructed the Twelve to examine sites for Mormon expansion in California, which in that day extended eastward to the Rocky Mountains. Allen and Leonard, *The Story of the Latter-day Saints*, 184.

9. Although no direct reference to a plural marriage between Jonathan Crosby and Amelia Althea Stevens is found in any of Caroline's memoirs, an undated record of such a union is documented in the Church of Jesus Christ of Latter-day Saints Nauvoo Temple Index. The Nauvoo Temple Endowment Register, compiled by the Church of Jesus Christ of Latter-day Saints in 1974, records on page 169 as unverified an endowment received by Amelia Althea Stevens on 21 Jan 1846. Although there is no record of a temple marriage sealing, an earlier manual card file called the "Temple Index Bureau," used before the current (2000) "Ordinance Index" version 1.02, does indeed note that she was married to Jonathan Crosby. (Note that on that same date the sealing of Jonathan and Caroline was "solemnized.") In addition, Elvira Stevens wrote of her sister: "She married, first, Jonathan Crosby in the Temple at Nauvoo, Ill." (Barney, *The Stevens Genealogy*, 239). Caroline was fully committed to the principle of plural marriage. She probably did not more openly acknowledge the relationship in these later reminiscences because the young woman did not choose to go with them when they moved west from Nauvoo. Perhaps the relationship failed when Amelia did not become pregnant. And perhaps over the time with Caroline and Jonathan, Amelia realized their relationship was too close for her to fit in—or possibly it was Jonathan's illness and poverty that discouraged them both. Whatever the reasons, the relationship apparently ended amicably. Amelia kept a cordial correspondence with Jonathan in the ensuing years.

10. The exodus of some 15,000 Mormons from Nauvoo began in February 1846 when Brigham Young's advance party, calling itself the "Camp of Israel," pioneered routes and travel methods, reaching Winter Quarters four months later. The leaders had determined in April, while camped by Locust Creek (when William Clayton wrote his immortal "Come Come Ye Saints") to make their winter encampment on the Missouri River rather than attempting to go on to the Rocky Mountains. William G. Hartley, "Mormons and

Early Iowa History (1838 to 1858)," *The Annals of Iowa* 59 (summer 2000): 232.

11. Elvira and her twin brother Barnard, born May 1832, were the youngest of the orphaned children of Samuel and Minerva Stevens. A partial biographical sketch of Elvira, who reappears often in Caroline's journals, is presented in Part 5 of her book, *The Stevens Genealogy.*

12. There were three separate waves of departure from Nauvoo in 1846, the first being the winter exodus of Brigham Young's advance party and the second being the much larger spring exodus, which included Louisa Barnes Pratt with her four daughters. The final departures occurred in September when armed mobs drove the remaining few hundred Saints from Nauvoo, although most were too ill or unequipped for the trek across Iowa. This included the so-called "Poor Camp" the Crosbys joined. See note 15. Hartley, "Mormons and Early Iowa History," 240.

13. The situation proved as serious as the rumors and uncertainties implied. See Flanders, *Nauvoo,* 326–341.

14. Hartley, "Mormons and Early Iowa History," 242.

15. In mid-September there were between 600 and 700 Saints camped by Potter's Slough, on the west side of the Mississippi river, about a mile north of Montrose. Many had moved out by the time diarist Thomas Bullock counted 17 tents and 8 wagons in camp on October 4, "and most of those are the poorest of the Saints. [There is] not a tent or Wagon but [has] sickness in it, and nearly all don't know which way they shall get to the main camp." When Bullock composed his list of "Persons who Volunteer to Go" to Winter Quarters with the relief train sent by Brigham Young, Jonathan Crosby was listed as having a wagon but no animals. Will Bagley, ed., *The Pioneer Camp of the Saints: The 1846 and 1847 Mormon Trail Journals of Thomas Bullock,* Kingdom in the West, The Mormons and the American Frontier, vol. 1 (Spokane: The Arthur H. Clark Company, 1997), 72, 75.

16. After Joseph Smith's death, Joseph L. Heywood, Almon Babbitt, Joseph Coolidge and John Fullmer were appointed trustees-in-trust of the LDS church at Nauvoo. Their responsibilities were to stay behind, disposing of the property of the Mormons. Heywood directly assisted Jonathan Crosby and later was a guest in the Crosby home in San Francisco. JC, 17.

17. Jonathan was probably referring to an event of October 9, 1846, known as the "Miracle of the Quail." Large flocks of exhausted quail flopped into the camp, landing on and under wagons and in tents. "Every man, woman and child had quails to eat for their dinner," wrote Thomas Bullock. Hartley, "Mormons and Early Iowa History," 241; Bagley, *Pioneer Camp of the Saints,* 76.

18. Bentonsport, a small Iowa village on the Des Moines River, was once an important port-of-call for river steamers and boasts today (2004) of several buildings in its National Historic District as being constructed by Mormon craftsmen soliciting work on their trek west.

19. Jonathan's memoirs indicate the family started west the spring following their move to Bentonsport, but the family remained in Iowa through 1847, emigrating in the spring of 1848.

Chapter 5

1. Council Bluffs, Iowa. The winter of 1846–47 saw thousands of westward-moving Saints locating in temporary encampments on both sides of the Missouri

River. The heart of the Mormon settlement in Iowa, on the east side of the river, from July 1846 to the spring of 1852, was Kanesville, now part of Council Bluffs. Allen and Leonard, *The Story of the Latter-day Saints*, 234–36.

2.   This was probably part of the cooperative farming effort to start cultivating fields that would be tended by Saints passing through.

3.   Prior to the Crosbys' arrival in early June 1848, the "gathering up of Zion," eventually totaling 2,408 people in 923 wagons, was organized into three great companies led by Brigham Young, Heber C. Kimball, and Willard Richards, assisted by Amasa Lyman, who had all returned from the Great Salt Lake Valley that fall. The Crosbys would be in the third company. JH, 5, 6, 8, 16 June 1848. Bagley, *Pioneer Camp of the Saints*, 321. In December 1847 the Mormons constructed a huge log building for their meeting hall. The Kanesville Tabernacle could seat 1,000 people. Hartley, "Mormons and Early Iowa History," 244.

4.   Louisa Pratt and her four daughters, who had been living at Winter Quarters since the fall of 1846, were in Brigham Young's company, which led the 1848 march, leaving Winter Quarters on 26 May 1848.

5.   Twice-widowed Marial Thompson Crosby Bent married William Draper at Winter Quarters, Nebraska in 1848. David Harland, son of David and Marial Crosby, was born in 1837 in Massachusetts.

6.   Winter Quarters, on the west side of the Missouri river, was renamed Florence, Nebraska in 1854.

7.   Dr. Willard Richards had been sick in bed at Winter Quarters. His fellow members of the Mormon First Presidency, Brigham Young and Heber C. Kimball, had already left for the West, instructing him to solicit funds and equipment to follow when he had recovered. Richards was still convalescing in mid-June, but, as a physician, understood the need to get out of the unhealthful environment of the river bottom. He was finally ready to travel on 5 July. JH, 30 May, 15, 27 June 1848.

8.   Thomas Bullock secured one hundred copies of William Clayton's *Emigrants' Guide,* published in St. Louis that same year, and peddled them among members of the forward camps. The mileages given here by the editors are taken from the guidebook, to which Caroline referred during her journey. W. Clayton, *The Latter-day Saints' Emigrants' Guide: Being a Table of Distances, from Council Bluffs to the Valley of the Great Salt Lake* (St. Louis: Chambers & Knapp, 1848).

9.   Where the earlier companies had taken days to ferry across the river, by the time the Richards and Lyman groups arrived the water was low enough for the wagons to be pulled through.

10.   Amasa M. Lyman, who along with Young, Kimball and some others, had already been to Salt Lake Valley the previous summer, had recently come from the American South with a company of Latter-day Saints from that region. This was a close-knit group, many of whom later accompanied Lyman to San Bernardino, California. When the group was approached to have some volunteers join Richards' company to equalize the numbers, none expressed willingness to do so. The two companies soon agreed to travel closely together. JH, 7 July 1848.

11.   The combined companies totaled 502 white members and 24 African-American slaves. There were 169 wagons, 70 horses and mules, 515 oxen, 426 cows and loose cattle, 369 sheep, 63 pigs, 44 dogs and 170 chickens. JH, 9 July 1848.

12. "Old Pawnee village, burned fall of 1846" Clayton, *Emigrants' Guide*, 3.

13. This was William Crosby, a "Mississippi Saint" and future bishop of San Bernardino. He was no relation to Jonathan.

14. These hunters, who were consistently successful providing their company with fresh meat, negligently allowed their horses to get away. Stranded in the heat without water, they were compelled to walk. It took Lyman days to recover. JH, 19, 20 July 1848.

15. These ex-Mormon Battalion boys were apparently heading back to their families still in Iowa. There was some dissension when Brigham Young failed to bring their families to the Salt Lake Valley as promised when their advance pay had been utilized to purchase teams and wagons.

16. That day the two companies essentially subdivided into three, then further spread out into groups of ten wagons each, led by "Captains of Ten." Andrew Cunningham had earlier been selected as captain of the 6th ten of Amasa Lyman's larger group.

17. The Saints used the term "wolf" to refer to both coyotes (*Canis latrans*) and wolves (*Canis lupis*). Bagley, *Pioneer Camp of the Saints*, 132.

18. After traveling 306 miles from Winter Quarters, Clayton noted that "you will find no more timber on the north side the river for two hundred miles, except one lone tree. Your only dependence for fuel will be buffalo chips and drift wood." Clayton, *Emigrants' Guide*, 8.

19. Caroline refers to Clayton's *Emigrants' Guide* here and again on 31 August.

20. Apparently, the two ladies had little fear of the rattlesnakes Clayton warned were "lurking around, concealed in the clefts of the bluffs."

21. Clayton described traveling over four and ½ miles of dark, red sand along the steep banks of the La Bonte River, with doubtful water. He also advised: "Look out for toads with horns and tails." Clayton, *Emigrants' Guide*, 16.

22. Caroline apparently had little time to examine Independence Rock, the most noted landmark on the Mormon Trail west of Fort Laramie. She had been duly occupied earlier, gathering saleratus, or baking soda (sodium bicarbonate). Thomas Bullock had advised the Saints that when they came to the small lake east of Independence Rock, to "gather one or two hundred pounds weight for family use; this stuff is what you will rise your bread with, and the soda in the same lake is excellent to wash with." She did have the opportunity to explore Devil's Gate, which is actually 370 feet deep and 1,500 feet long, and is considered one of the most beautiful spots on the Mormon Trail. Bagley, *Pioneer Camp of the Saints*, 198–99.

23. Here President Richards preached—at least to his company—and praised them for their "faithfulness and strict attendance to duty." The groups were several days apart at this point, but all appeared to be doing well, though many animals were weak.

24. Caroline made no note of crossing the Continental Divide at South Pass, nor of her first view of water flowing toward the Pacific Ocean.

25. Louisa Pratt and girls arrived in Salt Lake on 20 September 1848. Eight days later, Addison Pratt arrived from California to rejoin the family he had left behind in Nauvoo for his mission to the Society Islands and from whom he had been separated for over five years.

26. Jedediah M. Grant and three associates took 9 yoke of oxen, 6 mules and two wagons to assist those who were struggling along the last leg of the journey. Willard Richards had "tarried near the Weber River while his wife Sarah gave birth to a healthy son." They entered the Valley on 19 October.

Claire Noall, *Intimate Disciple: A Portrait of Willard Richards* (Salt Lake City: University of Utah Press, 1957), 554.

27. The Crosbys had entered Little Emigration Canyon and now had "to ascend the highest mountain you cross in the whole journey." Clayton, *Emigrants' Guide*, 29.

28. Philip B. Lewis's lifelong friendship with Addison Pratt's family began with his generous contribution to outfit the missionaries to the Society Islands in 1843. He married Caroline and Louisa's cousin Jane Stevens on 11 May 1848, at Winter Quarters.

Chapter 6

1. John Eagar of Auburn, New York had traveled to California on the ship *Brooklyn* in 1846. He served as Sam Brannan's clerk, was also a printer and for a time associate editor of the *California Star,* San Francisco's first newspaper. His mother had been excommunicated from the church during the voyage and wished to remove her children from Mormon influences, but John did not apostatize and came to Utah with Addison Pratt in 1848. Hubert Howe Bancroft, "California Pioneer Register and Index, 1542–1848," extracted from *The History of California*, 7 vols., 1886 (Baltimore: Regional Publishing Co., 1964), 127–28.

2. Zina Diantha Huntington Jacobs, wife of Brigham Young, whose friendship with Caroline, begun in Nauvoo, continued through their later correspondence.

3. John D. Unruh, Jr. offers a brief description of John Eagar and Brigham Young's "Emigrant Guide" in *The Plains Across: The Overland Emigrants and the Trans-Mississippi West, 1840–60* (Urbana: University of Illinois, 1979), 265. It was the unidentified "Mormon Guide Book" referred to in Lorenzo Sawyer's *Way Sketches, Across the Plains in 1850*, published in 1926.

4. James S. Brown and Hiram H. Blackwell were appointed to the Society Islands mission with Addison Pratt. They left Salt Lake with the Jefferson Hunt party on 4 October 1849.

5. "I built a small house on the side of the hill or bench east of President B Youngs habitation, on what is cald south Temple street." JC, 20.

6. Elders appointed to the Society Island mission at the General Conference included Uriah B. Powell, Simeon A. Dunn, Julian Moses, Thomas Tompkins, Sidney Alvarus Hanks, George Pitkin, Joseph Busby, and Jonathan Crosby. JH, 13 April 1850.

7. Louisa described her sister's response: "She had a pleasant home, and was comfortable. Her home must be sold to make the necessary preparations. She was tranquil and unmoved." It was doubtless Sister Pratt's selfish insistence which had Jonathan re-included in the missionary list. The Crosbys were later informed while living in California how much the property they had possessed had appreciated in value. LPB, 107.

Chapter 7

1. A number of the missionaries called to the Society Islands traveled together with a company of men bound for the California gold mines. The missionary families included, along with the Crosbys, the following: named in charge, Thomas Tompkins, his wife and two girls; Louisa Pratt with her four

daughters; Joseph Busby and wife; Simeon A. Dunn; Julian Moses; Sidney Alvarus Hanks; and Hiram E. W. Clark, a fourteen-year-old boy traveling with the Pratts. JH, 7 May 1850.

2. Louisa and her girls had departed earlier from their adobe home in the Old Fort, calling at Brigham Young's, where supper was waiting, and then drove on to Warm Springs, in the northwestern portion of the city, accompanied by several friends who spent the evening. LBP, 110.

3. William D. Huntington led the last officially sanctioned company of Mormon gold miners to leave Utah. All together there were fifty-one people in the company, including his father-in-law, Hiram Clark, on his way to the Sandwich Islands to preside over the mission there. The elder Clark was apparently no relation to the young boy who was accompanying the Pratts per the request of Louisa's friend, Emmeline B. Wells. J. Kenneth Davies, *Mormon Gold, The Story of California's Mormon Argonauts* (Salt Lake City: Olympus Publishing Company, 1984), 244.

4. Lieutenant John W. Gunnison of the U. S. Army, under the command of Captain Howard Stansbury, was completing the first scientific survey of the Salt Lake Valley region. During this period, he wrote a treatise called *The Mormons, or, Latter-day Saints, in the Valley of the Great Salt Lake* which was published a year before his death in a massacre in Utah Territory in 1853. Brigham D. Madsen, ed., *Exploring the Great Salt Lake: The Stansbury Expedition of 1849–50* (Salt Lake City: University of Utah Press, 1989).

5. Caroline's sister was more forthright in her critcism of the non-Mormon hangers-on who attached themselves to the company. "Badir the Socialist has made trouble in the camp by coming without supplies. Mr Mills the phrenologist who hired his passage with him, is now destitute; likewise a family he engaged to take through. Although the two men above mentioned are not of our faith, the brethren will not see them want for food." LBP, 114.

6. The company had just traversed the important Salt Lake Road, or Cutoff, the second of two major contributions to the California Trail forged in 1848 by the eastward-headed company of Mormons who were the first to take wagons from City of Rocks (Steeple Rocks) to Great Salt Lake City. Their first major accomplishment was the creation of the road over the Carson Pass, at the western end of the trail, thus avoiding crossing the Truckee River some twenty-seven times. Will Bagley, ed., *A Road from El Dorado, the 1848 Trail Journal of Ephraim Green* (Salt Lake City: Prairie Dog Press, 1991).

7. First known as Ogden's River, then Mary's River, John C. Fremont gave the Humboldt river its final name in 1845, but travelers were slow to adopt the change. Dale L. Morgan, *The Humboldt: Highroad of the West* (New York: Farrar and Rinehart, 1943).

8. Louisa credited her guardian angel being very near in her account of this incident. She wrote: "My cow was grazing a little way off, an impression came to me, as if some one had whispered 'walk out where your cow is, and look at her.' I did so, and while I was standing there I heard a report like a canon fired. I returned immediately, found my stove blown over the top of a covered wagon! It was crushed, as with a sledge hammer." LBP, 112.

9. The "First Principles" referred to the Mormon position on faith, repentance, baptism, and the gift of the Holy Ghost. Elders were encouraged to teach only "first principles" and to leave alone the "mysteries" and less comprehensible details. S. George Ellsworth, "History of Mormon Missions," 50.

10. The Salmon Trout River was an appellation applied to both the Truckee and the Carson Rivers. The Truckee River, which bears the name of the Indian who led the Stevens Party to it in 1844, was titled the Salmon Trout River by Fremont. This name appeared on Bancroft's map as late as 1858. Ira J. Willis's popular waybill, "Best Guide to the Gold Mines," handwritten in 1849, identified the Salmon Trout as the Carson River, which was the route opened to the south of the Truckee on the Mormons' eastward trek in 1848. The Crosbys would have followed the Carson River, as did the vast majority of westward travelers after 1849. Erwin G. Gudde, *California Place Names*, 4th ed. (Berkeley: University of California Press, 1998), 345. William E. Hill, *The California Trail Yesterday & Today* (Boulder, Colorado: Pruett Publishing Company, 1986), 35–36.

11. Carson Valley included for a time a church colony named Mormon Station, now Genoa, Nevada.

12. Brigham Young publicly charged Moses Martin with adultery and lying at the General Conference at Salt Lake City in April 1850, likening him to "a wild bull in the net." A unanimous vote was taken to excommunicate him from the church. JH 6 April 1850. (Moses traveled to the gold fields with his wife Julia Priscilla Smith, whom he married in 1837 in New York. Plural wife Emma, whom Moses married during a church mission to England in 1846, came later with their two daughters to California.)

13. Generally, thievery was the only danger from Indians to which the vast majority of overlanders were exposed. The Shoshones, along the upper Humboldt, were unwarlike, and, though they had no scruples against stealing, were not greatly to be feared. The Northern Paiutes of the middle Humboldt were more aggressive and would kill or cripple livestock so that the beasts would be left behind for the Indians to consume. There were, of course, fatal encounters, such as the one at Tragedy Springs, discussed below. For an analysis of the relatively small number of Indian-related pillages and killings, see John D. Unruh, Jr., *The Plains Across*, 141–48.

14. Addison Pratt described in vivid detail the gruesome discovery on 19 July 1848 of the grave of the three men sent out about ten days earlier from Pleasant Valley (see note 17 below) to scout the road ahead. Opening the Indian burial mound they were dismayed to find the bodies of their friends, with skulls broken and "entirely divested of evry article of clothing, and bearing marks of horrid violence." Since Pratt wrongly named one of the Mormon men in his journal as Nelson Allen, he would not have been the carver. The inscription, still legible on the tree today, reads: "To the Memory of Daniel Browett, Ezrah H. Allen, and Henderson Cox, Who was Supposed to have Been Murdered and Buried by Indians On the Night of the 27th of June, 1848." AP, 344–45.

15. Louisa identified these two as "good Spanish boys." LBP 116.

16. A brief description of gold camp dwellings referred to as "greenies."

17. About 50 miles from Sutter's Fort, Pleasant Valley was the gathering place for the Mormons to assemble and organize their memorable trek to the Salt Lake valley in the summer of 1848. They named the spot and whiled away idle time by washing gold, with good success, according to Henry Bigler. Erwin G. Gudde, *Bigler's Chronicle of the West, The Conquest of California, Discovery of Gold, and Mormon Settlement as Reflected in Henry William Bigler's Diaries* (Berkeley: University of California Press, 1962), 112.

18.   Louis C. Bidamon, who married the widow of the prophet Joseph Smith in Nauvoo in December 1847, came to California eighteen months later with his brother John and, "by the hardest of labour," apparently prospered in the mines, according to letters he sent Emma Smith. Davies, *Mormon Gold*, 248–49. Newell and Avery, *Mormon Enigma*, 252.

19.   In the fall of 1849 Brigham Young directed Apostles Amasa Lyman and later Charles C. Rich to go to the gold fields of California to determine if a gathering place could be established and try to win back those who had strayed from the church. The First Presidency in addition expressed interest in "a chain of settlements" extending from Salt Lake City to the coast. Prior to their arrival in Pleasant Valley in mid-July 1850, Lyman and Rich traveled with other church brethren to San Pedro and concluded that a Mormon colony should be planted in southern California rather than in closer proximity to the gold fields. Edward Leo Lyman, *San Bernardino, The Rise and Fall of a California Community* (Salt Lake City: Signature Books, 1996), 27.

20.   LBP, 116.

21.   The sizeable mining camp of Weberville at the confluence of Weber and Hangtown [Placerville] creeks in El Dorado County was often mistakenly named Weaverville. Erwin G. Gudde and Elisabeth K. Gudde, eds. *California Gold Camps* (Berkeley: University of California Press, 1975), 366.

22.   Louisa identified Mr. Brown in her entry for the 16th July: "Camped in an oak grove near Brown's a fictitious name for Porter Rockwell." Mormon scout and one-time bodyguard for Joseph Smith, Rockwell would well have not wanted his identity known in the gold fields as he was widely suspected of having attempted to assassinate the ex-Missouri governor Lillburn Boggs. His notoriety would plague him among Missourians and southern sympathizers throughout his life. LBP 116. See also Harold Schindler, *Orrin Porter Rockwell, Man of God, Son of Thunder* (Salt Lake City: University of Utah Press, 1966), 190–97.

23.   Asahel Lathrop had been a Captain of Ten in the Mormon migration of 1847, and probably came to California with Lyman and Rockwell in the spring of 1849. His Mormon Tavern, established a few miles west of Porter Rockwell's settlement, served as a base of operations for Apostles Rich and Lyman in 1850. Davies, *Mormon Gold*, 370–71.

24.   Caroline would have been acquainted with Henry Jacobs in Nauvoo, as he was the first husband of her friend and correspondent Zina Diantha Huntington.

25.   Jeremiah Root had his establishment at Brighton, on the South Fork of the American River, in the vicinity of Five and Six Mile Houses. Davies, *Mormon Gold*, 356.

26.   This lyrical morsel of poetry may have been Caroline's own, though her sister was the one recognized for her poetic achievements. Louisa narrated in prose the plight of the gentleman who was determined to lodge with his wife in the Ladies' cabin but was ravaged by the mosquitoes and fled out to the deck. LBP, 119.

27.   Benicia, California's state capitol in 1853, marked the bottle-neck opening to San Francisco Bay, "situated on the north side of the Strait of Carquinez, where the channel is little more than a mile wide, and at which place are a government dock-yard and naval stores." Frank Soulé, John H. Gihon, and James Nisbet, *The Annals of San Francisco* (New York: D. Appleton &

Company, 1855; facsimile edition, Berkeley: Berkeley Hills Books, 1998), 153.

Chapter 8

1. "The *Bark* had been baffling about in the bay for two weeks" while the steamer *Hartford* with its seventeen passengers, including Louisa Pratt, had made the trip to San Francisco overnight, arriving 5 August 1850. They were currently visiting at Mission San Jose in the east bay, where Caroline and Jonathan would later reside. LBP, 121.
2. Fannie Corwin, mother-in-law to Samuel Brannan, and widow Lucy Buell Eagar were fellow travelers on the *Brooklyn*, becoming good friends despite the fact Brannan disfellowshipped Mrs. Eagar from the church during the voyage, citing "lascivious conduct." Mrs. Corwin and Mrs. Eagar helped set the social tone for early San Francisco Yankee society with such amusements as all-night dances. Joseph T. Downey, *Filings from an Old Saw, Reminiscences of San Francisco and California's Conquest,* edited by Fred Blackburn Rogers, (San Francisco: John Howell, 1956), 140.
3. Here began what was to be an ongoing relationship with Horace Austin and Laura Farnsworth Skinner and their son James Horace, *Brooklyn* passengers who farmed in what is today Fremont in the East Bay, removed to San Bernardino in southern California, and went on to Beaver, Utah, crossing paths with the Crosbys throughout their lives.
4. George and Hanna Winner arrived on the *Brooklyn* with seven children, having buried another at sea. Their daughter Elizabeth's wedding was the first to take place in San Francisco under the protection of the American flag. John H. Brown, *Reminiscences and Incidents of Early Days of San Francisco* (1886; reprint, Oakland: Biobooks, 1949), 34. With the eventual excommunication of Samuel Brannan, Winner became the branch president in San Francisco. By 1852 he joined with the many Brooklyn Saints who helped establish San Bernardino as the largest pioneer Mormon settlement outside of Salt Lake City.
5. Caroline would later spend much time in Upper California with Barton and Ruth Mowry and their grown sons, while Theodore Thorp would move *Brooklyn* arrival Caroline Warner with her children to San Bernardino where she died January 1854.
6. When the Crosbys and their associates arrived in Tahiti they were among the first Latter-day Saint missionary couples ever to serve in an environment so foreign and lacking in amenities customary to them. While fervently welcomed by people previously converted by Addison Pratt and Benjamin F. Grouard, this aspect of the work would never again be quite so successful, even though the missionaries proved dedicated to their cause.
7. Benjamin F. Grouard was one of the original missionaries sent from Nauvoo to the Society Islands. He and Addison Pratt, both former sailors, proved by far the most effective in proselytizing among the islanders. He became head of the mission when Pratt departed for America. He married a native woman and had a daughter by her; and upon her death he married another and had three sons. Grouard dedicated nine years to the Pacific mission before returning to the states, accompanied by his wife and children. Co-editor S. George Ellsworth praised Pratt and Grouard: "These two men, by dogged efforts, had anchored their church's position

      in the Pacific and thereby given it a universality only theoretical before."
AP, 501.

8.   The Tahitian language has only 13 letters. "B" in Tahitian is pronounced and written as "P". *Fare pure raa* is "church house." Caroline sometimes spells Tubuai as Tu*p*uai. She also writes Pomutu for Tuamotu. John Davies, *A Tahitian and English Dictionary with Introductory Remarks on the Polynesian Language, and a Short Grammar of the Tahitian Dialect.* (Tahiti: London Missionary Society's Press, 1851; reprint, AMS Press, New York, 1978.) Tahitian, Hawaiian, Maori, Samoan, and Tongan are all the same language and understandable to each other. The various Polynesian dialects have many sounds that cannot accurately be put into our modern language sounds. There are only eight consonants in Tahitian, including variations of the same sound such as H or F for WH, B for P, V for W, L for R, etc. William A. Cole and Elwin W. Jensen, *Israel in the Pacific* (Salt Lake City: Polynesian Department of the Genealogical Society of the Church of Jesus Christ of Latter-day Saints, 1961), 24, 27.

9.   James S. Brown, a former Mormon Battalion captain, had figured prominently in securing army pay from the government, some of which purchased the beginning nucleus of Ogden, Utah. Brown proved to possess a strong, and occasionally abrasive, personality that eventually did much damage to future prospects for the Tahitian mission.

10.   Benjamin Grouard directed the construction of the mission ship, christened *Ravaai* (the Fisherman), with Jonathan Crosby erecting the schooner's cabin. The craft played a central role in the mission by transporting elders and raising financial support for the missionaries by partially engaging in inter-island commerce under Captain Grouard.

11.   Thomas Whitaker spent fourteen years as a sailor and was conversant in seven languages, including Tahitian. He was baptised into the Latter-day Saint church in San Francisco in 1849. He later brought his Polynesian wife to San Bernardino where he worked as a carpenter. Eventually the wife returned to the islands for a visit and the couple never saw each other again.

12.   A longstanding cordial relationship between the royal family and the Mormon church is evidenced in Addison Pratt's journal. He wrote in July 1844: "This man is the best friend I have among the natives, outside of the family I live with." In August he added: "King Tommatooa and his wife came over to see me, said as soon as his wife could see her way clear they should both join the church." AP, 176, 186.

13.   Mahu, village on the south side of Tubuai, where the *Ravaai* was being built.

14.   The family reunion was an emotional one for Addison, who stated "it was about 16 months since my eyes had been blessed with such a sight. 'But the effect' I will not try to describe. Let the curious, under similar circumstances, try it, and they will know for themselves." AP, 465.

15.   Missionaries were requested to make a written statement to the governor of their intentions of their missions. They replied, among other things, that their intent was to "preach the everlasting Gospel," while also pledging to obey the laws under which they then dwelled. To the specific inquiries concerning how the missionary families were to be sustained economically, they affirmed no intention to "lean on the natives" for support. The Americans were specifically directed to limit their instruction to "preaching their religion without interfering in any, or under any pre-text with political or

civil matters." S. George Ellsworth and Kathleen C. Perrin, *Seasons of Faith and Courage, The Church of Jesus Christ of Latter-day Saints in French Polynesia: A Sesquicentennial History, 1843–1993* (Sandy, Utah: Yves R. Perrin, 1994), 19–21.

16. Captain Jo[h]son's wife, Mereama, mother of Mary Ann, was the widow of John Cane, native of Ireland, who died on Tubuai in 1845. AP 464. Luna Williams was the daughter of "Tummy," whose father was probably Anglo-American and whose mother was likely the Polynesian, Teofai. Since the girl is referred to as "quadroon," her mother would doubtless be Polynesian as well. CBC, 18 February 1852. Maria Ellsworth was probably incorrect when she identified her as the daughter of a sea captain in "The First Mormon Missionary Women in the Pacific, 1850–1852," in *Voyages of Faith, Explorations in Mormon Pacific History*, ed. Grant Underwood (Provo: Brigham Young University Press, 2000), 39.

17. There were not sufficient church members on Tubuai to pull so heavy a craft so far, and the missionaries had to bargain for additional assistance. The non-Mormon Tahitians secured permission for a native dance and celebration not usually condoned by church members. It took four days of alternate dancing and pulling the mission ship to get the *Ravaai* properly launched. It sailed well.

18. The ignominy of this situation may have severely unbalanced the man's life. Hiram Clark returned to San Francisco, and, in 1853, he removed to San Bernardino where he took his own life.

19. Raivavae, part of the Austral Islands, is located just south and east of Tubuai. Various spellings include Lavavai and Livewy and reflect the difficulty in describing the Polynesian sound, "a sort of rolling R, halfway between an R and an L." Cole and Jensen, *Israel in the Pacific*, 24. Jonathan left for his mission assignment on 10 May 1851 and did not reunite with Caroline until 22 August. The notably isolated wife was thus without her husband's company for a hundred days.

20. As usual, the contrast between these Barnes sisters was dramatic. Louisa considered her time in Tahiti "dull, dull, dull." She also longed for more stimulating company—presumably for more conversation than the Tahitians could provide. For a discussion of the activities of the two sisters and how the monotony of island life affected them, see Maria S. Ellsworth, "First Mormon Missionary Women," 33–47; S. George Ellsworth and Perrin, *Faith and Courage*, 25.

21. Addison Pratt's friendship with Mr. Bourne dated back to his arrival at Mataura in May 1844. Pratt identifies him as "the oldest man of the American company." The other four Americans on Tubuai at that time were Charles Hill, John Layton, William F. Bowen and Ambrose Alexander, all of whom became Mormon converts. AP 159, 161.

22. The queen was sufficiently impressed with the educational progress of the native children under the charge of the Sisters Pratt and Crosby that she requested the latter to take her son into her home. Darius was the same age as Alma and appeared to be an apt pupil himself. The sisters conducted the weekly women's prayer meeting, and it was to their eventual satisfaction that they did learn the language sufficiently well to read scripture, sing hymns, and pray in Tahitian. AP, 477, ed. note.

23. Thus the teaching of the Tahitian sisters by the Barnes sisters remained mostly by example. They kept their houses and dooryards particularly clean "to encourage the native women to clean theirs." They also taught by

example family relations, care and schooling of children, personal dress, manners and such needlework as sewing, knitting and quilting. The influence of these missionary women cannot be underestimated because it endured to future generations on the islands. Maria Ellsworth cites two such examples: 1) the tradition on Tubuai of saints keeping their yards clean, going beyond their own property into the street and down to the ocean; 2) the unusual practice on Tubuai of making and giving quilts to important visitors as parting gifts. Maria S. Ellsworth, "First Mormon Missionary Women," 45.

24.   S. George Ellsworth stated forty-five years ago, "Brown lacked the finesse of relationships with potential antagonists that saved Pratt and Grouard so many troubles." S. George Ellsworth, "Zion in Paradise: Early Mormons in the South Seas" (Twenty-First Faculty Honor Lecture, Utah State University, 1959), 27. In Brown's personal conversations, promptly reported by the four Catholic priests in the vicinity, he displayed the American flag, recounted his Mormon Battalion exploits, and sympathized with the islanders' complaints about being under the French "yoke." These were clearly in violation of the agreements the missionaries had made with the French governor. Brown's lack of good judgment and diplomacy early did much to end the Latter-day Saint missionary efforts in the Society Islands. Another seemingly reliable authority on Tahiti during its early contact with foreigners, presumably drawing from non-Mormon sources, stated the following: "James Brown . . . built up his own version of local government on Ana'a by appointing converts to run the districts under the American flag, which was hoisted as a symbol of loyalty to the church and resistance to the French." He was arrested for this clearly subversive (and unwise) behavior. Colin Newbury, *Tahiti Nui: Change and Survival in French Polynesia, 1767–1945* (Honolulu: University Press of Hawaii, 1980), 143.

25.   Pratt and Grouard met with William H. Kelly, the American consul in the islands, along with some French officials. It was finally decided that James S. Brown would be released from custody with the strict understanding that he would be taken to some island outside of the French domain. Grouard subsequently took him to Raivavae, the Austral Islands at that time filling that requirement, but matters got progressively worse for all the missionaries thereafter.

26.   Caroline's initial entry in her journal history, begun in Tubuai, is dated "Jan 1851," which seems to contradict her statement here. More likely, she was referring to her activity over the past year as she had been faithfully keeping a periodic record, which became an almost lifelong habit, while concurrently writing in her "back journal."

27.   Initial Latter-day Saint missionary work was a phenomenal success. The delay of the church in sending reinforcements, however, gave the civil and religious opposition time to get organized and somewhat thwart their achievements.

28.   Louisa Pratt labored diligently to acquire a facility with the Tahitian language. Caroline never gained much confidence in using the language, particularly in comparison with Ellen and her mother.

29.   Author George Combe (1788–1856) became the leading spokesman on phrenology, fashionable in Britain and America in the 1820s and after. Combe's essays and lectures were very popular, and his book *The Constitution of Man*, ranked fourth in the list of Victorian best sellers during the era.

30. Benjamin F. Grouard appeared to be pressuring Nahina into accompanying him by keeping the children with him. They included Sophronia, the daughter by his first native wife, Tearo, and three boys by Nahina—Benjamin Franklin, Ephraim, and a baby.

31. Addison Pratt attributed his daughter's ill health to emotional disturbances. "As she is of a nervous temprament, our protracted stay [on Tubuai] had produced a bad effect on her mind, and had now began to disorder her system." Caroline was concerned with her niece's frequent episodes of illness, but never commented upon the cause with the frankness of Frances's father. AP, 494–95.

32. "A Voice of Warning and Instruction to all People, containing a Declaration of the Faith and Doctrine of the Church of Jesus Christ of Latter-day Saints, commonly called Mormons" was written and first published by Parley P. Pratt in 1837. It was one of the most successful and perennially employed Mormon proselyting tracts. Another popular publication was "Evidences in Proof of the Book of Mormon," written by Charles B. Thompson and published in 1841. S. George Ellsworth, "History of Mormon Missions," 213, 434.

33. Alfred Tahinevai Layton was the seven-year-old son of missionary John Layton and his Polynesian wife Aeata. He would remain under Caroline's charge for a time in California.

34. Caroline maintained an almost continuous list of foster children in her home, but much to her frustration, none permanently.

Chapter 9

1. The Mission San Jose was founded by Franciscan father Fermin LaSuén in 1797, on the southeast plains of San Francisco Bay, in what is present-day Fremont, Alameda County, California. The former mission lands secularized in 1834 became known as Washington Township and were settled largely by Latter-day Saints in 1848 and should not be confused with the Pueblo, now City, of San Jose, located 15 miles to the south. For a more comprehensive treatment of the American colonization and contributions of the Latter-day Saints to the development of the East Bay lands of Ex-Mission San Jose, which Caroline and other diarists called San Jose Valley, see Lorin K. Hansen and Lila J. Bringhurst, *Let This Be Zion: Mormon Pioneers and Modern Saints in Southern Alameda California* (Salt Lake City: Publishers Press, 1996), 1–5.

2. The Mowry [Morey, Mowrey] Family were representative of the various means by which immigrating Latter-day Saints arrived in California. Charles Barton Mowry and his wife Ruth sailed to California on the ship *Brooklyn* with their sons Origin [Origan] and Rinaldo [Rhanaldo]. They left New York in February 1846 with some 230 Latter-day Saints, including about 100 children, under the leadership of Samuel Brannan, who was instructed by Brigham Young to set up a colony at the Bay of San Francisco. The youngest brother, Harley, came to California in January 1847 with the Mormon Battalion, an enlistment of 500 Mormon volunteers joining Col. Stephen Kearney's "Army of the West," recruited on the plains of Iowa at the outset of the Mexican War. Hansen and Bringhurst, *Let This Be Zion*, 33, 76.

3. Quartus S. Sparks was a school teacher on Long Island, New York before coming to California on the *Brooklyn* with his wife and mother-in-law and

infant son. He was reputed to have "only a very ordinary, common school education and no learning as a lawyer," but a "gift of oratory" which established him as a notable preacher and eventually an attorney in San Bernardino. John Brown, Jr. and James Boyd, *History of San Bernardino and Riverside Counties,* vol. 1 (Chicago: Lewis Publishing Co., 1922), 121–22.

4.   Welsh convert Thomas Morris came to California with the Mormon Battalion. He, along with other "Battalion boys" was one of the first into the gold fields. Morris wrote the "Mormon Battalion Song" with which Daniel Tyler concluded his chronicle history of the volunteer force. Upon his return from missionary service on Molokai in the Sandwich Islands in 1852, Morris settled in Centerville and worked as John Horner's gardener. He eventually returned to Salt Lake City and served as "market gardener" to Brigham Young. Daniel Tyler, *A Concise History of the Mormon Battalion in the Mexican War, 1846–1847* (Salt Lake City, 1881), 375. David L. Bigler and Will Bagley, eds., *Army of Israel: Mormon Battalion Narratives* (Logan: Utah State University Press, 2000), 447–48.

5.   Born in Bavaria in 1825, John C. Naile [Naegle] emigrated to America with his family and became a Mormon convert in Nauvoo. A private in the Mormon Battalion, he settled on the Mission San Jose lands after a successful period in the gold fields. He bought 250 acres of farmland about three miles north and west of the old mission, in what became known as Centerville, presently the location of the California State School for the Deaf and Blind. His large, two-story adobe home served as church meeting place, school, and social center. The Crosbys occupied the Naile property while he went back east to bring his parents west. Hansen and Bringhurst, *Let This be Zion,* 62.

6.   The Mowrys kept a home in San Francisco while Origin and his father Barton kept their sailing vessel *Neptune* at what soon became known as Mowry's Landing, a flourishing district and active shipping point for grain from all parts of Washington Township. The narrow water passageway through the tidal swamplands was only navigable at high tide to the landing. Their farm was at the west end of what is now Mowry Avenue in Fremont. The family eventually separated over the issue of religion. Ruth and her sons Rinaldo and Harley returned to Utah while Barton and Origin continued to practice spiritualism and remained in California. Country Club of Washington Township Research Committee. *History of Washington Township* (1904; 2nd ed., Stanford: Stanford University Press, 1950), 114, 119.

7.   *Brooklyn* passengers Horace A. Skinner and his wife Laura Ann Farnsworth, along with her uncle Alfonzo Farnsworth, farmed in the region of Clear Lake, just west of the Naile Ranch.

8.   The redwood schoolhouse was built in Centerville by John M. Horner in 1850, about halfway between Mission San Jose and Union City. The schoolhouse functioned as the first English-language school in what is now Alameda County as well as the first public structure built for Latter-day Saint services in the region. *History of Washington Township,* 88–89.

9.   Joseph and Jerusha Nichols came on the *Brooklyn,* their two-year-old son being the first of ten deaths on board the ship. At the end of the voyage, Jerusha gave birth to another son, the first Anglo-American child born in Yerba Buena, soon-to-be San Francisco. They bought property and established a fruit farm in what is today Niles, just east of the civic center of Fremont. Joseph was a stone mason by trade. The redwood-frame house he

built with its stone foundation still stands (in 2004), although precariously dilapidated after nearly a century of neglect and abuse.

10. Hannah Evans came to San Francisco with her husband William on the *Brooklyn,* where they established the first tailor shop in the community. Widowed with five children in 1851, she continued offering her home for church meetings and room and board for traveling missionaries as well as carrying on the tailoring business. Kate B. Carter, *Our Pioneer Heritage,* vol. 3 (Salt Lake City: Daughters of Utah Pioneers, 1960), 539–41.

11. John M. Horner was the first of the Latter-day Saints to settle in Washington Township. An experienced farmer from New Jersey, he and his bride Elizabeth arrived on the *Brooklyn* and spent a short time in the gold fields before moving to Washington Corners (Irvington). By the end of 1852, he had surveyed and fenced 10,000 acres of former mission lands, had laid out some of the main roads, which remain today, and had started the towns of Centerville and Union City. Given the title of "First Farmer of California" at the initial state agricultural fair in 1852, John Horner proved that grain and vegetables, especially potatoes and tomatoes, could be profitably grown in California. For an autobiographical sketch, see John M. Horner, "Adventures of a Pioneer," *Improvement Era* 7 (May to November 1904).

12. John Jacob Riser came to California with the Mormon Battalion. He returned to Salt Lake City where he met and married Helen Allen, who had come overland to Salt Lake Valley with her parents. She lost her mother during the first winter in Utah and her father during the third. The Risers returned to California and worked for John Naile before settling a farm of their own in the area of Centerville. Her brother Charles drove the stage coach from Mission San Jose to Union City for John Horner. *History of Washington Township,* 93. Hansen and Bringhurst, *Let This be Zion,* 63.

13. Harvey (Hervey) Green lost twin sons and his wife to exposure during the persecutions in Missouri in 1837. He married Charles C. Rich's sister Jane that same fall. He taught school for a while in Utah, then traveled to the California gold fields with his two older sons, Henry and Ammon. He then came to the San Jose Valley to farm for John Horner and to teach in the Horner school. Hansen and Bringhurst, *Let This be Zion,* 64.

14. Henry Jacobs had a history of irresolution in marital matters. First married to Zina D. Huntington in Nauvoo, he was never reconciled to the dissolution of their union even after she was sealed as a plural wife first to Joseph Smith, and then to Brigham Young. Henry lived for a time in the gold fields in Northern California with another wife whom he brought back from his mission to England in 1846. Family tradition indicates he married again in 1850. He continued to write heartrending letters to Zina until September 1852. He married the widow Clawson in January 1853, only to leave her when his English wife reappeared. Martha S. Bradley and Mary Brown F. Woodward, "Plurality, Patriarchy, and the Priestess: Zina D. H. Young's Nauvoo Marriages," *Journal of Mormon History* 20 (spring 1994): 107–11.

15. Dolly Stevens Barnes died in Dunham, Quebec, Canada on 27 January 1852, according to church burial records. (LDS temple records at St. George, Utah list the date as 1 February 1851.) Caroline's diary entry here would indicate the year was, indeed, 1852. All Saints Anglican Church, Dunham, register for the year 1852, folio 2, Quebec National Archives microfilm #124.2.

16. Alexander Badlam, brother-in-law to Samuel Brannan, came to the gold fields in 1849. That winter he returned to the states, complaining in a letter to Brigham Young that Brannan hadn't helped him enough financially. Brigham Young arranged for Badlam to accompany a missionary party from Utah to San Bernardino in 1852, and a year later he and his family were settled in Sacramento. He acted for a time as an agent for Mormon interests in California. His son, Alexander Jr. was a successful politician and businessman in California and served as Samuel Brannan's business agent in his declining years. Bagley, *Scoundrel's Tale*, 304–5.

17. Addison and Louisa Pratt moved to San Bernardino with their two youngest daughters, Lois and Ann Louise, and their adopted Anglo-Tahitian child, Sophronia, in December 1852.

18. Caroline's cousin Elvira Stevens married John Stillman Woodbury in December 1850. He served several missions in the Hawaiian Islands beginning in 1851, and she spent eleven months there with her sister Jane and brother-in-law Philip B. Lewis, president of the Sandwich Islands mission, before returning to San Francisco in November 1852.

19. The *Jenny Lind* steamer was en route from Alviso to San Francisco with about one hundred and twenty-five passengers on board when a steam-pipe explosion killed thirty-one persons. Ellen Pratt was one of the passengers on the *Union* which came to the aid of the survivors. She described the horrific scene to her mother in her letter dated 17 April 1853. Frank Soulé, *Annals of San Francisco*, 444. Addison Pratt Family Papers, S. George Ellsworth Collection, Special Collections and Archives, (Merrill Library, Utah State University, Logan, Utah), box 5, fd. 15, hereinafter APFP.

20. Cyrus Ira was on the *Brooklyn* and among the first to appear at Mormon Island, site of California's initial gold rush on the south fork of the American River. Louisa called him a "comical fellow," but Caroline became his confidante as he exposed his troubles to her and sought answers concerning his life and faith. LBP, 205.

21. In a letter to Ellen dated 1 June [1853] Frances described her home: "Oh Ellen you do not know how pretty the house looks it is all papered and painted so pretty the paint is pale lilack to corespond with the paper. my room has got the pretty light coulered paper in it the clothes press is torn away from where it was and put at the foot of the bed and I have got my table and toy shelf where that was, and a nice little book case over the door you had better believe it looks nice and feels nice to when I come in and sit down of a hot afternoon after my dinner work is done." APFP, box 7, fd. 13.

22. James Jones Dyer, suitor and eventual husband of Frances Pratt.

23. Ebenezer W. Dyer, born about 1829 in Maine, settled in San Lorenzo, Alameda County, where he died 2 April 1861. It is probable he and his brother James Jones Dyer, were related to non-Mormon brothers Ephraim and Ebenezer Herrick Dyer, prominent pioneer settlers of Alameda County, who came from Sullivan, Hancock County, Maine. *History of Alameda County* (Oakland: M. W. Wood, publisher, 1883), 878–79, 881.

24. Levi Dougherty was in the same company as the Crosbys in the journey from Salt Lake City to California in 1850. There is no known record confirming that he crossed the plains in their company five years earlier.

25. The year 1852 had been so profitable for the farmers that no one could foresee the overplanting and resultant glut of potatoes on the market the

following year. Unfortunately, it did not even pay for Jonathan to dig up his harvest. *Improvement Era* 7, July 1904, 668.

26. The Australian Mission of the Church of Jesus Christ of Latter-day Saints was organized in 1851 with the arrival in Sydney of the first American missionaries. Mission president Charles W. Wandell, later associated with the Crosbys at San Bernardino and at Beaver, Utah, led the first emigration of Mormon converts from Australia aboard the *Envelope,* arriving in San Francisco 8 July 1853 with 29 passengers. Marjorie Newton, *Southern Cross Saints: The Mormons in Australia* (Laie, Hawaii: The Institute for Polynesian Studies, Brigham Young University, Hawaii, 1991), 136.
27. Battalion veteran Zacheus Cheney was a brickmaker in San Francisco when he met Mary Ann Fisher, a passenger on the *Brooklyn.* The two first had to go to the gold fields to find an authorized Mormon elder to marry them before setting up a home and farm on Mission Creek, near Mission San Jose. She died a week after the birth of their daughter Mary on Christmas day 1850. Zacheus married Amanda Evans, also a passenger on the *Brooklyn,* on 10 January 1853.
28. Thomas S. Williams would become an independent-minded Salt Lake City merchant. Caroline would later (1860) note his death at the hand of Indians in Southern California.
29. Future husband of Caroline's eldest niece Ellen Pratt, William McGary was born in Montreal, Canada in 1832. His parents joined the Mormons and settled in Ogden, Utah by 1850. S. George Ellsworth, *Dear Ellen, Two Mormon Women and Their Letters* (Salt Lake City: University of Utah Library, 1974), 21n.
30. This is the first mention of Andrew Vanhorn Patten and his wife, with whom Caroline would later be much involved at San Bernardino.
31. Elvira Stevens's sister Jane, apparently afflicted with tuberculosis, faced the dilemma of leaving her husband, mission president Philip B. Lewis, to hopefully improve her condition in California.
32. The federal land laws devised for California initially favored Anglo-American "squatters," but eventually court decisions upheld many old Hispanic land grant claims—after much litigation. Both Horner's property and the San Bernardino rancho were affected by this situation. E. L. Beard, a non-Mormon original settler, and Horner had purchased a large part of the ex-mission lands together, with some titles remaining unsettled until 1866. *Improvement Era* 7 (July 1904): 669–71.
33. John Naile had been courting Frances Pratt before he left for the East. A contributing factor to Frances's illness could well have been the news of his marriage to childhood friend Mary Louisa Kepple while on his trip home to Indiana. Naile left his parents and bride in Salt Lake City before returning to California.
34. Andrew Jackson Davis is known as a main spokesman of early American spiritualism. It was probably *The Great Harmonia* (1850–1852) that Caroline was reading and in which he expounded upon "the everlasting and unchangeable teachings of Nature, Reason and Intuition."
35. A month and a day later, Hiram Clark, noted to be somewhat unbalanced since his mission, slit his throat in a field in San Bernardino and died in the presence of a horrified son.
36. Indeed, the mission was abandoned for lack of funds as well as because of oppressive Franco-American relations. Pratt and Grouard remained in San

Francisco some four months after placing Grouard's Polynesian wife and baby aboard a ship for Tahiti, leaving behind her other two sons. AP, 506; LBP, 212–15.

37.   John M. Horner and his brother William Yeats Horner had recently purchased from Jose de Jesus Noe, the Rancho San Miguel, paying $200,000 for 5,250 acres of land adjoining the city of San Francisco. A portion of this land, some six hundred acres, was subdivided and called Horner's Addition, just south and west of the mission San Francisco de Asis, better known as Mission Dolores. Among the streets he laid out and named, there still exists today Elizabeth Street, named after his wife. John Meirs Horner, *Personal History* (Honolulu, Hawaiian Gazette Co., 1898), 263.

Chapter 10

1.   Agnes Coolbrith Smith was formerly the wife of Don Carlos Smith, brother to the prophet Joseph Smith. Widowed in 1841, she married lawyer and printer William Pickett who removed her with her two young daughters from Nauvoo in 1846. Pickett brought his family, now increased by twin boys, to California in 1851, establishing a printing shop in San Francisco before moving south in 1855 to open a law practice in Los Angeles. Josephine DeWitt Rhodehamel and Raymund Francis Wood, *Ina Coolbrith, Librarian and Laureate of California* (Provo: Brigham Young University Press, 1973), 25–29.

2.   Between the post office at Kearny and Clay streets at Portsmouth Plaza, San Francisco's city center, a new omnibus line, the first regular transportation in the city, operated on a thirty-minute schedule, charging a fare of fifty cents on week days and one dollar on Sundays. Just as the plank toll road to Mission Dolores, when first completed, had proved a stimulus to real estate and building activities, so did the omnibus line. The pattern of growth in San Francisco, westward and southward and up the slopes of many hills, was to be shaped largely by transit lines, as John M. Horner no doubt anticipated with his tract of land adjoining the city limits of San Francisco and known as Ex Mission Dolores. Mel Scott, *The San Francisco Bay Area: A Metropolis in Perspective* (Berkeley: University of California Press, 1959), 35.

3.   In his *Circular to the Citizens of San Francisco and Vicinity*, dated 20 December 1853, one of the first inducements John M. Horner made to solicit purchasers of his lots at Ex Mission Dolores was to select a choice spot for a park and endeavor to beautify it at once with fencing and planting shrubbery. Copy in S. George Ellsworth Papers, Merrill Library, Special Collections, Logan: Utah State University.

4.   It was here at Mountain Lake, known by the Spaniards as Laguna de Loma Alta (Lake of the High Hill), where Juan Bautista de Anza camped in 1776. Situated at the edge of the Presidio, the spring-fed fresh-water lagoon was the site of the first water works company in San Francisco. Gladys Hansen, *San Francisco Almanac* (San Francisco: Chronicle Books, 1975), 128. Soule, *Annals of San Francisco*, 342, 448.

5.   Actually, Almon Babbitt was the Utah delegate to Congress.

6.   In her letter to her sister and nieces Caroline described her new accomodations: "There are ten large rooms, the house is 100 and 20 feet in length. We have 3 rooms on the ground and as much as we want in the

chamber, free of rent. I have two wooden rooms Frances, larger than that dining room where you left us, and one front addobie, larger than either." Caroline Barnes Crosby to Louisa Barnes Pratt, 26 March 1854. Caroline and Jonathan Crosby Papers, folder 10, Utah State Historical Society, Salt Lake City, Utah.

7. William McBride had recently returned from a mission to the Sandwich Islands with Nathan Tanner, George Q. Cannon, William Farrer, James Hawkins and Henry W. Bigler. During his second presidency in San Francisco, Parley P. Pratt was aided in his missionary work by McBride, who started a branch of the church in Santa Clara, south of San Francisco.

8. Well known in California as the ranking Latter-day Saint officer in the Mormon Battalion, Captain Jefferson Hunt had been a leading instigator in persuading Brigham Young to approve the San Bernardino colony venture. Hunt, subsequently elected one of the assemblymen from Los Angeles County, was instrumental in creating a separate San Bernardino County in 1853. He remained in the state assemby three more years.

9. Since attending a Mormon sermon in San Francisco two years previous, Eleanor McComb McLean had been seeking the consent of her husband, Hector H. McLean, to be baptized in the Latter-day Saint church. When Parley P. Pratt arrived in 1854, Mrs. McLean helped care for his ill wife Elizabeth, and at this time she became romantically involved with the church leader. Steven Pratt, "Eleanor McLean and the Murder of Parley P. Pratt." *BYU Studies* 15 (winter 1975): 225–56.

10. It is worth noting that it was Jonathan Crosby, and not Caroline, who answered the correspondence from Amelia Stevens, who doubtless lived with the couple as Jonathan's plural wife for a short time in Nauvoo.

11. Agnes (17) was the elder daughter of Don Carlos Smith, and Josephine Donna (13) the younger. It would be just seven years later that Josephine would turn her back on the past, adopt the pen name Ina Coolbrith and eventually become California's first poet laureate.

12. The Lake House was a well-known "out of town" resort. Starting near present-day Elizabeth Street, the excursion party most likely followed the Old San Jose Road (San Jose Avenue) to Ocean House Road (Ocean Avenue) to the north-east side of Lake Merced, where the Ocean House can be located on an 1861 map of San Francisco drawn by V. Wackenreuder, C. E., #FN–25307 of the map collection of the California Historical Society. Nearby, the "Lake House was prettily situated on the banks above a lagoon near the beach." Ray Siemeys, ed. "Vicissitudes of Dwellings and Localities," *San Francisco Historical Records Index* (1987) 25–26.

13. Yerba Buena Cemetery, situated out in the sand hills nearly midway between the town and Mission Dolores, occupied a triangular lot bounded by McAllister, Market and Larkin streets. Today this is the heart of San Francisco's Civic Center. From the beginning of 1850 to January 1854, 5,770 burials were recorded in the city, 4,450 of which were interred at Yerba Buena Cemetery. Soulé, *Annals of San Francisco*, 593–96.

14. Hiram Blackwell had traveled to southern California with Addison Pratt in 1849 and remained peripherally involved in the family's lives until his own ended at the Pratt home much later at Beaver, Utah. LBP, 307–8.

15. Joseph F. Smith was only five when his father, Hyrum, and his uncle, the prophet Joseph Smith, were shot and killed. He became the sixth president of the Church of Jesus Christ of Latter-day Saints nearly half a century

later. Richard O. Cowan and William E. Homer, *California Saints, A 150-Year Legacy In The Golden State* (Salt Lake City: Bookcraft, 1996), 192–93.

16. *Imlay* was Elizabeth Horner's maiden name.

17. The prediction proved tragically false. Parley P. Pratt married Mrs. McLean in plural marriage and within two years the husband would kill the popular apostle.

18. David Seely, president of the San Bernardino stake.

19. John Thomas Caine was called in April 1854, with a number of others, to take a mission to the Hawaiian Islands. The company traveled first to San Bernardino under the leadership of Parley P. Pratt and then by steamer from San Pedro to San Francisco, arriving on 10 July. Caroline had occasion to meet several of the missionaries during the fall, including elders Joseph F. Smith, Edward Partridge, William W. Cluff, Henry P. Richards, Orson K. Whitney, Sixtus E. Johnson, Joseph A. Peck, Washington Rogers and George Spiers.

20. In the fall of 1852, Benjamin F. Grouard had gone to Salt Lake City, where he was sealed in marriage to Louisa Maria Hardy by President Young. He brought his new wife to San Bernardino and, the following year, allowed his Polynesian wife to return to Tahiti.

21. This was the crisis time Horner later recalled: "Lock-Jaw came upon me with a heavy fever, which lasted a long time. My life was despaired of by my physicians and friends. . . . My recovery was slow and my sickness left me with but little use of my legs; for weeks, I used a crutch when moving around." *Improvement Era* 7 (September 1904): 849.

22. Parley P. Pratt returned to Upper California in July 1854 with instructions from Brigham Young to formally establish a colony in the Mission San Jose area, but only if John Horner would donate land for the purpose. The years 1851–53 had been positive ones for the Saints living in Centerville. Horner's redwood church-schoolhouse built here was almost certainly the first place of worship constructed for the Latter-day Saints in California. The biannual conferences alternated their meetings between San Francisco and Centerville. However, John Horner had put his money into so many ventures and so much property that he was unable to overcome the onslaught of the gold panic and economic depression that swept over the region after 1853. The death of his daughter and the failure of his land deals marked a turning point in the life of Horner and, by extension, not only thwarted Mormon colonization efforts in Upper California but also ended any hopes of a quick resolution to the mortgage on the church lands in San Bernardino, which he had pledged to help repay. Hansen and Bringhurst, *Let This Be Zion,* 70–73. Lyman, *San Bernardino,* 126.

23. William Jones was a skilled stone mason who brought his family overland to California. His wife Elizabeth, with their daughters Sarah and Anna, ran a modest rooming house and entertained church members and former friends from Nauvoo.

24. Icarians were followers of the Frenchman Etienne Cabet, who wrote several books including a novel of a utopian community, *A Voyage into Icaria.* Forced to leave France because of their communistic political beliefs, the colonists came to the United States and moved to Nauvoo in March 1849. Dissension among the followers led to the eventual disbandment of the commune in Nauvoo in 1860.

25. The Ambrose Moses family went to live at the Mission Dolores after their arrival on the *Brooklyn.* Their daughter, Ann Frances, married Eustaqueo

Valencia, heir to vast ranchlands south of San Francisco. When she died in 1859 she was the first non-Catholic to be buried in the mission cemetery. Carter, *Our Pioneer Heritage*, 3:563.

26.   This is the first instance of an underline drawn in a noticeably different-colored ink and a duplicated date entered above the line. The writing appears to be that of Caroline, but somewhat unsteady, indicating she probably reviewed her journal and marked the dates at a much later time. From this point forward, there are occasional similarly-marked entries. We have included the underlines and have denoted the text as [*added later*].

27.   Amelia Althea Stevens married Eugene F. Trouslot, a Frenchman ten years her senior, on 15 October 1854 in Nauvoo, Illinois. In 1860 she was living in De Kalb County, Illinois with her husband, a carpenter, and his two sons from a previous marriage. Their only child, a son Rollin, was born a year later. Illinois Marriage Index, 1851–1900. U. S. Census, 1860 and 1870, DeKalb Co., Illinois.

28.   Spanish *potrero,* "pasture." Two areas were set aside in the early 1830s for the common use of the inhabitants of Yerba Buena. The land Horner planned to develop, west of the *potrero nuevo*, was largely goat farms adjoining what is still known today as the "Potrero District."

29.   Caroline made note of her Sunday excursions to the fashionable districts south of Market Street. Rincon Point, today the western terminus of the Oakland-Bay Bridge, was home to numerous elegant structures—the predecessor to San Francisco's Nob Hill. On 14 January and 4 February 1855 she visited newly-developed South Park, with its two-story brick homes crowded around an oval garden copied after the elite areas of London and bounded today by Second, Third, Bryant and Brannan Streets. Albert Shumate, *Rincon Hill and South Park* (Sausalito, California: Windgate Press), 10.

30.   *Biographical Sketches of Joseph Smith, the Prophet and His Progenitors for Many Generations*, by Lucy Mack Smith, was published by S. W. Richards in Liverpool, England, 1853.

31.   This note gives us an idea of the journey Caroline herself was taking into the past as she recorded her memoirs. Begun in 1851 in Tubuai, our journalist had been alternately keeping a daily or weekly log as well as recalling her childhood and young adult years. Now, in May 1855, four years after beginning her "back journal," she has reached the time when she and Jonathan committed themselves to the church and moved to Kirtland, Ohio.

32.   Having brought his family from San Francisco to San Bernardino in March 1853, apostate Quartus Sparks would eventually be charged with multiple "affairs" in a divorce trial in which Caroline would attest to being acquainted while in San Francisco with a lady purported to be his mistress.

Chapter 11

1.   After serving four years as a missionary in the Sandwich Islands, George Q. Cannon came to California at Parley P. Pratt's request to publish the Book of Mormon in Hawaiian and to assist him in publishing his newpaper, the *Western Standard*. Elder Pratt set Cannon apart as his successor, to preside over the Pacific Mission, subject to the Twelve Apostles' directives. There were at the time three apostles residing in the area. Orson Hyde, president of the Quorum of Twelve, was to preside over a colony in Carson Valley (on the California-Nevada border); Amasa Lyman and Charles C. Rich were in

San Bernardino. Elder Cannon completed his Hawaiian translation of the Book of Mormon in January 1856. He and his wife, Elizabeth, proofread the entire text letter by letter, the type setters not knowing the language. Two thousand copies were then printed. See George Q. Cannon, *Writings From the WESTERN STANDARD Published in San Francisco, California* (Liverpool: George Q. Cannon, 1864), v–vii as cited in Cowan and Homer, *California Saints,* 196–97. See also Roger Robin Ekins, ed. *Defending Zion: George Q. Cannon and the California Mormon Newspaper Wars of 1856–1857,* Kingdom in the West, the Mormons and the American Frontier, vol. 5 (Spokane: The Arthur H. Clark Co., 2002).

2.   Joseph L. Heywood had provided food for the Crosbys when help was most needed in Nauvoo. Here was an opportunity for them to reciprocate.

3.   Abraham Coombs brought his wife Olive and three children (one, a daughter from a previous marriage) on the *Brooklyn,* settling for a while in the Napa valley north of San Francisco. This was the first of numerous encounters Caroline would later have with the Coombs children during their stay in San Bernardino and later in Utah.

4.   Among the men from San Bernardino who accompanied Amasa Lyman and David Seely on their quest through Upper California to procure funds to pay the debt on the Rancho were Thomas Holliday, Henry Boyle, Peter Nielson, and William Warren.

5.   Benjamin F. Grouard had been disfellowshipped that year for defying church authority by independently seeking political office in San Bernardino County. He was already deep into spiritualist activity, and thus this former great Mormon missionary was permanently lost from the church.

6.   William Tait, born in Ireland, became a Mormon convert in 1841. He joined the Queen's service in India, where he married college graduate Elizabeth Xavier, a native of Bombay and daughter of a high-ranking, wealthy family. William sailed for America in 1855 and brought their young son John with him to the west coast. His trust in Caroline was well placed. She would have the boy even longer later at San Bernardino, when he would leave him to board for an extended time while traveling to Salt Lake City to await his wife's arrival by handcart over the plains from Iowa, after crossing the ocean from England. Carter, *Our Pioneer Heritage,* 1:318–20.

7.   A former Methodist minister and early Mormon missionary to England, Theodore Turley was a member of the Council of Fifty at Nauvoo, and would be equally prominent at San Bernardino.

8.   Like the *Deseret News,* which began publication as a weekly newspaper in Salt Lake City in 1850, *The Mormon* was published weekly from February 1855 to September 1857.

9.   Many of the streets south of Market are named after builders of the first homes in that area, including Samuel Brannan. A large landowner in Happy Valley, at the foot of Rincon Hill, he built his home just off Mission Street on 2nd Street, between Minna and Natoma. Shumate, *Rincon Hill and South Park,* 20, 110.

10. President of the mission to the Hawaiian Islands, Phillip B. Lewis returned to California too late to rejoin his wife, Jane, who died of tuberculosis two months prior in the mountains above San Bernardino.

11. John's mother, Lucy Eagar, had been excommunicated from the church by Sam Brannan while on the *Brooklyn.* John was the only member of his

family to emigrate to Utah. For a time he boarded in Salt Lake City with the Crosbys. CBC, 25 October 1848.

12. William Smith's career as a Mormon leader at Nauvoo was erratic at best. In 1842, when the local high council investigated a prominent contemporary figure, John C. Bennett, for seductions during the previous year, two women identified William as among the friends of the accused who also made visits for immoral purposes. Later, after Joseph and Hyrum's deaths, William practiced and performed plural marriages in the East in a manner considered unwise by Brigham Young and his associates. D. Michael Quinn, *The Mormon Hierarchy: Origins of Power* (Salt Lake City: Signature Books, 1994), 214, 220.

Chapter 12

1. There was no federal law against polygamy until 1862—some time after this conversation. Some states may have had such statutes, but not in the West. In California most political leaders desired Latter-day Saint support and there had never been any open controversy on the subject in the state. In fact, it was fairly common knowledge that the Mormon assemblyman, Jefferson Hunt, had more than one wife.
2. Two of many off-shoot groups from the original Church of Jesus Christ of Latter-day Saints arising from the confusion following the assassination of Joseph Smith.
3. Charles Hill, James Kipp and Ed Dennis were Anglo-American men who, like Benjamin F. Grouard, were married to Polynesian women. They became alienated from the Mormon community and formed their own spiritualist settlement several miles west of town. Lyman, *San Bernardino*, 297–99.
4. William Crosby was a Mormon convert from Mississippi, no relation to Jonathan.
5. William J. Cox was president of the San Bernardino stake since the previous June. Though not dynamic, he was efficient and supportive of a wife who was chronically ill and would become Caroline's neighbor at Beaver, Utah.
6. Bishop William Crosby's residence was an exception to the modest-sized houses in San Bernardino. His was large enough to serve as a hotel as well as a boarding house for at least a half-dozen former slaves still working for his family. These African-Americans simply chose to remain with their former owners for this period. Almost all would move to Los Angeles within the next year. Lyman, *San Bernardino*, 131–32.
7. Among the dozen or so men in San Bernardino openly involved in polygamous relationships at this time were Charles Rich with three wives in California, and Amasa Lyman with four. General acceptance of plural households by Caroline and others contrasted with that of some of the women in branches in the San Francisco Bay area, who opposed vocally the church doctrine of "celestial marriage" or polygamy. The practice had not been publicly announced until 1852.
8. The other popular boarding house-hotel in the community was that of Edward and Nancy Daley, daughter of Jefferson Hunt.
9. Mr. Grinelle, a non-Mormon from Northern California, left a five-year-old daughter, whom he had taken from his estranged wife, in the care of Louisa Pratt. The notably sweet little girl was exposed to whooping cough through

a neighbor child and slowly grew weaker and died at the Pratt home. Louisa's account of her death is most touching. See LBP, 220.

10. Orrin Smith and his wife Mary Ann were accompanied by their children, including Eliza and Amelia, on the ship *Brooklyn* and resided briefly in San Bernardino on their way from Northern California to Utah.

11. The original San Bernardino cemetery was in a swampy area just south of the present Pioneer Cemetery. Caroline's cousin, Jane Stevens Lewis, recently deceased from tuberculosis, was buried there next to her young son. Her husband, Phillip, ordered a stone marker for the gravesite prior to leaving San Bernardino. It was placed there 17 February by Elvira Stevens's husband, J. S. Woodbury, Alma and Jonathan Crosby. For further study of possible remains of other Mormon settlers, see Philip L. Walker and Patricia M. Lambert, *Human Skeletal Remains from the Historic Cemetery and Seccombe Park, San Bernardino, California* (Department of Anthropology, University of California, Santa Barbara, 1991).

12. The *Western Standard* was the only west coast Mormon publication. Jonathan had sold subscriptions to the weekly newspaper before coming to Southern California.

13. In April 1854, Amasa Lyman and others brought part of the Lytle Creek stream flow into San Bernardino from the west. William J. Cox was appointed watermaster to not only oversee water delivery, but to assure that the property owners dug the essential collateral ditches to irrigate their lots. Alma Crosby was engaged in this labor. Later trees would typically be planted along these to assure shade in the community. Amasa M. Lyman Journal (LDS Church Archives, Salt Lake City, Utah), 10–30 April 1854. The only purported physical remnant left of Mormon San Bernardino is a small portion of a hand-laid irrigation ditch in the north end of the city. Arda Haenszel, "Mormons in San Bernardino," *San Bernardino County Museum Association* (Summer 1992): 21.

14. Frances Clark, former wife of church leader Heber C. Kimball, was suffering greatly from the death of her children and both Caroline and Louisa Pratt, still grieving Emma Grinelle, were sympathetic to her pain. LBP, 221.

15. Caroline's typical circumspection in referring to pregnancy and childbirth.

16. Jonathan Crosby, an increasingly accomplished woodworker and finish carpenter, was employed part of each of his two years in San Bernardino at the first sawmill in lower Waterman Canyon, owned by Charles Crismon. The millworks obviously included some planing and other finishing machinery.

17. The interest in New York-born spiritualism had become widespread throughout California. In San Bernardino mayor Amasa Lyman was in part initiated into such practices by Jonathan Crosby's former business partner Calvin Reed. There were at least a dozen other San Bernardino Mormons who were then dabbling in spiritualist activities, including Benjamin F. Grouard and his Polynesian associates. For an explanation of the appeal spiritualism held for many Mormons—namely direct communication with the unseen world—see Davis Bitton, "Mormonism's Encounter with Spiritualism," *Journal of Mormon History* (spring 1974); revised and republished in *Ritualization of Mormon History and Other Essays* (Urbana: University of Illinois Press, 1994), 83–97.

18. Jones and Eben Dyer's place, west of San Bernardino toward the main channel of Lytle Creek, was situated near the home of Thomas Tompkins and family, who had arrived from Mission San Jose in December 1852.

19. The main meeting place for worship services was the "council house" which was thirty feet wide and sixty feet long. However, the building was hardly suited for a congregation of potentially 2,000 souls. The men usually sat outside and tried to listen to the words of the speakers through the doors. The women and children inside, as Caroline, were often uncomfortable. Later Amasa Lyman chided the local saints for not building a more adequate facility.

20. "Bishop" Albert W. Collins was actually a counselor to Bishop William Crosby. However, as the ward entailed all of the city of San Bernardino, it became too large for one man to handle all of the tithing paid in farm produce, lumber and labor. Collins had responsibility for the segment of the ward where the Crosbys resided.

21. San Bernardino became during this period a major stopping place for Latter-day Saint converts from Australia, who arrived by ship at San Francisco, then made their way to the Mormon colony, which was intended from the beginning to be part of a chain of settlements from Salt Lake City to the Pacific coast for the gathering of the Saints from abroad. Newton, *Southern Cross Saints*, 153.

22. The apochrypha are books of the Old Testament not found in Hebrew and thus not accepted by Jewish nor most Protestant scholars. Eleven such books are contained in some Roman Catholic versions of the Bible.

23. Philemon was a former slave to Daniel Thomas, Mormon merchant and justice of the peace. He was a good musician, who often assisted Louisa Pratt with household tasks in exchange for a taste of liquor. He later recounted to Caroline his earlier life and experiences in slavery. See CBC, 11 August 1856.

24. Judge Alden A. M. Jackson, an officer in the war with Mexico, converted to Mormonism and married Carolyn Joyce, an accomplished vocal and instrumental musician. Their home adjacent to Lytle Creek became the principal plant nursery as well as a gathering center for social and musical functions.

25. Addison Pratt was to travel to the South Pacific with the Laytons, who were returning to the Sandwich Islands, and with Sister Thomas Whitaker, a Tahitian woman, who would never see her husband again. Caroline's reluctance to take part in the toast typified some confusion regarding the church teachings concerning liquor during this period. The Word of Wisdom, a revelation given to Joseph Smith in 1833, proscribed abstinence from strong drink. Tea and coffee were also implied, but Caroline had no such reservations about their use. The Word of Wisdom became much more a test of faithfulness toward the end of the 19th century.

26. The family register shows Willard Barnes, born 16 April 1766, died 31 December 1849, aged 83. Church burial records in Dunham list the following: "Willard Barnes, born the fifteenth day of April One thousand Seven hundred & Sixty Six, died on the thirtieth day of December one thousand eight hundred & forty eight, in the eighty third year of his age." All Saints Anglican Church in Dunham, register for the year 1849, folio 1, Quebec National Archives microfilm #124.2. Caroline's mother's burial record shows Dolly Stevens Barnes's death on 27 January 1852 (see chapter 9, n. 15).

27. Eliza Roxcy Snow was the most honored Mormon woman of her era, partly for the poetry she wrote, sometimes set to music in significant church hymns. Caroline probably knew her fairly well earlier in Kirtland and Nauvoo.

28.   These items of clothing may well have been worn at the weekly prayer meetings the Crosby couple attended fairly regularly, which would have replicated some aspects of Latter-day Saint temple worship they experienced briefly at Nauvoo.

29.   Returning missionaries John S. Eldredge and James Graham were among the 28 Saints aboard the *Julia Ann* when the Australian vessel bound for California struck a coral reef two hundred miles west of Tahiti on the night of October 3, 1855. With heroic courage, one of the crew fastened a rope to the coral, and one by one women and children were ferried to calmer water inside the reef while the ship broke apart. Only two women and three children drowned. With daylight, the survivors were able to move to a small island a few miles distant with the use of the one remaining damaged but serviceable boat. The company survived for two months on brackish water filtered through the sand, on turtles and wild fowl, fish and coconuts. It was six weeks before the small boat was sufficiently repaired so that the captain and crew could row some two hundred miles east to Huahine, and eight weeks before the company was taken off in a whaling schooner sent to their rescue. Newton, *Southern Cross Saints*, 145–47.

30.   The term "ward" never referred to an ecclesiastical subdivision in San Bernardino, which was all one unwieldy congregation. It was used to designate irrigation districts or blocks taking turns utilizing the water needed for yards and gardens. It also connoted districts of families to which block teachers such as Jonathan Crosby were assigned to visit with regularity.

31.   There were at least six different Jewish mercantile establishments in San Bernardino at this time, including Glaser's and Jackson's and Ephraim's, all of which Caroline patronized.

32.   At the time of her marriage, Ellen Pratt McGary began a correspondence with her intimate friend Ellen Spencer Clawson. The surviving letters of the next two years, published by S. George Ellsworth in *Dear Ellen, Two Mormon Women and Their Letters*, are remarkable for their insight into the hearts and minds of the young married women and the dilemmas they faced in a polygamous society.

33.   An unquestionably scandalous divorce trial between attorney Quartus Sparks and his estranged wife, Mary Hamilton, was precipitated when, after she sued for divorce, alleging the former church orator and county official had kept a mistress for almost a year, he counter-sued, charging she had been "too free in the company with one Dr. Beems [Ira Burrus?]." The trial was said to have featured such explicit language that women hesitated to attend, while male jurors found the proceedings "considerable sport." Although Sparks mounted an elaborate defense, he was found guilty and failed to prove a case against his wife. The trial involved a fight over property, including a newly-completed home in the city. Judge Benjamin Hayes ruled against Sparks and ordered his mistress arrested for keeping items belonging to the wife. San Bernardino County District Court Case No. 4.5, *Sparks vs. Sparks*, 1856.

34.   Jonathan was only employed at Crismon's mill during the seasons of sufficient stream-flow to propel the machinery, although for a time a steam engine was utilized. Ebenezer Hanks was a part-owner of the San Bernardino gristmill, which had a more consistent millrace tapping Warm Creek spring water.

35.   The Grouard children, Sophronia and Benjamin, stayed with their father after his Polynesian wife returned to Tahiti in 1853. Ephraim was adopted

by Louisa Pratt. Sophronia was left with Ellen when Benjamin F. Grouard and his new wife Louisa moved from San Bernardino a few months later. LBP, 393.

36. The relationship between these two remained close throughout their lives. Elvira Stevens had been an intimate companion to her sister Jane and her brother-in-law Philip B. Lewis since the three left Winter Quarters together and crossed the plains to the Great Salt Lake Valley in 1848. She traveled with them to California in 1851, and spent 11 months in the Sandwich Islands during his mission there. Philip, already twice a widower, remarried in the winter of 1858 and moved to St. George and then to Kanab, Utah. Barney, *The Stevens Genealogy*, 238–39, 261–66. See also CBC, 2 April 1856 for Elvira Stevens's probable disclosure of a marital offense which led to her divorcing John S. Woodbury.

37. The initial prosperity of the California gold rush led by 1854 to a very serious regional economic depression in which a high percentage of formerly flourishing businesses did not survive. John Horner's complex combination of good intentions, generosity and perhaps a measure of irresponsibility cost him most of his former fortune as well. This certainly hurt the Crosbys who had worked for him and were not paid nearly all of their due.

38. Caroline Joyce Jackson, known as "the Mormon nightingale," purchased the first melodeon brought to San Francisco, much to the disappointment of competing ministers' wives. This small keyboard organ drew air past metal reeds through pedal-operated bellows. In San Bernardino the center of music-making, both choir practice and special parties, was the beautifully furnished Jackson parlor where a "singing school" was held in the evenings. Carter, *Heart Throbs of the West* (Salt Lake City: Daughters of Utah Pioneers), 8:395–98. Lyman, *San Bernardino*, 276–77.

39. While the May Day and Fourth of July celebrations had involved the entire community, these festivities were for the benefit of two specific groups—the San Bernardino Rangers, a semi-official posse unit whose leaders were almost all former Mormon Battalion members, and Latter-day Saint pioneers celebrating the anniversary of their arrival in Salt Lake Valley in 1847.

40. Caroline was mistaken here. Only one of Rollins' wives was Mother Walker's daughter, although she had another in town, Dionetia Lyman.

41. Ed Dennis had been a metal dealer earlier in the Sandwich Islands. Married to Hakuole, a Hawaiian woman, he may have had insights into Addison Pratt's dissatisfaction and eventual dissociation from the church, since he was the recent recipient of the former missionary's letter, the probable reason for Caroline's visit to the Dennis's. For an account of Hakuole's discontent with the "dreariness" of the land and climate compared to her former home, and her candid impressions of the California Mormon community, see Jules Remy and Julius Benchly, *A Journey to Great Salt Lake City* (London: W. Jeffs, 1861), 459–60.

42. Caroline's church attendance during the hot summer months was not at all regular. This was probably due in part to the discomfort of the meeting place, although her favorite preacher, Amasa Lyman, was absent in Utah the first nine months of the year. See CBC, 5 October 1856.

43. Erysipelas, an acute febrile disease associated with intense edema and inflammation of the skin.

44. Caroline was simply being informed that as the "Mormon Reformation," which commenced in mid-1856, reached San Bernardino, Jonathan was

being offered another opportunity to demonstrate his spiritual priorities over worldy ones—which the Crosbys had consistently done.

45. For the Latter-day Saints' commitment to education in San Bernardino, including the establishment of a circulating library years before Los Angeles or San Diego, see Lyman, *San Bernardino,* 272–73.

46. These people were doubtless curious about his darker complexion, his mother having been born in India.

47. Actually, Louisa Pratt did not learn directly of her daughter's wedding until she received a letter from Frances in mid-November, "containing intelligence of her marriage" and creating "surprise and excitement." LBP, 237.

48. Kanaka, a common term for Hawaiians, as were Sisters Kipp, Hill and Dennis.

49. Jonathan Crosby purchased two one-acre city lots "together with the tenements and appurtenances thereon" from Amasa Lyman, Charles C. Rich, and Ebenezer Hanks for $250.00. A copy of the original deed, dated 26 November 1856, was re-recorded on 24 January 1888, identifying the lots of land "known on the official map of said City as lots number (3) three and (4) four in Block 12 twelve." This places their lots on the east side of present-day F Street between 2nd and 3rd Streets. San Bernardino County Archives, Deeds, Book 65, 590–91.

50. It was a tradition at San Bernardino on election day for politicians to engage Hispanic serenaders, most likely from the Santa Ana riverbed community of Agua Mansa, to add a holiday atmosphere to the occasion.

51. Reminiscent of the Nauvoo Relief Society, Caroline and other sisters with older children, along with some of the yet unmarried younger women, participated in an unofficial network of caring for the ill. This explains Sister Crosby's feeling of chagrin at not hearing of a case with which she should have been involved.

52. The incomplete house had no roof nor eaves, so that the adobe bricks would wash away quite rapidly. The boards were probably placed on the windward side, which was receiving altogether too much moisture to remain a stable wall.

53. Here began what would be a lengthy and disappointing relationship between Caroline and Helen Coombs, 14-year-old daughter of Abraham Coombs and his wife Olive Curtis, passengers on the *Brooklyn.* Caroline encountered Olive in San Francisco when she was attempting to bring her family from Napa to San Bernardino, and would be briefly associated with her again at Beaver, Utah.

54. Amasa Lyman was clearly stressing the dedication and discipline expected during the "Mormon Reformation." It may well be that he was denouncing a certain kind of dancing rather than an absolute prohibition on that activity as the Christmas holidays approached. It is almost inconceivable that either stake president William J. Cox or Caroline Crosby would have acted in any manner defiant to the highest church authority in the community. See CBC, 10 December 1856.

55. A kind of cloth made from mulberry bark, of Polynesian origin. Many houses had a fabric hung as part of the ceiling.

56. The "Mormon Reformation" featured careful scrutiny of the faithfulness of church members, which was partly demonstrated by their willingness to answer prying questions about behavior and belief and through being

"rebaptised." This movement had reached San Bernardino late in the year, with Jonathan and Alma submitting to the cold ordeal of complete immersion in water five days before Caroline finally complied with the requirement.

Chapter 13

1. This was a most significant personal account of sensations during the last major slippage along the infamous San Andreas faultline. See Ward M. McAfee, "A Social History of the Great Quake of 1857," *Southern California Quarterly* 74 (summer 1992): 125–40.
2. Elizabeth Tait's perseverence in joining her husband was beset by hardship and tragedy. In India their younger son had died of cholera, and in immigrating to the United States, she joined the ill-fated Willie's handcart company of late 1856, at about the time their infant daughter also died. After a brief reunion in Salt Lake City, the Taits moved to Cedar City, where Caroline later became acquainted with Elizabeth and admired her greatly. Carter, *Our Pioneer Heritage*, 1:318–20.
3. Plunge Creek is in the previously uncultivated northeast section of the San Bernardino Valley. The creek is between City Creek and the Santa Ana River, all flowing south from the San Bernardino Mountains.
4. John Tobin, son-in-law to Charles C. Rich and soldier in the U. S. Army, was one of three men attacked while camping along the Santa Clara River in southern Utah as they traveled toward California. Many believed the attack was by Mormons enforcing prohibitions on church members leaving the area without permission. See *Los Angeles Star,* 7 March 1857.
5. Eleanor Morse, plural wife of Justus Morse, was one of several unhappily married sisters Caroline attempted to comfort. Her husband gave her some assistance for returning to Utah.
6. Lyman and Rich were leaving San Bernardino to fulfill church missions in Great Britain. Their abrupt departure from the colony came as a shock to many. Some anti-Mormons threatened to detain them for whatever purposes, but failed partly because of this show of strength. George William and Helen Pruitt Beattie, *Heritage of the Valley: San Bernardino's First Century* (Pasadena: San Pasqual Press, 1939), 269–70.
7. Addison Pratt probably never accepted plural marriage nor several other Mormon doctrines, and probably never fully recovered from the outrageous neglect he and his companions suffered while on their amazingly successful missions in Tahiti. He was an especially honest and complex individual. As co-editor George Ellsworth has well argued, God alone can properly judge a man who had done so much as one of the first and most successful foreign missionaries in the history of the Church of Jesus Christ of Latter-day Saints.
8. Typically, the Mormon irrigation arrangement allowed each lot so much time per water turn. One could borrow such turns with special permission.
9. This year's May Day celebration was not as methodically organized as the one in 1856, but was also very festive. Some 200 citizens participated in the picnic at the mouth of City Creek Canyon before returning to town to enjoy an all-night ball at Ed Daley's Star Hotel. Lyman, *San Bernardino*, 261–62.
10. Here is one of the rare instances of complaint by this notably uncomplaining lady.

11.   There was some difference of opinion between Brigham Young and those trying to fulfill all ranch payment obligations. In fact, correspondence from Brigham Young to President William J. Cox dated 4 June 1857 offered ambiguous advice to build up San Bernardino "not as a permanent abode." Lyman, *San Bernardino*, 382.

12.   The former Sister Repsher had been sealed in the Nauvoo temple to a respected Latter-day Saint. She probably left him for her current husband. Church leaders, including Orson Pratt, editor of *The Seer*, would not be encouraging about the future status of such a woman in the hereafter.

13.   As shown by Caroline's cross-out, she may have had some question of who was sharing the brandy with Olive Coombs. Emily was just eight years old, having been born 27 August 1849.

14.   This was the end of a rather unsuccessful attempt to better the lot of a mismatched couple and their children, although Caroline would again become involved in the tragic circumstances of the family in Utah.

15.   Friends of the Pratts and the Crosbys since Nauvoo, Agnes Coolbrith Smith, now married to attorney William Pickett, would, at his insistence, raise her family apart from the Church of Jesus Christ of Latter-day Saints. This was to be about the last positive contact the family had with the church. Rhodehamel and Wood, *Ina Coolbrith*, 27.

16.   This was the culmination of a great deal of bitterness between Latter-day Saints and apostate Mormons. Perkins was known to be intoxicated and had let it be known he was going to beat up the Independent Party extremist McDonald, who was preparing to take his business out of town. McDonald actually was defending himself and eventually was acquitted of all charges in the local court. Beattie, *Heritage of the Valley*, 272–74.

17.   Discipline—or the lack thereof—of the Tahitian boy was one of several sources of conflict between the Pratts. Ephraim Pratt's future as a famous Indian scout was partly the result of the natural independence of spirit motivating him to run away. At 15, he left for Montana as a teamster and disappeared. Not until 1876 would Louisa eventually hear what had become of her "lost boy." LBP, 364–65. He changed his name to Frank Grouard, and soon was employed by the government as guide and scout under General Crook in his campaign against the Sioux. First published in 1894, his exploits as he related to the author are fully treated by Joe DeBarthe, *The Life and Adventures of Frank Grouard* (rev. ed., Norman: University of Oklahoma Press, 1958).

18.   Parley P. Pratt had welcomed the Crosbys to room with him in early Kirtland. They had renewed their acquaintance with him while living in San Francisco, where Caroline had socialized with both his wife Elizabeth and with the murderer's ex-wife, Eleanor McLean, who had recently become Pratt's new plural wife. Will Bagley, *Blood of the Prophets: Brigham Young and the Mountain Meadows Massacre* (Norman: University of Oklahoma Press, 2002), 68–72. See also Pratt, "Eleanor McLean," 225–56.

19.   Jonathan apparently installed a detached shower-bathroom referred to by Caroline as a "pattentright bathing establishment." The room became a showplace of the new Crosby home, much admired by all who saw it. Caroline would never have mentioned the separate "privy," which would have been kept well away from the house.

20.   George Day's farm west of San Bernardino was among the swamplands of Lytle Creek, which enabled him to divert a small stream right through his

dairy house, keeping the building relatively cool through the hot summer months. Lyman, *San Bernardino*, 231.

21.   Former neighbors of the Crosbys at Mission San Jose, Isaac Goodwin, who lost his first wife Laura aboard the *Brooklyn*, moved his six children and his second wife Mary down to San Bernardino with the Tompkins and others in 1852. He was among the first alfalfa growers in the San Bernardino valley, and one of the first to grow alfalfa hay in Utah. Carter, *Our Pioneer Heritage*, 3:543–45.

22.   Generous offerings of fresh fruit was standard procedure in Mormon San Bernardino. Melons, peaches and grapes were community property to be enjoyed in numerous "feasts" by all who wished to partake—and some partook of the fruited wines as well.

23.   This is a less-than-accurate first mention of the infamous Mountain Meadows Massacre which had much to do with the demise of Mormon San Bernardino. Until that point Latter-day Saints were relatively well accepted by most Californians. However, a vast increase in bitterness toward all Mormondom characterized the state citizenry thereafter. Lyman, *San Bernardino*, 361–69.

24.   The escalating conflict with the U. S. government at Salt Lake City would continue as the so-called Utah War. President James Buchanan appointed a new governor to Utah to challenge the firm control the church leaders held over the territorial government. At this time, a 2,500-man military expedition escorting the new governor, Alfred Cumming, was enroute to Utah. The Mormons proved determined to resist by force if necessary.

25.   William Matthews and Sidney Tanner were San Bernardino citizens who happened to be the mail carriers from Utah that month. William Hyde was a recently-returned missionary from Australia. The three passed directly through the massacre site. Juanita Brooks, *The Mountain Meadows Massacre* (rev. ed., Norman: University of Oklahoma Press, 1991), 85.

26.   The Latter-day Saints in Northern California received definite word they should return to Utah before Southern California church members accepted similar instruction.

27.   A total of 449 Latter-day Saint converts left the Australian colonies between 1853 and 1859. Absalom P. Dowdle, president of the Australian Mission in 1856–57, brought this final sizeable company of immigrants from Australia to the San Bernardino valley prior to most traveling to Utah. Newton, *Southern Cross Saints*, 33.

28.   By this time it was common knowledge that President Buchanan had sent troops toward Utah. Brigham Young and the Mormon militia impressively delayed the progress of the troops, but probably could not have long hindered their entrance into Salt Lake City. Negotiations eventually allowed them in but only to camp some distance from the church population.

29.   Co-editor Edward Leo Lyman has made a good case that Brigham Young disliked the San Bernardino colony from the beginning and, when he had the opportunity, ordered it disbanded. That occasion was the supposed need for all faithful church members to return to Utah to assist in the crisis against the invading army. See Lyman, *San Bernardino*, 392–95.

30.   Potter claimed to be the Savior or his direct messenger. All indications were that he was unbalanced, and he was not in the vicinity for long.

31.   The Crosbys apparently traded their new house for two yoke of oxen, a good wagon and perhaps a few provisions. This was the fifth or sixth time they

546   Notes, Pages 499–505

had sacrificed the comforts of an established home for their perceived obligations to their religion. Perhaps the most impressive aspect of the entire diary of Caroline Barnes Crosby has been the absence of any complaint about these sacrifices. However, she would express doubts in her journal once enroute to Utah.

32.   In 1864, 80-year-old Andrew V. Patten paid taxes on the assessed value of lots 3 and 4 in Block 12, the two acres valued at $100 and improvements thereon of $200. Four years later, he sold the property for $450.00. San Bernardino County Archives, Assessment Roll 1864 A (Book 7), 298. Book of Deeds H, 187.

33.   In fact, 3,000 head of livestock perished and another 1,100 were either stolen or ran off. Donald R. Moorman, *Camp Floyd and the Mormons: The Utah War* (Salt Lake City: University of Utah Press, 1992), 26–30.

34.   Caroline's thorough preparation for this trip actually caused them some difficulty enroute. Their wagon was too heavily laden, forcing delays and dependence on others to get over the mountain pass. Their late departure left them stranded in Las Vegas, (then New Mexico Territory), without an oxen team and surrounded by thieving Indians.

35.   Sister Patten apparently followed that course, most likely leaving with the family willing to take her in exchange for her midwife services (CBC, 12 December 1857). Caroline met her there when she herself finally arrived in Utah.

BIBLIOGRAPHY

Allen, James B., and Glen M. Leonard. *The Story of the Latter-day Saints*. Salt Lake City: Deseret Book Company, 1976.

Arrington, Leonard J. and Davis Bitton. *The Mormon Experience, A History of the Latter-day Saints*. New York: Alfred A. Knopf, 1979.

Bagley, Will. *Blood of the Prophets: Brigham Young and the Mountain Meadows Massacre*. Norman: University of Oklahoma Press, 2002.

————, ed. *A Road from El Dorado, the 1848 Trail Journal of Ephraim Green*. Salt Lake City: Prairie Dog Press, 1991.

————, ed. *The Pioneer Camp of the Saints: The 1846 and 1847 Mormon Trail Journals of Thomas Bullock*. Kingdom in the West, The Mormons and the American Frontier, vol. 1. Spokane: The Arthur H. Clark Co., 1997.

————, ed. *Scoundrel's Tale, The Samuel Brannan Papers*. Kingdom in the West, The Mormons and the American Frontier, vol. 3. Spokane: The Arthur H. Clark Co., 1999.

Bancroft, Hubert Howe. "California Pioneer Register and Index, 1542–1848," extracted from *The History of California*. 7 vols. 1886. Baltimore: Regional Publishing Co., 1964.

Barney, Elvira Stevens. *The Stevens Genealogy: Embracing Branches of the Family Descended from Puritan Ancestry, New England Families Not Traceable to Puritan Ancestry and Miscellaneous Branches Wherever Found*. Salt Lake City: Skelton Publishing Co., 1907.

Baugh, Alexander L. "A Call to Arms: The 1838 Mormon Defense of Northern Missouri." Ph.D. diss., Brigham Young University, Provo, Utah, 1996. Reprint, 2000.

Beattie, George William and Helen Pruitt Beattie. *Heritage of the Valley: San Bernardino's First Century*. Pasadena: San Pasqual Press, 1939.

Bigler, David L. and Will Bagley, eds. *Army of Israel: Mormon Battalion Narratives*. Logan: Utah State University Press, 2000.

Bitton, Davis. *Guide to Mormon Diaries and Autobiographies*. Provo: Brigham Young University Press, 1977.

————. "Kirtland as a Center of Missionary Activity, 1830–1838." *BYU Studies* 11 (fall 1971).

————. "Mormonism's Encounter with Spiritualism," *Journal of Mormon History* (spring 1974); revised and republished in *Ritualization of Mormon History and Other Essays*. Urbana: University of Illinois Press, 1994.

Bradley, Martha S. and Mary Brown F. Woodward. "Plurality, Patriarchy, and the Priestess: Zina D. H. Young's Nauvoo Marriages." *Journal of Mormon History* (spring 1994).

Brooks, Juanita. *The Mountain Meadows Massacre.* Rev. ed., Norman: University of Oklahoma Press, 1991.

Brown, John H. *Reminiscences and Incidents of Early Days of San Francisco.* 1886. Reprint, Oakland: Biobooks, 1949.

Brown, John, Jr. and James Boyd. *History of San Bernardino and Riverside Counties,* Vol. 1. Chicago: Lewis Publishing Co., 1922.

Carter, Kate B., ed. *Heart Throbs of the West.* 12 vols. Salt Lake City: Daughters of Utah Pioneers, 1947.

————, ed. *Our Pioneer Heritage.* 20 vols. Salt Lake City: Daughters of Utah Pioneers, 1958–77.

Clayton, William. *The Latter-day Saints Emigrants' Guide.* St. Louis: Republican Steam Power Press, Chambers & Knapp, 1848.

Cole, William A. and Elwin W. Jensen. *Israel in the Pacific.* Salt Lake City: Polynesian Department of the Genealogical Society of the Church of Jesus Christ of Latter-day Saints, 1961.

Country Club of Washington Township Research Committee. *History of Washington Township.* 1904. 2d ed., Stanford: Stanford University Press, 1950.

Cowan, Richard O. and Homer, William E. *California Saints, A 150-Year Legacy in the Golden State.* Salt Lake City: Bookcraft, 1996.

Crosby, Jonathan. *A Biographical Sketch of the Life of Jonathan Crosby Written by Himself.* Holograph. Jonathan Crosby Papers, Utah State Historical Society. Typescript, bound in with journal-memoir of his wife, Caroline Barnes Crosby, in possession of editors.

Davies, J. Kenneth. *Mormon Gold, The Story of California's Mormon Argonauts.* Salt Lake City: Olympus Publishing Company, 1984.

Davies, John. *A Tahitian and English Dictionary with Introductory Remarks on the Polynesian Language, and a Short Grammar of the Tahitian Dialect.* Tahiti: London Missionary Society's Press, 1851. Reprint, New York: AMS Press, 1978.

DeBarthe, Joe. *The Life and Adventures of Frank Grouard.* Rev. ed. Norman: University of Oklahoma Press, 1958.

Downey, Joseph T. *Filings From an Old Saw, Reminiscences of San Francisco and California's Conquest.* Edited by Fred Blackburn Rogers. San Francisco: John Howell, publisher, 1956.

Ekins, Roger Robin, ed. *Defending Zion: Cannon and the Newspaper Wars.* Kingdom in the West, The Mormons and the American Frontier, vol. 5. Spokane: The Arthur H. Clark Co., 2002.

Ellsworth, Maria S. "The First Mormon Missionary Women in the Pacific, 1850–1852." In *Voyages of Faith, Explorations in Mormon Pacific History,* edited by Grant Underwood. Provo: Brigham Young University Press, 2000.

Ellsworth, S. George. "A History of Mormon Missions in the United States and Canada, 1830–1860." Ph.D. diss., University of California, Berkeley, 1951.

————. "Zion in Paradise: Early Mormons in the South Seas." Twenty-First Faculty Honor Lecture, Utah State University, 1959.

————, ed. *The Journals of Addison Pratt: Being a Narrative of Yankee Whaling in the Eighteen Twenties, A Mormon Mission to the Society Islands, and of Early California and Utah in the Eighteen Forties and Fifties.* Salt Lake City: University of Utah Press, 1990.

————, ed. *The History of Louisa Barnes Pratt, Being the Autobiography of A Mormon Missionary Widow and Pioneer.* Logan: Utah State University Press, 1998.

————, ed. *Dear Ellen: Two Mormon Women and Their Letters.* Salt Lake City: University of Utah Library, 1974.

Ellsworth, S. George and Kathleen C. Perrin. *Seasons of Faith and Courage, The Church of Jesus Christ of Latter-day Saints in French Polynesia. A Sesquicentennial History, 1843–1993.* Sandy, Utah: Yves R. Perrin, publisher, 1994.

Faragher, John Mack. *Women and Men on the Overland Trail.* New Haven, Connecticut: Yale University Press, 1979.

Flanders, Robert Bruce. *Nauvoo: Kingdom on the Mississippi.* Urbana: University of Illinois Press, 1965.

Gentry, Leland H. "The Mormon Way Stations: Garden Grove and Mt. Pisgah." *BYU Studies* 21 (fall 1981): 445–61.

Gudde, Erwin G. *Bigler's Chronicle of the West: The Conquest of California, Discovery of Gold, and Mormon Settlement as Reflected in Henry William Bigler's Diaries.* Berkeley: University of California Press, 1962.

————. *California Place Names,* 4th ed., Berkeley: University of California Press, 1998.

Gudde, Erwin G. and Elisabeth K. Gudde, eds. *California Gold Camps.* Berkeley: University of California Press, 1975.

Haenszel, Arda. "Mormons in San Bernardino." *San Bernardino County Museum Association* (summer 1992).

Hansen, Gladys. *San Francisco Almanac.* San Francisco: Chronicle Books, 1975.

Hansen, Lorin K. and Lila J. Bringhurst. *Let This Be Zion: Mormon Pioneers and Modern Saints in Southern Alameda California.* Salt Lake City: Publishers Press, 1996.

Hartley, William G. "Mormons and Early Iowa History (1838 to 1858): Eight Distinct Connections." *The Annals of Iowa* 59 (Summer 2000).

Hill, William E. *The California Trail Yesterday & Today.* Boulder, Colorado: Pruett Publishing Company, 1986.

History of Alameda County. Oakland, California: M. W. Wood, publisher, 1883.

Horner, John M. "Adventures of a Pioneer," *Improvement Era* 7 (May to December 1904).

————. *Personal History,* (Honolulu: Hawaiian Gazette Co., 1898.

Journal History of the Church of Jesus Christ of Latter-day Saints, 1830–1972. Historical Department of the Church, Salt Lake City, Utah.

Leonard, Glen M. *Nauvoo: A Place of Peace, A People of Promise.* Salt Lake City: Deseret Book Company, 2002.

Los Angeles Star, 7 March 1857.

Lyman, Amasa M. Journal. LDS Church Archives, Salt Lake City, Utah.

Lyman, Edward Leo. *San Bernardino: The Rise and Fall of a California Community.* Salt Lake City: Signature Books, 1996.

Madsen, Brigham D., ed. *Exploring the Great Salt Lake: The Stansbury Expedition of 1849–50.* Salt Lake City: University of Utah Press, 1989.

McAfee, Ward M. "A Social History of the Great Quake of 1857." *Southern California Quarterly* 74 (Summer 1992): 125–40.

Moorman, Donald R. *Camp Floyd and the Mormons: The Utah War.* Salt Lake City: University of Utah Press, 1992.

Morgan, Dale L. *The Humboldt: Highroad of the West.* New York: Farrar and Rinehart, 1943.

Newbury, Colin. *Tahiti Nui: Change and Survival in French Polynesia, 1767–1945.* Honolulu: University of Hawaii Press, 1980.

Newell, Linda King, and Valeen Tippets Avery. *Mormon Enigma: Emma Hale Smith, Prophet's Wife, "Elect Lady," Polygamy's Foe.* New York: Doubleday, 1984.

Newton, Marjorie. *Southern Cross Saints: The Mormons in Australia.* Laie, Hawaii: The Institute for Polynesian Studies, Brigham Young University-Hawaii, 1991.

Owens, Kenneth N. *Gold Rush Saints: California Mormons and the Great Rush for Riches.* Kingdom in the West, The Mormons and the American Frontier, vol. 7. Spokane: The Arthur H. Clark Co., 2004.

Noall, Claire. *Intimate Disciple: A Portrait of Willard Richards.* Salt Lake City: University of Utah Press, 1957.

Pratt, Steven. "Eleanor McLean and the Murder of Parley P. Pratt." *BYU Studies,* 15 (winter 1975): 225–56.

Quinn, D. Michael. *The Mormon Hierarchy: Origins of Power.* Salt Lake City: Signature Books, 1994.

Remy, Jules and Julius Benchly. *A Journey to Great Salt Lake City.* London: W. Jeffs, 1861.

Rhodehamel, Josephine DeWitt, and Raymond Francis Wood. *Ina Coolbrith, Librarian and Laureate of California.* Provo: Brigham Young University Press, 1973.

Roberts, Brigham H., ed. *History of the Church of Jesus Christ of Latter-day Saints.* 7 vols. Salt Lake City: Deseret Book Company, 1902–32.

Rudolph, L. C. *Hoosier Faiths, A History of Indiana Churches and Religious Groups.* Bloomington: Indiana University Press, 1995.

Schindler, Harold. *Orrin Porter Rockwell, Man of God, Son of Thunder.* Salt Lake City, University of Utah Press, 1966.

Schlissel, Lillian. *Women's Diaries of the Westward Journey.* New York: Shocken Books, 1992.

Scott, Mel. *The San Francisco Bay Area: A Metropolis in Perspective.* Berkeley: University of California Press, 1959.

Shumate, Albert. *Rincon Hill and South Park, San Francisco's Early Fashionable Neighborhood.* Sausalito: Windgate Press, 1988.

Siemers, Ray, ed. "Vicissitudes of Dwellings and Localities," *San Francisco Historic Records Index* (1987).

Soulé, Frank, John H. Gihon, and James Nisbet. *The Annals of San Francisco.* New York: D. Appleton & Company, 1855. Facsimile edition, Berkeley: Berkeley Hills Books, 1998.

Stegner, Wallace. *The Gathering of Zion: The Story of the Mormon Trail.* New York: McGraw-Hill Book Company, 1971.

Thomas, C. *Contributions to the History of the Eastern Townships: A Work Containing an Account of the Early Settlement of St. Armand, Dunham, Sutton, Brome, Potton, and Bolton.* Montreal: John Lovell, St. Nicholas Street, 1866.

Tyler, Daniel. *A Concise History of the Mormon Battalion.* Salt Lake City, 1881.

Unruh, John D., Jr. *The Plains Across: The Overland Emigrants and the Trans-Mississippi West, 1840–60.* Urbana: University of Illinois, 1979.

Walker, Philip L. and Patricia M. Lambert. *Human Skeletal Remains from the Historic Cemetery and Seccombe Park, San Bernardino, California.* Department of Anthropology, University of California, Santa Barbara, 1991.

INDEX

Page numbers in italics refer to illustrations, including maps.

Curtis, Sister, 347, 348

Dack family, 71
Dagroot, Sister, 336, 337, 341, 353
daguerreotype, *8, 179,* 244, 363, *364,* 388, 426, 473, 478
Daily Alta Californian, 248
daily log, 6
dairy, 239, 488, 544
Dalee, Mr., 426
Daley (child), 385
Daley Hotel, 378, 379, 416, 421, 444, 454, 455, 464, 466
Daley, Adeline, 395, 396, 420, 469, 470, 484, 502
Daley, Brother, 373, 406
Daley, Celia, 470
Daley, Ed, 378, 379, 411, 416, 421, 433, 439, 444, 454, 455, 464, 466, 470, 537
Daley, Nancy Hunt, 390, 393, 400, 402, 466, 477, 489, 496
Daley, Phineas, 385, 394, 395, 424, 449, 469, 470, 471, 503
dancing, 374, 375, 379, 387, 429, 433, 444, 453, 454, 459, 461, 462, 464, 466, 475, 486; children, 175, 404; Christmas, 298; cotillion, 177, 208, 297, 429, 434, 502; 502; country, 177; Cox opposes, 495; fandango, 176, 180; French fours, 208, 234; Lyman preaches against, 440; parties, 178, 186, 188, 198, 206, 228, 229, 405, 421, 428, 434; Parley Pratt speaks on propriety of, 316; in San Francisco, 168, 309, 317; waltzes, 177, 185, 234, 452, 502
Danforth, Amelia, 322
Darius (prince), 133, 135, 138, 139, 140, 141, 142, 148, 150
Dart, Brother, 471, 434
David, Brother, 381, 455, 470, 473
David, Sister, 381
Davis, A. J., 221, 224
Davis, Brother, 346, 349, 387, 393, 396, 420, 425, 448, 449, 451, 452, 456, 468, 469, 473, 485, 493, 499
Davis, H., 202, 217
Davis, Meuriel C., 40
Davis, Sister, 347, 348, 349, 350, 387, 389, 396, 434, 454, 459, 479, 485
Day, George, 487, 488, 544
Day, Mr., 364
Day, William C., 274
Deer Creek, 82
deer, 485
Delin, Sister, 412, 430
Dell, Sarah Milikin, 379, 388
Denis, Mr., 215
Dennis (black man), 349, 354, 355, 360, 362
Dennis, Ed, 395, 404, 423, 439
Dennis, Mary, 399

Dennis, Sister, 379, 398
Denton, Brother, 58
Des Moines River, 69, 86
Deseret News, 240, 257, 322, 405, 408, 427, 431, 439, 444, 447, 449, 451, 454, 464, 469, 470, 479, 491, 495, 496, 501
Devil's Gate, 83
Dewel. *See* Duell
Dewey, Elzira, 409, 426, 454, 480
Dewey, F., 281
Dewey, Frank, 427, 480
Dickey, Doctor, 503
Dikes, G. P., 420
Dire. *See* Dyer
Dixon, Mary, 427
Doctrine and Covenants, 53, 513n. 20
Dodge, Brother, 276, 317, 320, 321, 338, 340, 341, 466, 468, 476; to San Bernardino, 357
Dodge, Sister, 320, 321, 382
Dodson, Mr., 507
dogs, 128, 220, 246, 248, 260
Dolon, Mr., 246
Doniphan, Catherine, 265, 266, 268, 274, 277, 278, 290, 298, 301, 308, 310, 318, 331, 332, 333, 336, 337
Dougherty, Levi, 113, 194, 196, 197, 198, 206, 207, 210, 212, 217, 222, 278, 306
Dougherty, Sister, 195, 199
Dowdle, Absolom, 495, 497
Dragoons, San Bernardino, 420, 425
Drakesville, Iowa, 70
Draper, Brother, 72
Drury, Joel, 33
Drury, M. S., 29
Drury, Ruth, 46
Drury, Sister, 46
Duell, Brother, 493
Duell, Sister, 482, 483, 485, 489, 492, 501
duff (pudding), 482, 485
Duke, Jimmy, 70, 71
Duncan, Chapman, 43, 58, 205, 206, 208, 217, 236, 237, 239, 242, 243, 250, 251, 252, 310; mission to China, 180, 212
Duncan, Homer, 82
Duncan's Chinese Sales Room, 288
Dunham, Canada: Crosbys move to, 17; *18;* Allsaints Church, 21
Dunham, Mr., 313
Duning, Elizabeth, 28, 29
Dunn, Simeon, A., 95, 100, 114, 117, 127; cow washed downstream, 106
Dustin, Bechias, 191, 207, 212, 216; 283, 289, 290, 295, 299, 302, 303, 304, 305, 309, 310; death of child, 210–11, 303; to San Bernardino, 311
Dyer, Ebenezer, 194, 209, 215, 230, 357, 361, 362, 369, 372, 379, 383, 388, 394, 397, 466, 488

Whipple, Miss, 316, 317, 318
Whipple, Sister, 471, 473
Whitaker, Sister, 158 378, 379, 392, 397
Whitaker, Thomas W., 122, 126, 127, 132, 152, 154, 158, 160, 161, 162, 167, 375, 378, 388, 391, 392, 393, 396, 397, 470, 480, 491; correspondence with, 241, 249, 260, 272, 346
white foreigners, 123
White, Brother, 431, 441
White, Mrs., 112
Whitit, Brother, 297
Whitmer, David, 512n. 16
Whitney, Orson, 271, 272, 274, 275, 276, 454
Wilber, Benjamin S., 49, 50, 59
Wilber, Melvin, 67
Wilkie, Brother, 334, 335, 336, 337, 353, 360, 363
Wilkins, Henry, 191, 253, 254, 282, 283, 287, 288, 301, 302, 304, 308, 311, 317, 322, 325, 327, 328, 330, 333, 337, 340, 342, 353, 356, 373; to San Bernardino, 357
Williams, Dr. Frederick G., 44
Williams, Luna, 125, 131, 139, 141, 144, 150, 157
Williams, Mr., 373
Williams, Thomas S., 206, 212
Willis, Mr., 181, 256, 272, 299, 300
wind storms, 70–71, 72, 77, 82, 98, 107, 121, 132, 135, 180, 210, 224, 232, 241, 243, 244, 251, 260, 262, 263, 275, 299, 334, 433, 454, 459, 464, 485, 489, 497
Winner, George K., 119
Winner, Hanna, 119
Winslow, Dr., 223, 241
Winter Quarters, Nebraska, 65; Crosbys arrive, 5, 73
Wixom, Brother, 337, 421

Wixom, Sister, 377
wood finishing mill, 392, 393
Woodbury, Elvira Stevens: Brigham Young grants divorce, 412; at Mission San Jose, 183–84, 191, 207, 210, 212, 225; in San Francisco, 243, 258, 259, 279, 287, 293, 304, 305, 317, 320, 334, 336, 337, 339, 343, 344, 345, 346, 349, 352, 356, 364; news of sister's death, 347; in San Bernardino, 377, 380, 388, 390, 391, 395, 399. *See also* Stevens, Elvira
Woodbury, John Stillman, 346, 351, 352, 375, 376, 377, 379, 384, 388, 391, 392, 395, 396; to San Bernardino, 356; to Utah, 399
wood-gathering bee, 440
Woods, Mr., 19
Worcester, Ohio, 102
Worden, William, 464, 466
Worth, Captain, 136
writing school, 462, 464

Young, Brigham, 315, 322, 405, 412, 498, 501, 505, 508; assumes church presidency, 63; disbands San Bernardino, 9; family blessing meeting, 43, 44; at Kirtland, 44; at Pleasant Garden, 55; at Salt Lake Valley, 87, 90; says "troops cannot come in," 495
Young, Father, 43
Young, John, 409
Young, Joseph, 47, 91, 322, 379, 409, 512n. 8
Young, Phineas, 72
Young, Zina D. Huntington, 88, 89, 91, 280, 282, 415; wife of Henry Jacobs, 177

Zion, 35, 42, 53, 105; gathering to, 4, 9, 508, 511n. 4